Entrepreneur® MAGAZINE'S
ULTIMATE
BOOK OF FRANCHISES

From the Franchise Experts at
Entrepreneur *Magazine*

RIEVA LESONSKY
and MARIA ANTON-CONLEY

EP
Entrepreneur®
Press

Editorial director: Jere L. Calmes
Managing editor: Maria Anton-Conley
Cover design: Beth Hansen-Winter
Interior design and production: Eliot House Productions

This publication is designed to provide accurate and authoritative information in regard to the subject matter covered. It is sold with the understanding that the publisher is not engaged in rendering legal, accounting or other professional services. If legal advice or other expert assistance is required, the services of a competent professional person should be sought.

Library of Congress Cataloging-in-Publication Data

Lesonsky, Rieva.

Entrepreneur magazine's ultimate book of franchises: from the franchise experts at Entrepreneur magazine/Rieva Lesonsky and Maria Anton-Conley.

p.   cm.

ISBN 1-932156-86-0

1. Franchises (Retail trade) I. Title: Ultimate book of franchises. II. Title: Book of franchises. III. Anton, Maria. IV. Entrepreneur (Irvine, Calif.) V. Title.

HF5429.23.L47 2004

658.8'708--dc22

2004040584

Printed in Canada

09 08 07 06 05

10 9 8 7 6 5 4 3

Table of Contents

SECTION ONE
How To Buy a Franchise

Acknowledgments

THERE ARE MANY BOOKS THAT TELL YOU about franchising, but this is the only one to incorporate *Entrepreneur* magazine's acclaimed Franchise 500®, making *Entrepreneur Magazine's Ultimate Book of Franchises* the most comprehensive book about buying a franchise available anywhere.

It takes a talented, dedicated group of people to create a work of this magnitude, so we are grateful to all who have contributed. Thanks to Chuck Fuller, Entrepreneur.com's vice president of business development, for his support; to *Entrepreneur* magazine's creative director Mark Kozak for his expert guidance, and to Marla Markman, *Entrepreneur's* managing editor, for her insight and advice. We appreciate the efforts of *Entrepreneur's* listing assistant Tracy Stapp and the talent of independent book designer Karen Billipp, who created a book that's so chock-full of information yet so easy to use.

There are three *Entrepreneur* magazine staffers who went well above and beyond their job duties to make this book possible. So for all their help and hard work, a special thank you to senior designer Matt Samarin and projects editor Maggie Iskander. There aren't enough words to properly thank articles editor Janean Chun, who helped conceive this book's format and edited it with her usual flair.

Every aspiring or current business owner needs a good accountant, someone he or she can trust without hesitation. And we have one. Many thanks to CPA David R. Juedes, who, as the former CFO of a franchise company, is especially qualified to review and rate the financials of the franchises in the listing section.

Many years ago, when *Entrepreneur's* Franchise 500® was still young, we were lucky enough to meet Andrew A. Caffey, who, at the time, was an attorney for the International Franchise Association. Today, from his law practice in Washington, DC, Andy is a frequent contributor to *Entrepreneur,* using his years of experience as a franchise and business opportunity attorney to demystify the franchise buying process. The first section of the *Ultimate Book of Franchises* is adapted from Andy's book, *Franchise & Business Opportunities*. Without Andy's contribution, this book would not be worthy of the word "ultimate."

Maria Anton-Conley
Rieva Lesonsky

Introduction

IF YOU ARE LIKE MOST AMERICANS, CHANCES are you and/or some member of your family spend time—and money—in a franchise nearly every week. Doubt it? Well, do you ever get gas? Stay in a hotel or motel? Get a cup of coffee at a place other than Starbucks? Pick up a fast meal at the drive-thru? Go to a staffing service in search of a job? Have your house (or office) cleaned? Grab a sandwich or ice cream cone on the run? Think about buying or selling a house? Well, you get my point—franchising is a central part of our everyday lives. In fact, as an industry it generates more than $200 billion in annual revenue.

Since you purchased the *Ultimate Book of Franchises*, you must want to be part of it. Or you've at least considered buying a franchise. That's a good start, but to be a successful franchisee, you need to do more than just think about it—you need to actually get started. I can guess what you're thinking: "There are so many franchises to choose from, where do I even begin?" The obvious answer: right here. You can't start a business without doing your homework. Consider this book your cheat sheet—we've done a lot of the work for you.

First, a word about franchising. A type of business opportunity, franchises are essentially business packages that enable you to, as the franchisors say, be in business for yourself, but not by yourself. All franchises are offered with the same premise: "We (the franchisor) have already developed a successful business program. For your investment, we will provide you with all the tools you need to own and operate a successful business." All business start-ups entail some risk. But franchises generally are less risky to start: After all, you are buying a proven system. That's not to say there is no risk in franchising; obviously, there is. But you can mitigate that risk by knowing what to expect from franchisors, by understanding the rules and regulations that govern franchising and by getting the inside scoop on the hundreds of franchise opportunities available. And that's where we come in.

We are the folks who publish *Entrepreneur* magazine, and for more than 26 years we've been telling people how to start and grow their own businesses. For 25 years, we've produced *Entrepreneur*'s Franchise 500°, the most authoritative and comprehensive ranking of franchise opportunities in the world. And we've taken the many months of research that go into the Franchise 500 and applied it to this book.

Ultimate Book of Franchises is divided into two sections. In the first section, "How To Buy a Franchise," Andrew A. Caffey, a franchise attorney, internationally recognized specialist in franchise and business opportunity law and former general counsel of the International Franchise Association, provides you with an overall look at the world of franchising. Here you'll find information on everything from researching a franchise on the Internet to negotiating your franchise agreements.

An in-depth statistical overview of hundreds of franchises makes up the rest of the book. Organized by Maria Anton-Conley, Maggie Iskander and Tracy Stapp, here you'll find the 411 on opportunities ranging from the tried and true, like McDonald's, Subway and Jiffy Lube, to newer franchises, like Mathnasium Learning Centers and Mama Fu's Noodle House.

While it's likely there is an opportunity just right for you, not all opportunities are suited for everyone. And chances are, you're going to invest a lot of your savings into your venture, so you need to invest wisely. As Chinese philosopher Laotzu said, "The journey of a thousand miles must begin with a single step." So turn the page, and put your best foot forward.

How To Buy a Franchise

CHAPTER 1

So You Want to Own Your Own Business?

A T THE AGE OF 30, SUCCESS WAS ELUDING *Jon, and he knew something was wrong. After a promising high school athletic career and a fair academic showing at his state's university, he bounced from one job to the next with no sense of purpose and without achieving the success he knew was in him. People liked him, and he was presentable, but his 30th birthday stopped him in his tracks. How and when was he going to realize his potential? He hungered for success but didn't quite know how to go about it. Somehow that part was not taught in school.*

BUSINESS OWNERSHIP
The Advantages

Owning your own business—a sparkling, elusive goal of the American dream. It wasn't until Jon began considering starting his own business that he felt some optimism about his life's goals.

Business ownership seems out of reach to many would-be entrepreneurs because it appears expensive, complicated and intimidating. Yet business ownership is the most common route taken by Americans to substantial wealth.

There are a number of advantages to owning a business:

- Small-business ownership can bring *independence*—no more punching a time clock and worrying whether your job will be there tomorrow.
- It can mean *flexibility* so that you are free to take time off and spend time with the ones you love.
- It can bring a *healthy variety* of daily tasks instead of the repetitive routines of so many workplace specialties.
- Business ownership can bring immense *pride in accomplishment.*
- Business owners make a *difference* in the lives of everyone involved, especially employees who depend on the owner's business savvy to keep their jobs.

- Owning your own business gives you the chance to do it *your way*. It gives you the chance to bring your pride, your style, your gifts to a business operation.
- Business ownership can bring *wealth*. You don't need to be Bill Gates to realize the rewards of starting your own business. Ownership gives you the opportunity to build equity value over time, so that once your business is up and running, it will have acquired a substantial value. It puts to shame the apparent value of a week-to-week paycheck after those taxes are taken out.

The Challenges

Given these benefits, why don't even more people own their own businesses? It takes an enormous amount of work, perseverance and drive to overcome the challenges of getting started. To many people, those challenges can seem insurmountable. Just take a look at what it was like for Jon:

Jon had a fevered panic dream: Look at this checklist of things I have to do! I can't do this! It's a mess. Borrow a quarter-million dollars? Who is going to lend me that kind of dough? Quit my job and launch out on my own? What if I fail? The national failure rates for small businesses are staggering. Am I nuts?! Even if I find the money, I will have to learn the traps of the business. Sure, there are lots of other businesses in my line I could talk to, but they are all competitors! No way are they going to tell me how to run one of these operations. I have to hire people, buy advertising, buy inventory … I don't know how to do that. I'll probably get ripped off at every turn and lose my shirt.

In some ways, Jon is right. It is difficult to find the information you need to set up and operate a business, create the trademark and graphics, and amass the cash and borrowed funds necessary to get going. As they say, if it were easy, everyone would do it.

But owning a successful business is possible, and there are many ways to go about doing it. One way is to buy a franchise. The franchise concept is designed to help the average person overcome the challenges of small-business ownership and get into a proven business, while providing the type of training and continued coaching that is not available anywhere else.

There are lots of ways to skin the business cat, of course. Whether you choose a franchise or something else entirely, it must be a program that fits your needs and gets you on the road to building wealth through small-business ownership.

SUMMARY NOTES

✓ Avenues to success are often not taught in our schools.

✓ Business ownership is a proven pathway to success and wealth.

✓ You can overcome the intimidating challenges of business ownership.

✓ A popular way to get into business is owning a franchise.

Action PLAN

Write down on a single sheet of paper three goals of a business you would start. How do you imagine it would change your life? Then write down three aspects of business that appeal to you. If you have any general ideas of the type of business that would appeal to you, note them on the same sheet. Keep this paper in a folder labeled "Business Planning"; you will want to refer to it again.

CHAPTER 2

Organizing for Business

O*NCE MERRY DECIDED TO GET INTO business for herself, she realized that she didn't know much about business organization. She had heard the horror stories: A friend's dad had lost everything in a stupid business concept, and because of the liabilities of the business failure, the friend and her family had to move out of their house and into an apartment when she was in high school. Merry was determined to be smart about her own business, protect herself as best she could and build an organization that could stand on its own feet. However, despite her firm resolve, she didn't even know what questions to ask to get started.*

ADVANTAGES AND DISADVANTAGES OF DIFFERENT BUSINESS ORGANIZATIONS

One of the early decisions all businesspeople have to make is how best to organize legally to be in business. Do you form a corporation?

Do you have to? Are there other choices? This can be confusing if you are new to business ownership. There are lots of choices and a number of concerns to consider as you sift through the options.

You can operate as a sole proprietor, a corporation, a partnership or a limited liability company. Even if you buy a franchise, you need to select a form of business organization. Take a look at each one.

The Sole Proprietorship

A sole proprietorship is a business owned directly by one person. This is the simplest type of business organization, and some may even find it hard to think of it as an "organization." However, some sole proprietorships may be large and complex with many employees. For now think of a sole proprietorship as one person running the business as both owner and manager.

The greatest advantage to running the sole proprietorship is the ease with which it is formed. There are no papers to file or meetings to hold in order to keep it in existence. From an organizational point of view, you may simply start doing business as a sole proprietor with no further legal maintenance required. Of course there may be licenses or permits required for the type of business you are starting, but the "organization" of your business is done.

The greatest disadvantage of the sole proprietorship is personal liability. The owner is required to repay any amount borrowed personally no matter what happens to the business. This means they could lose more than their initial investment. There is no distinction between business and personal assets. A bank or other creditor may try to collect any money owed from the sole proprietor's personal assets if the business fails. You may obtain liability insurance, but it will not cover you if your business fails.

Another serious limitation for a sole proprietor is the inability to take on investors or partners. This may be unimportant for many businesses but could make all the difference in financing others.

A lot of businesses start out as sole proprietorships and then morph into corporations or limited liability companies (LLCs). If you are buying a franchise, however, it may be important to consider forming a separate legal entity before you sign on to the franchised business, because it can be difficult to transfer the franchise rights to your new entity after you sign the franchise agreement.

Partnership

A partnership exists when two or more people agree to run a business together and share control and profits. Creating a partnership does not require any formal steps. The agreement to form a partnership may be either expressed or implied, oral or written. However, it is highly recommended that a written partnership agreement be prepared and signed by the partners.

The partnership agreement should cover such issues as the amount of each partner's contribution, how profits will be shared, what authority each partner has, and how interests may be transferred. If a partnership is formed without a written agreement, the law will impose a series of standard terms that may not be intended by the partners. If you wish to have a partnership agreement, it is recommended that you consult with an attorney licensed in your state with some experience in the area.

Business partners should understand the significance the law places on sharing control. They may act on behalf of one another and the partnership in making agreements, incurring debt, and taking any other action in the course of running the business. The obligations of the business become personal to all. State law will impose equally shared liability on each general partner, unless the partnership agreement states otherwise. For example, if your partner takes out a loan on behalf of the business and the business fails, the bank will seek repayment from both your partner *and* you. If your partner or the partnership has no assets to satisfy the debt, the creditor may look to you personally.

So far we have been discussing a general partnership; however, there is another form of partnership known as a limited partnership. A limited partnership has at least one general partner and one limited partner. The main difference between these two types of partners is that a limited partner has no liability for the debts of the partnership. Nor do they have rights to management or control of the business. The general partner controls the business and has unlimited liability. To form a limited partnership, you must carefully consult the laws of the state in which you do business and seek the assistance of a competent attorney. For accountability purposes, the partnership is required to report its income on IRS Form 1065.

Corporation

The corporation is radically different from the other forms of business organization. It is controlled by statute, and each state's laws vary to some extent. You should therefore contact the secretary of state's office in the state in which you incorporate for more information.

In the eyes of the law, a corporation is a legal entity separate and apart from its shareholders. It may buy, sell or inherit property; enter into contracts; and sue or be sued in court. It is also responsible for its own debts. If the corporation fails, creditors may not seek payment from investors in the company. The shareholder's liability is therefore limited to his or her initial investment.

Shareholders in a corporation are ultimately responsible for all corporate actions, somewhat like citizens in a democracy. Shareholders elect representatives to the board of directors and the board of directors appoints the officers of the corporation to handle its everyday affairs. This three-tier structure applies to nearly all corporations, from General Motors to the smallest one-owner, home-based corporation.

If you form a legal entity like a corporation or an LLC, make sure that whenever you enter a business contract or other important obligation, you bind the entity to the obligation and not to yourself. To do this, make sure you sign in your official capacity showing your title, such as "President" or "Member." Make sure your title appears under your name and that you are committing the entity to the obligation.

Subchapter S Corporation

Most smaller businesses will benefit from selecting the tax treatment of a subchapter S corporation. A subchapter S corporation receives special tax treatment under the Internal Revenue Code and has some distinct advantages. These include:

- **No Double Taxation.** A subchapter S corporation sidesteps the principal disadvantage of the corporate form of doing business by receiving tax treatment that is similar to a partnership. It is not taxed at the corporate level, but the income of the entity is passed through to the shareholders and reported on each individual's personal tax return.
- **Ease of Election.** A new corporation or an existing corporation may elect subchapter S corporation treatment simply by filing IRS Form 2553.

In order to qualify for subchapter S corporation treatment, the corporation must be a domestic (U.S.) entity with one class of stock and no more than 35 shareholders. Its shareholders must be individuals, estates or certain trusts and not other corporations. Finally, it may not have a nonresident alien among its shareholders. Most personally owned and family-owned businesses qualify for subchapter S corporation treatment and should seriously consider electing it.

The drawback to a subchapter S corporation is that many of the corporate perks of a regular corporation may not be realized. For instance, a regular corporation can pay for the health plan of its shareholders, but a subchapter S corporation may not. There may be other drawbacks, as well, which you should review with your attorney.

Limited Liability Company

The limited liability company is a recently developed concept in business organization that has a number of advantages for small-business owners. Like a subchapter S corporation, a limited liability company (LLC) offers the liability protection of a corporation and the tax benefits of a partnership but does not require compliance with the legal formalities that characterize a corporation.

Wyoming first adopted an LLC statute in 1977, but the concept really caught on in the 1980s. In

1988, the IRS ruled that an LLC under Wyoming law would receive tax treatment like a partnership (on a pass-through basis to individual managers), and its popularity has since soared.

An LLC has an enormous advantage over the corporation: flexibility in its management. Depending on the particular requirements of your state's law, an LLC is operated by either members or by appointed or elected managers. It may be structured for governance and economics by agreement of its owner-members, and there are few limitations on the way it is organized and operated. Most new business owners are well-advised to take a close look at the LLC concept.

For most small-business owners, the answer will be to stay a sole proprietor (and run whatever liability risks there may be), create a corporation and elect subchapter S treatment under the Tax Code, or form a limited liability company. Buying a franchise will accelerate your decision-making because the franchisor may demand you have your organization in place at the beginning of the franchise term.

CONCERNS UNDERLYING BUSINESS ORGANIZATIONS

In order to make the right choice of business organization, it is important to consider the following:

Personal Liability

If you do not form any legal entity to hold your business, you will be operating under your own name, as yourself, and putting your personal assets on the line. Your form of business ownership will be known as a "sole proprietor," and you will have no protection from claims anyone may have against your business.

Here's a quick example. You start a home business of buying and selling used video games. It takes off like a jack rabbit, and soon you are dealing in large wholesale lots of games. You enter into a contract with a new local games store to buy all of its used games for a year at a negotiated price, a contract that you estimate is worth $25,000. You do this because you have a buyer lined up who tells you he will buy as many games as you can produce for him.

One bleak day your buyer goes out of business and disappears. The games store expects you to continue buying from them, but you don't have the cash or the buyers to move the merchandise. When you don't buy the used games as required in your contract, the seller files a lawsuit on the contract, seeking $25,000 in damages. Your lawyer tells you that because you operate as a sole proprietor, all your personal assets are exposed to this claim, and you could lose your car and/or your house if you lose the case. If you operated as a corporation, he tells you, then it would be liable, and your personal assets would be out of your creditors' reach.

When someone talks about the disadvantages of operating under your own name, you need to weigh the potential liability that you could incur in the business. In large measure your decision depends on the type of business (will you be entering into contracts for substantial obligations?) and the state of your personal assets (can you absorb all potential losses of the business?).

Taxation

This is a biggie. There are dramatically different tax consequences depending on the form of business organization you use. Taxation concerns drive a lot of the business organization decisions, and some of the legal forms available strike a balance between liability and taxation.

If you operate as an individual sole proprietor, then your tax picture is straightforward. You simply add a Schedule C to your annual personal return.

Corporations have another story to tell. The law (and the IRS) recognize that a corporation is a separate entity and must pay its own taxes on its own net income. Then, when the corporation pays out a dividend to its owners, the owners must pay taxes on that income when they file their personal returns. In an important sense, a corporation is taxed twice:

once on its own revenue, and again when the owners take money out of the corporation.

A traditional answer to this double whammy is an IRS tax treatment as a "subchapter S corporation." This is a corporation that has met a series of qualifications (mostly as to size and the number of shareholders) and has elected to receive special tax treatment. As a result, the subchapter S corporation has the liability protection of a standard corporation but is not taxed twice. The IRS allows the corporation to pass through its revenues to its owners and the taxation on that revenue at the owners' level. The subchapter S corporation does not pay taxes separately. The result: one-time taxation. Problem solved.

A partnership has always been taxed directly to the individual partners; it is not considered a separate entity for liability or taxation purposes. Limited liability companies have also solved the taxation problem by receiving single tax treatment.

Flexibility

This concern becomes evident when you are told what directors and officers you must have and what annual meetings you must conduct in order to maintain a corporation. The law imposes rather extensive rules on the owners of a corporation, and if the rules are not followed, the liability shield effectiveness is lost. Partnerships are quite flexible. So are limited liability companies. Sole proprietorships are the most flexible of all, of course, because there is no organization to nurture along the way.

Flexibility has another dimension. Say you want to take in other owners and give them different shares of ownership. You cannot do that if you are a sole proprietor, but the other legal structures are designed for multiple owners.

SUMMARY NOTES
- ✓ Business organizations will change depending on the needs of the business itself and the organizers.
- ✓ Limiting personal liability, maximizing tax benefits and flexibility are principal concerns.
- ✓ Understand the major forms of business organization before consulting with an attorney; it will save you time and money.
- ✓ One of the most attractive new forms of business organization is the limited liability company. It is fast becoming the leading choice of small-business owners.

Action PLAN

Make a checklist of goals for your business as well as concerns you may have about things like ownership and liability. Take the list to a good attorney, and ask what you need to do to form a solid business entity for your business plan.

CHAPTER 3

Understanding the Franchise Concept

*P*AUL HAD ALWAYS WANTED TO OWN HIS *own business, but the opportunity had just never presented itself. On a fishing trip to Minnesota, he came across a business concept that he could not get out of his mind. It was new and fresh, and he thought it had a huge market potential. He wanted to get in on the business somehow and learned it was being offered as a new franchise program. This might mean he could bring the concept to his hometown and open a sensational business. He had never considered a franchise. Where should he start?*

INDEPENDENT OWNERSHIP

Start at the beginning. A business format franchise is a long-term business relationship in which the purchaser (the "franchisee") is granted the right to operate a business under the trademark of an established business owner (the "franchisor") and use its business techniques. This franchise relationship gives the franchisee the right to start up a business concept that the franchisor has already invented and perfected, using an established trademark and a comprehensive set of operating techniques.

Once licensed to use the franchisor's trademark and business system, the franchisee has the right to set up a business—usually under the franchisor's close scrutiny—that looks and operates *exactly* like other franchises in the franchise network. The magic in this formula—the simple fact that drives the success of the entire concept of business franchising—is that *the franchise owner remains an independent businessperson.* A franchisee is never an employee and is subject only to the limited control exercised by the franchisor under the franchise agreement. Independence means that if the franchisee is very successful in operating the business, he or she will reap the financial rewards. And the rewards can be substantial: Franchising has created an untold number of millionaires (think McDonald's and Holiday Inn). Of course, the converse also remains true: If the franchised business is not successful, the franchisee absorbs the loss.

THE BUSINESS OF FRANCHISING

Contrary to the impression conveyed nightly by the business press, it is small-business ownership, not big business, that is the bedrock strength of the American economy. Franchising gives the individual investor the opportunity to own their own small business without having to go it alone or invent and perfect a profitable retail concept that is, statistically at least, doomed to failure.

The franchise relationship we describe here has been adopted by hundreds of successful business programs, many of which are familiar cultural icons: Burger King, Dairy Queen, Holiday Inn, Jani-King, Jiffy Lube, McDonald's, Midas, Quality Inn, 7-Eleven and Subway stores. Many American towns have strip malls and mile-long commercial streets that are dominated by such franchised businesses.

While quick-service restaurants may be some of the best known franchises, the franchise concept has actually been applied in more than 50 different industry categories. These include everything from cellular telephone networks and formalwear rental businesses to automobile dent removal and paper shredding businesses.

Are gas station dealers and automobile dealers part of business franchising? Yes and no. Most systems are made up of independent dealers licensed to operate under a particular company's trademark and are said to own "product franchises," but they generally do not pay the franchise fees described here. The traditional practice in these industries is for dealers to buy product from the manufacturer at wholesale and sell it through their dealerships at retail. In contrast, the McDonald's restaurant franchisee does not buy any product from the franchisor—not even one

sesame seed. Supplies are bought exclusively from third-party suppliers approved by the company. Ray Kroc, the legendary founder of the McDonald's system, did not want any buyer/seller tension to creep into his relationship with franchise owners.

Franchising by itself is not an "industry," but a form of distribution. The franchisor is distributing products and services through licensed franchisees. This is important because two businesses may be franchised, say a convenience store and a hotel, but have absolutely nothing else in common.

In the past several years, there has also been an explosive growth in international franchising. The McDonald's trademark has become nothing short of a symbol of American culture, the restaurant's golden arches established now in more than 120 countries.

THE FRANCHISEE VIEW

Consider three important measures of a franchise system from the franchisee point of view: independence, training and money dynamics.

Independent Ownership

This concept energizes franchising because of the motivation, commitment and drive of an on-site owner. An employee manager working on an hourly wage is usually not motivated to work as hard or as long as an owner. It's that simple: An employee is involved; an owner is committed. It is the lesson taught when a pig and a chicken form a partnership to produce a ham and egg sandwich. The chicken is "involved," but the pig is *committed*.

Training Says It All

Training and support are keys to a strong business franchise. A well-established franchisor has something valuable to impart to the franchisee: know-how. It's one thing to perfect a business concept; it is quite another to transfer the essence of that concept to someone who knows nothing about the business and enable them to find success.

The strongest and best franchise programs are those able to convey know-how through rigorous training. Fresh-baked whole wheat bread franchisor Great Harvest Bread Co. requires that new franchisees spend one week in classroom training at its Montana headquarters and another two weeks doing hands-on training in an existing franchised bakery in their system. Additional in-store training takes place when the franchisee opens for business.

 IN*sight*

Among franchisors, the phrase "fast food" is discouraged. As commonly used, it has become a pejorative comment on the quality of the food. Preferred, more politically correct expressions in franchise circles include "quick service" food and "quality service" restaurants. We like "quick cuisine."

How the Money Works

How does the money work in a franchise relationship? While there are no hard and fast rules, the franchisee generally pays the franchisor in three ways: the initial franchise fee, royalties and advertising contributions.

The *initial franchise fee* is a lump sum paid when the contract is signed. This payment can range from a few thousand dollars to as high as $50,000 or more. A typical initial franchise fee for a restaurant franchise is in the $20,000 to $30,000 range. This fee generally covers the franchisor's cost of recruiting franchisees and of initial services, like site location and training.

The franchisee also pays the franchisor a continuing *royalty fee*. This is usually calculated as a percentage of the business's gross sales, somewhere in the range of 3 to 8 percent. It is important to understand the significance of the royalty fee being calculated on gross sales rather than on a net figure or a flat-fee basis, such as $500 per month. Calculating the royalty on gross sales means that the percentage is measured on every dollar that comes in the door. Gross sales are those that are made by the business before any expenses, salaries, rent or other overhead is paid. They have nothing to do with the profitability of the business or with the net income that the owner might take home. Naturally, the franchisor wants to see the gross sales of the franchise maximized, since this increases the level of royalties paid. However, the franchisee, like any business owner, wants to maximize profitability. The franchisor does not have a direct interest in seeing that the business is run efficiently or profitably. The cold reality is that the franchisor will be paid the royalty whether or not the business is profitable for the franchisee.

The royalty fee is similar to a rent calculation. Your commercial landlord cares little whether your operation is profitable; however, if the rent is partly calculated on gross sales, he cares a lot that the gross sales figures are high. Both franchisor and landlord leave the task of making the business profitable entirely to the franchisee. A franchisee may have annual sales of $500,000 and pay the franchisor $25,000 in royalties (5 percent of gross sales) but still be losing money. Obviously, the franchisor wants to see every franchisee running a profitable business because healthy, profitable franchisees stay in business and keep paying royalties, but the franchisee is the only business player in this game with a direct interest in profitability.

Finally, most franchisees pay *advertising fund contributions.* Many franchisors organize franchise owners in a particular market or region and have them pool their advertising money for coordinated expenditures that benefit all stores operating under the system trademarks. This fee is usually within a range of 1 to 4 percent of gross sales.

If those are all the fees paid to the franchisor, the rest of the business expenses must be assumed by the franchise owner, as with any other form of business. At the same time, the revenues from the business belong to the franchisee.

In business terms, then, a franchise is a form of joint venture, with the neophyte paying the experienced company for the right to conduct a business using all the techniques that made the experienced company successful. The franchisor has its arm around the shoulders of the franchisee, training and assisting, and showing exactly how to run the business. A good franchisor is a patient mentor, a relentless teacher and a demanding partner.

With such a robust market of franchisors, you can expect to find brand-new sparkling programs, fading giants, troubled systems with rebellious franchise owners, systems on the way up, and systems crumbling under the weight of competition.

Be on the lookout for fad franchises that sound snazzy but probably won't be around long enough for you to get any return on your investment. My all-time favorite is the freestanding bungee-jump tower franchise of a few years ago; a close second is the corrugated cardboard coffins dealerships spotted at a franchise trade show in the late 1980s. Other fads might include laser tag games, bagel stores and yogurt shops. Also look out for businesses that may be eclipsed by fundamental changes in equipment or the marketplace. How would you like to have a franchise for the best typewriter repair shop in town? The Internet is profoundly changing lots of businesses, such as travel agencies. Don't get stuck with a buggy-whip franchise. So before you invest in such a company, you owe it to yourself to do the research, just as you would before buying stock in a publicly traded corporation.

The underlying message here should be clear: You can get hurt financially if you invest in the wrong franchise.

THE ALL-AMERICAN HARD SELL

One feature of a robust franchise marketplace is that franchisors are under extreme pressure to make the franchise sale. They have invested heavily in their program (it takes a chunk of change to pull together the business organization and meet the legal requirements), and the sales process itself is difficult and time-consuming. The cost of the sale (representative's salary, trade show costs, advertising, promotional materials, etc.) can also be substantial. The result is often the all-American hard sell: sales representatives pressing too hard to move a vaguely interested prospect to make a commitment, selling a franchise to anyone with a heartbeat, and making untenable promises or inappropriate representations about the financial potential of the business. Many franchisor sales specialists will employ crude closing techniques that would make a used car salesman proud.

Never allow yourself to be stampeded into making a franchise investment decision because of urgencies created by the sales representative. "Buy today before the price increase"; "Territories are going fast. Get in on this or the prime markets will be taken"; and "We only have a couple territories left" are just some of the claims you might hear. In all likelihood, these statements are entirely false. If you could see behind the curtain, you would understand that the salesman is scrambling to make his sales numbers, probably paid

 IN*sight*

Many franchise sales representatives are paid a large portion of their salary on commission, and will sometimes bring an over-enthusiasm to their work that gets them in trouble with their employers, and sometimes with consumer protection agencies or franchise regulators.

on straight commission, and having a devil of a time closing on his leads. He wants to close you on his schedule, not yours.

Your best defense is to anticipate this hard sell and use it to your advantage. Learn to hear and appreciate a closing technique for what it is—a salesperson working hard to move you to commitment. Know that many franchise organizations would love to have you buy into their business concept, but in front of the curtain, they're cool about their eagerness. The better companies want to make sure that there is a great match between their concept and their franchisees and want to spend time exploring that match with a prospective investor. Ask them what qualifications they look for in a franchisee and what strengths among franchisees have led to success in their business. By listening closely during the sales process, you will learn a lot about the business of franchising.

Here is a little-known secret in franchising: The buyer has an enormous amount of control and power in the sales process. Many franchisors make buyers feel unworthy or poorly qualified to own and operate the franchise. They portray themselves as powerful trademark owners who control all aspects of their business, and they require detailed information in order for prospects to qualify for the right to buy a franchise. However, the prospective franchisee actually has the greater power since they can choose to invest or move on to the next opportunity. Experienced franchisors are aware of this; but you wouldn't know it from the noise surrounding most franchise sales.

The business of franchising is not slow, sedate and welcoming. It is fast, exciting, a hard sell and sometimes intimidating to the uninitiated. But read on. By the time you finish this book, you won't qualify as uninitiated anymore.

SUMMARY NOTES

✓ A business format franchise is a continuing relationship in which the franchisee is granted rights to operate under the trademark, business format and techniques owned by the franchisor.

✓ As a franchisee you are an independent business owner, never an employee. That includes risk and reward, success and failure.

✓ Franchisors like to say that in a franchise you are in business for yourself, not by yourself.

✓ Training is one key to a successful franchise program.

✓ Initial franchise fees, royalties and advertising fees define your money relationship with the franchisor.

✓ Franchising represents a huge marketplace, so it takes some research to find a solid program.

Action PLAN

Identify as many franchises in your immediate market as you can, and list them. Ask the managers if the business is a franchise and where you can learn more about the program. Look up the businesses on the Internet, and send away for franchise information of those business concepts you like.

CHAPTER 4

Buying Multiple Franchise Rights

*G*EORGE HAS THE HIGHEST CAREER AMBI-
*tions of anyone in his family. He
longs for a life of wealth and is determined to get there. Business ownership appeals to him, and he understands that
most millionaires in the United States own their
own businesses. He is interested in buying a
franchised business but is already looking down
the road to his second, fifth and 10th businesses. George never has done anything on a small
scale.*

Most investors like George and many franchise owners understand the real path to substantial personal wealth is ownership of multiple
retail businesses. Many ultrasuccessful franchisees establish a profitable franchised operation and then go on to develop or buy a
dozen other franchised businesses. Before
they know it, they have built an empire.

Multiple franchise development is a chal-
lenging part of the franchising business and
varies from one company to the next. Is it possible to purchase the right to develop an entire
state or region of the country? Do you need to
be a subfranchisor or master franchisee for a
region, or is there another way? What legal
rights are granted for multiple franchise ownership? What if the franchise owner wants to
purchase only two or three additional units?

TYPES OF MULTI-UNIT FRANCHISE PROGRAMS

Start with a look at some of the basic concepts
of multiple franchising.

Multiple Unit Ownership

This is when the same individual is granted
franchise rights at more than one location.
Most franchisors encourage multiple unit ownership once a franchisee shows they are capable
of operating a successful business. Everybody
wins under this arrangement. The franchisee
expands their business one step at a time, as

their resources grow. The franchisor enhances its relationship with successful franchise owners, rewarding those who prove themselves successful. The franchisor does not have the costs and risks associated with recruiting a new franchisee into the system. No special legal rights are created for multiple unit ownership. The franchisor simply grants standard unit franchise rights for newly identified locations or markets. Some companies will grant a right of first refusal, which says essentially, "We will give you the first shot at another franchise in this market if we want to grant one." Once George has established one restaurant, he requests the rights to another across town, and the franchisor decides to grant him a unit franchise agreement exactly like his first franchise. A year later he may want to go for a third.

Ask the sales representative what kind of multiple unit franchising the company has done in the past and what it offers now. You may find that a development agreement is included in the company's unit offering Uniform Franchise Offering Circular (UFOC). Other companies may have a separate UFOC for their multiple unit offering.

Area Franchise

Here the franchisor grants the franchisee, through a contract usually referred to as a development agreement, the right to develop a specified number of franchised units in a given territory. The development agreement details the time frame in which the units must be developed and opened for business, development quotas, the geographic area in which the franchisee has rights, and the fee obligations that apply. This type of development agreement is essentially an option agreement with a development schedule; it grants the developer option rights to enter into contracts in the future.

Master Franchise

With a master franchise agreement, the franchisor grants to a franchisee in its system the limited right to recruit new franchisees and to provide specified field support services to franchisees in a given area. In exchange, the master franchisee receives a commission on franchise sales made and a percentage of the royalty revenues generated among the franchisees it serves. George's franchisor appoints him to serve as a master franchisee in Texas. He runs advertising to generate interested investors in Texas and meets with all prospects who respond. Serious, qualified investors are sent to the franchisor's headquarters, where the sale is closed. George has a regular schedule for visiting all 19 Texas franchises twice a year and runs three regional meetings each year. In return, George receives 35 percent of the initial franchise fees of sales made through his efforts and 25 percent of all royalties paid by Texas franchisees.

Subfranchising

Under a subfranchising arrangement, the franchisor grants to another entity (a subfranchisor) the right to enter into unit franchise agreements with subfranchisees in a specified area. The franchisor usually dictates the terms on which unit franchises are granted. As a subfranchisor, George has near complete autonomy in the franchise sales process. He actually grants franchises, provides training and field support, and has the right to collect royalties and advertising contributions. George must pay to the franchisor 45 percent of all franchise revenue.

The most common of these types of multiple-unit programs is the area franchise. If an investor wants to secure the right to develop a large number of franchises in a favorite market, they should consider negotiating for a development agreement. A development agreement has the advantage of being relatively straightforward conceptually. It balances the aggression of the large developer with the franchisor's need to make sure that a designated market is fully developed in a timely manner.

The least common type of multiple-unit program is subfranchising. True subfranchising is relatively rare in the world of franchising.

PROTECTING YOUR DEVELOPMENT INVESTMENT

In order to balance these interests and risks financially, the developer usually pays upfront a substantial portion of the initial franchise fees of the units to be developed. Look at a quick example. Our ambitious George signs a development agreement and receives the right to open six restaurants in Salt Lake City over 10 years. He pays a nonrefundable, upfront development fee of $60,000, which represents half of the $20,000 per-store initial franchise fee for the six units. The development agreement promises that George will have exclusive rights to develop Salt Lake City for the next decade. He signs six standard unit franchise agreements within his development period and achieves his financial ambition. If George defaults under the development agreement and slips off the development schedule agreed upon, he may forfeit the unallocated portion of the upfront $60,000.

Clearly, multiple franchise development occurs at the higher financial end of franchising. It can be extremely expensive to secure the rights to multiple franchises, and the legal rights granted can be quite complicated.

If you are presented with an opportunity to purchase the rights to multiple franchises, be sure to take the program to your attorney for a detailed review of your rights and obligations. Developers, especially those who are inexperienced in the business being franchised or who are not well capitalized, can put a significant investment at risk by signing onto an aggressive development schedule. When negotiating the terms of development, it is vital that the build-out schedule is reasonable and that the exchange of fees is properly weighted for the risks being taken by both sides.

SUMMARY NOTES

✓ There are several ways that multiple-franchise rights are granted.
✓ Development fees may be paid upfront, so it is important to protect the investment by carefully negotiating your legal rights.

Action PLAN

Read a development contract for a complete understanding of its dynamics. Sketch out a business plan and projection of the money that might be required to develop an entire market.

CHAPTER 5

Franchise Sales Regulation

JIM THOUGHT HE WAS BEING HUSTLED. THE franchisor had not delivered any information about its program, and he was being pressured to sign a 40-page contract by the end of the week before it was offered to "the next person in line for the territory." It didn't feel right. Jim wondered "Isn't there a body of franchise law that protects the little guy?"

Given the early franchise success of companies like Holiday Inn and McDonald's and the sizzle that became associated with anything franchised ("Get in now—this is the next McDonald's!"), problems in the marketplace were perhaps inevitable.

In the 1970s, a number of fraudulent operators sold empty franchise opportunities that were all sizzle and no steak. Many people lost money investing in "can't lose" franchise propositions, and their shocking stories were told in the press. It wasn't long before state and federal regulators moved in. A dozen states and the FTC defined the franchise business concept in statutes and imposed a strict set of rules for franchising, based in large part on state and federal securities regulation. The rules are designed to counter the tendency in franchising to overhype the opportunity and to provide the prospective franchisee investor with key information on which to base a purchase decision. A number of states have also adopted regulations designed to protect franchise owners from the arbitrary termination of their rights.

The franchise laws are similar in many ways to the business opportunity laws discussed in earlier chapters and were adopted at about the same time. Both sets of laws require that the seller register the offering with state authorities and provide presale disclosure of material information to prospective investors. The similarities end there. The two business concepts are conceptually very different, and the disclosure document for franchising is far more extensive than the disclosure required for business opportunities.

Franchise regulation has a huge influence on how franchising is practiced. The following is a discussion of these rules of the franchise road.

HOW THE LAW DEFINES A FRANCHISE

How is a franchise defined under franchise laws? Ready for a little law school action? The law regulates a franchise transaction when three distinct elements are present:

1. The franchisor licenses the right to use its trademark in the operation of the business;

2. The franchisor prescribes in substantial part a marketing plan or provides significant assistance or control over the franchisee's business (some state definitions look for a "community of interest" between the franchisor and the franchisee); and

3. The franchisee is required to pay, directly or indirectly, a fee for the right to participate in the franchise program.

 **IN***sight*

As a prospective franchisee, you should have little concern about complying with the franchise investment laws. They impose no obligations on you. But recognizing a franchise when you see one could be an important asset in protecting yourself. If you see a franchise but someone tells you it is not one, ask why not, and listen carefully! You may want to share your notes with your attorney or the enforcement authorities in your state.

If one of these elements is missing, whatever the business transaction is, it is not regulated as a business franchise. In many circumstances the investment is then regulated as that close cousin, the "business opportunity."

It is quite possible to invest in a business program that enables you to start a business that is not a franchise. There are dozens and dozens of such programs available. You can spend a couple thousand dollars and receive a package of materials designed to teach you how to make money with a new business application of your computer. You are not granted the right to use a trademark, and you are expected to operate under your own name. It may be a business opportunity, but it is not a franchise.

THE CONSEQUENCES OF BEING A FRANCHISE

What if a transaction meets the franchise definition? Then there are three consequences:

1. ***Presale disclosure must be delivered.*** Under the FTC's Trade Regulation Rule on Franchising, if a franchise is offered anywhere in the United States, a franchisor must deliver a disclosure document to a prospective franchisee, using either the FTC's format or the Uniform Franchise Offering Circular (UFOC) format. The franchisor does not have to register or file anything with the FTC; complying with the disclosure requirements satisfies the requirements of the federal rule.

   The UFOC is a gold mine of information for the franchise investor. Ask for one early; it will help you evaluate the offering.

   When must the UFOC be delivered to the prospective franchisee? Either 1) at the first face-to-face personal meeting for the purpose of discussing the franchise sale, or 2) at least 10 business days (14 calendar days in Illinois) before money is paid for the franchise or a binding franchise agreement is signed by the franchisee, whichever comes first. That means that the franchisor is not required by law to deliver a UFOC until fairly far along in the sales process. Talking to a franchisor representative at a trade show exhibitor's booth is not considered to be a "first personal meeting" that would trigger disclosure obligations, even though it is "face to face." The disclosure obligation will trigger if the meeting is a detailed, extended discussion about the franchise opportunity.

2. ***The offering must comply with state law.*** Fourteen states require franchisors to file or register with the state officials prior to any offering activity taking place. The franchisor will submit its UFOC, adapted to meet the particular requirements of each state, along with an application form and the appropriate fees. State franchise examiners review the disclosure document to assure that it is complete. They do not determine if the offer is reasonable or exercise any judgment regarding whether it is a good deal, or fair. They only make sure that the franchisor has complied with the UFOC guidelines.

   When approved, the franchisor is authorized to sell franchises and must renew the registration at the end of the registration period. Some states will grant a registration period of a full calendar year; others such as California and Hawaii will automatically end the registration period a certain number of days after the end of the franchisor's fiscal year. That means a company with a fiscal year ending on December 31 remains registered in Hawaii until March 31 and in California until April 20.

3. ***Relationship laws may apply.*** A transaction meeting the franchise definition may also fall under the protections of the various state franchise relationship laws. These generally prohibit termination and nonrenewal of a franchise in the absence of "good cause."

So what does this mean for investors? Franchise investors receive a generous amount of valuable information in the disclosure document. If the franchisee is in one of the 14 registration states, it means that the franchisor has gone through the process of document review by state examiners and achieved registration, clearing an important hurdle in the life of a franchisor. It is not easy to become registered in these states, although some are tougher than others.

Registration is no guarantee for the investor, of course. It does not tell you anything about the company, and it is not a qualifier in any sense. It simply means that the company has taken an important step to comply with the law. It has filed its offering on the public record in that state and will remain under the annual scrutiny of the state officials.

If you live in one of the registration states (California, Hawaii, Illinois, Indiana, Maryland, Michigan, Minnesota, New York, North Dakota, Rhode Island, South Dakota, Virginia, Washington, Wisconsin), you should plan to call the appropriate agency (see appendix B) and confirm that the company is currently registered to offer and sell franchises.

SUMMARY NOTES

✓ If a business meets the legal definition of a franchise, it will be regulated as a franchise.

✓ The consequences of meeting the franchise definition include disclosure, registration in a number of states, and possible application of relationship laws.

✓ Registration under a state law is no guarantee of anything.

Action **PLAN**

Call the appropriate agencies to find out how franchising is regulated in your state. Keep addresses and phone numbers for key state officials on file so you can contact them later with specific questions.

CHAPTER 6

Make Sure You Are Well-Suited to Be a Franchisee

*B*ILL WAS EAGER TO GET INTO A GOOD BUSI-*ness and jumped at the chance to buy an established one in his home town when he heard it was up for sale. It was a holiday ham and sandwich shop, and Bill soon learned it was also franchised. This meant every aspect of the operation—from the cases used to display product to the uniforms worn by the counter staff—was dictated by the terms of an operating manual. He had always wanted to own a business in which he could express his own creativity and offbeat sense of humor. Looking at the detailed operational requirements, he now wondered whether he was cut out to be a franchisee.*

IS A FRANCHISE FOR EVERYONE?

Clearly, owning a franchise is not for everyone. A capable person in the wrong program is not likely to stay happy for very long. Buying into a franchise is especially risky since the investment can involve your life's savings and a long-term legal commitment.

Fiercely independent entrepreneurs are rarely happy in the franchise harness. If you are interested in running and designing every aspect of the operation, think twice before you buy that franchise. You might actually be better off with your own independent business. Most franchising programs impose a strict regimen on franchise owners, dictating everything from how to greet customers to how to prepare and present the product or service, and many people find the restrictions far too confining. They might be better off choosing a business opportunity program that offers more independence.

If you have been a secure employee of a large corporation for a long time, the jolt of small-business ownership can be difficult. Franchise owners have to put themselves completely into the daily operation of the business;

small-business owners do not delegate. They do whatever needs to be done. Remember the old line: You can always identify the owner of a small business—he or she is the one sweeping up after 6 o'clock.

Nevertheless, there are many downsized middle managers bringing a wealth of business savvy to the franchise market. They are at that stage in their careers where they have some capital to invest, are not interested in inventing a new (and risky) business concept, and yet are attracted to the dream of self-employment. For them, franchising may be the ticket.

QUESTIONS TO CONSIDER

A careful approach to deciding whether or not owning a franchise is for you starts with a self-examination and a brief planning exercise. Consider the following key questions:

- *Are you motivated to invest the time and energy—not to mention money—necessary for small-business ownership?* The first year of business can be especially trying; the time required to get a business up and running—even a sophisticated franchise—is intimidating. Your days of punching and watching the clock will be long gone. Small-business ownership requires a sea change in your mental attitudes toward work, and a new level of dedication and perseverance.

- *Is your family behind you?* Many businesses are designed for total family involvement. Even if you invest in one that is not, you cannot commit the time and energy needed without the full support of every member of your family. Have you discussed it in detail with them? Your spouse may be supportive but skeptical (which is healthy). Involve them in the decision-making process, and listen to all their doubts or concerns. Try to help your kids understand that they are part of the whole family effort. You may also want to seek out experienced businesspeople you know who can help make sure you are thinking straight and not just daydreaming. Ask them to serve on your informal board of advisors so you can turn to them with questions.

- *Have you evaluated your resources?* Take out a pad of paper and jot down all possible sources of investment capital. Include not only cash, securities and other liquid assets, but also insurance policies, the equity in your home and retirement funds. Don't forget what the bankers refer to as NAR and NAF ("nail a relative" and "nail a friend"): your well-heeled friends and relatives could make all the difference, especially if you need a cosignature or additional equity pledged as security when applying for financing. If your dear Aunt Edna once said she would back you in a business venture, now is the time to go see her.

  Consider that you may need to maintain a revenue stream while the new business is being established. Your spouse may want to land a job to make ends meet until your franchise is kicking out a salary, which may take a while. Talk to a banker and an accountant. Discuss what you are planning, and ask about sources of capital, loans, investors and angels.

- *Have you evaluated your dreams?* Dreams provide the courage and drive that new entrepreneurs need to make the leap of faith into business ownership. But you must transform your dreams into an action plan. If you dream of being wealthy and living in a million-dollar home, turn your attention to the steps it will take to get there. If you start with owning a retail business, research how much money such a business is likely to put in your pocket, and then determine how many of those businesses and how much time you will need to achieve your dream of a million-dollar house.

Use dollars in your calculations, and add time frames. Anticipate milestones along the path, and work back to where you are today. Make notes about what you need to accomplish to make it successfully to the next milestone, and before you know it you will have created what looks to others like a business plan, but to you is nothing more than your dream path.

- *Are you ready for the physical challenge?* This question surprises a lot of people. Depending, of course, on the type of business you get involved in, business ownership can be physically demanding. Your sleep patterns may change, and you may be on your feet for 12 hours or more a day. Daily frustrations and the heightened stress of responding to unfamiliar challenges will draw on your deepest energy resources. You will need physical stamina and a healthy, positive mental outlook. We strongly recommend that as part of your preparation for owning a business, you step up your exercise and stick to to a healthy diet. You will need every ounce of energy your personal fitness can deliver.

SUMMARY NOTES

✓ Owning a franchise is not for everyone. Strong-willed entrepreneurs who want to do things their own way may be unhappy owning a franchise.

✓ Before buying a franchise, consider the level of your motivation, how your family feels about the idea, your resources, how realistic your plans are, and whether you are ready for the physical challenge.

Action PLAN

Write out complete responses to the questions in the chapter (be honest here; no one else will see your answers), and file them in your business planning folder.

CHAPTER 7

Attending a Franchise Trade Show

*J*ENNIFER HAD NEVER BEEN TO A FRANCHISE *trade show before, but she was told it is a great place to get started in business and learn a bit about franchising and other packaged business programs. She had no plan or goals for the show, but she wanted to cruise through. However, she was overwhelmed by the atmosphere. "I got so wrapped up in the games and cookies offered at one booth, I never saw most of the exhibitors. Maybe I'll go again when it comes through town next year."*

Attending a franchise trade show is the quickest, most enlightening way to search for the franchise program that best suits your needs. It can also be fun.

However, it helps to understand what you can expect at the show and to go with a plan. As many as 300 companies may be standing at their booths ready to talk to investors about their programs. Up to 10,000 people could pass through the convention center, each exploring the idea of buying a franchise as the ticket to business success. The effect can be dazzling: so many concepts to evaluate and hardly enough time to see them all!

Of course, many of the investors attending the show, like Jennifer, are there out of curiosity and will have no focused plan. They may be lost in the crowd and have no clue as to how to get the most out of the show. We recommend that you be different.

PREPARE FOR THE SHOW

The first step in setting yourself apart from the crowd is to prepare and set goals for the session. Decide what types of businesses interest you. Are you fascinated by automobiles and interested in a business that is part of that industry? Do you want a high-end consumer products business that brings you into direct contact with your customers? What are your financial resources? Do you have the money and credit to establish a retail location, or would a lower-level investment be better, perhaps a business you can operate from home? Giving some thought to these questions will allow you to focus your time at the show on programs that fit your needs.

It's a good idea to leave your usual funky weekend attire at home and dress conservatively. Your goal is to show franchisor representatives that you are there for business. A casual business look is fine; a suit is optional, but be sure you look sharp. If possible, leave the kids at home and take personal business cards if you have them. If you don't, consider having some printed up. They are inexpensive, project a business-like impression, and relieve you of having to dictate your name, address and telephone number over and over. Don't forget your briefcase for the papers you collect, and take paper and pen for taking notes. You are not there just to pass a few idle hours and eat the free cookies. Show the representatives you meet that you are a serious prospect and there to consider their business program.

HOW TO DEVELOP AN EFFECTIVE METHOD OF ATTENDING

Plan to arrive early in the morning on one of the first days of the show. The typical franchise show lasts for three days, from Friday to Sunday. By Sunday, everyone is tired and spent, so try to be there on Friday (typically the least crowded day) or early Saturday (the most crowded day). This is when everyone involved should be fresh, with anticipation running high.

When you arrive at the convention center to register, take a few minutes with the show brochure to understand the floor layout, and review the list of companies that are exhibiting. Find a quiet corner with a cup of coffee and read what the show offers. Mark those companies whose offerings appeal to you and seem to fit your needs and financial resources. As you stop by their booths during the day, you can check them off and make sure you are covering all the promising companies on your list.

It is important to understand why the exhibitors are there. They consider the show a success if they collect the names of several serious, qualified candidates and come away with a list of leads for follow-up calls. We are told by franchisors that if they sell one or two franchises as the result of a trade show, they can cover all their exhibiting costs and make a profit. To get that list of hot leads, they have to make about 1,000 contacts a day.

Many franchise shows schedule seminars for investors on subjects like "How to Buy a Franchise" and "Financing Your Franchise Purchase." Mark the ones that look interesting, and schedule time to attend them. This may be the most valuable part of your day at the trade show, especially if you actually purchase a business package.

Try to approach the exhibit floor methodically. The franchise investment possibilities are virtually endless, and you may feel overwhelmed if you do not remember the interests you identified before attending the show. Stick to your plan, and find as many of the exhibitors you marked off earlier in the day as you can.

It is easy to underestimate the time needed to meet with all the interesting exhibitors on your list. You might spend as much as five or 10 minutes with each exhibitor and discover in a couple of hours that you have met with only 10 or 15 companies, a mere fraction of those on your list.

THE RIGHT QUESTIONS

The secret is not to spend time with exhibitors whose programs are inappropriate for you or out of your financial reach. Prepare three "knock-out" questions that will allow you to eliminate those companies quickly and move on to more promising conversations. What are those questions? That depends on you and your circumstances. If you have limited resources (and who doesn't?), try "What are the minimum financial qualifications for your applicants?" or "What kind of business experience do you require?" and "Are you looking for franchisees in my town?" The franchisor's answers will tell you quickly whether their program is within your reach. If it seems to be, stay and find out more. If there is no fit, move on.

If you want to find out more about a particular franchisor, here are a few more good queries to generate useful conversation:

- *How would you describe the culture in your franchise/business opportunity system?* This wonderfully open-ended probe should draw a variety of responses. Every franchise system has a cultural character. Is it clubby, friendly, chilly, all business or distant? Listen carefully to the answer. You will pick up some good information that does not appear in any glossy brochures.

- *What are your plans for growth in this region over the next three years?* The answer to this question will give you an idea of the effort and energy that the organization has committed to your market. If you get a vague answer or a grandiose statement suggesting that the company expects to take over the retail world in that modest time period, well, you've been forewarned.

- *May I take a complete set of promotional materials?* Many exhibitors will have a limited supply of full brochures behind the table and less expensive fliers out front for the hundreds of casual visitors who stop by. Express serious interest in the investment, and ask if there are other materials you can study at home. Request a copy of the company's Uniform Franchise Offering Circular. If it is not readily available, ask if the company can send you

one, along with a set of promotional materials and an application package.

- *Tell me about your training program.* Find out how long it is (i.e., two weeks at the company headquarters and 10 days in the field), where it takes place and the general subjects covered. Look for a well-organized plan that combines classroom time with field orientation. A solid training program is the mark of a careful franchisor who is interested in the business success of its franchise owners.

- *Tell me about your franchisee support program.* Good support from a franchisor can spell the difference between failure and success. Look for support from the very beginning, as soon as you start to write a business plan. Will the company help you find financing? Will people be available when you are opening for business? Will someone be at the other end of the phone when things get crazy?

A question you might expect to be on this list, but that isn't, is "How much money can I expect to make with one of your businesses?" This is a difficult question for a franchisor to answer. Most would like to boast about the potential of their franchise, but it is a subject that is closely regulated under the franchise laws. In addition, no franchisor knows how much you can expect to make in a franchised business. The variables—including your business acumen and industry—make such estimates impossible.

Slinging numbers at a trade show would be a misleading and unfair inducement by the seller to get you to purchase the franchise. Franchisors generally do know how their existing franchise owners have performed, and some companies will make this information available in the disclosure document. Our best advice: check it out for yourself. Go visit as many franchise owners as time and distances allow. Ask them how they have performed and whether, knowing what they now know, they would make the investment again. Their answers will be invaluable in your assessment of the franchise.

It is also important to understand that a franchise trade show event is designed to make an initial contact only. It is a meeting place that operates merely to introduce sellers to potential investors. The conversation on the floor of the trade show is preliminary and rarely delves deeply into the investment itself. The more in-depth discussion usually takes place in a follow-up meeting or sometimes in a nearby hospitality suite the seller has reserved. Leave behind one of your business cards so sellers may send you additional information. And make sure that you have contact information, either a contact listing in the program or the business card of the sales representative.

TRADE SHOW RED FLAGS

Risks abound in the search for a franchise. While at the trade show, keep alert to red flags that should tell you to avoid one company or another. Here are a few:

Shouting Performance Numbers

Dollar signs have no place at a franchise trade show. They can be the source of any number of legal problems for franchisors and should be avoided by well-disciplined companies. If performance information is discussed, check out item 19 in the company's UFOC, which you will see sometime after the show. Any big talk about what you will earn should be a warning sign that this is not an experienced or well-disciplined representative. The talk may also be totally misleading.

The Hard Sell

A solid franchise investment should sell itself. If you find yourself at the receiving end of a hard sell, back slowly away.

The Start-Up Rookie

A franchising company with no track record presents risks that you should carefully evaluate. You may determine that the program is new enough and exciting enough that the potential for success outweighs the risks, but protect yourself as best you can. A new franchisor cannot offer the most attractive features of the franchise concept: a business that has been proven in the marketplace and experience that can help you handle the challenges of the business.

The Franchise Fad

Fads come and go in the franchise community. Remember that your investment needs to survive for the long term. Look out for concepts that are the flavor of the month but may have little staying power.

Limited Regional Hits

Do not assume that because a shop can sell truckloads of fresh-baked whole wheat bread in Cincinnati, the same product will move as well in Palm Beach. It may not be true, and you can't afford to prove it with your life's savings.

The Poorly Financed Franchisor

Most franchise financial advisors will tell you that one of the most common business mistakes made in this field is for the franchisor not to have enough capital to finance its rapid growth. The resulting under-financed company is weak and may not be in a position to deliver on its promises to new franchisees. The best measure of the franchisor's financial standing is its audited financial statements, which you will find as part of the UFOC.

THE FOLLOW-UP

Expect a follow-up call or visit after the show from any company where you showed serious interest. Remember, the companies that prepared and

INsight

Your follow-up call may not come from the person you met at the show, but from a staff representative at the company's headquarters or a regional office. Find out who you are talking to, and get a good idea of where they fit into the company's organization.

staffed a booth invested heavily in finding you—a qualified and interested investor. The follow-up is your opportunity to dig into the investment and explore every question that might occur to you. Be diligent and skeptical in your evaluation of the information you collect from the franchisor.

A franchise trade show may be your first step toward an exciting new business future. Increase the odds of your personal success by preparing carefully for the show and evaluating the opportunities presented with a detailed—and realistic—eye.

SUMMARY NOTES

✓ A franchise trade show can be overwhelming if you are not prepared for it.

✓ Prepare for the show with a battle plan.

✓ Ask the right questions on the floor. If there is no fit with your plan, quickly move on down the aisle.

✓ Look for the red flags.

✓ Follow up with your show contacts to confirm you are serious about finding the right franchise program.

Action PLAN

Find out when a good franchise trade show is coming to a city near you. Read a current issue of *Entrepreneur* magazine and other business trade publications. Franchise trade show schedules from around the country are usually calendared there. Also try searching the Internet for trade show cities and dates. (See the next chapter for ideas on using the Internet.)

CHAPTER 8

Research on the Internet

MARCIE WAS DETERMINED TO FIND A business package that would allow her to work part-time at home around her young children and bring in more money for the family. Getting out of the house was difficult with the kids. She heard that a business opportunity and franchise show was coming to the downtown arena in a few weeks, and she wanted to find out a lot more about the whole concept of a home business. Marcie was a new Internet user but thought it would be a good place to start.

Enter the word "franchise" into any of the competent search engines on the Internet, and you may feel a bit like Alice falling down the rabbit hole.

A Google search kicks up 3,220,000 franchise listings; on Yahoo! 3.3 million. Head down any of these pathways, and you will quickly find yourself browsing through dozens of sites extolling the virtues of various franchises, touting association membership benefits and describing individual franchise investment benefits.

WHAT TO LOOK FOR

The Internet is an essential tool in the search for the right franchise. It has its strengths and weaknesses, of course, but you cannot afford to overlook it. Its greatest strength is that it gives you the ability to browse for ideas and prospects. If you have leads you want to check out or if you are curious about a particular franchise, a quick search will provide at least brochure-level information about the program.

The law has been slow to catch up to the franchise regulation implications of electronic commerce on the Internet. The FTC has promised to address the rules surrounding electronic distribution of the UFOC and the posting of disclosure information on a Web site, but the rules are not yet final. Under current law, with rare exception, a franchisor may not comply with disclosure requirements by delivering a document in electronic form. This may change as early as 2004. Some states have issued regulations telling franchisors what disclaimers they must put on their sites, and you will find them in the small print of well-managed sites. In essence, the disclaimer says that the information on the site does not constitute an offer in franchise registration states. Seeing this disclaimer conveys to the experienced eye a subtle but important message: The company is receiving, and paying attention to, informed legal advice. You should wonder about franchise company sites that do not have this legal disclaimer.

HANDLING THE HIGH HYPE-TO-FACT RATIO

The Internet's weakness is the low quality and reliability of the information at its busy commercial locations. Lists of available "franchises" are littered with nonfranchised business opportunity offerings, and much of the information you see is essentially sponsored advertising. If you understand this inescapable feature of the Internet and make allowances for it, you will not be misled.

 IN*sight*

The hype level tells you something about franchising sales. This is a market that enjoys a robust level of aggressive selling.

THE IMPORTANCE OF FOCUS

The FTC has assembled a surprisingly useful site for franchise investors (www.ftc.gov). Here you will find general information about franchising, the

federal laws that apply to a franchise sale, and current and recent investigations and legal actions taken by the FTC against offending franchisors.

Also, Entrepreneur.com offers a site specifically for franchise seekers—it includes franchise listings and in-depth articles. Another information-packed site is www.franchise.org, the site of the International Franchise Association.

These are just a start. The problem with the Internet, of course, is the sensation of trying to take a sip from a fire hose of information. The sites dedicated to franchising go on and on and may cause even an experienced Internet researcher to suffer from MEGO (my eyes glaze over) in no time.

The secret to effective use of the Internet for your franchise search is the same as with other kinds of franchise research: focus, focus, focus. Know your targets and general interest areas. Don't be distracted by the glitter, the pop-up ads, the eager virtual experts. Plan to use your computer connection for first-level contact and brochure-level information. Then roll up your sleeves and plan for person-to-person meetings and in-depth discussions about the franchise opportunity.

SUMMARY NOTES

✓ Use the Internet judiciously. There is a high hype-to-fact ratio at most information sites.
✓ The Internet is great for brochure-level information.
✓ Focus your search to your areas of interest.

Action **PLAN**

Spend some time on the Net and bookmark the sites that seem most helpful.

CHAPTER 9

Organizing the Information You Gather

AL WAS NOT WELL-ORGANIZED IN HIS JOB life, but then he never had a job that required him to be. He was determined to find a good franchise. He had the money to buy one, and he had been in contact with a couple dozen companies. The amount of paper generated in his search surprised him, and it had formed a few messy piles on the floor of his bedroom. Now he was going to a trade show and dreaded the prospect of taking more paper home to his piles. Maybe this wasn't for him.

The franchise search process can generate a lot of paper, and you will quickly become discouraged if you do not prepare to receive and keep it in an organized fashion. This is particularly true if you attend franchise trade shows, which are notorious for generating piles of promotional pieces of paper. (And you wondered why they handed you that big plastic bag with handles when you walked in!)

You may also receive a stack of promotional materials when you write to franchisors for information.

INsight

From the company's point of view, distributing glossy brochures is a cost of being a franchisor, and it can be quite expensive. More and more franchisors are putting their brochure money into Web site presentations. You may find that the quality of the brochures you receive will be modest, but the Web sites will be eye-popping.

SETTING UP A FILING SYSTEM

So get prepared before you go. Set up a few files, one for each seller with internal tabs or manila folders for different subjects. Take a quick trip to an office supply store, and buy a few packets of file folders, pocket files and tab labels.

Divide each seller's file into subsections, such as:

- **Promotional pieces.** Drop into this folder all the glossy brochures, fliers, handouts and form letters you pick up.
- **Letters, notes, contact information.** Take notes on each of the companies you visit at the trade show or elsewhere, and keep all the personalized letters they send you as well as copies of any letters you write. Staple into the file—or slide into a plastic sleeve—all the sales representatives' business cards you are handed.
- **UFOC.** After you read and mark up the UFOC with any questions or comments, drop it in the file for future use. If the franchisor is a serious prospect, you will want to take this document to your attorney and accountant. It is amazing how many people buy a franchise yet never read the UFOC. You must take the time to look through this important document. If you get serious about a program, take the documents to your attorney and your CPA for review.

- **Contracts.** Form contracts will be included in the UFOC, but other versions will be provided to you as you approach closing.
- **Site information, lease forms.** As you meet with landlords to review available sites for the business you have in mind, keep the information in its own section of your file.

With these files prepared ahead of time, you will be able to quickly file all the paperwork you bring home and have it easily accessible for follow-up reading.

Retain all your files until you have actually made a choice and invested in a franchise. Only then should you sort through them, keeping in your permanent records all of the documents relating to the business you purchase or remain interested in, and discarding the rest.

SUMMARY NOTES

✓ Prepare to organize informational materials before the franchise search begins.
✓ Set up labeled file folders so that you can file your papers when you get home from a trade show or other franchise or business opportunity meeting.

Action **PLAN**

Head to the supply store for the materials you will need to organize your franchise search files.

CHAPTER 10

Understanding the UFOC

ROBIN INQUIRED ABOUT A FRANCHISE PRO-
gram and received a heavy spiral-
bound book in the mail. It was at least
an inch and a half thick! She did not
know what it was or why they sent it. She
flipped through it but did not expect to spend
the time it would take to read it all.

WHAT IS A UFOC?

Robin didn't know it yet, but what she had
was the franchisee's bible: the Uniform
Franchise Offering Circular, or UFOC.

Like Robin, all prospective franchisees
receive detailed and extensive information
about the franchisor, the franchise being
offered and the franchise system. This gives
you a distinct advantage over other investors.
It contains sample forms of every contract
you will be asked to sign as well as a set of
audited financial statements for the franchisor. In franchise circles, the UFOC is also

referred to as a "franchise disclosure document" or an "offering prospectus."

The UFOC format and presentation is prescribed by state and federal law and is
designed to deliver key information about the
franchise investment. In it you will find 23
different items of information that are all
important to your investment decision. If
there is one piece of advice you take, it should
be to read the UFOC carefully. Sure, it may
read like an insurance policy in places, but it
is a treasure trove of details for the alert
investor. The good news is, all UFOC documents must be written in "plain English"—no
Latin phrases, no "hereinafters," no "wherein-
befores," and no run-on sentences that only a
lawyer could love. At least, that's the theory.

Does everyone get a UFOC? As a practical
matter, franchisors do not deliver a UFOC to
everyone who applies for a franchise. The typical UFOC runs from 75 to 350 pages in
length and can be expensive to reproduce in

INsight

Put yourself in the franchisor's shoes. You want to deliver a UFOC only to candidates who have been qualified and appear serious about the investment because each copy costs several dollars to reproduce. Let them know you are serious about their program and are genuinely interested in the information contained in their UFOC, and you increase your chances of receiving one early in the process.

large numbers. Expect to receive a copy as you progress through the evaluation process or if you visit the company's headquarters for a "first personal meeting," which will trigger the legal requirement that you receive a UFOC.

The best approach is to request a UFOC early in your discussions. If you are at all serious about a particular franchise, it makes no sense to spend time on it until you have a chance to read the UFOC.

THE SECTIONS OF THE UFOC

How do you read and comprehend a UFOC? Some sections are more important than others, but all are worth your attention.

Here is a short rundown of what to look for, section by section.

The Cover Page

This page shows the franchise logo. It also has a summary of the initial franchise fees and the total investment, followed by "Risk Factors" in all capitals. Most of the risk factors are boilerplate and address whether the franchise agreement requires the franchisee to litigate or arbitrate outside of the franchisee's home state. They also caution if the franchisor has little or no experience in business or

in franchising. Make a note to discuss any such risk factor with your attorney.

Item 1: The Franchisor, Its Predecessors and Affiliates

This is a concise overview of the franchisor, its formal corporate name and state of incorporation, and its background, business experience, predecessors and affiliates. It tells you how long the company has been offering franchises and gives a general description of the franchisee's potential competition. Read the franchisor's business record carefully.

Item 2: Business Experience

This section gives you a bare-bones five-year outline of the business experience of the franchisor's key executives. It's just the facts: title, employer, dates of employment and city. Note if there are any gaps in the employment history (such as might be created by some time out of work).

Item 3: Litigation

This section requires the franchisor to reveal details about specific types of litigation that may be "material" (important) to prospective franchisees. If in the past 10 years the company itself or any of its directors or officers listed in item 2 have been defendants in cases involving claims of franchise law, securities law, fraud, unfair or deceptive trade practices or comparable allegations, you will see it described here. You will also see arbitration actions listed in this section.

Don't be alarmed if there are one or two cases disclosed here. It is a rare franchisor, or one that has not been in the franchising business long, that has no litigation to disclose in item 3. In this great country anyone can file a lawsuit alleging anything, so the cases disclosed may not convey the right impression of the company or its dispute resolution style. On the other hand, an item 3 that discloses many cases may tell you a lot about the company.

The best approach is to make a note to discuss with your own attorney and your franchisor representative any questions you have about disclosures in this item. You may also want to ask any existing franchisees you interview about the company's litigation history. They can probably shed light on what the company's litigation style means to franchisees.

Item 4: Bankruptcy

If there is a bankruptcy in the 10-year background of the franchisor, its predecessors, affiliates, partners or officers, you will see it briefly described in item 4.

Item 5: Initial Franchise Fee

This section details all moneys paid to the franchisor prior to the time the franchisee opens for business. Typically, the franchisor imposes an initial franchise fee that is a lump sum payment—as much as $20,000, $30,000 or more—to be made at the time the franchise agreement is signed. Look for other fees, such as training fees, that may be included, and the circumstances in which they might be refundable.

Item 6: Other Fees

The chart in item 6 summarizes all the recurring or isolated fees that the franchisee must pay to the franchisor or its affiliates during the course of the franchise relationship. The royalty is listed, of course. The chart also includes any continuing advertising contributions to an advertising fund or otherwise, cooperative advertising organizations that charge advertising fees, transfer fees and audit costs.

Item 7: Initial Investment

This section of the UFOC is one of the most important for your planning purposes. In chart form, it summarizes the total initial expenses you can expect when opening the franchised business. It tells you what categories of expenses are typical, to whom payments are to be made, and when they are due. It also tells you whether payments are refundable under any circumstances. Use these figures when preparing your own business plan, but check with a good accountant and existing franchisees in the system to see if there are other expenses you should anticipate that are not included in item 7. For instance, if you borrow a substantial portion of the investment, you will have debt service to anticipate that will not appear in this disclosure document. Consider this item as the starting point in your financial planning.

Item 8: Restrictions on Sources of Products and Services

The area of product sourcing is one of the most important aspects of franchise operations, but it is often well-hidden. Imagine that you are considering a franchise for an ice cream shop that sells a premium ice cream that is manufactured especially for the franchise system. There is only one source of the product, the franchisor. You are required by the franchise agreement to purchase only from the designated source. Would you know whether $11.35 per tub is a reasonable price for ice cream inventory? What will you do if the franchisor raises its prices and cuts down your (already razor-thin) margins? Some franchisees feel trapped by a confining supply arrangement where they have no opportunity to seek out a competitive price. Supply arrangements are described in this item but may not paint the entire picture for you.

Item 9: Franchisee's Obligations

This item is nothing more than a cross-reference chart showing you where certain subjects are addressed in the franchise agreement.

Item 10: Financing

If the franchisor offers financing, either directly or indirectly, you will find it detailed here. It should lay out the terms of the financing in chart form and specify which portion of the purchase qualifies for the financing. Copies of any loan documents will be included as exhibits.

Item 11: Franchisor's Obligations

This provides a lengthy recital of the promises made by the franchisor, the services they will supply to you in the course of the franchise relationship, and details about some of the training and other programs offered. This is the longest section of the UFOC and it contains a wealth of information. Among the topics addressed are the pre-opening and post-opening services to be provided by the franchisor, the time that typically elapses between the date of signing the franchise agreement and opening the business, the specifications for any computerized cash registers or computers necessary in the business, and a detailed description of the training program.

Item 12: Territory

This is a description of any territorial rights granted as a part of the franchise agreement. It is fair to say that most, but not all, franchise systems include some form of territorial protection for the franchisee. The key point for the prospective franchisee is to read this section carefully and without the natural assumptions you may have of these intangible concepts. For instance, it may include a promise by the franchisor that says something like, "We will not develop ourselves or grant franchises to others to develop another franchise in your territory." Does this mean that you have absolute exclusivity in the territory? No. In fact, it is a rather narrow promise that prevents the establishment of competing units in your area but does not prevent the franchisor from selling product to customers in your territory. Ask your attorney to review the promises in this section so that you are clear on the nature of the rights you are receiving. They are important.

Item 13: Trademarks

It has been said that the trademark is the cornerstone of the franchise relationship. Item 13 provides some key details about the primary trademarks associated with the franchise package. First it tells you whether the trademark has been registered with the U.S. Patent and Trademark Office. While that registration is not necessary for a protectable trademark, it is an important step for the franchisor, and if it has not been done, it tells you and your attorney a lot. Having an unregistered mark may increase your risks that someone else with the same mark can claim superior legal rights and force you and the franchisor to find another trade name. If the franchisor has any litigation pending that pertains to the marks, it is described here, as are promises made by the franchisor to protect franchisees from claims of trademark infringement by third parties. Make sure that your attorney reviews item 13 and advises you of any apparent problems.

Item 14: Patents, Copyrights and Proprietary Information

The majority of UFOCs contain boilerplate language in this section because so few franchise programs have patent rights that pertain to the franchise. What is usually protected by copyright are the operations manual and other printed advertising and operating materials. There is also language in this section protecting the "trade secrets" and other "proprietary rights" of the franchisor in various aspects of the franchised business.

Item 15: Obligation to Participate in the Actual Operation of the Franchise Business

If the contract requires you to be present at the business for a certain number of hours each week, or that a trained manager supervise the operation at all times, it should be disclosed here.

Item 16: Restrictions on What the Franchisee May Sell

If you will be required to sell only approved products, or only those supplied to you by approved suppliers, it will say so here.

Item 17: Renewal, Termination, Transfer and Dispute Resolution

This multipage chart provides the reader with a full cross-reference to the franchise agreement along with a summary of the key legal provisions relating to renewal (what happens at the end of the contract term), termination (the circumstances under which you and the franchisor may choose to end the contract before its expiration), transfer (the restrictions on your right to sell all or part of your franchised business), and dispute resolution (where and how legal disputes will be resolved). These topics are the most legally intense sections of the franchise agreement and deserve careful review by your attorney.

Item 18: Public Figures

This section describes the terms of any endorsement or other involvement by a well-known figure who is promoting the franchise.

Item 19: Earnings Claims

This item may provide some of your most important clues to answering the question, "How much money does one of these babies make?" Franchisors are not required to supply any performance information about their program, but if they do, it must be disclosed here. Only about 20 percent of all UFOCs contain performance information. There could be a number of reasons for a company leaving this disclosure blank. It may be that they are concerned about potential misrepresentations and legal liability if they list performance figures for their existing franchisees. It may also be that the performance statistics do not tell a compelling story, and the company does not want to focus your attention on the low performance of its franchised businesses. If you do find performance information, be sure to use it when you prepare your business plan. Then supplement the bare statistics with franchisee interviews. If the company does not disclose anything, find out why, and press for performance information from other sources. Again, existing franchisees are the best place to start.

Item 20: List of Outlets

This section includes a series of charts about the growth or contraction of the franchise system for the prior three years as well as information about existing company-owned units and projected growth of the system during the coming year. There is an attached list of the names, addresses and telephone numbers of current franchisees, as well as a list of the names and the last-known addresses and telephone numbers of all franchisees who have left the system during the prior year or have not been in contact with the franchisor for at least 10 weeks. These lists are often attached as exhibits to the UFOC. Find out from these former franchise owners why they left and whether it was related to shortcomings in the program itself.

Item 21: Financial Statements

The law requires that a franchisor attach to the body of the UFOC as an exhibit a copy of its financial balance sheet and operating statements for the prior three years, all of which must be audited (or "certified") by a certified public accountant. If the franchisor has been in existence for less than three years or has only recently begun franchising, you may find fewer than three years of financial statements. However, the company is required to provide at least one certified statement, even if it is only an opening balance sheet. Make sure your accountant sees this information. You want to make sure the franchisor is on solid financial footing and in business for the long haul.

Item 22: Contracts

You will find a description of all the contracts you need to sign in order to purchase the franchise in this item. Copies of the contracts will also be attached to the UFOC as an exhibit. If the franchisor provides loan documents, equipment or real estate leases, they are also included in an exhibit, along with a sample franchise agreement form. Before you close on the transaction, make sure your attorney has a chance to review all these contracts.

Item 23: Receipt

The UFOC requires that two receipts be attached to it, one for the franchisee and the other for the franchisor. This is important for the franchisor in case they have to prove they delivered a disclosure document to you and that you received it. (Was it at least 10 business days before you signed the franchise agreement?) You must sign and date the receipt.

That's a lot of investment information in one document—and well worth reading through it.

SUMMARY NOTES

✓ The UFOC is a key document in your search for a franchise.

✓ READ the UFOC!

✓ Have professionals help you with parts of this document.

✓ Review the various sections of the UFOC. Some are more important than others.

✓ The UFOC does not contain *all* of the information you need to evaluate the franchise.

Action PLAN

Get a UFOC—any UFOC—and flip through it to see how it is organized and where to find key information.

CHAPTER 11

Five Great Questions *Not* Answered in the UFOC

*E*LLEN SLOGGED THROUGH THE UFOC FOR *the franchise she was interested in and was proud of herself. She had every reason to be impressed by the program and wondered if there was anything else she needed to dig into. Surely, she thought, this huge tome told her everything she needed to know. Right?*

THE UFOC DOES NOT DELIVER EVERYTHING

Ellen makes a mistake if she assumes that the UFOC will tell her everything she needs to know about the franchise investment. It is designed by regulators to deliver information that they consider "material" to the investment—that is, information that should be important to the investor. However, there are some gaping holes in the UFOC, key pieces of information it does not

convey that are material to your purchase decision. Take a look at five of the most important areas. There may be more, depending on the type of business you are buying.

- *Pricing/product distribution.* Item 8 of the UFOC delivers some of the product and pricing information you need, but the guidelines for franchisors to follow in preparing this section are complex and cumbersome, resulting in confusing disclosures that are not particularly helpful. After all, smooth product sourcing, the savings on prices available to franchisees based on large group purchases, and carefully considered product specifications are all fundamental business reasons for buying a franchise. If this part of the business is not working well, there may be little reason to go into the franchise.

  Make a point of exploring product dynamics with the franchisees you meet.

47

IN*sight*

We talked to a franchisee of an ice cream concept who was beside himself. He has an MBA and thought his business looked great on paper. He liked the taste of the product, the well-designed brand name, the modern look of the stores, the sales figures he had seen, and the location in an enclosed mall without a food court. What he didn't count on was the price of the premium ice cream, which, under the terms of the franchise agreement, could be purchased only from the franchisor. The price was way too high, but he didn't realize it until he got into the business and learned about wholesale ice cream prices. The president of the company told him that there was no UFOC because, they were "not a public company." "How was I to know about that?" he says. Now he is saddled with an expensive business that is breaking even but not making much of a profit, and he is embarrassed to admit this could happen to an MBA.

Press the franchisor representatives about purchasing arrangements, any buying cooperatives in your area and pricing strategies. Check the franchise agreement and any other paperwork from the franchisor describing product matters. In many franchises, this is the economic engine of the business. It never hurts to look under the hood and make sure it is running well.

- ***Franchisee associations.*** Nowhere in the UFOC is a franchisor required to disclose the existence of a franchisee association or advisory council. Yet this is an important aspect of the franchise program for a new investor. The presence of a strong association that is well-attended and governed by franchisees is an attractive asset of any franchise program.

I have long suspected that omitting any mention of a franchisee association in the UFOC is due to the swift internal political waters surrounding franchisee associations. Some associations are created by the franchisor and promoted by the company; others are "renegade associations" created by the franchisees and resented by the franchisor. Ask current franchisees about the role they play through an association or a franchisee council.

- ***Training.*** One of the keys to franchisee success is solid training. The UFOC will give you some of the basic facts, including a chart outlining the sections of the training, who teaches the sections, the experience of the trainers, how much time is devoted to each topic, and where the training takes place. However, you need assurances about the program that cannot be delivered in a disclosure document. Is the training effective? Do franchisees feel that they are well-prepared to run a successful

IN*sight*

A franchisee association or council organizes and provides to the franchisor and all franchisees a valuable franchisee viewpoint of the business. Franchisee associations generally meet on a regular basis, and the prudent franchisor listens carefully to the advice and recommendations offered. They can provide new investors with a knowledgeable perspective independent of the franchisor and an in-depth evaluation of the whole franchise organization.

business upon completing it? Is the training based on current thinking, and is it the best available in the field? Is it complete, and how much of it is hands-on, under supervision? Be sure you explore these ideas with franchisees and your franchisor representatives.

- *Market for product/service.* This is a basic but intangible question that is difficult to address in a disclosure document: Is the market for the product or service a strong one? Is the growth of the market for the business on the rise or decline?

- *Franchisor support.* The language in a franchise agreement that describes the level of the franchisor's continuing support may be surprising. You are likely to find something like: "The franchisor will provide such continuing advice and support as it deems appropriate in its absolute discretion."

How's that for reassurance?! Attorneys for franchisors learned decades ago that specific promises of support in the franchise agreement, such as quarterly meetings, monthly newsletters and regular telephone calls, would lead to legal trouble when the franchisor's business practices changed. And they always change. The result is the smallest, most flexible promise of support imaginable.

Even though the promises might be modest, the practice is important. Find out exactly—from franchisees and the franchisor's representatives—what the company does for its new franchisees when they are planning to locate the business, when they are hiring staff, and during the opening and start-up phase. Is help available? Is it responsive? Will the franchisor be there to help if and when things go wrong?

SUMMARY NOTES

✓ As lengthy as it is, the UFOC will not deliver all the information you need to know about a franchise program.

✓ Look to some key topics for more information: product distribution, franchisee associations, training, the market for the product and/or service, and franchisee support by the franchisor.

Action PLAN

Write a single-page list of questions and topics you want to discuss with any franchisor representative you meet. Ask your attorney and accountant if you should add other questions to your list.

CHAPTER 12

The Key Sections of the Franchise Agreement

*B*ILL RECEIVED HIS FRANCHISE AGREEMENT *and figured he'd just look it over himself. Why hire an attorney? He knew attorneys could be expensive. After all, the contract was in English and looked straightforward to him. Sure it was long and the language was a little dense, but it was registered under Bill's state franchise law and seemed to be fully described in the UFOC. What could go wrong?*

UNDERSTANDING THE BASIC DYNAMIC OF THE FRANCHISE AGREEMENT

Bill is setting himself up for an expensive lesson. The agreement that grants a franchisee the right to operate a business in the franchisor's system is a complex commercial contract. It is designed to create a continuing business relationship that could span 20 years or more. It grants a panoply of intangible "intellectual property" rights, describes

product and service standards, and sets the ground rules for the transfer, renewal and termination of the relationship.

This agreement is not an easy document to read or understand, and it makes sense to take it to an attorney who can help you understand it in detail. While the size, shape and style of franchise agreements are tailored to each system, many of their basic features are universal. You will be well ahead of the franchise game if you comprehend the basic legal dynamics of this complex contract.

KEY PROVISIONS CONSIDERED
Intellectual Property Rights

A franchise agreement has been described as a trademark license with overdrive. It grants to the franchisee the limited right to use the trademarks, techniques, procedures, trade dress and know-how that comprise the franchise system. These rights are "limited" so

IN*sight*

A franchise is, at its essence, the licensing of intellectual property. All the valuable information delivered to the franchisee, from the trademark, to the operating manuals, to the techniques taught in training, to the color designs of a retail franchise, is a form of intangible intellectual property.

that the franchisor can preserve its ownership rights of trademarks, copyrights and trade secrets.

Look closely at these terms:

- *Trademark.* This a word, name, phrase, symbol, logo, or in some cases a design that traditionally represents the source of a product or service. A leading example is McDonald's® brand sandwiches, including the famous Big Mac® sandwich. A trademark owner has the legal right to license other people to use the trademark, and those licenses generally require correct display of the mark. If the colors of red and yellow in the McDonald's golden arches brand name are a bit off—if they turn out maroon and gold—you can expect the trademark owner to object. A "service mark" is the same thing as a trademark, but it specifically identifies a service, not a product.

- *Franchise system techniques and procedures.* In a franchise system, these terms denote the specifications, equipment and routines that are part of the franchise rights and obligations. They are usually found in an operating manual provided by the franchisor. In a restaurant franchise, for instance, the operating manual details the preparation of all menu items and their components, as well as things such as the timing of cooking and the temperature of cooking oil. Equipment specifications

are included, as well as the uniform attire of employees. Many of these techniques that are not obvious to the public may be claimed by the franchisor as trade secrets, which are confidential and not to be disclosed. All franchisees need to be aware of claimed trade secrets and take steps to keep them confidential.

- *Trade dress.* This is a legal term that describes the appearance of a product, product packaging, or the distinctive style of a building or restaurant. Trade dress may be protected under the law in the same fashion as a trademark. What does this mean to a franchisee? If you operate a restaurant franchise in a building with a distinctive color design or roof line, those features may have to be changed if you leave the system because they are owned by the franchisor.

- *Know-how.* This is often used to describe the knowledge and entire set of techniques that go into a franchise system. It includes the franchisor's experience in business and its knowledge of the bumps and bruises of the marketplace and how to avoid them, and it is imparted to the franchisee in a healthy franchise system.

- *Copyright.* This is the legal protection of an original work that is fixed in a tangible form, including books, songs, plays, software and all printed material. The legal copyright protects the author's exclusive right to use and exploit the value of the work. It cannot be published, copied or used without the author's permission. An author—and this is important—cannot protect an idea but can claim a copyright for the original expression of an idea (like a novel or a franchise operations manual). The franchise system's operations manual, advertising and other printed material may be copyright-protected by the franchisor. As a franchisee, you may be restricted in the ways you can use and exploit these materials for your own purposes.

- **Patent.** A patent is a property right, secured in the U.S. Constitution, protecting the rights to an invention, new device or innovation. As with a trademark, the owner has the right to license the use of his or her patented device to other people.

- **License rights.** The franchisee receives the right to use and display the trademark, or a family of trademarks, only as the franchisor authorizes, and only during the term of the franchise agreement. This means that all signs displaying the mark, and all printed materials, vehicles and even Web locations used by the franchisee, must be approved in form, color and design by the franchisor.

Although this is a point of some contention in the franchise community, the "goodwill" of the franchised business represented by the trademark—which is to say much of the goodwill of the business itself—remains in the ownership of the franchisor, not the franchisee. In that sense, a franchise agreement is similar to a commercial lease: At the end of the lease term, the property that is granted reverts completely to the owner, not the tenant.

The same may be said of any of the other intellectual property of the franchise system. Its use is licensed only in the manner prescribed and only for the term of the franchise agreement. When the franchise agreement is expired or terminated, all rights to use the trademarks, copyrighted material, patents and/or trade secrets will also cease.

Contract Flexibility Over Time

How does the franchise relationship handle the marketplace changes that occur in the franchise system over a number of years? The changed appearance of American business establishments in the past 20 years, or even 10 years, is dramatic. Look at a picture of a McDonald's restaurant or a Holiday Inn from the 1980s. They've definitely changed!

Franchise relationships must allow for change over time, and they do it by incorporating a reference in the contract to a living, changing set of policies, standards, guidance and know-how contained in a confidential set of documents, usually called operating manuals. The manuals are typically updated as changes in the system occur or new policies are adopted.

The franchise agreement also usually describes a dynamic franchise system that changes over time. The parties stipulate that many aspects of the franchise will require alteration as the years go by.

Franchise agreements accommodate changes over time by expressly anticipating them, while assuring the franchisee that the fundamental rights of the contract will not change. While franchisees clearly want to receive their full contract rights and the undiluted benefit of their bargain, they also want the franchisor to take the lead in keeping their business concept fresh and competitive in the marketplace. Obviously, this creates something of a dynamic legal tension for the franchisee and franchisor. What is fundamental and what is allowed to change over time?

While there is no easy answer, the courts and franchise systems ask whether a particular change is "material" to the franchisee's business. Is a proposed change so important (or fundamental) that it would have affected the franchisee's decision to purchase the franchise if they had known that such a change would be made to the program? If it is material or fundamental to the franchise, it may be in violation of the contract's promises to the franchisee.

Product Standards

The essential genius of franchising is the delivery of consistent products or services through independent businesses licensed to operate under a universal display mark. Isn't it remarkable that a Big Mac® sandwich purchased at a McDonald's in Bangor, Maine, tastes the same as one bought in Hawaii or Australia? What is more remarkable is that all the ingredients and sandwich components are provided by unaffiliated, third-party suppliers to the McDonald's system.

The franchise agreement addresses the requirements of product and service supply in one of several different ways, reflecting varying degrees of control that the company needs to exercise over the delivery of the products or services of the franchised business. In some systems, of course, the franchisor is the manufacturer of the product line carried by the franchisee, and the franchise is itself a "product franchise" through which independent franchisees distribute the line.

In most business format franchise programs, franchisees are required to purchase only from suppliers who have received the company's prior written approval. If the franchisee wants to buy product from a supplier who has not received approval, the franchise agreement requires that an application must be made to the franchisor. This way the franchisor can assure that all suppliers to the system are capable of delivering specialized product and that system standards are not eroded through poor supply selections (which are often driven by price considerations) made by franchisees.

An even-handed supplier approval process also allows the franchisor to control quality without unreasonably restricting supplier access to its system of franchise buyers, which could have serious antitrust implications for the franchisor. An unreasonably restrictive supply arrangement might injure competition among suppliers to franchisees. Injury to competition is what antitrust laws were designed to combat.

Transfer

Can the franchisee build up the business and then sell it to another person? In most systems the franchisee can sell the business only if the franchisor issues written permission, and permission is generally granted by a franchisor only after reviewing the qualifications of the prospective buyer. Most franchisors apply the same standards of qualification on the proposed transferee (the buyer) as they apply to new applicants.

If the transferee does not measure up, the franchisor has every right to deny consent to the transfer. The courts have made it clear that a franchisor has a legitimate interest in preventing its franchised businesses from being owned by businesspeople who are undercapitalized, lack necessary levels of business experience or fail to meet the company's objective qualifications.

The transfer, or assignment, sections of the typical franchise agreement are the most lengthy and dense legalese of the entire contract but are also the most important to the value of the franchisee's business. Your ability to sell your business and pull out your sweat equity is essential to the original decision to purchase the franchise.

It surprises many franchisees to learn that the transfer language of the contract may cover events that do not amount to the sale of the business, such as taking in a new partner, granting stock in an existing corporation that is the franchisee, the death of a minority owner of a franchise, and shifting ownership of the unit's assets to a newly formed corporation or limited liability company. All these events require the prior written consent of the franchisor, if the contract's transfer provisions are typical.

CORPORATE OWNERSHIP
Private Corporations, Limited Liability Companies (LLCs) and Personal Guarantees

Most franchisors allow an individual investor to create these legal entities to serve as the formal franchisee under the franchise agreement. It often makes sense: Create an LLC to hold the franchise rights, sign the franchise agreement, hold the assets of the operation, and accommodate multiple ownership and various positions and roles. However, there is usually one catch, and it's a significant one: Under the franchise agreement, you will be asked to personally guarantee to the franchisor the obligations of your new legal entity.

"Wait a minute," you say. "My lawyer told me that the main reason for creating an LLC was to shield my personal assets from the liabilities of the business!" That's right. The personal guarantee, if required by the franchisor, defeats that objective, at least insofar as you wanted to be shielded from the claims of the franchisor. If it is narrowly drafted, the guarantee should not defeat your objective relating to other aspects of the business.

What does this personal guarantee mean as a practical matter? Suppose your business falls on difficult times and you are unable to pay the royalties, and perhaps the franchisor terminates your franchise or you close the business. The franchisor will have legal claim for royalties and other damages against the LLC *and* you personally, as well as others who have guaranteed the obligations of your legal entity.

Right of First Refusal

Many franchise agreements reserve to the franchisor a "right of first refusal." This means that if you receive a formal offer to purchase your business, you must present the offer to the franchisor and allow them the opportunity to purchase your business on the same terms. This allows the franchisor to maintain control over the buying and selling of its franchises, but also draws criticism from

 INsight

Most franchisors include a right of first refusal in their franchise agreements in order to control ownership of the franchised businesses and to buy out a franchisee if it fits with the company's business plans for that area. However, it is a right rarely exercised by a franchisor.

franchisees who believe that it hampers their ability to attract a serious buyer. What buyer wants to go through the effort of putting together a detailed purchase offer, only to have the franchisor take it out from under them?

Termination

Oh, the dreaded termination section! It seems to rattle on ad nauseam, listing dozens of situations in which the franchisor may terminate the relationship, while rarely including even one circumstance in which the franchisee may terminate the relationship. Franchisors generally have only one enforcement tool, the threat of termination. They describe it at length, but use it gingerly.

Here are some of the typical termination grounds you will see in a franchise agreement, with notes on what to look out for:

- **Business abandonment.** Make sure you understand how abandonment is defined. You don't want a spring vacation to amount to abandonment of your business.
- **Criminal conviction.** How is a crime defined here? Is it a felony or any crime? The franchisor wants to protect its reputation if the franchisee commits a crime.
- **Lying on the application.** If you mislead the company during the application process, it wants to reserve the right to terminate the relationship.
- **Bankruptcy.** If your business does declare bankruptcy, the franchisor wants to be able to terminate the contractual relationship. This termination provision is often set to occur "automatically" if bankruptcy is declared, but in fact a whole body of federal bankruptcy law will take effect immediately. Bankruptcy legal specialists caution that the law may not allow the franchisor to terminate after a bankruptcy, regardless of what the contract says.
- **Termination after notice.** Most franchise agreements allow the franchisor to terminate

INsight

Many franchise agreements also include the broader termination grounds of the franchisee committing an act that injures the goodwill of the trademark. Plan to discuss this provision with your attorney.

the relationship if the franchisee receives notice of any default and does not correct the problem within a reasonable amount of time. The typical time to cure is 30 days, but it certainly could be a longer or shorter period, depending on the nature of the default.

Termination after notice is how most franchise terminations occur. If you receive a default notice that warns of the possible termination of your franchise rights, do not file it away. Respond to it immediately.

The franchise agreement, drafted by lawyers in the interests of franchisors, allows them to protect their trademarks, systems and other intellectual property if a franchisee abuses, misuses or misappropriates any portion of the franchised business. At the same time, exacting termination language allows the franchisor to protect other franchisees.

Look at it this way: If a franchisee on the other side of your small town is running a slovenly or dirty operation, your *own* business will suffer. That is the other sharp blade of the two-edged sword of franchising: You operate under the same trademark as many other operators; their businesses are indistinguishable from yours in the eye of the customer.

Most franchisees dislike the seemingly overbearing language of their own franchise agreement but are the first to insist that the franchisor use those rights to enforce system standards against another owner who is not doing the job.

The franchise laws of about 19 jurisdictions impose standards of termination that preempt conflicting language of a franchise agreement, allowing for termination or failure to renew only when the franchisor has good cause, as that term is defined in the statute. These statutes come into play if you get into a tangle with the franchisor and they notify you that your franchise is or will be canceled.

DISPUTE RESOLUTION PROVISIONS

The truth is, franchising tends to generate disputes. The interests of franchisor and franchisee are fundamentally at odds in a number of ways. Remember, the franchisor receives royalties based on a percentage of the gross sales of the business, *before* expenses are paid; franchisees take money home at the end of the day if they maximize profits, *after* expenses are paid. Franchisors therefore push for higher sales; franchisees for better profits.

One measure of excellence in franchising is the ability of the franchisor to avoid the courtroom when they must enforce the terms of its franchise agreements. The contract may contain a provision that requires the parties to submit all disputes to an arbitration process before any lawsuit may be filed. Where must that arbitration take place? Many franchise agreements specify that the process take place at the American Arbitration Association office closest

INsight

Franchisors have additional motivation to avoid a courtroom or an arbitration procedure: disclosure. The UFOC requires that a franchisor disclose in item 3 certain lawsuits and arbitration procedures during the prior 10 years as well as the terms of any settlement of those actions.

to the franchisor headquarters. That means you have to travel to the franchisor's backyard in order to resolve a dispute.

Even if there is no arbitration language in place, the franchise agreement may specify where a lawsuit must be filed if either party makes a legal claim under the contract. Franchisee attorneys generally resist accepting language mandating that legal actions must be filed in the home jurisdiction of the franchisor.

Remember, no prospective franchisee should attempt to fully comprehend a franchise agreement without the benefit of legal counsel. Your attorney is far more familiar with the complexities and limitations of contract law and can advise you about the obligations and rights it stipulates.

For all the attention the contract receives at the start of the relationship, it should not loom large in your daily business. When everything is going well, the franchised business is succeeding, and your relationship with the franchisor is on solid footing, that carefully evaluated franchise agreement—the foundation of your business investment—will not even come out of the drawer. All solid foundations are supposed to work that way.

SUMMARY NOTES

- ✓ Take the proposed franchise agreement to an attorney. It's important.
- ✓ It is also important to understand some of the basic dynamics of a franchise agreement, such as intellectual property, license rights, product standards, transfer and termination.
- ✓ If the business works out well, the contract will not come out of the drawer. If problems arise, it is the key to resolving any disputes.

Action PLAN

Look immediately for a good attorney. Ask current franchisees or friends in business who they use, or contact your state bar association.

CHAPTER 13

Franchisor Financial Information in the UFOC

(and How Do I Read This Gobbledegook?)

ERIC NEVER HAD A HEAD FOR NUMBERS BUT thought he was pretty good at judging the financial status of a company by its balance sheets. Now the UFOC gave him an opportunity to do just that for the home health-care franchise he was evaluating. But he had never seen a franchisor balance sheet and operating statement before and was not sure what to make of them. So he decided to take them to his accountant. Something told him this was too important to be left to his amateur accounting skills.

FRANCHISOR FINANCIAL DISCLOSURES

Eric's instincts are serving him well. Item 21 of the UFOC requires franchisors to supply two years of audited balance sheets and three years of audited operational statements. This is extremely important information for a prospective franchisee and should not be left to an amateur evaluation. It shows whether the franchisor is well-capitalized, how well they are managing their cash flow, and whether the company is healthy and profitable. In short, it is a snapshot of the franchisor's finances, and it is invaluable to you.

You are considering entering into a five-, 10- or even 20-year relationship when you execute a franchise agreement. You want to know whether the franchisor has staying power and will be there for the duration.

AUDITS ACCORDING TO GAAP

What does it mean that a financial statement is " audited"? It means that a certified public accounting firm has independently reviewed the company's books and expressed its professional opinion in writing that the financial statements accurately reflect the company's financial position and have been prepared in accordance with

 IN*sight*

The auditors must consent to the inclusion of their report in the UFOC. They go through a rigorous process of inspecting the company's records for the period they are auditing, as required by the standards of the accounting profession. A Compilation Report or Review Report does not involve that level of accounting scrutiny.

Generally Accepted Accounting Principles (GAAP)—the standard financial statement rules.

This audit opinion is a big deal in the world of accountants. It is the highest level of review that a CPA conducts (the other two are a Compilation Report and a Review Report), and it is as close as you're going to get to an independent third party approving the accuracy of a set of financials. You can usually rely on the accuracy of an audited statement.

So you peek at the exhibits in the back of your UFOC and there they are, the franchisor's financials. They are a sea of numbers. Now what do you do? Well, it goes without saying that most people have not made a study of how to read a financial statement. Now is not the time to start. Take the UFOC to an accountant, preferably a CPA, and have them conduct a review. You are going to need the services of a good accountant anyway when it comes time to plan the business, make some projections and create a business road map, so asking for a quick review of a set of financials is a good first step. Talk to the accountant about what it is you need and how much it will cost. Can't afford the full Cadillac review? Then ask how much half an hour of time costs. Present the financials, and ask the accountant to go over them slowly and explain what they mean to an experienced eye.

ACCOUNTANT'S ANALYSIS TIPS

We asked Roger Heymann of Heymann, Suissa and Stone P.C. of Rockville, Maryland—one of the leading small-business accounting firms on the East Coast—to summarize some of the lingo you may encounter in this session and to recommend what to listen for and what to ask. Here is what Heymann says:

"For a prospective franchisee, there are three major points to keep in mind when looking at financial statements. These are: Look at the relevant ratio analyses, pay close attention to footnotes, and conduct an industry analysis.

"Qualitative information from financial statements can be gathered by performing a ratio analysis, which expresses the relationship among selected financial statement data. As a franchisee, you want to pay close attention to relevant ratios, which may include the current ratio, quick ratio, inventory turnover, and return on assets ratio. Current ratio and quick ratio measure short-term debt-paying ability. Inventory turnover presents the liquidity of inventory. Return on assets ratio measures the overall profitability of assets.

"The second major point is to pay close attention to the footnotes to the financial statement. These provide the additional key information that supplements the principal financial statement. There are two types of footnotes. First, the major accounting policies of the business have to be identified and explained. They tell an investor what method the company chooses to present its accounts in the financial statement. For example, the cost of goods sold expense method will be included in this type of footnote. The second kind of footnote provides additional information that cannot be placed in the main body of the financial statement. For example, the maturity date or interest rate of a particular loan will be stated in the footnotes.

"The last major point is to conduct an industry analysis. A company's financial statements can tell you how well the business ran in the past, but not how well it has been doing in the context of a specific industry. Therefore, an industry analysis is needed to put the figures in perspective."

EVALUATING THE FRANCHISOR'S FINANCIAL STANDING

Now that an accountant has advised you about the franchisor's financial standing, how do you evaluate it in your investment decisions? Take a look at a common example. Say the franchisor is a subsidiary of a well-known corporation but is showing only a small net worth on an opening balance sheet with no operating history. What do you make of that?

First, understand why you are looking at a franchisor with a small net worth. When a well-established corporation considers franchising for the first time, the attorneys explain that it will need to provide a set of audited financial statements for the UFOC. If the company has never prepared an audited statement in the past, this can pose an extremely expensive problem. Auditors have to go over the corporation's old books in painful detail, and probably charge the corporation an arm and a leg. On top of that, the company is concerned about litigation arising out of the franchise program and figures that a subsidiary corporation will add an additional level of protection for the corporation. So the company decides it will be cheaper and smarter to create a new corporation to serve as the franchisor. A newly formed franchisor must provide only an audited opening balance sheet, which is a relatively simple matter for the auditor to complete. If the franchise program results in litigation, the assets of the established corporation are shielded.

This is perfectly legal, and quite common in franchising. When a thinly capitalized franchisor files in one of the registration states, however, it will probably be required to provide a surety bond to the state or make some other protective financial arrangement for investors as a condition of registration.

What does a surety bond do for franchisees? Imagine you have paid a $30,000 initial franchise fee, and the franchisor tells you that it cannot provide the promised training because it is low on funds and the training managers have quit. You request your money back, and the franchisor says it does not have that amount of cash in its accounts. In that situation, you would probably qualify to apply to be reimbursed under the surety bond on file with state authorities. It makes it relatively easy to be reimbursed for the investment of an initial fee if the franchisor goes out of business or is otherwise unable to perform basic obligations because it has no substantial assets. Without a protection like a surety bond, you may have no recourse at all, except filing a lawsuit against the franchisor and its principals.

Whether or not you are in a registration state, a low franchisor net worth increases the risks you are taking when you invest in a franchised business. If you are looking at a young program that has not been in operation very long, it may have an extremely low net worth. The profit potential of buying a franchise from a new concept may be high, but the concomitant risks should be part of your calculation when you evaluate any franchise investment.

The regulation of franchise sales is not designed to make all franchise investments safe. In order not to interfere unnecessarily in the marketplace, franchise regulation is designed to deliver all pertinent information into the hands of the investor, and then step back so that the investor can make an informed decision. That leaves a substantial burden on the prospective franchisee to consider all the relevant information.

SUMMARY NOTES

✓ The UFOC requires the inclusion of the franchisor's audited financial statements.

✓ Audits are generally presented by independent accountants, and they confirm that the numbers are prepared and presented according to the standards adopted in the business accounting industry known as Generally Accepted Accounting Principles (GAAP).

✓ Accountants conduct a ratio analysis and industry analysis and review the footnotes to the statements.

✓ A low net worth or otherwise shaky financial statement increases the risk that the company may not be there for the long term.

Action PLAN

Find a good accountant by asking current franchisees and friends or contacts already in business who they use. Check the Yellow Pages, or search for a local CPA at the American Institute of Certified Public Accountants Web site (www.aicpa.org).

CHAPTER 14

The Top 10 Warning Signs in Franchise Investments

CHRIS WAS HAVING TROUBLE EVALUATING a restaurant franchise. The company would not give her a UFOC, its answers to her questions were confusing, and franchisees were giving a mixed review on some key issues. At what point, she wondered, should she back away from the program?

DON'T GET SNAGGED

As exciting as it may be to purchase a franchise, this business requires all buyers to exercise caution. Regulations require franchisors to give you a UFOC, that's all. Once you have this document in hand, it is your responsibility to review it carefully and to ask more questions of the franchisor and as many franchisees as you can.

KEY WARNING SIGNS

Even if you follow this advice, how do you know if there are problems with a franchise you have your eye on? Although there is no way to be absolutely certain about a given investment, you can improve your odds of success if you keep an eye out for some of these key warning signs:

10. ***Weak financial statements.*** The UFOC contains three years of the franchisor's audited financial statements. Review them carefully, and take them to a knowledgeable CPA. If the franchisor is in a weak financial condition, it will raise the risk levels for your investment. You may find some terrific programs being offered by thinly capitalized franchisors or start-up companies, but understand that your risks as a franchisee are magnified by the company's weak financial standing.

9. ***No answers.*** If you do not get all your questions answered by the franchisor, or if you start getting the feeling that the company is being evasive, move on.

8. *The hustle.* Buying a franchise is a substantial investment. It might wipe out your life savings and put you on a financial bubble. If the seller is hurrying you along, telling you that the window of opportunity is closing, or using any other tried and true closing techniques, be prepared to walk away from the deal. This is too important to rush.

7. *Product price squeeze.* Product supply is the ticklish underbelly of franchise relationships. If you are buying a business that is designed to distribute the franchisor's product line, then you had better make sure the pricing of the product will allow you to be competitive in the marketplace. Ask other franchise owners how the pricing structure works for them. If you are going into a "business format" program where product is supplied by third parties, or some is supplied by the franchisor, make sure that it runs well. Have the franchisees established a buying cooperative? Do franchisees have input on the supply arrangements? Make sure this key aspect of your business will not frustrate you.

6. *High turnover rates.* Check item 20 of the UFOC and confirm how many franchisees have left the system in the past three years. There is no rule of thumb to determine when the number is too high; this depends largely on the type of business. Lower-investment franchises generally have a higher turnover rate than more expensive businesses. If anything looks out of line, ask the franchisor what's going on.

5. *Attorney avoidance.* The franchisor discourages you from getting a lawyer involved, telling you it will unnecessarily complicate and slow the process.

4. *Too many lawsuits.* Ours has become a litigious society, of course, and most franchisors reflect that fact. Item 3 of the UFOC will reveal the 10-year history of "material" lawsuits and/or arbitration cases filed against the company. If you see a heavy litigation history, find out what has been going on. Ask your attorney's opinion. It could mean that franchisees are fundamentally unhappy in the business.

3. *Earnings claims mumbo jumbo.* Ask the seller's representative: "How much money can I make with this franchise?" If it is not in the UFOC, the company must decline to answer the question. If they say, "We are prohibited by federal law from answering the question," realize that although that may be true, it may also be because the earnings picture is not a pretty one.

2. *No UFOC.* All franchisors are required by federal law and many state laws to deliver a UFOC before you pay any money for the franchise or sign a franchise agreement. If you do not receive one, don't even think about buying the franchised business.

And the number-one warning sign in franchise investments:

1. *Consistently bad reports from current franchisees.* If you make the effort to visit with some current franchisees of the company, and each one tells you they are unhappy or would not make the investment in this franchise again, think long and hard about your own decision. There is no stronger or more trustworthy source of information about the company than those independents who are in the trenches. If they feel that the franchisor has let them down or has a flawed program, it will tell you to look more carefully before you take the plunge.

These warning signs should prompt you to ask more questions. If you don't like the answers you receive, and your gut (or your professional advisor) tells you to head for the door, this is probably not the program for you. Take the time to look around at other programs. For a decision as important as this one, you owe it to yourself and your family to be confident that it is the right business investment for you.

SUMMARY NOTES ————————

✓ Look for red flags indicating problems in the franchise program.

✓ The decision about whether to invest in a particular franchise is yours, and no one knows better than you what will fit with your needs. Carefully consider anything else that appears to be a red flag in your own judgment.

Action **PLAN**

Move on if you encounter any serious problems regarding a franchise that are not cleared up to your satisfaction.

CHAPTER 15

Closing on Your Franchise Purchase

*N*OW *IT WAS GETTING EXCITING FOR Kevin. He had gone through all the steps with the franchisor, lined up the financing he needed to develop the new business, and was ready to close the transaction. In just a few days he would launch a new chapter of personal success in his life. What did he need to know going into the closing meeting?*

Once the franchisor has thoroughly checked out the applicant's qualifications, and the applicant has reviewed all documents, seen an accountant and an attorney, scraped together the money necessary to buy the franchise, and completed all necessary discussions, it is time to close on the transaction.

Purchasing the franchise rights for a business that has not yet been built is not a complicated transaction, and the closing involves nothing more than signing a few contracts and sliding a check across the table for the initial franchise fee. Most "closings" for franchise sales do not take place in a room face to face with the franchisor. They take place through the mail. The company sends you a final package with tabs showing where your signature is needed and a cover letter stating the amount of the initial franchise fee. You sign and return, and it is done.

A CHECKLIST FOR CLOSING

However, you should pay attention to the following before you sign on the dotted line:

The Franchise Agreement

This contract should have been in your hands with all blanks filled in for at least five business days before you sign and date it. That is a requirement imposed on the franchisor by state and federal law; it is not the franchisee's responsibility to see that this is met. Make sure your attorney has reviewed the contract and signed off on it. If you have requested any changes to be made to accommodate you, make sure they appear in the final form of the contract.

Many companies ask you to sign two originals and return them to the company. The franchisor then executes them and returns one original to you for your records.

Always Date Your Signature

Begin the habit of adding a date to any legal document that contains your signature. If the signature form does not have a space to show the date, simply jot it immediately after your signature. Dates are important in the regulation of franchise sales, and you may be called upon to swear as to a series of dated events. The date of delivery of the UFOC, the date you first had a face-to-face meeting with the franchisor, the date on which you received a completed franchise agreement, and the date on which you signed the franchise agreement are all important.

Never backdate a document, even if asked to do so by the franchisor; it will only confuse your recollection of events. Make sure your document record is clear on the dates.

Other Contracts

You may be presented with other contracts to sign that are ancillary to the franchise agreement. All such documents should be included in the UFOC and should not come as a surprise at closing. If you do receive a surprise contract, check it with your attorney. Ancillary contracts may include a site selection agreement (if you do not have a site selected yet), an agreement regarding necessary lease terms, and an acknowledgment of the training schedule.

UFOC

If you have not received the franchisor's UFOC at least 10 business days before you are asked to sign the franchise agreement, stop. Don't sign the contract, and don't send any money. This could indicate a mere oversight, or it could mean that you have a more serious problem. Contact your franchisor representative.

Lease Paperwork

If you have selected a location for the franchised business, you probably have received a proposed lease from the landlord. Make sure that your attorney sees this lease form and that you understand what requirements the franchisor might impose on the lease terms. It probably will not hold up the closing if this is not resolved, but you want to give all parties—and their attorneys—as much notice as possible regarding the potential terms of any lease.

Bank Paperwork

If you have arranged a loan from a bank or other lending institution, it will want to receive a copy of the franchise agreement (and every other piece of paper related to the franchise) as soon as possible. Talk to your banker about the steps necessary to provide the money you are borrowing and when it will be available. Make sure all is in order before you close.

SUMMARY NOTES

✓ Prepare paperwork as you approach the closing.
✓ Prepare a checklist for the closing so that nothing is dropped. Confirm the list with your attorney.
✓ You should have checklist items for the contracts, the UFOC, your lease paperwork and financing paperwork.

Action **PLAN**

Plan ahead so that you are sure of your costs and obligations before the closing. Meet with your attorney to consider all contingencies.

CHAPTER 16

When Things Don't Work Out
Resolving Franchisor/Franchisee Legal Disputes

ACCORDING TO JEFF, "IT SEEMED LIKE A good idea at the time." Jeff had carefully selected a franchise—an Italian restaurant—and it would be the first and the best in his town. He found a strip mall location and threw his heart into it. He borrowed $350,000 and worked at the business 12 hours a day, seven days a week. He mopped floors after closing and managed the buying, hiring and money. He personally welcomed his customers and spent a fortune on build-out and grand-opening advertising. Six months after the opening, the restaurant just wasn't cutting it, and Jeff was nearly out of operating cash. He stopped paying his royalties, telling the company that the program was not working in his town, and that he would pay the royalties as soon as the business made some money. Rather than come in to help, the franchisor sent a letter on lawyer's letterhead threatening termination for failure to pay royalties if the account was not brought up-to-date in 30 days.

"Now what do I do?" a bewildered Jeff asked.

The termination of a franchise agreement has been a legal flash point since the earliest days of franchising. Nowhere are the divergent interests of franchisors and franchisees brought into sharper focus, and no other feature of the franchise relationship has generated more disputes, arbitration and litigation. When you combine the complexities of the typical franchise agreement, the regulation of franchise sales, the perception that big corporations (franchisors) are against the little guy (franchisees), and the substantial amounts of money invested, it presents a ready-made formula for legal disputes.

Attorneys are building lucrative careers helping franchisors and franchisees resolve these disputes. There are more than 2,000 members of the Forum on Franchising of the American Bar Association, and the number is growing.

LINES OF DEFENSE: CONTRACT TERMS AND PROTECTIVE LAWS

Franchisees do have some tools, however. The first is the franchise agreement.

The Contract

The first line of defense for the franchisee, and the fundamental legal guideline for any termination for the franchisor, is the franchise agreement. The contract spells out the conditions under which either party may terminate the relationship. Typically the franchisor will reserve the right to terminate on a series of grounds, some based on the franchisee's failure to cure a default after a written notice is delivered, and others based on incurable violations that lead to immediate or automatic termination.

If a termination occurs in violation of the terms of the franchise agreement, the franchisee has the right to bring a lawsuit against the franchisor under state law, seeking either a court order that the termination be stopped, or damages, or both.

State Relationship Laws

The franchise relationship laws are state laws that regulate terminations, nonrenewals and some franchising practices. There are 19 U.S. jurisdictions that have adopted some form of franchise relationship law (see the list at Appendix A). The typical relationship law requires that a franchisor have "good cause" before it moves to terminate a franchisee. This protects a franchisee from arbitrary or baseless terminations and creates a right to sue the franchisor for damages if the standard is violated.

These laws were adopted in response to perceived widespread abuses in franchising. Unjust terminations and the absence of renewal rights seemed to be depriving franchisees of the value of the businesses they had built. Other abuses, such as

no right of assignment, restricted right of association, unreasonable performance standards and encroachment (placing another unit too close to a franchised unit), also led to the legislative attempt to level the playing field.

If the franchisee has an argument that a state relationship law supersedes the contract, there may be an opportunity to seek court relief under that law. The state relationship laws allow termination where the franchisor has "good cause" to terminate the franchise. What is "good cause"?

GENERAL STANDARD. Where the state law does define the concept, "good cause" means "failure of the franchisee to comply substantially with the requirements imposed by the franchisor." In other words, it means a breach of the franchise agreement.

STATUTORY GROUNDS. Here are some of the additional statutory grounds where termination is lawful:

- Voluntary abandonment
- Criminal conviction of the franchisee on a charge related to the franchised business
- The franchisee's insolvency or declaration of bankruptcy
- Failure to pay the franchisor sums due
- Loss of the right to occupy the franchisee's business premises
- A material misrepresentation by the franchisee relating to the business
- Franchisee conduct that materially impairs the goodwill of the franchised business or the franchisor's trademark
- The franchisee's repeated noncompliance with the requirements of the franchise
- Imminent danger to public health or safety
- Failure to act in good faith and in a commercially reasonable manner
- A written agreement to terminate
- The franchisee's failure to comply with any law applicable to the operation of the franchise

- Government seizure of the franchised business or foreclosure by a creditor

DISPUTE RESOLUTION TOOLBOX

Obviously, there are lots of land mines on the path to franchise success. Given the strong interests and even stronger feelings among franchisors and franchisees over termination issues, resolving the inevitable disputes is something of an art form. As a franchisee, you need to understand the tools in your dispute resolution toolbox.

There are four distinct types of dispute resolution tools, and each of them can be used in the franchise context.

1. *Negotiation.* It has been said that negotiation and compromise are the oils that smooth the gears of business. Negotiation is the process of give and take that results in an acceptable solution for the parties involved. It takes a willingness to explore the possibilities with the other side and benefits from face-to-face discussions.

   What could our franchisee, Jeff, negotiate for in his situation? Perhaps he could seek a royalty concession until his business is on its feet, or propose to sign a promissory note for the amount of royalty owing with an installment repayment schedule. Or he could begin negotiations to either sell the business to a more aggressive owner or to the franchisor, or close the business with both parties working to minimize the financial impact on Jeff. The principal advantage of an effective negotiation is that it quickly embraces creative, business-oriented resolutions. With clever businesspeople working in good faith, a negotiated resolution of a difficult situation offers the greatest hope for a solution that is fair to all involved.

2. *Mediation.* Mediation is professionally assisted negotiation. Where franchisor and franchisee are unable to negotiate a satisfactory solution, they may choose to bring into the discussion a professional mediator. This is someone trained in the mediation process and possibly experienced in the franchised business, who can use their skills to help the parties fashion a creative resolution. Often the most effective mediators are retired civil court judges. Mediation is nonbinding unless and until the parties find an agreeable solution; then they may commit to binding terms. Disputing parties can turn to the American Arbitration Association or national private organizations like JAMS for mediation services. Of particular interest to franchisors is the fact that a franchisor/franchisee dispute that is taken through a mediation process need not be disclosed in item 3 of the UFOC.

3. *Arbitration.* Arbitration is a more formal dispute resolution process that results in a final, nonappealable decision made by an arbitrator or a panel of three arbitrators. Think of arbitration as litigation without the courtroom. The result is just as binding on the parties as a court decision, and it must be disclosed in item 3 of the UFOC, just as with court cases.

 IN*sight*

Franchise disputes can often be resolved if they are recognized and handled at an early moment in the dispute. Many franchisors express frustration that their contracts give them only one response to a serious problem—termination—and it is an atomic bomb. Mediation has become popular among franchisors and their lawyers as an effective technique for resolving business disputes without resorting to nuclear weaponry.

If your franchise agreement contains a provision that commits all disputes to binding arbitration, then you will not have the right to sue in a court of law. Except in rather extreme cases of fraud in the formation of the contract, the arbitration provision is almost always enforced by a court if challenged by one of the parties. The Federal Arbitration Act and court decisions of the past 50 years have created an extremely strong policy in favor of enforcing arbitration agreements. The policy reduces the crushing case load in our public courts and allows private parties to resolve their disputes privately. It is not entirely private, however, because disputes submitted to arbitration must be disclosed in item 3 of the franchisor's UFOC.

4. *Litigation.* A franchisee can always sue a franchisor in court to enforce the terms of the franchise agreement and try to stop a threatened termination. Of course, the franchisor can also sue to enforce the payment requirements or other terms of the franchise agreement. Of all the dispute resolution tools available to franchisors and franchisees, litigation is by far the most expensive and time-consuming.

One of your most important objectives in business is to avoid litigation, and to a lesser degree arbitration. Use these tools only as a last resort. It is a rare business owner who finds litigation satisfactory as a dispute resolution process.

SUMMARY NOTES

✓ In franchising, disputes happen.
✓ Your first line of defense as a franchisee is the franchise agreement. Look to the terms and conditions articulated in the contract, and ask your attorney for assistance.
✓ The second line of defense are specific standards adopted in the various franchise relationship laws.
✓ Dispute resolution techniques are important tools in your franchise business life. Familiarize yourself with the basic advantages and disadvantages of negotiation, mediation, arbitration and litigation.

Action **PLAN**

Talk to your attorney about alternate forms of dispute resolution, and ask how dispute resolution is addressed in the contract. Discuss with the franchisor how you both will handle a dispute if and when it arises.

CHAPTER 17

Renewing Your Franchise Rights

SAM REALIZED WITH A START ONE DAY THAT his franchise agreement was due to expire in a year. "Where has the time gone?" he thought. The foreseeable arrival of the expiration date means that Sam has some decisions to make. "Do I want to sign on for another five years? If I don't re-up, what will happen to my business? If I have a buyer for my business walk in tomorrow, what do I have to sell? What hoops do I have to jump through to renew the franchise rights? Will the renewal contract be on the same terms as my current contract?"

CONTRACT TERMS AND RENEWAL RIGHTS

The franchise agreement is a long-term arrangement that can last more than 20 years. Many of the earliest McDonald's franchise agreements from the 1960s and 1970s have completed their initial 20-year terms

and have been renewed for another 20 years. We suspect some of those may even be coming around again.

Think of a franchise agreement as you would a lease for real estate. The lease/franchise agreement grants the tenant/franchisee the right to use the company's property (the building/franchise system) for a period of years and then, when the time is up, the relationship ends. The tenant/franchisee moves out and both parties go their separate ways.

As with many commercial leases, the franchise agreement often grants the franchisee the conditional right to renew the relationship for another term of years, and the renewal right usually depends on meeting a short list of preconditions.

Before looking at those preconditions, it is necessary to understand the overall structure of the franchise agreement term. Current practice and conventional wisdom among franchisors suggest that you are not likely to find a full 20-year term granted at the outset of the relationship. Why? Because things change too much over such a long period of time. When circumstances change, or when the franchise system itself changes, the franchisor does not want to be locked into contracts that cannot keep up with these changes.

For instance, say that in its first 15 franchise agreements, a franchisor designated that the franchisee had an exclusive territory covering a radius of 30 miles from the store location. But then things change: The franchise system expands at an astonishing rate so there are lots of new locations; the company develops smaller, mobile locations, for the service that can be flexible and nimble in following the market for the franchise product; the company develops a catalog to offer products directly to the customer; the company increases its standard royalty rate from 4 to 5 percent; the Internet is invented; and so on. The franchisor wants to be able to respond to such changes, so it structures the franchise agreement to be for a five-year initial term with the option to renew for three additional terms of five years each.

The effect of such a multiterm structure is to allow the franchisor to present the franchisee with a new form of franchise agreement every five years, and each form can adapt the system to the current market circumstances. The franchisor wants to reduce the size of the exclusive territory and modify the concept of exclusivity. The franchisor can make those changes only if the terms of renewal allow the changes. The renewal also gives the franchisee a chance to evaluate the continuing value of participating in the franchise program. The franchisee can always walk away at the date of expiration. Today terms are shorter, and there are more renewals than in the past. That's why contract renewal is an important topic for any franchisee looking at a new franchise agreement.

RENEWAL CONDITIONS

Renewal by the franchisee is typically articulated as a "right" or "option," but it always comes with conditions to be met. As with any legal contract, read the fine print to understand the steps necessary to satisfy the conditions and enjoy the full rights under the agreement.

What sorts of conditions will you encounter at renewal time? Here are the most common:

Give Written Notice to the Franchisor

This provision usually requires a written notice no less than x months and no more than y months prior to the date of expiration. It is designed this way so that renewal paperwork can be prepared and the franchisor can comply with state laws that may require a franchisor to give a certain amount of notice before failing to renew a franchise.

No Defaults and In Full Compliance

Look for a provision that says something like "You must not currently be in default under the franchise agreement and must have remained in compliance during its term." What if you cured a minor default in your first year—are you in full compliance?

Sign a New Form of Franchise Agreement

This is the most sensitive of the renewal conditions. Does the contract allow the substitution of a new form of agreement and advise you that the terms of the renewal agreement may be substantially different from the current agreement? That allows the franchisor to increase your royalty rates, alter your grant of territorial protections, and change other features that might directly affect the value of your business. Some franchise agreements specify that royalty rates and territories will not be changed but that other provisions may be changed on renewal. This is a step in the right direction. Be sure to go over this provision with your attorney.

INsight

Some franchise relationship laws (see Appendix A) require that a franchisor give at least 180 days notice to the franchisee of its intention not to renew a franchise agreement.

Sign a Release of Claims

Why does the franchisor require you to release legal claims as a condition of renewal? It has everything to do with the company's opportunity to cut off problems that might have occurred during the expiring term. This way, the franchisor can begin the new term on a new slate without concern that it will renew the contract and then get hit with a lawsuit over something that occurred in the earlier term. One idea that is usually acceptable to the franchisor: Make the release mutual, so that the franchisor also releases any claims it may have against the franchisee under the expiring contract. Discuss this provision and any claims you may have under the current contract with your legal counsel.

Pay a Renewal Fee

A minority of franchise agreements require a renewal fee. Most don't, because franchisors generally want to impose no impediment to renewal. They want the franchisee to re-up. The franchisee represents an exceedingly valuable revenue stream

for the franchisor, which would be expensive to replace if the franchisee did not renew.

Renewal is the strongest vote for the value of the franchise program that a franchisee can make. You will find that most franchisors generally want you to renew and will make renewal as easy and favorable as possible. A renewed franchise is far less expensive than finding, training and establishing a new franchisee.

The answers to most of the questions Sam was pondering at the beginning of this chapter should be answered in his franchise agreement and by the renewal policies of the particular franchise system. Many of the franchise relationship laws discussed in Chapter 19 apply the "good cause" standard to a franchisor's failure to renew a franchise agreement and may therefore preempt the renewal terms laid out in your franchise agreement. Check with your attorney to consider any applicable statutory renewal standards.

SUMMARY NOTES

✓ Like a commercial lease, a franchise agreement typically grants a term of years with conditional renewal rights.

✓ The duration of franchise agreement terms is getting shorter. This offers flexibility to franchisor and franchisee alike.

✓ The conditions imposed on renewal may include notice, contract compliance, a new form of franchise agreement, a release of claims and payment of a renewal fee.

Action PLAN

Keep these renewal concerns in mind when analyzing the initial franchise agreement. Ask the franchisor representative about renewal rights. Make sure your attorney is comfortable with the contract renewal language.

CHAPTER 18

International Franchising

*E*NRIQUE LIVES IN MEXICO CITY, BUT HE *has traveled to the United States many times. He is excited about bringing an American restaurant concept to Mexico because his cosmopolitan city has never seen anything like it. Enrique contacted the franchisor in Minneapolis, thinking it was a long shot, and was surprised to find that the company has an active international franchising department with a Spanish-speaking specialist in Latin America. Things are looking up for Enrique.*

THE GLOBALIZATION OF FRANCHISING

The global expansion of U.S. franchisors is one of the most interesting business success stories of the past 30 years. The American franchise concept has dispersed its various familiar brand names in large and small countries around the world at an astonishing rate.

 IN*sight*

The history of international franchise expansion has not been—as they say in the United Kingdom—all beer and skittles. In the 1980s, McDonald's restaurants reported enormous difficulties in establishing their foods supply organization in foreign locations like Russia and Asia. Other franchisors have had their international expansion plans frustrated at huge expense by national laws restricting money transfer, trademark pirates and poorly enforced intellectual property laws, poor reception of their products because of cultural concerns, and communications problems.

McDonald's has been a global franchise expansion leader. It has established over 30,000 restaurants in more than 120 countries. The company says that 80 percent of its restaurants worldwide are franchised. The InterContinental Hotels Group, a franchisor of Holiday Inn hotels and other brands, has opened hotels in nearly 100 countries.

Franchise regulation has been growing as well. The countries with a form of presale disclosure requirements for franchisors include Australia, Brazil, Canada (Ontario and Alberta), China, France, Indonesia, Italy, Japan, Malaysia, Mexico, South Africa, South Korea, Spain and the United States. Buy a franchise in one of these countries, and you will likely receive a presale disclosure statement presenting some of the key information you will need to evaluate the proposed franchise investment.

KEYS TO FOREIGN-BASED FRANCHISES

The international expansion of franchising has now come full circle as franchisors from other lands expand into the U.S. market. If you are interested in purchasing an international franchise, located in the U.S. market or another country, make sure you consider the following:

Find out if the company has taken steps to comply with all the laws on franchising in this country. Does the company have a UFOC or other disclosure statement? Is it complete? Has the company registered its offering in the U.S. registration states? If it has complied with these laws, that tells you the company has made a substantial investment in seeking successful franchisees in the U.S. market. If it has sidestepped these requirements, it is trying to cut some important corners, and you should be careful. You could be the next corner.

Is the program a regional offering or limited to one market? Will you receive rights for several markets or multiple states? Many companies new to the U.S. market divide up the country into separate, multistate regions so that penetrating such a huge commercial country is manageable.

How is the U.S. expansion going to be managed? Is there a regional manager or a master franchisee? Make sure you understand how the relationships are set up so that you know who will provide things like training and services. This may not be clear after you review the UFOC, so plan to discuss it with the sales representatives you meet.

One of the largest challenges of international franchising is effective communication. Will the company be communicating directly with the U.S. franchisees, or will it go through its regional managers/master franchisees? Find out if regular meetings will be held, and where. If they are overseas, be sure that you include these costs in your budgeting. Ask if the franchisor will assist with any meeting expenses.

Trademark protection can be a challenge for a franchisor from outside the United States. Be sure to check item 13 of the UFOC describing the U.S. registration status of the principal trademark. If it is not registered with the U.S. Patent and Trademark Office, exercise extreme caution and have your attorney check it out.

Is the cultural fit of the business a good one? Has the product/service been tested in the U.S. market, or are you the test? If you are the pioneer for this program, make sure you will not be too badly hurt if the product/service flops. It does happen. And it will happen regardless of the level of your enthusiasm and industry. Make sure your lawyer takes steps to protect you in the event the project goes south.

Don't shy away from an opportunity just because it is a franchisor from another country. The UFOC will tell you a lot about the company and how it is organized to service the U.S. market. Ask for the UFOC early on. If it does not exist, always proceed with extreme caution.

SUMMARY NOTES

✓ An international franchise can make an exciting investment, and more and more foreign-based franchisors tackle the U.S. market.

✓ Protect yourself by looking into the three key areas of an international relationship: control, communication and commitment.

✓ Find out how the market will be managed. Is there a regional manager or a U.S. master franchisee, or will the company manage its franchisees directly?

✓ Make sure that the program will be successful in the U.S. market. Foreign success does not always translate to the U.S. market.

Action PLAN

Contact and meet with managers responsible for franchising an international brand in your area. Locate other franchisees of the system in your area.

CHAPTER 19

Negotiating Franchise Agreements

*M*ARIA DISLIKES BUYING CARS FOR ONE *reason: She hates having to negotiate aggressively on the price to get a fair deal. Now that she is buying a franchise, she has the same feeling as she gets closer to closing the transaction. Is it supposed to be like buying a car? Is she expected to negotiate? Maria wonders if she has enough information to negotiate on this purchase but remembers her dad always saying, "Everything is negotiable."*

The purchase of a franchise can be an intimidating process. Most Americans have never seen, let alone signed, a contract of such length and complexity as a typical business format franchise agreement. Signing one under any circumstances takes an act of courage and a leap of faith.

The lesson that Maria's dad taught her is always true in business, and it applies with equal force to franchises. Don't miss the opportunity to negotiate your purchase.

NEGOTIATING A FRANCHISE AGREEMENT

Signing a franchise agreement comes at the end of a lengthy process, highlighted by the delivery of a UFOC, promotional brochures, other system literature and personal interviews. Pressing for favorable contract terms may be the last thought on your mind. However, with some planning and understanding of the franchisor's position, you can cut a far better legal and financial deal.

WHY IS THE FRANCHISE AGREEMENT SO ONE-SIDED?

Franchise agreements have always been weighted in the franchisor's favor for one simple reason: The franchisor is not only your partner in this venture; it is the system-wide enforcer. It is in everyone's interests—the franchisor's, yours, and other franchisees'—that all franchisees operate in a manner that meets the highest system standards. In a retail system, all stores must be clean and well-run. If the store closest to you is dirty, slow or run-down, it affects your business directly and dramatically. Both units operate under the same trademark; if your neighbor is injuring the local reputation of the mark, you pay the price. Customers who have visited the dirty store will naturally assume that your store is in the same condition and stay away in droves. To paraphrase the great Yogi Berra, "If people don't want to come to your store, how are you going to stop them?"

As the system standards enforcer, the franchisor must reserve draconian enforcement rights in the franchise agreement. These may strike you as overbearing, but they are designed to allow the franchisor to take action if a franchisee's operation is subpar. In a sense, the enforcement provisions are there to protect you as well. When your neighbor's careless operation starts to hurt your business, you will be the first one to request that the franchisor do something to correct the situation. The franchisor had better have tough enforcement provisions in the franchise agreement, or it will be powerless to do anything. Negotiating some of these provisions will be tough.

UNDERSTANDING THE SELLER'S POSITION

Powerful financial forces drive the franchisor to complete the franchise transaction. It is difficult, time-consuming and expensive for a franchisor to locate a qualified franchisee. Selling a franchise is the ultimate hard sell; the sales cycle is measured in months, not days. Most franchisors devote tens of thousands of dollars a year to recruiting franchisees, and once a qualified applicant shows an interest, the franchisor is highly motivated to complete the sale. A new franchisee in the system means

IN*sight*

The power of your position is expressed in your attitude: You are interested in buying but not overeager. You let the seller know that you are interested, but there are lots of other investments you are evaluating (even if in your heart you know this is the one). Negotiation expert Herb Cohen says the best negotiating attitude says to the other side: "I care about making this commitment, but not that much."

a stream of revenue that will last for years and continued growth for the system.

Franchise sales representatives are often paid in whole or in part on commission. They are extremely motivated to see the transaction close; if you walk away, they lose money.

The point is that you are in a position of considerable power when it comes to negotiating a franchise agreement. Use that power to your advantage.

TAKE IT OR LEAVE IT?

How easy is it to negotiate the terms of a franchise agreement? While it complicates the life of franchisors, it is a well-known secret in the franchisor community that these contracts are negotiated all the time. You may hear from a franchisor that franchise law prohibits negotiation (it doesn't), or the company does not want to negotiate the terms that are offered to you, but you should not understand that to mean that the company *cannot* change its contract for you.

In fact, even the law of California—the toughest jurisdiction on negotiated changes in a franchise offering—allows franchisors to negotiate the terms of a franchise, but imposes a series of disclosure and registration obligations on a franchisor who changes the terms of its standard, registered offer. At the other end of the legal spectrum, the franchise law in the Commonwealth of Virginia states that a franchise agreement may be voided by the franchisee within a short time if it is not negotiated by the franchisor.

A franchisor can change the standard contract terms for you if it chooses to make the changes.

NEGOTIATING RULES

Steven B. Wiley, founder of the Wiley Group in Gettysburg, Pennsylvania, and one of the country's leading motivators and instructors of top corporate executives in matters of building partnerships and negotiating techniques, has some key suggestions for your negotiation. "First, there is no substitute for doing your homework," says Wiley. "Talk to other franchisees and find out where the company has shown flexibility in the past; talk to an experienced franchise lawyer; ask the franchisor for as much background information as you can. When you meet with the company to talk about the terms of the franchise agreement, you want to know as much as you can about that contract. You will be prepared, and you will not be thrown off balance when the give and take starts."

Keep in mind that you are about to commence a long-term business relationship with the franchisor. It is in your and the franchisor's best interests that both parties are happy with the deal struck and comfortable with any changes you agree to make. If you are not happy with any aspect of the contract, or there is a provision that you do not understand, you need to make your position known to the franchisor representatives.

According to Steve Wiley, the number-one negotiating principle to keep in mind is to "start high." "I teach corporate managers at the largest companies in the world that they need to start with an aggressive opening position," says Wiley. "Not because they should be greedy—rather, it is so that

INsight

Check item 5 of the UFOC ("Initial Franchise Fee"). If the initial franchise fee is not uniform, the company is required to disclose a formula or actual initial fees paid in the prior fiscal year. If the company cut some deals on the initial franchise fee, they will be at least mentioned here.

they can make concessions along the way of the discussion and work toward their target position. If you open at what you consider a fair position, you will have no room to maneuver when the other side asks you for something."

A prospective franchisee negotiating the franchise agreement should always be prepared to walk away from the deal. "This is the real strength of any negotiator," says Wiley. "Your neutral attitude says to the other side that you are not overeager to conclude the deal, that you want the deal but only if it is on reasonable terms. Even if you think this is the opportunity of a lifetime that will make you wealthy beyond your wildest dreams, never show it to the other side, or you will not conclude the deal on your terms."

FRANCHISORS' INFLEXIBLE POSITIONS

Many provisions of the franchise agreement can be negotiated, but there are a few areas where franchisors can be expected to dig in their heels:

Trademarks

As the owner of the trademarks, a franchisor will not be at all willing to water down their legal rights to control the display of the mark or protect the mark through enforcement actions. There is usually some wiggle room in the degree to which a franchisor is willing to stand behind the mark if the franchisee is attacked legally for its use of the mark. Look for language by which the company "indemnifies" (will pay) the franchisee for legal expenses incurred where the franchisee has properly used the marks and comes under legal attack by someone claiming infringement.

Royalty Rates

Conventional wisdom in the franchisor community suggests that all franchisees should pay the same rate of royalty whenever possible. This keeps everyone in the system on the same footing and avoids creating different classes of franchise citizens in the system. So if the standard royalty rate is set at 5 percent, don't expect the company to accept your suggestion that you pay a royalty rate of 4 percent.

There may be extenuating circumstances where you would be allowed to pay a lower rate for a period of time, but those are relatively rare. If you are taking over a store that has been poorly managed and the customer base is depleted, you may want to suggest a break in the royalty rate for your first year while you turn around the operation.

Assignment/Termination Controls

Franchisors will do their best to exercise control over the people who are allowed to own and operate their franchises. They have a direct interest; all those franchises are flying a flag owned by the company. If a weak operator is allowed to come in through a sale, or someone comes in who does not have the capital to run the business successfully, it creates a threat of business failure. That hurts the reputation of the system and indirectly all franchisees.

If an operator is not following the program or their operations are not clean or they are otherwise hurting the system's reputation, the company has little choice but to take corrective steps. For these reasons, franchisors are not likely to give on

suggested changes to the assignment or termination provisions.

FRANCHISORS' FLEXIBLE POSITIONS

Franchisors tend to have more flexibility in other areas of the contract:

Initial Fee

The franchisor has great flexibility when it comes to the initial fee. If it is set at $30,000, you may be able to argue for a reduction of that amount or a plan by which you defer payment over time. Try suggesting that you pay $15,000 upfront and the balance over the first 18 months of your operation of the business.

There may be some resistance to this concept, of course. Perhaps the company needs the upfront fee to pay a commission to the broker or for its own operating expenses. Franchisors are also reluctant to make any changes that require additional disclosure. If there are variations in the initial fee, the company may have to disclose that fact in item 5 of its UFOC. If the company offers financing, it may be required to disclose those terms as well as in item 10. Ask anyway; it's your money, after all.

Territorial Rights

This is ticklish in some systems, but well worth exploring in negotiations. What are the dimensions of the territory you are granted? Can you request an expansion of that area or ask for an option right on an adjoining territory? Perhaps you could request additional time and territorial protection during the first few years of your franchise. It may take a bit of creativity on your part, but it is well worth exploring if there are ways that you can structure the territorial rights to your own needs.

Marketing Contributions

This topic, and the franchisor's flexibility on it, will be determined by the type and the circumstances of the business. You may suggest that a local marketing fee be waived because of the unusual location: If you are building a retail store on the grounds of a popular theme park, you should not be paying marketing fees to increase foot traffic to your location. Your rent rate may be higher precisely because you have a premium location where foot traffic is delivered by the park's own promotion.

Never forget the fundamental impulse of good negotiators: It never hurts to ask. Build a win-win franchise agreement going in, and your relationship will be that much stronger for the long term.

SUMMARY NOTES

✓ Get creative when buying a franchise or business opportunity. Propose price reductions and payment terms that fit your needs.

✓ When you first read a franchise agreement, it may strike you as one-sided. But there are reasons for that. There are other players here; this is not merely a two-party agreement.

✓ Position yourself for negotiation. Gather as much information as you can about deals the franchisor has granted to others.

✓ It's legal in all states to negotiate a franchise agreement.

✓ Remember some of the key rules of negotiation: do your homework, "start high," be willing to walk on the deal, and "it never hurts to ask."

✓ There are some areas (initial fees, territory, advertising contributions) where a franchisor is more likely to give than other areas (trademark, royalties and transfer rights).

Action PLAN

Become a good negotiator. Take a seminar on negotiation skills, or head to the library or the bookstore for a book on negotiation, such as the classic *You Can Negotiate Anything* by Herb Cohen (Bantam Books).

CHAPTER 20

Working with Lawyers and Accountants

*B*OBBY IS A PRO AT COACHING HIGH *school kids but is lost when it comes to reading a balance sheet or understanding dense legal language in a contract. He had* what he considered an excellent franchise invest-*ment opportunity but knew he needed some professional help. Could he afford it? Could he afford not to get help?*

USING LEGAL SERVICES

Anyone buying a franchise today is well-advised to retain the services of an experienced attorney to review the franchise agreement and any related contracts. Business opportunity buyers, depending on the size of the investment, may need an attorney's help as well. The objection is right on the tip of your tongue, isn't it? "How can I afford a lawyer? I am putting this business together on a shoestring as it is. A lawyer's going to cost me a fortune."

In the first place, using the services of an attorney need not cost a fortune, and you can work out in advance what fees are likely to be involved. Most lawyers still charge for their services by the hour, but many are willing to set a quoted fee or agree to a cap on the fee for a simple project like the review of a franchise agreement and UFOC. If it takes a lawyer two hours to review the document and another hour to meet with you to discuss it, that suggests

 IN*sight*

Attorneys know their clients are concerned about legal fees and generally encourage discussion of the subject at the first meeting. Gone are the days when attorneys thought it unprofessional to discuss money.

a legal fee—assuming a $150 hourly rate—that does not exceed $500. Hiring an attorney is like buying insurance. And as insurance goes, $500 is not expensive at all. You can expect to purchase casualty insurance, health coverage for your employees, and unemployment compensation insurance that will put the cost of your modest attorney fees to shame.

What can you expect to receive for your legal fees? At a minimum you want to hear from your learned counsel whether there are any provisions in the proposed contract that run distinctly against your interests. You also want to know about provisions that put your investment in a precarious position. For instance, what if the franchisor reserves the right to terminate the relationship with no advance notice if you fail to follow the standards in the operating manuals? Your lawyer should advise you that this is way too broad and threatens your business in an unacceptable manner. They may suggest that language be added that gives you the right to receive at least 30 days' written notice of the infraction and an opportunity to cure it without threatening your entire investment in the program.

You also want to hear from your lawyer if there are any other aspects of the franchise documents that cause concern or call for further investigation. If you live in one of the several states requiring a franchisor to register under a franchise law or file for an exemption under a state business opportunity law, your lawyer should make the phone call to check on the company's status. Ask your attorney to tell you if your state's law protects you from an arbitrary or groundless termination by the franchisor. They should be able to give you a copy of any such law.

DO YOU NEED A SPECIALIST?

In this age of professional specialization, how do you find a lawyer experienced enough to be of help reviewing a franchise agreement? Referrals are by far the most effective way to locate the right lawyer. As you meet franchise owners in the system you are investigating, ask them who they use. Every state has

a lawyer referral system you can look up in your phone book. Ask your friends and business acquaintances for referrals. You don't want the name of a cousin's brother-in-law who just graduated from law school in another state, but you do want to hear about lawyers a person has used and knows are experienced. Get familiar with the *Martindale-Hubbell Law Directory*, available in every law library and most public libraries, and online (www.martindale.com). This directory lists lawyers by state and town, and many entries include a short description of their professional background. It even offers a rating system of lawyers.

USING ACCOUNTING SERVICES

The other professional assistance you should consider hiring is a competent accountant. Accountants are worth their weight in Big Mac sandwiches if you are planning to go into business and are evaluating a franchise or business opportunity investment.

First and foremost, your accountant can put together a detailed projection for your business and help you consider how to finance the total investment. The projection will tell you a lot about the business. It should show where your break-even points will be, the number of customers you will need in order to generate your revenue, and the amount of your investment plus financing costs. It will also give you an idea of the return you can expect on your investment.

In short, your accountant can help you decide whether you would be better off financially buying the franchise or business opportunity or getting a job and putting your money in treasury bonds.

Your accountant can also look over the franchisor's three years of audited financial statements contained in the UFOC. These tell you a lot about the staying power of the company. Will it be there for the long haul? Do the statements show healthy growth or stagnating losses? Your accountant should be able to provide a professional opinion about the standing of the franchisor.

A full review by a CPA can be expensive, running into a few thousand dollars rather quickly. Talk to your accountant about what you need and what it's going to cost. Then figure out a way to do it.

WHAT TO ASK YOUR LEGAL AND ACCOUNTING ADVISORS

Some Great Questions for Your Attorney

Plan to explore these basic topics with your attorney, and add to the list whatever you think is appropriate for the franchise you are reviewing:

- How does this franchise agreement compare to others you have reviewed?
- Are there any provisions in this agreement that I should not agree to under any circumstances ("deal breakers")? Do you have any suggested changes for the agreement, and would they be accepted by the franchisor?
- Have you checked with state authorities to confirm that the company is registered to sell franchises or business opportunities in this state?
- How do the termination provisions stack up under this state's franchise laws or case law on termination? What exactly are my transfer rights under the agreement?
- Do any of the litigation or arbitration cases disclosed in item 3 concern you?
- What protections do I need when buying this business opportunity? Should I defer payments or otherwise structure the transaction? Are there any surety bonds, escrow arrangements or trust accounts in place in this state to protect buyers of this program?

Some Great Questions for Your Accountant/CPA

- What is the seller's net worth? How does this amount relate to the size of my total investment in the franchise? Should I be concerned about it?
- Can you tell from the financial statement whether the seller's business is profitable? How would you describe the seller's financial health?
- Does the financial statement show the average annual royalty payment received from a franchisee? Can we extrapolate any average sales figures from that?
- Is there a surety bond, escrow account or deferred payment in place in this state? Is there another entity that guarantees the obligations of the seller for this program?
- How do the item 7 figures strike you compared to other small businesses you have advised? Do they look reasonable?
- What is the break-even point for this business? What revenues will I need to cover my expenses and make the franchise or business opportunity profitable?

SUMMARY NOTES

✓ Ask franchisees you meet who they use for legal services. Do your research and find a good lawyer with experience representing small businesses.

✓ Think of legal and accounting expenses as part of your insurance costs.

✓ Get organized in your use of legal and accounting services. Know what questions you want answered in the preliminary review process.

Action PLAN

Interview a few attorneys and accountants to determine their individual styles, experience and capabilities. Be sure to confirm in advance that you will not be billed for the interview.

CHAPTER 21

Questions for Franchisees

NANCY KNEW SHE NEEDED TO TALK TO some franchisees in the ham store business she was investigating but was a bit intimidated. Was she imposing on them? Would she offend these experienced businesspeople with her intrusive call? What would she say?

THE KEY TO YOUR RESEARCH

Current franchisees are without a doubt the best source of information you will find on the benefits, drawbacks and strengths of the business you are investigating. They can also generally provide some great insights and advice. It takes a bit of gumption to approach a business owner, but you should not hesitate. Here are some thoughts on the approach.

First, check out the business as a customer. If it is a retail operation, go to the unit, sit for a while, and observe the operation. Return to do this again during different times of the day. Learn to be a keen observer on these visits: Count customers as they come in the door, observe how the employees handle their jobs (what do they say at the counter when they greet a customer?), note the amount of the purchases made by customers to get a rough estimate of the "average ticket" spent in the store, and observe what you can of the work going on out back.

The next step is to make arrangements to talk to the owner. Remember that retail business owners are extremely busy at certain times of the day. It's best to call ahead and find a good time to visit. When the owner does meet with you, be sensitive to the time you spend. If you requested a 20-minute interview, stick to it. If it is a busy lunch hour at a restaurant, you may want to find a better time of day.

FRANCHISE QUESTIONS

It also helps to have a set of questions prepared. Don't try to wing it. Here is a checklist of franchise questions to ask:

- Is the training program worthwhile? Did it leave you well-prepared to run this business?
- Has the franchisor's support been steady? Are they there when you need them?
- What is the culture of the franchise system? Are franchisees friendly with one another? Is it encouraging or discouraging to be with the franchisor?
- Is the business seasonal? What are the strongest and weakest times of the year?
- Does the franchisor provide continuing training?
- Is the market for this business a strong one? Is it growing or slowing?
- Is there a franchisee association or council? Do franchisees have a real role in the franchisor's decision-making process?
- Did you have a good year last year? Do you recall what your gross sales were? Will this year be stronger or weaker?
- How is product supply arranged for franchisees? Does it work well?
- What questions do you wish you had asked going into your franchise investment?
- Knowing what you now know, would you buy this franchise again?

INsight

Most franchise owners will discuss the performance of their business once you establish a rapport with them. They need to know you are not a competitor or a potential competitor but someone serious about making the same investment decision they made. Most want to help.

Don't hesitate to take notes during your conversations. It tells the franchisees you value their words and experience. And resist the urge to get too chatty or argumentative. Your objective is to gather information. If you hear comments that concern you, by all means follow up with the franchisor.

SUMMARY NOTES

- ✓ When approaching a franchisee, be respectful of time and business demands.
- ✓ Visit the business as a customer.
- ✓ Prepare a set of questions to discuss. Don't wing it.
- ✓ Take notes, and follow up with the franchisor if you hear answers that concern you.

Action PLAN

Create a list of owner questions for each franchise you investigate. Make full notes after each interview and drop them in your file.

CHAPTER 22

Skill Sets of the Successful Franchisee

*AROLYN PLANS TO BUY A RETAIL BUSI-
ness because she has always dreamed
about having a stream of customers
whom she pleases with scrumptious
teas, cakes and other treats. She enjoys meeting her customers face to face and looks forward to owning her own shop. She wonders
what else she will need to know to be successful. Are there skills that she could learn that
will help in her business?*

Carolyn is asking the right questions,
because all successful small-business owners
develop a distinct skill set. At the heart of any
franchised business are some basic elements
of business operation and business development that must be mastered. Falter on these
basics, and your business may have some serious problems. The most successful business
owners develop these skill sets and drill them
into their employees.

THE ART OF THE SALE

Business is selling. All businesses boil down
quickly to this realization; franchises are no
exception. It does not matter whether you are
a junior manager in the world's largest organization or the owner of your own small business; the engine of both businesses is driven
by sales activity.

Remember this basic truth of business:
"Nothing happens in business until someone,
somewhere makes a sale."

It follows that your key to success is to
become a student of the sale; become an
expert in the process and the techniques used
by the best salespeople. Try to learn the basic
rules for presenting features and benefits,
overcoming objections and closing techniques. Park yourself in the business book
section of your local library, and crawl
through a few books on selling. There are
dozens of titles available. Drink them in.

COUNTER MAGIC

One of the most fascinating aspects of retail business is the study of what happens at the counter, that magic place where the front-line representatives of your business meet your customers. When I say the "counter" of your business, I mean it literally and metaphorically. All businesses meet customers, whether it is on the telephone, over the Internet, or at the customer's residence or place of business. In a traditional retail business, it will literally be a countertop at your location. Successful franchise organizations have pioneered and perfected the techniques at the counter that can have enormous payoffs in business.

No one has taught us more than the great Ray Kroc of McDonald's restaurants. He insisted that counter workers greet all customers with a smile and a cheery "Welcome to McDonald's!" The company reinforced the message with advertising showing the warm smiles of perky counter people welcoming you to McDonald's. "We love to see you smile."

Kroc also drove billions of dollars in sales, and propelled his organization to prominence, by teaching all counter people to say six simple words to every customer: "Would you like fries with that?" The resulting sales figures changed the landscape of American business.

Whatever franchised business you manage, study what is happening at the counter. Put your training resources to work on the exchange. Make sure your employees follow your example and stick to your counter procedures. Study and watch their performance and try new ideas. Keep your counter fresh, enthusiastic and fun, and your customers will come back time and again for more.

YOUR PROFITS ARE IN THE DETAILS

One thundering lesson of business ownership is just how small is the portion of gross revenue that actually falls into your pocket as profit. These small "margins" can represent vast fortunes, of course, when a business is run on a modestly large scale. Even at a large scale, though, the details determine whether the business comes out on the profitable side of the small margins or on the loss side of the profit/loss measure.

You have no choice but to become a student of the details of your franchised business. A few cents break on the price of your wholesale inventory, the lower costs of office supplies when purchased in bulk, the small incremental costs of condiments, managing the costs of labor—these details make all the difference.

BECOME A BEAN COUNTER

Money is the language of business, and accountants are the interpreters of the language. As a business owner, you must master the language and become conversant in balance sheets and monthly operations statements. If problems are brewing in your business, they will show up first in the monthly numbers. You will get to know intimately your percentages of food costs, labor, administrative costs and gross profit. This takes some study, so cozy up

 **IN***sight*

Pete and Laura Wakeman, founders of Great Harvest Bread Co., a whole-wheat bakery franchise, developed an entire marketing program based on their teachings of what should happen at the customer counter, which is vital to all Great Harvest bakeries today. Their counter techniques teach franchisees and their employees the value of smiling and generosity of spirit, and ways to personally connect with the customer.

to your favorite accountant and tell them that you think this is the beginning of a beautiful friendship.

BE A SKILLED NEGOTIATOR

It often surprises people coming from a job into business ownership just how much of small-business dealings are subject to a fluid marketplace, where prices and terms are determined by the give and take of negotiation. It takes a spot of courage to ask for a better price or payment terms or faster delivery, but it gives you the edge you need in your business. Your suppliers and business customers expect many aspects of the sale to be negotiated, so be prepared to jump in.

 IN*sight*

In all negotiations, know beforehand how long you will go before you stop negotiating, and what you consider your target. When opening your discussion, "start high" and then be prepared to make concessions as the other side (starting low) pulls you down toward your target endpoint. Asking for more than you will settle for will not insult anyone. It will leave you some room to make concessions to the other side. That will put you in the give and take of business—right where you need to be.

PEOPLE MANAGEMENT

Small-business ownership is little more than the management of employees. Keep them happy, well-paid and motivated, and your business will be on solid ground. Give no personal attention, underpay, and discourage them with a punishing attitude, and you will experience high turnover and low productivity. Given typically low margins in small businesses, this can make the difference between a profitable business and a troubled one.

BUILD AN ORGANIZATION

It's been said that the owner does not build a business; they build an organization of people and the organization builds the business. Think about building a team of talented people, look for the best you can find, and try to stay out of their way as they build your business.

BE AN A+ FRANCHISEE

If your business is a franchise, follow the rules of the system. Part of being a top-performing franchised business is full and careful compliance with all aspects of the franchise program. That means paying royalties on time, showing up for meetings and taking educational opportunities as they come along. Be a leader among franchise owners who do their best to promote the brand. Not only is this good business, but it will also add to the value of your business and may open opportunities down the road for expansion. The franchisor will naturally look to its A+ franchisees when new opportunities present themselves.

COLLECTING MONEY

The biggest challenge you face as a small-business owner is the collection of money owed to you. For all businesses, successful collection is a combination of smart routine business practice and persistence.

When do you know you have a collection problem? Here are the symptoms:

- An unacceptably high level of accounts receivable
- No office policy on collections
- Too many bad checks
- No information on the customer who pays on credit (including by check!)

- An inability to be decisive and move promptly against the deadbeat
- No way to recover the expenses associated with debt collection, such as attorney's fees, interest and late charges

No one likes collection problems. If you are new to business, the reluctance of your customers to pay their bills can be a surprise. After all, you have always paid your mortgage, utility bills, credit card statements and household expenses on time. Why can't your customers do the same?

Often the reason they do not pay in a timely fashion is *you*. Your routine credit extension practices, the information you gather on your customers, and the way you respond to slow payment all dictate the success you have at getting paid.

The best advice is to create a written policy statement that details exactly how credit will be extended or how a new customer account will be set up. Give a copy of the policy to the customer. The policy should spell out all credit procedures and collection policies. For your internal use, develop form letters that you use when a customer is late, and prepare to respond immediately.

Use some form of credit application that gathers this basic information about the account: name, address, telephone number (work and residence), Social Security number (this is essential), place of employment, bank account information, and property ownership information (automobiles and homes). If you are extending credit to a corporation, be sure to obtain the formal corporate name, the date and state of incorporation and the employer identification number. Without this basic information, collections can be a nightmare. The following are some tips for smart collection practices:

Don't Accept Bad Checks

Examine all checks carefully. A quick way to spot a forged check is to look for the perforations. Most forged checks are produced on plain paper stock with no perforated edges. Real check paper stock allows the check to be removed from a perforated edge. Bank tellers are trained to look for this distinctive feature.

Is the date correct? If the date is old (generally more than three or four weeks) or if it has been postdated, do not accept it.

Is the amount properly stated? Does the numerical figure agree with the written dollar amount? If the number, the written amount or the payee (you) is illegible, written over or hard to read in any way, do not take the check.

Be careful accepting a two-party check. A two-party check is made to one person, and that person offers to endorse the check to you. Unless you know both parties, you run a risk that the original maker will stop payment on the check.

Look out for checks that show a low sequence number. This indicates a recently opened account since most banks begin numbering a new checking account at #101. Just be more cautious when the number is low.

Do Not Put Off Collecting on the Debt

The longer you wait to take action, the more difficult it will be to collect on an overdue account. An account receivable that is more than 90 days old should be turned over for collection, either to a collection agency, which will handle the matter for a hefty percentage of the outstanding bill, or to your attorney.

Use a Credit Agreement

You cannot collect interest, late fees or attorney's fees without the written agreement of the customer. A credit agreement also spells out the terms of the credit being extended and shows you take this account, the credit and collections seriously.

SUMMARY NOTES ──────────

✓ Running your business is the ultimate challenge. Brush up on the skills that are essential to all business operations: master the art of the sale, manage details, count beans, negotiate, manage people effectively, build an organization, be an A+ franchisee, and collect the money you are owed.

Action **PLAN**

Take a course at a local college, university or business school to learn more about areas of business that are mystifying to you.

CHAPTER 23

Make It Happen

*S*EAN HAS TOYED WITH THE IDEA OF START-*ing his own business for more than five years. Since he was a boy, he has dreamed of building a successful business. He works up to a point of getting serious about an opportunity and then backs off and stays in the comfortable routine of his job. He is beginning to wonder if he will ever make the commitment.*

Starting a business, whether it is an independent one or a franchise, takes an enormous amount of initiative. If you have not done it before, it is easy not to start. That's Sean's problem. There are mental obstacles at every turn. You can fall into a trap of indecision, where you constantly search for the exact business of your dreams but never seem to find it. People you love and respect can talk you out of it. You can be discouraged by the doom and gloom of the popular press. You can decide that your route to wealth is working your way up to middle management. There are a thousand reasons not to start.

But you know in your heart that the world rewards courage and persistence.

So start! Make that call. Contact your support team. Start lining up your money resources. Go to that trade show. Ask those questions, and present yourself in the finest light possible to your new business contacts.

You will be pleasantly surprised at how your hard work and persistence pays off, and the interesting places your initiative can lead you. If the words in this book help you take that first step, then you have made my day.

Good luck in your new business!

Action **PLAN**

There is no substitute for taking action. No amount of dreaming, planning or talking takes its place. If you want to be in business for yourself, you must make it happen. Take action today.

Ultimate Franchise Directory

Understanding the Directory

SECTION TWO OF OUR BOOK DETAILS THE basic start-up information of 1,069 franchise opportunities. Use this information as a first step toward buying a franchise of your own.

This directory is not intended to endorse, advertise or recommend any particular franchise(s). It is solely a research tool you can use to compare franchise operations. You should always conduct your own independent investigation before you invest money in a franchise. If you haven't already, make sure you read Section One of this book.

KEY TO THE LISTINGS
Franchise 500® ranking

As an additional research tool, we've included the rankings of companies in *Entrepreneur* magazine's 2004 Franchise 500®. Rankings are based on objective factors, including financial stability of the system, growth rate and size of the system, years in business, length of time franchising, start-up costs, litigation, percentage of terminations and whether the company provides financing. For more information regarding the methodology used in these rankings, go to www.entrepreneur.com/franchise500.

Financial rating

$$$$: Exceeded our standards
$$$: Met all our standards
$$: Met most of our standards
$: Met our minimal standards
0: Did not meet our minimal standards

An important step in researching a franchise opportunity is determining the financial strength of the company. If a franchise company is in a weak financial condition, it could raise the risk levels for your investment.

For our financial ratings, we examined, among other things, liquidity ratios, debt to net worth, revenue or sales volume, and profitability. This information was taken from the financial information provided in the companies' Uniform Franchise Offering Circulars (UFOCs).

We strongly suggest that, when researching a franchise, you have your accountant read the financial statements included in the UFOC and ask for a more detailed opinion of the financial condition of the company.

Franchise units

Besides providing data on the number of units in a system, we tell you where the company's current units are concentrated and where the company wants to expand this year. Here you'll also learn whether the franchise can be run from home or from a kiosk.

Exclusive territories

The majority of franchise companies offer exclusive territories to their franchisees. Territory size typically is based on population size or by geographic area.

Absentee ownership

Many franchise companies require their franchisees to be hands-on owners. Here you can see whether absentee ownership is allowed.

Costs

Total cost: the initial investment necessary to open the franchise. This amount includes costs for equipment, location, leasehold improvements, initial supplies, business licenses, signage, working capital as well as the initial franchise fee.

Franchise fee: a lump sum payment made at the time the franchise agreement is signed. This fee generally covers the franchisor's cost of recruiting franchisees and of initial services like site location and training.

Royalty fee: typically a monthly fee paid by the franchisee to the franchisor, which is either calculated as a percentage of the franchisee's gross sales or on a flat-fee basis.

Term of agreement: the length of time the franchisee is granted the right to operate under the franchise system. When the time is up, most franchise companies offer a right to renew either for a fee or for free.

Franchisees required to buy multiple units? While many franchise companies encourage franchisees to buy more than one unit at a time, there are franchisors that require multiple franchise ownership.

Financing

Types of financing provided by the franchisor are listed under the "in-house" heading.

When the franchisor has developed a relationship with an outside lender to provide financing to its franchisees, the types of financing are listed under the "3rd party" heading.

Qualifications, Training, Business support, Marketing support

We provide additional information on these factors to help you make an informed decision.

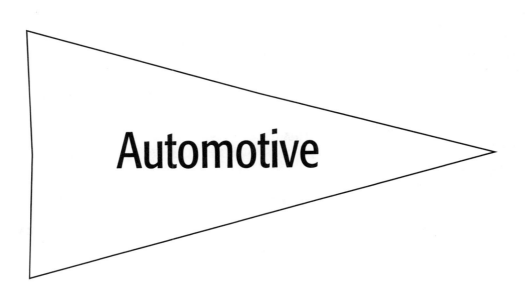

Automotive

AUTOMOTIVE   *Appearance Services*

AERO COLOURS INC.

Ranked #398 in Entrepreneur Magazine's 2004 Franchise 500

Financial rating: 0

6971 Washington Ave. S., #102
Minneapolis, MN 55439
Ph: (800)696-2376/(952)942-0490
Fax: (952)942-0628
www.aerocolours.com
Mobile automotive paint repair
Began: 1985, Franchising since: 1993
Headquarters size: 8 employees
Franchise department: 8 employees

U.S. franchises: 219
Canadian franchises: 0
Other foreign franchises: 2
Company-owned: 5
Units concentrated in all U.S.

Seeking: All U.S.
Seeking in Canada? Yes
Exclusive territories? Yes
Homebased option? Yes
Kiosk option? No
Employees needed to run franchise: 4
Absentee ownership? Yes

COSTS
Total cost: $56.4K-164.4K
Franchise fee: $25K-125K
Royalty fee: 7%
Term of agreement: 10 years renewable
    for $1K
Franchisees required to buy multiple
    units? No

FINANCING
In-house: Franchise fee
3rd-party: Equipment, franchise fee

QUALIFICATIONS
Net worth: $100K
Cash liquidity: $50K
Experience:
    General business experience
    Marketing skills

TRAINING
At headquarters: 2 weeks
At franchisee's location: 2 weeks

BUSINESS SUPPORT
Newsletter
Meetings
Toll-free phone line
Internet
Security/safety procedures
Field operations/evaluations

MARKETING SUPPORT
Ad slicks

COLORS ON PARADE

Ranked #160 in Entrepreneur Magazine's 2004 Franchise 500　　　　*Financial rating: $$$$*

642 Century Cir.
Conway, SC 29526
Ph: (800)726-5677
Fax: (843)347-0349
www.colorsfranchise.com
Mobile automotive appearance
　　services
Began: 1989, Franchising since: 1991
Headquarters size: 15 employees
Franchise department: 2 employees

U.S. franchises: 272
Canadian franchises: 0
Other foreign franchises: 0
Company-owned: 12
Units concentrated in CA, FL, TX, VA

Seeking: All U.S.
Seeking in Canada? Yes
Exclusive territories? Yes
Homebased option? Yes
Kiosk option? No
Employees needed to run franchise: 0
Absentee ownership? No

COSTS
Total cost: $50K-594K
Franchise fee: $5.5K-15.5K
Royalty fee: 7-30%
Term of agreement: 10 years renewable
Franchisees required to buy multiple
　　units? Outside the U.S. only

FINANCING
In-house: None
3rd-party: Equipment, inventory

QUALIFICATIONS
Net worth: $50K-500K
Cash liquidity: $15K-200K
Experience:
　　General business experience
　　Marketing skills
　　Love of cars helpful

TRAINING
At headquarters: 2 weeks
At franchisee's location: 3 months
Ongoing technical training

BUSINESS SUPPORT
Newsletter
Meetings
Toll-free phone line
Grand opening
Internet
Security/safety procedures
Field operations/evaluations

MARKETING SUPPORT
Co-op advertising
Ad slicks
Recruitment seminars

DENT DOCTOR

Ranked #497 in Entrepreneur Magazine's 2004 Franchise 500　　　　*Financial rating: $$$*

11301 W. Markham
Little Rock, AR 72211
Ph: (501)224-0500
Fax: (501)224-0507
www.dentdoctor.com
Paint-free dent repair
Began: 1986, Franchising since: 1990
Headquarters size: 6 employees
Franchise department: 3 employees

U.S. franchises: 37
Canadian franchises: 1
Other foreign franchises: 1
Company-owned: 3
Units concentrated in all U.S.

Seeking: All U.S.
Focusing on: CA, FL, NY
Seeking in Canada? Yes
Exclusive territories? Yes
Homebased option? No
Kiosk option? No
Employees needed to run franchise: 3
Absentee ownership? Yes

COSTS
Total cost: $47.5K-84.9K
Franchise fee: $19.9K+
Royalty fee: 6%
Term of agreement: 10 years renewable
　　at no charge
Franchisees required to buy multiple
　　units? No

FINANCING
In-house: None
3rd-party: Equipment, franchise fee,
　　inventory, start-up costs

QUALIFICATIONS
Net worth: $75K
Cash liquidity: $10K
Experience:
　　General business experience

TRAINING
At headquarters: 4 weeks
At franchisee's location: 4 weeks

BUSINESS SUPPORT
Newsletter
Meetings
Toll-free phone line
Grand opening
Internet
Security/safety procedures
Field operations/evaluations
Purchasing cooperatives

MARKETING SUPPORT
Co-op advertising
Ad slicks
Regional marketing
Local advertising plan

MAACO AUTO PAINTING & BODYWORKS
Ranked #126 in Entrepreneur Magazine's 2004 Franchise 500   *Financial rating: $$$$*

381 Brooks Rd.
King of Prussia, PA 19406
Ph: (800)296-2226
Fax: (610)337-6176
www.franchise.maaco.com
Automotive painting & body repair
Began: 1972, Franchising since: 1972
Headquarters size: 120 employees
Franchise department: 5 employees

U.S. franchises: 458
Canadian franchises: 38
Other foreign franchises: 6
Company-owned: 2
Units concentrated in all U.S.

Seeking: All U.S.
Seeking in Canada? Yes
Exclusive territories? No
Homebased option? No
Kiosk option? No
Employees needed to run franchise:
    7-8
Absentee ownership? No

COSTS
Total cost: $249K
Franchise fee: $30K
Royalty fee: 8%
Term of agreement: 15 years renewable
    at no charge
Franchisees required to buy multiple
    units? No

FINANCING
In-house: None
3rd-party: Equipment, franchise fee,
    inventory, start-up costs

QUALIFICATIONS
Net worth: $250K
Cash liquidity: $65K
Experience:
    General business experience
    Marketing skills

TRAINING
At headquarters: 3 weeks
At franchisee's location: 4 weeks

BUSINESS SUPPORT
Newsletter
Meetings
Toll-free phone line
Grand opening
Internet
Security/safety procedures
Field operations/evaluations
Purchasing cooperatives

MARKETING SUPPORT
Ad slicks
National media campaign
Regional marketing

MARS INT'L. INC.

Financial rating: $$$

2001 E. Division, #101
Arlington, TX 76001
Ph: (800)909-6277
Fax: (800)230-2859
www.marsinternational.com
Cosmetic automotive reconditioning
Began: 1987, Franchising since: 1998
Headquarters size: 17 employees
Franchise department: 5 employees

U.S. franchises: 137
Canadian franchises: 0
Other foreign franchises: 0
Company-owned: 0
Units concentrated in AK, AL, AR, AZ,
    CA, CO, CT, DE, FL, GA, IA, ID,
    KS, KY, LA, MA, ME, MO, MS, MT,
    NC, NE, NH, NJ, NM, NV, OH,
    OK, OR, PA, SC, TN, TX, UT, VT,
    WY

Seeking: All U.S.
Focusing on: States where units are
    concentrated (see above)
Seeking in Canada? No

Exclusive territories? No
Homebased option? Yes
Kiosk option? No
Employees needed to run franchise: 1+
Absentee ownership? Yes

COSTS
Total cost: $44K
Franchise fee: $15K
Royalty fee: 8%
Term of agreement: 5 years renewable
    for 50% of current franchise fee
Franchisees required to buy multiple
    units? No

FINANCING
In-house: None
3rd-party: Equipment, franchise fee,
    inventory, start-up costs

QUALIFICATIONS
Info not provided

TRAINING
At headquarters: 2 weeks
At franchisee's location: 2 weeks

BUSINESS SUPPORT
Newsletter
Meetings
Toll-free phone line
Internet

MARKETING SUPPORT
Ad slicks
National media campaign
Online business development center

MIRACLE AUTO PAINTING INC.

Ranked #442 in Entrepreneur Magazine's 2004 Franchise 500   *Financial rating: $$$$*

3157 Corporate Pl.
Hayward, CA 94545
Ph: (877)647-2253/(510)887-2211
Fax: (510)887-3092
www.miracleautopainting.com
Automotive painting & body repair
Began: 1953, Franchising since: 1964
Headquarters size: 10 employees
Franchise department: 2 employees

U.S. franchises: 27
Canadian franchises: 0
Other foreign franchises: 0
Company-owned: 3
Units concentrated in AZ, CA, NV, TX

Seeking: All U.S.
Focusing on: AZ, CA, NV, TX
Seeking in Canada? No
Exclusive territories? Yes
Homebased option? No
Kiosk option? No
Employees needed to run franchise: 10
Absentee ownership? No

COSTS
Total cost: $216K-273K
Franchise fee: $35K
Royalty fee: 5%
Term of agreement: 10 years renewable
    for $1.5K
Franchisees required to buy multiple
    units? No

FINANCING
In-house: None
3rd-party: Equipment, franchise fee,
    inventory, start-up costs

QUALIFICATIONS
Net worth: $500K
Cash liquidity: $100K
Experience:
    General business experience
    Automotive experience

TRAINING
At headquarters: 2 weeks
At franchisee's location: 2 weeks
At existing franchise location: 2 weeks

BUSINESS SUPPORT
Newsletter
Meetings
Toll-free phone line
Grand opening
Internet
Lease negotiations
Security/safety procedures
Field operations/evaluations
Purchasing cooperatives

MARKETING SUPPORT
Co-op advertising
Ad slicks
Regional marketing

NOVUS AUTO GLASS

Ranked #240 in Entrepreneur Magazine's 2004 Franchise 500   *Financial rating: $$*

10425 Hampshire Ave. S.
Minneapolis, MN 55438
Ph: (800)944-6811
Fax: (952)946-0481
www.novusglass.com
Windshield repair/replacement
Began: 1972, Franchising since: 1985
Headquarters size: 40 employees
Franchise department: 13 employees

U.S. franchises: 377
Canadian franchises: 43
Other foreign franchises: 2,113
Company-owned: 2
Units concentrated in all U.S.

Seeking: All U.S.
Seeking in Canada? No
Exclusive territories? Info not provided
Homebased option? Yes
Kiosk option? No
Employees needed to run franchise:
    2-3
Absentee ownership? Yes

COSTS
Total cost: $37K-170K
Franchise fee: $7.5K
Royalty fee: 7-8%
Term of agreement: 10 years renewable
    for $2.5K
Franchisees required to buy multiple
    units? No

FINANCING
In-house: None
3rd-party: Equipment, franchise fee,
    inventory, start-up costs

QUALIFICATIONS
Net worth: $50K/100K
Cash liquidity: 25% of initial invest-
    ment
Experience:
    General business experience
    Marketing skills

TRAINING
At headquarters: 8 days initial
At franchisee's location: 1 week follow-
    up
At regional center: 2 weeks; Advanced
    training in glass replacement

BUSINESS SUPPORT
Newsletter
Meetings
Toll-free phone line
Internet
Security/safety procedures
Field operations/evaluations

MARKETING SUPPORT
Co-op advertising
Ad slicks
National media campaign
Regional marketing
Web locator
Brand awareness program

PAINT MEDIC

Financial rating: 0

3111 Walden Ave.
Depew, NY 14043
Ph: (866)446-2277
Fax: (905)788-1939
www.paintmedic.com
Vehicle paint touch-up services
Began: 1990, Franchising since: 1995
Headquarters size: 10 employees
Franchise department: 8 employees

U.S. franchises: 1
Canadian franchises: 19
Other foreign franchises: 0
Company-owned: 2

Seeking: All U.S.
Seeking in Canada? No
Exclusive territories? Yes
Homebased option? Yes
Kiosk option? No
Employees needed to run franchise:
    0 -15
Absentee ownership? No

COSTS
Total cost: $39.6K-71.3K
Franchise fee: $25K-50K
Royalty fee: 5%
Term of agreement: 5 years renewable
Franchisees required to buy multiple
    units? No

FINANCING
No financing available

QUALIFICATIONS
Cash liquidity: $50K-75K
Experience:
    General business experience
    Marketing skills

TRAINING
At headquarters: 3 weeks
At franchisee's location: 1 week

BUSINESS SUPPORT
Newsletter
Meetings
Toll-free phone line
Internet
Security/safety procedures
Field operations/evaluations
Purchasing cooperatives

MARKETING SUPPORT
Regional marketing

THE SHINE FACTORY

Current financial data not available

320 Monument Pl. S.E.
Calgary, AB Canada T2A 1X3
Ph: (403)243-3030
Fax: (403)243-3031
www.shinefactory.ca
Automotive appearance services
Began: 1979, Franchising since: 1979
Headquarters size: 4 employees
Franchise department: Info not
    provided

U.S. franchises: 0
Canadian franchises: 31
Other foreign franchises: 0
Company-owned: 0

Not available in the U.S.
Seeking in Canada? Yes
Exclusive territories? Yes
Homebased option? No
Kiosk option? No
Employees needed to run franchise:
    4-5
Absentee ownership? No

COSTS
Total cost: $125K
Franchise fee: $10K-50K
Royalty fee: 8%
Term of agreement: 5 years renewable
    at no charge
Franchisees required to buy multiple
    units? No

FINANCING
No financing available

QUALIFICATIONS
Net worth: $100K
Cash liquidity: $60K
Experience:
    General business experience

TRAINING
At headquarters: 1 week
At franchisee's location: 1 week
Ongoing

BUSINESS SUPPORT
Toll-free phone line
Grand opening
Lease negotiations
Field operations/evaluations

MARKETING SUPPORT
Ad slicks

SUPER CLEAN YACHT SERVICE FRANCHISING INC.

Current financial data not available

910 W. Coast Hwy.
Newport Beach, CA 92663
Ph: (949)646-2990
Fax: (949)646-9311
www.supercleanyachtservice.com
Pleasure boat cleaning & detailing
Began: 1984, Franchising since: 1999
Headquarters size: 12 employees
Franchise department: 3 employees

U.S. franchises: 2
Canadian franchises: 0
Other foreign franchises: 0
Company-owned: 1
Units concentrated in CA

Seeking: All U.S.
Focusing on: CA, FL, TX
Seeking in Canada? No
Exclusive territories? Yes
Homebased option? Yes
Kiosk option? No
Employees needed to run franchise: 4
Absentee ownership? Yes

COSTS
Total cost: $12.7K-50.8K
Franchise fee: $7.5K-25K
Royalty fee: $500/mo.
Term of agreement: 5 years renewable
    for $1.5K
Franchisees required to buy multiple
    units? No

FINANCING
In-house: Franchise fee
3rd-party: None

QUALIFICATIONS
Net worth: $15.5K+
Cash liquidity: $2.5K
Experience:
    Marketing skills

TRAINING
At headquarters: 11 days
At franchisee's location: 1 day

BUSINESS SUPPORT
Newsletter
Meetings
Toll-free phone line
Grand opening
Internet
Security/safety procedures
Field operations/evaluations
Purchasing cooperatives

MARKETING SUPPORT
Co-op advertising
Ad slicks
Regional marketing

SUPERGLASS WINDSHIELD REPAIR

Ranked #287 in Entrepreneur Magazine's 2004 Franchise 500　　　*Financial rating: $$*

6101 Chancellor Dr., #200
Orlando, FL 32809
Ph: (407)240-1920
Fax: (407)240-3266
www.sgwr.com
Windshield repair
Began: 1992, Franchising since: 1993
Headquarters size: 5 employees
Franchise department: 2 employees

U.S. franchises: 201
Canadian franchises: 1
Other foreign franchises: 8
Company-owned: 0

Seeking: All U.S.
Seeking in Canada? No
Exclusive territories? Yes
Homebased option? Yes
Kiosk option? No
Employees needed to run franchise: 1
Absentee ownership? Yes

COSTS
Total cost: $9.9K-31K
Franchise fee: $9.5K+
Royalty fee: 3-4%
Term of agreement: 10 years renewable
    for $1K
Franchisees required to buy multiple
    units? Outside the U.S. only

FINANCING
In-house: Franchise fee, start-up costs
3rd-party: None

QUALIFICATIONS
Net worth: $15K
Cash liquidity: $15K
Experience:
    People skills
    Must enjoy working outdoors

TRAINING
At headquarters: 5 days
At franchisee's location: 5 days

BUSINESS SUPPORT
Newsletter
Meetings
Toll-free phone line
Grand opening
Internet
Security/safety procedures
Field operations/evaluations
Purchasing cooperatives

MARKETING SUPPORT
Co-op advertising
Ad slicks
National media campaign
Regional marketing
Phone support w/B2B accounts

ZIEBART

Ranked #374 in Entrepreneur Magazine's 2004 Franchise 500   *Financial rating: $$$$*

1290 E. Maple Rd.
Troy, MI 48007-1290
Ph: (800)877-1312/(248)588-4100
Fax: (248)588-0718
www.ziebart.com
Auto appearance services/accessories
    & auto glass
Began: 1954, Franchising since: 1963
Headquarters size: 60 employees
Franchise department: 2 employees

U.S. franchises: 174
Canadian franchises: 56
Other foreign franchises: 162
Company-owned: 29
Units concentrated in Midwest

Seeking: All U.S.
Seeking in Canada? Yes
Exclusive territories? No
Homebased option? No
Kiosk option? No
Employees needed to run franchise: 4
Absentee ownership? No

COSTS
Total cost: to $190K
Franchise fee: $25K
Royalty fee: 8%
Term of agreement: 10 years renewable
    for $3.9K
Franchisees required to buy multiple
    units? No

FINANCING
No financing available

QUALIFICATIONS
Net worth: $239K
Cash liquidity: $100K-150K
Experience:
    General business experience

TRAINING
At headquarters: 3-6 weeks
At franchisee's location: 1 day

BUSINESS SUPPORT
Newsletter
Meetings
Toll-free phone line
Grand opening
Internet
Security/safety procedures
Field operations/evaluations

MARKETING SUPPORT
Co-op advertising
Ad slicks
National media campaign
Regional marketing

AUTOMOTIVE   *Rentals & Sales*

AFFILIATED CAR RENTAL LC

Ranked #295 in Entrepreneur Magazine's 2004 Franchise 500   *Financial rating: $$$*

96 Freneau Ave., #2
Matawan, NJ 07747
Ph: (800)367-5159
Fax: (732)290-8305
www.sensiblecarrental.com
Car rentals
Began: 1987, Franchising since: 1987
Headquarters size: 7 employees
Franchise department: 7 employees

U.S. franchises: 142
Canadian franchises: 0
Other foreign franchises: 0
Company-owned: 0

Seeking: All U.S.
Seeking in Canada? No
Exclusive territories? Yes
Homebased option? No
Kiosk option? No
Employees needed to run franchise:
    2-3
Absentee ownership? Yes

COSTS
Total cost: $46.4K-69.5K
Franchise fee: $6K-10.8K
Royalty fee: Varies
Term of agreement: Perpetual
Franchisees required to buy multiple
    units? No

FINANCING
In-house: None
3rd-party: Inventory

QUALIFICATIONS
Experience:
    General business experience

TRAINING
At headquarters: 2 days
At franchisee's location: 2 days

BUSINESS SUPPORT
Newsletter
Meetings
Toll-free phone line
Internet
Security/safety procedures
Field operations/evaluations
Purchasing cooperatives

MARKETING SUPPORT
Co-op advertising
Ad slicks

EAGLERIDER MOTORCYCLE RENTAL
Ranked #474 in Entrepreneur Magazine's 2004 Franchise 500   *Financial rating: $$$*

11860 S. La Cienega Blvd.
Hawthorne, CA 90250-3461
Ph: (310)536-6777
Fax: (310)536-6770
www.eaglerider.com
Harley-Davidson rentals & tours
Began: 1992, Franchising since: 1997
Headquarters size: 25 employees
Franchise department: 4 employees

U.S. franchises: 16
Canadian franchises: 0
Other foreign franchises: 2
Company-owned: 5
Units concentrated in CA

Seeking: All U.S.
Seeking in Canada? Yes
Exclusive territories? Yes
Homebased option? No
Kiosk option? No
Employees needed to run franchise: 5
Absentee ownership? No

COSTS
Total cost: $219.5K-674K
Franchise fee: $15K-35K
Royalty fee: 5%/10%
Term of agreement: 10 years renewable
    at no charge
Franchisees required to buy multiple
    units? No

FINANCING
In-house: Inventory
3rd-party: Accounts receivable, equip-
    ment, franchise fee, payroll, start-
    up costs

QUALIFICATIONS
Net worth: $350K
Cash liquidity: $100K
Experience:
    Industry experience
    General business experience
    Marketing skills
    Understanding of travel industry

TRAINING
At headquarters: 14 days
At franchisee's location: 3 days

BUSINESS SUPPORT
Newsletter
Meetings
Toll-free phone line
Grand opening
Internet
Security/safety procedures
Field operations/evaluations
Purchasing cooperatives

MARKETING SUPPORT
Ad slicks
National media campaign
Regional marketing
International advertising & promo-
    tions

J.D. BYRIDER SYSTEMS INC.
Ranked #247 in Entrepreneur Magazine's 2004 Franchise 500   *Financial rating: $$$$*

12802 Hamilton Crossing Blvd.
Carmel, IN 46032
Ph: (800)947-4532/(317)249-3000
Fax: (317)249-3001
www.jdbyrider.com
Auto sales & auto financing
Began: 1979, Franchising since: 1989
Headquarters size: 135 employees
Franchise department: 83 employees

U.S. franchises: 121
Canadian franchises: 0
Other foreign franchises: 0
Company-owned: 11
Units concentrated in all U.S.

Seeking: All U.S.
Seeking in Canada? Yes
Exclusive territories? Yes
Homebased option? No
Kiosk option? No
Employees needed to run franchise:
    10-15
Absentee ownership? Yes

COSTS
Total cost: $289.2K-2.5M
Franchise fee: $50K
Royalty fee: 3.5%
Term of agreement: 10 years renewable
    at no charge
Franchisees required to buy multiple
    units? No

FINANCING
In-house: None
3rd-party: Accounts receivable, equip-
    ment, inventory, start-up costs

QUALIFICATIONS
Net worth: $2M
Cash liquidity: $750K-1M
Experience:
    General business experience

TRAINING
At headquarters: 7 days
At franchisee's location: 1 week pre-
    opening
Franchise meetings: 3 times per year

BUSINESS SUPPORT
Newsletter
Meetings
Toll-free phone line
Grand opening
Internet
Security/safety procedures
Field operations/evaluations

MARKETING SUPPORT
Ad slicks
National media campaign
Regional marketing
POS support
TV commercials

PAYLESS CAR RENTAL SYSTEM INC.

Financial rating: $$$$

2350-N 34th St. N.
St. Petersburg, FL 33713
Ph: (800)729-5255/(727)321-6352
Fax: (727)323-6856
www.paylesscarrental.com
Auto rentals/sales
Began: 1971, Franchising since: 1971
Headquarters size: 55 employees
Franchise department: 5 employees

U.S. franchises: 51
Canadian franchises: 1
Other foreign franchises: 35
Company-owned: 2
Units concentrated in all U.S.

Seeking: All U.S.
Seeking in Canada? No
Exclusive territories? Yes
Homebased option? No
Kiosk option? No
Employees needed to run franchise:
    4 -20
Absentee ownership? Yes

COSTS
Total cost: $217.9K-6.3M
Franchise fee: $15K-500K
Royalty fee: 5%
Term of agreement: 5 years renewable
    for $2K
Franchisees required to buy multiple
    units? No

FINANCING
No financing available

QUALIFICATIONS
Net worth: $500K-1M
Cash liquidity: $50K-150K
Experience:
    Industry experience
    General business experience

TRAINING
At headquarters: 3 days
At franchisee's location: 3 days
Ongoing

BUSINESS SUPPORT
Newsletter
Meetings
Toll-free phone line
Grand opening
Internet
Security/safety procedures
Field operations/evaluations
Purchasing cooperatives

MARKETING SUPPORT
National media campaign
Internet marketing

PRICELESS RENT-A-CAR

Financial rating: $$$$

10324 S. Dolfield Rd.
Owings Mills, MD 21117
Ph: (800)662-8322
Fax: (410)581-1566
www.pricelesscar.com
Car rentals & leasing
Began: 1997, Franchising since: 1997
Headquarters size: 10 employees
Franchise department: 2 employees

U.S. franchises: 131
Canadian franchises: 0
Other foreign franchises: 1
Company-owned: 0
Units concentrated in all U.S.

Seeking: All U.S.
Seeking in Canada? Yes
Exclusive territories? Yes
Homebased option? No
Kiosk option? No
Employees needed to run franchise: 2
Absentee ownership? Yes

COSTS
Total cost: $30.9K-175K
Franchise fee: $2.5K-37K
Royalty fee: $30/car/mo.
Term of agreement: 10 years renewable
    at no charge
Franchisees required to buy multiple
    units? Outside the U.S. only

FINANCING
In-house: None
3rd-party: Accounts receivable, equip-
    ment, franchise fee, inventory, pay-
    roll, start-up costs

QUALIFICATIONS
Experience:
    General business experience
    Marketing skills

TRAINING
At headquarters: 1 week
At franchisee's location: Varies

BUSINESS SUPPORT
Newsletter
Meetings
Toll-free phone line
Grand opening
Internet
Lease negotiations
Security/safety procedures
Field operations/evaluations
Purchasing cooperatives

MARKETING SUPPORT
Co-op advertising
Ad slicks
National media campaign
Regional marketing

RENT-A-WRECK

Financial rating: $$$$

10324 S. Dolfield Rd.
Owings Mills, MD 21117
Ph: (410)581-5755
Fax: (410)581-1566
www.rentawreck.com
Auto rentals & leasing
Began: 1970, Franchising since: 1977
Headquarters size: 35 employees
Franchise department: 7 employees

U.S. franchises: 431
Canadian franchises: 0
Other foreign franchises: 27
Company-owned: 0
Units concentrated in all U.S.

Seeking: All U.S.
Seeking in Canada? Yes
Exclusive territories? Yes
Homebased option? No
Kiosk option? No
Employees needed to run franchise: 2
Absentee ownership? Yes

COSTS
Total cost: $32.8K-207K+
Franchise fee: $5K-74K+
Royalty fee: $30/car/mo.
Term of agreement: 10 years renewable
    at no charge
Franchisees required to buy multiple
    units? No

FINANCING
In-house: None
3rd-party: Accounts receivable, equip-
    ment, franchise fee, inventory, pay-
    roll, start-up costs

QUALIFICATIONS
Experience:
    General business experience
    Marketing skills

TRAINING
At headquarters: 1 week
At franchisee's location: Varies
At counter classes, marketing seminar
    & via newsletter

BUSINESS SUPPORT
Newsletter
Meetings
Toll-free phone line
Grand opening
Internet
Lease negotiations
Security/safety procedures
Field operations/evaluations
Purchasing cooperatives

MARKETING SUPPORT
Co-op advertising
Ad slicks
National media campaign
Regional marketing

THRIFTY CAR SALES INC.

Ranked #368 in Entrepreneur Magazine's 2004 Franchise 500

Financial rating: $$$$

5310 E. 31st St., CIMS 1130
Tulsa, OK 74135
Ph: (877)289-2583
Fax: (918)669-2654
www.thriftycarsales.com
Used car sales
Began: 1998, Franchising since: 1998
Headquarters size: 20 employees
Franchise department: 5 employees

U.S. franchises: 51
Canadian franchises: 0
Other foreign franchises: 0
Company-owned: 0
Units concentrated in AL, AZ, CA, CT,
    FL, GA, ID, LA, MS, MT, NC, NE,
    NM, OH, RI, SC, TN, TX, WV

Seeking: All U.S.
Seeking in Canada? No
Exclusive territories? Yes
Homebased option? No
Kiosk option? No
Employees needed to run franchise:
    10-14
Absentee ownership? Yes

COSTS
Total cost: $765K-4M
Franchise fee: $35K
Royalty fee: $110+/vehicle
Term of agreement: 5 years renewable
    for $2.5K
Franchisees required to buy multiple
    units? No

FINANCING
No financing available

QUALIFICATIONS
Net worth: $500K
Cash liquidity: $125K
Experience:
    Industry experience

TRAINING
Thrifty University

BUSINESS SUPPORT
Newsletter
Meetings
Internet
Field operations/evaluations
Purchasing cooperatives

MARKETING SUPPORT
Ad slicks
Marketing & media analysis
Design services
PR assistance

U-SAVE AUTO RENTAL OF AMERICA INC.
Ranked #324 in Entrepreneur Magazine's 2004 Franchise 500   *Financial rating: $$$$*

4780 I-55 N., #300
Jackson, MS 39211
Ph: (800)438-2300/(601)713-4333
Fax: (601)713-4330
www.usave.net
New & used auto rentals
Began: 1979, Franchising since: 1979
Headquarters size: 30 employees
Franchise department: 15 employees

U.S. franchises: 320
Canadian franchises: 0
Other foreign franchises: 5
Company-owned: 10
Units concentrated in all U.S.

Seeking: All U.S.
Seeking in Canada? No
Exclusive territories? Yes
Homebased option? No
Kiosk option? No
Employees needed to run franchise: 3
Absentee ownership? Yes

COSTS
Total cost: $56.5K-103.5K
Franchise fee: $20K
Royalty fee: $34/car/mo.
Term of agreement: 10 years renewable
at no charge
Franchisees required to buy multiple
units? No

FINANCING
In-house: None
3rd-party: Inventory

QUALIFICATIONS
Net worth: $250K
Cash liquidity: $60K
Experience:
General business experience
Marketing skills

TRAINING
At headquarters: 1 week
Follow-up visits: 3 days each

BUSINESS SUPPORT
Newsletter
Meetings
Toll-free phone line
Internet
Security/safety procedures
Field operations/evaluations

MARKETING SUPPORT
Ad slicks
Marketing training
Marketing materials

AUTOMOTIVE ◄ *Repair Services*

AAMCO TRANSMISSIONS INC.
Ranked #80 in Entrepreneur Magazine's 2004 Franchise 500   *Financial rating: $$$$*

One Presidential Blvd.
Bala Cynwyd, PA 19004
Ph: (800)223-8887/(610)668-2900
Fax: (610)538-0004
www.aamcotransmissions.com
Transmission repair & services
Began: 1963, Franchising since: 1963
Headquarters size: Info not provided
Franchise department: 10 employees

U.S. franchises: 681
Canadian franchises: 23
Other foreign franchises: 0
Company-owned: 0
Units concentrated in CA, FL, TX

Seeking: All U.S.
Seeking in Canada? Yes
Exclusive territories? No
Homebased option? No
Kiosk option? No
Employees needed to run franchise: 5
Absentee ownership? No

COSTS
Total cost: $187.5K-207K
Franchise fee: $30K
Royalty fee: 7%
Term of agreement: 15 years renewable
at no charge
Franchisees required to buy multiple
units? No

FINANCING
In-house: None
3rd-party: Equipment, inventory,
start-up costs

QUALIFICATIONS
Net worth: $250K
Cash liquidity: $75K
Experience:
General business experience
Marketing skills

TRAINING
Total training: 5 weeks

BUSINESS SUPPORT
Newsletter
Meetings
Toll-free phone line
Grand opening
Internet
Security/safety procedures
Field operations/evaluations
Purchasing cooperatives

MARKETING SUPPORT
Ad slicks
National media campaign
Regional marketing
Marketing guides & tools
Sales assistance

ALL TUNE AND LUBE

Ranked #302 in Entrepreneur Magazine's 2004 Franchise 500   *Financial rating: $$*

8334 Veterans Hwy.
Millersville, MD 21108
Ph: (800)935-8863/(410)987-1011
Fax: (410)987-9080
www.alltuneandlube.com
Total car care
Began: 1985, Franchising since: 1985
Headquarters size: 60 employees
Franchise department: 60 employees

U.S. franchises: 250
Canadian franchises: 1
Other foreign franchises: 0
Company-owned: 1
Units concentrated in all U.S. except
   AK, HI

Seeking: All U.S.
Seeking in Canada? No
Exclusive territories? Yes
Homebased option? No
Kiosk option? No
Employees needed to run franchise: 5
Absentee ownership? No

COSTS
Total cost: $125K
Franchise fee: $25K
Royalty fee: 7%
Term of agreement: 15 years renewable
   at no charge
Franchisees required to buy multiple
   units? No

FINANCING
In-house: Franchise fee
3rd-party: Equipment, franchise fee,
   inventory, start-up costs

QUALIFICATIONS
Net worth: $100K
Cash liquidity: $32K
Experience:
   General business experience

TRAINING
At headquarters: 2 weeks
At franchisee's location: 1-2 weeks

BUSINESS SUPPORT
Newsletter
Meetings
Toll-free phone line
Grand opening
Security/safety procedures
Field operations/evaluations
Purchasing cooperatives

MARKETING SUPPORT
Co-op advertising
Ad slicks
Regional marketing

AUTOMOTIVE MAINTENANCE SOLUTIONS

Current financial data not available

1404 7th Ave. E.
Hendersonville, NC 28792
Ph: (866)845-9611/(828)696-9611
Fax: (828)693-0823
www.amscarcare.com
Automotive maintenance services
Began: 1962, Franchising since: 2002
Headquarters size: 4 employees
Franchise department: 2 employees

U.S. franchises: 0
Canadian franchises: 0
Other foreign franchises: 0
Company-owned: 1

Seeking: All U.S.
Seeking in Canada? No
Exclusive territories? Yes
Homebased option? No
Kiosk option? No
Employees needed to run franchise:
   3-4
Absentee ownership? Yes

COSTS
Total cost: $118.1K-175.6K
Franchise fee: $25K
Royalty fee: 7%/mo.
Term of agreement: Renewable term at
   no charge
Franchisees required to buy multiple
   units? No

FINANCING
No financing available

QUALIFICATIONS
Net worth: $150K
Cash liquidity: $50K
Experience:
   General business experience
   Marketing skills

TRAINING
At headquarters: 2 weeks
At franchisee's location: 2 weeks

BUSINESS SUPPORT
Newsletter
Meetings
Toll-free phone line
Grand opening
Internet
Lease negotiations
Security/safety procedures
Field operations/evaluations
Purchasing cooperatives

MARKETING SUPPORT
Info not provided

BIG O TIRES INC.

Ranked #60 in Entrepreneur Magazine's 2004 Franchise 500

Financial rating: $$$$

12650 E. Briarwood Ave., #2D
Englewood, CO 80112
Ph: (800)622-2446
Fax: (303)728-5700
www.bigotires.com
Tires/wheels/related under-car services
Began: 1962, Franchising since: 1962
Headquarters size: 100 employees
Franchise department: 10 employees

U.S. franchises: 558
Canadian franchises: 35
Other foreign franchises: 0
Company-owned: 0
Units concentrated in AZ, CA, CO, IA,
    ID, IN, KS, KY, MI, MO, MT, NE,
    NM, NV, OH, OK, OR, SD, TX,
    UT, WA WY

Seeking: Southeast, Southwest, West
Seeking in Canada? No
Exclusive territories? Yes
Homebased option? No
Kiosk option? No
Employees needed to run franchise: 8
Absentee ownership? Yes

COSTS
Total cost: $150K-1.5M
Franchise fee: $27.5K
Royalty fee: 2%
Term of agreement: 10 years renewable
    for $1.5K
Franchisees required to buy multiple
    units? No

FINANCING
In-house: None
3rd-party: Accounts receivable, equip-
    ment, franchise fee, inventory, pay-
    roll, start-up costs

QUALIFICATIONS
Net worth: $300K
Cash liquidity: $100K-150K
Experience:
    Strong management skills

TRAINING
At headquarters: 5 weeks
At franchisee's location: 2 weeks
At national training center &
    in-market: 7 weeks

BUSINESS SUPPORT
Newsletter
Meetings
Grand opening
Internet
Security/safety procedures
Field operations/evaluations
Purchasing cooperatives

MARKETING SUPPORT
Co-op advertising
Ad slicks
National media campaign
Regional marketing

CAR-X AUTO SERVICE

Ranked #189 in Entrepreneur Magazine's 2004 Franchise 500

Financial rating: $$$$

1414 Baronial Plaza Dr.
Toledo, OH 43615
Ph: (800)359-2359/(419)865-6900
Fax: (419)865-7343
www.carx.com
Auto repair & maintenance services
Began: 1971, Franchising since: 1973
Headquarters size: 22 employees
Franchise department: 7 employees

U.S. franchises: 150
Canadian franchises: 0
Other foreign franchises: 0
Company-owned: 29
Units concentrated in IA, IL, IN, KS,
    KY, MN, MO, TX, WI

Seeking: Midwest, Southwest
Focusing on: IL, KS, OH, TX, WI
Seeking in Canada? No
Exclusive territories? Yes
Homebased option? No
Kiosk option? No
Employees needed to run franchise: 5
Absentee ownership? No

COSTS
Total cost: $232K-341.5K
Franchise fee: $25K
Royalty fee: 5%
Term of agreement: 15 years renewable
    at no charge
Franchisees required to buy multiple
    units? No

FINANCING
In-house: None
3rd-party: Equipment, inventory,
    start-up costs

QUALIFICATIONS
Net worth: $200K
Cash liquidity: $75K
Experience:
    General business experience
    Management skills

TRAINING
At headquarters
At franchisee's location

BUSINESS SUPPORT
Meetings
Toll-free phone line
Grand opening
Internet
Lease negotiations
Security/safety procedures
Field operations/evaluations
Purchasing cooperatives

MARKETING SUPPORT
Ad slicks
Regional marketing

COTTMAN TRANSMISSION SYSTEMS LLC
Ranked #92 in Entrepreneur Magazine's 2004 Franchise 500　　　　*Financial rating: $$$$*

240 New York Dr.
Ft. Washington, PA 19034
Ph: (800)374-6116/(215)643-5885
Fax: (215)643-2519
www.cottman.com
Transmission repair & services
Began: 1962, Franchising since: 1964
Headquarters size: Info not provided
Franchise department: Info not
  provided

U.S. franchises: 362
Canadian franchises: 4
Other foreign franchises: 2
Company-owned: 7
Units concentrated in all U.S.

Seeking: All U.S.
Seeking in Canada? Yes
Exclusive territories? No
Homebased option? No
Kiosk option? No
Employees needed to run franchise: 3
Absentee ownership? No

COSTS
Total cost: $155K-221K
Franchise fee: $31.5K
Royalty fee: 7.5%
Term of agreement: Renewable term at
  no charge
Franchisees required to buy multiple
  units? No

FINANCING
3rd-party: Equipment, franchise fee,
  inventory, start-up costs
Other: Working capital, leasehold
  improvements

QUALIFICATIONS
Net worth: $150K
Cash liquidity: $45K-50K

TRAINING
At headquarters: 3 weeks
At franchisee's location: 1 week
Ongoing

BUSINESS SUPPORT
Newsletter
Meetings
Toll-free phone line
Grand opening
Internet
Lease negotiations
Security/safety procedures
Field operations/evaluations
Purchasing cooperatives

MARKETING SUPPORT
Co-op advertising
Ad slicks
National media campaign
Regional marketing

EXPRESS OIL CHANGE
Ranked #194 in Entrepreneur Magazine's 2004 Franchise 500　　　　*Financial rating: $$$$*

190 W. Valley Ave.
Birmingham, AL 35209
Ph: (205)945-1771
Fax: (205)940-6025
www.expressoil.com
Oil changes, transmission, brakes, tire
  services
Began: 1979, Franchising since: 1983
Headquarters size: 30 employees
Franchise department: 10 employees

U.S. franchises: 130
Canadian franchises: 0
Other foreign franchises: 0
Company-owned: 13
Units concentrated in AL, FL, GA,
  MS, TN

Seeking: South, Southeast
Focusing on: AL, FL, GA, LA, MS, NC,
  SC, TN, TX
Seeking in Canada? No
Exclusive territories? Yes
Homebased option? No
Kiosk option? No

Employees needed to run franchise:
  6-8
Absentee ownership? Yes

COSTS
Total cost: $114.5K-149.5K
Franchise fee: $17.5K
Royalty fee: 5%
Term of agreement: 10 years renewable
  at no charge
Franchisees required to buy multiple
  units? No

FINANCING
3rd-party: Equipment, franchise fee,
  inventory, start-up costs
Other: Build-to-suit option

QUALIFICATIONS
Net worth: $500K
Cash liquidity: $200K
Experience:
  General business experience

TRAINING
At headquarters: 2 days
At franchisee's location: Varies
At training centers: 4-8 weeks

BUSINESS SUPPORT
Newsletter
Meetings
Toll-free phone line
Grand opening
Internet
Lease negotiations
Security/safety procedures
Field operations/evaluations
Purchasing cooperatives

MARKETING SUPPORT
Co-op advertising
Ad slicks
Regional marketing

GREASE MONKEY INT'L. INC.

Ranked #274 in Entrepreneur Magazine's 2004 Franchise 500

Financial rating: $$

633 17th St., #400
Denver, CO 80202
Ph: (800)364-0352/(303)308-1660
Fax: (303)308-5908
www.greasemonkeyintl.com
Preventive maintenance & quick lube
Began: 1978, Franchising since: 1979
Headquarters size: 31 employees
Franchise department: 3 employees

U.S. franchises: 190
Canadian franchises: 0
Other foreign franchises: 33
Company-owned: 13
Units concentrated in CA, CO, IN,
   NC, NJ, PA, SC, WA

Seeking: All U.S.
Seeking in Canada? No
Exclusive territories? Yes
Homebased option? No
Kiosk option? No
Employees needed to run franchise: 8
Absentee ownership? Yes

COSTS
Total cost: $120K-220K+
Franchise fee: $28K
Royalty fee: 5%
Term of agreement: 15 years renewable
   for $5K
Franchisees required to buy multiple
   units? No

FINANCING
In-house: None
3rd-party: Equipment, franchise fee,
   inventory, start-up costs

QUALIFICATIONS
Net worth: $300K
Cash liquidity: $120K-220K
Experience:
   General business experience
   Marketing skills

TRAINING
At headquarters: 5 days
At franchisee's location: As needed

BUSINESS SUPPORT
Newsletter
Meetings
Toll-free phone line
Grand opening
Security/safety procedures
Field operations/evaluations
Purchasing cooperatives

MARKETING SUPPORT
Co-op advertising
Ad slicks
Regional marketing

JIFFY LUBE INT'L. INC.

Ranked #11 in Entrepreneur Magazine's 2004 Franchise 500

Financial rating: $$$$

P.O. Box 4427
Houston, TX 77210-4427
Ph: (800)327-9532
Fax: (713)546-8762
www.jiffylube.com
Fast oil change
Began: 1979, Franchising since: 1979
Headquarters size: 200 employees
Franchise department: 60 employees

U.S. franchises: 1,735
Canadian franchises: 44
Other foreign franchises: 0
Company-owned: 434
Units concentrated in all U.S.

Seeking: All U.S.
Seeking in Canada? Yes
Exclusive territories? No
Homebased option? No
Kiosk option? No
Employees needed to run franchise: 10
Absentee ownership? Yes

COSTS
Total cost: $174K-194K
Franchise fee: $35K
Royalty fee: to 5%
Term of agreement: 20 years renewable
   for $17.5K
Franchisees required to buy multiple
   units? No

FINANCING
In-house: None
3rd-party: Equipment, franchise fee,
   inventory, start-up costs

QUALIFICATIONS
Net worth: $450K
Cash liquidity: $150K
Experience:
   General business experience

TRAINING
At headquarters: 2-4 weeks
At franchisee's location
Additional training available

BUSINESS SUPPORT
Newsletter
Meetings
Toll-free phone line
Grand opening
Internet
Security/safety procedures
Field operations/evaluations
Purchasing cooperatives

MARKETING SUPPORT
Co-op advertising
Ad slicks
National media campaign
Regional marketing
Reminder mailings
Research tie-ins

LEE MYLES TRANSMISSIONS

Ranked #275 in Entrepreneur Magazine's 2004 Franchise 500   *Financial rating: $$$$*

140 Rte. 17 N.
Paramus, NJ 07652
Ph: (800)533-6953/(201)262-0555
Fax: (201)262-5177
www.leemyles.com
Transmission repair center
Began: 1947, Franchising since: 1964
Headquarters size: 13 employees
Franchise department: 4 employees

U.S. franchises: 91
Canadian franchises: 0
Other foreign franchises: 0
Company-owned: 0
Units concentrated in AZ, CA, CT, FL,
    MA, MD, NJ, NY, OH, PA, RI, TX,
    WA, WV

Seeking: All U.S.
Focusing on: AK, AL, CO, GA, KS, MI,
    MN, MS, NC, OH, SC, VA
Seeking in Canada? No
Exclusive territories? No
Homebased option? No
Kiosk option? No

Employees needed to run franchise: 4
Absentee ownership? No

COSTS
Total cost: $126.2K-169.1K
Franchise fee: $27.5K
Royalty fee: 7%
Term of agreement: 15 years renewable
    for 15% of current franchise fee
Franchisees required to buy multiple
    units? No

FINANCING
In-house: None
3rd-party: Equipment, franchise fee,
    inventory, start-up costs

QUALIFICATIONS
Net worth: $125K-150K
Cash liquidity: $70K
Experience:
    Industry experience
    General business experience
    Marketing skills

TRAINING
At headquarters: 1-2 weeks
At franchisee's location: Ongoing visits

BUSINESS SUPPORT
Newsletter
Meetings
Toll-free phone line
Grand opening
Internet
Security/safety procedures
Field operations/evaluations

MARKETING SUPPORT
Co-op advertising
Ad slicks
National media campaign
Regional marketing

LENTZ U.S.A. SERVICE CENTERS

Current financial data not available

1001 Riverview Dr.
Kalamazoo, MI 49048
Ph: (800)354-2131/(269)342-2200
Fax: (269)342-9461
www.lentzusa.com
Brakes/mufflers/chassis
Began: 1983, Franchising since: 1989
Headquarters size: 10 employees
Franchise department: 10 employees

U.S. franchises: 15
Canadian franchises: 0
Other foreign franchises: 0
Company-owned: 11
Units concentrated in FL, MI

Seeking: All U.S.
Focusing on: FL, IN, MI, NC, SC, TX
Seeking in Canada? Yes
Exclusive territories? Yes
Homebased option? No
Kiosk option? No
Employees needed to run franchise: 3
Absentee ownership? No

COSTS
Total cost: $114K-130K
Franchise fee: $20K
Royalty fee: to 7%
Term of agreement: 10 years renewable
    for 25% of original franchise fee
Franchisees required to buy multiple
    units? No

FINANCING
In-house: None
3rd-party: Accounts receivable, equip-
    ment, franchise fee, inventory,
    start-up costs

QUALIFICATIONS
Net worth: $150K
Cash liquidity: $50K
Experience:
    Marketing skills

TRAINING
At headquarters: 2 weeks
At franchisee's location: 1 week
At existing location: As needed

BUSINESS SUPPORT
Newsletter
Toll-free phone line
Grand opening
Internet
Field operations/evaluations
Purchasing cooperatives

MARKETING SUPPORT
Co-op advertising
Ad slicks
Individual programs

MEINEKE CAR CARE CENTERS

Ranked #49 in Entrepreneur Magazine's 2004 Franchise 500   *Financial rating: $$$$*

128 S. Tryon, #900
Charlotte, NC 28202
Ph: (800)634-6353
Fax: (704)358-4706
www.ownameineke.com
Exhaust systems/shocks/brakes/struts
Began: 1972, Franchising since: 1972
Headquarters size: 77 employees
Franchise department: 13 employees

U.S. franchises: 818
Canadian franchises: 23
Other foreign franchises: 16
Company-owned: 21
Units concentrated in all U.S.

Seeking: All U.S.
Seeking in Canada? Yes
Exclusive territories? Yes
Homebased option? No
Kiosk option? No
Employees needed to run franchise:
    4-5
Absentee ownership? Yes

COSTS
Total cost: $180K-365K
Franchise fee: $30K
Royalty fee: 2.5-7%
Term of agreement: 15 years renewable
    for $2.5K
Franchisees required to buy multiple
    units? Outside the U.S. only

FINANCING
In-house: None
3rd-party: Equipment, franchise fee,
    inventory, start-up costs

QUALIFICATIONS
Cash liquidity: $50K
Experience:
    Industry experience
    General business experience
    Marketing skills

TRAINING
At headquarters: 4 weeks
At franchisee's location: 4+ days
    per year
Ongoing technical hotline

BUSINESS SUPPORT
Newsletter
Meetings
Toll-free phone line
Grand opening
Internet
Security/safety procedures
Field operations/evaluations

MARKETING SUPPORT
Co-op advertising
Ad slicks
National media campaign
Regional marketing
Yellow Pages

MERLIN'S FRANCHISING INC.

Ranked #257 in Entrepreneur Magazine's 2004 Franchise 500   *Financial rating: $$$$*

1 N. River Ln., #206
Geneva, IL 60134
Ph: (800)652-9900/(630)208-9900
Fax: (630)208-8601
www.merlins.com
Brakes/exhaust/suspension/oil & lube
Began: 1975, Franchising since: 1975
Headquarters size: 25 employees
Franchise department: 9 employees

U.S. franchises: 66
Canadian franchises: 0
Other foreign franchises: 0
Company-owned: 4
Units concentrated in IL, TX

Seeking: Midwest, Southeast,
    Southwest
Focusing on: GA, IL, IN, MI, TX, WI
Seeking in Canada? No
Exclusive territories? Yes
Homebased option? No
Kiosk option? No
Employees needed to run franchise: 5
Absentee ownership? No

COSTS
Total cost: $183.6K-315.9K
Franchise fee: $26K-30K
Royalty fee: 4.9-6.9%
Term of agreement: 20 years renewable
    at no charge
Franchisees required to buy multiple
    units? No

FINANCING
3rd-party: Equipment, franchise fee,
    inventory, start-up costs
Other: Equity-assistance programs

QUALIFICATIONS
Net worth: $50K
Cash liquidity: $25K-45K
Experience:
    Industry experience
    General business experience
    Marketing skills
    Management experience
    Customer service skills

TRAINING
At headquarters: 6 weeks
At corporate training center: Varies

BUSINESS SUPPORT
Newsletter
Meetings
Toll-free phone line
Grand opening
Internet
Lease negotiations
Security/safety procedures
Field operations/evaluations
Purchasing cooperatives

MARKETING SUPPORT
Co-op advertising
Ad slicks
Regional marketing
Local marketing programs

MIDAS AUTO SERVICE EXPERTS

Ranked #29 in Entrepreneur Magazine's 2004 Franchise 500　　　*Financial rating: $$$$*

1300 Arlington Heights Rd.
Itasca, IL 60143
Ph: (800)621-0144/(630)438-3000
Fax: (630)438-3700
www.midasfran.com
Auto repair & maintenance services
Began: 1956, Franchising since: 1956
Headquarters size: 1,900 employees
Franchise department: 82 employees

U.S. franchises: 1,615
Canadian franchises: 233
Other foreign franchises: 755
Company-owned: 111
Units concentrated in all U.S.

Seeking: All U.S.
Seeking in Canada? Yes
Exclusive territories? No
Homebased option? No
Kiosk option? No
Employees needed to run franchise: 9
Absentee ownership? No

COSTS
Total cost: $379.4K-528K
Franchise fee: $20K
Royalty fee: 10%
Term of agreement: 20 years renewable
　　for 50% of franchise fee
Franchisees required to buy multiple
　　units? No

FINANCING
No financing available

QUALIFICATIONS
Net worth: $300K
Cash liquidity: $100K
Experience:
　　General business experience
　　Financially capable

TRAINING
At headquarters: 3 weeks
At franchisee's location: 1-2 weeks self-
　　study
In-shop assignment: 1-2 weeks

BUSINESS SUPPORT
Newsletter
Meetings
Toll-free phone line
Grand opening
Internet
Security/safety procedures
Field operations/evaluations

MARKETING SUPPORT
Co-op advertising
Ad slicks
National media campaign
Regional marketing

MILEX TUNE-UP & BRAKES

Ranked #457 in Entrepreneur Magazine's 2004 Franchise 500　　　*Financial rating: $$$$*

4444 W. 147th St.
Midlothian, IL 60445
Ph: (800)377-9247/(708)389-5922
Fax: (708)389-9882
www.milextuneupbrake.com
Automotive tune-up & brakes
Began: 1978, Franchising since: 1979
Headquarters size: 35 employees
Franchise department: 2 employees

U.S. franchises: 12
Canadian franchises: 0
Other foreign franchises: 0
Company-owned: 0
Units concentrated in CT, IL, IN, TX

Seeking: All U.S.
Seeking in Canada? No
Exclusive territories? No
Homebased option? No
Kiosk option? No
Employees needed to run franchise:
　　3-4
Absentee ownership? Yes

COSTS
Total cost: $149K
Franchise fee: $27.5K
Royalty fee: 7%
Term of agreement: 20 years renewable
　　at no charge
Franchisees required to buy multiple
　　units? No

FINANCING
In-house: None
3rd-party: Equipment, franchise fee,
　　inventory

QUALIFICATIONS
Net worth: $150K-300K
Cash liquidity: $35K
Experience:
　　General business experience
　　Marketing skills

TRAINING
At headquarters: 1 week
At franchisee's location: 3 weeks

BUSINESS SUPPORT
Newsletter
Meetings
Toll-free phone line
Grand opening
Internet
Lease negotiations
Security/safety procedures
Field operations/evaluations
Purchasing cooperatives

MARKETING SUPPORT
Co-op advertising
Ad slicks
National media campaign
Regional marketing

MISTER TRANSMISSION INT'L. LTD.

Current financial data not available

9675 Yonge St., 2nd FL
Richmond Hill, ON Canada L4C 1V7
Ph: (905)884-1511
Fax: (905)884-4727
www.mistertransmission.com
Transmission repair & services
Began: 1963, Franchising since: 1969
Headquarters size: 11 employees
Franchise department: 4 employees

U.S. franchises: 0
Canadian franchises: 88
Other foreign franchises: 0
Company-owned: 0
Units concentrated in Canada

Not available in the U.S.
Focusing on: All Canadian provinces
Exclusive territories? No
Homebased option? No
Kiosk option? No
Employees needed to run franchise: 5
Absentee ownership? No

COSTS
Total cost: $100K-125K
Franchise fee: $25K
Royalty fee: 7%
Term of agreement: 10 years renewable
    at no charge
Franchisees required to buy multiple
    units? No

FINANCING
In-house: None
3rd-party: Equipment

QUALIFICATIONS
Net worth: $300K
Cash liquidity: $75K
Experience:
    Industry experience
    General business experience
    Marketing skills

TRAINING
At headquarters: 1 week
At franchisee's location: Varies

BUSINESS SUPPORT
Newsletter
Meetings
Toll-free phone line
Grand opening
Internet
Lease negotiations
Field operations/evaluations

MARKETING SUPPORT
Co-op advertising
Ad slicks
National media campaign
Regional marketing

MR. TRANSMISSION

Ranked #228 in Entrepreneur Magazine's 2004 Franchise 500

Financial rating: $$$$

4444 W. 147th St.
Midlothian, IL 60445
Ph: (800)377-9247/(708)389-5922
Fax: (708)389-9882
www.mrtransmission.com
Transmission repair & services
Began: 1956, Franchising since: 1976
Headquarters size: 35 employees
Franchise department: 2 employees

U.S. franchises: 121
Canadian franchises: 0
Other foreign franchises: 0
Company-owned: 0
Units concentrated in Midwest, South,
    Northeast

Seeking: All U.S.
Focusing on: South, Southwest, FL
Seeking in Canada? No
Exclusive territories? No
Homebased option? No
Kiosk option? No
Employees needed to run franchise:
    3-5
Absentee ownership? Yes

COSTS
Total cost: $149K
Franchise fee: $27.5K
Royalty fee: 7%
Term of agreement: 20 years renewable
    at no charge
Franchisees required to buy multiple
    units? No

FINANCING
In-house: None
3rd-party: Equipment, franchise fee,
    inventory

QUALIFICATIONS
Net worth: $150K-300K
Cash liquidity: $35K
Experience:
    General business experience
    Marketing skills

TRAINING
At headquarters: 2 weeks
At franchisee's location: 3 weeks

BUSINESS SUPPORT
Newsletter
Meetings
Toll-free phone line
Grand opening
Internet
Lease negotiations
Security/safety procedures
Field operations/evaluations
Purchasing cooperatives

MARKETING SUPPORT
Co-op advertising
Ad slicks
National media campaign
Regional marketing

MULTISTATE TRANSMISSIONS

Ranked #449 in Entrepreneur Magazine's 2004 Franchise 500

Financial rating: $$$$

4444 W. 147th St.
Midlothian, IL 60445
Ph: (800)377-9247/(708)389-5922
Fax: (708)389-9882
www.moranindustries.com
Transmission repair & services
Began: 1973, Franchising since: 1973
Headquarters size: 35 employees
Franchise department: 2 employees

U.S. franchises: 26
Canadian franchises: 0
Other foreign franchises: 0
Company-owned: 0
Units concentrated in Midwest

Seeking: Midwest, Northeast
Focusing on: Midwest
Seeking in Canada? No
Exclusive territories? No
Homebased option? No
Kiosk option? No
Employees needed to run franchise:
    3-5
Absentee ownership? Yes

COSTS
Total cost: $149K
Franchise fee: $27.5K
Royalty fee: 7%
Term of agreement: 20 years renewable
    at no charge
Franchisees required to buy multiple
    units? No

FINANCING
In-house: None
3rd-party: Equipment, franchise fee,
    inventory

QUALIFICATIONS
Net worth: $150K-300K
Cash liquidity: $35K
Experience:
    General business experience
    Marketing skills

TRAINING
At headquarters: 2 weeks
At franchisee's location: 3 weeks

BUSINESS SUPPORT
Newsletter
Meetings
Toll-free phone line
Grand opening
Internet
Lease negotiations
Security/safety procedures
Field operations/evaluations
Purchasing cooperatives

MARKETING SUPPORT
Co-op advertising
Ad slicks
National media campaign
Regional marketing

OIL BUTLER INT'L. CORP.

Ranked #385 in Entrepreneur Magazine's 2004 Franchise 500

Financial rating: $$

1599 Rte. 22 W.
Union, NJ 07083
Ph: (908)687-3283
Fax: (908)687-7617
www.oilbutlerinternational.com
Mobile oil change/quick lube/wind-
    shield repair
Began: 1987, Franchising since: 1991
Headquarters size: 6 employees
Franchise department: 4 employees

U.S. franchises: 141
Canadian franchises: 3
Other foreign franchises: 17
Company-owned: 1
Units concentrated in all U.S.

Seeking: All U.S.
Seeking in Canada? Yes
Exclusive territories? Yes
Homebased option? Yes
Kiosk option? No
Employees needed to run franchise: 0
Absentee ownership? Yes

COSTS
Total cost: $28K-40.7K
Franchise fee: $15K
Royalty fee: 7%
Term of agreement: 10 years renewable
    for $1K
Franchisees required to buy multiple
    units? No

FINANCING
In-house: None
3rd-party: Equipment, franchise fee,
    inventory, start-up costs

QUALIFICATIONS
Cash liquidity: $15K

TRAINING
At headquarters: 4 days

BUSINESS SUPPORT
Newsletter
Toll-free phone line
Grand opening
Internet
Security/safety procedures
Field operations/evaluations

MARKETING SUPPORT
Co-op advertising
Ad slicks
National media campaign
Regional marketing
Weekly contact sheet evaluations

OIL CAN HENRY'S

Current financial data not available

1200 N.W. Naito Pkwy., #690
Portland, OR 97209
Ph: (800)765-6244/(503)243-6311
Fax: (503)228-5227
www.oilcanhenry.com
Automotive lubrication & filter maintenance
Began: 1972, Franchising since: 1988
Headquarters size: 12 employees
Franchise department: Info not provided

U.S. franchises: 59
Canadian franchises: 0
Other foreign franchises: 0
Company-owned: 5
Units concentrated in AZ, CA, CO, ID, MN, NV, OR, TX, WA

Focusing on: AZ, CA, CO, ID, MN, NV, OR, TX, WA
Seeking in Canada? No
Exclusive territories? Yes
Homebased option? No
Kiosk option? No

Employees needed to run franchise:
 3 -12
Absentee ownership? Yes

COSTS
Total cost: $137K-203K
Franchise fee: $35K
Royalty fee: 5.5%
Term of agreement: 10 years renewable at no charge
Franchisees required to buy multiple units? No

FINANCING
In-house: None
3rd-party: Equipment, inventory, start-up costs

QUALIFICATIONS
Net worth: $500K
Cash liquidity: $150K
Experience:
 General business experience
 Marketing skills

TRAINING
At headquarters: 5 weeks
At franchisee's location: 10 days
Additional training available

BUSINESS SUPPORT
Newsletter
Meetings
Toll-free phone line
Grand opening
Internet
Lease negotiations
Security/safety procedures
Field operations/evaluations

MARKETING SUPPORT
Ad slicks
Regional marketing

OILSTOP-DRIVE THRU OIL CHANGE CENTERS

Current financial data not available

6111 Redwood Dr.
Rohnert Park, CA 94928
Ph: (707)586-1399
Fax: (707)586-2296
www.oilstopinc.com
Automotive lubrication & services
Began: 1987, Franchising since: 1998
Headquarters size: 15 employees
Franchise department: 5 employees

U.S. franchises: 15
Canadian franchises: 0
Other foreign franchises: 0
Company-owned: 12
Units concentrated in AZ, CA, NM, OR, TN, TX, VA

Seeking: South, Southwest, West
Focusing on: AZ, CA, NM, OR, TN, TX, VA
Seeking in Canada? No
Exclusive territories? Yes
Homebased option? No
Kiosk option? No
Employees needed to run franchise: 8
Absentee ownership? Yes

COSTS
Total cost: $266.1K-995.1K
Franchise fee: $24.5K-35K
Royalty fee: 5%
Term of agreement: 20 years renewable at no charge
Franchisees required to buy multiple units? No

FINANCING
No financing available

QUALIFICATIONS
Net worth: $1M
Cash liquidity: $200K
Experience:
 General business experience

TRAINING
At headquarters: 12 weeks
At franchisee's location: 1 week
Ongoing

BUSINESS SUPPORT
Newsletter
Meetings
Toll-free phone line
Grand opening
Internet
Lease negotiations
Security/safety procedures
Field operations/evaluations
Purchasing cooperatives

MARKETING SUPPORT
Ad slicks
Regional marketing
TV & print ads

PRECISION TUNE AUTO CARE

Financial rating: $$$$

748 Miller Dr. S.E.
Leesburg, VA 20175
Ph: (800)438-8863/(703)669-2311
Fax: (703)669-1539
www.precisiontune.com
Auto maintenance & engine
    performance
Began: 1975, Franchising since: 1978
Headquarters size: 32 employees
Franchise department: 3 employees

U.S. franchises: 324
Canadian franchises: 0
Other foreign franchises: 108
Company-owned: 0
Units concentrated in all U.S.

Seeking: All U.S.
Seeking in Canada? Yes
Exclusive territories? Yes
Homebased option? No
Kiosk option? No
Employees needed to run franchise:
    5-8
Absentee ownership? Info not provided

COSTS
Total cost: $142.3K-208.1K
Franchise fee: $25K
Royalty fee: 7.5%
Term of agreement: Renewable term
Franchisees required to buy multiple
    units? No

FINANCING
In-house: Franchise fee
3rd-party: Accounts receivable, equip-
    ment, inventory, start-up costs

QUALIFICATIONS
Net worth: $150K-200K
Experience:
    General business experience

TRAINING
At headquarters: 2 weeks
At franchisee's location: 1 day-
    2 weeks+
Additional training available

BUSINESS SUPPORT
Newsletter
Meetings
Toll-free phone line
Grand opening
Internet
Lease negotiations
Security/safety procedures
Field operations/evaluations

MARKETING SUPPORT
Co-op advertising
Ad slicks
National media campaign
Regional marketing
TV, Yellow Pages & coupon advertising

SAF-T AUTO CENTERS

Current financial data not available

121 N. Plains Industrial Rd.
Wallingford, CT 06492
Ph: (800)382-7238
Fax: (203)269-2532
www.saftauto.com
Suspension/brakes/exhaust/steering/m
    inor repairs
Began: 1978, Franchising since: 1986
Headquarters size: 4 employees
Franchise department: 4 employees

U.S. franchises: 6
Canadian franchises: 0
Other foreign franchises: 0
Company-owned: 1
Units concentrated in CT

Seeking: All U.S.
Focusing on: CT
Seeking in Canada? No
Exclusive territories? Yes
Homebased option? No
Kiosk option? No
Employees needed to run franchise: 3
Absentee ownership? No

COSTS
Total cost: $85K-100K
Franchise fee: $15K
Royalty fee: $500/mo.
Term of agreement: 5 years renewable
    at no charge
Franchisees required to buy multiple
    units? Outside the U.S. only

FINANCING
In-house: None
3rd-party: Equipment, inventory

QUALIFICATIONS
Net worth: $100K
Cash liquidity: $20K
Experience:
    Industry experience

TRAINING
At headquarters: 1 week
At franchisee's location: 1 week

BUSINESS SUPPORT
Newsletter
Meetings
Toll-free phone line
Internet
Lease negotiations
Field operations/evaluations
Purchasing cooperatives

MARKETING SUPPORT
Co-op advertising
Ad slicks

SPEEDY TRANSMISSION CENTERS

Financial rating: 0

74 N.E. 4th Ave., #1
Delray Beach, FL 33483
Ph: (800)336-0310/(561)274-0445
Fax: (561)274-6456
www.speedytransmission.com
Transmission repair
Began: 1983, Franchising since: 1984
Headquarters size: 4 employees
Franchise department: 1 employee

U.S. franchises: 25
Canadian franchises: 0
Other foreign franchises: 0
Company-owned: 0
Units concentrated in FL, GA

Seeking: South, Southeast
Focusing on: Southeast
Seeking in Canada? No
Exclusive territories? Yes
Homebased option? No
Kiosk option? No
Employees needed to run franchise: 4
Absentee ownership? Yes

COSTS
Total cost: $53.5K-96.9K
Franchise fee: $19.5K
Royalty fee: 7%
Term of agreement: 20 years renewable
    for 50% of initial franchise fee
Franchisees required to buy multiple
    units? Outside the U.S. only

FINANCING
In-house: None
3rd-party: Equipment

QUALIFICATIONS
Net worth: $150K
Cash liquidity: $50K
Experience:
    General business experience
    Marketing skills

TRAINING
At headquarters: 3 weeks
At franchisee's location: Varies
Weekend classes

BUSINESS SUPPORT
Newsletter
Meetings
Toll-free phone line
Grand opening
Internet
Field operations/evaluations

MARKETING SUPPORT
Ad slicks
Regional marketing

TECHZONE AIRBAG SERVICE

Financial rating: $$$$

9675 S.E. 36th St., #100
Mercer Island, WA 98040
Ph: (800)224-7224/(206)275-4105
Fax: (206)275-4112
www.airbagservice.com
Airbag diagnostic & repair services
Began: 1992, Franchising since: 1995
Headquarters size: 12 employees
Franchise department: 5 employees

U.S. franchises: 32
Canadian franchises: 0
Other foreign franchises: 1
Company-owned: 1
Units concentrated in all U.S.

Seeking: All U.S.
Seeking in Canada? No
Exclusive territories? Yes
Homebased option? Yes
Kiosk option? No
Employees needed to run franchise: 2
Absentee ownership? Yes

COSTS
Total cost: $45.9K-116.3K
Franchise fee: $25K-35K
Royalty fee: 8.5%
Term of agreement: 15 years renewable
Franchisees required to buy multiple
    units? No

FINANCING
In-house: None
3rd-party: Equipment

QUALIFICATIONS
Net worth: $75K
Cash liquidity: $50K
Experience:
    Industry experience
    General business experience
    Marketing skills
    Automotive experience

TRAINING
At headquarters: 3 weeks

BUSINESS SUPPORT
Newsletter
Meetings
Toll-free phone line
Grand opening
Internet
Lease negotiations
Security/safety procedures
Field operations/evaluations
Purchasing cooperatives

MARKETING SUPPORT
Co-op advertising
Ad slicks
National media campaign
Regional marketing
Industry trade shows

TILDEN CAR CARE CENTERS
Ranked #423 in Entrepreneur Magazine's 2004 Franchise 500

Financial rating: $$$$

1325 Franklin Ave., #165
Garden City, NY 11530
Ph: (800)845-3367
Fax: (516)746-1288
www.tildencarcare.com
Full-service automotive repair
Began: 1923, Franchising since: 1996
Headquarters size: 5 employees
Franchise department: 2 employees

U.S. franchises: 53
Canadian franchises: 0
Other foreign franchises: 0
Company-owned: 0
Units concentrated in CO, FL, GA,
    MA, NH, NJ, NY, PA, TX

Seeking: All U.S.
Seeking in Canada? Yes
Exclusive territories? Yes
Homebased option? No
Kiosk option? No
Employees needed to run franchise: 4
Absentee ownership? Info not provided

COSTS
Total cost: $131.5K-171.2K
Franchise fee: $25K
Royalty fee: 6%
Term of agreement: 20 years
Franchisees required to buy multiple
    units? No

FINANCING
In-house: None
3rd-party: Equipment, franchise fee,
    start-up costs

QUALIFICATIONS
Net worth: $150K
Cash liquidity: $60K

TRAINING
At headquarters: 2 weeks
At franchisee's location: 1 week

BUSINESS SUPPORT
Toll-free phone line
Grand opening
Internet
Lease negotiations
Field operations/evaluations
Purchasing cooperatives

MARKETING SUPPORT
Info not provided

TIRE WAREHOUSE

Current financial data not available

492 Main St., P.O. Box 486
Keene, NH 03431
Ph: (603)352-4478
Fax: (603)358-6620
www.tirewarehouse.net
Tires, auto parts & accessories
Began: 1971, Franchising since: 1989
Headquarters size: 50 employees
Franchise department: 2 employees

U.S. franchises: 25
Canadian franchises: 0
Other foreign franchises: 0
Company-owned: 27
Units concentrated in MA, ME, NH,
    RI, VT

Seeking: Northeast
Focusing on: MA, ME, NH, RI, VT
Seeking in Canada? No
Exclusive territories? No
Homebased option? No
Kiosk option? No
Employees needed to run franchise: 4
Absentee ownership? No

COSTS
Total cost: $100K-342K
Franchise fee: $15K
Royalty fee: 3%
Term of agreement: 7 years renewable
    for $1.5K
Franchisees required to buy multiple
    units? No

FINANCING
In-house: None
3rd-party: Equipment, inventory

QUALIFICATIONS
Net worth: $50K+
Cash liquidity: $50K+
Experience:
    General business experience
    Marketing skills

TRAINING
At headquarters: 5 weeks

BUSINESS SUPPORT
Newsletter
Meetings
Toll-free phone line
Grand opening
Internet
Lease negotiations
Security/safety procedures
Field operations/evaluations

MARKETING SUPPORT
Ad slicks

TUFFY ASSOCIATES CORP.

Ranked #168 in Entrepreneur Magazine's 2004 Franchise 500　　　*Financial rating: $$$$*

1414 Baronial Plaza Dr.
Toledo, OH 43615
Ph: (800)228-8339/(419)865-6900
Fax: (419)865-7343
www.tuffy.com
Exhaust/brakes/auto services
Began: 1970, Franchising since: 1971
Headquarters size: 39 employees
Franchise department: 39 employees

U.S. franchises: 236
Canadian franchises: 0
Other foreign franchises: 0
Company-owned: 13
Units concentrated in all U.S.

Seeking: Midwest, South, Southeast
Focusing on: All U.S.
Seeking in Canada? No
Exclusive territories? Yes
Homebased option? No
Kiosk option? No
Employees needed to run franchise:
    4-5
Absentee ownership? No

COSTS
Total cost: $209K-317K
Franchise fee: $25K
Royalty fee: 5%
Term of agreement: 15 years renewable
    at no charge
Franchisees required to buy multiple
    units? No

FINANCING
In-house: None
3rd-party: Equipment, inventory,
    start-up costs

QUALIFICATIONS
Net worth: $200K
Cash liquidity: $90K
Experience:
    General business experience

TRAINING
At headquarters: 3 weeks
At franchisee's location: 2 weeks
At existing store: 1 week

BUSINESS SUPPORT
Newsletter
Meetings
Toll-free phone line
Grand opening
Internet
Lease negotiations
Security/safety procedures
Field operations/evaluations
Purchasing cooperatives

MARKETING SUPPORT
Co-op advertising
Ad slicks
National media campaign
Regional marketing

TUNEX AUTOMOTIVE SPECIALISTS

Ranked #443 in Entrepreneur Magazine's 2004 Franchise 500　　　*Financial rating: $$$$*

556 E. 2100 South
Salt Lake City, UT 84106
Ph: (800)448-8639/(801)486-8133
Fax: (801)484-4740
www.tunex.com
Automotive diagnostics & related serv-
    ices
Began: 1972, Franchising since: 1974
Headquarters size: 5 employees
Franchise department: 4 employees

U.S. franchises: 26
Canadian franchises: 0
Other foreign franchises: 0
Company-owned: 2
Units concentrated in AZ, CO, ID,
    NV, UT

Seeking: All U.S.
Seeking in Canada? No
Exclusive territories? Yes
Homebased option? No
Kiosk option? No
Employees needed to run franchise: 4
Absentee ownership? Yes

COSTS
Total cost: $125K-166K
Franchise fee: $19K
Royalty fee: 5%
Term of agreement: 10 years renewable
    for $200
Franchisees required to buy multiple
    units? No

FINANCING
In-house: None
3rd-party: Equipment, franchise fee,
    inventory

QUALIFICATIONS
Net worth: $200K
Experience:
    General business experience

TRAINING
At headquarters: 1 week
At franchisee's location: 1 week

BUSINESS SUPPORT
Newsletter
Meetings
Toll-free phone line
Grand opening
Internet
Lease negotiations
Security/safety procedures
Field operations/evaluations
Purchasing cooperatives

MARKETING SUPPORT
Co-op advertising
Regional marketing

VALVOLINE INSTANT OIL CHANGE

Ranked #56 in Entrepreneur Magazine's 2004 Franchise 500 *Financial rating: $$$$*

P.O. Box 14046
Lexington, KY 40512
Ph: (800)622-6846
Fax: (859)357-7049
www.viocfranchise.com
Quick-lube service center
Began: 1986, Franchising since: 1988
Headquarters size: 800 employees
Franchise department: 21 employees

U.S. franchises: 375
Canadian franchises: 0
Other foreign franchises: 0
Company-owned: 355
Units concentrated in all U.S.

Seeking: All U.S.
Seeking in Canada? No
Exclusive territories? No
Homebased option? No
Kiosk option? No
Employees needed to run franchise: 4
Absentee ownership? Yes

COSTS
Total cost: $107.8K-1M
Franchise fee: $30K
Royalty fee: 6%
Term of agreement: 15 years renewable
    at no charge
Franchisees required to buy multiple
    units? No

FINANCING
In-house: None
3rd-party: Equipment, franchise fee,
    inventory, payroll, start-up costs

QUALIFICATIONS
Net worth: $200K
Cash liquidity: $150K
Experience:
    General business experience

TRAINING
At headquarters: 3 weeks
At franchisee's location: Ongoing

BUSINESS SUPPORT
Newsletter
Meetings
Toll-free phone line
Grand opening
Security/safety procedures
Field operations/evaluations

MARKETING SUPPORT
Ad slicks
Ad agency
PR assistance
Corporate marketing manager

WALT'S AUTO WORLD INC.

Current financial data not available

1506 S. Byrne Rd.
Toledo, OH 43614
Ph: (419)382-1333
Fax: (419)382-7056
www.waltsautoworld.com
Auto care services
Began: 1981, Franchising since: 2000
Headquarters size: 6 employees
Franchise department: 2 employees

U.S. franchises: 1
Canadian franchises: 0
Other foreign franchises: 0
Company-owned: 0
Units concentrated in all U.S.

Seeking: All U.S.
Seeking in Canada? No
Exclusive territories? Yes
Homebased option? No
Kiosk option? No
Employees needed to run franchise:
    3-4
Absentee ownership? Yes

COSTS
Total cost: $135K
Franchise fee: $15K
Royalty fee: 4%
Term of agreement: 10 years renewable
    for $1K
Franchisees required to buy multiple
    units? No

FINANCING
No financing available

QUALIFICATIONS
Info not provided

TRAINING
At headquarters: 30 days
At franchisee's location: 30 days
Ongoing

BUSINESS SUPPORT
Newsletter
Meetings
Toll-free phone line
Grand opening
Internet
Security/safety procedures
Field operations/evaluations
Purchasing cooperatives

MARKETING SUPPORT
Co-op advertising
Ad slicks

AUTOMOTIVE   *Miscellaneous*

ALTA MERE INDUSTRIES
Ranked #482 in Entrepreneur Magazine's 2004 Franchise 500   *Financial rating: $$$$*

4444 W. 147th St.
Midlothian, IL 60445
Ph: (800)377-9247/(708)389-5922
Fax: (708)389-9882
www.altamere.com
Window tinting, auto alarms & auto imaging
Began: 1986, Franchising since: 1993
Headquarters size: 35 employees
Franchise department: 2 employees

U.S. franchises: 26
Canadian franchises: 0
Other foreign franchises: 0
Company-owned: 0
Units concentrated in Sunbelt states

Seeking: South, Southeast, Southwest
Focusing on: Sunbelt states
Seeking in Canada? No
Exclusive territories? No
Homebased option? No
Kiosk option? No
Employees needed to run franchise:
    3-4
Absentee ownership? Yes

COSTS
Total cost: $93K
Franchise fee: $27.5K
Royalty fee: 7%
Term of agreement: 20 years renewable at no charge
Franchisees required to buy multiple units? No

FINANCING
In-house: None
3rd-party: Equipment, franchise fee, inventory

QUALIFICATIONS
Net worth: $100K-150K
Cash liquidity: $25K
Experience:
    General business experience
    Marketing skills

TRAINING
At headquarters: 1 week
At franchisee's location: 3 weeks

BUSINESS SUPPORT
Newsletter
Meetings
Toll-free phone line
Grand opening
Internet
Lease negotiations
Security/safety procedures
Field operations/evaluations
Purchasing cooperatives

MARKETING SUPPORT
Co-op advertising
Ad slicks
National media campaign
Regional marketing

LINE-X
Ranked #152 in Entrepreneur Magazine's 2004 Franchise 500   *Financial rating: Financial data n/a*

2400 S. Garnsey St.
Santa Ana, CA 92707
Ph: (800)831-3232
Fax: (714)850-8759
www.linexcorp.com
Spray-on truck bed liners & industrial coatings
Began: 1993, Franchising since: 1999
Headquarters size: 18 employees
Franchise department: 18 employees

U.S. franchises: 223
Canadian franchises: 18
Other foreign franchises: 22
Company-owned: 0
Units concentrated in all U.S.

Seeking: All U.S.
Seeking in Canada? Yes
Exclusive territories? Yes
Homebased option? No
Kiosk option? No
Employees needed to run franchise: 2
Absentee ownership? Yes

COSTS
Total cost: $70.2K-157.5K
Franchise fee: $20K-30K
Royalty fee: 0
Term of agreement: 5 years renewable at no charge
Franchisees required to buy multiple units? No

FINANCING
In-house: None
3rd-party: Accounts receivable, equipment, franchise fee, inventory, payroll, start-up costs

QUALIFICATIONS
Net worth: $50K
Cash liquidity: $25K
Experience:
    General business experience
    Marketing skills

TRAINING
At headquarters: Up to 7 days
At franchisee's location: Up to 7 days

BUSINESS SUPPORT
Newsletter
Purchasing cooperatives

MARKETING SUPPORT
Co-op advertising
Ad slicks
National media campaign

MIGHTY DISTRIB. SYSTEM OF AMERICA

Ranked #450 in Entrepreneur Magazine's 2004 Franchise 500   *Financial rating: $$$$*

650 Engineering Dr.
Norcross, GA 30092
Ph: (800)829-3900/(770)448-3900
Fax: (770)446-8627
www.mightyfranchise.com
Wholesale distribution of auto parts
Began: 1963, Franchising since: 1970
Headquarters size: 48 employees
Franchise department: 6 employees

U.S. franchises: 115
Canadian franchises: 0
Other foreign franchises: 1
Company-owned: 7

Seeking: All U.S.
Seeking in Canada? Yes
Exclusive territories? Yes
Homebased option? No
Kiosk option? No
Employees needed to run franchise:
    Info not provided
Absentee ownership? Yes

COSTS
Total cost: $150K-200K
Franchise fee: $12.9K-34.8K
Royalty fee: 5%
Term of agreement: 10 years renewable
    for 20% of current license fee
Franchisees required to buy multiple
    units? No

FINANCING
No financing available

QUALIFICATIONS
Net worth: $300K+
Cash liquidity: $75K
Experience:
    Industry experience
    General business experience

TRAINING
At headquarters: 4-5 days
At franchisee's location: 5-10 days

BUSINESS SUPPORT
Newsletter
Meetings
Toll-free phone line
Grand opening
Internet
Field operations/evaluations

MARKETING SUPPORT
Co-op advertising
Ad slicks
National media campaign
Regional marketing

SPOT-NOT CAR WASHES

Current financial data not available

2950 East Division
Springfield, MO 65802
Ph: (800)682-7629/(417)781-6233
Fax: (417)781-3906
www.spot-not.com
Automatic & self-serve car wash
Began: 1968, Franchising since: 1985
Headquarters size: Info not provided
Franchise department: Info not
    provided

U.S. franchises: 24
Canadian franchises: 0
Other foreign franchises: 0
Company-owned: 0
Units concentrated in AR, IL, MO

Seeking: All U.S.
Focusing on: IL, IN, MO
Seeking in Canada? No
Exclusive territories? Yes
Homebased option? No
Kiosk option? No
Employees needed to run franchise: 5
Absentee ownership? No

COSTS
Total cost: $622K-1.1M
Franchise fee: $25K
Royalty fee: 5%
Term of agreement: 10 years renewable
Franchisees required to buy multiple
    units? No

FINANCING
In-house: None
3rd-party: Equipment

QUALIFICATIONS
Net worth: $300K
Cash liquidity: $200K
Experience:
    General business experience

TRAINING
At headquarters: 3 weeks
At franchisee's location: 2 weeks

BUSINESS SUPPORT
Newsletter
Meetings
Toll-free phone line
Grand opening
Internet
Security/safety procedures
Field operations/evaluations

MARKETING SUPPORT
Co-op advertising
Ad slicks
National media campaign
Regional marketing

SUPER WASH
Ranked #110 in Entrepreneur Magazine's 2004 Franchise 500　　　　*Financial rating: $$$$*

707 W. Lincolnway
Morrison, IL 61270
Ph: (815)772-2111
Fax: (815)772-7160
www.superwash.com
Coin-operated self-serve automatic
　　car washes
Began: 1982, Franchising since: 2001
Headquarters size: 70 employees
Franchise department: 3 employees

U.S. franchises: 248
Canadian franchises: 0
Other foreign franchises: 0
Company-owned: 60
Units concentrated in IA, IL, IN, OH,
　　SD, WI

Seeking: All U.S.
Seeking in Canada? No
Exclusive territories? No
Homebased option? No
Kiosk option? No
Employees needed to run franchise:
　　3-4
Absentee ownership? Yes

COSTS
Total cost: $391.3K-1M
Franchise fee: $9K
Royalty fee: Varies
Term of agreement: 10 years renewable
　　at no charge
Franchisees required to buy multiple
　　units? No

FINANCING
In-house: None
3rd-party: Equipment, franchise fee,
　　inventory, start-up costs

QUALIFICATIONS
Net worth: $500K
Cash liquidity: $100K
Experience:
　　General business experience

TRAINING
At headquarters
At franchisee's location
Ongoing

BUSINESS SUPPORT
Newsletter
Meetings
Toll-free phone line
Grand opening
Field operations/evaluations

MARKETING SUPPORT
Ad slicks
Individual promotions
Radio

AUTOMOTIVE ▶ *Other Franchises*

AL & ED'S AUTOSOUND
*Ranked #430 in Entrepreneur
　　Magazine's 2004 Franchise 500*
6855 Hayvenhurst Ave.
Van Nuys, CA 91406
Ph: (818)908-5700
www.al-eds.com
Mobile electronics sales & installation

ALTRACOLOR SYSTEMS
*Ranked #472 in Entrepreneur
　　Magazine's 2004 Franchise 500*
113 23rd St.
Kenner, LA 70062
Ph: (800)727-6567
www.altracolor.com
Mobile auto painting & plastic repair

BRAKE DEPOT SYSTEMS INC.
840 B. St., #200
San Diego, CA 92101
Ph: (619)696-0200
www.brakedepot.com
Brake repair

BRAKE MASTERS SYSTEMS INC.
6179 E. Broadway
Tucson, AZ 85711
Ph: (800)888-5545/(520)512-0000
www.brakemasters.com
Brake & under-car services

CARSTAR FRANCHISE SYSTEMS INC.
8400 110th St., #200
Overland Park, KS 66210
Ph: (800)999-1949/(913)451-1294
www.carstar.com
Automotive collision repair

THE COLLISION SHOP
2899 E. Big Beaver Rd., #318
Troy, MI 48083
Ph: (800)219-3113
www.collisionfranchise.com
Body paint specialist

KING BEAR AUTO SERVICE CENTER
130-29 Merrick Blvd.
Springfield Gardens, NY 11434
Ph: (800)311-5464/(718)527-1252
www.kingbearauto.com
Automotive tire & service center

MISTER FRONT END
192 N. Queen St.
Etobicoke, ON Canada M9C 1A8
Ph: (416)622-9999
Alignment/suspension/springs/brakes

POWER WINDOW REPAIR EXPRESS
7675 Dixie Hwy.
Louisville, KY 40258
Ph: (877)797-3977
www.pwrexpress.com
Mobile power window repair

RYAN ENGINE EXCHANGE
2465 W. Evans Ave.
Denver, CO 80219
Ph: (303)232-0012
www.ryanengineexchange.com
Remanufactured engine installation

Business Services

BUSINESS   *Advertising*

ADVENTURES IN ADVERTISING FRANCHISE INC.

Current financial data not available

400 Crown Colony Dr.
Quincy, MA 02169
Ph: (800)432-6332
Fax: (617)472-9976
www.discoveraia.com
Promotional products/advertising specialties
Began: 1982, Franchising since: 1994
Headquarters size: 45 employees
Franchise department: 45 employees

U.S. franchises: 518
Canadian franchises: 8
Other foreign franchises: 0
Company-owned: 0

Seeking: All U.S.
Seeking in Canada? Yes
Exclusive territories? No
Homebased option? Yes
Kiosk option? No
Employees needed to run franchise: 1-2
Absentee ownership? No

COSTS
Total cost: $11.9K-47.7K
Franchise fee: $5K-27.5K
Royalty fee: 6-7%
Term of agreement: 5 years renewable for $2.5K
Franchisees required to buy multiple units? No

FINANCING
In-house: Franchise fee
3rd-party: None

QUALIFICATIONS
Experience:
    Industry experience
    General business experience
    Marketing skills

TRAINING
At headquarters: 1-1/2 weeks
Regional meetings & annual convention for 1-5 days

BUSINESS SUPPORT
Newsletter
Meetings
Toll-free phone line
Internet
Security/safety procedures
Field operations/evaluations

MARKETING SUPPORT
Regional marketing

AMERICAN TOWN MAILER

Financial rating: $$$

P.O. Box 31240
Mesa, AZ 85275
Ph: (480)649-0344
Fax: (480)464-1025
Co-op direct mail advertising
Began: 1976, Franchising since: 2000
Headquarters size: 6 employees
Franchise department: 2 employees

U.S. franchises: 2
Canadian franchises: 0
Other foreign franchises: 0
Company-owned: 0
Units concentrated in AZ, MN

Seeking: All U.S.
Seeking in Canada? No
Exclusive territories? Yes
Homebased option? Yes
Kiosk option? No
Employees needed to run franchise: 1
Absentee ownership? Yes

COSTS
Total cost: $23.9K-37.2K
Franchise fee: $20K
Royalty fee: 0
Term of agreement: 10 years renewable
for $1K
Franchisees required to buy multiple
units? No

FINANCING
No financing available

QUALIFICATIONS
Experience:
General business experience
Marketing skills

TRAINING
At headquarters: 1 week
At franchisee's location: 1 week

BUSINESS SUPPORT
Newsletter
Meetings
Toll-free phone line

MARKETING SUPPORT
Info not provided

AROUND TOWN COMMUNITY MAGAZINE INC.

Financial rating: $

1025 Rose Creek Dr., #340
Woodstock, GA 30189
Ph: (770)516-7105
Fax: (770)516-4809
www.aroundtowncm.com
Direct-mail community magazine
Began: 1996, Franchising since: 2003
Headquarters size: 6 employees
Franchise department: 6 employees

U.S. franchises: 0
Canadian franchises: 0
Other foreign franchises: 0
Company-owned: 2

Seeking: Southeast
Seeking in Canada? No
Exclusive territories? Yes
Homebased option? Yes
Kiosk option? No
Employees needed to run franchise:
1-2
Absentee ownership? No

COSTS
Total cost: $32.5K-42.9K
Franchise fee: $25K
Royalty fee: 5%
Term of agreement: 5 years renewable
for 20% of then-current fee
Franchisees required to buy multiple
units? No

FINANCING
No financing available

QUALIFICATIONS
Info not provided

TRAINING
At headquarters: 10 days
At franchisee's location: 5 days

BUSINESS SUPPORT
Grand opening
Field operations/evaluations

MARKETING SUPPORT
Info not provided

BILLBOARD CONNECTION INC.

Financial rating: $$$

590 Huiet Dr.
McDonough, GA 30253
Ph: (770)472-7500
Fax: (678)583-1605
www.billboardconnection.com
Ad agency specializing in outdoor
  media
Began: 1997, Franchising since: 2003
Headquarters size: 4 employees
Franchise department: 3 employees

U.S. franchises: 1
Canadian franchises: 0
Other foreign franchises: 0
Company-owned: 1
Units concentrated in GA

Seeking: All U.S.
Seeking in Canada? No
Exclusive territories? Yes
Homebased option? Yes
Kiosk option? No
Employees needed to run franchise: 1
Absentee ownership? Yes

COSTS
Total cost: $19.5K-26.5K
Franchise fee: $19.5K
Royalty fee: 2.5%
Term of agreement: 20 years renewable
  for $1K
Franchisees required to buy multiple
  units? No

FINANCING
No financing available

QUALIFICATIONS
Net worth: $45K+
Cash liquidity: $45K
Experience:
   Industry experience
   Marketing skills

TRAINING
At headquarters: 1 week
At franchisee's location: 1 week

BUSINESS SUPPORT
Newsletter
Meetings
Grand opening
Internet

MARKETING SUPPORT
Ad slicks
Regional marketing

BINGO BUGLE NEWSPAPER

Financial rating: $$$

P.O. Box 527
Vashon, WA 98070
Ph: (800)327-6437/(206)463-5656
Fax: (206)463-5630
www.bingobugle.com
Specialty newspaper
Began: 1981, Franchising since: 1983
Headquarters size: 3 employees
Franchise department: 2 employees

U.S. franchises: 61
Canadian franchises: 1
Other foreign franchises: 0
Company-owned: 0
Units concentrated in all U.S.

Seeking: Midwest, Northeast, South,
  Southeast
Focusing on: FL, MO, NC, NE, NJ, NY,
  PA, RI, SC, WV
Seeking in Canada? Yes
Exclusive territories? Yes
Homebased option? Yes
Kiosk option? No
Employees needed to run franchise: 1
Absentee ownership? No

COSTS
Total cost: $5.1K-11.5K
Franchise fee: $1.5K-10K
Royalty fee: 8%
Term of agreement: 5 years renewable
  at no charge
Franchisees required to buy multiple
  units? No

FINANCING
No financing available

QUALIFICATIONS
Cash liquidity: $5K
Experience:
   Outgoing personality

TRAINING
At franchisee's location: 2 days
At headquarters or w/regional
  manager

BUSINESS SUPPORT
Newsletter
Meetings
Toll-free phone line
Internet

MARKETING SUPPORT
Co-op advertising
Ad slicks

COFFEE NEWS

Current financial data not available

P.O. Box 8444
Bangor, ME 04402-8444
Ph: (207)941-0860
Fax: (207)941-0860
www.coffeenewsusa.com
Weekly restaurant newspaper
Began: 1988, Franchising since: 1994
Headquarters size: 7 employees
Franchise department: 2 employees

U.S. franchises: 200
Canadian franchises: 54
Other foreign franchises: 150
Company-owned: 4
Units concentrated in CA, FL, ME, MS, NC, TX

Seeking: All U.S.
Seeking in Canada? Yes
Exclusive territories? Yes
Homebased option? Yes
Kiosk option? No
Employees needed to run franchise: 1
Absentee ownership? Yes

COSTS
Total cost: $4K
Franchise fee: $3.5K/2K
Royalty fee: $20-75/wk.
Term of agreement: 4 years renewable at no charge
Franchisees required to buy multiple units? No

FINANCING
No financing available

QUALIFICATIONS
Experience:
General business experience
Marketing skills
Sales & advertising experience

TRAINING
At headquarters: 3 days
Mentor program

BUSINESS SUPPORT
Newsletter
Meetings
Internet
Purchasing cooperatives

MARKETING SUPPORT
Ad slicks

DISCOVERY MAP INT'L.

Financial rating: $

P.O. Box 1278
Anacortes, WA 98221
Ph: (877)820-7827/(360)588-0144
Fax: (360)588-8344
www.discoverymap.com
Specialty map advertising system
Began: 1987, Franchising since: 1999
Headquarters size: 9 employees
Franchise department: 2 employees

U.S. franchises: 14
Canadian franchises: 0
Other foreign franchises: 0
Company-owned: 6
Units concentrated in AZ, CO, ID, MT, NM, WY

Seeking: All U.S.
Focusing on: AZ, CA, MT, OR, SD, UT
Seeking in Canada? No
Exclusive territories? Yes
Homebased option? Yes
Kiosk option? No
Employees needed to run franchise: 1
Absentee ownership? Yes

COSTS
Total cost: $32.3K-36.3K
Franchise fee: $18K
Royalty fee: 0
Term of agreement: 10 years renewable for 33% of franchise fee
Franchisees required to buy multiple units? No

FINANCING
No financing available

QUALIFICATIONS
Experience:
General business experience
Marketing skills

TRAINING
At headquarters: 5 days
At franchisee's location: 1 day

BUSINESS SUPPORT
Newsletter
Meetings
Toll-free phone line
Internet
Field operations/evaluations

MARKETING SUPPORT
Co-op advertising
Regional marketing

EASYCHAIR MEDIA LLC

Current financial data not available

800 Third St.
Windsor, CO 80550-5424
Ph: (800)741-6308
Fax: (800)438-2150
www.easychairmedia.com
Regional/city publications
Began: 2000, Franchising since: 2002
Headquarters size: 12 employees
Franchise department: 3 employees

U.S. franchises: 1
Canadian franchises: 0
Other foreign franchises: 0
Company-owned: 3

Seeking: All U.S.
Seeking in Canada? Yes
Exclusive territories? Yes
Homebased option? Yes
Kiosk option? No
Employees needed to run franchise:
    1-2
Absentee ownership? Yes

COSTS
Total cost: $32.7K-36.7K
Franchise fee: $10K-20K
Royalty fee: 0
Term of agreement: 10 years renewable
    for 25% of original franchise fee
Franchisees required to buy multiple
    units? No

FINANCING
No financing available

QUALIFICATIONS
Experience:
    Marketing skills
    Sales, publishing & direct mail

TRAINING
At headquarters: 1-2 weeks
At franchisee's location

BUSINESS SUPPORT
Newsletter
Meetings
Toll-free phone line

MARKETING SUPPORT
Info not provided

GOTCHA MOBILE MEDIA

Current financial data not available

2020 Fieldstone Pkwy, #900-180
Franklin, TN 37069
Ph: (615)309-7666
Fax: (615)250-4913
www.ad-motionbillboards.com
Mobile billboard advertising
Began: 1975, Franchising since: 2001
Headquarters size: Info not provided
Franchise department: Info not
    provided

U.S. franchises: 6
Canadian franchises: 0
Other foreign franchises: 0
Company-owned: 0
Units concentrated in AZ, FL, GA, IA,
    IL, MO, NJ

Seeking: All U.S.
Seeking in Canada? No
Exclusive territories? Yes
Homebased option? Yes
Kiosk option? No
Employees needed to run franchise: 2
Absentee ownership? Yes

COSTS
Total cost: $49K-100K
Franchise fee: $20K-42.5K
Royalty fee: Varies
Term of agreement: 10 years renewable
    for 40% of current franchise fee
Franchisees required to buy multiple
    units? No

FINANCING
In-house: Franchise fee
3rd-party: Equipment

QUALIFICATIONS
Net worth: $100K+
Cash liquidity: $50K
Experience:
    Marketing skills

TRAINING
At headquarters: 5-7 days
Semi-annual training: 1-3 days

BUSINESS SUPPORT
Newsletter
Meetings
Internet

MARKETING SUPPORT
Sales & promotional materials

HOMES & LAND MAGAZINE

Ranked #261 in Entrepreneur Magazine's 2004 Franchise 500   *Financial rating: $$$$*

1600 Capital Cir. S.W.
Tallahassee, FL 32310
Ph: (850)574-2111
Fax: (850)574-2525
www.homesandland.com
Real estate advertising magazine
Began: 1973, Franchising since: 1984
Headquarters size: 25 employees
Franchise department: 3 employees

U.S. franchises: 187
Canadian franchises: 3
Other foreign franchises: 0
Company-owned: 6

Seeking: All U.S.
Seeking in Canada? Yes
Exclusive territories? Yes
Homebased option? Yes
Kiosk option? No
Employees needed to run franchise: 2
Absentee ownership? Yes

COSTS
Total cost: $48K-104K
Franchise fee: $25K
Royalty fee: Varies
Term of agreement: 10 years renewable
    for $1K
Franchisees required to buy multiple
    units? No

FINANCING
No financing available

QUALIFICATIONS
Experience:
    General business experience
    Marketing skills

TRAINING
At headquarters: 2 weeks
In-field training

BUSINESS SUPPORT
Newsletter
Meetings
Toll-free phone line
Internet
Field operations/evaluations
Purchasing cooperatives

MARKETING SUPPORT
Co-op advertising
Ad slicks
National media campaign
Regional marketing

MONEY MAILER LLC

Ranked #140 in Entrepreneur Magazine's 2004 Franchise 500   *Financial rating: $$$$*

14271 Corporate Dr.
Garden Grove, CA 92843
Ph: (888)446-4648
Fax: (714)265-8311
www.moneymailer.net
Direct-mail advertising
Began: 1979, Franchising since: 1980
Headquarters size: 280 employees
Franchise department: 20 employees

U.S. franchises: 250
Canadian franchises: 0
Other foreign franchises: 0
Company-owned: 13
Units concentrated in CA, IL, NJ

Seeking: All U.S.
Seeking in Canada? No
Exclusive territories? Yes
Homebased option? Yes
Kiosk option? No
Employees needed to run franchise: 0
Absentee ownership? No

COSTS
Total cost: $48.7K-88.3K
Franchise fee: $30.5K-41.5K
Royalty fee: Varies
Term of agreement: 10 years renewable
    for $2K
Franchisees required to buy multiple
    units? No

FINANCING
Printing & mailing services

QUALIFICATIONS
Cash liquidity: $50K
Experience:
    Marketing skills
    Sales experience
    Strong communication skills
    Good credit

TRAINING
At headquarters: 6 days
At franchisee's location: 11 days
Ongoing

BUSINESS SUPPORT
Newsletter
Meetings
Internet
Field operations/evaluations
Purchasing cooperatives

MARKETING SUPPORT
Co-op advertising
Ad slicks
Local advertising

THE PERFECT WEDDING GUIDE INC.
Ranked #431 in Entrepreneur Magazine's 2004 Franchise 500

Financial rating: $$

1206 N. C.R. 427
Longwood, FL 32750
Ph: (888)222-7433/(407)331-6212
Fax: (888)933-3404
www.thepwg.com
Wedding guide
Began: 1991, Franchising since: 1998
Headquarters size: 25 employees
Franchise department: 21 employees

U.S. franchises: 86
Canadian franchises: 0
Other foreign franchises: 0
Company-owned: 2
Units concentrated in all U.S.

Seeking: All U.S.
Seeking in Canada? Yes
Exclusive territories? Yes
Homebased option? Yes
Kiosk option? No
Employees needed to run franchise: 2
Absentee ownership? Yes

COSTS
Total cost: $39K-49K
Franchise fee: $25K-35K
Royalty fee: 6%
Term of agreement: 10 years renewable
　　at no charge
Franchisees required to buy multiple
　　units? No

FINANCING
In-house: Franchise fee
3rd-party: None

QUALIFICATIONS
Net worth: $75K
Cash liquidity: $39K-49K
Experience:
　　General business experience
　　Marketing skills

TRAINING
At headquarters: 5 days
At franchisee's location: 5 days

BUSINESS SUPPORT
Newsletter
Meetings
Toll-free phone line
Internet
Purchasing cooperatives

MARKETING SUPPORT
Co-op advertising
Ad slicks
National media campaign

PROFIT-TELL INT'L.

Financial rating: $$$

15 Spinning Wheel Rd., #114
Hinsdale, IL 60521
Ph: (888)366-4653
Fax: (630)655-4542
www.profit-tell.com
Telephone "on-hold" marketing system
Began: 1993, Franchising since: 2001
Headquarters size: 7 employees
Franchise department: 7 employees

U.S. franchises: 5
Canadian franchises: 0
Other foreign franchises: 0
Company-owned: 1
Units concentrated in all U.S.

Seeking: All U.S.
Seeking in Canada? No
Exclusive territories? No
Homebased option? Yes
Kiosk option? No
Employees needed to run franchise: 1
Absentee ownership? No

COSTS
Total cost: $27.4K-45.3K
Franchise fee: $19.5K
Royalty fee: 0
Term of agreement: 20 years renewable
　　for $1K
Franchisees required to buy multiple
　　units? No

FINANCING
No financing available

QUALIFICATIONS
Cash liquidity: $23.7K
Experience:
　　General business experience
　　Sales experience

TRAINING
At headquarters: 6 days
At franchisee's location: As needed

BUSINESS SUPPORT
Newsletter
Meetings
Toll-free phone line
Internet
Field operations/evaluations

MARKETING SUPPORT
Ad slicks
Regional marketing
Ad funds & support

PRSTORE LLC

Financial rating: 0

2108 South Blvd., #107
Charlotte, NC 28203
Ph: (704)333-2200
Fax: (704)332-0100
www.prstore.biz
B2B marketing services
Began: 2001, Franchising since: 2002
Headquarters size: 7 employees
Franchise department: 2 employees

U.S. franchises: 2
Canadian franchises: 0
Other foreign franchises: 0
Company-owned: 1
Units concentrated in MI, NC

Seeking: All U.S.
Focusing on: GA, KY, NC, TX
Seeking in Canada? No
Exclusive territories? No
Homebased option? No
Kiosk option? No
Employees needed to run franchise: 1
Absentee ownership? No

COSTS
Total cost: $100.96K-181.3K
Franchise fee: $25K-40K
Royalty fee: 2-6%
Term of agreement: 5 years renewable
    at no charge
Franchisees required to buy multiple
    units? No

FINANCING
No financing available

QUALIFICATIONS
Net worth: $250K
Cash liquidity: $50K
Experience:
    Industry experience

TRAINING
At headquarters: 3 weeks
At franchisee's location: Up to 10 days

BUSINESS SUPPORT
Newsletter
Meetings
Grand opening
Internet
Lease negotiations
Field operations/evaluations

MARKETING SUPPORT
Co-op advertising
Ad slicks
National media campaign
Regional marketing

REZCITY.COM

Ranked #372 in Entrepreneur Magazine's 2004 Franchise 500

Financial rating: $$$$

560 Sylvan Ave.
Englewood Cliffs, NJ 07632
Ph: (800)669-9000/(201)567-8500
Fax: (201)567-3265
www.rezcity.biz
Online local city guides & travel store
Began: 2002, Franchising since: 2002
Headquarters size: 18 employees
Franchise department: 8 employees

U.S. franchises: 215
Canadian franchises: 0
Other foreign franchises: 0
Company-owned: 2
Units concentrated in all U.S.

Seeking: All U.S.
Seeking in Canada? No
Exclusive territories? Yes
Homebased option? Yes
Kiosk option? No
Employees needed to run franchise: 1
Absentee ownership? Yes

COSTS
Total cost: $6.7K-61.2K
Franchise fee: $1K-50K
Royalty fee: 0
Term of agreement: 5 years renewable
Franchisees required to buy multiple
    units? No

FINANCING
In-house: Franchise fee
3rd-party: Equipment

QUALIFICATIONS
Net worth: $20K
Cash liquidity: $5K-25K
Experience:
    General business experience
    Marketing skills

TRAINING
At headquarters: 2 days
Web conference training

BUSINESS SUPPORT
Newsletter
Meetings
Toll-free phone line
Grand opening
Internet

MARKETING SUPPORT
Co-op advertising
Ad slicks
National media campaign
E-mail clubs

SUPER COUPS

Ranked #265 in Entrepreneur Magazine's 2004 Franchise 500   *Financial rating: $$$*

180 Bodwell St.
Avon, MA 02322
Ph: (800)626-2620
Fax: (508)588-3347
www.supercoups.com
Co-op direct-mail advertising
Began: 1982, Franchising since: 1983
Headquarters size: 130 employees
Franchise department: 3 employees

U.S. franchises: 227
Canadian franchises: 0
Other foreign franchises: 0
Company-owned: 0
Units concentrated in AL, AR, AZ, CA,
    CO, CT, FL, GA, IN, KY, MA, MD,
    ME, MN, NC, NH, NJ, OH, PA, RI,
    TX, VA & Puerto Rico

Seeking: All U.S.
Seeking in Canada? No
Exclusive territories? Yes
Homebased option? Yes
Kiosk option? No
Employees needed to run franchise: 1
Absentee ownership? No

COSTS
Total cost: $34.95K-53.5K
Franchise fee: $29K
Royalty fee: Varies
Term of agreement: 10 years renewable
    for $1K
Franchisees required to buy multiple
    units? No

FINANCING
No financing available

QUALIFICATIONS
Net worth: $100K
Cash liquidity: $29K
Experience:
    General business experience
    Sales & sales management
    experience

TRAINING
At headquarters: 1 week
At franchisee's location: 2 weeks

BUSINESS SUPPORT
Meetings
Internet
Security/safety procedures
Field operations/evaluations

MARKETING SUPPORT
Ad slicks
Franchisee marketing committee

UNITED MARKETING SOLUTIONS INC.

Current financial data not available

7644 Dynatech Ct.
Springfield, VA 22153-2811
Ph: (800)368-3501/(703)644-0200
Fax: (703)455-8519
www.unitedol.com
Direct-mail advertising, direct market-
    ing, Internet marketing
Began: 1981, Franchising since: 1982
Headquarters size: 60 employees
Franchise department: 8 employees

U.S. franchises: 40
Canadian franchises: 0
Other foreign franchises: 0
Company-owned: 0
Units concentrated in AL, FL, MA,
    MD, PA, VA

Seeking: All U.S.
Seeking in Canada? No
Exclusive territories? Yes
Homebased option? Yes
Kiosk option? No
Employees needed to run franchise: 0
Absentee ownership? No

COSTS
Total cost: $30.4K-59.3K
Franchise fee: $24K-28K
Royalty fee: 0
Term of agreement: 10 years renewable
    for 5% of current license fee
Franchisees required to buy multiple
    units? No

FINANCING
In-house: Franchise fee
3rd-party: None

QUALIFICATIONS
Experience:
    General business experience
    Marketing skills
    Sales experience

TRAINING
At headquarters: 10 days
At franchisee's location: 5 days+
Additional training available

BUSINESS SUPPORT
Newsletter
Meetings
Toll-free phone line
Grand opening
Internet
Field operations/evaluations

MARKETING SUPPORT
Brochures
Promotional materials
Samples
Mailings

VAL-PAK DIRECT MARKETING SYSTEMS INC.

Ranked #349 in Entrepreneur Magazine's 2004 Franchise 500   *Financial rating: $$$$*

8605 Largo Lakes Dr.
Largo, FL 33773
Ph: (800)237-6266
Fax: (727)392-0049
www.valpak.com
Co-op direct-mail advertising
Began: 1968, Franchising since: 1988
Headquarters size: 1,200 employees
Franchise department: 32 employees

U.S. franchises: 183
Canadian franchises: 22
Other foreign franchises: 0
Company-owned: 5
Units concentrated in all U.S.

Seeking: All U.S.
Seeking in Canada? Yes
Exclusive territories? Yes
Homebased option? Yes
Kiosk option? No
Employees needed to run franchise: 2
Absentee ownership? No

COSTS
Total cost: $48.7K-81.3K
Franchise fee: $12K
Royalty fee: 0
Term of agreement: 10 years renewable
    at no charge
Franchisees required to buy multiple
    units? No

FINANCING
3rd-party: Franchise fee, start-up costs
Other: Territory fee

QUALIFICATIONS
Experience:
    General business experience
    Sales skills
    Management skills

TRAINING
At headquarters: 1 week
At franchisee's location: 4 weeks
At headquarters: Ongoing

BUSINESS SUPPORT
Newsletter
Meetings
Toll-free phone line
Grand opening
Internet
Field operations/evaluations

MARKETING SUPPORT
Co-op advertising
Ad slicks
National media campaign

BUSINESS   *Business Brokerages*

SUNBELT BUSINESS ADVISORS NETWORK

Ranked #74 in Entrepreneur Magazine's 2004 Franchise 500   *Financial rating: $$$*

474 Wando Park Blvd., #204
Mt. Pleasant, SC 29464
Ph: (800)771-7866
Fax: (843)284-2419
www.sunbeltnetwork.com
Business brokerage
Began: 1979, Franchising since: 1993
Headquarters size: 10 employees
Franchise department: 10 employees

U.S. franchises: 359
Canadian franchises: 10
Other foreign franchises: 20
Company-owned: 0
Units concentrated in all U.S.

Seeking: All U.S.
Seeking in Canada? Yes
Exclusive territories? Yes
Homebased option? No
Kiosk option? No
Employees needed to run franchise:
    2-5
Absentee ownership? No

COSTS
Total cost: $51K-100K
Franchise fee: $15K-25K
Royalty fee: $3K/2x/yr.
Term of agreement: 10 years renewable
    at no charge
Franchisees required to buy multiple
    units? No

FINANCING
In-house: None
3rd-party: Accounts receivable, equip-
    ment, franchise fee, inventory, pay-
    roll, start-up costs

QUALIFICATIONS
Net worth: $150K
Cash liquidity: $25K
Experience:
    General business experience

TRAINING
At headquarters: 1 week
Regional training

BUSINESS SUPPORT
Newsletter
Meetings
Toll-free phone line
Internet

MARKETING SUPPORT
Co-op advertising
National media campaign

VR BUSINESS BROKERS

Current financial data not available

2601 E. Oakland Pk. Blvd., #301
Ft. Lauderdale, FL 33306
Ph: (800)377-8722/(954)565-1555
Fax: (954)565-6855
www.vrbusinessbrokers.com
Business brokerage/mergers & acquisitions
Began: 1979, Franchising since: 1979
Headquarters size: 10 employees
Franchise department: 2 employees

U.S. franchises: 110
Canadian franchises: 0
Other foreign franchises: 10
Company-owned: 0
Units concentrated in all U.S.

Seeking: All U.S.
Seeking in Canada? Yes
Exclusive territories? Yes
Homebased option? No
Kiosk option? No
Employees needed to run franchise: 1
Absentee ownership? Yes

COSTS
Total cost: $32.1K-58.8K
Franchise fee: $17.5K
Royalty fee: 6%
Term of agreement: 10 years renewable for 33% of current franchise fee
Franchisees required to buy multiple units? No

FINANCING
In-house: None
3rd-party: Equipment, franchise fee, inventory, start-up costs

QUALIFICATIONS
Net worth: $250K
Cash liquidity: $100K
Experience:
    General business experience

TRAINING
At headquarters: 10 days
At franchisee's location: As needed

BUSINESS SUPPORT
Newsletter
Meetings
Toll-free phone line
Grand opening
Internet
Field operations/evaluations
Purchasing cooperatives

MARKETING SUPPORT
Co-op advertising
Ad slicks
National media campaign

BUSINESS ▶ *Consulting*

ACCUTRAK INVENTORY SPECIALISTS

Financial rating: 0

1818C Hwy. 17 N., #320
Surfside Beach, SC 29575
Ph: (843)293-8274
Fax: (843)293-5075
www.accutrakinventory.com
Inventory consulting
Began: 1993, Franchising since: 2000
Headquarters size: 5 employees
Franchise department: 5 employees

U.S. franchises: 36
Canadian franchises: 0
Other foreign franchises: 2
Company-owned: 1
Units concentrated in all U.S.

Seeking: All U.S.
Seeking in Canada? Yes
Exclusive territories? Yes
Homebased option? Yes
Kiosk option? No
Employees needed to run franchise: 1
Absentee ownership? Yes

COSTS
Total cost: $30K-43K
Franchise fee: $22.5K
Royalty fee: 7%
Term of agreement: 15 years renewable at no charge
Franchisees required to buy multiple units? No

FINANCING
In-house: Franchise fee
3rd-party: None

QUALIFICATIONS
Net worth: $125K
Cash liquidity: $30K
Experience:
    General business experience
    Marketing skills

TRAINING
At headquarters: 4 days
At franchisee's location: Varies
At franchisee training site: 4 days

BUSINESS SUPPORT
Newsletter
Meetings
Grand opening
Internet
Security/safety procedures
Field operations/evaluations
Purchasing cooperatives

MARKETING SUPPORT
Co-op advertising
Ad slicks
Regional marketing

ACTION INT'L.

Ranked #69 in Entrepreneur Magazine's 2004 Franchise 500   *Financial rating: $$$*

5670 Wynn Rd., #C
Las Vegas, NV 89118
Ph: (702)795-3188
Fax: (702)795-3183
www.action-international.com
Business coaching, consulting, training
Began: 1993, Franchising since: 1997
Headquarters size: 7 employees
Franchise department: Info not provided

U.S. franchises: 115
Canadian franchises: 81
Other foreign franchises: 359
Company-owned: 28
Units concentrated in GA, NJ, OH

Seeking: All U.S.
Seeking in Canada? Yes
Exclusive territories? Yes
Homebased option? Yes
Kiosk option? No
Employees needed to run franchise: 1
Absentee ownership? Yes

COSTS
Total cost: $52.2K-79K
Franchise fee: $25K-40K
Royalty fee: $1.5K/mo.
Term of agreement: 5 years renewable
    for $2.5K
Franchisees required to buy multiple
    units? No

FINANCING
In-house: None
3rd-party: Accounts receivable, equipment, franchise fee, inventory, payroll, start-up costs

QUALIFICATIONS
Net worth: $100K
Cash liquidity: $60K
Experience:
    General business experience
    Marketing skills

TRAINING
At headquarters: 10 days
At various locations: 10 days

BUSINESS SUPPORT
Newsletter
Meetings
Toll-free phone line
Internet
Field operations/evaluations

MARKETING SUPPORT
Co-op advertising
Ad slicks
National media campaign
Regional marketing

THE ALTERNATIVE BOARD TAB

Ranked #475 in Entrepreneur Magazine's 2004 Franchise 500   *Financial rating: 0*

225 E. 16th Ave., #580
Denver, CO 80203-1622
Ph: (800)727-0126
Fax: (800)420-7055/(303)839-0012
www.tabboards.com
Peer advisory boards & business
    services
Began: 1990, Franchising since: 1996
Headquarters size: 19 employees
Franchise department: 3 employees

U.S. franchises: 77
Canadian franchises: 6
Other foreign franchises: 1
Company-owned: 16
Units concentrated in all U.S.

Seeking: All U.S.
Seeking in Canada? Yes
Exclusive territories? Yes
Homebased option? Yes
Kiosk option? No
Employees needed to run franchise: 1
Absentee ownership? No

COSTS
Total cost: $27.9K-57.9K
Franchise fee: $9.9K-39.9K
Royalty fee: 0
Term of agreement: 10 years renewable
    for $1.5K
Franchisees required to buy multiple
    units? No

FINANCING
In-house: Franchise fee
3rd-party: None

QUALIFICATIONS
Net worth: $100K
Cash liquidity: $75K
Experience:
    Industry experience
    General business experience
    Marketing skills
    Minimum 10 years of business
    executive experience

TRAINING
At headquarters: 1 week
At franchisee's location: 2 weeks

BUSINESS SUPPORT
Newsletter
Meetings
Toll-free phone line
Grand opening
Internet
Field operations/evaluations
Purchasing cooperatives

MARKETING SUPPORT
Co-op advertising
Regional marketing

BUSINESS ROUND TABLE

Current financial data not available

37 Chandler Crescent
Moncton, NB Canada E1E 3W6
Ph: (506)857-8177
Fax: (506)858-5553
www.business-round-table.com
Mentoring groups for small businesses
Began: 1991, Franchising since: 1998
Headquarters size: 2 employees
Franchise department: 1 employee

U.S. franchises: 0
Canadian franchises: 2
Other foreign franchises: 0
Company-owned: 1

Not available in the U.S.
Seeking in Canada? Yes
Exclusive territories? Yes
Homebased option? Yes
Kiosk option? No
Employees needed to run franchise: 2
Absentee ownership? No

COSTS
Total cost: $20K
Franchise fee: $20K
Royalty fee: 5-10%
Term of agreement: 10 years renewable
　　for $1K
Franchisees required to buy multiple
　　units? No

FINANCING
No financing available

QUALIFICATIONS
Net worth: $100K
Cash liquidity: $25K
Experience:
　　General business experience
　　Marketing skills

TRAINING
At franchisee's location: 1 week

BUSINESS SUPPORT
Newsletter
Meetings
Toll-free phone line
Internet
Field operations/evaluations

MARKETING SUPPORT
Ad slicks

THE ENTREPRENEUR'S SOURCE

Ranked #81 in Entrepreneur Magazine's 2004 Franchise 500

Financial rating: $$$$

900 Main St. S., Bldg. 2
Southbury, CT 06488
Ph: (800)289-0086
Fax: (203)264-3516
www.franchiseexperts.com
Franchise consulting & development
　　services
Began: 1984, Franchising since: 1997
Headquarters size: 12 employees
Franchise department: Info not pro-
　　vided

U.S. franchises: 245
Canadian franchises: 3
Other foreign franchises: 1
Company-owned: 0
Units concentrated in all U.S.

Seeking: All U.S.
Seeking in Canada? Yes
Exclusive territories? No
Homebased option? Yes
Kiosk option? No
Employees needed to run franchise: 0
Absentee ownership? No

COSTS
Total cost: $71K-79K
Franchise fee: $45K
Royalty fee: 0
Term of agreement: 10 years renewable
　　for $5K
Franchisees required to buy multiple
　　units? Outside the U.S. only

FINANCING
No financing available

QUALIFICATIONS
Net worth: $100K
Cash liquidity: $50K

TRAINING
At headquarters: 8 days
Ongoing

BUSINESS SUPPORT
Newsletter
Meetings
Internet

MARKETING SUPPORT
Ad slicks
National media campaign
Regional marketing

EWF INT'L.

Current financial data not available

4900 Richmond Sq., #105
Oklahoma City, OK 73118
Ph: (405)843-3934
Fax: (405)843-3933
www.ewfinternational.com
Peer support groups for women business owners & execs
Began: 1998, Franchising since: 2002
Headquarters size: 3 employees
Franchise department: 1 employee

U.S. franchises: 0
Canadian franchises: 0
Other foreign franchises: 0
Company-owned: 1

Seeking: All U.S.
Focusing on: Midwest & Southwest
Seeking in Canada? Yes
Exclusive territories? Yes
Homebased option? Yes
Kiosk option? No
Employees needed to run franchise: 1
Absentee ownership? No

COSTS
Total cost: $30K-35K
Franchise fee: $25K
Royalty fee: 15%
Term of agreement: 3 years renewable at no charge
Franchisees required to buy multiple units? No

FINANCING
No financing available

QUALIFICATIONS
Experience:
　　General business experience
　　Marketing skills

TRAINING
At headquarters: 20 hours
At franchisee's location: 2 days

BUSINESS SUPPORT
Meetings
Toll-free phone line
Internet

MARKETING SUPPORT
Ad slicks
On-site visits

THE GROWTH COACH

Current financial data not available

4338 Glendale-Milford Rd.
Cincinnati, OH 45242
Ph: (888)292-7992
Fax: (513)563-2691
www.thegrowthcoach.com
Small business coaching & mentoring
Began: 2002, Franchising since: 2003
Headquarters size: 8 employees
Franchise department: 8 employees

U.S. franchises: 6
Canadian franchises: 0
Other foreign franchises: 0
Company-owned: 0
Units concentrated in KY, NJ, OH

Seeking: All U.S.
Seeking in Canada? No
Exclusive territories? Yes
Homebased option? Yes
Kiosk option? No
Employees needed to run franchise: 0
Absentee ownership? No

COSTS
Total cost: $22.5K-34.9K
Franchise fee: $17.9K
Royalty fee: 6%
Term of agreement: 10 years renewable at no charge
Franchisees required to buy multiple units? No

FINANCING
In-house: Franchise fee
3rd-party: None

QUALIFICATIONS
Cash liquidity: $10K
Experience:
　　General business experience

TRAINING
At headquarters: 5 days
Ongoing

BUSINESS SUPPORT
Newsletter
Meetings
Toll-free phone line
Grand opening
Internet

MARKETING SUPPORT
Ad slicks
Marketing strategies

INNER CIRCLE INT'L. LTD.

Financial rating: 0

3320 Louisiana Ave. S., #305
Minneapolis, MN 55426
Ph: (952)933-6629
Fax: (952)935-5269
www.theinnercircle.com
Peer advisory groups for business
   owners
Began: 1985, Franchising since: 1997
Headquarters size: 4 employees
Franchise department: 4 employees

U.S. franchises: 5
Canadian franchises: 0
Other foreign franchises: 0
Company-owned: 0
Units concentrated in all U.S.

Seeking: All U.S.
Seeking in Canada? Yes
Exclusive territories? No
Homebased option? Yes
Kiosk option? No
Employees needed to run franchise: 1
Absentee ownership? Yes

COSTS
Total cost: $67K-84K
Franchise fee: $56K
Royalty fee: 15%
Term of agreement: 20 years renewable
   at then-current franchise fee
Franchisees required to buy multiple
   units? No

FINANCING
No financing available

QUALIFICATIONS
Net worth: $500K
Cash liquidity: $80K
Experience:
   General business experience

TRAINING
At headquarters: 2 weeks
At franchisee's location: 3 days
Annual symposium; monthly confer-
   ence calls

BUSINESS SUPPORT
Newsletter
Meetings
Internet

MARKETING SUPPORT
National media campaign

INTERNATIONAL MERGERS AND ACQUISITIONS

Current financial data not available

4300 N. Miller Rd., #230
Scottsdale, AZ 85251
Ph: (480)990-3899
Fax: (480)990-7480
www.ima-world.com
Mergers/acquisitions consulting &
   services
Began: 1970, Franchising since: 1979
Headquarters size: 3 employees
Franchise department: 2 employees

U.S. franchises: 30
Canadian franchises: 0
Other foreign franchises: 3
Company-owned: 0
Units concentrated in all U.S.

Seeking: All U.S.
Seeking in Canada? Yes
Exclusive territories? No
Homebased option? Yes
Kiosk option? No
Employees needed to run franchise: 1
Absentee ownership? No

COSTS
Total cost: $15K
Franchise fee: $15K
Royalty fee: $375/quarter
Term of agreement: Perpetual
Franchisees required to buy multiple
   units? No

FINANCING
No financing available

QUALIFICATIONS
Cash liquidity: $25K-50K
Experience:
   Industry experience
   General business experience

TRAINING
At headquarters: As needed
Orientation & workshops

BUSINESS SUPPORT
Newsletter
Meetings
Internet

MARKETING SUPPORT
Web sessions
Creative work sessions
Hotlines
Manuals

LOTUSEA FRANCHISING GROUP INC.

Financial rating: Current financial data not available

150 View Bend
Johnson City, TN 37601
Ph: (866)915-5944/(423)915-0852
Fax: (423)915-0852
www.lotusea.com
Corporate wellness programs
Began: 1990, Franchising since: 2000
Headquarters size: 13 employees
Franchise department: 1 employee

U.S. franchises: 2
Canadian franchises: 0
Other foreign franchises: 0
Company-owned: 1
Units concentrated in all U.S.

Seeking: All U.S.
Seeking in Canada? No
Exclusive territories? Yes
Homebased option? Yes
Kiosk option? No
Employees needed to run franchise: 2
Absentee ownership? No

COSTS
Total cost: $56.8K-96.2K
Franchise fee: $35K
Royalty fee: 7-8%
Term of agreement: 10 years renewable
for 20% of franchise fee
Franchisees required to buy multiple
units? No

FINANCING
In-house: Franchise fee
3rd-party: None

QUALIFICATIONS
Experience:
General business experience
Marketing skills
Health-care experience

TRAINING
At headquarters: 1 week
At franchisee's location: 2 weeks

BUSINESS SUPPORT
Meetings
Toll-free phone line
Grand opening
Internet

MARKETING SUPPORT
Ad slicks
National media campaign
Regional marketing

MANUFACTURING MANAGEMENT ASSOCIATES

Current financial data not available

700 Commerce Dr., 5th Fl.
Oak Brook, IL 60523
Ph: (630)574-0300
Fax: (630)574-0309
www.consult-mma.com
Consulting to small- & medium-sized
manufacturing businesses
Began: 1982, Franchising since: 1990
Headquarters size: 20 employees
Franchise department: 3 employees

U.S. franchises: 5
Canadian franchises: 2
Other foreign franchises: 0
Company-owned: 0
Units concentrated in IL, MI, OH

Seeking: All U.S.
Seeking in Canada? No
Exclusive territories? No
Homebased option? No
Kiosk option? No
Employees needed to run franchise: 3
Absentee ownership? No

COSTS
Total cost: to $25K
Franchise fee: $10K-15K
Royalty fee: 5%
Term of agreement: 10 years renewable
Franchisees required to buy multiple
units? No

FINANCING
In-house: Franchise fee
3rd-party: None

QUALIFICATIONS
Net worth: $100K+
Cash liquidity: $25K
Experience:
Industry experience
General business experience

TRAINING
At headquarters: 5-7 days
At franchisee's location: 3-5 days

BUSINESS SUPPORT
Newsletter
Meetings
Internet
Field operations/evaluations

MARKETING SUPPORT
Co-op advertising
Internet

PRO: PRESIDENT'S RESOURCE ORGANIZATION

Financial rating: $

100 E. Bellevue #4E
Chicago, IL 60611
Ph: (312)337-3658
Fax: (312)944-6815
www.propres.com
Peer advisory boards
Began: 1993, Franchising since: 1999
Headquarters size: 2 employees
Franchise department: 2 employees

U.S. franchises: 1
Canadian franchises: 0
Other foreign franchises: 0
Company-owned: 3
Units concentrated in all U.S.

Seeking: All U.S.
Seeking in Canada? No
Exclusive territories? Yes
Homebased option? Yes
Kiosk option? No
Employees needed to run franchise:
    Info not provided
Absentee ownership? Yes

COSTS
Total cost: $18.9K-63K
Franchise fee: $8.5K-35K
Royalty fee: 10-15%
Term of agreement: Info not provided
Franchisees required to buy multiple
    units? No

FINANCING
In-house: Franchise fee
3rd-party: None

QUALIFICATIONS
Net worth: $100K+
Cash liquidity: $35K+
Experience:
    Industry experience
    General business experience
    Marketing skills

TRAINING
At headquarters: 5 days
At franchisee's location: 5 days

BUSINESS SUPPORT
Newsletter
Toll-free phone line
Grand opening
Internet
Field operations/evaluations

MARKETING SUPPORT
Direct mail
Telemarketing

RENAISSANCE EXECUTIVE FORUMS INC.

Financial rating: $

7855 Ivanhoe Ave., #300
La Jolla, CA 92037
Ph: (858)551-6600
Fax: (858)551-8777
www.executiveforums.com
Business advisory boards & consulting
    services
Began: 1994, Franchising since: 1994
Headquarters size: 12 employees
Franchise department: 2 employees

U.S. franchises: 31
Canadian franchises: 1
Other foreign franchises: 3
Company-owned: 0
Units concentrated in all U.S.

Seeking: All U.S.
Seeking in Canada? Yes
Exclusive territories? Yes
Homebased option? Yes
Kiosk option? No
Employees needed to run franchise: 0
Absentee ownership? No

COSTS
Total cost: $44.4K-59.9K
Franchise fee: $29.5K
Royalty fee: 20%
Term of agreement: 10 years renewable
    for $3K
Franchisees required to buy multiple
    units? No

FINANCING
No financing available

QUALIFICATIONS
Net worth: $500K
Cash liquidity: $60K
Experience:
    General business experience
    Marketing skills
    People skills

TRAINING
At headquarters: 1 week
At franchisee's location: 2 days
Online training

BUSINESS SUPPORT
Newsletter
Meetings
Toll-free phone line
Grand opening
Internet
Security/safety procedures
Field operations/evaluations
Purchasing cooperatives

MARKETING SUPPORT
Ad slicks
Regional marketing
Intranet
Mentor program

SCHOOLEY MITCHELL TELECOM CONSULTANTS

Ranked #181 in Entrepreneur Magazine's 2004 Franchise 500　　　*Financial rating: $$$$*

187 Ontario St.
Stratford, ON Canada N5A 3H3
Ph: (800)465-4145/(519)275-3339
Fax: (519)273-7979
www.schooleymitchell.com
Telecommunications consulting
Began: 1983, Franchising since: 1997
Headquarters size: 35 employees
Franchise department: 35 employees

U.S. franchises: 101
Canadian franchises: 47
Other foreign franchises: 0
Company-owned: 0
Units concentrated in all U.S.

Seeking: All U.S.
Seeking in Canada? Yes
Exclusive territories? No
Homebased option? Yes
Kiosk option? No
Employees needed to run franchise: 0
Absentee ownership? No

COSTS

Total cost: $37.5K-50K
Franchise fee: $37.5K
Royalty fee: 8%
Term of agreement: 10 years renewable
　　for $2.5K
Franchisees required to buy multiple
　　units? No

FINANCING

No financing available

QUALIFICATIONS

Net worth: $125K
Cash liquidity: $75K
Experience:
　　General business experience
　　Marketing skills

TRAINING

At headquarters: 11 days
At franchisee's location: 5 days
Annual training conference: 7 days

BUSINESS SUPPORT

Newsletter
Meetings
Toll-free phone line
Grand opening
Internet
Security/safety procedures
Field operations/evaluations
Purchasing cooperatives

MARKETING SUPPORT

Ad slicks
National media campaign
Regional marketing
Various programs

WE THE PEOPLE FORMS & SERVICE CENTERS USA INC.

Ranked #156 in Entrepreneur Magazine's 2004 Franchise 500　　　*Financial rating: $$$*

1501 State St.
Santa Barbara, CA 93101
Ph: (805)962-4100
Fax: (805)962-9602
www.wethepeopleusa.com
Paralegal services
Began: 1985, Franchising since: 1996
Headquarters size: 50 employees
Franchise department: 1 employee

U.S. franchises: 107
Canadian franchises: 0
Other foreign franchises: 0
Company-owned: 1
Units concentrated in AK, AZ, CA,
　　CO, CT, FL, GA, HI, ID, IL, KY,
　　MD, MN, MO, NC, NE, NJ, NV,
　　NY, OH, PA, TN, TX

Seeking: All U.S.
Focusing on: IN, WI & states where
　　units are concentrated (see above)
Seeking in Canada? No
Exclusive territories? Yes
Homebased option? No
Kiosk option? No

Employees needed to run franchise:
　　1-2
Absentee ownership? Yes

COSTS

Total cost: $115.5K-151.5K
Franchise fee: $89.5K
Royalty fee: 0
Term of agreement: 10 years renewable
　　at no charge
Franchisees required to buy multiple
　　units? No

FINANCING

In-house: Franchise fee
3rd-party: None

QUALIFICATIONS

Net worth: $250K
Cash liquidity: $132K
Experience:
　　Marketing skills
　　Sales skills

TRAINING

At headquarters: 1 week
At franchisee's location: 1 week
Ongoing

BUSINESS SUPPORT

Newsletter
Meetings
Internet
Lease negotiations
Field operations/evaluations

MARKETING SUPPORT

Co-op advertising
Ad slicks
TV ads

BUSINESS *Shipping*

UNISHIPPERS

Financial rating: $$$$

746 E. Winchester, #200
Salt Lake City, UT 84107
Ph: (800)999-8721/(801)487-0600
Fax: (801)487-0623
www.unishippers.com
Discounted express & freight shipments
Began: 1987, Franchising since: 1987
Headquarters size: 60 employees
Franchise department: 2 employees

U.S. franchises: 284
Canadian franchises: 0
Other foreign franchises: 13
Company-owned: 0
Units concentrated in all U.S.

Sold out in U.S.; resales available only
Seeking in Canada? Yes
Exclusive territories? Yes
Homebased option? Yes
Kiosk option? No
Employees needed to run franchise: 2
Absentee ownership? Yes

COSTS
Total cost: $31K+
Franchise fee: $10K
Royalty fee: 16.5%
Term of agreement: 5 years renewable for $5K
Franchisees required to buy multiple units? Outside the U.S. only

FINANCING
No financing available

QUALIFICATIONS
Info not provided

TRAINING
At headquarters: 1 week
At franchisee's location: 2 days

BUSINESS SUPPORT
Newsletter
Meetings
Toll-free phone line
Internet
Security/safety procedures
Field operations/evaluations

MARKETING SUPPORT
Co-op advertising
Ad slicks
National media campaign

UNITED SHIPPING SOLUTIONS

Financial rating: $$$$

6985 Union Park Ctr., #565
Salt Lake City, UT 84047
Ph: (866)744-7486/(801)352-0012
Fax: (801)352-0339
www.usshipit.com
Discount air express & freight services
Began: 2002, Franchising since: 2002
Headquarters size: 6 employees
Franchise department: 1 employee

U.S. franchises: 64
Canadian franchises: 0
Other foreign franchises: 0
Company-owned: 0
Units concentrated in all U.S.

Seeking: All U.S.
Seeking in Canada? No
Exclusive territories? Yes
Homebased option? Yes
Kiosk option? No
Employees needed to run franchise: 1
Absentee ownership? Yes

COSTS
Total cost: $22.5K-65K
Franchise fee: $18K-25K
Royalty fee: 6%
Term of agreement: 5 years renewable
Franchisees required to buy multiple units? No

FINANCING
No financing available

QUALIFICATIONS
Experience:
    General business experience
    Marketing skills

TRAINING
At headquarters: 1 week
At franchisee's location: Up to 1 week
Ongoing

BUSINESS SUPPORT
Newsletter
Meetings
Toll-free phone line
Internet
Field operations/evaluations
Purchasing cooperatives

MARKETING SUPPORT
Regional marketing
Sales support

WORLDWIDE EXPRESS
Ranked #186 in Entrepreneur Magazine's 2004 Franchise 500   *Financial rating: $$$$*

2501 Cedar Springs Rd., #450
Dallas, TX 75201
Ph: (800)758-7447
Fax: (214)720-2446
www.wwex.com
Discounted air express services
Began: 1991, Franchising since: 1994
Headquarters size: 12 employees
Franchise department: 7 employees

U.S. franchises: 149
Canadian franchises: 0
Other foreign franchises: 0
Company-owned: 5
Units concentrated in all U.S.

Seeking: All U.S.
Seeking in Canada? No
Exclusive territories? Yes
Homebased option? Yes
Kiosk option? No
Employees needed to run franchise: 1
Absentee ownership? Yes

COSTS
Total cost: $40.7K-295.3K+
Franchise fee: $20K-266K
Royalty fee: 6%
Term of agreement: 5 years renewable
Franchisees required to buy multiple
    units? No

FINANCING
In-house: None
3rd-party: Accounts receivable, equip-
    ment, franchise fee, inventory,
    start-up costs

QUALIFICATIONS
Net worth: $50K
Cash liquidity: $50K
Experience:
    General business experience
    Marketing skills

TRAINING
At headquarters
At franchisee's location

BUSINESS SUPPORT
Newsletter
Meetings
Toll-free phone line

MARKETING SUPPORT
Info not provided

BUSINESS   *Signs*

FASTSIGNS INT'L. INC.
Ranked #111 in Entrepreneur Magazine's 2004 Franchise 500   *Financial rating: $$$*

2550 Midway Rd., #150
Carrollton, TX 75006
Ph: (800)827-7446/(214)346-5600
Fax: (972)248-8201
www.fastsigns.com
Signs & graphic solutions
Began: 1985, Franchising since: 1986
Headquarters size: 85 employees
Franchise department: 6 employees

U.S. franchises: 385
Canadian franchises: 7
Other foreign franchises: 53
Company-owned: 0
Units concentrated in all U.S.

Seeking: All U.S.
Seeking in Canada? Yes
Exclusive territories? Yes
Homebased option? No
Kiosk option? No
Employees needed to run franchise:
    3-8
Absentee ownership? No

COSTS
Total cost: $152.3K-225K
Franchise fee: $20K
Royalty fee: 6%
Term of agreement: 20 years renewable
    at no charge
Franchisees required to buy multiple
    units? No

FINANCING
In-house: None
3rd-party: Equipment, franchise fee,
    inventory, start-up costs

QUALIFICATIONS
Net worth: $240K
Cash liquidity: $75K
Experience:
    General business experience
    Marketing skills

TRAINING
At headquarters: 4 weeks
At franchisee's location: 2 weeks
2-3 visits per year; regional & annual
    convention

BUSINESS SUPPORT
Newsletter
Meetings
Toll-free phone line
Grand opening
Internet
Lease negotiations
Security/safety procedures
Field operations/evaluations
Purchasing cooperatives

MARKETING SUPPORT
Co-op advertising
Ad slicks
National media campaign
Regional marketing
Research & development

SIGN-A-RAMA INC.

Ranked #76 in Entrepreneur Magazine's 2004 Franchise 500   *Financial rating: $$$$*

1801 Australian Ave.
West Palm Beach, FL 33409
Ph: (800)286-8671/(561)640-5570
Fax: (561)478-4340
www.signarama.com
Signs
Began: 1986, Franchising since: 1987
Headquarters size: 40 employees
Franchise department: 5 employees

U.S. franchises: 494
Canadian franchises: 27
Other foreign franchises: 155
Company-owned: 0
Units concentrated in all U.S.

Seeking: All U.S.
Seeking in Canada? Yes
Exclusive territories? No
Homebased option? No
Kiosk option? No
Employees needed to run franchise:
    2-4
Absentee ownership? No

COSTS

Total cost: $47.6K-179.1K
Franchise fee: $37.5K
Royalty fee: 6% w/cap
Term of agreement: 35 years renewable
    for $1.5K
Franchisees required to buy multiple
    units? Outside the U.S. only

FINANCING

In-house: None
3rd-party: Accounts receivable, equip-
    ment, franchise fee, inventory,
    start-up costs

QUALIFICATIONS

Net worth: $75K+
Cash liquidity: $50K-75K
Experience:
    General business experience
    Marketing skills

TRAINING

At headquarters: 2 weeks
At franchisee's location: 2 weeks
At mentor store: 1 week

BUSINESS SUPPORT

Newsletter
Meetings
Toll-free phone line
Grand opening
Internet
Lease negotiations
Security/safety procedures
Field operations/evaluations
Purchasing cooperatives

MARKETING SUPPORT

Co-op advertising
Ad slicks
National media campaign
Regional marketing
Phone support
Quarterly seminars

SIGNS BY TOMORROW

Ranked #154 in Entrepreneur Magazine's 2004 Franchise 500   *Financial rating: $$$*

6460 Dobbin Rd.
Columbia, MD 21045
Ph: (800)765-7446/(410)992-7192
Fax: (410)992-7675
www.signsbytomorrow.com
One-day retail sign stores
Began: 1986, Franchising since: 1987
Headquarters size: 22 employees
Franchise department: 3 employees

U.S. franchises: 156
Canadian franchises: 0
Other foreign franchises: 0
Company-owned: 1

Seeking: All U.S.
Seeking in Canada? No
Exclusive territories? Yes
Homebased option? No
Kiosk option? No
Employees needed to run franchise: 4
Absentee ownership? No

COSTS

Total cost: $97.5K-179K
Franchise fee: $24.5K
Royalty fee: 3-6%
Term of agreement: 20 years renewable
    at no charge
Franchisees required to buy multiple
    units? No

FINANCING

No financing available

QUALIFICATIONS

Net worth: $150K
Cash liquidity: $40K
Experience:
    General business experience
    Marketing skills

TRAINING

At headquarters: 2 weeks
At franchisee's location: 2 weeks
At various locations: 2-4 days

BUSINESS SUPPORT

Newsletter
Meetings
Toll-free phone line
Grand opening
Internet
Lease negotiations
Security/safety procedures
Field operations/evaluations
Purchasing cooperatives

MARKETING SUPPORT

Co-op advertising
Ad slicks
Sales training

SIGNS FIRST

Current financial data not available

813 Ridge Lake Blvd., #495
Memphis, TN 38120
Ph: (800)852-2163
Fax: (901)682-2475
www.signsfirst.com
Computerized one-day sign store
Began: 1966, Franchising since: 1989
Headquarters size: 7 employees
Franchise department: 7 employees

U.S. franchises: 30
Canadian franchises: 0
Other foreign franchises: 0
Company-owned: 0
Units concentrated in AR, CO, LA,
    MS, NC, TN, TX

Seeking: All U.S.
Seeking in Canada? No
Exclusive territories? Yes
Homebased option? No
Kiosk option? No
Employees needed to run franchise: 2
Absentee ownership? Yes

COSTS
Total cost: $30K-118K
Franchise fee: $7.5K-17.5K
Royalty fee: 6%
Term of agreement: 20 years renewable
    for $3K
Franchisees required to buy multiple
    units? No

FINANCING
In-house: None
3rd-party: Accounts receivable, equip-
    ment, franchise fee, inventory,
    start-up costs

QUALIFICATIONS
Cash liquidity: 25% of investment
Experience:
    General business experience

TRAINING
At headquarters: 2 weeks
At franchisee's location
At regional locations

BUSINESS SUPPORT
Newsletter
Meetings
Toll-free phone line
Grand opening
Internet
Lease negotiations
Security/safety procedures
Field operations/evaluations
Purchasing cooperatives

MARKETING SUPPORT
Co-op advertising
Ad slicks
Regional marketing
Local promotions

SIGNS NOW CORP.

Ranked #303 in Entrepreneur Magazine's 2004 Franchise 500

Financial rating: $$$$

4900 Manatee Ave. W., #201
Bradenton, FL 34209
Ph: (800)356-3373/(941)747-7747
Fax: (941)750-8604
www.signsnow.com
Signs & graphics services
Began: 1983, Franchising since: 1986
Headquarters size: 36 employees
Franchise department: 3 employees

U.S. franchises: 215
Canadian franchises: 17
Other foreign franchises: 10
Company-owned: 2

Seeking: All U.S.
Seeking in Canada? No
Exclusive territories? No
Homebased option? No
Kiosk option? No
Employees needed to run franchise: 3
Absentee ownership? No

COSTS
Total cost: $132.3K-160K
Franchise fee: $25K
Royalty fee: 5%
Term of agreement: 20 years renewable
    at percentage of current fee
Franchisees required to buy multiple
    units? Outside the U.S. only

FINANCING
In-house: None
3rd-party: Equipment, franchise fee,
    inventory, start-up costs

QUALIFICATIONS
Net worth: $150K-175K
Cash liquidity: $55K-75K
Experience:
    Marketing skills
    Management experience

TRAINING
At headquarters: 3 weeks
At franchisee's location: 2 weeks

BUSINESS SUPPORT
Newsletter
Meetings
Toll-free phone line
Grand opening
Internet
Security/safety procedures
Field operations/evaluations
Purchasing cooperatives

MARKETING SUPPORT
Ad slicks
Yellow Pages
Marketing programs
Vendor purchasing

ACCOUNTANTS INC.

Ranked #425 in Entrepreneur Magazine's 2004 Franchise 500   *Financial rating: $$$$*

111 Anza Blvd., #400
Burlingame, CA 94010
Ph: (800)491-9411/(650)579-1111
Fax: (650)579-1927
www.accountantsinc.com
Accounting & finance staffing services
Began: 1986, Franchising since: 1994
Headquarters size: 44 employees
Franchise department: 2 employees

U.S. franchises: 16
Canadian franchises: 0
Other foreign franchises: 0
Company-owned: 14
Units concentrated in all U.S.

Seeking: All U.S.
Seeking in Canada? No
Exclusive territories? Yes
Homebased option? No
Kiosk option? No
Employees needed to run franchise: 4
Absentee ownership? No

COSTS
Total cost: $185.8K-259K
Franchise fee: $30K
Royalty fee: 10%
Term of agreement: Renewable term at
    50% of current franchise fee
Franchisees required to buy multiple
    units? No

FINANCING
In-house: Accounts receivable, payroll
3rd-party: None

QUALIFICATIONS
Cash liquidity: $80K
Experience:
    Industry experience
    General business experience
    Marketing skills
    Customer service skills
    Human resources experience

TRAINING
At headquarters: 1 week
At franchisee's location: 1 week

BUSINESS SUPPORT
Newsletter
Meetings
Toll-free phone line
Grand opening
Internet
Field operations/evaluations

MARKETING SUPPORT
National media campaign
Regional marketing
Internet partnership with
    Monster.com

AHEAD HUMAN RESOURCES (PEO)

Current financial data not available

2209 Heather Ln.
Louisville, KY 40218
Ph: (502)485-1000
Fax: (502)485-0801
www.aheadhr.com
PEO & HR outsourcing
Began: 1996, Franchising since: 2000
Headquarters size: 40 employees
Franchise department: 2 employees

U.S. franchises: 5
Canadian franchises: 0
Other foreign franchises: 0
Company-owned: 1
Units concentrated in all U.S.

Seeking: All U.S.
Seeking in Canada? No
Exclusive territories? Yes
Homebased option? Yes
Kiosk option? No
Employees needed to run franchise: 1
Absentee ownership? No

COSTS
Total cost: $118.9K-172.7K
Franchise fee: $13.7K
Royalty fee: Varies
Term of agreement: 5 years renewable
    at no charge
Franchisees required to buy multiple
    units? No

FINANCING
No financing provided

QUALIFICATIONS
Cash liquidity: $13.7K

TRAINING
At headquarters: 2 weeks
At franchisee's location: As necessary
At branch office: As needed

BUSINESS SUPPORT
Toll-free phone line
Grand opening
Internet
Security/safety procedures
Field operations/evaluations

MARKETING SUPPORT
Ad slicks

AHEAD HUMAN RESOURCES (STAFFING)

Current financial data not available

2209 Heather Ln.
Louisville, KY 40218
Ph: (502)485-1000
Fax: (502)485-0801
www.aheadhr.com
Staffing services
Began: 1995, Franchising since: 2000
Headquarters size: 35 employees
Franchise department: 30 employees

U.S. franchises: 5
Canadian franchises: 0
Other foreign franchises: 0
Company-owned: 2
Units concentrated in all U.S.

Seeking: All U.S.
Seeking in Canada? Yes
Exclusive territories? Yes
Homebased option? No
Kiosk option? No
Employees needed to run franchise: 1
Absentee ownership? No

COSTS
Total cost: $80.1K-120.95K
Franchise fee: $13.7K
Royalty fee: Varies
Term of agreement: 5 years renewable
  at no charge
Franchisees required to buy multiple
  units? No

FINANCING
No financing provided

QUALIFICATIONS
Cash liquidity: $35K

TRAINING
At headquarters: 2-3 weeks
Field visits

BUSINESS SUPPORT
Toll-free phone line
Internet
Field operations/evaluations

MARKETING SUPPORT
Ad slicks

ATWORK PERSONNEL SERVICES

Ranked #445 in Entrepreneur Magazine's 2004 Franchise 500

Financial rating: $$$$

1470 Main St., P.O. Box 989
White Pine, TN 37890
Ph: (800)233-6846
Fax: (865)674-8780
www.atworkpersonnel.com
Permanent & temporary staffing
  services
Began: 1990, Franchising since: 1992
Headquarters size: 20 employees
Franchise department: 20 employees

U.S. franchises: 51
Canadian franchises: 0
Other foreign franchises: 0
Company-owned: 0
Units concentrated in all U.S.

Seeking: All U.S.
Seeking in Canada? Yes
Exclusive territories? No
Homebased option? No
Kiosk option? No
Employees needed to run franchise:
  2-4
Absentee ownership? No

\COSTS
Total cost: $59.5K-105K
Franchise fee: $11.5K
Royalty fee: 1.4-6.1%
Term of agreement: 10 years renewable
  at no charge
Franchisees required to buy multiple
  units? No

FINANCING
In-house: Accounts receivable, payroll
3rd-party: Accounts receivable, payroll

QUALIFICATIONS
Cash liquidity: $25K
Experience:
    Industry experience
    Marketing skills
    Collections experience
    HR experience

TRAINING
At headquarters: 5 days+
At franchisee's location: 3-5 days+
Meetings: 2 days

BUSINESS SUPPORT
Newsletter
Meetings
Toll-free phone line
Grand opening
Internet
Security/safety procedures
Field operations/evaluations
Purchasing cooperatives

MARKETING SUPPORT
Co-op advertising
Ad slicks
Regional marketing

CAREERS USA

Current financial data not available

6501 Congress Ave., #200
Boca Raton, FL 33487
Ph: (888)227-3375/(561)995-7000
Fax: (561)995-7001
www.careersusa.com
Temporary & permanent staffing
    services
Began: 1981, Franchising since: 1988
Headquarters size: 30 employees
Franchise department: 4 employees

U.S. franchises: 5
Canadian franchises: 0
Other foreign franchises: 0
Company-owned: 16
Units concentrated in IL, NJ

Seeking: All U.S.
Seeking in Canada? No
Exclusive territories? Yes
Homebased option? No
Kiosk option? No
Employees needed to run franchise:
    3-4
Absentee ownership? Yes

COSTS
Total cost: $110.9K-159.6K
Franchise fee: $14.5K
Royalty fee: Varies
Term of agreement: 10 years renewable
    at no charge
Franchisees required to buy multiple
    units? No

FINANCING
In-house: Accounts receivable, payroll
3rd-party: None

QUALIFICATIONS
Net worth: $150K-250K
Cash liquidity: $100K-150K
Experience:
    General business experience
    Marketing skills

TRAINING
At headquarters: 2 weeks
At franchisee's location: 1 week
Ongoing

BUSINESS SUPPORT
Newsletter
Meetings
Toll-free phone line
Grand opening
Internet
Field operations/evaluations
Purchasing cooperatives

MARKETING SUPPORT
Co-op advertising
Ad slicks

EXPRESS PERSONNEL SERVICES

Ranked #95 in Entrepreneur Magazine's 2004 Franchise 500

Financial rating: $$$$

8516 Northwest Expwy.
Oklahoma City, OK 73162
Ph: (877)652-6400/(405)840-5000
Fax: (405)717-5665
www.expresspersonnel.com
Staffing & executive-search services
Began: 1983, Franchising since: 1985
Headquarters size: 190 employees
Franchise department: 5 employees

U.S. franchises: 386
Canadian franchises: 15
Other foreign franchises: 9
Company-owned: 0

Seeking: All U.S.
Seeking in Canada? Yes
Exclusive territories? Yes
Homebased option? No
Kiosk option? No
Employees needed to run franchise: 5
Absentee ownership? No

COSTS
Total cost: $120K-160K
Franchise fee: $17.5K-20.5K
Royalty fee: 6-9%
Term of agreement: 5 years renewable
    at no charge
Franchisees required to buy multiple
    units? No

FINANCING
In-house: Payroll
3rd-party: None

QUALIFICATIONS
Net worth: $100K+
Cash liquidity: $50K
Experience:
    General business experience
    Marketing skills

TRAINING
At headquarters: 3 weeks
At franchisee's location: 2 weeks
In-field training (twice a year):
    1-2 days

BUSINESS SUPPORT
Newsletter
Meetings
Toll-free phone line
Grand opening
Internet
Security/safety procedures
Field operations/evaluations
Purchasing cooperatives

MARKETING SUPPORT
Co-op advertising
Ad slicks
National media campaign
Regional marketing
Intranet & extranet support

FORTUNE PERSONNEL CONSULTANTS (FPC)

Current financial data not available

1140 Ave. of the Americas
New York, NY 10036
Ph: (800)886-7839/(212)302-1141
Fax: (212)302-2422
www.fpcnational.com
Middle-management & executive
    recruiting
Began: 1959, Franchising since: 1973
Headquarters size: Info not provided
Franchise department: Info not pro-
    vided

U.S. franchises: 83
Canadian franchises: 0
Other foreign franchises: 0
Company-owned: 0
Units concentrated in all U.S.

Seeking: All U.S.
Seeking in Canada? No
Exclusive territories? Info not provided
Homebased option? No
Kiosk option? No
Employees needed to run franchise: 3
Absentee ownership? No

COSTS
Total cost: $83K-128K
Franchise fee: $40K
Royalty fee: 7%
Term of agreement: 20 years renewable
    at no charge
Franchisees required to buy multiple
    units? No

FINANCING
In-house: Franchise fee
3rd-party: None

QUALIFICATIONS
Net worth: $250K
Cash liquidity: $100K
Experience:
    Industry experience
    General business experience

TRAINING
At headquarters
At franchisee's location

BUSINESS SUPPORT
Newsletter
Meetings
Toll-free phone line
Grand opening
Internet
Lease negotiations
Security/safety procedures
Field operations/evaluations
Purchasing cooperatives

MARKETING SUPPORT
Co-op advertising
Ad slicks
National media campaign
Regional marketing

GLOBAL RECRUITERS NETWORK

Financial rating: $$$$

2001 Butterfield Rd., #102
Downers Grove, IL 60516
Ph: (866)476-8200/(630)663-1900
Fax: (630)663-1919
www.grncorp.net
Executive-search services
Began: 2003, Franchising since: 2003
Headquarters size: 24 employees
Franchise department: 3 employees

U.S. franchises: 13
Canadian franchises: 0
Other foreign franchises: 1
Company-owned: 0

Seeking: All U.S.
Seeking in Canada? Yes
Exclusive territories? Yes
Homebased option? No
Kiosk option? No
Employees needed to run franchise:
    2-5
Absentee ownership? Yes

COSTS
Total cost: $107.5K-116.4K
Franchise fee: $67.5K
Royalty fee: 6.5%
Term of agreement: 10-25 years
    renewable
Franchisees required to buy multiple
    units? No

FINANCING
In-house: None
3rd-party: Equipment, franchise fee,
    start-up costs

QUALIFICATIONS
Net worth: $175K+
Cash liquidity: $50K
Experience:
    General business experience
    Marketing skills

TRAINING
At headquarters: 3 weeks
At franchisee's location: 2 weeks+
Videoconferencing network

BUSINESS SUPPORT
Newsletter
Meetings
Toll-free phone line
Internet
Field operations/evaluations
Purchasing cooperatives

MARKETING SUPPORT
National media campaign

INTERIM HEALTHCARE
Ranked #180 in Entrepreneur Magazine's 2004 Franchise 500   *Financial rating: $$$$*

1601 Sawgrass Corporate Pkwy.
Sunrise, FL 33323
Ph: (800)338-7786
Fax: (954)858-2870
www.interimhealthcare.com
Home health care & medical-staffing
    services
Began: 1966, Franchising since: 1966
Headquarters size: Info not provided
Franchise department: Info not pro-
    vided

U.S. franchises: 267
Canadian franchises: 0
Other foreign franchises: 2
Company-owned: 20

Seeking: All U.S.
Seeking in Canada? Yes
Exclusive territories? Info not provided
Homebased option? No
Kiosk option? No
Employees needed to run franchise:
    2-3
Absentee ownership? No

COSTS
Total cost: $123K-404K
Franchise fee: $5K-30K
Royalty fee: 5%
Term of agreement: 5 years renewable
    at no charge
Franchisees required to buy multiple
    units? No

FINANCING
No financing available

QUALIFICATIONS
Net worth: $250K-750K
Cash liquidity: $100K-250K
Experience:
    General business experience
    Marketing skills

TRAINING
At headquarters: Up to 10 days
At franchisee's location: Up to 10 days
Regional training: Up to 5 days

BUSINESS SUPPORT
Newsletter
Meetings
Toll-free phone line
Grand opening
Internet
Lease negotiations
Security/safety procedures
Field operations/evaluations
Purchasing cooperatives

MARKETING SUPPORT
Co-op advertising
Ad slicks
National media campaign
Regional marketing

JASNEEK STAFFING
Current financial data not available

9840 N. Michigan Rd.
Carmel, IN 46032
Ph: (866)527-6335
Fax: (317)872-4563
www.jasneek.com
Medical-staffing services
Began: 1996, Franchising since: 2000
Headquarters size: 16 employees
Franchise department: 4 employees

U.S. franchises: 8
Canadian franchises: 0
Other foreign franchises: 0
Company-owned: 0
Units concentrated in CT, IN, KY, MA,
    NY, OH, RI

Seeking: All U.S.
Seeking in Canada? No
Exclusive territories? Yes
Homebased option? No
Kiosk option? No
Employees needed to run franchise: 3
Absentee ownership? Yes

COSTS
Total cost: $54K-186K
Franchise fee: $17K
Royalty fee: 5.5%
Term of agreement: 10 years renewable
    at no charge
Franchisees required to buy multiple
    units? No

FINANCING
No financing available

QUALIFICATIONS
Net worth: $200K
Cash liquidity: $50K
Experience:
    General business experience
    Sales skills

TRAINING
At headquarters: Approx. 2 weeks
At franchisee's location: 1 week
At franchisor location: 1 week

BUSINESS SUPPORT
Meetings
Grand opening
Internet
Lease negotiations
Field operations/evaluations
Purchasing cooperatives

MARKETING SUPPORT
Co-op advertising
Ad slicks
Regional marketing

LABOR FINDERS

Ranked #167 in Entrepreneur Magazine's 2004 Franchise 500   *Financial rating: $$$$*

3910 RCA Blvd., #1001
Palm Beach Gardens, FL 33410
Ph: (561)627-6507
Fax: (561)627-6556
www.laborfinders.com
Industrial-staffing services
Began: 1975, Franchising since: 1975
Headquarters size: 20 employees
Franchise department: 4 employees

U.S. franchises: 168
Canadian franchises: 0
Other foreign franchises: 0
Company-owned: 12
Units concentrated in South, Sunbelt
    states

Seeking: Midwest, Northeast, West
Focusing on: Northeast, Midwest,
    Northwest
Seeking in Canada? No
Exclusive territories? Yes
Homebased option? No
Kiosk option? No
Employees needed to run franchise:
    2-3

Absentee ownership? Yes

COSTS
Total cost: $67.1K-111.6K
Franchise fee: $10K
Royalty fee: Varies
Term of agreement: 10 years renewable
    at no charge
Franchisees required to buy multiple
    units? No

FINANCING
In-house: Payroll
3rd-party: None

QUALIFICATIONS
Net worth: $500K+
Cash liquidity: $100K
Experience:
    General business experience
    Marketing skills

TRAINING
At headquarters: 1 week
At franchisee's location: Ongoing
Regional training: 1-2 weeks

BUSINESS SUPPORT
Newsletter
Toll-free phone line
Internet
Security/safety procedures
Field operations/evaluations
Purchasing cooperatives

MARKETING SUPPORT
Co-op advertising
Ad slicks
National media campaign
Regional marketing

LINK STAFFING SERVICES

Financial rating: $$

1800 Bering, #800
Houston, TX 77057
Ph: (800)848-5465/(713)784-4400
Fax: (713)784-4454
www.linkstaffing.com
Temporary-staffing services
Began: 1980, Franchising since: 1994
Headquarters size: 45 employees
Franchise department: 5 employees

U.S. franchises: 29
Canadian franchises: 0
Other foreign franchises: 0
Company-owned: 11
Units concentrated in CA, FL, TX

Seeking: All U.S.
Seeking in Canada? No
Exclusive territories? Yes
Homebased option? No
Kiosk option? No
Employees needed to run franchise:
    2-3
Absentee ownership? Yes

COSTS
Total cost: $85.5K-156K
Franchise fee: $17K
Royalty fee: Varies
Term of agreement: 10 years renewable
    at no charge
Franchisees required to buy multiple
    units? No

FINANCING
In-house: Accounts receivable, payroll
3rd-party: None

QUALIFICATIONS
Net worth: $200K+
Cash liquidity: $60K+
Experience:
    General business experience
    Sales & marketing skills
    Management skills
    Customer service skills
    Communication skills

TRAINING
At headquarters: 1 week
At franchisee's location: 1 week
At field office & support center: 5 days
    at each

BUSINESS SUPPORT
Newsletter
Meetings
Toll-free phone line
Grand opening
Internet
Security/safety procedures
Field operations/evaluations
Purchasing cooperatives

MARKETING SUPPORT
Co-op advertising
Ad slicks
National media campaign
Regional marketing
Management, budgeting, billing &
    technical assistance

LLOYD PERSONNEL SYSTEMS INC.

Current financial data not available

445 Broadhollow Rd., #119
Melville, NY 11747
Ph: (888)292-6678/(631)777-7600
Fax: (631)777-7620
www.lloydstaffing.com
Staffing services
Began: 1971, Franchising since: 1986
Headquarters size: 175 employees
Franchise department: 17 employees

U.S. franchises: 7
Canadian franchises: 0
Other foreign franchises: 0
Company-owned: 7
Units concentrated in CT, FL, MD, NJ, NY, PA

Seeking: West
Focusing on: CA, GA, NC, TX, VA
Seeking in Canada? No
Exclusive territories? Yes
Homebased option? No
Kiosk option? No
Employees needed to run franchise: 4
Absentee ownership? No

COSTS
Total cost: $93.5K-155.3K
Franchise fee: $20K
Royalty fee: 7-40%
Term of agreement: 10 years renewable at no charge
Franchisees required to buy multiple units? No

FINANCING
No financing available

QUALIFICATIONS
Cash liquidity: $150K
Experience:
    Industry experience
    General business experience
    Marketing skills

TRAINING
At headquarters: 7-10 days
At franchisee's location: Ongoing
Annual conference

BUSINESS SUPPORT
Newsletter
Meetings
Toll-free phone line
Grand opening
Internet
Lease negotiations
Security/safety procedures
Field operations/evaluations

MARKETING SUPPORT
Ad slicks
Regional marketing
Job fairs
Additional support as needed

MADDEN INDUSTRIAL CRAFTSMEN INC.

Current financial data not available

1800 N.W. 169th Pl., #A-200
Beaverton, OR 97006
Ph: (503)690-0641
Fax: (503)690-9815
www.mici.com
Staffing services for manufacturing & construction-skilled labor
Began: 1988, Franchising since: 2002
Headquarters size: 15 employees
Franchise department: 3 employees

U.S. franchises: 0
Canadian franchises: 0
Other foreign franchises: 0
Company-owned: 2
Units concentrated in WA

Seeking: All U.S.
Seeking in Canada? No
Exclusive territories? Yes
Homebased option? No
Kiosk option? No
Employees needed to run franchise: 3
Absentee ownership? No

COSTS
Total cost: $95K-138K
Franchise fee: $15K
Royalty fee: 3%
Term of agreement: 5 years renewable for $1.5K
Franchisees required to buy multiple units? No

FINANCING
In-house: Accounts receivable, payroll
3rd-party: None

QUALIFICATIONS
Net worth: $150K
Cash liquidity: $50K-75K
Experience:
    Industry experience
    General business experience
    Marketing skills

TRAINING
At headquarters: 1 week
At franchisee's location: 1 week
Ongoing

BUSINESS SUPPORT
Newsletter
Grand opening
Internet
Security/safety procedures
Field operations/evaluations

MARKETING SUPPORT
Co-op advertising
Ad slicks

MANAGEMENT RECRUITERS/SALES CONSULTANTS/MRI WORLDWIDE
Ranked #43 in Entrepreneur Magazine's 2004 Franchise 500   *Financial rating: $$$$*

200 Public Sq., 31st Fl.
Cleveland, OH 44114-2301
Ph: (800)875-4000/(216)696-1122
Fax: (216)696-6612
www.brilliantpeople.com
Personnel placement; search & recruiting services
Began: 1957, Franchising since: 1965
Headquarters size: 80 employees
Franchise department: 20 employees

U.S. franchises: 1,088
Canadian franchises: 2
Other foreign franchises: 246
Company-owned: 0
Units concentrated in CA, FL, NC, NJ, TX

Seeking: All U.S.
Seeking in Canada? No
Exclusive territories? Yes
Homebased option? No
Kiosk option? No
Employees needed to run franchise: 3-4
Absentee ownership? No

COSTS
Total cost: $115.6K-160.4K
Franchise fee: $79K
Royalty fee: 7-7.5%
Term of agreement: 10-20 years renewable at no charge
Franchisees required to buy multiple units? No

FINANCING
In-house: Accounts receivable, inventory, payroll
3rd-party: Equipment, franchise fee, start-up costs

QUALIFICATIONS
Net worth: $250K
Cash liquidity: $100K
Experience:
    Industry experience
    Sales/sales management background

TRAINING
At headquarters: 15 days
At franchisee's location: Up to 10 days

BUSINESS SUPPORT
Newsletter
Meetings
Toll-free phone line
Grand opening
Internet
Field operations/evaluations
Purchasing cooperatives

MARKETING SUPPORT
Co-op advertising
Ad slicks
National media campaign
Regional marketing
National & local PR campaign

PERSONET-THE PERSONNEL NETWORK

Current financial data not available

33907 U.S. 19 North
Palm Harbor, FL 34684
Ph: (727)781-2983
Fax: (727)781-3023
www.personet.com
Staffing, payroll & P.E.O. services
Began: 1994, Franchising since: 1994
Headquarters size: Info not provided
Franchise department: Info not provided

U.S. franchises: 9
Canadian franchises: 0
Other foreign franchises: 0
Company-owned: 0
Units concentrated in FL, IA, IN, MI, TX

Seeking: All U.S.
Seeking in Canada? No
Exclusive territories? Yes
Homebased option? No
Kiosk option? No
Employees needed to run franchise: 2-3
Absentee ownership? No

COSTS
Total cost: $35.2K-100K+
Franchise fee: $15K-60K
Royalty fee: Varies
Term of agreement: 10 years renewable at no charge
Franchisees required to buy multiple units? No

FINANCING
In-house: Accounts receivable, payroll
3rd-party: None

QUALIFICATIONS
Net worth: $100K
Cash liquidity: $50K
Experience:
    General business experience

TRAINING
At headquarters
At franchisee's location
Ongoing

BUSINESS SUPPORT
Newsletter
Internet
Field operations/evaluations

MARKETING SUPPORT
Info not provided

PMA FRANCHISE SYSTEMS

Financial rating: $$

1950 Spectrum Cir., #B-310
Marietta, GA 30067
Ph: (800)466-7822
Fax: (770)916-1429
www.pmasearch.com
Management-recruiting services
Began: 1985, Franchising since: 1998
Headquarters size: Info not provided
Franchise department: Info not provided

U.S. franchises: 7
Canadian franchises: 0
Other foreign franchises: 0
Company-owned: 1
Units concentrated in all U.S.

Seeking: All U.S.
Seeking in Canada? No
Exclusive territories? Yes
Homebased option? No
Kiosk option? No
Employees needed to run franchise:
    1-3
Absentee ownership? No

COSTS
Total cost: $43.3K-70K+
Franchise fee: $35K
Royalty fee: 10-8%
Term of agreement: 10 years renewable
    for $5K
Franchisees required to buy multiple
    units? No

FINANCING
In-house: Franchise fee
3rd-party: None

QUALIFICATIONS
Net worth: $100K
Cash liquidity: $50K
Experience:
    General business experience

TRAINING
At headquarters: 4 weeks
At franchisee's location: 2-3 days
Ongoing

BUSINESS SUPPORT
Newsletter
Meetings
Toll-free phone line
Internet
Field operations/evaluations

MARKETING SUPPORT
Co-op advertising

SANFORD ROSE ASSOCIATES
Ranked #454 in Entrepreneur Magazine's 2004 Franchise 500

Financial rating: $$$

3737 Embassy Pkwy., #200
Akron, OH 44333
Ph: (800)731-7724/(330)670-9797
Fax: (330)670-9798
www.franchisesra.com
Executive-search services
Began: 1959, Franchising since: 1970
Headquarters size: 7 employees
Franchise department: 7 employees

U.S. franchises: 52
Canadian franchises: 0
Other foreign franchises: 5
Company-owned: 1
Units concentrated in CA, IL, OH

Seeking: All U.S.
Seeking in Canada? No
Exclusive territories? Yes
Homebased option? No
Kiosk option? No
Employees needed to run franchise:
    2-5
Absentee ownership? No

COSTS
Total cost: $63.5K-103.5K
Franchise fee: $45K
Royalty fee: 7-5%
Term of agreement: 7 years renewable
    at no charge
Franchisees required to buy multiple
    units? No

FINANCING
In-house: Franchise fee
3rd-party: None

QUALIFICATIONS
Cash liquidity: $70.3K-98.1K
Experience:
    Industry experience
    General business experience
    Marketing skills

TRAINING
At headquarters: 12 days
At franchisee's location: 3 days

BUSINESS SUPPORT
Newsletter
Meetings
Toll-free phone line
Internet
Field operations/evaluations
Purchasing cooperatives

MARKETING SUPPORT
Info not provided

ULTIMATE STAFFING SERVICES

Financial rating: $$$$

333 City Blvd. W.
Orange, CA 92868
Ph: (714)919-5214
Fax: (714)939-8014
www.ultimatestaffingfranchise.com
Staffing services
Began: 1994, Franchising since: 2002
Headquarters size: 55 employees
Franchise department: 3 employees

U.S. franchises: 3
Canadian franchises: 0
Other foreign franchises: 0
Company-owned: 61
Units concentrated in AK, GA,
   OH, TX

Seeking: All U.S.
Seeking in Canada? No
Exclusive territories? Yes
Homebased option? No
Kiosk option? No
Employees needed to run franchise:
   Info not provided
Absentee ownership? Yes

COSTS
Total cost: $120K-198K
Franchise fee: $17.5K
Royalty fee: Varies
Term of agreement: 10 years renewable
   at no charge
Franchisees required to buy multiple
   units? No

FINANCING
In-house: Accounts receivable, payroll
Equipment, start-up costs

QUALIFICATIONS
Net worth: $250K
Cash liquidity: $60K
Experience:
   General business experience
   Marketing skills

TRAINING
At headquarters: 2 weeks
At franchisee's location: 1 week

BUSINESS SUPPORT
Newsletter
Meetings
Toll-free phone line
Internet
Field operations/evaluations
Purchasing cooperatives

MARKETING SUPPORT
Ad slicks
Mailing list development

BUSINESS ▶ *Training*

CRESTCOM INT'L. LTD.

Ranked #241 in Entrepreneur Magazine's 2004 Franchise 500

Financial rating: $$$$

6900 E. Belleview Ave.
Greenwood Village, CO 80111
Ph: (303)267-8200
Fax: (303)267-8207
www.crestcom.com
Management, sales & office-personnel
   training
Began: 1987, Franchising since: 1991
Headquarters size: 15 employees
Franchise department: 12 employees

U.S. franchises: 56
Canadian franchises: 11
Other foreign franchises: 72
Company-owned: 0

Seeking: All U.S.
Seeking in Canada? Yes
Exclusive territories? Yes
Homebased option? Yes
Kiosk option? No
Employees needed to run franchise:
   1-2
Absentee ownership? Yes

COSTS
Total cost: $47.8K-78.5K
Franchise fee: $39.5K/58.5K
Royalty fee: 1.5%
Term of agreement: 7 years renewable
   for $500
Franchisees required to buy multiple
   units? No

FINANCING
In-house: Franchise fee
3rd-party: Franchise fee

QUALIFICATIONS
Experience:
   General business experience
   Marketing skills

TRAINING
At headquarters: 7-10 days

BUSINESS SUPPORT
Newsletter
Meetings
Internet
Security/safety procedures

MARKETING SUPPORT
Info not provided

DALE CARNEGIE TRAINING
Ranked #310 in Entrepreneur Magazine's 2004 Franchise 500　　　　　*Financial rating: $$$$*

290 Motor Pkwy.
Hauppauge, NY 11788
Ph: (631)415-9300
Fax: (631)415-9358
www.dalecarnegie.com
Sales & human-development training
Began: 1912, Franchising since: 1999
Headquarters size: 40 employees
Franchise department: 10 employees

U.S. franchises: 115
Canadian franchises: 5
Other foreign franchises: 66
Company-owned: 3
Units concentrated in all U.S.

Seeking: Northeast, West
Seeking in Canada? No
Exclusive territories? Yes
Homebased option? No
Kiosk option? No
Employees needed to run franchise:
　2-10
Absentee ownership? No

COSTS
Total cost: $32.7K-221.9K
Franchise fee: $25K
Royalty fee: 12%
Term of agreement: 15 years renewable
　for $10K
Franchisees required to buy multiple
　units? Outside the U.S. only

FINANCING
No financing available

QUALIFICATIONS
Cash liquidity: $100K
Experience:
　General business experience
　Sales background
　Managerial background
　Established business network

TRAINING
At headquarters: 1 week
At franchisee's location: 10 days

BUSINESS SUPPORT
Newsletter
Meetings
Internet
Security/safety procedures
Field operations/evaluations

MARKETING SUPPORT
Co-op advertising
Ad slicks
Regional marketing
Catalog
Web support

SANDLER SALES INSTITUTE
Ranked #288 in Entrepreneur Magazine's 2004 Franchise 500　　　　　*Financial rating: $$$$*

10411 Stevenson Rd.
Stevenson, MD 21153
Ph: (800)669-3537/(410)653-1993
Fax: (410)358-7858
www.sandler.com
Sales & sales-management training
Began: 1967, Franchising since: 1983
Headquarters size: 28 employees
Franchise department: 2 employees

U.S. franchises: 149
Canadian franchises: 13
Other foreign franchises: 3
Company-owned: 0
Units concentrated in all U.S.

Seeking: All U.S.
Seeking in Canada? No
Exclusive territories? No
Homebased option? Yes
Kiosk option? No
Employees needed to run franchise: 1
Absentee ownership? No

COSTS
Total cost: $56.5K-73.3K
Franchise fee: $50K
Royalty fee: $1.2K/mo.
Term of agreement: 5 years renewable
　at no charge
Franchisees required to buy multiple
　units? No

FINANCING
No financing available

QUALIFICATIONS
Net worth: $100K
Cash liquidity: $56.5K-73.3K
Experience:
　Sales experience

TRAINING
At headquarters: 1 week

BUSINESS SUPPORT
Newsletter
Meetings
Toll-free phone line
Internet
Field operations/evaluations

MARKETING SUPPORT
Ad slicks
Regional marketing

TURBO LEADERSHIP SYSTEMS

Current financial data not available

36280 N.E. Wilsonville Rd.
Newberg, OR 97132
Ph: (503)625-1867
Fax: (503)625-2699
www.turboleadershipsystems.com
Leadership development & training
Began: 1985, Franchising since: 1995
Headquarters size: 6 employees
Franchise department: 6 employees

U.S. franchises: 1
Canadian franchises: 0
Other foreign franchises: 0
Company-owned: 1
Units concentrated in AZ, OR

Seeking: All U.S.
Seeking in Canada? Yes
Exclusive territories? Yes
Homebased option? Yes
Kiosk option? No
Employees needed to run franchise: 2
Absentee ownership? No

COSTS
Total cost: $29K-36K
Franchise fee: $29K
Royalty fee: 10%
Term of agreement: 10 years renewable
    at no charge
Franchisees required to buy multiple
    units? Outside the U.S. only

FINANCING
No financing available

QUALIFICATIONS
Net worth: $150K
Cash liquidity: $40K
Experience:
    Industry experience
    General business experience
    Marketing skills
    Communication skills

TRAINING
At headquarters: 30 days

BUSINESS SUPPORT
Newsletter
Meetings
Toll-free phone line
Grand opening
Internet
Field operations/evaluations

MARKETING SUPPORT
Co-op advertising
Ad slicks

BUSINESS ▸ *Miscellaneous*

BEVINCO BAR SYSTEMS LTD.

Ranked #256 in Entrepreneur Magazine's 2004 Franchise 500

Financial rating: $$$$

510-505 Consumers Rd.
Toronto, ON Canada M2J 4V8
Ph: (888)238-4626/(416)490-6266
Fax: (416)490-6899
www.bevinco.com
Liquor inventory-control service
Began: 1987, Franchising since: 1990
Headquarters size: 9 employees
Franchise department: 3 employees

U.S. franchises: 170
Canadian franchises: 25
Other foreign franchises: 28
Company-owned: 1

Seeking: All U.S.
Seeking in Canada? Yes
Exclusive territories? Yes
Homebased option? Yes
Kiosk option? No
Employees needed to run franchise:
    0-1
Absentee ownership? No

COSTS
Total cost: $41.5K-45K
Franchise fee: $34.9K
Royalty fee: $12/audit
Term of agreement: 5 years renewable
    for $1K
Franchisees required to buy multiple
    units? Outside the U.S. only

FINANCING
No financing available

QUALIFICATIONS
Net worth: $50K
Cash liquidity: $30K

TRAINING
At headquarters: 10 days
At franchisee's location: 1 week

BUSINESS SUPPORT
Newsletter
Meetings
Toll-free phone line
Internet

MARKETING SUPPORT
Co-op advertising
National media campaign

BUSINESS PRODUCTS EXPRESS

Ranked #492 in Entrepreneur Magazine's 2004 Franchise 500

Financial rating: 0

18500 Von Karman Ave., #140
Irvine, CA 92612
Ph: (949)225-1524
Fax: (949)225-1525
www.officesupplyfranchise.com
Office supply products
Began: 1996, Franchising since: 1999
Headquarters size: 7 employees
Franchise department: 3 employees

U.S. franchises: 14
Canadian franchises: 0
Other foreign franchises: 0
Company-owned: 0
Units concentrated in all U.S.

Seeking: All U.S.
Seeking in Canada? No
Exclusive territories? Yes
Homebased option? Yes
Kiosk option? No
Employees needed to run franchise: 1
Absentee ownership? Yes

COSTS
Total cost: $49.99K-100K
Franchise fee: $24.99K+
Royalty fee: 4%
Term of agreement: 10 years renewable
at no charge
Franchisees required to buy multiple
units? No

FINANCING
In-house: Franchise fee
3rd-party: Accounts receivable, start-
up costs

QUALIFICATIONS
Net worth: $100K
Cash liquidity: $50K
Experience:
General business experience
Marketing skills
Sales professional

TRAINING
At headquarters: 10 days
At franchisee's location: 2 days
Ongoing

BUSINESS SUPPORT
Newsletter
Meetings
Toll-free phone line
Internet
Field operations/evaluations
Purchasing cooperatives

MARKETING SUPPORT
Co-op advertising
Ad slicks
National media campaign
Internet

FOLIAGE DESIGN SYSTEMS

Financial rating: $$$$

4496 35th St.
Orlando, FL 32811
Ph: (800)933-7351/(407)245-7776
Fax: (407)245-7533
www.foliagedesign.com
Interior foliage & plant maintenance
Began: 1971, Franchising since: 1980
Headquarters size: 7 employees
Franchise department: 7 employees

U.S. franchises: 33
Canadian franchises: 0
Other foreign franchises: 0
Company-owned: 3
Units concentrated in all U.S.

Seeking: All U.S.
Seeking in Canada? No
Exclusive territories? Yes
Homebased option? Yes
Kiosk option? No
Employees needed to run franchise: 5
Absentee ownership? No

COSTS
Total cost: $49.4K-144.4K
Franchise fee: $25K-100K
Royalty fee: 6%
Term of agreement: 4-5 years renew-
able
Franchisees required to buy multiple
units? No

FINANCING
No financing available

QUALIFICATIONS
Net worth: $250K
Cash liquidity: $33.95K-124.6K
Experience:
General business experience
Marketing skills
Sales experience

TRAINING
At headquarters: 8-10 days
At franchisee's location: 3 days

BUSINESS SUPPORT
Newsletter
Meetings
Toll-free phone line
Internet
Security/safety procedures
Field operations/evaluations

MARKETING SUPPORT
Ad slicks
National media campaign
Regional marketing
Leads

HYDRO PHYSICS PIPE INSPECTION CORP.

Financial rating: 0

1855 W. Union Ave., #N
Englewood, CO 80110
Ph: (800)781-3164
Fax: (303)781-0477
www.hydrophysics.org
Pipe inspection & locating services
Began: 1991, Franchising since: 1996
Headquarters size: 4 employees
Franchise department: 1 employee

U.S. franchises: 8
Canadian franchises: 0
Other foreign franchises: 0
Company-owned: 1
Units concentrated in all U.S.

Seeking: All U.S.
Seeking in Canada? No
Exclusive territories? Yes
Homebased option? Yes
Kiosk option? No
Employees needed to run franchise: 1
Absentee ownership? No

COSTS
Total cost: $70K-95K
Franchise fee: $22.5K
Royalty fee: 7.5%
Term of agreement: 10 years renewable
    for $1.00
Franchisees required to buy multiple
    units? No

FINANCING
No financing available

QUALIFICATIONS
Net worth: $150K
Cash liquidity: $25K
Experience:
    General business experience
    Marketing skills

TRAINING
At headquarters: 2 weeks
At franchisee's location: As needed

BUSINESS SUPPORT
Newsletter
Meetings
Toll-free phone line
Grand opening
Internet
Security/safety procedures
Field operations/evaluations
Purchasing cooperatives

MARKETING SUPPORT
Co-op advertising
Ad slicks
National media campaign
Regional marketing

ITEX

Financial rating: 0

2880 Meade Ave., #204
Las Vegas, NV 89102
Ph: (866)839-4839
Fax: (702)220-8031
www.itex.com
Retail trade & barter exchange
Began: 1982, Franchising since: 2002
Headquarters size: Info not provided
Franchise department: 5 employees

U.S. franchises: 3
Canadian franchises: 0
Other foreign franchises: 0
Company-owned: 5

Seeking: All U.S.
Seeking in Canada? No
Exclusive territories? No
Homebased option? No
Kiosk option? No
Employees needed to run franchise:
    1-10
Absentee ownership? Yes

COSTS
Total cost: $15.9K-31K
Franchise fee: $10K
Royalty fee: Varies
Term of agreement: 5 years renewable
    at no charge
Franchisees required to buy multiple
    units? No

FINANCING
No financing available

QUALIFICATIONS
Experience:
    General business experience

TRAINING
At headquarters: 1 week
At various locations: 3 days

BUSINESS SUPPORT
Meetings
Toll-free phone line
Internet

MARKETING SUPPORT
Co-op advertising
Ad slicks
National media campaign
Regional marketing

MR. PLANT

Current financial data not available

1106 2nd St.
Encinitas, CA 92024
Ph: (888)677-5268
Fax: (760)295-5629
www.mrplant.com
Interior plant maintenance
Began: 1980, Franchising since: 1990
Headquarters size: 6 employees
Franchise department: 3 employees

U.S. franchises: 40
Canadian franchises: 0
Other foreign franchises: 0
Company-owned: 1
Units concentrated in all U.S.

Seeking: All U.S.
Seeking in Canada? Yes
Exclusive territories? Info not provided
Homebased option? Yes
Kiosk option? No
Employees needed to run franchise: 2
Absentee ownership? Yes

COSTS
Total cost: $14.95K-25K
Franchise fee: $14.95K
Royalty fee: Varies
Term of agreement: 5 years renewable
  for $1K
Franchisees required to buy multiple
  units? No

FINANCING
No financing available

QUALIFICATIONS
Net worth: $25K
Cash liquidity: $20K

TRAINING
At headquarters: 5 days
Home study course

BUSINESS SUPPORT
Newsletter
Toll-free phone line
Internet
Purchasing cooperatives

MARKETING SUPPORT
Co-op advertising
Ad slicks
Yellow Pages

NATIONAL TENANT NETWORK INC.

Current financial data not available

P.O. Box 1664
Lake Grove, OR 97035
Ph: (503)635-1118
Fax: (503)638-2450
www.ntnnet.com
Tenant performance reporting &
  screening
Began: 1981, Franchising since: 1987
Headquarters size: 10 employees
Franchise department: 10 employees

U.S. franchises: 23
Canadian franchises: 0
Other foreign franchises: 0
Company-owned: 2
Units concentrated in all U.S.

Seeking: All U.S.
Seeking in Canada? Yes
Exclusive territories? Yes
Homebased option? Yes
Kiosk option? No
Employees needed to run franchise: 3
Absentee ownership? No

COSTS
Total cost: $65K
Franchise fee: $45K
Royalty fee: 10%
Term of agreement: 10 years renewable
  for $15K-25K
Franchisees required to buy multiple
  units? No

FINANCING
In-house: Franchise fee
3rd-party: None

QUALIFICATIONS
Cash liquidity: $100K
Experience:
  General business experience
  Marketing skills

TRAINING
At franchisee's location: 2 weeks
Additional training available

BUSINESS SUPPORT
Newsletter
Meetings
Toll-free phone line
Grand opening
Internet
Security/safety procedures
Field operations/evaluations
Purchasing cooperatives

MARKETING SUPPORT
Co-op advertising
Ad slicks
National media campaign
Regional marketing

PROFORMA

Ranked #94 in Entrepreneur Magazine's 2004 Franchise 500   *Financial rating: $$$$*

8800 E. Pleasant Valley Rd.
Cleveland, OH 44131
Ph: (800)825-1525/(216)520-8400
Fax: (216)520-8474
www.proforma.com
Printing & promotional products
Began: 1978, Franchising since: 1985
Headquarters size: 120 employees
Franchise department: 10 employees

U.S. franchises: 560
Canadian franchises: 44
Other foreign franchises: 1
Company-owned: 0
Units concentrated in all U.S.

Seeking: All U.S.
Seeking in Canada? Yes
Exclusive territories? No
Homebased option? Yes
Kiosk option? No
Employees needed to run franchise: 0
Absentee ownership? No

COSTS

Total cost: $4.5K-34.1K
Franchise fee: to $14.9K
Royalty fee: 6-8%
Term of agreement: 10 years renewable
    for $1K
Franchisees required to buy multiple
    units? No

FINANCING

In-house: Accounts receivable
3rd-party: None

QUALIFICATIONS

Net worth: $50K-100K
Cash liquidity: $10K-20K
Experience:
    General business experience
    Marketing skills
    Sales background

TRAINING

At headquarters: 1 week
At franchisee's location: Quarterly
At regional/annual convention: 2-4
    days

BUSINESS SUPPORT

Newsletter
Meetings
Toll-free phone line
Internet
Field operations/evaluations
Purchasing cooperatives

MARKETING SUPPORT

National media campaign
Regional marketing
Product promotions, direct mail
    campaigns
Direct-mail campaigns

PROSHRED SECURITY INT'L.

Current financial data not available

2470 Huntley Rd.
Stittsville, ON Can. K2S 1B8
Ph: (877)360-8876
Fax: (613)838-5590
www.proshred.com
Mobile document destruction
Began: 1984, Franchising since: 1987
Headquarters size: 50 employees
Franchise department: 5 employees

U.S. franchises: 4
Canadian franchises: 35
Other foreign franchises: 0
Company-owned: 1
Units concentrated in CT, GA, MA,
    NY, WI

Seeking: All U.S.
Focusing on: CA, FL, IL, NE, TX, WY
Seeking in Canada? Yes
Exclusive territories? Yes
Homebased option? Yes
Kiosk option? No
Employees needed to run franchise: 2
Absentee ownership? Yes

COSTS

Total cost: $55K-150K
Franchise fee: $35K
Royalty fee: 6.5%
Term of agreement: 10 years renewable
Franchisees required to buy multiple
    units? Outside the U.S. only

FINANCING

In-house: None
3rd-party: Equipment

QUALIFICATIONS

Net worth: $250K
Cash liquidity: $50K-100K
Experience:
    General business experience
    Marketing skills

TRAINING

At headquarters: 1 week
At franchisee's location: 1 week
Ongoing

BUSINESS SUPPORT

Newsletter
Meetings
Toll-free phone line
Grand opening
Internet
Lease negotiations
Security/safety procedures
Field operations/evaluations
Purchasing cooperatives

MARKETING SUPPORT

Co-op advertising
Ad slicks
National media campaign
Regional marketing

SAVE IT NOW!

Financial rating: $$$

9100 Keystone Crossing, #750
Indianapolis, IN 46240
Ph: (317)208-4800
Fax: (317)581-9348
www.saveitnow.com
Group buying program for business
    products & services
Began: 1986, Franchising since: 2002
Headquarters size: 25 employees
Franchise department: 3 employees

U.S. franchises: 1
Canadian franchises: 0
Other foreign franchises: 0
Company-owned: 0
Units concentrated in GA, NC

Seeking: All U.S.
Focusing on: Great Lakes states,
    Midwest, Northeast, Mid-Atlantic
Seeking in Canada? No
Exclusive territories? Yes
Homebased option? Yes
Kiosk option? No
Employees needed to run franchise: 1
Absentee ownership? Yes

COSTS
Total cost: $58.5K-167.9K
Franchise fee: $32.5K
Royalty fee: 6%
Term of agreement: 10 years renewable
    at no charge
Franchisees required to buy multiple
    units? No

FINANCING
In-house: None
3rd-party: Accounts receivable, equip-
    ment, franchise fee, inventory, pay-
    roll, start-up costs

QUALIFICATIONS
Net worth: $75K
Cash liquidity: $53.5K
Experience:
    General business experience
    Sales or sales management experience

TRAINING
At headquarters: 12 days
At franchisee's location: 6 days+
Advanced training: 7 days
Web training

BUSINESS SUPPORT
Meetings
Toll-free phone line
Grand opening
Internet
Field operations/evaluations
Purchasing cooperatives

MARKETING SUPPORT
Co-op advertising
Ad slicks
E-mail support
Telemarketing

SHANE'S OFFICE SUPPLY

Financial rating: $$$

2717 Curtiss St.
Downers Grove, IL 60515
Ph: (800)258-6055
Fax: (630)435-3970
www.eshanes.com/franchise/index.htm
Commercial office supplies
Began: 1989, Franchising since: 2003
Headquarters size: 28 employees
Franchise department: 2 employees

U.S. franchises: 0
Canadian franchises: 0
Other foreign franchises: 0
Company-owned: 1
Units concentrated in all U.S.

Seeking: All U.S.
Focusing on: IA, IL, IN, MI, MO, WI
Seeking in Canada? No
Exclusive territories? Yes
Homebased option? No
Kiosk option? No
Employees needed to run franchise: 3
Absentee ownership? Yes

COSTS
Total cost: $76K-137K
Franchise fee: $26K
Royalty fee: 2-6%
Term of agreement: 6 years renewable
    at no charge
Franchisees required to buy multiple
    units? Info not provided

FINANCING
No financing available

QUALIFICATIONS
Net worth: $150K
Cash liquidity: $50K-75K
Experience:
    General business experience
    Marketing skills
    Sales & management skills

TRAINING
At headquarters: 3 weeks
At franchisee's location

BUSINESS SUPPORT
Toll-free phone line
Field operations/evaluations
Purchasing cooperatives

MARKETING SUPPORT
Co-op advertising
Ad slicks
Catalogs
Flyers

ZLAND BUSINESS CENTERS

Financial rating: $$$$

131 Innovation Dr.
Irvine, CA 92612
Ph: (877)682-0922
Fax: (949)255-8400
www.namg.zland.com
Financial & business application software
Began: 1996, Franchising since: 2002
Headquarters size: 25 employees
Franchise department: 8 employees

U.S. franchises: 44
Canadian franchises: 0
Other foreign franchises: 0
Company-owned: 0
Units concentrated in all U.S.

Seeking: All U.S.
Seeking in Canada? No
Exclusive territories? No
Homebased option? Yes
Kiosk option? No
Employees needed to run franchise:
    5-10
Absentee ownership? Yes

COSTS
Total cost: $67.3K-137.99K
Franchise fee: $19.5K
Royalty fee: 0
Term of agreement: 7 years renewable
Franchisees required to buy multiple
    units? No

FINANCING
No financing available

QUALIFICATIONS
Net worth: $50K
Cash liquidity: $15K-20K
Experience:
    General business experience
    Marketing skills
    Sales skills

TRAINING
At headquarters: 13 days

BUSINESS SUPPORT
Meetings
Grand opening
Internet
Field operations/evaluations

MARKETING SUPPORT
Info not provided

BUSINESS *Other Franchises*

AUTOWRAPS INC.
53 W. 36th St., #402
New York, NY 10018
Ph: (646)733-9000
www.autowraps.com
Mobile advertising & promotional
    programs

BUSINESS AMERICA
2120 Greentree Rd.
Pittsburgh, PA 15220
Ph: (412)276-7701
www.pghbiznet.com
Business & franchise brokerage

CLICKTOWN INT'L. LLC
20 Hoiles Dr.
Kenilworth, NJ 07033
Ph: (908)259-0500
www.clicktown.com
Online city guides

HR FIRST CONTACT
12750 Merit Dr., #1215
Dallas, TX 75251
Ph: (972)404-4479
www.hrfirstcontact.com
Pre-employment screening

LEADERSHIP MANAGEMENT INC.
*Ranked #133 in Entrepreneur
    Magazine's 2004 Franchise 500*
4567 Lake Shore Dr.
Waco, TX 76710
Ph: (800)568-1241
www.lmi-bus.com
Executive & management training

REMEDYTEMP INC.
101 Enterprise
Aliso Viejo, CA 92656
Ph: (800)828-3726/(949)425-7600
www.remedystaff.com
Temporary-staffing services

RSVP PUBLICATIONS
1156 N.E. Cleveland St.
Clearwater, FL 33755
Ph: (800)360-7787/(727)442-4000
www.rsvppublications.com
Direct-mail advertising

SPHERION CORP.
925 N. Point Pkwy.
Alpharetta, GA 30005
Ph: (888)241-5725
www.spherion.com
Full-time & temporary staffing
    services

STRATIS BUSINESS CENTERS
555 North Point Centre E., 4th Fl.
Alpharetta, GA 30022
Ph: (888)778-7284
www.stratisnet.com
Office space & business-support
    services

Children's Businesses

CHILD CARE CHOICES

Financial rating: 0

P.O. Box 4
Spring City, PA 19475
Ph: (877)748-4968
Fax: (610)792-3709
www.childcarechoicesinc.com
Child-care referral network
Began: 1998, Franchising since: 1999
Headquarters size: 8 employees
Franchise department: 3 employees

U.S. franchises: 11
Canadian franchises: 0
Other foreign franchises: 0
Company-owned: 10
Units concentrated in DE, NJ, PA

Seeking: All U.S.
Focusing on: DE, NJ, NY, PA & most
    other East Coast states
Seeking in Canada? No
Exclusive territories? Yes
Homebased option? Yes
Kiosk option? No
Employees needed to run franchise: 1
Absentee ownership? No

COSTS
Total cost: $23.5K-46.6K
Franchise fee: $19K
Royalty fee: 6%
Term of agreement: 15 years renewable
    at no charge
Franchisees required to buy multiple
    units? No

FINANCING
In-house: None
3rd-party: Franchise fee, start-up costs

QUALIFICATIONS
Net worth: $50K
Cash liquidity: $20K
Experience:
    Industry experience
    General business experience
    Marketing skills

TRAINING
At headquarters
At franchisee's location: 5 days

BUSINESS SUPPORT
Newsletter
Meetings
Toll-free phone line
Grand opening
Internet
Purchasing cooperatives

MARKETING SUPPORT
Co-op advertising
Ad slicks
National media campaign
Regional marketing

CHILDREN'S LIGHTHOUSE FRANCHISE CORP.

Current financial data not available

101 S. Jennings, #209
Fort Worth, TX 76104
Ph: (888)338-4466/(817)338-1332
Fax: (817)338-2716
www.childrenslighthouse.com
Child-care services
Began: 1997, Franchising since: 1999
Headquarters size: 6 employees
Franchise department: 6 employees

U.S. franchises: 3
Canadian franchises: 0
Other foreign franchises: 0
Company-owned: 8
Units concentrated in TX

Seeking: All U.S.
Seeking in Canada? Yes
Exclusive territories? Yes
Homebased option? No
Kiosk option? No
Employees needed to run franchise: 25
Absentee ownership? Yes

COSTS
Total cost: $250K-1.5M
Franchise fee: $50K
Royalty fee: 7%
Term of agreement: 15 years renewable
   at no charge
Franchisees required to buy multiple
   units? Yes

FINANCING
In-house: None
3rd-party: Accounts receivable, equipment, inventory, start-up costs

QUALIFICATIONS
Net worth: $150K
Cash liquidity: $50K
Experience:
   Industry experience
   General business experience
   Marketing skills

TRAINING
At headquarters: 4 weeks
At franchisee's location: 4 weeks
Unlimited for the first year

BUSINESS SUPPORT
Meetings
Toll-free phone line
Grand opening
Internet
Security/safety procedures
Field operations/evaluations
Purchasing cooperatives

MARKETING SUPPORT
Co-op advertising
Ad slicks
Regional marketing

GODDARD SYSTEMS INC.

Ranked #143 in Entrepreneur Magazine's 2004 Franchise 500

Financial rating: $$$$

1016 W. Ninth Ave.
King of Prussia, PA 19406
Ph: (610)265-8510
Fax: (610)265-6931
www.goddardschool.com
Preschool/child-care center
Began: 1986, Franchising since: 1988
Headquarters size: Info not provided
Franchise department: Info not provided

U.S. franchises: 145
Canadian franchises: 0
Other foreign franchises: 0
Company-owned: 1
Units concentrated in all U.S.

Seeking: All U.S.
Seeking in Canada? No
Exclusive territories? No
Homebased option? No
Kiosk option? No
Employees needed to run franchise: 20
Absentee ownership? No

COSTS
Total cost: $350K
Franchise fee: $60K
Royalty fee: 7%
Term of agreement: 15 years renewable
   at no charge
Franchisees required to buy multiple
   units? No

FINANCING
3rd-party: Equipment, franchise fee,
   start-up costs
Other: Working capital

QUALIFICATIONS
Net worth: $350K
Cash liquidity: $90K
Experience:
   General business experience

TRAINING
At headquarters: 3 weeks
At franchisee's location: At opening

BUSINESS SUPPORT
Newsletter
Meetings
Grand opening
Internet
Lease negotiations
Security/safety procedures
Field operations/evaluations

MARKETING SUPPORT
Co-op advertising
Ad slicks
National media campaign
Regional marketing

KIDDIE ACADEMY CHILD CARE LEARNING CENTERS

Ranked #290 in Entrepreneur Magazine's 2004 Franchise 500   *Financial rating: $$$$*

108 Wheel Rd.
Bel Air, MD 21015
Ph: (800)554-3343
Fax: (410)569-2729
www.kiddieacademy.com
Child-care learning center
Began: 1979, Franchising since: 1991
Headquarters size: 24 employees
Franchise department: 3 employees

U.S. franchises: 60
Canadian franchises: 0
Other foreign franchises: 0
Company-owned: 11
Units concentrated in all U.S.

Seeking: All U.S.
Seeking in Canada? Yes
Exclusive territories? Yes
Homebased option? No
Kiosk option? No
Employees needed to run franchise: 20
Absentee ownership? No

COSTS
Total cost: $233.3K-606.6K
Franchise fee: $50K
Royalty fee: 7.5%
Term of agreement: 10 years renewable
for $1K per 5-year term
Franchisees required to buy multiple
units? Outside the U.S. only

FINANCING
In-house: None
3rd-party: Accounts receivable, equipment, franchise fee, inventory, payroll, start-up costs

QUALIFICATIONS
Net worth: $250K
Cash liquidity: $70K
Experience:
People & management skills

TRAINING
At headquarters: 2 weeks
At franchisee's location: 1 week

BUSINESS SUPPORT
Newsletter
Meetings
Toll-free phone line
Grand opening
Internet
Security/safety procedures
Field operations/evaluations
Purchasing cooperatives

MARKETING SUPPORT
Ad slicks
Regional marketing
Marketing plans

THE LEARNING EXPERIENCE

Financial rating: $$$

2740 Rt. 10 W.
Morris Plains, NJ 07950
Ph: (973)539-5392
Fax: (973)539-5979
www.thelearningexperience.net
Child-care services
Began: 1979, Franchising since: 2003
Headquarters size: 20 employees
Franchise department: 10 employees

U.S. franchises: 0
Canadian franchises: 0
Other foreign franchises: 0
Company-owned: 5

Seeking: Northeast
Seeking in Canada? Yes
Exclusive territories? Yes
Homebased option? No
Kiosk option? No
Employees needed to run franchise: 23
Absentee ownership? Yes

COSTS
Total cost: $275K
Franchise fee: $50K
Royalty fee: 3-6%
Term of agreement: 15 years renewable
at no charge
Franchisees required to buy multiple
units? Info not provided

FINANCING
In-house: Franchise fee
3rd-party: Equipment, inventory,
start-up costs

QUALIFICATIONS
Net worth: $350K
Cash liquidity: $100K
Experience:
General business experience
Marketing skills

TRAINING
At headquarters: 1 month
At training facility: 2 weeks

BUSINESS SUPPORT
Newsletter
Meetings
Toll-free phone line
Grand opening
Internet
Security/safety procedures
Field operations/evaluations
Purchasing cooperatives

MARKETING SUPPORT
Co-op advertising
Ad slicks
Regional marketing

LEGACY ACADEMY FOR CHILDREN

Current financial data not available

4536-A Nelson Brogdon Blvd.
Sugar Hill, GA 30518
Ph: (770)932-0091
Fax: (770)932-3805
www.legacyacademy.com
Child-care center
Began: 1997, Franchising since: 1998
Headquarters size: 8 employees
Franchise department: 1 employee

U.S. franchises: 10
Canadian franchises: 0
Other foreign franchises: 0
Company-owned: 0

Seeking: South
Seeking in Canada? No
Exclusive territories? Yes
Homebased option? No
Kiosk option? No
Employees needed to run franchise: 25
Absentee ownership? No

COSTS
Total cost: $2.1M-2.5M
Franchise fee: $40K
Royalty fee: 5%
Term of agreement: 24 years renewable
Franchisees required to buy multiple
  units? No

FINANCING
In-house: None
3rd-party: Equipment, inventory

QUALIFICATIONS
Net worth: $200K
Cash liquidity: $200K
Experience:
  General business experience

TRAINING
At headquarters: 1 month
At franchisee's location: 1 month

BUSINESS SUPPORT
Newsletter
Meetings
Toll-free phone line
Grand opening
Internet
Security/safety procedures
Field operations/evaluations
Purchasing cooperatives

MARKETING SUPPORT
Co-op advertising
Ad slicks
Regional marketing

MONDAY MORNING MOMS

Current financial data not available

276 White Oak Ridge Rd.
Bridgewater, NJ 08807-1532
Ph: (800)335-4666/(908)685-0060
Fax: (908)526-3156
www.mondayam.com
Child-care management services
Began: 1981, Franchising since: 1989
Headquarters size: 3 employees
Franchise department: Info not pro-
  vided

U.S. franchises: 7
Canadian franchises: 0
Other foreign franchises: 0
Company-owned: 0
Units concentrated in CO, HI, MD, NJ,
  OH, TX

Seeking: All U.S.
Seeking in Canada? No
Exclusive territories? Yes
Homebased option? Yes
Kiosk option? No
Employees needed to run franchise:
  0-1
Absentee ownership? No

COSTS
Total cost: $24.2K-31.2K
Franchise fee: $12K
Royalty fee: 4-6%
Term of agreement: 5 years renewable
  at no charge
Franchisees required to buy multiple
  units? No

FINANCING
No financing available

QUALIFICATIONS
Net worth: $200K
Cash liquidity: $25K
Experience:
  Industry experience
  General business experience
  Marketing skills

TRAINING
At headquarters: 8 days
At franchisee's location: 4 days per
  year

BUSINESS SUPPORT
Newsletter
Toll-free phone line
Internet
Field operations/evaluations

MARKETING SUPPORT
Info not provided

PRIMROSE SCHOOL FRANCHISING CO.

Ranked #294 in Entrepreneur Magazine's 2004 Franchise 500   *Financial rating: $$$$*

3660 Cedarcrest Rd.
Acworth, GA 30101
Ph: (800)745-0677/(770)529-4100
Fax: (770)529-1551
www.primroseschools.com
Educational child-care facility
Began: 1982, Franchising since: 1988
Headquarters size: 33 employees
Franchise department: 3 employees

U.S. franchises: 106
Canadian franchises: 0
Other foreign franchises: 0
Company-owned: 1
Units concentrated in GA, TX

Seeking: All U.S.
Focusing on: AL, AZ, CO, FL, GA, KS,
    NC, NE, OH, OK, TN, TX, VA
Seeking in Canada? No
Exclusive territories? Yes
Homebased option? No
Kiosk option? No
Employees needed to run franchise: 30
Absentee ownership? No

COSTS
Total cost: $200K-250K
Franchise fee: $50K
Royalty fee: 7%
Term of agreement: 10 years renewable
    at no charge
Franchisees required to buy multiple
    units? No

FINANCING
In-house: None
3rd-party: Equipment, franchise fee,
    inventory, start-up costs

QUALIFICATIONS
Net worth: $500K
Cash liquidity: $200K-250K
Experience:
    General business experience
    Marketing skills
    People skills

TRAINING
At headquarters: 1 week
At franchisee's location: 1 week
At existing location: 1 week

BUSINESS SUPPORT
Newsletter
Meetings
Toll-free phone line
Grand opening
Internet
Security/safety procedures
Field operations/evaluations
Purchasing cooperatives

MARKETING SUPPORT
Co-op advertising
Ad slicks
National media campaign
Regional marketing
Radio

RAINBOW STATION INC.

Current financial data not available

3307 Church Rd., #205
Richmond, VA 23233
Ph: (888)747-1552
Fax: (804)747-8016
www.rainbowstation.org
Child-care services
Began: 1988, Franchising since: 1999
Headquarters size: 4 employees
Franchise department: 1 employee

U.S. franchises: 1
Canadian franchises: 0
Other foreign franchises: 0
Company-owned: 3
Units concentrated in TX

Seeking: All U.S.
Seeking in Canada? No
Exclusive territories? Yes
Homebased option? No
Kiosk option? No
Employees needed to run franchise: 50
Absentee ownership? No

COSTS
Total cost: $256.1K-924.2K
Franchise fee: $30K
Royalty fee: 6%
Term of agreement: 10 years renewable
    for $5K
Franchisees required to buy multiple
    units? No

FINANCING
In-house: None
3rd-party: Equipment, franchise fee,
    start-up costs

QUALIFICATIONS
Net worth: $750K
Cash liquidity: $250K+
Experience:
    Industry experience
    General business experience
    Marketing skills

TRAINING
At headquarters: 2 weeks
At franchisee's location: 1 week

BUSINESS SUPPORT
Newsletter
Toll-free phone line
Grand opening
Internet
Security/safety procedures
Field operations/evaluations

MARKETING SUPPORT
Co-op advertising

SUNBROOK ACADEMY

Financial rating: 0

2933 Cherokee St.
Kennesaw, GA 30144
Ph: (770)426-0619
Fax: (770)426-0724
www.sunbrookacademy.com
Child-care centers
Began: 1984, Franchising since: 1999
Headquarters size: 7 employees
Franchise department: 7 employees

U.S. franchises: 2
Canadian franchises: 0
Other foreign franchises: 0
Company-owned: 4
Units concentrated in GA

Seeking: Southeast
Focusing on: GA
Seeking in Canada? No
Exclusive territories? Yes
Homebased option? No
Kiosk option? No
Employees needed to run franchise: 25
Absentee ownership? No

COSTS
Total cost: $271.2K-2.1M
Franchise fee: $40K
Royalty fee: 6%
Term of agreement: 15 years renewable
for $1K
Franchisees required to buy multiple
units? No

FINANCING
In-house: None
3rd-party: Accounts receivable, equipment, franchise fee, inventory, payroll, start-up costs

QUALIFICATIONS
Net worth: $500K
Cash liquidity: $150K-250K
Experience:
General business experience
Marketing skills
Must enjoy working with children

TRAINING
At headquarters: 21 days
At franchisee's location: 1 mo. after
opening

BUSINESS SUPPORT
Meetings
Grand opening
Internet
Lease negotiations
Security/safety procedures
Field operations/evaluations

MARKETING SUPPORT
Ad slicks

TUTOR TIME LEARNING CENTERS LLC
Ranked #340 in Entrepreneur Magazine's 2004 Franchise 500

Financial rating: $$$

621 N.W. 53rd St., #115
Boca Raton, FL 33487
Ph: (800)275-1235/(561)994-6226
Fax: (561)237-3466
www.tutortime.com
Child-care learning center
Began: 1979, Franchising since: 1989
Headquarters size: 65 employees
Franchise department: 2 employees

U.S. franchises: 123
Canadian franchises: 1
Other foreign franchises: 10
Company-owned: 63
Units concentrated in AZ, CA, CT, FL,
GA, IN, MI, MN, MO, NC, NJ, NY,
OH, TX

Seeking: All U.S.
Focusing on: AZ, CA, CT, DE, FL, GA,
IN, MO, NC, NJ, NY, OH, TX
Seeking in Canada? Yes
Exclusive territories? No
Homebased option? No
Kiosk option? No
Employees needed to run franchise: 15
Absentee ownership? Yes

COSTS
Total cost: $355K-2.8M
Franchise fee: $50K
Royalty fee: 6%
Term of agreement: 15 years renewable
for $5K
Franchisees required to buy multiple
units? No

FINANCING
No financing available

QUALIFICATIONS
Net worth: $1M
Cash liquidity: $350K
Experience:
General business experience
Marketing skills

TRAINING
At headquarters: 2 weeks
At franchisee's location: 2 weeks
At operating facility: 2-4 weeks

BUSINESS SUPPORT
Newsletter
Meetings
Toll-free phone line
Grand opening
Internet
Lease negotiations
Security/safety procedures
Field operations/evaluations

MARKETING SUPPORT
Co-op advertising
National media campaign
Regional marketing

CHILDREN'S *Fitness*

BABY POWER

Current financial data not available

P.O. Box 526
Annandale, NJ 08801
Ph: (800)365-4847
Fax: (908)713-6547
www.babypower.com
Parent/child play program
Began: 1973, Franchising since: 1996
Headquarters size: 4 employees
Franchise department: 4 employees

U.S. franchises: 4
Canadian franchises: 0
Other foreign franchises: 0
Company-owned: 1
Units concentrated in NJ

Seeking: All U.S.
Seeking in Canada? Yes
Exclusive territories? Yes
Homebased option? No
Kiosk option? No
Employees needed to run franchise: 3
Absentee ownership? Yes

COSTS
Total cost: $45K-65K
Franchise fee: $18.5K
Royalty fee: 5%
Term of agreement: 10 years renewable
    for $5K
Franchisees required to buy multiple
    units? No

FINANCING
In-house: None
Equipment, start-up costs

QUALIFICATIONS
Net worth: $100K
Cash liquidity: $50K
Experience:
    General business experience

TRAINING
At headquarters: 5 days
At franchisee's location: 5 days

BUSINESS SUPPORT
Meetings
Toll-free phone line
Grand opening
Internet
Security/safety procedures
Field operations/evaluations

MARKETING SUPPORT
Co-op advertising
Ad slicks

GYMBOREE
Ranked #77 in Entrepreneur Magazine's 2004 Franchise 500

Financial rating: $$$$

700 Airport Blvd., #200
Burlingame, CA 94010
Ph: (800)520-7529/(650)579-0600
Fax: (650)696-7452
www.gymboree.com
Parent/child play program
Began: 1976, Franchising since: 1978
Headquarters size: 230 employees
Franchise department: 20 employees

U.S. franchises: 329
Canadian franchises: 19
Other foreign franchises: 172
Company-owned: 18
Units concentrated in all U.S.

Seeking: All U.S.
Seeking in Canada? Yes
Exclusive territories? Yes
Homebased option? No
Kiosk option? No
Employees needed to run franchise:
    3-4
Absentee ownership? No

COSTS
Total cost: $76.7K-214.2K
Franchise fee: $35K
Royalty fee: 6%
Term of agreement: 10 years renewable
    at no charge
Franchisees required to buy multiple
    units? Outside the U.S. only

FINANCING
In-house: None
3rd-party: Equipment, inventory,
    start-up costs

QUALIFICATIONS
Net worth: $150K
Cash liquidity: $40K
Experience:
    General business experience

TRAINING
At headquarters: 7 days
At regional location: 2 days/twice a
    year

BUSINESS SUPPORT
Newsletter
Meetings
Toll-free phone line
Grand opening
Internet
Field operations/evaluations
Purchasing cooperatives

MARKETING SUPPORT
Co-op advertising
Ad slicks
National media campaign
Regional marketing

JUMPBUNCH INC.

Financial rating: 0

302 Annapolis St.
Annapolis, MD 21401
Ph: (410)703-2300
Fax: (928)441-7838
www.jumpbunch.com
Preschool sports & fitness programs
Began: 2002, Franchising since: 2002
Headquarters size: Info not provided
Franchise department: Info not provided

U.S. franchises: 1
Canadian franchises: 0
Other foreign franchises: 0
Company-owned: 1
Units concentrated in MD

Seeking: All U.S.
Seeking in Canada? Yes
Exclusive territories? Yes
Homebased option? Yes
Kiosk option? No
Employees needed to run franchise:
    Info not provided
Absentee ownership? No

COSTS
Total cost: $14K-45K
Franchise fee: $7.5K-17.5K
Royalty fee: 8%
Term of agreement: Renewable term at
    25% of then-current franchise fee
Franchisees required to buy multiple
    units? No

FINANCING
No financing available

QUALIFICATIONS
Net worth: $40K
Cash liquidity: $10.5K
Experience:
    General business experience

TRAINING
At headquarters: 2 days

BUSINESS SUPPORT
Newsletter
Meetings
Toll-free phone line
Internet
Security/safety procedures

MARKETING SUPPORT
Co-op advertising
Ad slicks
National media campaign
Regional marketing

J.W. TUMBLES, A CHILDREN'S GYM

Current financial data not available

12750 Carmel Country Rd., #A-102
San Diego, CA 92130
Ph: (800)886-2532
Fax: (858)794-0398
www.jwtumbles.com
Children's gym & parties
Began: 1985, Franchising since: 1993
Headquarters size: 5 employees
Franchise department: 3 employees

U.S. franchises: 8
Canadian franchises: 0
Other foreign franchises: 0
Company-owned: 1
Units concentrated in AZ, CA

Seeking: All U.S.
Seeking in Canada? No
Exclusive territories? Yes
Homebased option? No
Kiosk option? No
Employees needed to run franchise: 6
Absentee ownership? Info not provided

COSTS
Total cost: $115.5K-142.2K
Franchise fee: $30K
Royalty fee: $500/mo.
Term of agreement: Info not provided
Franchisees required to buy multiple
    units? No

FINANCING
No financing available

QUALIFICATIONS
Net worth: $200K
Experience:
    General business experience
    Marketing skills

TRAINING
At headquarters: 4 weeks

BUSINESS SUPPORT
Meetings
Toll-free phone line
Grand opening
Internet
Lease negotiations

MARKETING SUPPORT
Co-op advertising
Ad slicks

KINDERDANCE INT'L. INC.

Ranked #298 in Entrepreneur Magazine's 2004 Franchise 500   *Financial rating: $$$$*

268 N. Babcock St.
Melbourne, FL 32935
Ph: (800)554-2334/(321)242-0590
Fax: (321)254-3388
www.kinderdance.com
Children's movement/educational
  programs
Began: 1979, Franchising since: 1985
Headquarters size: 7 employees
Franchise department: 3 employees

U.S. franchises: 88
Canadian franchises: 1
Other foreign franchises: 3
Company-owned: 1
Units concentrated in all U.S.

Seeking: All U.S.
Seeking in Canada? No
Exclusive territories? Yes
Homebased option? Yes
Kiosk option? No
Employees needed to run franchise:
  1-2
Absentee ownership? No

COSTS
Total cost: $9.95K-27.1K
Franchise fee: $7K-21K
Royalty fee: 6-15%
Term of agreement: 10 years renewable
  for 10% of current franchise fee
Franchisees required to buy multiple
  units? No

FINANCING
In-house: Franchise fee
3rd-party: None

QUALIFICATIONS
Net worth: $10K+
Cash liquidity: $6.4K+
Experience:
  Energetic
  Enjoy working with kids

TRAINING
At headquarters: 6 days
At franchisee's location: As needed
Annual conference: 2-3 days

BUSINESS SUPPORT
Newsletter
Meetings
Toll-free phone line
Grand opening
Internet
Security/safety procedures
Field operations/evaluations
Purchasing cooperatives

MARKETING SUPPORT
Co-op advertising
Ad slicks
National media campaign
Regional marketing
PR releases

MY GYM CHILDREN'S FITNESS CENTER

Ranked #166 in Entrepreneur Magazine's 2004 Franchise 500   *Financial rating: $$$$*

15300 Ventura Blvd., #423
Sherman Oaks, CA 91403
Ph: (800)469-4967
Fax: (818)907-0735
www.my-gym.com
Children's early learning & fitness
  program
Began: 1983, Franchising since: 1995
Headquarters size: 20 employees
Franchise department: 4 employees

U.S. franchises: 102
Canadian franchises: 0
Other foreign franchises: 1
Company-owned: 6
Units concentrated in CA, FL, IL

Seeking: All U.S.
Seeking in Canada? Yes
Exclusive territories? Yes
Homebased option? No
Kiosk option? No
Employees needed to run franchise:
  6-10
Absentee ownership? Yes

COSTS
Total cost: $120K-200K
Franchise fee: $42.5K
Royalty fee: 6%
Term of agreement: 12 years renewable
  at no charge
Franchisees required to buy multiple
  units? Outside the U.S. only

FINANCING
In-house: None
3rd-party: Accounts receivable, equipment, inventory, start-up costs

QUALIFICATIONS
Cash liquidity: $35K-50K
Experience:
  Industry experience
  General business experience
  Marketing skills

TRAINING
At headquarters: 21 days
At franchisee's location: Ongoing

BUSINESS SUPPORT
Newsletter
Meetings
Toll-free phone line
Grand opening
Internet
Security/safety procedures
Field operations/evaluations

MARKETING SUPPORT
Co-op advertising
Ad slicks
Regional marketing

PEE WEE WORKOUT

Current financial data not available

34976 Aspenwood Ln.
Willoughby, OH 44094
Ph: (800)356-6261/(440)946-7888
Fax: (440)946-7888
www.peeweeworkout.com
Preschool fitness program
Began: 1986, Franchising since: 1988
Headquarters size: 3 employees
Franchise department: 1 employee

U.S. franchises: 19
Canadian franchises: 0
Other foreign franchises: 2
Company-owned: 1

Seeking: All U.S.
Seeking in Canada? Yes
Exclusive territories? No
Homebased option? Yes
Kiosk option? No
Employees needed to run franchise:
    Info not provided
Absentee ownership? Yes

COSTS
Total cost: $2.7K
Franchise fee: $2K
Royalty fee: 10%
Term of agreement: 5 years renewable
    for $250
Franchisees required to buy multiple
    units? No

FINANCING
No financing available

QUALIFICATIONS
Net worth: $2.2K
Cash liquidity: $2.2K
Experience:
    Industry experience
    General business experience
    Marketing skills

TRAINING
Video-based training program

BUSINESS SUPPORT
Newsletter
Toll-free phone line
Internet
Purchasing cooperatives

MARKETING SUPPORT
Ad slicks
Press releases

STRETCH-N-GROW INT'L. INC.

Ranked #260 in Entrepreneur Magazine's 2004 Franchise 500

Financial rating: $$$

P.O. Box 7955
Seminole, FL 33775
Ph: (727)596-7614
Fax: (727)596-7633
www.stretch-n-grow.com
On-site children's fitness program
Began: 1992, Franchising since: 1993
Headquarters size: 4 employees
Franchise department: 4 employees

U.S. franchises: 130
Canadian franchises: 4
Other foreign franchises: 25
Company-owned: 0
Units concentrated in all U.S.

Seeking: All U.S.
Seeking in Canada? Yes
Exclusive territories? Yes
Homebased option? Yes
Kiosk option? No
Employees needed to run franchise: 1
Absentee ownership? No

COSTS
Total cost: $15K-20K
Franchise fee: $14.6K-19.6K
Royalty fee: $100/mo.
Term of agreement: Info not provided
Franchisees required to buy multiple
    units? No

FINANCING
No financing available

QUALIFICATIONS
Experience:
    Must enjoy working with children

TRAINING
At headquarters: 4 days
Additional training in Tampa, FL

BUSINESS SUPPORT
Newsletter
Meetings
Toll-free phone line
Internet

MARKETING SUPPORT
National media campaign
Trade print ads

CHILDREN'S *ID Services*

IDENT-A-KID SERVICES OF AMERICA
Ranked #207 in Entrepreneur Magazine's 2004 Franchise 500

Financial rating: $$

2810 Scherer Dr., #100
St. Petersburg, FL 33716
Ph: (727)577-4646
Fax: (727)576-8258
www.ident-a-kid.com
Child identification products & services
Began: 1986, Franchising since: 2000
Headquarters size: Info not provided
Franchise department: Info not provided

U.S. franchises: 210
Canadian franchises: 0
Other foreign franchises: 0
Company-owned: 0
Units concentrated in all U.S.

Seeking: All U.S.
Seeking in Canada? Yes
Exclusive territories? Yes
Homebased option? Yes

Kiosk option? No
Employees needed to run franchise:
    0-3
Absentee ownership? No

COSTS
Total cost: $29.5K-64.96K
Franchise fee: $29.5K
Royalty fee: 0
Term of agreement: 10 years renewable at no charge
Franchisees required to buy multiple units? No

FINANCING
No financing available

QUALIFICATIONS
Experience:
    General business experience
    Marketing skills

TRAINING
At franchisee's location: 3 days
By phone

BUSINESS SUPPORT
Newsletter
Meetings
Toll-free phone line
Internet

MARKETING SUPPORT
National media campaign

MCGRUFF SAFE KIDS TOTAL IDENTIFICATION SYSTEM

Financial rating: $$

15500 Wayzata Blvd., #812
Wayzata, MN 55391
Ph: (888)209-4218
Fax: (727)781-9863
www.mcgruff-safe-kids.com
Computerized children's identification system
Began: 2001, Franchising since: 2002
Headquarters size: Info not provided
Franchise department: Info not provided

U.S. franchises: 24
Canadian franchises: 0
Other foreign franchises: 0
Company-owned: 0
Units concentrated in CT, FL, GA, MD, SD, TX, UT

Seeking: All U.S.
Seeking in Canada? Yes
Exclusive territories? Yes
Homebased option? Yes
Kiosk option? Yes
Employees needed to run franchise:
    Info not provided
Absentee ownership? No

COSTS
Total cost: $28.8K-42K
Franchise fee: $25K
Royalty fee: 0
Term of agreement: 3 years renewable for $3K
Franchisees required to buy multiple units? No

FINANCING
In-house: Franchise fee
3rd-party: None

QUALIFICATIONS
Net worth: $35K
Cash liquidity: $15K
Experience:
    General business experience

TRAINING
At franchisee's location: 16 hours
In Tampa, FL: 16 hours

BUSINESS SUPPORT
Newsletter
Toll-free phone line
Grand opening
Internet
Field operations/evaluations

MARKETING SUPPORT
Ad slicks
National media campaign

SAFE KIDS CARD

Financial rating: $

17100-B Bear Valley Rd., PMB #238
Victorville, CA 92392
Ph: (909)496-9982
Fax: (760)249-5751
www.myfamilycd.com
Child, adult & pet identification
    system
Began: 2002, Franchising since: 2003
Headquarters size: 2 employees
Franchise department: 1 employee

U.S. franchises: 12
Canadian franchises: 0
Other foreign franchises: 0
Company-owned: 0
Units concentrated in AZ, CA, DC, FL,
    NC, NJ, PA, TX, VA, WI

Seeking: All U.S.
Seeking in Canada? Yes
Exclusive territories? Yes
Homebased option? Yes
Kiosk option? No
Employees needed to run franchise:
    Info not provided
Absentee ownership? Yes

COSTS
Total cost: $20.4K-51.6K
Franchise fee: $18.9K
Royalty fee: $75/mo.
Term of agreement: 10 years renewable
    for $1K
Franchisees required to buy multiple
    units? No

FINANCING
In-house: Franchise fee
3rd-party: Start-up costs

QUALIFICATIONS
Net worth: $20K
Cash liquidity: $7K+
Experience:
    General business experience
    Marketing skills
    Must like children

TRAINING
1-2 days of training available

BUSINESS SUPPORT
Newsletter
Internet
Security/safety procedures
Purchasing cooperatives

MARKETING SUPPORT
Co-op advertising

CHILDREN'S **Learning Programs**

DRAMA KIDS INT'L. INC.

Ranked #364 in Entrepreneur Magazine's 2004 Franchise 500

Financial rating: $$$

3225-B Corporate Ct.
Ellicott City, MD 21042
Ph: (410)480-2015
Fax: (410)480-2026
www.dramakids.com
After-school children's drama program
Began: 1979, Franchising since: 1989
Headquarters size: 8 employees
Franchise department: 3 employees

U.S. franchises: 24
Canadian franchises: 0
Other foreign franchises: 93
Company-owned: 2
Units concentrated in all U.S.

Seeking: All U.S.
Seeking in Canada? No
Exclusive territories? Yes
Homebased option? Yes
Kiosk option? No
Employees needed to run franchise: 2
Absentee ownership? No

COSTS
Total cost: $33.4K-39.6K
Franchise fee: $25K
Royalty fee: 10%
Term of agreement: 5 years renewable
    for $2K
Franchisees required to buy multiple
    units? No

FINANCING
No financing available

QUALIFICATIONS
Net worth: $50K
Cash liquidity: $25K
Experience:
    General business experience

TRAINING
At headquarters: 5 days
At franchisee's location: 5 days
Regional training: 1 day
Annual conference

BUSINESS SUPPORT
Newsletter
Meetings
Toll-free phone line
Grand opening
Internet
Security/safety procedures
Field operations/evaluations

MARKETING SUPPORT
Co-op advertising
Ad slicks
National media campaign
Regional marketing

FASTRACKIDS INT'L. LTD.

Ranked #215 in Entrepreneur Magazine's 2004 Franchise 500   *Financial rating: $$$$*

6900 E. Belleview Ave.
Greenwood Village, CO 80111
Ph: (303)224-0200
Fax: (303)224-0222
www.fastrackids.com
Enrichment education for young children
Began: 1998, Franchising since: 1998
Headquarters size: 12 employees
Franchise department: 10 employees

U.S. franchises: 42
Canadian franchises: 8
Other foreign franchises: 120
Company-owned: 0

Seeking: All U.S.
Seeking in Canada? Yes
Exclusive territories? Yes
Homebased option? No
Kiosk option? No
Employees needed to run franchise:
    1-2
Absentee ownership? Yes

COSTS
Total cost: $20.9K-39.7K
Franchise fee: $15K
Royalty fee: 1.5%
Term of agreement: 5 years renewable
    for $1K
Franchisees required to buy multiple
    units? No

FINANCING
In-house: Franchise fee
3rd-party: Franchise fee

QUALIFICATIONS
Experience:
    Industry experience
    General business experience
    Marketing skills

TRAINING
At headquarters: 3-4 days

BUSINESS SUPPORT
Newsletter
Meetings
Internet

MARKETING SUPPORT
Info not provided

HIGH TOUCH-HIGH TECH

Ranked #341 in Entrepreneur Magazine's 2004 Franchise 500   *Financial rating: $$$*

12352 Wiles Rd.
Coral Springs, FL 33076
Ph: (800)444-4968
Fax: (954)755-1242
www.hightouch-hightech.com
Science activities for schools/children's
    parties
Began: 1990, Franchising since: 1993
Headquarters size: 9 employees
Franchise department: 3 employees

U.S. franchises: 68
Canadian franchises: 9
Other foreign franchises: 11
Company-owned: 2
Units concentrated in CT, FL, GA,
    MA, NJ, TX

Seeking: All U.S.
Seeking in Canada? Yes
Exclusive territories? Yes
Homebased option? Yes
Kiosk option? No
Employees needed to run franchise: 4
Absentee ownership? Yes

COSTS
Total cost: $20.1K
Franchise fee: $15K
Royalty fee: 7%
Term of agreement: 10 years renewable
    for $2.5K
Franchisees required to buy multiple
    units? No

FINANCING
In-house: Franchise fee
3rd-party: None

QUALIFICATIONS
Experience:
    General business experience
    Marketing skills
    Education/teaching experience

TRAINING
At headquarters: 5 days

BUSINESS SUPPORT
Newsletter
Meetings
Toll-free phone line
Internet
Security/safety procedures
Field operations/evaluations

MARKETING SUPPORT
Ad slicks

THE HONORS LEARNING CENTER

Current financial data not available

P.O. Box 24055
Chattanooga, TN 37422-4055
Ph: (423)892-1803
Fax: (423)892-1803
www.honorslearningcenter.com
Supplemental educational services &
  academic testing
Began: 1987, Franchising since: 1991
Headquarters size: 2 employees
Franchise department: 2 employees

U.S. franchises: 1
Canadian franchises: 0
Other foreign franchises: 0
Company-owned: 0
Units concentrated in TN

Seeking: All U.S.
Focusing on: AL, FL, GA, TN
Seeking in Canada? No
Exclusive territories? Yes
Homebased option? No
Kiosk option? No
Employees needed to run franchise: 10
Absentee ownership? No

COSTS
Total cost: $48.5K-53.7K
Franchise fee: $15K
Royalty fee: $2K/mo.
Term of agreement: 10 years renewable
Franchisees required to buy multiple
  units? No

FINANCING
No financing available

QUALIFICATIONS
Net worth: $100K
Cash liquidity: $50K
Experience:
  Marketing skills
  Degree in education

TRAINING
At headquarters: 2 weeks
At franchisee's location: 1 week

BUSINESS SUPPORT
Newsletter
Meetings
Grand opening
Internet
Security/safety procedures
Field operations/evaluations

MARKETING SUPPORT
Ad slicks
Radio & TV ads

HUNTINGTON LEARNING CENTERS INC.

Ranked #196 in Entrepreneur Magazine's 2004 Franchise 500

Financial rating: $$$$

496 Kinderkamack Rd.
Oradell, NJ 07649
Ph: (800)653-8400/(201)261-8400
Fax: (201)261-3233
www.huntingtonlearning.com
Educational services
Began: 1977, Franchising since: 1985
Headquarters size: 60 employees
Franchise department: 7 employees

U.S. franchises: 180
Canadian franchises: 0
Other foreign franchises: 0
Company-owned: 32
Units concentrated in all U.S.

Seeking: All U.S.
Seeking in Canada? Yes
Exclusive territories? No
Homebased option? No
Kiosk option? No
Employees needed to run franchise: 3
Absentee ownership? No

COSTS
Total cost: $155.3K-206.6K
Franchise fee: $38K
Royalty fee: 8%
Term of agreement: 10 years renewable
  at to $19K
Franchisees required to buy multiple
  units? No

FINANCING
In-house: None
3rd-party: Equipment, inventory,
  start-up costs

QUALIFICATIONS
Net worth: $250K
Cash liquidity: $50K
Experience:
  General business experience

TRAINING
At headquarters: 3-1/2 weeks
At various locations: 2-3 days/twice a
  year

BUSINESS SUPPORT
Newsletter
Meetings
Toll-free phone line
Internet
Field operations/evaluations
Purchasing cooperatives

MARKETING SUPPORT
Co-op advertising
Ad slicks
National media campaign

KIDSTAGE

Current financial data not available

P.O. Box 1072
Appleton, WI 54912
Ph: (877)543-1234
Fax: (920)913-1193
www.kidstagefranchise.com
Children's theater program
Began: 1997, Franchising since: 2003
Headquarters size: 2 employees
Franchise department: Info not
   provided

U.S. franchises: 0
Canadian franchises: 0
Other foreign franchises: 0
Company-owned: 2

Seeking: All U.S.
Seeking in Canada? No
Exclusive territories? Yes
Homebased option? Yes
Kiosk option? No
Employees needed to run franchise:
   0-5
Absentee ownership? Yes

COSTS
Total cost: $8.5K-18.5K
Franchise fee: $8.5K
Royalty fee: 6%
Term of agreement: 5 years renewable
   at no charge
Franchisees required to buy multiple
   units? No

FINANCING
No financing available

QUALIFICATIONS
Experience:
   General business experience
   Desire to work with kids

TRAINING
At headquarters: 4 days

BUSINESS SUPPORT
Toll-free phone line
Internet

MARKETING SUPPORT
Info not provided

KIDZART

Financial rating: $$$

1327 Dime Box Cir.
New Braunfels, TX 78130
Ph: (800)379-8302
Fax: (800)379-8302
www.kidzart.us
Drawing program for all ages
Began: 1997, Franchising since: 2002
Headquarters size: 2 employees
Franchise department: 2 employees

U.S. franchises: 19
Canadian franchises: 1
Other foreign franchises: 0
Company-owned: 2
Units concentrated in all U.S. except
   HI, IN, ND, RI, SD, WI

Seeking: All U.S.
Seeking in Canada? Yes
Exclusive territories? Yes
Homebased option? Yes
Kiosk option? No
Employees needed to run franchise:
   1-5
Absentee ownership? No

COSTS
Total cost: $16.6K-22.4K
Franchise fee: $14.9K-16.4K
Royalty fee: 7%
Term of agreement: 10 years renewable
   at no charge
Franchisees required to buy multiple
   units? No

FINANCING
No financing available

QUALIFICATIONS
Net worth: $50K-100K
Cash liquidity: $20K
Experience:
   General business experience
   Marketing skills
   Teaching experience
   Creativity-oriented

TRAINING
At headquarters: 4-5 days
Ongoing

BUSINESS SUPPORT
Meetings
Toll-free phone line
Grand opening
Internet

MARKETING SUPPORT
Regional marketing
PR support

KNOWLEDGEPOINTS

Current financial data not available

12600 S.W. 68th Ave.
Portland, OR 99223
Ph: (866)204-4222
Fax: (503)620-4700
www.knowledgepoints.com
Tutoring in reading, math & study
  skills
Began: 1998, Franchising since: 2000
Headquarters size: 10 employees
Franchise department: 10 employees

U.S. franchises: 100
Canadian franchises: 0
Other foreign franchises: 0
Company-owned: 0
Units concentrated in all U.S.

Seeking: All U.S.
Seeking in Canada? No
Exclusive territories? Yes
Homebased option? Yes
Kiosk option? No
Employees needed to run franchise: 4
Absentee ownership? No

COSTS
Total cost: $175K-201K
Franchise fee: $50K+
Royalty fee: 12.5%
Term of agreement: 10 years renewable
  for $1 cent/person within territory
Franchisees required to buy multiple
  units? Yes

FINANCING
No financing available

QUALIFICATIONS
Net worth: $500K
Cash liquidity: $75K-100K
Experience:
    General business experience
    Marketing skills
    Strong people & relationship-
    building skills

TRAINING
At headquarters: 3 days
Unit manager training: 1 week

BUSINESS SUPPORT
Meetings
Toll-free phone line
Grand opening
Internet
Security/safety procedures
Field operations/evaluations
Purchasing cooperatives

MARKETING SUPPORT
Ad slicks
Direct mail collateral materials
Grand opening support

KUMON MATH & READING CENTERS

Ranked #16 in Entrepreneur Magazine's 2004 Franchise 500

Financial rating: $$$$

300 Frank W. Burr Blvd., 5th Fl.
Teaneck, NJ 07666
Ph: (866)633-0740/(201)928-0444
Fax: (201)928-0044
www.kumon.com
Supplemental education
Began: 1958, Franchising since: 1958
Headquarters size: 400 employees
Franchise department: 12 employees

U.S. franchises: 1,082
Canadian franchises: 322
Other foreign franchises: 22,000
Company-owned: 23
Units concentrated in all U.S.

Seeking: All U.S.
Seeking in Canada? Yes
Exclusive territories? No
Homebased option? No
Kiosk option? No
Employees needed to run franchise:
  2-3
Absentee ownership? No

COSTS
Total cost: $8K-30K
Franchise fee: $1K
Royalty fee: $30+/student/mo.
Term of agreement: 2 years renewable
  at no charge
Franchisees required to buy multiple
  units? No

FINANCING
No financing available

QUALIFICATIONS
Experience:
    General business experience
    Marketing skills
    Good math & reading skills
    Communication skills

TRAINING
At headquarters: Over 3-month period
At franchisee's location: Ongoing
At regional offices

BUSINESS SUPPORT
Newsletter
Meetings
Toll-free phone line
Grand opening
Internet

MARKETING SUPPORT
Co-op advertising
Regional marketing

THE MAD SCIENCE GROUP

Ranked #209 in Entrepreneur Magazine's 2004 Franchise 500   *Financial rating: $$$$*

8360 Bougainville St., #201
Montreal, PQ Canada H4P 2G1
Ph: (800)586-5231
Fax: (514)344-6695
www.madscience.org
Science activities for children
Began: 1985, Franchising since: 1995
Headquarters size: 30 employees
Franchise department: 3 employees

U.S. franchises: 102
Canadian franchises: 21
Other foreign franchises: 33
Company-owned: 0
Units concentrated in all U.S.

Seeking: All U.S.
Seeking in Canada? Yes
Exclusive territories? Yes
Homebased option? Yes
Kiosk option? No
Employees needed to run franchise:
    3-30
Absentee ownership? No

COSTS
Total cost: $36.9K-78.5K
Franchise fee: $10K-23.5K
Royalty fee: 8%
Term of agreement: 25 years renewable
    at no charge
Franchisees required to buy multiple
    units? No

FINANCING
In-house: None
3rd-party: Franchise fee, start-up costs

QUALIFICATIONS
Net worth: $50K
Cash liquidity: $23.5K
Experience:
    Industry experience
    General business experience
    Marketing skills

TRAINING
At headquarters: 5 days
At franchisee's location: 5 days

BUSINESS SUPPORT
Newsletter
Meetings
Toll-free phone line
Internet
Security/safety procedures
Field operations/evaluations

MARKETING SUPPORT
Co-op advertising
Regional marketing

MATHNASIUM LEARNING CENTERS

Financial rating: $$$

468 N. Camden Dr., #200
Beverly Hills, CA 90210
Ph: (310)943-6100
Fax: (310)943-6123
www.mathnasium.com
After-school math-only learning cen-
    ters
Began: 2002, Franchising since: 2003
Headquarters size: 6 employees
Franchise department: 4 employees

U.S. franchises: 0
Canadian franchises: 0
Other foreign franchises: 0
Company-owned: 1

Seeking: All U.S.
Seeking in Canada? Yes
Exclusive territories? No
Homebased option? No
Kiosk option? No
Employees needed to run franchise: 1
Absentee ownership? No

COSTS
Total cost: $27.1K-65.3K
Franchise fee: $3.1K
Royalty fee: Varies
Term of agreement: 3 years renewable
    at no charge
Franchisees required to buy multiple
    units? No

FINANCING
No financing available

QUALIFICATIONS
Cash liquidity: $27.1K
Experience:
    General business experience
    Marketing skills
    Must enjoy math & teaching

TRAINING
At headquarters: 10 days

BUSINESS SUPPORT
Meetings
Toll-free phone line
Internet
Field operations/evaluations

MARKETING SUPPORT
Ad slicks

ODYSSEY ART CENTERS

Current financial data not available

Box 512
Tarrytown, NY 10591
Ph: (914)631-7148
Fax: (914)631-8337
www.odysseyart.com
Art classes
Began: 1974, Franchising since: 1995
Headquarters size: Info not provided
Franchise department: Info not
provided

U.S. franchises: 2
Canadian franchises: 0
Other foreign franchises: 0
Company-owned: 1
Units concentrated in NY

Seeking: All U.S.
Seeking in Canada? No
Exclusive territories? Yes
Homebased option? Yes
Kiosk option? No
Employees needed to run franchise:
0-1
Absentee ownership? Yes

COSTS
Total cost: $28.7K-56.2K
Franchise fee: $24K
Royalty fee: 6%
Term of agreement: Info not provided
Franchisees required to buy multiple
units? No

FINANCING
No financing available

QUALIFICATIONS
Experience:
Artistic & nurturing skills

TRAINING
At headquarters: 2 weeks
At franchisee's location: Periodic visits

BUSINESS SUPPORT
Newsletter
Meetings
Field operations/evaluations

MARKETING SUPPORT
Info not provided

OXFORD LEARNING CENTRES INC.

Current financial data not available

747 Hyde Park Rd., #230
London, ON Canada N6H 3S3
Ph: (888)559-2212
Fax: (519)473-6086
www.oxfordlearning.com
Educational learning centers
Began: 1982, Franchising since: 1989
Headquarters size: 22 employees
Franchise department: 2 employees

U.S. franchises: 10
Canadian franchises: 63
Other foreign franchises: 0
Company-owned: 9
Units concentrated in AZ, DE, NJ, NY,
TX, VA

Seeking: All U.S.
Focusing on: AZ, CA, DE, IL, MD, NJ,
NY, TX, VA
Seeking in Canada? Yes
Exclusive territories? Yes
Homebased option? No
Kiosk option? No
Employees needed to run franchise:
3-10
Absentee ownership? Yes

COSTS
Total cost: $125K-250K
Franchise fee: $39.5K
Royalty fee: 10%
Term of agreement: Info not provided
Franchisees required to buy multiple
units? Yes

FINANCING
No financing available

QUALIFICATIONS
Info not provided

TRAINING
At headquarters: 12 days

BUSINESS SUPPORT
Newsletter
Meetings
Field operations/evaluations
Purchasing cooperatives

MARKETING SUPPORT
Info not provided

SYLVAN LEARNING CENTERS
Ranked #46 in Entrepreneur Magazine's 2004 Franchise 500

Financial rating: $$$$

1001 Fleet St.
Baltimore, MD 21202
Ph: (800)284-8214/(410)843-8000
Fax: (410)843-6265
www.sylvanfranchise.com
Supplemental education
Began: 1979, Franchising since: 1980
Headquarters size: 97 employees
Franchise department: 32 employees

U.S. franchises: 765
Canadian franchises: 83
Other foreign franchises: 3
Company-owned: 129
Units concentrated in all U.S.

Seeking: All U.S.
Seeking in Canada? Yes
Exclusive territories? Yes
Homebased option? No
Kiosk option? No
Employees needed to run franchise:
2-4
Absentee ownership? No

COSTS
Total cost: $142.1K-220.3K
Franchise fee: $38K/46K
Royalty fee: 8-9%
Term of agreement: 10 years renewable
for $1K
Franchisees required to buy multiple
units? No

FINANCING
In-house: None
3rd-party: Accounts receivable, equipment, inventory, start-up costs

QUALIFICATIONS
Net worth: $150K
Cash liquidity: $75K
Experience:
Industry experience
General business experience
Marketing skills
Education background

TRAINING
At headquarters: 1 week
At franchisee's location: During open-
ing
At regional locations: 5 days

BUSINESS SUPPORT
Newsletter
Meetings
Toll-free phone line
Grand opening
Internet
Field operations/evaluations

MARKETING SUPPORT
Co-op advertising
Ad slicks
National media campaign

TUTORING CLUB
Ranked #190 in Entrepreneur Magazine's 2004 Franchise 500

Financial rating: $$$$

6964 Almaden Expy.
San Jose, CA 95120
Ph: (888)674-6425/(925)513-7784
Fax: (925)513-8443
www.tutoringclub.com
Individualized instruction for K-12
students
Began: 1991, Franchising since: 1999
Headquarters size: 10 employees
Franchise department: 7 employees

U.S. franchises: 72
Canadian franchises: 0
Other foreign franchises: 0
Company-owned: 2
Units concentrated in all U.S.

Seeking: All U.S.
Seeking in Canada? No
Exclusive territories? Yes
Homebased option? No
Kiosk option? No
Employees needed to run franchise: 4
Absentee ownership? Yes

COSTS
Total cost: $56.8K-97.9K
Franchise fee: $29.5K
Royalty fee: 10%
Term of agreement: 20 years renewable
at no charge
Franchisees required to buy multiple
units? No

FINANCING
In-house: None
3rd-party: Accounts receivable, equipment, franchise fee, inventory, payroll, start-up costs

QUALIFICATIONS
Info not provided

TRAINING
At headquarters: 1 week
At franchisee's location: 1-4 days
Discovery Bay, CA: 1 week

BUSINESS SUPPORT
Newsletter
Meetings
Toll-free phone line
Grand opening
Internet
Lease negotiations
Security/safety procedures
Field operations/evaluations
Purchasing cooperatives

MARKETING SUPPORT
Co-op advertising
Ad slicks
Regional marketing

THE WHOLE CHILD LEARNING CO.

Current financial data not available

921 Belvin St.
San Marcos, TX 78666
Ph: (888)317-3535/(512)396-2740
Fax: (512)392-7820
www.wholechild.com
Children's enrichment programs
Began: 1996, Franchising since: 1999
Headquarters size: 3 employees
Franchise department: 1 employee

U.S. franchises: 9
Canadian franchises: 0
Other foreign franchises: 0
Company-owned: 8

Seeking: All U.S.
Seeking in Canada? Yes
Exclusive territories? Yes
Homebased option? Yes
Kiosk option? No
Employees needed to run franchise: 1
Absentee ownership? No

COSTS
Total cost: $17.5K
Franchise fee: $17.5K
Royalty fee: 6%
Term of agreement: 5 years renewable
    at no charge
Franchisees required to buy multiple
    units? No

FINANCING
In-house: Franchise fee
3rd-party: None

QUALIFICATIONS
Net worth: $8K
Cash liquidity: $7.5K
Experience:
    Industry experience
    General business experience
    Marketing skills

TRAINING
At headquarters: 3 days
At franchisee's location: 5 days

BUSINESS SUPPORT
Newsletter
Meetings
Toll-free phone line
Grand opening
Internet
Field operations/evaluations

MARKETING SUPPORT
Co-op advertising
Regional marketing

YOUNG REMBRANDTS FRANCHISE INC.

Current financial data not available

23 N. Union St.
Elgin, IL 60123
Ph: (847)742-6966
Fax: (847)742-7197
www.youngrembrandts.com
Art classes for children 3 to 12
Began: 1988, Franchising since: 1997
Headquarters size: Info not provided
Franchise department: Info not pro-
    vided

U.S. franchises: 11
Canadian franchises: 0
Other foreign franchises: 0
Company-owned: 1

Seeking: All U.S.
Seeking in Canada? No
Exclusive territories? Yes
Homebased option? Yes
Kiosk option? No
Employees needed to run franchise:
    2-20
Absentee ownership? No

COSTS
Total cost: $36K-45.5K
Franchise fee: $28.5K
Royalty fee: Varies
Term of agreement: 15 years renewable
    at no charge
Franchisees required to buy multiple
    units? No

FINANCING
No financing available

QUALIFICATIONS
Cash liquidity: $75K
Experience:
    General business experience
    Marketing skills
    Teaching skills
    Art skills
    Experience working with children

TRAINING
At headquarters: 5 days

BUSINESS SUPPORT
Meetings
Toll-free phone line
Internet
Field operations/evaluations

MARKETING SUPPORT
Co-op advertising
Ad slicks
Full marketing package

CHILDREN'S   *Miscellaneous*

BABIES 'N' BELLS INC.

Financial rating: $

4489 Mira Vista Dr.
Frisco, TX 75034
Ph: (888)418-2229
Fax: (469)384-0138
www.babiesnbells.com
Invitations & announcements
Began: 1996, Franchising since: 1997
Headquarters size: 6 employees
Franchise department: 2 employees

U.S. franchises: 59
Canadian franchises: 0
Other foreign franchises: 0
Company-owned: 30
Units concentrated in all U.S.

Seeking: All U.S.
Seeking in Canada? No
Exclusive territories? Yes
Homebased option? Yes
Kiosk option? No
Employees needed to run franchise: 1
Absentee ownership? No

COSTS
Total cost: $16.7K-28.9K
Franchise fee: $9K
Royalty fee: 8%
Term of agreement: 5 years renewable
    for $2K
Franchisees required to buy multiple
    units? No

FINANCING
No financing available

QUALIFICATIONS
Net worth: $15K
Cash liquidity: $15K
Experience:
    General business experience

TRAINING
At headquarters: 1 week

BUSINESS SUPPORT
Newsletter
Meetings
Toll-free phone line
Internet

MARKETING SUPPORT
Co-op advertising
National media campaign

CHILDREN'S ORCHARD
Ranked #435 in Entrepreneur Magazine's 2004 Franchise 500

Financial rating: $$$$

2100 S. Main St., #B
Ann Arbor, MI 48103
Ph: (734)994-9199
Fax: (734)994-9323
www.childrensorchard.com
Children's products resale stores
Began: 1980, Franchising since: 1985
Headquarters size: 8 employees
Franchise department: 1 employee

U.S. franchises: 85
Canadian franchises: 0
Other foreign franchises: 0
Company-owned: 1
Units concentrated in all U.S.

Seeking: All U.S.
Seeking in Canada? Yes
Exclusive territories? Yes
Homebased option? No
Kiosk option? No
Employees needed to run franchise: 2
Absentee ownership? No

COSTS
Total cost: $69.5K-144.95K
Franchise fee: $19.5K
Royalty fee: 5%
Term of agreement: 10 years renewable
    for $3K
Franchisees required to buy multiple
    units? No

FINANCING
In-house: None
3rd-party: Accounts receivable, equip-
    ment, franchise fee, inventory, pay-
    roll, start-up costs

QUALIFICATIONS
Net worth: $100K
Cash liquidity: $30K
Experience:
    Customer service experience

TRAINING
At headquarters: 12 days
At franchisee's location: 4 days

BUSINESS SUPPORT
Newsletter
Meetings
Toll-free phone line
Grand opening
Internet
Lease negotiations
Security/safety procedures
Field operations/evaluations
Purchasing cooperatives

MARKETING SUPPORT
Co-op advertising
Ad slicks
Regional marketing
Monthly promotions

EDUCATIONAL OUTFITTERS

Financial rating: $$$

8002 E. Brainerd Rd.
Chattanooga, TN 37421
Ph: (877)814-1222/(423)894-1222
Fax: (423)894-9222
www.educationaloutfitter.com
School uniforms
Began: 1998, Franchising since: 2001
Headquarters size: 7 employees
Franchise department: 2 employees

U.S. franchises: 6
Canadian franchises: 0
Other foreign franchises: 0
Company-owned: 2
Units concentrated in GA, MN, NC, SC, TN

Seeking: All U.S.
Seeking in Canada? No
Exclusive territories? Yes
Homebased option? No
Kiosk option? No
Employees needed to run franchise: 2
Absentee ownership? No

COSTS
Total cost: $72.2K-172.2K
Franchise fee: $25K
Royalty fee: 5%
Term of agreement: 10 years renewable at no charge
Franchisees required to buy multiple units? No

FINANCING
No financing available

QUALIFICATIONS
Net worth: $300K
Cash liquidity: $75K
Experience:
    General business experience
    Marketing skills

TRAINING
At headquarters: 1 week
At franchisee's location: 1 week

BUSINESS SUPPORT
Newsletter
Meetings
Toll-free phone line
Grand opening
Internet
Field operations/evaluations
Purchasing cooperatives

MARKETING SUPPORT
Co-op advertising
Ad slicks
Regional marketing

KID TO KID

Ranked #483 in Entrepreneur Magazine's 2004 Franchise 500

Financial rating: $$

452 E. 500 South
Salt Lake City, UT 84111
Ph: (888)543-2543/(801)359-0071
Fax: (801)359-3207
www.kidtokid.com
New & used children's & maternity clothing & products
Began: 1992, Franchising since: 1994
Headquarters size: 5 employees
Franchise department: 1 employee

U.S. franchises: 31
Canadian franchises: 0
Other foreign franchises: 1
Company-owned: 6
Units concentrated in all U.S.

Seeking: All U.S.
Seeking in Canada? Yes
Exclusive territories? Yes
Homebased option? No
Kiosk option? No
Employees needed to run franchise: 4
Absentee ownership? No

COSTS
Total cost: $96.8K-127.1K
Franchise fee: $25K
Royalty fee: 5%
Term of agreement: 10 years renewable for 25% of franchise fee
Franchisees required to buy multiple units? Outside the U.S. only

FINANCING
In-house: None
3rd-party: Equipment, franchise fee, inventory, payroll, start-up costs

QUALIFICATIONS
Net worth: $100K
Cash liquidity: $30K-40K
Experience:
    General business experience
    Knowledge of children's products

TRAINING
At headquarters: 11 days
At franchisee's location: 3 days
Other store location: 5 days

BUSINESS SUPPORT
Newsletter
Meetings
Toll-free phone line
Grand opening
Lease negotiations
Security/safety procedures
Field operations/evaluations

MARKETING SUPPORT
Co-op advertising
Ad slicks
Regional marketing
Customized marketing materials

LEARNING EXPRESS

Ranked #464 in Entrepreneur Magazine's 2004 Franchise 500   *Financial rating: $$$$*

29 Buena Vista St.
Ayer, MA 01432
Ph: (978)889-1000
Fax: (978)889-1010
www.learningexpress.com
Specialty toy store
Began: 1987, Franchising since: 1987
Headquarters size: 18 employees
Franchise department: 16 employees

U.S. franchises: 117
Canadian franchises: 0
Other foreign franchises: 0
Company-owned: 0
Units concentrated in all U.S.

Seeking: All U.S.
Seeking in Canada? Yes
Exclusive territories? Yes
Homebased option? No
Kiosk option? No
Employees needed to run franchise:
    8-12
Absentee ownership? No

COSTS
Total cost: $185K-290K
Franchise fee: $30K
Royalty fee: 5%
Term of agreement: 10 years renewable
    for 10% of then current fee
Franchisees required to buy multiple
    units? No

FINANCING
No financing available

QUALIFICATIONS
Net worth: $300K
Cash liquidity: 50% of investment
Experience:
    General business experience
    People skills

TRAINING
At headquarters: 1 week
At franchisee's location: 3 weeks
Ongoing

BUSINESS SUPPORT
Newsletter
Meetings
Toll-free phone line
Grand opening
Internet
Lease negotiations
Field operations/evaluations

MARKETING SUPPORT
Ad slicks
Regional marketing
National catalog

ONCE UPON A CHILD

Ranked #380 in Entrepreneur Magazine's 2004 Franchise 500   *Financial rating: $$$$*

4200 Dahlberg Dr., #100
Minneapolis, MN 55422-4837
Ph: (800)445-1006/(763)520-8490
Fax: (763)520-8501
www.ouac.com
Used/new children's clothing, equip-
    ment, furniture & toys
Began: 1984, Franchising since: 1992
Headquarters size: 100 employees
Franchise department: 5 employees

U.S. franchises: 198
Canadian franchises: 18
Other foreign franchises: 0
Company-owned: 1
Units concentrated in AK, AR, AZ, CA,
    CO, CT, DE, FL, GA, IA, ID, IL, IN,
    KS, KY, MD, MI, MN, MO, MS,
    NC, ND, NE, NV, NY, OH, OR, PA,
    SC, SD, TN, TX, VA, VT, WA, WI,
    WV, WY

Seeking: All U.S.
Seeking in Canada? Yes
Exclusive territories? Yes

Homebased option? No
Kiosk option? No
Employees needed to run franchise: 7
Absentee ownership? No

COSTS
Total cost: $133.9K-218.1K
Franchise fee: $20K
Royalty fee: 5%
Term of agreement: 10 years renewable
    for $5K
Franchisees required to buy multiple
    units? No

FINANCING
No financing available

QUALIFICATIONS
Net worth: $200K
Cash liquidity: $40K-60K
Experience:
    General business experience
    Marketing skills

TRAINING
At headquarters: 2 weeks

BUSINESS SUPPORT
Newsletter
Meetings
Toll-free phone line
Grand opening
Internet
Lease negotiations
Security/safety procedures
Field operations/evaluations
Purchasing cooperatives

MARKETING SUPPORT
Co-op advertising
Ad slicks

PUMP IT UP

Financial rating: $$

1233 Quarry Ln., #100
Pleasanton, CA 94588
Ph: (925)249-2273
Fax: (925)249-0375
www.pumpitupparty.com
Children's party facilities
Began: 2000, Franchising since: 2001
Headquarters size: 10 employees
Franchise department: 10 employees

U.S. franchises: 6
Canadian franchises: 0
Other foreign franchises: 0
Company-owned: 1

Seeking: All U.S.
Seeking in Canada? No
Exclusive territories? Yes
Homebased option? No
Kiosk option? No
Employees needed to run franchise: 20
Absentee ownership? Yes

COSTS
Total cost: $164.5K-259K
Franchise fee: $25K
Royalty fee: 6%
Term of agreement: 10 years renewable
   for 25% of franchise fee
Franchisees required to buy multiple
   units? No

FINANCING
In-house: Inventory
3rd-party: Available

QUALIFICATIONS
Net worth: $300K
Cash liquidity: $70K
Experience:
   Must love children

TRAINING
At headquarters: 1 week
At franchisee's location: 2 days

BUSINESS SUPPORT
Newsletter
Meetings
Toll-free phone line
Grand opening
Internet
Lease negotiations
Security/safety procedures
Field operations/evaluations
Purchasing cooperatives

MARKETING SUPPORT
Co-op advertising
Ad slicks

STORK NEWS OF AMERICA INC.

Current financial data not available

1305 Hope Mills Rd., #A
Fayetteville, NC 28304
Ph: (800)633-6395/(910)426-1357
Fax: (910)426-2473
www.storknews.com
Newborn announcement services &
   products
Began: 1983, Franchising since: 1984
Headquarters size: 10 employees
Franchise department: 3 employees

U.S. franchises: 130
Canadian franchises: 0
Other foreign franchises: 0
Company-owned: 1
Units concentrated in all U.S.

Seeking: All U.S.
Seeking in Canada? Yes
Exclusive territories? Yes
Homebased option? Yes
Kiosk option? No
Employees needed to run franchise: 1
Absentee ownership? Yes

COSTS
Total cost: $10K-18K
Franchise fee: $5K-10K
Royalty fee: $500-1.5K/yr.
Term of agreement: Info not provided
Franchisees required to buy multiple
   units? No

FINANCING
In-house: None
3rd-party: Accounts receivable, equip-
   ment, franchise fee, inventory, pay-
   roll, start-up costs

QUALIFICATIONS
Cash liquidity: $3K
Experience:
   General business experience
   Marketing skills

TRAINING
At headquarters: 2 days
At franchisee's location: 3-5 days

BUSINESS SUPPORT
Newsletter
Toll-free phone line
Field operations/evaluations

MARKETING SUPPORT
National media campaign

USA BABY

Ranked #348 in Entrepreneur Magazine's 2004 Franchise 500

Financial rating: $$$

857 N. Larch Ave.
Elmhurst, IL 60126
Ph: (630)832-9880
Fax: (630)832-0139
www.usababy.com
Baby/children's furniture & accessories
Began: 1975, Franchising since: 1986
Headquarters size: 15 employees
Franchise department: 3 employees

U.S. franchises: 63
Canadian franchises: 0
Other foreign franchises: 3
Company-owned: 0
Units concentrated in all U.S.

Seeking: All U.S.
Seeking in Canada? Yes
Exclusive territories? Yes
Homebased option? No
Kiosk option? No
Employees needed to run franchise: 8
Absentee ownership? No

COSTS
Total cost: $344K-650K
Franchise fee: $23.4K-60.2K
Royalty fee: 3%
Term of agreement: 10 years renewable
    at no charge
Franchisees required to buy multiple
    units? No

FINANCING
In-house: None
3rd-party: Equipment, franchise fee,
    inventory, start-up costs

QUALIFICATIONS
Net worth: $175K
Cash liquidity: $145K
Experience:
    General business experience

TRAINING
At headquarters: 14 days
At franchisee's location: 10 days

BUSINESS SUPPORT
Newsletter
Meetings
Toll-free phone line
Grand opening
Internet
Lease negotiations
Security/safety procedures
Field operations/evaluations
Purchasing cooperatives

MARKETING SUPPORT
Ad slicks
Regional marketing
Direct mail

CHILDREN'S — Other Franchises

CHIP - THE REMARKABLE CHILD I.D. PROGRAM
15300 Devonshire St., #4
Mission Hills, CA 91345
Ph: (818)894-4784
www.4childid.com
Child identification & school safety
    program

CREATIVE PLAYTHINGS
33 Loring Dr.
Framingham, MA 01702
Ph: (800)444-0901
www.creativeplaythings.com
Residential wooden swingsets

HEAD OVER HEELS FRANCHISE SYSTEM INC.
280 Snow Dr., #2
Homewood, AL 35209
Ph: (800)850-3547/(205)940-3547
Children's gymnastics & motor-skills
    development system

WEBBY DANCE COMPANY
7275-C Dixie Hwy.
Fairfield, OH 45014
Ph: (513)942-0100
www.webbydancecompany.com
On-site children's dance program

WOODPLAY
2101 Harrod St.
Raleigh, NC 27604
Ph: (800)966-3752
www.woodplay.com
Residential playground equipment

Financial Services

FINANCIAL *Business Services*

CFO TODAY
Ranked #281 in Entrepreneur Magazine's 2004 Franchise 500

Financial rating: $$

401 St. Francis St.
Tallahassee, FL 32301
Ph: (888)643-1348/(850)681-1941
Fax: (850)561-1374
www.cfotoday.com
Accounting, tax & financial services
Began: 1989, Franchising since: 1990
Headquarters size: 8 employees
Franchise department: 8 employees

U.S. franchises: 244
Canadian franchises: 2
Other foreign franchises: 0
Company-owned: 1
Units concentrated in all U.S.

Seeking: All U.S.
Seeking in Canada? Yes
Exclusive territories? Yes
Homebased option? Yes
Kiosk option? No
Employees needed to run franchise: 1
Absentee ownership? Yes

COSTS
Total cost: $24.4K-40K
Franchise fee: $24K
Royalty fee: Varies
Term of agreement: 10 years renewable
   for $4.8K
Franchisees required to buy multiple
   units? No

FINANCING
In-house: Franchise fee
3rd-party: None

QUALIFICATIONS
Experience:
   General business experience

TRAINING
At headquarters: 5 days
At franchisee's location: 1 day

BUSINESS SUPPORT
Newsletter
Meetings
Toll-free phone line
Internet
Field operations/evaluations
Purchasing cooperatives

MARKETING SUPPORT
Co-op advertising
Ad slicks
National media campaign
Regional marketing

COMMISSION EXPRESS

Ranked #452 in Entrepreneur Magazine's 2004 Franchise 500

Financial rating: $

8306 Professional Hill Dr.
Fairfax, VA 22031
Ph: (703)560-5500
Fax: (703)560-5502
www.commissionexpress.com
Real estate commission factoring
Began: 1992, Franchising since: 1996
Headquarters size: 4 employees
Franchise department: 3 employees

U.S. franchises: 50
Canadian franchises: 0
Other foreign franchises: 0
Company-owned: 1
Units concentrated in CA, FL, IL, MD, TX, VA

Seeking: All U.S.
Focusing on: KS, MD, UT, WI
Seeking in Canada? No
Exclusive territories? Yes
Homebased option? No
Kiosk option? No
Employees needed to run franchise: 1
Absentee ownership? No

COSTS
Total cost: $85.3K-172.5K
Franchise fee: $10K-40K
Royalty fee: Varies
Term of agreement: 10 years renewable
Franchisees required to buy multiple units? No

FINANCING
In-house: Franchise fee
3rd-party: None

QUALIFICATIONS
Cash liquidity: $85.3K-172.5K
Experience:
　General business experience

TRAINING
At headquarters: 1 week

BUSINESS SUPPORT
Newsletter
Meetings
Toll-free phone line
Internet
Field operations/evaluations

MARKETING SUPPORT
Co-op advertising
Ad slicks
National media campaign
Regional marketing
Trade shows

FIDUCIAL INC.

Ranked #67 in Entrepreneur Magazine's 2004 Franchise 500

Financial rating: $$$$

10480 Little Patuxent Pkwy., 3rd Fl.
Columbia, MD 21044
Ph: (800)323-9000
Fax: (410)910-5903
www.fiducial.com
Tax, accounting, payroll & financial services
Began: 1999, Franchising since: 1999
Headquarters size: 70 employees
Franchise department: 13 employees

U.S. franchises: 673
Canadian franchises: 0
Other foreign franchises: 0
Company-owned: 26
Units concentrated in all U.S. except AR, ND

Seeking: All U.S.
Seeking in Canada? No
Exclusive territories? No
Homebased option? No
Kiosk option? No
Employees needed to run franchise: 1-4
Absentee ownership? No

COSTS
Total cost: $44.4K-115.6K
Franchise fee: $12.5K-25K
Royalty fee: 1.5-6%
Term of agreement: 10 years renewable for $5K
Franchisees required to buy multiple units? No

FINANCING
No financing available

QUALIFICATIONS
Net worth: $150K
Cash liquidity: $25K-75K
Experience:
　Industry experience
　General business experience
　Marketing skills

TRAINING
At headquarters: 10 days
At franchisee's location: 2-3 days
At existing location: 5 days

BUSINESS SUPPORT
Newsletter
Meetings
Toll-free phone line
Grand opening
Internet
Field operations/evaluations
Purchasing cooperatives

MARKETING SUPPORT
Co-op advertising
Ad slicks
National media campaign
Regional marketing
Telemarketing
National accounts

INTERFACE FINANCIAL CORP.

Ranked #441 in Entrepreneur Magazine's 2004 Franchise 500　　　　*Financial rating: $$*

2182 Dupont Dr., #221
Irvine, CA 92612-1320
Ph: (800)387-0860
Fax: (866)475-8688
www.interfacefinancial.com
Invoice discounting
Began: 1971, Franchising since: 1991
Headquarters size: 7 employees
Franchise department: 5 employees

U.S. franchises: 62
Canadian franchises: 48
Other foreign franchises: 0
Company-owned: 2
Units concentrated in all U.S.

Seeking: All U.S.
Seeking in Canada? Yes
Exclusive territories? No
Homebased option? Yes
Kiosk option? No
Employees needed to run franchise: 0
Absentee ownership? No

COSTS
Total cost: $77.1K-128.3K
Franchise fee: $25K
Royalty fee: 0.8%
Term of agreement: 10 years renewable
　　at no charge
Franchisees required to buy multiple
　　units? Outside the U.S. only

FINANCING
No financing available

QUALIFICATIONS
Net worth: $250K
Cash liquidity: $75K
Experience:
　　General business experience

TRAINING
At franchisee's location: 3-5 days

BUSINESS SUPPORT
Newsletter
Toll-free phone line
Internet
Field operations/evaluations

MARKETING SUPPORT
Co-op advertising
Ad slicks
Telemarketing

PADGETT BUSINESS SERVICES USA INC.

Ranked #272 in Entrepreneur Magazine's 2004 Franchise 500　　　　*Financial rating: $$$*

160 Hawthorne Pk.
Athens, GA 30606
Ph: (800)323-7292/(706)548-1040
Fax: (800)548-1040
www.smallbizpros.com
Financial, payroll, consulting & tax
　　services
Began: 1965, Franchising since: 1975
Headquarters size: 45 employees
Franchise department: 3 employees

U.S. franchises: 278
Canadian franchises: 91
Other foreign franchises: 0
Company-owned: 1
Units concentrated in all U.S.

Seeking: All U.S.
Seeking in Canada? Yes
Exclusive territories? No
Homebased option? Yes
Kiosk option? No
Employees needed to run franchise: 1
Absentee ownership? No

COSTS
Total cost: $53K-54.5K
Franchise fee: $25K
Royalty fee: 4.5-9%
Term of agreement: 20 years renewable
　　for 5% of then-current fee
Franchisees required to buy multiple
　　units? No

FINANCING
In-house: None
3rd-party: Franchise fee, start-up costs

QUALIFICATIONS
Net worth: $50K
Cash liquidity: $20K
Experience:
　　Industry experience

TRAINING
At headquarters: 10 days
At franchisee's location: 6 days
At annual marketing convention & tax
　　seminar

BUSINESS SUPPORT
Newsletter
Meetings
Toll-free phone line
Internet
Purchasing cooperatives

MARKETING SUPPORT
Ad slicks
Marketing materials

PAID INC.

Current financial data not available

4800 W. Waco Dr., #100
Waco, TX 76710
Ph: (254)772-8131
Fax: (254)772-4642
www.paidinc.com
Electronic payments & E-commerce
    financial services
Began: 1998, Franchising since: 1999
Headquarters size: 4 employees
Franchise department: 4 employees

U.S. franchises: 17
Canadian franchises: 0
Other foreign franchises: 0
Company-owned: 0
Units concentrated in all U.S.

Seeking: All U.S.
Seeking in Canada? No
Exclusive territories? Yes
Homebased option? Yes
Kiosk option? No
Employees needed to run franchise: 0
Absentee ownership? Yes

COSTS
Total cost: $24.5K
Franchise fee: $24.5K
Royalty fee: 0
Term of agreement: 15 years renewable
    for $2.5K
Franchisees required to buy multiple
    units? No

FINANCING
No financing available

QUALIFICATIONS
Net worth: $100K+
Cash liquidity: $50K
Experience:
    General business experience
    Marketing skills

TRAINING
At headquarters: 3 days

BUSINESS SUPPORT
Toll-free phone line
Field operations/evaluations

MARKETING SUPPORT
Ad slicks
Onsite sales help

FINANCIAL ▶ *Check Cashing*

ACE AMERICA'S CASH EXPRESS
Ranked #59 in Entrepreneur Magazine's 2004 Franchise 500   *Financial rating: $$$*

1231 Greenway Dr., #600
Irving, TX 75038
Ph: (800)713-3338
Fax: (972)582-1409
www.acecashexpress.com
Check cashing & related financial
    services
Began: 1968, Franchising since: 1996
Headquarters size: 240 employees
Franchise department: 9 employees

U.S. franchises: 200
Canadian franchises: 0
Other foreign franchises: 0
Company-owned: 968

Seeking: All U.S.
Seeking in Canada? Yes
Exclusive territories? Yes
Homebased option? No
Kiosk option? Yes
Employees needed to run franchise: 2
Absentee ownership? Yes

COSTS
Total cost: $118.2K-259.1K
Franchise fee: $15K-30K
Royalty fee: 6%
Term of agreement: 10 years renewable
    for $500
Franchisees required to buy multiple
    units? No

FINANCING
In-house: None
3rd-party: Equipment, inventory,
    start-up costs

QUALIFICATIONS
Net worth: $150K
Cash liquidity: $80K
Experience:
    General business experience

TRAINING
At headquarters: 2 weeks
At franchisee's location: 5 days

BUSINESS SUPPORT
Newsletter
Meetings
Toll-free phone line
Grand opening
Internet
Security/safety procedures
Field operations/evaluations
Purchasing cooperatives

MARKETING SUPPORT
Co-op advertising
Ad slicks

CASH NOW

Current financial data not available

3100 Steeles Ave. E., #201
Toronto, ON Canada L3R 8T9
Ph: (866)778-2996
Fax: (905)470-0084
www.cashnow-usa.com
Payday-based loan services & check
    cashing
Began: 1999, Franchising since: 2001
Headquarters size: 20 employees
Franchise department: 6 employees

U.S. franchises: 50
Canadian franchises: 41
Other foreign franchises: 10
Company-owned: 2
Units concentrated in all U.S.

Seeking: All U.S.
Seeking in Canada? Yes
Exclusive territories? Yes
Homebased option? Yes
Kiosk option? Yes
Employees needed to run franchise:
    1-2
Absentee ownership? Yes

COSTS
Total cost: $120.1K-363.5K
Kiosk cost: $15K
Franchise fee: $34.5K
Royalty fee: 5%
Term of agreement: 5 years renewable
    at no charge
Franchisees required to buy multiple
    units? No

FINANCING
In-house: None
3rd-party: Accounts receivable, equip-
    ment, franchise fee, inventory, pay-
    roll, start-up costs

QUALIFICATIONS
Net worth: $80K
Cash liquidity: $60K
Experience:
    General business experience

TRAINING

At headquarters: 3 days
Ongoing online assistance

BUSINESS SUPPORT
Newsletter
Meetings
Toll-free phone line
Grand opening
Internet
Security/safety procedures
Field operations/evaluations
Purchasing cooperatives

MARKETING SUPPORT
Co-op advertising
Ad slicks
National media campaign
Regional marketing

CASH PLUS INC.
Ranked #318 in Entrepreneur Magazine's 2004 Franchise 500

Financial rating: $$$

3002 Dow Ave., #120
Tustin, CA 92780
Ph: (888)707-2274/(714)731-2274
Fax: (714)731-2099
www.cashplusinc.com
Check cashing & related services
Began: 1985, Franchising since: 1988
Headquarters size: 8 employees
Franchise department: 3 employees

U.S. franchises: 68
Canadian franchises: 1
Other foreign franchises: 0
Company-owned: 3
Units concentrated in CA, FL, LA,
    MD, MI, NV, TX, WA

Seeking: Midwest, South, Southeast,
    Southwest, West
Focusing on: CO, OH, VA
Seeking in Canada? Yes
Exclusive territories? Yes
Homebased option? No
Kiosk option? No
Employees needed to run franchise: 3
Absentee ownership? Yes

COSTS
Total cost: $123.7K-200.7K
Franchise fee: $22.5K
Royalty fee: 5-6%
Term of agreement: 10 years renewable
    for $2K
Franchisees required to buy multiple
    units? No

FINANCING
In-house: None
3rd-party: Accounts receivable, equip-
    ment, inventory, start-up costs

QUALIFICATIONS
Net worth: $250K
Cash liquidity: $60K
Experience:
    General business experience
    People skills
    Employee supervisory experience

TRAINING
At headquarters: 1 week
At franchisee's location: 1 week
Additional training: 90 days

BUSINESS SUPPORT
Newsletter
Meetings
Toll-free phone line
Grand opening
Internet
Lease negotiations
Security/safety procedures
Field operations/evaluations
Purchasing cooperatives

MARKETING SUPPORT
Co-op advertising
Ad slicks
National media campaign
National sweepstakes

UNICASH FINANCIAL CENTRES

Ranked #496 in Entrepreneur Magazine's 2004 Franchise 500   *Financial rating: $$$*

5075 Yonge St., #401
Toronto, ON Canada M2N 6C6
Ph: (416)250-8661
Fax: (416)250-1078
www.unicash.com
Check cashing & related services
Began: 1992, Franchising since: 1998
Headquarters size: 10 employees
Franchise department: 3 employees

U.S. franchises: 0
Canadian franchises: 14
Other foreign franchises: 0
Company-owned: 7
Units concentrated in ON

Not available in the U.S.
Seeking in Canada? Yes
Exclusive territories? Yes
Homebased option? No
Kiosk option? No
Employees needed to run franchise: 2
Absentee ownership? No

COSTS
Total cost: $110K-150K
Franchise fee: $25K
Royalty fee: 5%
Term of agreement: 10 years renewable
    for $12.5K Canadian
Franchisees required to buy multiple
    units? No

FINANCING
In-house: None
3rd-party: Equipment, inventory

QUALIFICATIONS
Net worth: $300K
Cash liquidity: $100K
Experience:
    General business experience

TRAINING
At headquarters: 1 week
At franchisee's location: 1 week

BUSINESS SUPPORT
Meetings
Grand opening
Internet
Lease negotiations
Security/safety procedures
Field operations/evaluations
Purchasing cooperatives

MARKETING SUPPORT
Co-op advertising

UNITED FINANCIAL SERVICES GROUP

Ranked #130 in Entrepreneur Magazine's 2004 Franchise 500   *Financial rating: $$$$*

400 Market St., #1030
Philadelphia, PA 19106
Ph: (800)626-0787
Fax: (215)238-9056
www.unitedfsg.com
Financial services
Began: 1977, Franchising since: 1991
Headquarters size: 20 employees
Franchise department: 20 employees

U.S. franchises: 122
Canadian franchises: 0
Other foreign franchises: 0
Company-owned: 3
Units concentrated in NJ, PA

Seeking: All U.S.
Seeking in Canada? No
Exclusive territories? Yes
Homebased option? No
Kiosk option? No
Employees needed to run franchise: 2
Absentee ownership? Yes

COSTS
Total cost: $194.7K
Franchise fee: $27.5K
Royalty fee: 0.2%
Term of agreement: 15 years renewable
    for 25% of then-current fee
Franchisees required to buy multiple
    units? No

FINANCING
In-house: Accounts receivable, inven-
    tory, payroll
3rd-party: Equipment, franchise fee,
    start-up costs

QUALIFICATIONS
Net worth: $200K
Cash liquidity: $75K

TRAINING
At headquarters: 1-1/2 weeks
At franchisee's location: 1 week

BUSINESS SUPPORT
Newsletter
Meetings
Toll-free phone line
Grand opening
Internet
Lease negotiations
Security/safety procedures
Field operations/evaluations

MARKETING SUPPORT
Co-op advertising
Ad slicks
Regional marketing

FINANCIAL ▶ *Tax Services*

BLACK AMERICAN INCOME TAX SERVICE

Current financial data not available

4650 S. Hampton, #122
Dallas, TX 75232
Ph: (888)289-2831
Fax: (214)333-1411
www.americantaxandfinancialgroup.
    com
Tax preparation & electronic filing
    services
Began: 1997, Franchising since: 2003
Headquarters size: 3 employees
Franchise department: 3 employees

U.S. franchises: 0
Canadian franchises: 0
Other foreign franchises: 0
Company-owned: 1

Seeking: All U.S.
Seeking in Canada? No
Exclusive territories? Yes
Homebased option? No
Kiosk option? No
Employees needed to run franchise: 4
Absentee ownership? Yes

COSTS
Total cost: $33.6K-43K
Franchise fee: $20K
Royalty fee: 15%
Term of agreement: 5 years renewable
    for $2.5K
Franchisees required to buy multiple
    units? No

FINANCING
In-house: Franchise fee
3rd-party: None

QUALIFICATIONS
Net worth: $40K
Cash liquidity: $40K
Experience:
    Strong commitment to customer
    service

TRAINING
At headquarters: 5 days

BUSINESS SUPPORT
Toll-free phone line
Grand opening
Internet
Security/safety procedures
Field operations/evaluations

MARKETING SUPPORT
Ad slicks
Regional marketing

ECONOTAX

Ranked #345 in Entrepreneur Magazine's 2004 Franchise 500

Financial rating: $$$

5846 Ridgewood Rd., #B-101,
Box 13829
Jackson, MS 39236
Ph: (800)748-9106/(601)956-0500
Fax: (601)956-0583
www.econotax.com
Tax services
Began: 1965, Franchising since: 1968
Headquarters size: 6 employees
Franchise department: 6 employees

U.S. franchises: 61
Canadian franchises: 0
Other foreign franchises: 1
Company-owned: 0
Units concentrated in AL, FL, KS, LA,
    MA, MS, WA

Seeking: All U.S.
Seeking in Canada? No
Exclusive territories? Yes
Homebased option? No
Kiosk option? No
Employees needed to run franchise: 3
Absentee ownership? No

COSTS
Total cost: $15.4K-33K
Franchise fee: $10K
Royalty fee: 15%
Term of agreement: 5 years renewable
    at no charge
Franchisees required to buy multiple
    units? No

FINANCING
In-house: Franchise fee
3rd-party: None

QUALIFICATIONS
Experience:
    Customer service experience
    Computer skills

TRAINING
At headquarters: 1 week
Continuing education seminars

BUSINESS SUPPORT
Meetings
Toll-free phone line
Internet

MARKETING SUPPORT
Co-op advertising
Ad slicks
Regional marketing

ELECTRONIC TAX FILERS

Current financial data not available

P.O. Box 2077
Cary, NC 27512-2077
Ph: (919)469-0651
Fax: (919)460-5935
www.electronictaxfilers.com
Electronic filing of financial data
Began: 1990, Franchising since: 1991
Headquarters size: Info not provided
Franchise department: Info not provided

U.S. franchises: 42
Canadian franchises: 0
Other foreign franchises: 0
Company-owned: 2
Units concentrated in all U.S.

Seeking: All U.S.
Seeking in Canada? No
Exclusive territories? Yes
Homebased option? No
Kiosk option? Info not provided
Employees needed to run franchise:
    2-3
Absentee ownership? No

COSTS
Total cost: $22K
Franchise fee: $9K
Royalty fee: 8%
Term of agreement: 3 years renewable
    for $15K
Franchisees required to buy multiple
    units? No

FINANCING
No financing available

QUALIFICATIONS
Net worth: $25K
Cash liquidity: $20K
Experience:
    General business experience

TRAINING
At headquarters: 1 week +
At franchisee's location: Varies

BUSINESS SUPPORT
Meetings
Toll-free phone line
Grand opening
Lease negotiations
Security/safety procedures
Field operations/evaluations
Purchasing cooperatives

MARKETING SUPPORT
Co-op advertising
Ad slicks
Regional marketing

EXPRESS TAX

Ranked #487 in Entrepreneur Magazine's 2004 Franchise 500

Financial rating: $$$

3412 Kori Rd.
Jacksonville, FL 32257
Ph: (888)417-4461
Fax: (904)262-2864
www.expresstaxservice.com
Tax preparation & electronic-filing
    services
Began: 1997, Franchising since: 2002
Headquarters size: 8 employees
Franchise department: 3 employees

U.S. franchises: 145
Canadian franchises: 0
Other foreign franchises: 0
Company-owned: 1
Units concentrated in CA, CO, FL, GA,
    IL, KY, MI, NE, TX, WA

Seeking: All U.S.
Seeking in Canada? No
Exclusive territories? Yes
Homebased option? No
Kiosk option? Yes
Employees needed to run franchise: 2
Absentee ownership? No

COSTS
Total cost: $9.4K-16.1K
Kiosk cost: Same as total cost
Franchise fee: $4.5K
Royalty fee: $12/return
Term of agreement: 10 years renewable
    for $1K
Franchisees required to buy multiple
    units? No

FINANCING
No financing available

QUALIFICATIONS
Cash liquidity: $9.4K-16.1K
Experience:
    General business experience
    Marketing skills

TRAINING
At headquarters: 3 days
Annual conference: 2 days

BUSINESS SUPPORT
Newsletter
Meetings
Toll-free phone line
Internet

MARKETING SUPPORT
Co-op advertising
Ad slicks
Regional marketing

JACKSON HEWITT TAX SERVICE

Ranked #5 in Entrepreneur Magazine's 2004 Franchise 500   *Financial rating: $$$$*

7 Sylvan Way
Parsippany, NJ 07054
Ph: (800)475-2904
Fax: (973)496-2760
www.jacksonhewitt.com
Tax preparation services
Began: 1960, Franchising since: 1986
Headquarters size: 322 employees
Franchise department: 19 employees

U.S. franchises: 3,709
Canadian franchises: 0
Other foreign franchises: 0
Company-owned: 516
Units concentrated in all U.S.

Seeking: All U.S.
Seeking in Canada? No
Exclusive territories? Yes
Homebased option? No
Kiosk option? Yes
Employees needed to run franchise:
    Info not provided
Absentee ownership? Yes

COSTS
Total cost: $47.4K-75.2K
Kiosk cost: $2.5K-4K
Franchise fee: $25K
Royalty fee: 15%
Term of agreement: 10 years renewable
    at no charge
Franchisees required to buy multiple
    units? No

FINANCING
In-house: Franchise fee
3rd-party: Equipment, franchise fee,
    inventory, start-up costs

QUALIFICATIONS
Net worth: $100K-200K
Cash liquidity: $50K

TRAINING
At headquarters: 5 days
Regional training: 2 days

BUSINESS SUPPORT
Newsletter
Meetings
Toll-free phone line
Grand opening
Internet
Security/safety procedures
Field operations/evaluations
Purchasing cooperatives

MARKETING SUPPORT
Co-op advertising
Ad slicks
National media campaign
Regional marketing
800 locator number, Web site
Web site

LIBERTY TAX SERVICE

Ranked #28 in Entrepreneur Magazine's 2004 Franchise 500   *Financial rating: $$$$*

4575 Bonney Rd.
Virginia Beach, VA 23462
Ph: (800)790-3863/(757)493-8855
Fax: (757)493-0694
www.libertytax.com
Income-tax preparation services
Began: 1972, Franchising since: 1973
Headquarters size: 100 employees
Franchise department: 15 employees

U.S. franchises: 727
Canadian franchises: 257
Other foreign franchises: 0
Company-owned: 13
Units concentrated in CA, FL, GA, IL,
    NC, VA

Seeking: All U.S.
Seeking in Canada? Yes
Exclusive territories? Yes
Homebased option? No
Kiosk option? Yes
Employees needed to run franchise:
    5-10
Absentee ownership? Yes

COSTS
Total cost: $38.1K-49.1K
Kiosk cost: $30K-35K
Franchise fee: $25K
Royalty fee: Varies
Term of agreement: Perpetual renew-
    able at no charge
Franchisees required to buy multiple
    units? No

FINANCING
In-house: Equipment, franchise fee,
    payroll, start-up costs
3rd-party: Equipment, franchise fee,
    payroll, start-up costs

QUALIFICATIONS
Cash liquidity: $50K
Experience:
    General business experience
    Marketing skills
    Customer service experience

TRAINING
At headquarters: 1 week
At franchisee's location: 1 day
In various cities: 2 days

BUSINESS SUPPORT
Newsletter
Meetings
Toll-free phone line
Grand opening
Internet
Lease negotiations
Field operations/evaluations
Purchasing cooperatives

MARKETING SUPPORT
Co-op advertising
Ad slicks
Regional marketing
Local marketing plans

FINANCIAL *Miscellaneous*

ACFN

Financial rating: $$$

96 N. 3rd St., #680
San Jose, CA 95112
Ph: (888)794-2236
Fax: (888)708-8600
www.acfnfranchised.com
ATM machines
Began: 1986, Franchising since: 2003
Headquarters size: 12 employees
Franchise department: 6 employees

U.S. franchises: 1
Canadian franchises: 0
Other foreign franchises: 0
Company-owned: 1
Units concentrated in CA, FL, NJ

Seeking: All U.S.
Seeking in Canada? No
Exclusive territories? Info not provided
Homebased option? Yes
Kiosk option? No
Employees needed to run franchise: 1
Absentee ownership? Yes

COSTS
Total cost: $71.2K
Franchise fee: $29K
Royalty fee: 0
Term of agreement: 10 years renewable
for $5K
Franchisees required to buy multiple
units? No

FINANCING
No financing available

QUALIFICATIONS
Info not provided

TRAINING
At headquarters: 1 week

BUSINESS SUPPORT
Newsletter
Meetings
Toll-free phone line
Internet

MARKETING SUPPORT
Co-op advertising
Ad slicks
Market research

ACS INT'L.

Ranked #486 in Entrepreneur Magazine's 2004 Franchise 500

Financial rating: $$

41743 Enterprise Cir. N., #204
Temecula, CA 92590
Ph: (909)694-9394
Fax: (909)694-4300
www.acscorp.us
Accounts-receivable management
services
Began: 1984; Franchising since: 2000
Headquarters size: 40 employees
Franchise department: 4 employees

U.S. franchises: 15
Canadian franchises: 0
Other foreign franchises: 0
Company-owned: 0
Units concentrated in CA, FL

Seeking: All U.S.
Seeking in Canada? Yes
Exclusive territories? Yes
Homebased option? Yes
Kiosk option? No
Employees need to run franchise: 0
Absentee ownership: No

COSTS
Total cost: $38.4K-43.8K
Franchise fee: $35K
Royalty fee: 10%
Term of agreement: 10 years renewable
for 1/3 of current franchise fee
Franchisees required to buy multiple
units? No

FINANCING
No financing available

QUALIFICATIONS
Experience:
General business experience
Mid-level management skills for
outside B2B sales

TRAINING
At headquarters: 1 week
As needed

BUSINESS SUPPORT
Newsletter
Meetings
Toll-free phone line
Internet
Security/safety procedures

MARKETING SUPPORT
Co-op advertising
In-house print shop

BROOKE FRANCHISE CORP.
Ranked #136 in Entrepreneur Magazine's 2004 Franchise 500

Financial rating: $$$

10950 Grandview Dr., Bldg. 34, 6th Fl.
Overland Park, KS 66210
Ph: (800)642-1872
Fax: (888)292-4196
www.brookecorp.com
Insurance & financial services
Began: 1986, Franchising since: 1988
Headquarters size: 200 employees
Franchise department: 150 employees

U.S. franchises: 206
Canadian franchises: 0
Other foreign franchises: 0
Company-owned: 1
Units concentrated in AZ, CO, FL, KS, MO, TX

Seeking: Midwest, South, Southeast, Southwest, West
Focusing on: AZ, CA, CO, FL, GA, IA, IL, KS, LA, MS, NE, NM, NV, OK, TN, TX
Seeking in Canada? No
Exclusive territories? No
Homebased option? No
Kiosk option? No

Employees needed to run franchise: Info not provided
Absentee ownership? Yes

COSTS
Total cost: $25.9K-47.1K
Franchise fee: $25K
Royalty fee: 15%
Term of agreement: 5 years renewable at no charge
Franchisees required to buy multiple units? Yes

FINANCING
In-house: Accounts receivable, franchise fee, equipment, inventory, payroll, start-up costs
3rd-party: None

QUALIFICATIONS
Experience:
    Industry experience
    General business experience
    Marketing skills

TRAINING
At headquarters: 24 hours
At franchisee's location: 30 hours

BUSINESS SUPPORT
Meetings
Security/safety procedures
Field operations/evaluations
Purchasing cooperatives

MARKETING SUPPORT
Co-op advertising
Ad slicks
Regional marketing

CAPITAL BONDING

Financial rating: $$$

525 Penn St.
Reading, PA 19601
Ph: (610)372-8811, Fax: (610)372-4076
www.capitalbonding.com
Retail bail bonds
Began: 1988, Franchising since: 2001
Headquarters size: 75 employees
Franchise department: 2 employees

U.S. franchises: 9
Canadian franchises: 0
Other foreign franchises: 0
Company-owned: 19
Units concentrated in FL, GA, NC

Seeking: All U.S.
Focusing on: AL, AZ, CA, CO, IA, ID, IN, KS, LA, MI, MO, NV, SC
Seeking in Canada? No
Exclusive territories? Yes
Homebased option? No
Kiosk option? No
Employees needed to run franchise: 1-5
Absentee ownership? Yes

COSTS
Total cost: $58K-87K
Franchise fee: $25K
Royalty fee: 0
Term of agreement: 10 years renewable for 10% of franchise fee
Franchisees required to buy multiple units? No

FINANCING
No financing available

QUALIFICATIONS
Cash liquidity: $50K-59.99K
Experience:
    General business experience
    Marketing skills

TRAINING
At headquarters: 1 week
At franchisee's location: 1 week
At existing location: 1 week

BUSINESS SUPPORT
Newsletter
Internet
Lease negotiations
Field operations/evaluations

MARKETING SUPPORT
Co-op advertising
National media campaign
Templates for flyers & store sign layout

COMMERCIAL UNION INC.

Current financial data not available

3127 E. Otero Cir.
Littleton, CO 80122
Ph: (303)689-0867
Fax: (303)689-0870
www.cuatm.com
ATM machines
Began: 2000, Franchising since: 2002
Headquarters size: 1 employee
Franchise department: 1 employee

U.S. franchises: 6
Canadian franchises: 0
Other foreign franchises: 0
Company-owned: 1

Seeking: All U.S.
Seeking in Canada? Yes
Exclusive territories? No
Homebased option? Yes
Kiosk option? No
Employees needed to run franchise: 0
Absentee ownership? No

COSTS
Total cost: $30K
Franchise fee: $30K
Royalty fee: 0
Term of agreement: 10 years renewable
  at no charge
Franchisees required to buy multiple
  units? No

FINANCING
In-house: Franchise fee
3rd-party: None

QUALIFICATIONS
None

TRAINING
At franchisee's location: 20 hours

BUSINESS SUPPORT
Meetings
Toll-free phone line
Internet
Security/safety procedures
Field operations/evaluations
Purchasing cooperatives

MARKETING SUPPORT
Collateral materials

ELLIOTT & COMPANY APPRAISERS

Financial rating: $$$$

3316-A Battleground Ave.
Greensboro, NC 27410
Ph: (800)854-5889
Fax: (336)854-7734
www.appraisalsanywhere.com
Real estate appraisals
Began: 1980, Franchising since: 1993
Headquarters size: 18 employees
Franchise department: 1 employee

U.S. franchises: 7
Canadian franchises: 0
Other foreign franchises: 0
Company-owned: 3
Units concentrated in NC

Seeking: All U.S.
Seeking in Canada? No
Exclusive territories? Yes
Homebased option? Yes
Kiosk option? No
Employees needed to run franchise:
  1-2
Absentee ownership? No

COSTS
Total cost: $3.65K-18.9K
Franchise fee: $900-9.9K
Royalty fee: 8-18%
Term of agreement: 5 years renewable
  for $500
Franchisees required to buy multiple
  units? No

FINANCING
No financing available

QUALIFICATIONS
Experience:
  Industry experience
  General business experience
  Marketing skills
  Real estate appraiser's license

TRAINING
At headquarters: 1 days
At franchisee's location: 1 day
State-required continuing education
  annually

BUSINESS SUPPORT
Newsletter
Meetings
Toll-free phone line
Grand opening
Internet
Security/safety procedures
Field operations/evaluations

MARKETING SUPPORT
Co-op advertising
Ad slicks
National media campaign
Regional marketing
Specialty advertising

FED USA INSURANCE/FINANCIAL SERVICES

Current financial data not available

4161 N.W. 5th St.
Plantation, FL 33317
Ph: (888)440-6875
Fax: (954)316-9201
www.fedusa.com
Insurance & financial services/tax
    preparation
Began: 2000, Franchising since: 2000
Headquarters size: 120 employees
Franchise department: 5 employees

U.S. franchises: 38
Canadian franchises: 0
Other foreign franchises: 0
Company-owned: 22
Units concentrated in FL

Seeking: All U.S.
Seeking in Canada? No
Exclusive territories? Yes
Homebased option? No
Kiosk option? Info not provided
Employees needed to run franchise:
    1-4
Absentee ownership? No

COSTS
Total cost: $30K-40K
Franchise fee: $14.95K
Royalty fee: 7%
Term of agreement: 10 years renewable
    for $3K
Franchisees required to buy multiple
    units? No

FINANCING
In-house: None
3rd-party: Equipment, franchise fee,
    start-up costs

QUALIFICATIONS
Net worth: $75K
Cash liquidity: $20K
Experience:
    General business experience
    Ability to manage finances
    Enjoy dealing with public

TRAINING
At headquarters: 1 week
At training facility: 3 weeks

BUSINESS SUPPORT
Newsletter
Meetings
Toll-free phone line
Grand opening
Internet
Lease negotiations
Security/safety procedures
Field operations/evaluations
Purchasing cooperatives

MARKETING SUPPORT
Co-op advertising
Ad slicks
Regional marketing
Local marketing

NATIONAL HOME BUYERS ASSISTANCE

Financial rating: $$$$

6600 E. Hampden Ave.
Denver, CO 80224
Ph: (303)703-6422
Fax: (303)779-6422
www.nhba.com
Lease-to-own home buying program
Began: 2001, Franchising since: 2003
Headquarters size: 25 employees
Franchise department: 20 employees

U.S. franchises: 21
Canadian franchises: 0
Other foreign franchises: 0
Company-owned: 0

Seeking: All U.S.
Seeking in Canada? No
Exclusive territories? No
Homebased option? Yes
Kiosk option? No
Employees needed to run franchise: 2
Absentee ownership? Yes

COSTS
Total cost: $105K
Franchise fee: $25K
Royalty fee: 2%
Term of agreement: 10 years renewable
    for $5K
Franchisees required to buy multiple
    units? No

FINANCING
No financing available

QUALIFICATIONS
Cash liquidity: $70K
Experience:
    General business experience
    Marketing skills

TRAINING
At headquarters: 5 days

BUSINESS SUPPORT
Newsletter
Meetings
Toll-free phone line
Internet
Security/safety procedures
Field operations/evaluations
Purchasing cooperatives

MARKETING SUPPORT
Co-op advertising
Ad slicks
National media campaign
Regional marketing

PROPERTY DAMAGE APPRAISERS
Ranked #206 in Entrepreneur Magazine's 2004 Franchise 500   *Financial rating: $$$$*

6100 Southwest Blvd., #200
Ft. Worth, TX 76109-3964
Ph: (817)731-5555
Fax: (817)731-5550
www.pdahomeoffice.com
Auto & property appraisals for insurance companies
Began: 1963, Franchising since: 1963
Headquarters size: 35 employees
Franchise department: 3 employees

U.S. franchises: 280
Canadian franchises: 0
Other foreign franchises: 0
Company-owned: 0
Units concentrated in all U.S.

Seeking: All U.S.
Seeking in Canada? No
Exclusive territories? No
Homebased option? No
Kiosk option? No
Employees needed to run franchise:
    Info not provided
Absentee ownership? No

COSTS
Total cost: $18.3K-35.95K
Franchise fee: $0
Royalty fee: 15%
Term of agreement: 3 years renewable
    at no charge
Franchisees required to buy multiple
    units? No

FINANCING
No financing available

QUALIFICATIONS
Experience:
    Industry experience

TRAINING
At headquarters: 4-1/2 days
At franchisee's location: 3 days
Ongoing

BUSINESS SUPPORT
Newsletter
Meetings
Toll-free phone line
Internet
Field operations/evaluations
Purchasing cooperatives

MARKETING SUPPORT
Regional marketing

FINANCIAL ▶ *Other Franchises*

COLBERT/BALL TAX SERVICE
2616 S. Loop W., #110
Houston, TX 77054
Ph: (713)592-5555
www.colbertballtax.com
Tax preparation & electronic filing
    services

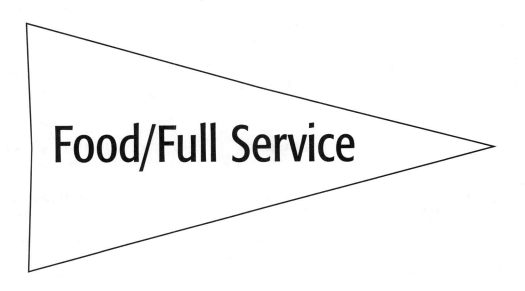

FULL SERVICE *Barbecue Restaurants*

BENNETT'S BAR-B-QUE INC.

Current financial data not available

6551 S. Revere Pkwy., #285
Englewood, CO 80111
Ph: (303)792-3088
Fax: (303)799-7941
Barbecue restaurant
Began: 1984, Franchising since: 1989
Headquarters size: 20 employees
Franchise department: 6 employees

U.S. franchises: 5
Canadian franchises: 0
Other foreign franchises: 0
Company-owned: 0
Units concentrated in CO, NC, TN

Seeking: Midwest, Northeast,
     Northwest, Southwest
Focusing on: All U.S.
Seeking in Canada? Yes
Exclusive territories? Yes
Homebased option? No
Kiosk option? No
Employees needed to run franchise: 50
Absentee ownership? Yes

COSTS
Total cost: $1.2M-2M
Franchise fee: $35K
Royalty fee: 3.5%
Term of agreement: 20 years renewable
     for $5K
Franchisees required to buy multiple
     units? No

FINANCING
No financing available

QUALIFICATIONS
Net worth: $1M
Cash liquidity: $300K
Experience:
     Industry experience
     General business experience
     Marketing skills

TRAINING
At headquarters: As needed
At franchisee's location: 8 weeks

BUSINESS SUPPORT
Newsletter
Meetings
Grand opening
Internet
Lease negotiations
Security/safety procedures
Field operations/evaluations

MARKETING SUPPORT
Ad slicks
Regional marketing

DAMON'S INT'L.

Financial rating: $$

4645 Executive Dr.
Columbus, OH 43220
Ph: (614)442-7900
Fax: (614)273-3121
www.damons.com
Barbecue ribs & casual dining
Began: 1979, Franchising since: 1982
Headquarters size: 60 employees
Franchise department: 20 employees

U.S. franchises: 105
Canadian franchises: 0
Other foreign franchises: 4
Company-owned: 33
Units concentrated in MI, OH, PA

Seeking: All U.S.
Seeking in Canada? Yes
Exclusive territories? Yes
Homebased option? No
Kiosk option? No
Employees needed to run franchise: 80
Absentee ownership? Yes

COSTS
Total cost: 941.5K-2.7M
Franchise fee: $50K
Royalty fee: 4%
Term of agreement: 10 years renewable
    at no charge
Franchisees required to buy multiple
    units? Yes

FINANCING
No financing available

QUALIFICATIONS
Net worth: $1M
Cash liquidity: $500K-750K
Experience:
    Industry experience

TRAINING
At headquarters: 2 weeks
At franchisee's location: 8 weeks

BUSINESS SUPPORT
Meetings
Toll-free phone line
Grand opening
Internet
Field operations/evaluations
Purchasing cooperatives

MARKETING SUPPORT
Co-op advertising
Ad slicks
Regional marketing

MISTER BAR-B-QUE

Current financial data not available

1134 Grove Dr.
Rockledge, FL 32955
Ph: (321)631-1742
Fax: (321)639-4318
www.digital.net/~mr-bbq
Barbecue restaurant
Began: 1988, Franchising since: 1997
Headquarters size: 7 employees
Franchise department: 2 employees

U.S. franchises: 0
Canadian franchises: 0
Other foreign franchises: 0
Company-owned: 1
Units concentrated in FL

Seeking: All U.S.
Seeking in Canada? Yes
Exclusive territories? Yes
Homebased option? No
Kiosk option? No
Employees needed to run franchise: 5
Absentee ownership? Yes

COSTS
Total cost: $159.9K-163.6K
Franchise fee: $15K
Royalty fee: 6%
Term of agreement: 10 years renewable
    for 20% of current franchise fee
Franchisees required to buy multiple
    units? Outside the U.S. only

FINANCING
No financing available

QUALIFICATIONS
Net worth: $170K
Cash liquidity: $163.6K
Experience:
    General business experience
    Marketing skills

TRAINING
At headquarters: 2 weeks
At franchisee's location: 1 week

BUSINESS SUPPORT
Toll-free phone line
Grand opening
Field operations/evaluations

MARKETING SUPPORT
Ad slicks

RED HOT & BLUE

Current financial data not available

1701 Clarendon Blvd., #105
Arlington, VA 22209
Ph: (703)276-8833
Fax: (703)528-4789
www.redhotandblue.com
Barbecue restaurant
Began: 1988, Franchising since: 1990
Headquarters size: 15 employees
Franchise department: 5 employees

U.S. franchises: 28
Canadian franchises: 0
Other foreign franchises: 0
Company-owned: 7
Units concentrated in all U.S.

Seeking: All U.S.
Seeking in Canada? No
Exclusive territories? Yes
Homebased option? No
Kiosk option? No
Employees needed to run franchise: 60
Absentee ownership? No

COSTS
Total cost: $380.7K-1M
Franchise fee: $45K
Royalty fee: 5%
Term of agreement: 20 years renewable
    at no charge
Franchisees required to buy multiple
    units? No

FINANCING
No financing available

QUALIFICATIONS
Net worth: $1M
Cash liquidity: $1M
Experience:
    Industry experience

TRAINING
At headquarters: 6 weeks
At franchisee's location: 2 weeks

BUSINESS SUPPORT
Newsletter
Meetings
Toll-free phone line
Grand opening
Field operations/evaluations

MARKETING SUPPORT
Ad slicks
National media campaign
Regional marketing

RIB CRIB BARBECUE

Current financial data not available

4271 W. Albany
Broken Arrow, OK 74012
Ph: (918)459-9999
Fax: (918)459-0699
www.ribcrib.com
Casual full-service barbecue restaurant
Began: 1992, Franchising since: 2000
Headquarters size: 20 employees
Franchise department: 10 employees

U.S. franchises: 9
Canadian franchises: 0
Other foreign franchises: 0
Company-owned: 20
Units concentrated in AZ, CA, FL, KS,
    MO, NM, OH, OK, TX

Seeking: All U.S.
Seeking in Canada? No
Exclusive territories? Yes
Homebased option? No
Kiosk option? No
Employees needed to run franchise: 50
Absentee ownership? Yes

COSTS
Total cost: $400K-1.3M
Franchise fee: $35K
Royalty fee: 4%
Term of agreement: 10 years renewable
    for $5K-10K
Franchisees required to buy multiple
    units? No

FINANCING
In-house: None
3rd-party: Accounts receivable, equip-
    ment, franchise fee, inventory, pay-
    roll, start-up costs

QUALIFICATIONS
Net worth: $1.6M
Cash liquidity: $250K
Experience:
    Industry experience
    General business experience
    Marketing skills

TRAINING
At headquarters: 8-12 weeks
In-store training: 8-10 weeks

BUSINESS SUPPORT
Newsletter
Meetings
Toll-free phone line
Grand opening
Internet
Lease negotiations
Security/safety procedures
Field operations/evaluations
Purchasing cooperatives

MARKETING SUPPORT
Co-op advertising
Ad slicks
Regional marketing
Graphic design services

FULL SERVICE ► *Family-Style Restaurants*

BIG BOY RESTAURANTS INT'L.

Ranked #371 in Entrepreneur Magazine's 2004 Franchise 500

Financial rating: $$$

4199 Marcy St.
Warren, MI 48091
Ph: (586)759-6000, Fax: (586)757-4737
www.bigboy.com
Family restaurant
Began: 1936, Franchising since: 1952
Headquarters size: 70 employees
Franchise department: 8 employees

U.S. franchises: 136
Canadian franchises: 0
Other foreign franchises: 93
Company-owned: 24
Units concentrated in AZ, CA, HI, MI,
  ND, OH

Seeking: All U.S.
Seeking in Canada? No
Exclusive territories? Yes
Homebased option? No
Kiosk option? No
Employees needed to run franchise: 60
Absentee ownership? Yes

COSTS
Total cost: $1.5M
Franchise fee: $40K
Royalty fee: 4%
Term of agreement: 20 years
Franchisees required to buy multiple
  units? No

FINANCING
In-house: None
3rd-party: Equipment

QUALIFICATIONS
Net worth: $500K
Cash liquidity: $250K
Experience:
    Industry experience
    General business experience

TRAINING
At headquarters: Up to 11 weeks
At franchisee's location: Up to 11
  weeks

BUSINESS SUPPORT
Newsletter
Meetings
Toll-free phone line
Grand opening
Internet
Security/safety procedures
Field operations/evaluations
Purchasing cooperatives

MARKETING SUPPORT
Co-op advertising
Ad slicks
Regional marketing

DENNY'S INC.

Ranked #52 in Entrepreneur Magazine's 2004 Franchise 500

Financial rating: $$$$

203 E. Main St.
Spartanburg, SC 29319
Ph: (800)304-0222
Fax: (864)597-7708
www.dennys.com
Full-service family restaurant
Began: 1953, Franchising since: 1984
Headquarters size: 295 employees
Franchise department: 9 employees

U.S. franchises: 1,024
Canadian franchises: 53
Other foreign franchises: 11
Company-owned: 563
Units concentrated in all U.S.

Seeking: All U.S.
Seeking in Canada? Yes
Exclusive territories? No
Homebased option? No
Kiosk option? No
Employees needed to run franchise: 80
Absentee ownership? No

COSTS
Total cost: $971K-1.8M
Franchise fee: $40K
Royalty fee: 4%
Term of agreement: 20 years not
  renewable
Franchisees required to buy multiple
  units? No

FINANCING
No financing available

QUALIFICATIONS
Net worth: $1M
Cash liquidity: $350K
Experience:
    Industry experience
    General business experience

TRAINING
At existing restaurant: Up to 10 weeks

BUSINESS SUPPORT
Newsletter
Meetings
Security/safety procedures
Field operations/evaluations

MARKETING SUPPORT
Co-op advertising
Ad slicks
National media campaign
Regional marketing

FRIENDLY'S RESTAURANTS FRANCHISE INC.

Ranked #219 in Entrepreneur Magazine's 2004 Franchise 500　　　*Financial rating: $$$$*

1855 Boston Rd.
Wilbraham, MA 01095
Ph: (413)543-2400, Fax: (413)543-2820
www.friendlys.com
Family-style restaurant/ice cream
Began: 1935, Franchising since: 1996
Headquarters size: Info not provided
Franchise department: Info not provided

U.S. franchises: 156
Canadian franchises: 0
Other foreign franchises: 0
Company-owned: 382
Units concentrated in DE, FL, MD,
　NC, NJ, NY, PA, SC, VA

Seeking: Midwest, Northeast, South,
　Southeast
Focusing on: DE, FL, MD, NC, NJ, NY,
　OH, PA, SC, VA
Seeking in Canada? No
Exclusive territories? Yes
Homebased option? No
Kiosk option? No
Employees needed to run franchise:
　Info not provided
Absentee ownership? No

COSTS
Total cost: $629.8K-1.9M
Franchise fee: $30K-35K
Royalty fee: 4%
Term of agreement: 20 years renewable
　for $5K
Franchisees required to buy multiple
　units? Yes

FINANCING
In-house: None
3rd-party: Available

QUALIFICATIONS
Net worth: $1.5M
Cash liquidity: $650K
Experience:
　Industry experience

TRAINING
At headquarters: 12 weeks

BUSINESS SUPPORT
Newsletter
Meetings
Toll-free phone line
Grand opening
Internet
Security/safety procedures
Field operations/evaluations

MARKETING SUPPORT
Ad slicks
National media campaign

GOLDEN GRIDDLE FAMILY RESTAURANTS

Current financial data not available

505 Consumers Rd., #1000
Willowdale, ON Canada M2J 4V8
Ph: (416)493-3800
Fax: (416)493-3889
www.goldengriddlecorp.com
Full-service family restaurant
Began: 1964, Franchising since: 1977
Headquarters size: 15 employees
Franchise department: 5 employees

U.S. franchises: 0
Canadian franchises: 37
Other foreign franchises: 0
Company-owned: 0

Seeking: All U.S.
Seeking in Canada? Yes
Exclusive territories? Yes
Homebased option? No
Kiosk option? No
Employees needed to run franchise:
　15-25
Absentee ownership? No

COSTS
Total cost: $150K-600K U.S.
Franchise fee: $25K U.S.
Royalty fee: 5%
Term of agreement: 10 years renewable
　at no charge
Franchisees required to buy multiple
　units? Yes

FINANCING
No financing available

QUALIFICATIONS
Net worth: $200K+
Cash liquidity: $100K
Experience:
　General business experience

TRAINING
At headquarters: 1 week
At franchisee's location: 1-2 weeks
At training store: 2-4 weeks

BUSINESS SUPPORT
Newsletter
Meetings
Internet
Field operations/evaluations

MARKETING SUPPORT
Co-op advertising
Ad slicks
Marketing planning

HUDDLE HOUSE

Ranked #370 in Entrepreneur Magazine's 2004 Franchise 500   *Current financial data not available*

2969 E. Ponce De Leon Ave.
Decatur, GA 30030
Ph: (800)868-5700, Fax: (404)377-0497
www.huddlehouse.com
24-hour restaurant
Began: 1964, Franchising since: 1966
Headquarters size: 120 employees
Franchise department: 9 employees

U.S. franchises: 330
Canadian franchises: 0
Other foreign franchises: 0
Company-owned: 24
Units concentrated in AL, AR, FL, GA,
  IL, IN, KY, LA, MO, MS, NC, OH,
  OK, SC, TN, TX, VA, WV

Seeking: Midwest, South, Southeast
Focusing on: AL, AR, FL, GA, IL, IN,
  KY, LA, MO, MS, NC, OH, OK, SC,
  TN, TX, VA, WV
Seeking in Canada? No
Exclusive territories? Yes
Homebased option? No

Kiosk option? No
Employees needed to run franchise: 24
Absentee ownership? Yes

COSTS
Total cost: $120K-800K
Franchise fee: $20K
Royalty fee: 4%
Term of agreement: 15 years renewable
Franchisees required to buy multiple
  units? No

FINANCING
In-house: None
3rd-party: Accounts receivable, equipment, franchise fee, inventory, payroll, start-up costs

QUALIFICATIONS
Net worth: $200K
Cash liquidity: $200K

TRAINING
At headquarters: 5 weeks

BUSINESS SUPPORT
Newsletter
Meetings
Toll-free phone line
Grand opening
Security/safety procedures
Field operations/evaluations
Purchasing cooperatives

MARKETING SUPPORT
Co-op advertising
Ad slicks
National media campaign

PERKINS RESTAURANT & BAKERY

Current financial data not available

6075 Poplar Ave., #800
Memphis, TN 38119
Ph: (800)877-7375/(901)766-6400
Fax: (901)766-6482
www.perkinsrestaurants.com
Full-service restaurant
Began: 1958, Franchising since: 1958
Headquarters size: 150 employees
Franchise department: 6 employees

U.S. franchises: 327
Canadian franchises: 14
Other foreign franchises: 0
Company-owned: 155
Units concentrated in all U.S.

Seeking: All U.S.
Seeking in Canada? Yes
Exclusive territories? Yes
Homebased option? No
Kiosk option? No
Employees needed to run franchise: 55
Absentee ownership? No

COSTS
Total cost: $1.7M-3M
Franchise fee: $40K
Royalty fee: 4%
Term of agreement: 20 years renewable
Franchisees required to buy multiple
  units? No

FINANCING
No financing available

QUALIFICATIONS
Net worth: $750K
Cash liquidity: $500K
Experience:
    Industry experience
    General business experience
    Marketing skills

TRAINING
At headquarters: 2 days
At franchisee's location: 4 weeks
At corporate store: 8-12 days

BUSINESS SUPPORT
Newsletter
Meetings
Toll-free phone line
Grand opening
Internet
Lease negotiations
Security/safety procedures
Field operations/evaluations
Purchasing cooperatives

MARKETING SUPPORT
Co-op advertising
Ad slicks
National media campaign
Regional marketing

FULL SERVICE   *Italian Restaurants*

AZPCO ARIZONA PIZZA COMPANY

Financial rating: $$

370 S.E. 15th Ave.
Pompano Beach, FL 33060
Ph: (954)942-9424
Fax: (954)783-5177
www.arizonapizzaco.com
Italian food & brick-oven pizza
Began: 1996, Franchising since: 2002
Headquarters size: 10 employees
Franchise department: 3 employees

U.S. franchises: 1
Canadian franchises: 0
Other foreign franchises: 0
Company-owned: 2

Seeking: All U.S.
Seeking in Canada? No
Exclusive territories? Yes
Homebased option? No
Kiosk option? No
Employees needed to run franchise: 20
Absentee ownership? Yes

COSTS
Total cost: $256.5K-397K
Franchise fee: $25K
Royalty fee: 4%
Term of agreement: 10 years
Franchisees required to buy multiple
    units? No

FINANCING
In-house: None
3rd-party: Equipment, franchise fee,
    inventory, start-up costs

QUALIFICATIONS
Experience:
    General business experience

TRAINING
At headquarters: 2 weeks
At franchisee's location: 2 weeks

BUSINESS SUPPORT
Meetings
Grand opening
Security/safety procedures
Field operations/evaluations
Purchasing cooperatives

MARKETING SUPPORT
Ad slicks
Regional marketing
Local marketing manual

BOSTON PIZZA

Ranked #376 in Entrepreneur Magazine's 2004 Franchise 500

Financial rating: 0

1501 LBJ Fwy., #450
Dallax, TX 75234
Ph: (972)484-9022
Fax: (972)484-7630
www.bostonpizza.com
Pizza & pasta family restaurant
Began: 1963, Franchising since: 1968
Headquarters size: 80 employees
Franchise department: 20 employees

U.S. franchises: 9
Canadian franchises: 166
Other foreign franchises: 1
Company-owned: 5
Units concentrated in TX, WA

Seeking: All U.S.
Seeking in Canada? Yes
Exclusive territories? Yes
Homebased option? No
Kiosk option? No
Employees needed to run franchise: 70
Absentee ownership? No

COSTS
Total cost: $1.5M-2.1M
Franchise fee: $35K/50K-65K
Royalty fee: 5%/7%
Term of agreement: 10 years renewable
    for 25% of current franchise fee
Franchisees required to buy multiple
    units? No

FINANCING
In-house: None
3rd-party: Equipment, inventory,
    start-up costs

QUALIFICATIONS
Net worth: $1M
Cash liquidity: $450K
Experience:
    General business experience

TRAINING
At headquarters: 10 weeks
At franchisee's location: As needed

BUSINESS SUPPORT
Newsletter
Meetings
Toll-free phone line
Grand opening
Internet
Lease negotiations
Security/safety procedures
Field operations/evaluations
Purchasing cooperatives

MARKETING SUPPORT
Co-op advertising
Ad slicks
National media campaign
Regional marketing

CICI'S PIZZA

Ranked #88 in Entrepreneur Magazine's 2004 Franchise 500   *Financial rating: $$$$*

1080 W. Bethel Rd.
Coppell, TX 75019
Ph: (972)745-4200, Fax: (972)745-4204
www.cicispizza.com
All-you-can-eat pizza buffet
Began: 1985, Franchising since: 1987
Headquarters size: 76 employees
Franchise department: 2 employees

U.S. franchises: 423
Canadian franchises: 0
Other foreign franchises: 0
Company-owned: 24
Units concentrated in AL, AR, FL, GA,
    IN, KS, KY, LA, MO, MS, NC, NM,
    OH, OK, SC, TN, TX, VA

Seeking: Midwest, South, Southeast,
    Southwest
Focusing on: AL, AR, FL, GA, IL, IN,
    KS, KY, LA, MI, MO, MS, NC, NM,
    OH, OK, SC, TN, TX, VA, WI
Seeking in Canada? No
Exclusive territories? Yes

Homebased option? No
Kiosk option? No
Employees needed to run franchise: 30
Absentee ownership? No

COSTS
Total cost: $391K-495K
Franchise fee: $30K
Royalty fee: 4%
Term of agreement: 10 years
Franchisees required to buy multiple
    units? No

FINANCING
No financing available

QUALIFICATIONS
Cash liquidity: $120.3K-182.1K
Experience:
    General business experience

TRAINING
14 weeks+ training available depend-
    ing on skill level

BUSINESS SUPPORT
Newsletter
Meetings
Security/safety procedures
Field operations/evaluations

MARKETING SUPPORT
Regional marketing
Local media advertising

DOUBLEDAVE'S PIZZAWORKS SYSTEMS INC.

Current financial data not available

3563 Far West Blvd., #104
Austin, TX 78731
Ph: (512)343-0330
Fax: (512)343-0248
www.doubledaves.com
Hand-rolled pizza buffet & delivery
Began: 1984, Franchising since: 1995
Headquarters size: 5 employees
Franchise department: 5 employees

U.S. franchises: 36
Canadian franchises: 0
Other foreign franchises: 0
Company-owned: 1
Units concentrated in OK, TX

Seeking: All U.S.
Focusing on: CO, NC, NM, OK,
    SC, TX
Seeking in Canada? No
Exclusive territories? Yes
Homebased option? No
Kiosk option? No
Employees needed to run franchise: 15
Absentee ownership? No

COSTS
Total cost: $295K-320K
Franchise fee: $25K
Royalty fee: 4%
Term of agreement: 10 years renewable
Franchisees required to buy multiple
    units? No

FINANCING
In-house: None
3rd-party: Accounts receivable, equip-
    ment, franchise fee, inventory, pay-
    roll, start-up costs

QUALIFICATIONS
Net worth: $300K
Cash liquidity: $300K
Experience:
    Industry experience
    General business experience
    Marketing skills

TRAINING
At headquarters: 3 weeks
At franchisee's location: 2 weeks

BUSINESS SUPPORT
Newsletter
Meetings
Toll-free phone line
Grand opening
Lease negotiations
Field operations/evaluations
Purchasing cooperatives

MARKETING SUPPORT
Co-op advertising
Ad slicks
Regional marketing

GOODFELLA'S OLD WORLD BRICK OVEN PIZZA

Financial rating: 0

101-1 Reon Ave.
Staten Island, NY 10314
Ph: (718)816-8111. Fax: (718)816-0141
www.goodfellas.com
Brick-oven pizza & Italian food
Began: 1993, Franchising since: 1997
Headquarters size: 5 employees
Franchise department: 5 employees

U.S. franchises: 10
Canadian franchises: 0
Other foreign franchises: 0
Company-owned: 1
Units concentrated in NJ, NY

Seeking: All U.S.
Focusing on: CA, DE, FL, GA, IN, MD,
    NC, PA, SC, VA
Seeking in Canada? Yes
Exclusive territories? Yes
Homebased option? No
Kiosk option? No
Employees needed to run franchise: 24
Absentee ownership? Yes

COSTS
Total cost: $247.2K-931K
Franchise fee: $22.5K/40K
Royalty fee: 5%
Term of agreement: 10 years renewable
    for 25% of current franchisee fee
Franchisees required to buy multiple
    units? No

FINANCING
In-house: None
3rd-party: Equipment, inventory,
    start-up costs

QUALIFICATIONS
Net worth: $500K-750K
Cash liquidity: $300K-500K
Experience:
    Industry experience
    General business experience

TRAINING
At headquarters: 3 weeks
At franchisee's location: 2 weeks

BUSINESS SUPPORT
Newsletter
Meetings
Grand opening
Internet
Lease negotiations
Security/safety procedures
Field operations/evaluations
Purchasing cooperatives

MARKETING SUPPORT
Co-op advertising
Ad slicks
National media campaign
Regional marketing

THE ITALIAN PIE FRANCHISE LLC

Financial rating: $

3701 Canal St.
New Orleans, LA 70119
Ph: (504)488-4441
Fax: (504)488-4474
www.italianpierestaurants.com
Casual Italian dining
Began: 1994, Franchising since: 1995
Headquarters size: 8 employees
Franchise department: 2 employees

U.S. franchises: 19
Canadian franchises: 0
Other foreign franchises: 0
Company-owned: 4
Units concentrated in AL, FL, LA, MS,
    NC, TX

Seeking: Southeast
Seeking in Canada? No
Exclusive territories? Yes
Homebased option? No
Kiosk option? No
Employees needed to run franchise: 30
Absentee ownership? No

COSTS
Total cost: $241.5K-351K
Franchise fee: $25K
Royalty fee: 5%
Term of agreement: 10 years renewable
    at no charge
Franchisees required to buy multiple
    units? Yes

FINANCING
No financing available

QUALIFICATIONS
Net worth: $500K+
Cash liquidity: $250K
Experience:
    Industry experience
    General business experience
    Marketing skills

TRAINING
At headquarters: 4 weeks
At franchisee's location: 10 days
Various programs

BUSINESS SUPPORT
Newsletter
Meetings
Grand opening
Internet
Lease negotiations
Security/safety procedures
Field operations/evaluations
Purchasing cooperatives

MARKETING SUPPORT
Co-op advertising
Ad slicks
National media campaign
Regional marketing

ROTELLI PIZZA & PASTA

Current financial data not available

9045 La Fontana Blvd., #B-1
Boca Raton, FL 33434
Ph: (561)477-8300
Fax: (561)451-1970
www.rotellipizzapasta.com
Italian restaurant
Began: 1999, Franchising since: 1999
Headquarters size: 7 employees
Franchise department: 2 employees

U.S. franchises: 30
Canadian franchises: 0
Other foreign franchises: 0
Company-owned: 0
Units concentrated in FL, NC, OH,
    PA, Puerto Rico

Seeking: All U.S.
Seeking in Canada? Yes
Exclusive territories? Yes
Homebased option? No
Kiosk option? No
Employees needed to run franchise:
    20-25
Absentee ownership? No

COSTS
Total cost: $310K-481K
Franchise fee: $25K
Royalty fee: 6%
Term of agreement: 10 years renewable
    for $5K
Franchisees required to buy multiple
    units? No

FINANCING
In-house: None
3rd-party: Equipment

QUALIFICATIONS
Net worth: $100K
Cash liquidity: $250K
Experience:
    General business experience

TRAINING
At headquarters: 2 weeks
At franchisee's location: 4 weeks

BUSINESS SUPPORT
Meetings
Toll-free phone line
Grand opening
Internet
Lease negotiations
Security/safety procedures
Field operations/evaluations

MARKETING SUPPORT
Co-op advertising
Ad slicks

SAMUEL MANCINO'S ITALIAN EATERY

Ranked #470 in Entrepreneur Magazine's 2004 Franchise 500   *Financial rating: $$$$*

1324 W. Milham
Portage, MI 49024
Ph: (616)226-4400
Fax: (616)226-4466
www.samuelmancinos.com
Italian food
Began: 1959, Franchising since: 1994
Headquarters size: 5 employees
Franchise department: 3 employees

U.S. franchises: 35
Canadian franchises: 0
Other foreign franchises: 0
Company-owned: 0
Units concentrated in all U.S.

Seeking: All U.S.
Seeking in Canada? Yes
Exclusive territories? Yes
Homebased option? No
Kiosk option? Yes
Employees needed to run franchise: 10
Absentee ownership? No

COSTS
Total cost: $234.5K-304.5K
    Kiosk cost: $100K
Franchise fee: $25K
Royalty fee: 5%
Term of agreement: 10 years renewable
    at no charge
Franchisees required to buy multiple
    units? No

FINANCING
In-house: None
3rd-party: Accounts receivable, equip-
    ment, franchise fee, inventory, pay-
    roll, start-up costs

QUALIFICATIONS
Net worth: $200K
Cash liquidity: $100K
Experience:
    Industry experience
    General business experience
    Marketing skills

TRAINING
At headquarters: 2-3 weeks
At franchisee's location: 2-3 weeks
At training store: 2-4 weeks

BUSINESS SUPPORT
Newsletter
Meetings
Toll-free phone line
Grand opening
Internet
Lease negotiations
Security/safety procedures
Field operations/evaluations
Purchasing cooperatives

MARKETING SUPPORT
Co-op advertising
Ad slicks
Regional marketing
Consultation & research

FULL SERVICE   *Steakhouses*

GOLDEN CORRAL FRANCHISING SYSTEMS INC.

Ranked #127 in Entrepreneur Magazine's 2004 Franchise 500   *Financial rating: $$$$*

5151 Glenwood Ave.
Raleigh, NC 27612
Ph: (800)284-5673, Fax: (919)881-5252
www.goldencorral.net
Family steakhouse/buffet & bakery
Began: 1973, Franchising since: 1987
Headquarters size: 180 employees
Franchise department: 10 employees

U.S. franchises: 348
Canadian franchises: 0
Other foreign franchises: 0
Company-owned: 122
Units concentrated in all U.S.

Seeking: All U.S.
Seeking in Canada? Yes
Exclusive territories? Yes
Homebased option? No
Kiosk option? No
Employees needed to run franchise: 100
Absentee ownership? No

COSTS
Total cost: $1.7M-3.9M
Franchise fee: $40K
Royalty fee: 4%
Term of agreement: 15 years renewable for $13.3K/5 years
Franchisees required to buy multiple units? No

FINANCING
In-house: None
3rd-party: Accounts receivable, equipment, franchise fee, inventory, payroll, start-up costs

QUALIFICATIONS
Net worth: $1.5M
Cash liquidity: $250K
Experience:
  Industry experience
  (or must have partner with industry experience)

TRAINING
At headquarters: 2 weeks
At company training location: 10 weeks

BUSINESS SUPPORT
Newsletter
Meetings
Toll-free phone line
Grand opening
Internet
Security/safety procedures
Field operations/evaluations
Purchasing cooperatives

MARKETING SUPPORT
Co-op advertising
Ad slicks
Regional marketing

WESTERN SIZZLIN

Ranked #488 in Entrepreneur Magazine's 2004 Franchise 500   *Financial rating: $$$*

P.O. Box 12167
Roanoke, VA 24023-2167
Ph: (540)345-3195, Fax: (540)345-0831
www.western-sizzlin.com
Family steakhouse
Began: 1962, Franchising since: 1965
Headquarters size: 22 employees
Franchise department: 8 employees

U.S. franchises: 166
Canadian franchises: 0
Other foreign franchises: 0
Company-owned: 7
Units concentrated in AL, AR, CO, FL, GA, IL, KS, KY, LA, MD, MS, MO, NM, NV, OH, OK, PA, SC, TN, TX, VA, WV

Seeking: All U.S.
Seeking in Canada? No
Exclusive territories? Yes
Homebased option? No
Kiosk option? No
Employees needed to run franchise: 40
Absentee ownership? Yes

COSTS
Total cost: $811K-2.3M
Franchise fee: $30K
Royalty fee: 3%
Term of agreement: 20 years renewable at no charge
Franchisees required to buy multiple units? No

FINANCING
No financing available

QUALIFICATIONS
Experience:
  Industry experience
  General business experience
  Marketing skills

TRAINING
At training centers: 6 weeks

BUSINESS SUPPORT
Newsletter
Meetings
Toll-free phone line
Grand opening
Internet
Security/safety procedures
Field operations/evaluations
Purchasing cooperatives

MARKETING SUPPORT
Ad slicks
Quarterly promotions

FULL SERVICE *Miscellaneous Restaurants*

THE ARROW NEIGHBORHOOD PUB GROUP

Current financial data not available

173 Woolwich St., #201
Guelph, ON Canada N1H 3V4
Ph: (519)836-3948
Fax: (519)836-6749
www.arrowpubs.com
Canadian pub-style restaurant
Began: 1990, Franchising since: 1996
Headquarters size: 4 employees
Franchise department: 2 employees

U.S. franchises: 0
Canadian franchises: 2
Other foreign franchises: 0
Company-owned: 1

Not available in the U.S.
Seeking in Canada? Yes
Exclusive territories? Yes
Homebased option? No
Kiosk option? No
Employees needed to run franchise: 20
Absentee ownership? No

COSTS
Total cost: $400K
Franchise fee: $35K
Royalty fee: 5%
Term of agreement: 7 years renewable
    for $2.8K maximum
Franchisees required to buy multiple
    units? No

FINANCING
No financing available

QUALIFICATIONS
Net worth: $500K
Cash liquidity: $150K
Experience:
    Industry experience
    General business experience
    Marketing skills
    People skills

TRAINING
At headquarters
At franchisee's location: 1 month

BUSINESS SUPPORT
Newsletter
Meetings
Grand opening
Field operations/evaluations
Purchasing cooperatives

MARKETING SUPPORT
Co-op advertising
Ad slicks

BEEF `O'BRADY'S

Ranked #386 in Entrepreneur Magazine's 2004 Franchise 500

Financial rating: $

5510 LaSalle, #200
Tampa, FL 33607
Ph: (813)226-2333, Fax: (813)226-0030
www.beefobradys.com
Family sports pub
Began: 1985, Franchising since: 1998
Headquarters size: 14 employees
Franchise department: 3 employees

U.S. franchises: 106
Canadian franchises: 0
Other foreign franchises: 0
Company-owned: 1
Units concentrated in AL, FL, GA, KY,
    MI, MS, NC, SC

Seeking: Southeast
Focusing on: AL, AR, FL, GA, KY, MI,
    MS, NC, OH, SC, TN
Seeking in Canada? No
Exclusive territories? Yes
Homebased option? No
Kiosk option? No
Employees needed to run franchise: 30
Absentee ownership? No

COSTS
Total cost: $300K-350K
Franchise fee: $30K
Royalty fee: 4%
Term of agreement: 10 years renewable
    at no charge
Franchisees required to buy multiple
    units? No

FINANCING
In-house: None
3rd-party: Equipment, franchise fee,
    inventory, payroll, start-up costs

QUALIFICATIONS
Net worth: $150K
Cash liquidity: $80K
Experience:
    Industry experience
    General business experience
    Marketing skills

TRAINING
At headquarters: 6 weeks
At franchisee's location: 2 weeks
Beef 'O'Brady's University; workshops

BUSINESS SUPPORT
Meetings
Toll-free phone line
Grand opening
Lease negotiations
Field operations/evaluations

MARKETING SUPPORT
Regional marketing

BENNIGAN'S GRILL & TAVERN

Current financial data not available

6500 International Pkwy., #1000
Plano, TX 75093
Ph: (800)543-9670
Fax: (972)588-5806
www.bennigans.com
Casual-theme restaurant
Began: 1976, Franchising since: 1995
Headquarters size: 150 employees
Franchise department: 10 employees

U.S. franchises: 102
Canadian franchises: 0
Other foreign franchises: 26
Company-owned: 173
Units concentrated in all U.S.

Seeking: All U.S.
Seeking in Canada? Yes
Exclusive territories? Yes
Homebased option? No
Kiosk option? No
Employees needed to run franchise:
    100
Absentee ownership? No

COSTS
Total cost: $1.4M-2.6M
Franchise fee: $65K
Royalty fee: 4%
Term of agreement: 15 years renewable
    at no charge
Franchisees required to buy multiple
    units? Yes

FINANCING
In-house: None
3rd-party: Equipment, inventory,
    start-up costs

QUALIFICATIONS
Net worth: $3M
Cash liquidity: $750K
Experience:
    Industry experience
    General business experience

TRAINING
At franchisee's location: Varies
At training restaurant for general
    manager: 13 weeks

BUSINESS SUPPORT
Meetings
Grand opening
Field operations/evaluations

MARKETING SUPPORT
Co-op advertising

BUFFALO'S SOUTHWEST CAFE

Current financial data not available

707 Whitlock Ave. S.W., #13
Marietta, GA 30064-3033
Ph: (800)459-4647/(770)420-1800
Fax: (770)420-1811
www.buffaloscafe.com
Buffalo-style chicken wings &
    Southwestern food
Began: 1985, Franchising since: 1990
Headquarters size: 15 employees
Franchise department: 2 employees

U.S. franchises: 38
Canadian franchises: 0
Other foreign franchises: 1
Company-owned: 9
Units concentrated in AL, FL, GA,
    MO, NC, NV, OH, SC, TX

Seeking: All U.S.
Focusing on: GA, NV, TX
Seeking in Canada? Yes
Exclusive territories? Yes
Homebased option? No
Kiosk option? No
Employees needed to run franchise:
    40-60
Absentee ownership? Yes

COSTS
Total cost: $309.3K-464.7K+
Franchise fee: $35K
Royalty fee: 5%
Term of agreement: 10 years renewable
Franchisees required to buy multiple
    units? Outside the U.S. only

FINANCING
No financing available

QUALIFICATIONS
Net worth: $400K
Cash liquidity: $200K
Experience:
    Industry experience
    General business experience

TRAINING
At headquarters: 28 days
At franchisee's location: 2 weeks
Ongoing seminars

BUSINESS SUPPORT
Newsletter
Meetings
Toll-free phone line
Grand opening
Internet
Lease negotiations
Security/safety procedures
Field operations/evaluations
Purchasing cooperatives

MARKETING SUPPORT
Co-op advertising
Ad slicks
Regional marketing

CAFE FONDUE FRANCHISE SYSTEMS INC.

Current financial data not available

281 W. 80th Pl.
Merrillville, IN 46410
Ph: (219)793-1511
Fax: (219)793-1511
www.cafefondue.net
Fondue-specialty restaurant
Began: 1996, Franchising since: 2003
Headquarters size: 2 employees
Franchise department: 2 employees

U.S. franchises: 0
Canadian franchises: 0
Other foreign franchises: 0
Company-owned: 1

Seeking: All U.S.
Seeking in Canada? No
Exclusive territories? No
Homebased option? No
Kiosk option? No
Employees needed to run franchise: 11
Absentee ownership? No

COSTS
Total cost: $136K-193K
Franchise fee: $50K
Royalty fee: 5%
Term of agreement: 10 years renewable
    for $2.5K
Franchisees required to buy multiple
    units? No

FINANCING
No financing available

QUALIFICATIONS
Experience:
    General business experience

TRAINING
At headquarters: 2 weeks
At franchisee's location: 1 week

BUSINESS SUPPORT
Grand opening
Security/safety procedures
Purchasing cooperatives

MARKETING SUPPORT
Co-op advertising

FAMOUS SAM'S INC.

Financial rating: $

1930 S. Alma School Rd., #C-105
Mesa, AZ 85210
Ph: (480)756-9800
Fax: (480)756-9884
www.famoussams.com
Sports bar & restaurant
Began: 1979, Franchising since: 1989
Headquarters size: 5 employees
Franchise department: 1 employee

U.S. franchises: 30
Canadian franchises: 0
Other foreign franchises: 0
Company-owned: 0
Units concentrated in AZ

Seeking: Southwest
Focusing on: AZ, CO, NV
Seeking in Canada? No
Exclusive territories? Yes
Homebased option? No
Kiosk option? No
Employees needed to run franchise:
    Info not provided
Absentee ownership? Info not provided

COSTS
Total cost: $573K-1.3M
Franchise fee: $30K
Royalty fee: 5%
Term of agreement: 20 years renewable
    at no charge
Franchisees required to buy multiple
    units? No

FINANCING
No financing available

QUALIFICATIONS
Net worth: $750K
Cash liquidity: $200K-250K
Experience:
    Industry experience
    General business experience

TRAINING
At headquarters: 2 weeks
At franchisee's location: Varies

BUSINESS SUPPORT
Newsletter
Meetings
Toll-free phone line
Field operations/evaluations

MARKETING SUPPORT
Co-op advertising

5 & DINER FRANCHISE CORP.

Financial rating: $$$

8700 E. Via De Ventura, #305
Scottsdale, AZ 85259
Ph: (480)778-9090
Fax: (480)778-1960
www.5anddiner.com
'50s-theme restaurant
Began: 1987, Franchising since: 1993
Headquarters size: 8 employees
Franchise department: 8 employees

U.S. franchises: 19
Canadian franchises: 0
Other foreign franchises: 0
Company-owned: 1
Units concentrated in AZ

Seeking: All U.S.
Seeking in Canada? No
Exclusive territories? Yes
Homebased option? No
Kiosk option? No
Employees needed to run franchise: 50
Absentee ownership? Yes

COSTS
Total cost: $300K-1M
Franchise fee: $35K
Royalty fee: 5%
Term of agreement: 15-20 years
     renewable for 25% of current fran-
     chise fee
Franchisees required to buy multiple
     units? No

FINANCING
In-house: None
3rd-party: Accounts receivable, equip-
     ment, franchise fee, inventory, pay-
     roll, start-up costs

QUALIFICATIONS
Net worth: $500K
Cash liquidity: $300K
Experience:
     Industry experience
     General business experience
     Marketing skills
     Past management experience

TRAINING
At headquarters: 5 weeks
At franchisee's location: 2 weeks
Ongoing

BUSINESS SUPPORT
Newsletter
Meetings
Grand opening
Internet
Security/safety procedures
Field operations/evaluations
Purchasing cooperatives

MARKETING SUPPORT
Co-op advertising
Ad slicks
National media campaign

FUDDRUCKERS

Ranked #447 in Entrepreneur Magazine's 2004 Franchise 500

Financial rating: $$$

66 Cherry Hill Dr., #200
Beverly, MA 01915
Ph: (978)778-1383
Fax: (978)778-1139
www.fuddruckers.com
Upscale hamburger restaurant
Began: 1980, Franchising since: 1983
Headquarters size: 35 employees
Franchise department: 9 employees

U.S. franchises: 93
Canadian franchises: 1
Other foreign franchises: 21
Company-owned: 111
Units concentrated in CA, MT, NJ, SC

Seeking: All U.S.
Focusing on: AL, CT, ID, IN, LA, NH,
     OR, WA, WY
Seeking in Canada? Yes
Exclusive territories? Yes
Homebased option? No
Kiosk option? No
Employees needed to run franchise: 40
Absentee ownership? No

COSTS
Total cost: $740K-1.5M
Franchise fee: $50K
Royalty fee: 5%
Term of agreement: 20 years renewable
     for $25K
Franchisees required to buy multiple
     units? No

FINANCING
No financing available

QUALIFICATIONS
Net worth: $1.5M
Cash liquidity: $550K
Experience:
     Industry experience
     General business experience

TRAINING
6-weeks training available

BUSINESS SUPPORT
Newsletter
Meetings
Grand opening
Internet
Field operations/evaluations

MARKETING SUPPORT
Regional marketing

GARFIELD'S RESTAURANT & PUB

Financial rating: $$

1220 S. Santa Fe
Edmond, OK 73003
Ph: (405)705-5000
Fax: (405)705-5004
www.eats-inc.com
Casual-dining restaurant
Began: 1984, Franchising since: 1987
Headquarters size: 51 employees
Franchise department: 1 employee

U.S. franchises: 10
Canadian franchises: 0
Other foreign franchises: 0
Company-owned: 45
Units concentrated in FL, IN

Seeking: All U.S.
Seeking in Canada? No
Exclusive territories? Yes
Homebased option? No
Kiosk option? No
Employees needed to run franchise: 75
Absentee ownership? No

COSTS
Total cost: $1.2M-1.96M
Franchise fee: $30K
Royalty fee: 4%
Term of agreement: 20 years renewable
    at no charge
Franchisees required to buy multiple
    units? Yes

FINANCING
In-house: None
3rd-party: Equipment

QUALIFICATIONS
Net worth: $1M+
Cash liquidity: $300K-500K
Experience:
    Industry experience
    General business experience
    Marketing skills

TRAINING
At headquarters: 6-8 weeks
At opening: 2 weeks

BUSINESS SUPPORT
Newsletter
Meetings
Toll-free phone line
Grand opening
Internet
Security/safety procedures
Field operations/evaluations
Purchasing cooperatives

MARKETING SUPPORT
Co-op advertising
Ad slicks
Regional marketing

HAMBURGER MARY'S BAR & GRILLE

Financial rating: 0

P.O. Box 456
Corona Del Mar, CA 92625
Ph: (888)834-6279/(949)729-8000
Fax: (949)675-9979
www.hamburgermarys.net
Full-service restaurant
Began: 1972, Franchising since: 1999
Headquarters size: 2 employees
Franchise department: 1 employee

U.S. franchises: 13
Canadian franchises: 0
Other foreign franchises: 0
Company-owned: 1
Units concentrated in AZ, CA, DC,
    FL, NV, OH, PA, TX

Seeking: All U.S.
Focusing on: CO, HI, IL, LA, MN,
    NY, WI
Seeking in Canada? No
Exclusive territories? Yes
Homebased option? No
Kiosk option? No
Employees needed to run franchise: 35
Absentee ownership? No

COSTS
Total cost: $250K-1M
Franchise fee: $45K
Royalty fee: 5%
Term of agreement: 5 years renewable
Franchisees required to buy multiple
    units? No

FINANCING
In-house: Accounts receivable, equip-
    ment, inventory, payroll, start-up
    costs
3rd-party: Accounts receivable, equip-
    ment, inventory, payroll, start-up
    costs

QUALIFICATIONS
Net worth: $200K
Cash liquidity: $75K
Experience:
    Industry experience
    Marketing skills
    Bar/restaurant-management expe-
    rience

TRAINING
At headquarters: 21 days+
At franchisee's location: 2 weeks
Additional training in California

BUSINESS SUPPORT
Newsletter
Meetings
Toll-free phone line
Grand opening
Internet
Lease negotiations
Security/safety procedures
Field operations/evaluations

MARKETING SUPPORT
Co-op advertising
Ad slicks
National media campaign
Regional marketing

HUHOT MONGOLIAN GRILL

Current financial data not available

10167 Miller Creek Rd.
Missoula, MT 59803
Ph: (406)251-4303
Fax: (406)251-4575
www.huhot.com
Mongolian grill restaurant
Began: 1999, Franchising since: 2001
Headquarters size: 6 employees
Franchise department: 4 employees

U.S. franchises: 4
Canadian franchises: 0
Other foreign franchises: 0
Company-owned: 1
Units concentrated in CO, IA, MT,
    ND, NE, SD, WA

Seeking: All U.S.
Seeking in Canada? No
Exclusive territories? Yes
Homebased option? No
Kiosk option? No
Employees needed to run franchise: 50
Absentee ownership? Yes

COSTS
Total cost: $327K-622K
Franchise fee: $30K
Royalty fee: 5%
Term of agreement: 15 years renewable
    at no charge
Franchisees required to buy multiple
    units? No

FINANCING
No financing available

QUALIFICATIONS
Net worth: $500K
Cash liquidity: $200K
Experience:
    General business experience

TRAINING
At headquarters: 3 weeks
At franchisee's location: Varies

BUSINESS SUPPORT
Grand opening
Internet
Lease negotiations
Security/safety procedures
Field operations/evaluations

MARKETING SUPPORT
Co-op advertising
Ad slicks
Regional marketing

INDIGO JOE'S SPORTS PUB & RESTAURANT

Financial rating: $$

132 N. El Camino Real, #384
Encinitas, CA 92024
Ph: (888)303-5637/(760)635-9020
Fax: (760)633-3563
www.indigojoes.com
Family sports pub restaurant
Began: 1994, Franchising since: 2002
Headquarters size: 5 employees
Franchise department: 1 employee

U.S. franchises: 0
Canadian franchises: 0
Other foreign franchises: 0
Company-owned: 1
Units concentrated in CA

Seeking: All U.S.
Focusing on: AZ, CA, NV
Seeking in Canada? Yes
Exclusive territories? Yes
Homebased option? No
Kiosk option? No
Employees needed to run franchise: 15
Absentee ownership? No

COSTS
Total cost: $332.8K-554.5K
Franchise fee: $25K
Royalty fee: 5%
Term of agreement: 10 years renewable
    for $10K
Franchisees required to buy multiple
    units? Outside the U.S. only

FINANCING
No financing available

QUALIFICATIONS
Cash liquidity: $50K-100K

TRAINING
At headquarters: 6 weeks

BUSINESS SUPPORT
Meetings
Toll-free phone line
Grand opening
Internet
Security/safety procedures
Field operations/evaluations
Purchasing cooperatives

MARKETING SUPPORT
Co-op advertising
Ad slicks
Regional marketing

JOEY'S ONLY SEAFOOD RESTAURANT

Current financial data not available

514 42nd Ave. S.E.
Calgary, AB Canada T2G 1Y6
Ph: (800)661-2123/(403)243-4584
Fax: (403)243-8989
www.joeys-only.com
Seafood, rotisserie chicken, ribs
Began: 1985, Franchising since: 1985
Headquarters size: 20 employees
Franchise department: 2 employees

U.S. franchises: 11
Canadian franchises: 88
Other foreign franchises: 0
Company-owned: 0
Units concentrated in all U.S.

Seeking: All U.S.
Seeking in Canada? Yes
Exclusive territories? Yes
Homebased option? No
Kiosk option? Yes
Employees needed to run franchise: 15
Absentee ownership? Yes

COSTS
Total cost: $121K-327.8K
Kiosk cost: $121K-156.5K
Franchise fee: $20K-25K
Royalty fee: 4.5%
Term of agreement: 10 years renewable
for $5K
Franchisees required to buy multiple
units? No

FINANCING
No financing available

QUALIFICATIONS
Net worth: $200K
Cash liquidity: $80K+
Experience:
General business experience

TRAINING
At headquarters: 4-5 weeks
At franchisee's location: Approx. 2
weeks

BUSINESS SUPPORT
Newsletter
Meetings
Toll-free phone line
Grand opening
Internet
Lease negotiations
Security/safety procedures
Field operations/evaluations
Purchasing cooperatives

MARKETING SUPPORT
Co-op advertising
Ad slicks
National media campaign
Regional marketing
POS materials

JOHNNY ROCKETS GROUP INC.

Ranked #367 in Entrepreneur Magazine's 2004 Franchise 500

Financial rating: $$

26970 Aliso Viejo Pkwy., #100
Aliso Viejo, CA 92656
Ph: (949)643-6100
Fax: (949)643-6200
www.johnnyrockets.com
1940s-style hamburger malt shop
Began: 1986, Franchising since: 1987
Headquarters size: 20 employees
Franchise department: 4 employees

U.S. franchises: 87
Canadian franchises: 0
Other foreign franchises: 12
Company-owned: 42
Units concentrated in all U.S.

Seeking: All U.S.
Focusing on: DC, FL, MD, NY, VA
Seeking in Canada? Yes
Exclusive territories? Yes
Homebased option? No
Kiosk option? No
Employees needed to run franchise:
48-53
Absentee ownership? No

COSTS
Total cost: $581K-877K
Franchise fee: $45K
Royalty fee: 5%
Term of agreement: 10 years w/two 5-
year options renewable at no
charge
Franchisees required to buy multiple
units? Yes

FINANCING
In-house: None
3rd-party: Equipment, inventory,
start-up costs

QUALIFICATIONS
Net worth: $1M+
Experience:
5 years restaurant-operations expe-
rience

TRAINING
At headquarters: 1 day
At franchisee's location: 10 days
At training store: 4-6 weeks

BUSINESS SUPPORT
Meetings
Grand opening
Field operations/evaluations

MARKETING SUPPORT
National media campaign
Regional marketing
Advertising support

THE MELTING POT RESTAURANTS INC.

Ranked #245 in Entrepreneur Magazine's 2004 Franchise 500　　　　　*Financial rating: $$$$*

8810 Twin Lakes Blvd.
Tampa, FL 33614
Ph: (800)783-0867, ext. 108
Fax: (813)889-9361
www.meltingpot.com
Fondue-specialty restaurant
Began: 1975, Franchising since: 1984
Headquarters size: 22 employees
Franchise department: 15 employees

U.S. franchises: 61
Canadian franchises: 0
Other foreign franchises: 0
Company-owned: 4

Seeking: All U.S.
Seeking in Canada? Yes
Exclusive territories? Yes
Homebased option? No
Kiosk option? No
Employees needed to run franchise:
　Info not provided
Absentee ownership? No

COSTS
Total cost: $595.8K-1M
Franchise fee: $32K
Royalty fee: 4.5%
Term of agreement: 10 years renewable
　for 50% of current franchise fee
Franchisees required to buy multiple
　units? No

FINANCING
In-house: None
3rd-party: Accounts receivable, equipment, franchise fee, inventory, payroll, start-up costs

QUALIFICATIONS
Cash liquidity: $125K-200K+
Experience:
　General business experience

TRAINING
At headquarters
At franchisee's location

BUSINESS SUPPORT
Newsletter
Meetings
Toll-free phone line
Grand opening
Internet
Security/safety procedures
Field operations/evaluations
Purchasing cooperatives

MARKETING SUPPORT
Co-op advertising
Ad slicks
Local marketing
Media planning services

PEPE'S MEXICAN RESTAURANTS

Ranked #499 in Entrepreneur Magazine's 2004 Franchise 500　　　　　*Financial rating: $$$$*

1325 W. 15th St.
Chicago, IL 60608
Ph: (312)733-2500
Fax: (312)733-2564
www.pepes.com
Mexican restaurant
Began: 1967, Franchising since: 1967
Headquarters size: 12 employees
Franchise department: 12 employees

U.S. franchises: 52
Canadian franchises: 0
Other foreign franchises: 0
Company-owned: 0
Units concentrated in IL, IN

Seeking: Midwest, Northeast,
　Southeast
Focusing on: Midwest
Seeking in Canada? No
Exclusive territories? Yes
Homebased option? No
Kiosk option? No
Employees needed to run franchise: 10
Absentee ownership? No

COSTS
Total cost: $145.1K-316K
Franchise fee: $15K
Royalty fee: 4%
Term of agreement: 20 years renewable
　at no charge
Franchisees required to buy multiple
　units? No

FINANCING
No financing available

QUALIFICATIONS
Experience:
　General business experience

TRAINING
At headquarters: 2 weeks
At franchisee's location: 2 weeks

BUSINESS SUPPORT
Newsletter
Meetings
Grand opening
Field operations/evaluations
Purchasing cooperatives

MARKETING SUPPORT
Co-op advertising
Ad slicks
National media campaign
Regional marketing

PIZZERIA UNO CHICAGO BAR & GRILL
Ranked #220 in Entrepreneur Magazine's 2004 Franchise 500   *Financial rating: $$$$*

100 Charles Park Rd.
Boston, MA 02132
Ph: (617)218-5325
Fax: (617)218-5376
www.unos.com
Full-service restaurant
Began: 1943, Franchising since: 1980
Headquarters size: 118 employees
Franchise department: 5 employees

U.S. franchises: 74
Canadian franchises: 0
Other foreign franchises: 2
Company-owned: 116
Units concentrated in all U.S.

Seeking: All U.S.
Seeking in Canada? Yes
Exclusive territories? Yes
Homebased option? No
Kiosk option? No
Employees needed to run franchise:
    Info not provided
Absentee ownership? Info not provided

COSTS
Total cost: $778K-1.7M
Franchise fee: $35K
Royalty fee: 5%
Term of agreement: Info not provided
Franchisees required to buy multiple
    units? Yes

FINANCING
3rd-party: Equipment
Other: Leasehold improvements, site

QUALIFICATIONS
Net worth: $3M
Cash liquidity: $750K
Experience:
    Industry experience

TRAINING
At headquarters: 16 weeks
At franchisee's location: 2-4 weeks

BUSINESS SUPPORT
Newsletter
Meetings
Toll-free phone line
Grand opening
Internet
Security/safety procedures
Field operations/evaluations
Purchasing cooperatives

MARKETING SUPPORT
Co-op advertising
Ad slicks
National media campaign
Regional marketing
FSIs

VAN HOUTTE INC.
Current financial data not available

8300 19th Ave.
Montreal, PQ Canada H1Z 4J8
Ph: (514)593-7711
Fax: (514)593-9582
www.vanhoutte.com
Cafe/bistro
Began: 1919, Franchising since: 1983
Headquarters size: 60 employees
Franchise department: 15 employees

U.S. franchises: 0
Canadian franchises: 64
Other foreign franchises: 0
Company-owned: 3
Units concentrated in Canada

Not available in the U.S.
Seeking in Canada? Yes
Exclusive territories? No
Homebased option? No
Kiosk option? No
Employees needed to run franchise:
    8-10
Absentee ownership? No

COSTS
Total cost: $225K
Franchise fee: $25K
Royalty fee: 5%
Term of agreement: 10 years renewable
    at no charge
Franchisees required to buy multiple
    units? No

FINANCING
No financing available

QUALIFICATIONS
Net worth: $70K
Cash liquidity: $70K
Experience:
    General business experience

TRAINING
At headquarters: 4 weeks

BUSINESS SUPPORT
Meetings
Grand opening
Field operations/evaluations
Purchasing cooperatives

MARKETING SUPPORT
Co-op advertising
Regional marketing

WINGER'S

Current financial data not available

404 E. 4500 South, #A12
Salt Lake City, UT 84107
Ph: (801)261-3700
Fax: (801)261-1615
www.wingersdiner.com
Casual-theme restaurant
Began: 1993, Franchising since: 1997
Headquarters size: 18 employees
Franchise department: 8 employees

U.S. franchises: 17
Canadian franchises: 0
Other foreign franchises: 1
Company-owned: 9
Units concentrated in ID, NV, OR,
    UT, WY

Seeking: Midwest, Northwest,
    Southwest, West
Seeking in Canada? No
Exclusive territories? Yes
Homebased option? No
Kiosk option? No
Employees needed to run franchise: 35
Absentee ownership? Yes

COSTS
Total cost: $124.5K-1.1M
Franchise fee: $30K
Royalty fee: 4%
Term of agreement: 15 years renewable
    for 10% of current franchise fee
Franchisees required to buy multiple
    units? No

FINANCING
No financing available

QUALIFICATIONS
Net worth: $400K
Cash liquidity: $200K
Experience:
    Industry experience
    General business experience
    Marketing skills

TRAINING
At headquarters: 1 day
At franchisee's location: 2-3 weeks at
    opening
At company diner: 6 weeks

BUSINESS SUPPORT
Meetings
Grand opening
Security/safety procedures
Field operations/evaluations
Purchasing cooperatives

MARKETING SUPPORT
Ad slicks
Regional marketing
Advertising materials

ZYNG ASIAN GRILL

Financial rating: $$$

132 King St.
Alexandria, VA 22314
Ph: (703)837-5175
Fax: (703)549-0740
www.zyng.com
Asian-style restaurant
Began: 1997, Franchising since: 1999
Headquarters size: 12 employees
Franchise department: 4 employees

U.S. franchises: 1
Canadian franchises: 6
Other foreign franchises: 0
Company-owned: 2
Units concentrated in CA, DC, GA,
    IN, KS, OH, VA

Seeking: All U.S.
Seeking in Canada? Yes
Exclusive territories? Yes
Homebased option? No
Kiosk option? No
Employees needed to run franchise: 24
Absentee ownership? Yes

COSTS
Total cost: $212K-480K
Franchise fee: $25K
Royalty fee: 5%
Term of agreement: 10 years renewable
Franchisees required to buy multiple
    units? Yes

FINANCING
In-house: None
3rd-party: Accounts receivable, equip-
    ment, franchise fee, inventory, pay-
    roll, start-up costs

QUALIFICATIONS
Net worth: $700K
Cash liquidity: $150K
Experience:
    Industry experience
    General business experience
    Marketing skills

TRAINING
At headquarters: 4 weeks
At franchisee's location: 2 weeks
Additional training

BUSINESS SUPPORT
Newsletter
Meetings
Toll-free phone line
Grand opening
Internet
Lease negotiations
Security/safety procedures
Field operations/evaluations
Purchasing cooperatives

MARKETING SUPPORT
Co-op advertising
Ad slicks
National media campaign
Regional marketing

FULL SERVICE *Other Franchises*

CHEEBURGER CHEEBURGER
15951 McGregor Blvd., #2A
Ft. Myers, FL 33908
Ph: (800)487-6211/(239)437-1611
www.cheeburger.com
Theme restaurant w/gourmet burgers

DIAMOND DAVE'S MEXICAN RESTAURANTS
201 S. Clinton St., #281
Iowa City, IA 52240
Ph: (319)337-7690
www.diamonddaves.com
Mexican restaurant

DICKEY'S BARBECUE PIT RESTAURANTS
4514 Cole Ave., #1000
Dallas, TX 75205-4177
Ph: (972)248-9899
www.dickeys.com
Texas-style barbecue restaurant

GREEN MILL RESTAURANTS
*Ranked #436 in Entrepreneur
    Magazine's 2004 Franchise 500*
4105 Lexington Ave. N., #240
Arden Hills, MN 55126
Ph: (651)203-3100
www.greenmill.com
Upscale pizza restaurant

TONY ROMA'S
9304 Forest Ln., #200
Dallas, TX 75243-8953
Ph: (214)343-7800
www.tonyromas.com
Barbecued ribs-specialty restaurant

TUMBLEWEED INC.
2301 River Rd., #200
Louisville, KY 40206
Ph: (502)893-0323
www.tumbleweedrestaurants.com
Southwestern-style restaurant

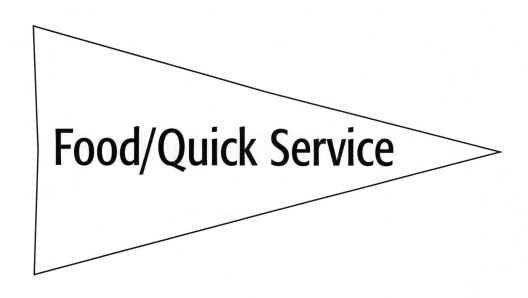

QUICK SERVICE *Asian*

EDO JAPAN INC.

Current financial data not available

4838 32nd St. S.E.
Calgary, AB Canada T2B 2S6
Ph: (403)215-8800
Fax: (403)215-8801
www.edojapan.com
Japanese fast food
Began: 1977, Franchising since: 1986
Headquarters size: 10 employees
Franchise department: 6 employees

U.S. franchises: 34
Canadian franchises: 53
Other foreign franchises: 3
Company-owned: 4
Units concentrated in AZ, CA, CO, FL,
     HI, ID, MD, NM, NV, OR, TX, UT,
     WA

Seeking: All U.S.
Focusing on: AZ, CA, CO, FL, HI, ID,
     MD, NM, NV, OR, TX, UT, WA
Seeking in Canada? No
Exclusive territories? No
Homebased option? No

Kiosk option? Yes
Employees needed to run franchise: 6
Absentee ownership? Yes

COSTS
Total cost: $150K-287K
Kiosk cost: Same as total cost
Franchise fee: $20K
Royalty fee: 6%
Term of agreement: 10 years renewable
     for 25% of franchise fee
Franchisees required to buy multiple
     units? No

FINANCING
No financing available

QUALIFICATIONS
Experience:
     Industry experience
     General business experience

TRAINING
At headquarters: 10 days
At franchisee's location: 10 days

BUSINESS SUPPORT
Newsletter
Grand opening
Lease negotiations
Field operations/evaluations

MARKETING SUPPORT
Regional marketing

KOYA JAPAN

Current financial data not available

207-720 Broadway Ave.
Winnipeg, MB Canada R3G 0X1
Ph: (888)569-2872/(204)783-4433
Fax: (204)783-1749
www.koyajapan.com
Japanese fast food
Began: 1985, Franchising since: 1986
Headquarters size: 4 employees
Franchise department: 3 employees

U.S. franchises: 2
Canadian franchises: 27
Other foreign franchises: 0
Company-owned: 1
Units concentrated in CO

Seeking: All U.S.
Seeking in Canada? Yes
Exclusive territories? Yes
Homebased option? No
Kiosk option? Info not provided
Employees needed to run franchise: 6
Absentee ownership? Yes

COSTS
Total cost: $213.7K-335.1K
Franchise fee: $25K
Royalty fee: 6%
Term of agreement: Renewable term
Franchisees required to buy multiple
    units? No

FINANCING
No financing available

QUALIFICATIONS
Experience:
    General business experience

TRAINING
At headquarters: Up to 1 week
At franchisee's location: Up to 1
    month

BUSINESS SUPPORT
Toll-free phone line
Grand opening
Lease negotiations
Field operations/evaluations

MARKETING SUPPORT
National media campaign
Regional marketing

MADE IN JAPAN TERIYAKI EXPERIENCE

Current financial data not available

700 Kerr St.
Oakville, ON Canada L6K 3W5
Ph: (905)337-7777
Fax: (905)337-0331
www.donatogroup.com
Japanese fast food
Began: 1986, Franchising since: 1987
Headquarters size: 25 employees
Franchise department: Info not pro-
    vided

U.S. franchises: 0
Canadian franchises: 59
Other foreign franchises: 11
Company-owned: 2
Units concentrated in Canada

Seeking: All U.S.
Seeking in Canada? Yes
Exclusive territories? Yes
Homebased option? No
Kiosk option? No
Employees needed to run franchise:
    Info not provided
Absentee ownership? Yes

COSTS
Total cost: $183K-229.8K
Franchise fee: $25K
Royalty fee: 6%
Term of agreement: 10 years renewable
    for $1K per year
Franchisees required to buy multiple
    units? No

FINANCING
No financing available

QUALIFICATIONS
Cash liquidity: $80K

TRAINING
At headquarters: 18 days
At franchisee's location: 1 week

BUSINESS SUPPORT
Newsletter
Meetings
Toll-free phone line
Grand opening
Internet
Security/safety procedures
Field operations/evaluations
Purchasing cooperatives

MARKETING SUPPORT
Co-op advertising
Ad slicks
National media campaign
Regional marketing

MANCHU WOK

Ranked #408 in Entrepreneur Magazine's 2004 Franchise 500   *Financial rating: 0*

12912 Meadow Breeze Dr.
Wellington, FL 33414
Ph: (561)798-7800
Fax: (561)333-6663
www.manchuwok.com
Chinese fast food
Began: 1981, Franchising since: 1989
Headquarters size: 47 employees
Franchise department: 4 employees

U.S. franchises: 92
Canadian franchises: 69
Other foreign franchises: 0
Company-owned: 42
Units concentrated in CA, FL, GA, IL
NY, TX, VA

Seeking: All U.S.
Focusing on: CA, CO, MN, NY, TX,
WA
Seeking in Canada? Yes
Exclusive territories? Yes
Homebased option? No
Kiosk option? No
Employees needed to run franchise: 12
Absentee ownership? Yes

COSTS
Total cost: $268.6K-332.8K
Franchise fee: $20K
Royalty fee: 7%
Term of agreement: 5 years renewable
for $3K per year
Franchisees required to buy multiple
units? No

FINANCING
In-house: Franchise fee, equipment,
start-up costs
3rd-party: Equipment inventory, payroll

QUALIFICATIONS
Net worth: $100K
Cash liquidity: $80K
Experience:
Industry experience
General business experience
Marketing skills

TRAINING
At headquarters: 3 weeks

BUSINESS SUPPORT
Newsletter
Meetings
Toll-free phone line
Grand opening
Security/safety procedures
Field operations/evaluations
Purchasing cooperatives

MARKETING SUPPORT
Co-op advertising
Ad slicks
National media campaign
Regional marketing
Local marketing

SAMURAI SAM'S TERIYAKI GRILL

Current financial data not available

7730 E. Greenway Dr., #104
Scottsdale, AZ 85260
Ph: (480)443-0200
Fax: (480)483-4621
www.samuraisams.net
Japanese fast food
Began: 1994, Franchising since: 1995
Headquarters size: 7 employees
Franchise department: 7 employees

U.S. franchises: 57
Canadian franchises: 0
Other foreign franchises: 0
Company-owned: 1
Units concentrated in AZ, CA, CO,
WA

Seeking: All U.S.
Seeking in Canada? No
Exclusive territories? Yes
Homebased option? No
Kiosk option? Yes
Employees needed to run franchise:
10-25
Absentee ownership? Yes

COSTS
Total cost: $118.5K-199.5K
Kiosk cost: To be determined
Franchise fee: $30K
Royalty fee: 6%
Term of agreement: 15 years renewable
for $5K
Franchisees required to buy multiple
units? No

FINANCING
No financing available

QUALIFICATIONS
Net worth: $250K
Cash liquidity: $50K
Experience:
General business experience

TRAINING
At headquarters: 2 weeks
At franchisee's location: 1 week

BUSINESS SUPPORT
Newsletter
Meetings
Toll-free phone line
Grand opening
Security/safety procedures
Field operations/evaluations
Purchasing cooperatives

MARKETING SUPPORT
Co-op advertising
Ad slicks
Regional marketing

ARIZONA BREAD COMPANY

Current financial data not available

8700 E. Via De Ventura, #305
Scottsdale, AZ 85258
Ph: (480)778-9090
Fax: (480)778-1960
www.azbread.com
Bakery & sandwiches
Began: 1994, Franchising since: 2002
Headquarters size: 10 employees
Franchise department: 10 employees

U.S. franchises: 0
Canadian franchises: 0
Other foreign franchises: 0
Company-owned: 2

Seeking: All U.S.
Seeking in Canada? No
Exclusive territories? Yes
Homebased option? No
Kiosk option? No
Employees needed to run franchise:
    13-15
Absentee ownership? Yes

COSTS
Total cost: $149K-341.5K
Franchise fee: $25K
Royalty fee: 5%
Term of agreement: 20 years renewable
    for 50% of current franchise fee
Franchisees required to buy multiple
    units? Yes

FINANCING
In-house: None
3rd-party: Accounts receivable, equip-
    ment, franchise fee, inventory, pay-
    roll, start-up costs

QUALIFICATIONS
Net worth: $300K
Cash liquidity: $75K-100K
Experience:
    Management skills

TRAINING
At headquarters: 4 weeks
At franchisee's location: 2 weeks

BUSINESS SUPPORT
Meetings
Toll-free phone line
Grand opening
Internet
Lease negotiations
Security/safety procedures
Field operations/evaluations
Purchasing cooperatives

MARKETING SUPPORT
Co-op advertising
Ad slicks
Regional marketing
Menu rollouts

ATLANTA BREAD CO.

Ranked #393 in Entrepreneur Magazine's 2004 Franchise 500   *Financial rating: $$$*

1200-A Wilson Wy., #100
Smyrna, GA 30082
Ph: (770)432-0933
Fax: (770)444-9082
www.atlantabread.com
Bakery/cafe
Began: 1993, Franchising since: 1995
Headquarters size: 65 employees
Franchise department: 5 employees

U.S. franchises: 147
Canadian franchises: 0
Other foreign franchises: 0
Company-owned: 11
Units concentrated in FL, GA, NC, SC

Seeking: All U.S.
Seeking in Canada? No
Exclusive territories? Yes
Homebased option? No
Kiosk option? No
Employees needed to run franchise:
    15-18
Absentee ownership? No

COSTS
Total cost: $629.7K-806.3K
Franchise fee: $40K-30K
Royalty fee: 5%
Term of agreement: 10 years renewable
    for $30K
Franchisees required to buy multiple
    units? No

FINANCING
No financing available

QUALIFICATIONS
Net worth: $650K
Cash liquidity: $300K-400K
Experience:
    General business experience
    Marketing skills
    Restaurant experience

TRAINING
At headquarters: 10 days
At franchisee's location: 5 weeks

BUSINESS SUPPORT
Newsletter
Meetings
Toll-free phone line
Grand opening
Internet
Lease negotiations
Security/safety procedures
Field operations/evaluations
Purchasing cooperatives

MARKETING SUPPORT
Co-op advertising
Ad slicks
Regional marketing

BETWEEN ROUNDS BAKERY SANDWICH CAFE

Financial rating: 0

19A John Fitch Blvd., Rte. 5
South Windsor, CT 06074
Ph: (860)291-0323
Fax: (860)289-2732
Bagels, baked goods, deli items, catering
Began: 1990, Franchising since: 1992
Headquarters size: 4 employees
Franchise department: 2 employees

U.S. franchises: 3
Canadian franchises: 0
Other foreign franchises: 0
Company-owned: 3
Units concentrated in CT, MA

Seeking: Northeast
Focusing on: CT, MA, NY, RI
Seeking in Canada? No
Exclusive territories? Yes
Homebased option? No
Kiosk option? No
Employees needed to run franchise: 8
Absentee ownership? No

COSTS
Total cost: $168K-215K
Franchise fee: $18K-25K
Royalty fee: 4%
Term of agreement: 10 years renewable
for $3.6K
Franchisees required to buy multiple
units? No

FINANCING
No financing available

QUALIFICATIONS
Net worth: $200K
Cash liquidity: $80K-100K
Experience:
Industry experience
General business experience
Marketing skills

TRAINING
At headquarters: 2 weeks
At franchisee's location: 1 week

BUSINESS SUPPORT
Meetings
Grand opening
Lease negotiations
Security/safety procedures
Field operations/evaluations
Purchasing cooperatives

MARKETING SUPPORT
Co-op advertising
Ad slicks
Regional marketing

BIG APPLE BAGELS

Ranked #293 in Entrepreneur Magazine's 2004 Franchise 500

Financial rating: $$$$

8501 W. Higgins Rd., #320
Chicago, IL 60631
Ph: (800)251-6101
Fax: (773)380-6183
www.babcorp.com
Bagels, sandwiches, gourmet coffee,
muffins
Began: 1993, Franchising since: 1993
Headquarters size: 22 employees
Franchise department: 7 employees

U.S. franchises: 165
Canadian franchises: 0
Other foreign franchises: 8
Company-owned: 4
Units concentrated in IL, MI, WI

Seeking: All U.S.
Seeking in Canada? Yes
Exclusive territories? Yes
Homebased option? No
Kiosk option? Yes
Employees needed to run franchise: 15
Absentee ownership? Yes

COSTS
Total cost: $174.8K-349.5K
Kiosk cost: $10K
Franchise fee: $25K
Royalty fee: 5%
Term of agreement: 10 years renewable
for $2.5K
Franchisees required to buy multiple
units? Outside the U.S. only

FINANCING
No financing available

QUALIFICATIONS
Net worth: $300K+
Cash liquidity: $60K
Experience:
General business experience

TRAINING
At headquarters: 11 days
At franchisee's location: 5 days
Additional training available

BUSINESS SUPPORT
Newsletter
Meetings
Toll-free phone line
Grand opening
Internet
Lease negotiations
Security/safety procedures
Field operations/evaluations

MARKETING SUPPORT
Ad slicks
Regional marketing
In-store POP

BREADSMITH

Financial rating: $$

409 E. Silver Spring Dr.
Whitefish Bay, WI 53217
Ph: (414)962-1965
Fax: (414)962-5888
www.breadsmith.com
Hearth-baked breads
Began: 1993, Franchising since: 1993
Headquarters size: 8 employees
Franchise department: 2 employees

U.S. franchises: 32
Canadian franchises: 0
Other foreign franchises: 0
Company-owned: 1
Units concentrated in Midwest

Seeking: All U.S.
Seeking in Canada? No
Exclusive territories? No
Homebased option? No
Kiosk option? No
Employees needed to run franchise: 20
Absentee ownership? No

COSTS
Total cost: $217.5K-416K
Franchise fee: $30K
Royalty fee: 7%
Term of agreement: 15 years renewable
for $500
Franchisees required to buy multiple
units? No

FINANCING
No financing available

QUALIFICATIONS
Net worth: $500K
Cash liquidity: $50K
Experience:
General business experience
Marketing skills

TRAINING
At headquarters: 3 weeks
At franchisee's location: 2 weeks

BUSINESS SUPPORT
Newsletter
Meetings
Toll-free phone line
Grand opening
Internet
Lease negotiations
Field operations/evaluations

MARKETING SUPPORT
Co-op advertising
Ad slicks
Posters
POP
Annual promotions

CINDY'S CINNAMON ROLLS

Current financial data not available

P.O. Box 1480
Fallbrook, CA 92028
Ph: (800)468-7655/(760)723-1121
Fax: (760)723-4143
Specialty bakery
Began: 1985, Franchising since: 1986
Headquarters size: 5 employees
Franchise department: 3 employees

U.S. franchises: 27
Canadian franchises: 0
Other foreign franchises: 5
Company-owned: 0
Units concentrated in all U.S.

Seeking: All U.S.
Seeking in Canada? Yes
Exclusive territories? No
Homebased option? No
Kiosk option? Yes
Employees needed to run franchise: 8
Absentee ownership? Yes

COSTS
Total cost: $69K-130.5K
Kiosk cost: $135K
Franchise fee: $25K
Royalty fee: 5%
Term of agreement: 10 years renewable
at no charge
Franchisees required to buy multiple
units? No

FINANCING
No financing available

QUALIFICATIONS
Net worth: $150K
Cash liquidity: $25K
Experience:
General business experience

TRAINING
At headquarters: 1 week
At franchisee's location: 4 days

BUSINESS SUPPORT
Newsletter
Toll-free phone line
Grand opening
Lease negotiations
Security/safety procedures
Field operations/evaluations
Purchasing cooperatives

MARKETING SUPPORT
Ad slicks

CINNABON INC.

Current financial data not available

6 Concourse Pkwy., #1700
Atlanta, GA 30328
Ph: (800)639-3826
Fax: (770)353-3093
www.cinnabon.com
Cinnamon rolls
Began: 1969, Franchising since: 1986
Headquarters size: 50 employees
Franchise department: 3 employees

U.S. franchises: 361
Canadian franchises: 23
Other foreign franchises: 149
Company-owned: 83
Units concentrated in CA, FL, IL, MD,
NV, NY, OH, TX, WA

Seeking: All U.S.
Focusing on: AL, AR, ID, KS, LA, MO,
MS, MT, ND, NY, OR, VA, VT
Seeking in Canada? Yes
Exclusive territories? Yes
Homebased option? No
Kiosk option? Info not provided
Employees needed to run franchise:
8-10
Absentee ownership? Yes

COSTS
Total cost: $232.5K-333.5K
Franchise fee: $30K-35K
Royalty fee: 5%
Term of agreement: 10-20 years
renewable for 50% of current fran-
chise fee
Franchisees required to buy multiple
units? Yes

FINANCING
No financing available

QUALIFICATIONS
Net worth: $600K
Cash liquidity: $300K
Experience:
Industry experience
General business experience
Marketing skills

TRAINING
At headquarters: 3 weeks
At franchisee's location: 3-5 days

BUSINESS SUPPORT
Newsletter
Meetings
Toll-free phone line
Grand opening
Internet
Lease negotiations
Security/safety procedures
Field operations/evaluations
Purchasing cooperatives

MARKETING SUPPORT
Co-op advertising
Ad slicks
Regional marketing

CINNAMON CITY

Current financial data not available

P.O. Box 490, 2265 W. Railway St.
Abbotsford, BC Canada V2S 5Z5
Ph: (604)852-8771
Fax: (604)859-1711
www.shefieldgourmet.com
Cinnamon rolls & baked goods
Began: 1992, Franchising since: 1996
Headquarters size: Info not provided
Franchise department: 2 employees

U.S. franchises: 0
Canadian franchises: 13
Other foreign franchises: 0
Company-owned: 1
Units concentrated in Canada

Not available in the U.S.
Seeking in Canada? Yes
Exclusive territories? Yes
Homebased option? No
Kiosk option? Yes
Employees needed to run franchise: 4
Absentee ownership? Yes

COSTS
Total cost: $79.9K-119.90K
Kiosk cost: $79K-100K
Franchise fee: $25K
Royalty fee: 6%
Term of agreement: 5 years renewable
at no charge
Franchisees required to buy multiple
units? Info not provided

FINANCING
No financing available

QUALIFICATIONS
Net worth: $100K
Cash liquidity: $40K
Experience:
General business experience

TRAINING
At franchisee's location: 2 weeks

BUSINESS SUPPORT
Newsletter
Meetings
Toll-free phone line
Grand opening
Lease negotiations
Field operations/evaluations

MARKETING SUPPORT
Co-op advertising
Ad slicks
National media campaign
Regional marketing

CINNZEO

Current financial data not available

6910 Farrell Rd. S.E.
Calgary, AB T2H Canada 0T1
Ph: (403)255-4556
Fax: (403)259-5124
www.cinnzeo.com
Cinnamon rolls
Began: 1987, Franchising since: 1998
Headquarters size: 12 employees
Franchise department: 3 employees

U.S. franchises: 4
Canadian franchises: 16
Other foreign franchises: 14
Company-owned: 6
Units concentrated in AZ, CA, FL

Seeking: All U.S.
Focusing on: CA, TX
Seeking in Canada? Yes
Exclusive territories? Yes
Homebased option? No
Kiosk option? No
Employees needed to run franchise: 15
Absentee ownership? Yes

COSTS
Total cost: $214K-621K
Franchise fee: $15K
Royalty fee: 7%
Term of agreement: 10 years renewable
    for $4K
Franchisees required to buy multiple
    units? No

FINANCING
No financing available

QUALIFICATIONS
Net worth: $500K
Cash liquidity: $200K
Experience:
    Industry experience
    General business experience
    Marketing skills

TRAINING
At headquarters: 3 weeks
At franchisee's location: 2 weeks

BUSINESS SUPPORT
Newsletter
Meetings
Toll-free phone line
Grand opening
Internet
Lease negotiations
Security/safety procedures
Field operations/evaluations

MARKETING SUPPORT
Info not provided

COOKIE FACTORY BAKERY

Ranked #312 in Entrepreneur Magazine's 2004 Franchise 500   *Financial rating: $$$$*

1010 W. St. Maartens Dr.
St. Joseph, MO 64506
Ph: (816)364-1088
Fax: (816)364-3739
www.thecookiefactorybakery.com
Cookies & bakery products
Began: 1970, Franchising since: 1991
Headquarters size: 15 employees
Franchise department: 2 employees

U.S. franchises: 23
Canadian franchises: 0
Other foreign franchises: 0
Company-owned: 2
Units concentrated in IL, MO

Seeking: Midwest
Focusing on: IA, IL, KS, MI, MO, NE
Seeking in Canada? No
Exclusive territories? Yes
Homebased option? No
Kiosk option? Yes
Employees needed to run franchise: 12
Absentee ownership? Yes

COSTS
Total cost: $98K-237.5K
    Kiosk cost: $25K-50K
Franchise fee: $15K
Royalty fee: 5%
Term of agreement: 15 years renewable
    for 25% of then-current fee
Franchisees required to buy multiple
    units? No

FINANCING
In-house: None
3rd-party: Equipment

QUALIFICATIONS
Net worth: $350K
Cash liquidity: $100K

TRAINING
At headquarters: 2 weeks
At franchisee's location: During first
    week

BUSINESS SUPPORT
Meetings
Toll-free phone line
Grand opening
Internet
Field operations/evaluations

MARKETING SUPPORT
Ad slicks

CRESCENT CITY BEIGNETS

Financial rating: $

3272 Westheimer, #1
Houston, TX 77098
Ph: (713)524-0012
Fax: (713)594-7642
www.crescentcitybeignets.com
French pastries/New Orleans-style
    coffeehouse
Began: 1997, Franchising since: 1999
Headquarters size: 12 employees
Franchise department: 8 employees

U.S. franchises: 10
Canadian franchises: 0
Other foreign franchises: 0
Company-owned: 1
Units concentrated in TX

Seeking: All U.S.
Seeking in Canada? Yes
Exclusive territories? Yes
Homebased option? No
Kiosk option? Yes
Employees needed to run franchise: 10
Absentee ownership? Yes

COSTS
Total cost: $250K-300K
    Kiosk cost: $150K-200K
Franchise fee: $25K
Royalty fee: 5%
Term of agreement: 10 years renewable
    for 15% of current franchise fee
Franchisees required to buy multiple
    units? Yes

FINANCING
In-house: None
3rd-party: Equipment, franchise fee,
    inventory, start-up costs

QUALIFICATIONS
Net worth: $1M
Cash liquidity: $200K
Experience:
    General business experience

TRAINING
At headquarters: 15 days
At franchisee's location: 14 days

BUSINESS SUPPORT
Newsletter
Grand opening
Internet
Lease negotiations
Security/safety procedures
Field operations/evaluations
Purchasing cooperatives

MARKETING SUPPORT
Co-op advertising
Ad slicks
Regional marketing
Advertising & graphic guideline CD-
    ROM

DUNKIN' DONUTS
Ranked #9 in Entrepreneur Magazine's 2004 Franchise 500

Financial rating: $$$$

14 Pacella Park Dr.
Randolph, MA 02368
Ph: (800)777-9983
Fax: (781)961-4207
www.dunkindonuts.com
Donuts & baked goods
Began: 1950, Franchising since: 1955
Headquarters size: Info not provided
Franchise department: Info not pro-
    vided

U.S. franchises: 4,255
Canadian franchises: 108
Other foreign franchises: 1,472
Company-owned: 0
Units concentrated in MA, NY, RI

Seeking: All U.S.
Seeking in Canada? Yes
Exclusive territories? No
Homebased option? No
Kiosk option? Yes
Employees needed to run franchise:
    Info not provided
Absentee ownership? No

COSTS
Total cost: $255.7K-1.1M
Kiosk cost: Varies
Franchise fee: $50K
Royalty fee: 5.9%
Term of agreement: Info not provided
Franchisees required to buy multiple
    units? No

FINANCING
No financing available

QUALIFICATIONS
Net worth: $900K
Cash liquidity: $450K
Experience:
    Industry experience
    General business experience
    Marketing skills

TRAINING
At headquarters: Varies

BUSINESS SUPPORT
Newsletter
Meetings
Toll-free phone line
Grand opening
Security/safety procedures
Field operations/evaluations

MARKETING SUPPORT
Regional marketing

GREAT AMERICAN COOKIES

Current financial data not available

2855 E. Cottonwood Pkwy., #400
Salt Lake City, UT 84121
Ph: (800)348-6311/(801)736-5600
Fax: (801)736-5936
www.greatamericancookies.com
Cookies
Began: 1977, Franchising since: 1977
Headquarters size: 150 employees
Franchise department: 25 employees

U.S. franchises: 224
Canadian franchises: 0
Other foreign franchises: 2
Company-owned: 60
Units concentrated in all U.S.

Seeking: All U.S.
Seeking in Canada? No
Exclusive territories? No
Homebased option? No
Kiosk option? Info not provided
Employees needed to run franchise:
    Info not provided
Absentee ownership? Info not provided

COSTS
Total cost: $118.3K-305.5K
Franchise fee: $30K
Royalty fee: 7%
Term of agreement: Co-terminus with
    lease, renewable
Franchisees required to buy multiple
    units? Outside the U.S. only

FINANCING
No financing available

QUALIFICATIONS
Net worth: $150K
Cash liquidity: $75K

TRAINING
At headquarters: 4 days
In Atlanta, GA

BUSINESS SUPPORT
Meetings
Toll-free phone line
Internet
Field operations/evaluations

MARKETING SUPPORT
Ad slicks

GREAT HARVEST FRANCHISING INC.

Ranked #234 in Entrepreneur Magazine's 2004 Franchise 500

Financial rating: $$$$

28 S. Montana St.
Dillon, MT 59725
Ph: (800)442-0424/(406)683-6842
Fax: (406)683-5537
www.greatharvest.com
Bread bakery
Began: 1976, Franchising since: 1978
Headquarters size: 28 employees
Franchise department: 28 employees

U.S. franchises: 171
Canadian franchises: 0
Other foreign franchises: 0
Company-owned: 1
Units concentrated in CO, IL, MI,
    MN, NC, OR, TX, UT, WA

Seeking: All U.S.
Seeking in Canada? Yes
Exclusive territories? Yes
Homebased option? No
Kiosk option? No
Employees needed to run franchise:
    5-7
Absentee ownership? No

COSTS
Total cost: $107.6K-352.3K
Franchise fee: $8K-30K
Royalty fee: 4-7%
Term of agreement: 10 years renewable
    at no charge
Franchisees required to buy multiple
    units? No

FINANCING
In-house: None
3rd-party: Equipment, franchise fee,
    inventory, start-up costs

QUALIFICATIONS
Net worth: $250K+
Cash liquidity: $80K
Experience:
    General business experience

TRAINING
At headquarters: 1 week
At franchisee's location: 1 week
At existing locations: 2 weeks

BUSINESS SUPPORT
Newsletter
Meetings
Toll-free phone line
Grand opening
Internet
Lease negotiations
Security/safety procedures
Field operations/evaluations
Purchasing cooperatives

MARKETING SUPPORT
Co-op advertising
Ad slicks
Regional marketing
Opening PR campaign
Monthly marketing promotions
Annual marketing plan

HOUSE OF BREAD

Financial rating: 0

858 Higuera St.
San Luis Obispo, CA 93401
Ph: (800)545-5146
Fax: (805)542-0257
www.houseofbread.com
Specialty bread, muffins, scones
Began: 1996, Franchising since: 1998
Headquarters size: 18 employees
Franchise department: 4 employees

U.S. franchises: 8
Canadian franchises: 0
Other foreign franchises: 0
Company-owned: 2
Units concentrated in CA, CO, CT,
    NV, TX, UT

Seeking: All U.S.
Seeking in Canada? No
Exclusive territories? Yes
Homebased option? No
Kiosk option? Yes
Employees needed to run franchise: 8
Absentee ownership? Yes

COSTS
Total cost: $99K-249K
Kiosk cost: $10K
Franchise fee: $24K
Royalty fee: 6%
Term of agreement: 10 years renewable
    for $5K
Franchisees required to buy multiple
    units? No

FINANCING
No financing available

QUALIFICATIONS
Net worth: $150K
Cash liquidity: $24K

TRAINING
At headquarters: 10 days
At franchisee's location: 10 days

BUSINESS SUPPORT
Newsletter
Meetings
Toll-free phone line
Grand opening
Internet
Lease negotiations
Security/safety procedures
Field operations/evaluations
Purchasing cooperatives

MARKETING SUPPORT
Co-op advertising
Ad slicks
Regional marketing

KETTLEMAN'S BAGEL CORP.

Current financial data not available

12 Inverary Dr.
Ottawa, ON Canada K2K 2R9
Ph: (613)592-2211
Fax: (613)592-9162
www.kettlemansbagel.com
Bagels
Began: 1992, Franchising since: 1996
Headquarters size: 5 employees
Franchise department: 1 employee

U.S. franchises: 0
Canadian franchises: 5
Other foreign franchises: 0
Company-owned: 1
Units concentrated in Canada

Seeking in Canada? Yes
Exclusive territories? Yes
Homebased option? No
Kiosk option? No
Employees needed to run franchise: 12
Absentee ownership? No

COSTS
Total cost: $300K-450K
Franchise fee: $25K
Royalty fee: 6%
Term of agreement: 10 years renewable
    for $6.25K
Franchisees required to buy multiple
    units? Outside the U.S. only

FINANCING
In-house: None
Equipment, start-up costs

QUALIFICATIONS
Net worth: $500K
Cash liquidity: $150K
Experience:
    Industry experience
    General business experience
    Marketing skills
    People skills

TRAINING
At headquarters: 6 weeks
At franchisee's location: 4 weeks

BUSINESS SUPPORT
Meetings
Toll-free phone line
Grand opening
Internet
Lease negotiations
Field operations/evaluations
Purchasing cooperatives

MARKETING SUPPORT
Co-op advertising
Ad slicks
Regional marketing

MANHATTAN BAGEL

Current financial data not available

100 Horizon Center Blvd.
Hamilton, NJ 08691
Ph: (609)631-7029
Fax: (609)631-7067
www.manhattanbagel.com
Bagel bakery & deli
Began: 1987, Franchising since: 1988
Headquarters size: Info not provided
Franchise department: Info not provided

U.S. franchises: 189
Canadian franchises: 0
Other foreign franchises: 0
Company-owned: 0
Units concentrated in CA, DE, FL, GA, NC, NJ, NY, PA, VA

Seeking: All U.S.
Focusing on: CT, DC, DE, MA, MD, NJ, NY, PA, VA
Seeking in Canada? No
Exclusive territories? Yes
Homebased option? No
Kiosk option? Yes
Employees needed to run franchise: 10-14
Absentee ownership? Yes

COSTS
Total cost: $159K-300K
Kiosk cost: $30K-125K
Franchise fee: $20K
Royalty fee: 5%
Term of agreement: 10 years renewable for 50% of current franchise fee
Franchisees required to buy multiple units? No

FINANCING
In-house: None
3rd-party: Equipment, inventory, start-up costs

QUALIFICATIONS
Net worth: $300K
Cash liquidity: $200K
Experience:
    General business experience

TRAINING
At headquarters: 2 weeks

BUSINESS SUPPORT
Newsletter
Meetings
Toll-free phone line
Grand opening
Internet
Security/safety procedures
Field operations/evaluations

MARKETING SUPPORT
Co-op advertising
Ad slicks
National media campaign
Regional marketing

MONTANA MILLS BREAD CO.

Current financial data not available

2171 Monroe Ave.
Rochester, NY 14618
Ph: (716)242-7540
Fax: (716)442-1284
www.montanamills.com
Bread bakery & cafe
Began: 1996, Franchising since: 2002
Headquarters size: 20 employees
Franchise department: 10 employees

U.S. franchises: 0
Canadian franchises: 0
Other foreign franchises: 0
Company-owned: 30

Seeking: All U.S.
Seeking in Canada? Yes
Exclusive territories? Yes
Homebased option? No
Kiosk option? No
Employees needed to run franchise: 10-15
Absentee ownership? No

COSTS
Total cost: $226K-573K
Franchise fee: $30K
Royalty fee: 4.9%
Term of agreement: 10 years renewable for 50% of then-current fee
Franchisees required to buy multiple units? No

FINANCING
No financing available

QUALIFICATIONS
Net worth: $300K
Cash liquidity: $150K-200K
Experience:
    General business experience

TRAINING
At headquarters: 3-5 weeks

BUSINESS SUPPORT
Newsletter
Meetings
Toll-free phone line
Grand opening
Internet
Field operations/evaluations

MARKETING SUPPORT
Ad slicks
Regional marketing
Ongoing store-level marketing literature

MRS. FIELDS

Current financial data not available

2855 E. Cottonwood Pkwy., #400
Salt Lake City, UT 84121
Ph: (800)348-6311/(801)736-5600
Fax: (801)736-5936
www.mrsfieldsfranchise.com
Cookies & bakery products
Began: 1977, Franchising since: 1990
Headquarters size: 150 employees
Franchise department: 25 employees

U.S. franchises: 366
Canadian franchises: 0
Other foreign franchises: 81
Company-owned: 72
Units concentrated in all U.S.

Seeking: All U.S.
Seeking in Canada? Yes
Exclusive territories? No
Homebased option? No
Kiosk option? Info not provided
Employees needed to run franchise:
    Info not provided
Absentee ownership? Info not provided

COSTS
Total cost: $162.4K-247.1K
Franchise fee: $30K
Royalty fee: 6%
Term of agreement: 7 years renewable
Franchisees required to buy multiple
    units? Outside the U.S. only

FINANCING
No financing available

QUALIFICATIONS
Net worth: $150K
Cash liquidity: $75K

TRAINING
At headquarters: 9 days

BUSINESS SUPPORT
Meetings
Toll-free phone line
Internet
Field operations/evaluations

MARKETING SUPPORT
Ad slicks

NESTLE TOLL HOUSE CAFE BY CHIP

Ranked #424 in Entrepreneur Magazine's 2004 Franchise 500

Financial rating: $$

1900 Preston Rd., #267-314
Plano, TX 75093
Ph: (214)495-9533
Fax: (214)853-5347
www.nestlecafe.com
Cookies, baked goods, coffee
Began: 2000, Franchising since: 2000
Headquarters size: 5 employees
Franchise department: 2 employees

U.S. franchises: 25
Canadian franchises: 0
Other foreign franchises: 0
Company-owned: 0
Units concentrated in CA, CO, FL, IL,
    MI, NH, NV, OH, TX, VA

Seeking: All U.S.
Seeking in Canada? No
Exclusive territories? No
Homebased option? No
Kiosk option? Yes
Employees needed to run franchise:
    8-10
Absentee ownership? Yes

COSTS
Total cost: $177.1K-313.5K
Kiosk cost: $128.1K-230K
Franchise fee: $25K
Royalty fee: 7%
Term of agreement: 10 years renewable
Franchisees required to buy multiple
    units? No

FINANCING
In-house: None
3rd-party: Accounts receivable, equip-
    ment, franchise fee, inventory, pay-
    roll, start-up costs

QUALIFICATIONS
Net worth: $250K/location
Cash liquidity: $100K/location
Experience:
    Industry experience
    General business experience
    Marketing skills
    Absentee ownership allowed with
    an operating partner

TRAINING
At headquarters: 12 days
At store opening: 2-3 days

BUSINESS SUPPORT
Meetings
Grand opening
Internet
Lease negotiations
Security/safety procedures
Field operations/evaluations

MARKETING SUPPORT
Ad slicks

PANERA BREAD/SAINT LOUIS BREAD CO.

Ranked #48 in Entrepreneur Magazine's 2004 Franchise 500　　　*Financial rating: $$$$*

6710 Clayton Rd.
Richmond Heights, MO 63117
Ph: (314)633-7100
Fax: (314)633-7200
www.panerabread.com
Bakery/cafe
Began: 1987, Franchising since: 1993
Headquarters size: 120 employees
Franchise department: 10 employees

U.S. franchises: 389
Canadian franchises: 0
Other foreign franchises: 0
Company-owned: 146

Seeking: West
Seeking in Canada? No
Exclusive territories? Yes
Homebased option? No
Kiosk option? No
Employees needed to run franchise:
　40-60
Absentee ownership? No

COSTS
Total cost: $843K-1.5M
Franchise fee: $35K
Royalty fee: 5%
Term of agreement: 20 years renewable
Franchisees required to buy multiple
　units? Yes

FINANCING
In-house: None
3rd-party: Accounts receivable, equip-
　ment, franchise fee, inventory, pay-
　roll, start-up costs

QUALIFICATIONS
Net worth: $3M
Cash liquidity: $1.2M
Experience:
　Industry experience
　General business experience
　Marketing skills
　Multi-unit & development experi-
　ence

TRAINING
At headquarters: 8-12 weeks
At franchisee's location
Baker training

BUSINESS SUPPORT
Newsletter
Meetings
Toll-free phone line
Grand opening
Internet
Security/safety procedures
Field operations/evaluations

MARKETING SUPPORT
Co-op advertising
Ad slicks
National media campaign
Regional marketing

SAINT CINNAMON BAKERY LTD.

Current financial data not available

7181 Woodbine Ave., #222
Markham, ON Canada L3R 1A3
Ph: (905)470-1517
Fax: (905)470-8112
www.saintcinnamon.com
Cinnamon rolls & baked goods
Began: 1986, Franchising since: 1986
Headquarters size: 8 employees
Franchise department: Info not pro-
　vided

U.S. franchises: 3
Canadian franchises: 72
Other foreign franchises: 28
Company-owned: 3
Units concentrated in GA, KS, NC

Seeking: Midwest, Southeast
Focusing on: CA, FL, MN
Seeking in Canada? Yes
Exclusive territories? Yes
Homebased option? No
Kiosk option? Yes
Employees needed to run franchise:
　Info not provided
Absentee ownership? No

COSTS
Total cost: $144.1K-264.7K
Kiosk cost: $35K-125K
Franchise fee: $25K
Royalty fee: 6%
Term of agreement: 10 years renewable
Franchisees required to buy multiple
　units? No

FINANCING
No financing available

QUALIFICATIONS
Experience:
　General business experience

TRAINING
At headquarters: 10 days
At franchisee's location: 4 days

BUSINESS SUPPORT
Newsletter
Meetings
Toll-free phone line
Grand opening
Internet
Security/safety procedures
Field operations/evaluations

MARKETING SUPPORT
Co-op advertising
Ad slicks
Regional marketing

SOUTHERN MAID DONUT FLOUR CO.

Current financial data not available

3615 Cavalier Dr.
Garland, TX 75042-7599
Ph: (800)936-6887/(972)272-6425
Fax: (972)276-3549
www.southernmaiddonuts.com
Donuts & related products
Began: 1937, Franchising since: 1939
Headquarters size: 8 employees
Franchise department: 3 employees

U.S. franchises: 95
Canadian franchises: 0
Other foreign franchises: 0
Company-owned: 0
Units concentrated in AL, FL, LA, TX

Seeking: All U.S.
Seeking in Canada? Yes
Exclusive territories? Yes
Homebased option? No
Kiosk option? Yes
Employees needed to run franchise:
    2-3
Absentee ownership? Yes

COSTS
Total cost: $63.95K-226.95K
Kiosk cost: $35K
Franchise fee: $5K
Royalty fee: 0
Term of agreement: 10 years renewable
    for $500
Franchisees required to buy multiple
    units? No

FINANCING
In-house: Franchise fee
3rd-party: None

QUALIFICATIONS
Net worth: $89K
Cash liquidity: $35K

TRAINING
At franchisee's location: As needed

BUSINESS SUPPORT
Toll-free phone line
Grand opening
Internet
Lease negotiations
Field operations/evaluations

MARKETING SUPPORT
Ad slicks

T.J. CINNAMONS

Current financial data not available

1000 Corporate Dr.
Ft. Lauderdale, FL 33334
Ph: (800)592-6245/(954)351-5200
Fax: (954)351-5222
www.arbys.com
Cinnamon rolls & gourmet bakery
    products
Began: 1985, Franchising since: 1985
Headquarters size: 120 employees
Franchise department: 59 employees

U.S. franchises: 292
Canadian franchises: 0
Other foreign franchises: 0
Company-owned: 2
Units concentrated in all U.S.

Seeking: All U.S.
Seeking in Canada? No
Exclusive territories? Yes
Homebased option? No
Kiosk option? Yes
Employees needed to run franchise:
    Info not provided
Absentee ownership? Yes

COSTS
Total cost: $32.6K-47.2K
Kiosk cost: Varies
Franchise fee: $5K
Royalty fee: 4%
Term of agreement: 10 years renewable
    at then-current franchise fee
Franchisees required to buy multiple
    units? No

FINANCING
In-house: None
3rd-party: Accounts receivable, equip-
    ment, franchise fee, inventory, pay-
    roll, start-up costs

QUALIFICATIONS
Net worth: $1M
Cash liquidity: $500K
Experience:
    Industry experience
    General business experience
    Marketing skills

TRAINING
Training manual

BUSINESS SUPPORT
Newsletter
Meetings
Toll-free phone line
Grand opening
Internet
Security/safety procedures
Field operations/evaluations
Purchasing cooperatives

MARKETING SUPPORT
Ad slicks

TIM HORTONS

Current financial data not available

4150 Tuller Rd., #236
Dublin, OH 43017
Ph: (614)791-4200
Fax: (614)791-4235
www.timhortons.com
Coffee & baked goods
Began: 1964, Franchising since: 1965
Headquarters size: 747 employees
Franchise department: 3 employees

U.S. franchises: 134
Canadian franchises: 2,176
Other foreign franchises: 0
Company-owned: 63
Units concentrated in MI, NY, OH &
    Canada

Seeking: Midwest, Northeast
Focusing on: ME, MI, NY, OH, PA &
    Canada
Seeking in Canada? Yes
Exclusive territories? No
Homebased option? No
Kiosk option? Yes

Employees needed to run franchise:
    25-30
Absentee ownership? No

COSTS
Total cost: $46.1K-498.3K
    Kiosk cost: $30.15K-250.15K
Franchise fee: $35K
Royalty fee: 4.5%
Term of agreement: 10 years renewable
    at no charge
Franchisees required to buy multiple
    units? No

FINANCING
No financing available

QUALIFICATIONS
Cash liquidity: $55K-163K
Experience:
    General business experience
    Marketing skills
    Track record of success

TRAINING
At headquarters: 7 weeks
In franchisee's area: 2 weeks

BUSINESS SUPPORT
Meetings
Toll-free phone line
Grand opening
Security/safety procedures
Field operations/evaluations

MARKETING SUPPORT
Ad slicks
Regional marketing

QUICK SERVICE — *Chicken*

BOJANGLES' FAMOUS CHICKEN 'N BISCUITS
Ranked #107 in Entrepreneur Magazine's 2004 Franchise 500

Financial rating: $$$$

P.O. Box 240239
Charlotte, NC 28224
Ph: (704)527-2675; Fax: (704)523-6803
www.bojangles.com
Chicken & biscuits
Began: 1977, Franchising since: 1978
Headquarters size: 86 employees
Franchise department: 5 employees

U.S. franchises: 183
Canadian franchises: 0
Other foreign franchises: 2
Company-owned: 119

Seeking: All U.S.
Focusing on: AL, AR, FL, GA, KY,
    LA,MD, MO, NC, NY, PA, SC, TN,
    VA, WV
Seeking in Canada? No
Exclusive territories? Yes
Homebased option? No
Kiosk option? Yes
Employees needed to run franchise:
    25-30
Absentee ownership? No

COSTS
Total cost: $145K-558.8K
Kiosk cost: Same as total cost
Franchise fee: $15K-25K
Royalty fee: 4%
Term of agreement: 20 years renewable
    for 50% of original franchise fee
Franchisees required to buy multiple
    units? No

FINANCING
In-house: None
3rd-party: Accounts receivable, equip-
    ment, franchise fee, inventory, pay-
    roll, start-up costs

QUALIFICATIONS
Net worth: $800K
Cash liquidity: $300K
Experience:
    Industry experience
    General business experience

TRAINING
At headquarters: 6 weeks
At franchisee's location: 1 week

BUSINESS SUPPORT
Newsletter
Meetings
Toll-free phone line
Grand opening
Internet
Security/safety procedures
Field operations/evaluations
Purchasing cooperatives

MARKETING SUPPORT
Co-op advertising
Ad slicks
Regional marketing
Marketing manuals
Media buys

BUFFALO WILD WINGS
Ranked #179 in Entrepreneur Magazine's 2004 Franchise 500

Financial rating: $$$$

1600 Utica Ave. S., #700
Minneapolis, MN 55416
Ph: (800)499-9586
Fax: (952)593-9787
www.buffalowildwings.com
Buffalo wings & sandwiches
Began: 1982, Franchising since: 1991
Headquarters size: 60 employees
Franchise department: 4 employees

U.S. franchises: 141
Canadian franchises: 0
Other foreign franchises: 0
Company-owned: 75

Seeking: All U.S.
Seeking in Canada? No
Exclusive territories? Yes
Homebased option? No
Kiosk option? No
Employees needed to run franchise:
    40-60
Absentee ownership? No

COSTS
Total cost: $969K-1.5M
Franchise fee: $30K-40K
Royalty fee: 5%
Term of agreement: 10 years renewable
    for $5K
Franchisees required to buy multiple
    units? No

FINANCING
No financing available

QUALIFICATIONS
Net worth: $800K
Cash liquidity: $250K
Experience:
    General business experience
    Track record of success

TRAINING
At headquarters: 4 weeks
At franchisee's location: 2-3 weeks

BUSINESS SUPPORT
Newsletter
Meetings
Toll-free phone line
Grand opening
Internet
Security/safety procedures
Field operations/evaluations
Purchasing cooperatives

MARKETING SUPPORT
Co-op advertising
Ad slicks
National media campaign
Regional marketing
Advertising Advisory Committee

CHICKEN DELIGHT

Current financial data not available

395 Berry St.
Winnipeg, MB Canada R3J 1N6
Ph: (204)885-7570
Fax: (204)831-6176
www.chickendelight.com
Fried chicken, pizza, ribs, wings
Began: 1952, Franchising since: 1952
Headquarters size: 20 employees
Franchise department: 2 employees

U.S. franchises: 10
Canadian franchises: 15
Other foreign franchises: 2
Company-owned: 11

Seeking: Midwest, Northeast
Seeking in Canada? Yes
Exclusive territories? Yes
Homebased option? No
Kiosk option? No
Employees needed to run franchise: 10
Absentee ownership? Yes

COSTS
Total cost: $150K-350K
Franchise fee: $20K
Royalty fee: 5%
Term of agreement: 10 years renewable
Franchisees required to buy multiple
    units? Info not provided

FINANCING
No financing available

QUALIFICATIONS
Net worth: $150K-200K
Cash liquidity: $75K-100K
Experience:
    General business experience

TRAINING
At headquarters: 1 month

BUSINESS SUPPORT
Grand opening
Field operations/evaluations
Purchasing cooperatives

MARKETING SUPPORT
Ad slicks
Regional marketing
Menus
Radio, TV & newspaper ads
Posters & flyers

CHURCH'S CHICKEN

Current financial data not available

980 Hammond Dr., #1100
Atlanta, GA 30328
Ph: (800)639-3495
Fax: (770)512-3920
www.churchs.com
Southern fried chicken & biscuits
Began: 1952, Franchising since: 1972
Headquarters size: 128 employees
Franchise department: 20 employees

U.S. franchises: 966
Canadian franchises: 15
Other foreign franchises: 254
Company-owned: 283
Units concentrated in AL, CA, FL, GA,
     LA, TX

Seeking: All U.S.
Focusing on: CO, FL, IL, MI, OH, PA,
     SC, TN, VA
Seeking in Canada? No
Exclusive territories? No
Homebased option? No
Kiosk option? No
Employees needed to run franchise:
     15-20
Absentee ownership? Yes

COSTS
Total cost: $203K-750K
Franchise fee: $10K/15K
Royalty fee: 5%
Term of agreement: 20 years renewable
     for $3K
Franchisees required to buy multiple
     units? Yes

FINANCING
No financing available

QUALIFICATIONS
Net worth: $1M
Cash liquidity: $300K
Experience:
     Industry experience
     General business experience
     Marketing skills
     Restaurant experience

TRAINING
At headquarters: 4 weeks
At franchisee's location: 4 weeks
Ongoing

BUSINESS SUPPORT
Newsletter
Meetings
Toll-free phone line
Grand opening
Internet
Lease negotiations
Security/safety procedures
Field operations/evaluations
Purchasing cooperatives

MARKETING SUPPORT
Co-op advertising
Ad slicks
National media campaign
Regional marketing

EL POLLO LOCO

Current financial data not available

3333 Michelson Dr., #550
Irvine, CA 92612
Ph: (800)997-6556
Fax: (949)399-2025
www.elpolloloco.com
Flame-broiled chicken
Began: 1975, Franchising since: 1980
Headquarters size: 100 employees
Franchise department: 4 employees

U.S. franchises: 174
Canadian franchises: 0
Other foreign franchises: 0
Company-owned: 135
Units concentrated in AZ, CA, NV, TX

Seeking: All U.S.
Seeking in Canada? No
Exclusive territories? Yes
Homebased option? No
Kiosk option? No
Employees needed to run franchise:
     25-40
Absentee ownership? No

COSTS
Total cost: $504.98K-1.1M
Franchise fee: $40K
Royalty fee: 4%
Term of agreement: 20 years
Franchisees required to buy multiple
     units? Yes

FINANCING
No financing available

QUALIFICATIONS
Net worth: $1.5M
Cash liquidity: $750K
Experience:
     Industry experience
     General business experience
     Marketing skills
     Food-service franchise background

TRAINING
At headquarters: 1 week
At training store: 6 weeks

BUSINESS SUPPORT
Meetings
Toll-free phone line
Grand opening
Internet
Security/safety procedures
Field operations/evaluations

MARKETING SUPPORT
Ad slicks
Regional marketing

GOLDEN CHICK

Financial rating: $$$$

11488 Luna Rd., #100B
Dallas, TX 75234-9430
Ph: (972)831-0911
Fax: (972)831-0401
www.goldenchick.com
Fast-food chicken restaurant
Began: 1967, Franchising since: 1972
Headquarters size: 12 employees
Franchise department: 1 employee

U.S. franchises: 58
Canadian franchises: 0
Other foreign franchises: 0
Company-owned: 9
Units concentrated in OK, TX

Seeking: South, Southeast
Focusing on: AR, OK, TX
Seeking in Canada? No
Exclusive territories? No
Homebased option? No
Kiosk option? No
Employees needed to run franchise: 15
Absentee ownership? Info not provided

COSTS
Total cost: $442.6K-780.9K
Franchise fee: $15K
Royalty fee: 4%
Term of agreement: 20 yearss
Franchisees required to buy multiple
    units? No

FINANCING
No financing available

QUALIFICATIONS
Net worth: $300K
Cash liquidity: $100K
Experience:
    General business experience

TRAINING
At headquarters: 6 weeks
At franchisee's location: 1 week

BUSINESS SUPPORT
Newsletter
Meetings
Grand opening
Security/safety procedures
Field operations/evaluations
Purchasing cooperatives

MARKETING SUPPORT
Co-op advertising
Ad slicks
National media campaign
Regional marketing

KFC CORP.

Financial rating: $$$

1441 Gardiner Ln.
Louisville, KY 40213
Ph: (866)298-6986
Fax: (502)874-2283
www.yum.com
Chicken
Began: 1930, Franchising since: 1952
Headquarters size: Info not provided
Franchise department: Info not pro-
    vided

U.S. franchises: 4,144
Canadian/other foreign franchises:
    4,190
Company-owned: 2,857
Units concentrated in all U.S. except
    MT, UT

Seeking: All U.S.
Seeking in Canada? Yes
Exclusive territories? No
Homebased option? No
Kiosk option? Info not provided
Employees needed to run franchise:
    Info not provided
Absentee ownership? No

COSTS
Total cost: $1.1M-1.7M
Franchise fee: $25K
Royalty fee: 4%
Term of agreement: 20 years renewable
    for $4.9K
Franchisees required to buy multiple
    units? No

FINANCING
No financing available

QUALIFICATIONS
Net worth: $1M
Cash liquidity: $500K
Experience:
    Industry experience
    General business experience
    Marketing skills

TRAINING
Info not provided

BUSINESS SUPPORT
Info not provided

MARKETING SUPPORT
Info not provided

POPEYES CHICKEN & BISCUITS

Current financial data not available

5555 Glenridge Connector N.E., #300
Atlanta, GA 30342
Ph: (800)639-3780
Fax: (404)459-4523
www.popeyesfranchising.com
Cajun-style fried chicken & biscuits
Began: 1972, Franchising since: 1976
Headquarters size: 100 employees
Franchise department: 6 employees

U.S. franchises: 1,250
Canadian franchises: 20
Other foreign franchises: 326
Company-owned: 89
Units concentrated in all U.S.

Seeking: All U.S.
Seeking in Canada? Yes
Exclusive territories? Yes
Homebased option? No
Kiosk option? Info not provided
Employees needed to run franchise:
    20-25
Absentee ownership? Yes

COSTS
Total cost: $600K-1.2M
Franchise fee: $30K
Royalty fee: 5%
Term of agreement: 20 years renewable
    for $10K
Franchisees required to buy multiple
    units? Yes

FINANCING
No financing available

QUALIFICATIONS
Net worth: $1.2M
Cash liquidity: $600K
Experience:
    Industry experience
    General business experience
    Marketing skills
    Franchising experience

TRAINING
At headquarters: 4 weeks

BUSINESS SUPPORT
Newsletter
Meetings
Toll-free phone line
Grand opening
Internet
Security/safety procedures
Field operations/evaluations
Purchasing cooperatives

MARKETING SUPPORT
Co-op advertising
Ad slicks
National media campaign
Regional marketing

PUDGIE'S FAMOUS CHICKEN LTD.

Current financial data not available

5 Dakota Dr., #302
Lake Success, NY 11042
Ph: (516)358-0600
Fax: (516)358-5076
www.pudgiesfamous.com
Fast-food skinless chicken, ribs, fish
Began: 1981, Franchising since: 1989
Headquarters size: 100 employees
Franchise department: 7 employees

U.S. franchises: 32
Canadian franchises: 0
Other foreign franchises: 2
Company-owned: 0
Units concentrated in CT, NJ, NY

Seeking: All U.S.
Seeking in Canada? Yes
Exclusive territories? Yes
Homebased option? No
Kiosk option? No
Employees needed to run franchise:
    5-10
Absentee ownership? Yes

COSTS
Total cost: $197K-379.9K
Franchise fee: $30K
Royalty fee: 5%
Term of agreement: 10 years renewable
    at current fee
Franchisees required to buy multiple
    units? Info not provided

FINANCING
No financing available

QUALIFICATIONS
Net worth: $400K
Cash liquidity: $100K
Experience:
    Industry experience
    General business experience

TRAINING
At headquarters: 2 weeks
At franchisee's location: 1 week

BUSINESS SUPPORT
Newsletter
Meetings
Toll-free phone line
Grand opening
Field operations/evaluations
Purchasing cooperatives

MARKETING SUPPORT
Co-op advertising
Ad slicks
Regional marketing

RANCH 1

Current financial data not available

7730 E. Greenway Rd., #104
Scottsdale, AZ 85260
Ph: (480)443-0200
Fax: (480)443-1972
www.kahalacorp.com
Grilled & fried chicken
    sandwiches/products
Began: 1993, Franchising since: 1993
Headquarters size: 30 employees
Franchise department: 30 employees

U.S. franchises: 37
Canadian franchises: 0
Other foreign franchises: 2
Company-owned: 5

Seeking: All U.S.
Seeking in Canada? Yes
Exclusive territories? Yes
Homebased option? No
Kiosk option? Yes
Employees needed to run franchise: 8
Absentee ownership? Yes

COSTS
Total cost: $212.8K-392.2K
Kiosk cost: $7.5K
Franchise fee: $30K
Royalty fee: 6%
Term of agreement: 10 years renewable
    for 75% of then-current fee
Franchisees required to buy multiple
    units? No

FINANCING
No financing available

QUALIFICATIONS
Experience:
    Industry experience
    General business experience

TRAINING
At headquarters: 1 week
At franchisee's location: 2 weeks

BUSINESS SUPPORT
Newsletter
Meetings
Toll-free phone line
Grand opening
Internet
Security/safety procedures
Field operations/evaluations
Purchasing cooperatives

MARKETING SUPPORT
Co-op advertising
Ad slicks
National media campaign
Regional marketing

WING ZONE FRANCHISE CORP.

Ranked #208 in Entrepreneur Magazine's 2004 Franchise 500

Financial rating: $$$$

1720 Peachtree St., #940
Atlanta, GA 30309
Ph: (404)875-5045/(877)333-9464
Fax: (404)875-6631
www.wingzone.com
Buffalo wings take-out & delivery
Began: 1991, Franchising since: 1999
Headquarters size: 7 employees
Franchise department: 7 employees

U.S. franchises: 42
Canadian franchises: 0
Other foreign franchises: 0
Company-owned: 4

Seeking: Northeast, South, Southeast,
    Southwest
Seeking in Canada? No
Exclusive territories? Yes
Homebased option? No
Kiosk option? No
Employees needed to run franchise: 10
Absentee ownership? Yes

COSTS
Total cost: $144.5K-204.5K
Franchise fee: $25K
Royalty fee: 5%
Term of agreement: 10 years renewable
    for $10K
Franchisees required to buy multiple
    units? No

FINANCING
In-house: None
3rd-party: Accounts receivable, equip-
    ment, franchise fee, inventory, pay-
    roll, start-up costs

QUALIFICATIONS
Net worth: $150K
Cash liquidity: $50K-75K
Experience:
    Industry experience
    General business experience
    Marketing skills

TRAINING
At headquarters: 10 days
At franchisee's location: 10 days

BUSINESS SUPPORT
Meetings
Toll-free phone line
Grand opening
Internet
Security/safety procedures
Field operations/evaluations
Purchasing cooperatives

MARKETING SUPPORT
Ad slicks
Regional marketing

WINGSTOP RESTAURANTS INC.

Ranked #116 in Entrepreneur Magazine's 2004 Franchise 500　　　　　*Financial rating: $$$$*

1234 Northwest Hwy.
Garland, TX 75041
Ph: (972)686-6500, Fax: (972)686-6502
www.wingstop.com
Chicken wings
Began: 1994, Franchising since: 1998
Headquarters size: 12 employees
Franchise department: 2 employees

U.S. franchises: 113
Canadian franchises: 0
Other foreign franchises: 0
Company-owned: 2
Units concentrated in FL, GA, LA,
　　MO, OK, TX

Seeking: All U.S.
Focusing on: AZ, CA, FL, IL, IN, KS,
　　KY, MD, NC, NV, SC, TN, VA
Seeking in Canada? No
Exclusive territories? Yes
Homebased option? No
Kiosk option? No
Employees needed to run franchise:
　　8-10
Absentee ownership? Yes

COSTS
Total cost: $193.3K-286.5K
Franchise fee: $20K
Royalty fee: 5%
Term of agreement: 10 years renewable
　　at no charge
Franchisees required to buy multiple
　　units? Outside the U.S. only

FINANCING
In-house: None
3rd-party: Accounts receivable, equip-
　　ment, inventory, start-up costs

QUALIFICATIONS
Net worth: $100K
Cash liquidity: $60K-70K
Experience:
　　General business experience

TRAINING
At headquarters: 3 weeks
At franchisee's location: 1 week
Ongoing

BUSINESS SUPPORT
Meetings
Grand opening
Internet
Security/safety procedures
Field operations/evaluations
Purchasing cooperatives

MARKETING SUPPORT
Co-op advertising
Ad slicks
Regional marketing

QUICK SERVICE　　*Coffee*

BAD ASS COFFEE CO.

Ranked #378 in Entrepreneur Magazine's 2004 Franchise 500　　　　　*Financial rating: $$$$*

166 W. 2700 South
Salt Lake City, UT 84115
Ph: (888)422-3277/(801)463-1966
Fax: (801)463-2606
www.badasscoffee.com
Coffee & logo wear
Began: 1991, Franchising since: 1998
Headquarters size: 10 employees
Franchise department: 2 employees

U.S. franchises: 26
Canadian franchises: 3
Other foreign franchises: 0
Company-owned: 1
Units concentrated in all U.S.

Seeking: All U.S.
Seeking in Canada? No
Exclusive territories? Yes
Homebased option? No
Kiosk option? Yes
Employees needed to run franchise: 10
Absentee ownership? Yes

COSTS
Total cost: $200K
Franchise fee: $20K
Royalty fee: 6%
Term of agreement: 5 years renewable
　　for $2.5K
Franchisees required to buy multiple
　　units? No

FINANCING
No financing available

QUALIFICATIONS
Info not provided

TRAINING
At headquarters: 2 weeks
At franchisee's location: Available on
　　request

BUSINESS SUPPORT
Newsletter
Toll-free phone line
Grand opening
Internet
Security/safety procedures
Field operations/evaluations
Purchasing cooperatives

MARKETING SUPPORT
Co-op advertising
Ad slicks
Regional marketing

BARNIE'S COFFEE & TEA CO.
Ranked #439 in Entrepreneur Magazine's 2004 Franchise 500

Financial rating: $$$$

7001 Lake Ellenor Dr., #250
Orlando, FL 32809
Ph: (407)854-6600
Fax: (407)854-6666
www.barniescoffee.com
Specialty gourmet coffee, teas, related
    accessories
Began: 1980, Franchising since: 1981
Headquarters size: 50 employees
Franchise department: 3 employees

U.S. franchises: 16
Canadian franchises: 0
Other foreign franchises: 0
Company-owned: 69
Units concentrated in AL, FL, IN, OH,
    TN

Seeking: All U.S.
Seeking in Canada? Yes
Exclusive territories? Yes
Homebased option? No
Kiosk option? Yes
Employees needed to run franchise:
    10-20
Absentee ownership? Yes

COSTS
Total cost: $202K-350K
Kiosk cost: $60K-123K
Franchise fee: $20K
Royalty fee: 7%
Term of agreement: 10 years renewable
    for 50% of current franchise fee
Franchisees required to buy multiple
    units? Yes

FINANCING
In-house: None
3rd-party: Accounts receivable, equip-
    ment, franchise fee, inventory, pay-
    roll, start-up costs

QUALIFICATIONS
Info not provided

TRAINING
At headquarters: 4 weeks

BUSINESS SUPPORT
Newsletter
Grand opening
Lease negotiations
Field operations/evaluations

MARKETING SUPPORT
Ad slicks

BEANER'S GOURMET COFFEE

Financial rating: 0

115 W. Allegan, 6th Fl.
Lansing, MI 48933
Ph: (517)482-8145
Fax: (517)482-8625
www.beaners.com
Espresso bar, sandwiches, salads, baked
    goods
Began: 1994, Franchising since: 1999
Headquarters size: 6 employees
Franchise department: 1 employee

U.S. franchises: 16
Canadian franchises: 0
Other foreign franchises: 0
Company-owned: 9
Units concentrated in IN, OH, MI

Seeking: All U.S.
Focusing on: AL, CA, FL, IN, OH, MI
Seeking in Canada? No
Exclusive territories? Yes
Homebased option? No
Kiosk option? Yes
Employees needed to run franchise: 15
Absentee ownership? Yes

COSTS
Total cost: $225K
Kiosk cost: $110K-160K
Franchise fee: $22.5K
Royalty fee: 5%
Term of agreement: 10 years renewable
    for 10% of current franchise fee
Franchisees required to buy multiple
    units? No

FINANCING
No financing available

QUALIFICATIONS
Net worth: $250K
Cash liquidity: $70K

TRAINING
At headquarters: 4 weeks
At franchisee's location: 3 weeks
Ongoing quarterly training

BUSINESS SUPPORT
Meetings
Toll-free phone line
Grand opening
Internet
Lease negotiations
Security/safety procedures
Field operations/evaluations
Purchasing cooperatives

MARKETING SUPPORT
Co-op advertising
Ad slicks
National media campaign
Regional marketing

CAFE ALA CARTE
Ranked #448 in Entrepreneur Magazine's 2004 Franchise 500

Financial rating: $$

589 Slippery Rock Rd.
Weston, FL 33327
Ph: (954)349-1030
Fax: (954)349-3100
www.cafealacarte.com
Cappucino catering service
Began: 1996, Franchising since: 2000
Headquarters size: 11 employees
Franchise department: 2 employees

U.S. franchises: 2
Canadian franchises: 0
Other foreign franchises: 0
Company-owned: 20
Units concentrated in FL

Seeking: All U.S.
Seeking in Canada? Yes
Exclusive territories? Yes
Homebased option? Yes
Kiosk option? No
Employees needed to run franchise: 2
Absentee ownership? No

COSTS
Total cost: $56.2K-80.8K
Franchise fee: $25K
Royalty fee: 8-5%
Term of agreement: 10 years renewable
    at then-current franchise fee
Franchisees required to buy multiple
    units? Outside the U.S. only

FINANCING
In-house: None
3rd-party: Equipment

QUALIFICATIONS
Experience:
    Industry experience
    General business experience
    Marketing skills

TRAINING
At headquarters: 1 week
In Fort Lauderdale, FL: 1 week

BUSINESS SUPPORT
Toll-free phone line
Grand opening
Internet

MARKETING SUPPORT
Ad slicks
Internet

CAPRI COFFEE BREAK

Financial rating: $$$

1555 Main St., #A6
Windsor, CO 80550
Ph: (970)674-1835
Fax: (970)674-0345
www.capricoffee.com
Coffee, tea, pastries, smoothies
Began: 2000, Franchising since: 2002
Headquarters size: 10 employees
Franchise department: 10 employees

U.S. franchises: 10
Canadian franchises: 0
Other foreign franchises: 0
Company-owned: 1
Units concentrated in CO, FL, IN, NV

Seeking: Midwest, South, Southeast,
    Southwest, West
Focusing on: All U.S.
Seeking in Canada? No
Exclusive territories? Yes
Homebased option? No
Kiosk option? Yes
Employees needed to run franchise: 12
Absentee ownership? Yes

COSTS
Total cost: $110K-200K
    Kiosk cost: $70K-90K
Franchise fee: $30K
Royalty fee: 6%
Term of agreement: 10 years renewable
    for $1.5K
Franchisees required to buy multiple
    units? No

FINANCING
No financing available

QUALIFICATIONS
Net worth: $250K
Cash liquidity: $60K
Experience:
    Must be personable

TRAINING
At headquarters: 5 days
At franchisee's location: 5 days

BUSINESS SUPPORT
Newsletter
Meetings
Toll-free phone line
Grand opening
Internet
Lease negotiations
Security/safety procedures
Field operations/evaluations
Purchasing cooperatives

MARKETING SUPPORT
Ad slicks
Regional marketing

THE COFFEE BEANERY
Ranked #379 in Entrepreneur Magazine's 2004 Franchise 500   *Financial rating: $$*

3429 Pierson Pl.
Flushing, MI 48433
Ph: (800)728-2326
Fax: (810)733-1536
www.coffeebeanery.com
Gourmet coffees, desserts, accessories
Began: 1976, Franchising since: 1985
Headquarters size: 50 employees
Franchise department: 4 employees

U.S. franchises: 149
Canadian franchises: 0
Other foreign franchises: 10
Company-owned: 9
Units concentrated in MI, NJ, NY,
     TX, VA

Seeking: All U.S.
Seeking in Canada? No
Exclusive territories? Yes
Homebased option? No
Kiosk option? Yes
Employees needed to run franchise:
     12-15
Absentee ownership? Yes

COSTS
Total cost: $50.5K-384K
Kiosk cost: $75K-150K
Franchise fee: $5K-25K
Royalty fee: 6%
Term of agreement: 10-20 years
     renewable for 25% of original fee
Franchisees required to buy multiple
     units? Outside the U.S. only

FINANCING
In-house: None
3rd-party: Equipment, franchise fee,
     inventory, start-up costs

QUALIFICATIONS
Net worth: $250K
Cash liquidity: $50K
Experience:
     General business experience
     Retail experience

TRAINING
At headquarters: 21 days
At franchisee's location: 5-7 days

BUSINESS SUPPORT
Newsletter
Meetings
Toll-free phone line
Grand opening
Internet
Lease negotiations
Security/safety procedures
Field operations/evaluations

MARKETING SUPPORT
Co-op advertising
Ad slicks
National media campaign

DUNN BROS COFFEE
Ranked #328 in Entrepreneur Magazine's 2004 Franchise 500   *Financial rating: $$$*

111 3rd Ave. S., #160
Minneapolis, MN 55401
Ph: (612)334-9746
Fax: (612)334-9749
www.dunnbros.com
Coffeehouse
Began: 1987, Franchising since: 1994
Headquarters size: 10 employees
Franchise department: 5 employees

U.S. franchises: 26
Canadian franchises: 0
Other foreign franchises: 0
Company-owned: 5
Units concentrated in MN, TX, WI

Seeking: Midwest, Southwest
Focusing on: IA, MN, ND, SD, TX, WI
Seeking in Canada? No
Exclusive territories? Yes
Homebased option? No
Kiosk option? No
Employees needed to run franchise: 15
Absentee ownership? No

COSTS
Total cost: $143.8K-418K
Franchise fee: $30K
Royalty fee: 5%
Term of agreement: 10 years renewable
     for 25% of current franchise fee
Franchisees required to buy multiple
     units? No

FINANCING
No financing available

QUALIFICATIONS
Net worth: $500K
Cash liquidity: $50K
Experience:
     General business experience

TRAINING
At headquarters: 2-1/2 weeks

BUSINESS SUPPORT
Newsletter
Meetings
Grand opening
Internet
Lease negotiations
Security/safety procedures
Field operations/evaluations

MARKETING SUPPORT
Co-op advertising
Ad slicks
National media campaign

GLORIA JEAN'S GOURMET COFFEES FRANCHISING CORP.

Ranked #494 in Entrepreneur Magazine's 2004 Franchise 500   *Current financial data not available*

2144 Michelson Dr.
Irvine, CA 92612
Ph: (949)260-1600
Fax: (949)260-1610
www.gloriajeans.com
Gourmet coffee, teas, accessories
Began: 1979, Franchising since: 1986
Headquarters size: 40 employees
Franchise department: 4 employees

U.S. franchises: 142
Canadian franchises: 0
Other foreign franchises: 232
Company-owned: 10
Units concentrated in all U.S.

Seeking: All U.S.
Seeking in Canada? Yes
Exclusive territories? Yes
Homebased option? No
Kiosk option? Yes
Employees needed to run franchise:
    6-12
Absentee ownership? No

COSTS
Total cost: $25.2K-437K
Kiosk cost: $25.2K
Franchise fee: $15K/30K
Royalty fee: 6%
Term of agreement: 10 years renewable
    for 50% of current franchise fee
Franchisees required to buy multiple
    units? No

FINANCING
No financing available

QUALIFICATIONS
Net worth: $500K+
Cash liquidity: $125K
Experience:
    General business experience

TRAINING
At headquarters: 2 days
At company store: 3 weeks

BUSINESS SUPPORT
Newsletter
Meetings
Toll-free phone line
Grand opening
Internet
Lease negotiations
Security/safety procedures
Field operations/evaluations
Purchasing cooperatives

MARKETING SUPPORT
Co-op advertising
Ad slicks
National media campaign

GOURMET CUP

Current financial data not available

2265 W. Railway St., P.O. Box 490
Abbotsford, BC Canada V2S 5Z5
Ph: (604)852-8771
Fax: (604)859-1711
www.shefieldgourmet.com
Coffees, teas, accessories
Began: 1985, Franchising since: 1986
Headquarters size: 19 employees
Franchise department: 2 employees

U.S. franchises: 0
Canadian franchises: 26
Other foreign franchises: 0
Company-owned: 2
Units concentrated in Canada

Not available in the U.S.
Seeking in Canada? Yes
Exclusive territories? No
Homebased option? No
Kiosk option? Yes
Employees needed to run franchise:
    Info not provided
Absentee ownership? Yes

COSTS
Total cost: $120K-200K
Kiosk cost: $100K-150K
Franchise fee: $25K
Royalty fee: 8%
Term of agreement: 5 years renewable
    for $5K
Franchisees required to buy multiple
    units? No

FINANCING
No financing available

QUALIFICATIONS
Net worth: $100K
Experience:
    General business experience

TRAINING
At franchisee's location: 2 weeks

BUSINESS SUPPORT
Newsletter
Toll-free phone line
Grand opening
Internet
Lease negotiations
Security/safety procedures
Field operations/evaluations
Purchasing cooperatives

MARKETING SUPPORT
Co-op advertising
Ad slicks
National media campaign

HAWAII'S JAVA KAI

Current financial data not available

2955 Aukele St., #C
Lihue, HI 96766
Ph: (808)245-6704
Fax: (808)245-6503
www.javakai.com
Specialty cafe w/Hawaiian-theme retail items
Began: 1997, Franchising since: 2000
Headquarters size: 6 employees
Franchise department: 3 employees

U.S. franchises: 4
Canadian franchises: 0
Other foreign franchises: 0
Company-owned: 0
Units concentrated in CA, HI

Seeking: West
Focusing on: CA, HI, TX
Seeking in Canada? No
Exclusive territories? No
Homebased option? No
Kiosk option? No
Employees needed to run franchise: 10
Absentee ownership? No

COSTS
Total cost: $168.99K-355.9K
Franchise fee: $30K
Royalty fee: 6%
Term of agreement: 20 years renewable at no charge
Franchisees required to buy multiple units? No

FINANCING
In-house: Franchise fee
3rd-party: Equipment, inventory, start-up costs

QUALIFICATIONS
Net worth: $300K
Cash liquidity: $80K
Experience:
    General business experience

TRAINING
At headquarters: 2 weeks
At franchisee's location: 3 weeks

BUSINESS SUPPORT
Meetings
Toll-free phone line
Lease negotiations
Field operations/evaluations
Purchasing cooperatives

MARKETING SUPPORT
Co-op advertising
Ad slicks

IT'S A GRIND

Financial rating: 0

6272 E. Pacific Coast Hwy., #E
Long Beach, CA 90803
Ph: (562)594-5600
Fax: (562)594-4100
www.itsagrind.com
Coffeehouse
Began: 1995, Franchising since: 2000
Headquarters size: 12 employees
Franchise department: 12 employees

U.S. franchises: 24
Canadian franchises: 0
Other foreign franchises: 0
Company-owned: 6
Units concentrated in AZ, CA, CO, MI, NV, TX

Seeking: All U.S.
Focusing on: AZ, CA, CO, FL, GA, IL, MI, NV, OH, PA, TX
Seeking in Canada? No
Exclusive territories? Yes
Homebased option? No
Kiosk option? Yes
Employees needed to run franchise: 12-15
Absentee ownership? Yes

COSTS
Total cost: $227K-397.3K
Kiosk cost: $175K-250K
Franchise fee: $30K
Royalty fee: 6%
Term of agreement: 10 years renewable for $2.5K
Franchisees required to buy multiple units? No

FINANCING
3rd-party: Equipment, franchise fee, inventory, start-up costs
Other: Leasehold improvements

QUALIFICATIONS
Net worth: $375K
Cash liquidity: $100K
Experience:
    General business experience
    Strong people skills

TRAINING
At headquarters: 2 weeks
At franchisee's location: 10 days
Additional training available

BUSINESS SUPPORT
Newsletter
Meetings
Toll-free phone line
Grand opening
Internet
Lease negotiations
Security/safety procedures
Field operations/evaluations
Purchasing cooperatives

MARKETING SUPPORT
Co-op advertising
Ad slicks
Regional marketing
Franchisee advertising council
Grand opening

JO TO GO THE DRIVE THRU ESPRESSO BAR

Financial rating: 0

1263 Main St.
Green Bay, WI 54302
Ph: (920)884-6601
Fax: (920)435-5444
www.jotogo.com
Espresso-based drinks, tea, smoothies,
    bakery
Began: 1998, Franchising since: 2001
Headquarters size: 4 employees
Franchise department: 1 employee

U.S. franchises: 4
Canadian franchises: 0
Other foreign franchises: 0
Company-owned: 4
Units concentrated in WI

Seeking: All U.S.
Focusing on: IL, MI, MN, WI
Seeking in Canada? No
Exclusive territories? Yes
Homebased option? No
Kiosk option? No
Employees needed to run franchise: 7
Absentee ownership? Yes

COSTS
Total cost: $104.5K-782.1K
Franchise fee: $25K
Royalty fee: 7%
Term of agreement: 15 years renewable
Franchisees required to buy multiple
    units? No

FINANCING
No financing available

QUALIFICATIONS
Experience:
    General business experience

TRAINING
At headquarters: 1 week
At franchisee's location: 1 week
At corporate store: 1 week

BUSINESS SUPPORT
Newsletter
Meetings
Grand opening
Internet
Lease negotiations
Security/safety procedures
Field operations/evaluations
Purchasing cooperatives

MARKETING SUPPORT
Co-op advertising
Ad slicks
National media campaign
Regional marketing

MOCHA DELITES INC.

Ranked #458 in Entrepreneur Magazine's 2004 Franchise 500

Financial rating: $$$

3300 N.E. Expressway, #4-J
Atlanta, GA 30341
Ph: (770)451-0901
Fax: (770)451-0902
www.mochadelites.com
Coffeehouse
Began: 2000, Franchising since: 2001
Headquarters size: 8 employees
Franchise department: 5 employees

U.S. franchises: 22
Canadian franchises: 0
Other foreign franchises: 0
Company-owned: 4
Units concentrated in GA, KY, TX, VA

Seeking: All U.S.
Focusing on: FL, LA, NC, SC, TN
Seeking in Canada? No
Exclusive territories? Yes
Homebased option? No
Kiosk option? Yes
Employees needed to run franchise: 4
Absentee ownership? Yes

COSTS
Total cost: $53.5K-218K
Kiosk cost: $30K
Franchise fee: $22.5K
Royalty fee: 4%
Term of agreement: 5 years renewable
    for $10K
Franchisees required to buy multiple
    units? No

FINANCING
In-house: Franchise fee
3rd-party: Equipment

QUALIFICATIONS
Net worth: $100K
Cash liquidity: $70K
Experience:
    Industry experience
    General business experience
    Customer service skills

TRAINING
At headquarters: 1 week
At franchisee's location: 2 weeks

BUSINESS SUPPORT
Newsletter
Meetings
Toll-free phone line
Grand opening
Internet
Lease negotiations
Security/safety procedures
Field operations/evaluations

MARKETING SUPPORT
Co-op advertising

PJ'S COFFEE & TEA CO.

Financial rating: 0

2800 Hessmer Ave., #C
Metarie, LA 70002
Ph: (504)454-9459
Fax: (504)454-9460
www.pjscoffee.com
Specialty coffee, teas, salads, sand-
    wiches, pastries
Began: 1978, Franchising since: 1989
Headquarters size: 10 employees
Franchise department: 2 employees

U.S. franchises: 32
Canadian franchises: 0
Other foreign franchises: 0
Company-owned: 2
Units concentrated in AL, CA, FL, GA,
    LA, MD

Seeking: Northeast, South, Southeast,
    West
Focusing on: East Coast & Northeast
    plus AL, CA, LA, TN
Seeking in Canada? No
Exclusive territories? No
Homebased option? No
Kiosk option? Yes
Employees needed to run franchise: 7
Absentee ownership? Yes

COSTS
Total cost: $140K-270K
Franchise fee: $20K-45K
Royalty fee: 5%
Term of agreement: 10 years renewable
    at no charge
Franchisees required to buy multiple
    units? No

FINANCING
No financing available

QUALIFICATIONS
Net worth: $150K
Cash liquidity: $50K
Experience:
    General business experience

TRAINING
At headquarters: 4 days
At franchisee's location: 4 days

BUSINESS SUPPORT
Newsletter
Meetings
Toll-free phone line
Grand opening
Internet
Lease negotiations
Security/safety procedures
Field operations/evaluations

MARKETING SUPPORT
Co-op advertising
Ad slicks
National media campaign
Regional marketing

SEEKERS COFFEE HOUSE

Financial rating: $$

13365 Smith Rd.
Middleburg Heights, OH 44130
Ph: (440)884-0000
Fax: (440)888-8332
www.seekerscoffeehouse.com
Coffeehouse
Began: 2001, Franchising since: 2002
Headquarters size: 3 employees
Franchise department: 3 employees

U.S. franchises: 1
Canadian franchises: 0
Other foreign franchises: 0
Company-owned: 1
Units concentrated in OH

Seeking: All U.S.
Seeking in Canada? No
Exclusive territories? Yes
Homebased option? No
Kiosk option? No
Employees needed to run franchise:
    8-10
Absentee ownership? No

COSTS
Total cost: $189K-325K
Franchise fee: $15K
Royalty fee: 4%
Term of agreement: 10 years renewable
    at no charge
Franchisees required to buy multiple
    units? No

FINANCING
No financing available

QUALIFICATIONS
Net worth: $150K
Cash liquidity: $50K

TRAINING
At headquarters: 1 week
At franchisee's location: 1 week

BUSINESS SUPPORT
Newsletter
Meetings
Grand opening
Field operations/evaluations

MARKETING SUPPORT
Co-op advertising
Ad slicks
Regional marketing

ARTHUR TREACHER'S FISH & CHIPS

Current financial data not available

5 Dakota Dr., #302
Lake Success, NY 11042
Ph: (516)358-0600
Fax: (516)358-5076
www.arthurtreachersinc.com
Quick-service seafood restaurant
Began: 1969, Franchising since: 1970
Headquarters size: 100 employees
Franchise department: 7 employees

U.S. franchises: 202
Canadian franchises: 0
Other foreign franchises: 1
Company-owned: 0
Units concentrated in CT, MD, MI, NJ,
    NY, OH, PA, VA

Seeking: All U.S.
Seeking in Canada? Yes
Exclusive territories? Yes
Homebased option? No
Kiosk option? No
Employees needed to run franchise: 10
Absentee ownership? Yes

COSTS
Total cost: $145.5K-267.9K
Franchise fee: $30K
Royalty fee: 5%
Term of agreement: 10 years renewable
    at current franchise fee
Franchisees required to buy multiple
    units? Info not provided

FINANCING
No financing available

QUALIFICATIONS
Net worth: $350K
Cash liquidity: $100K
Experience:
    Industry experience
    General business experience

TRAINING
At headquarters: 2 weeks
At franchisee's location: 1 week

BUSINESS SUPPORT
Newsletter
Meetings
Grand opening
Field operations/evaluations

MARKETING SUPPORT
Co-op advertising
Ad slicks
Regional marketing
Promotions

CAPTAIN D'S SEAFOOD

Ranked #115 in Entrepreneur Magazine's 2004 Franchise 500   *Financial rating: $$$*

1717 Elm Hill Pike, A-10
Nashville, TN 37210
Ph: (800)550-4877/(615)231-2066
Fax: (615)231-2650
www.captainds.com
Quick-service seafood restaurant &
    drive-thru
Began: 1969, Franchising since: 1969
Headquarters size: 100 employees
Franchise department: 13 employees

U.S. franchises: 232
Canadian franchises: 0
Other foreign franchises: 1
Company-owned: 328
Units concentrated in AL, GA, KY, NC,
    TN, TX

Seeking: All U.S.
Seeking in Canada? No
Exclusive territories? No
Homebased option? No
Kiosk option? Yes
Employees needed to run franchise: 25
Absentee ownership? Yes

COSTS
Total cost: $223K-894K
Kiosk cost: $223K-451.5K
Franchise fee: $20K/10K
Royalty fee: 3.5%
Term of agreement: 20 years renewable
Franchisees required to buy multiple
    units? No

FINANCING
In-house: None
3rd-party: Accounts receivable, equip-
    ment, franchise fee, inventory, pay-
    roll, start-up costs

QUALIFICATIONS
Net worth: $400K
Cash liquidity: $150K
Experience:
    Industry experience
    General business experience

TRAINING
At headquarters: 6-8 weeks

BUSINESS SUPPORT
Newsletter
Meetings
Toll-free phone line
Grand opening
Internet
Security/safety procedures
Field operations/evaluations
Purchasing cooperatives

MARKETING SUPPORT
Co-op advertising
Ad slicks
National media campaign
Regional marketing

LONG JOHN SILVER'S RESTAURANTS INC.

Financial rating: $$$

P.O. Box 11988
Lexington, KY 40579
Ph: (800)545-8360
Fax: (859)543-6190
www.ljsilvers.com
Fish & chicken
Began: 1969, Franchising since: 1970
Headquarters size: 350 employees
Franchise department: 10 employees

U.S. franchises: 481
Canadian franchises: 0
Other foreign franchises: 29
Company-owned: 745
Units concentrated in IL, IN, KY, OH

Seeking: All U.S.
Seeking in Canada? Yes
Exclusive territories? No
Homebased option? No
Kiosk option? Info not provided
Employees needed to run franchise:
    Info not provided
Absentee ownership? No

COSTS
Total cost: $192K-2M
Franchise fee: $20K/50K
Royalty fee: 5-6%
Term of agreement: 20 years renewable
    at no charge
Franchisees required to buy multiple
    units? No

FINANCING
In-house: None
Equipment, start-up costs

QUALIFICATIONS
Net worth: $1M
Cash liquidity: $360K
Experience:
    Industry experience
    General business experience
    Marketing skills

TRAINING
At headquarters: 3-5 days
At training restaurant: 4 weeks

BUSINESS SUPPORT
Newsletter
Meetings
Toll-free phone line
Grand opening
Internet
Security/safety procedures
Field operations/evaluations
Purchasing cooperatives

MARKETING SUPPORT
Ad slicks
National media campaign
Regional marketing

QUICK SERVICE ▸ *Hamburgers*

A & W RESTAURANTS INC.

Financial rating: $$$

P.O. Box 11988
Lexington, KY 40579-1988
Ph: (866)298-6298
Fax: (859)543-7111
www.yum.com
Burgers, hot dogs, root beer
Began: 1919, Franchising since: 1925
Headquarters size: Info not provided
Franchise department: Info not pro-
    vided

U.S. franchises: 531
Canadian franchises: 0
Other foreign franchises: 182
Company-owned: 106
Units concentrated in CA, MI, TX, WI

Seeking: All U.S.
Seeking in Canada? Yes
Exclusive territories? No
Homebased option? No
Kiosk option? Info not provided
Employees needed to run franchise:
    Info not provided
Absentee ownership? No

COSTS
Total cost: $212K-1.4M
Franchise fee: $20K/50K
Royalty fee: 5-6%
Term of agreement: 20 years renewable
    at no charge
Franchisees required to buy multiple
    units? No

FINANCING
In-house: None
3rd-party: Equipment, start-up costs

QUALIFICATIONS
Net worth: $1M
Cash liquidity: $360K
Experience:
    Industry experience
    General business experience
    Marketing skills

TRAINING
At headquarters: 2 weeks

BUSINESS SUPPORT
Newsletter
Meetings
Toll-free phone line
Grand opening
Field operations/evaluations
Purchasing cooperatives

MARKETING SUPPORT
Co-op advertising
Ad slicks
Regional marketing

BACK YARD BURGERS INC.

Ranked #191 in Entrepreneur Magazine's 2004 Franchise 500   *Financial rating: $$$$*

1657 N. Shelby Oaks Dr., #105
Memphis, TN 38134
Ph: (901)367-0888, Fax: (901)367-0999
www.backyardburgers.com
Hamburgers & chicken sandwiches
Began: 1986, Franchising since: 1988
Headquarters size: 30 employees
Franchise department: 7 employees

U.S. franchises: 86
Canadian franchises: 0
Other foreign franchises: 0
Company-owned: 42

Seeking: Midwest, Northeast, South,
    Southeast
Focusing on: CO, CT, DE, FL, GA, IA,
    IL, IN, KY, MA, MD, MI, MN, NC,
    NE, NJ, NY, OH, OK, PA, RI, SC,
    TN, TX, VA, WI, WV
Seeking in Canada? No
Exclusive territories? Yes
Homebased option? No
Kiosk option? No
Employees needed to run franchise: 35
Absentee ownership? No

COSTS
Total cost: $800K-1.4M
Franchise fee: $25K
Royalty fee: 4%
Term of agreement: 10 years renewable
    for $1K
Franchisees required to buy multiple
    units? No

FINANCING
3rd-party: Accounts receivable, equip-
    ment, franchise fee, inventory, pay-
    roll, start-up costs
Other: Build-to-suit/sale leaseback

QUALIFICATIONS
Net worth: $500K
Cash liquidity: $200K
Experience:
    Industry experience
    General business experience
    Marketing skills

TRAINING
At headquarters: 6 weeks
At franchisee's location: 2 weeks

BUSINESS SUPPORT
Newsletter
Meetings
Toll-free phone line
Grand opening
Internet
Lease negotiations
Security/safety procedures
Field operations/evaluations
Purchasing cooperatives

MARKETING SUPPORT
Co-op advertising
Ad slicks
National media campaign
Regional marketing

BURGER KING CORP.

Ranked #21 in Entrepreneur Magazine's 2004 Franchise 500   *Financial rating: $$$$*

P.O. Box 020783
Miami, FL 33157
Ph: (305)378-7579
Fax: (305)378-7721
www.burgerking.com
Hamburgers, fries, breakfast foods &
    other items
Began: 1954, Franchising since: 1961
Headquarters size: Info not provided
Franchise department: Info not pro-
    vided

U.S. franchises: 7,252
Canadian franchises: 233
Other foreign franchises: 3,090
Company-owned: 1,150
Units concentrated in all U.S.

Seeking: All U.S.
Seeking in Canada? Yes
Exclusive territories? No
Homebased option? No
Kiosk option? No
Employees needed to run franchise:
    Info not provided
Absentee ownership? Info not provided

COSTS
Total cost: $294K-2.8M
Franchise fee: $50K
Royalty fee: 4.5%
Term of agreement: 20 years renewable
    for $50K
Franchisees required to buy multiple
    units? No

FINANCING
In-house: None
3rd-party: Accounts receivable, equip-
    ment, franchise fee, inventory, pay-
    roll, start-up costs

QUALIFICATIONS
Net worth: $1.5M
Cash liquidity: $500K
Experience:
    Industry experience
    General business experience
    Marketing skills

TRAINING
Training in local market: 700 hours

BUSINESS SUPPORT
Meetings
Toll-free phone line
Grand opening
Security/safety procedures
Field operations/evaluations

MARKETING SUPPORT
Co-op advertising
National media campaign
Regional marketing

CARL'S JR. RESTAURANTS

Ranked #63 in Entrepreneur Magazine's 2004 Franchise 500   *Financial rating: $$$*

3916 State St., #100
Santa Barbara, CA 93105
Ph: (866)253-7655
Fax: (805)898-4206
www.ckr.com
Hamburgers & chicken sandwiches
Began: 1941, Franchising since: 1984
Headquarters size: 840 employees
Franchise department: 4 employees

U.S. franchises: 508
Canadian franchises: 0
Other foreign franchises: 50
Company-owned: 442
Units concentrated West of the
    Mississippi River

Seeking: Southwest, West
Focusing on: CO, ID, TX, WA
Seeking in Canada? Yes
Exclusive territories? Yes
Homebased option? No
Kiosk option? No
Employees needed to run franchise:
    Info not provided
Absentee ownership? No

COSTS
Total cost: $783K-1.2M
Franchise fee: $35K
Royalty fee: 4%
Term of agreement: 20 years renewable
Franchisees required to buy multiple
    units? Yes

FINANCING
No financing available

QUALIFICATIONS
Experience:
    Industry experience
    General business experience
    Restaurant operations experience
    Business ownership experience

TRAINING
At headquarters
At franchisee's location

BUSINESS SUPPORT
Newsletter
Meetings
Toll-free phone line
Grand opening
Internet
Lease negotiations
Field operations/evaluations
Purchasing cooperatives

MARKETING SUPPORT
Co-op advertising
Ad slicks
National media campaign
Regional marketing

FARMER BOYS

Financial rating: $

3452 University Ave.
Riverside, CA 92501
Ph: (888)930-3276/(909)275-9900
Fax: (909)275-9930
www.farmerboys.com
Hamburgers
Began: 1981, Franchising since: 1997
Headquarters size: 22 employees
Franchise department: 2 employees

U.S. franchises: 17
Canadian franchises: 0
Other foreign franchises: 0
Company-owned: 11
Units concentrated in CA

Seeking: West
Seeking in Canada? No
Exclusive territories? Yes
Homebased option? No
Kiosk option? No
Employees needed to run franchise: 30
Absentee ownership? No

COSTS
Total cost: $732.4K-1.8M
Franchise fee: $35K
Royalty fee: 5%
Term of agreement: 20 years renewable
    at no charge
Franchisees required to buy multiple
    units? No

FINANCING
In-house: None
3rd-party: Accounts receivable, equip-
    ment, franchise fee, inventory, pay-
    roll, start-up costs

QUALIFICATIONS
Net worth: $500K
Cash liquidity: $250K
Experience:
    Industry experience
    General business experience

TRAINING
At headquarters: 10 weeks
At franchisee's location: 4 weeks

BUSINESS SUPPORT
Newsletter
Meetings
Toll-free phone line
Grand opening
Lease negotiations
Field operations/evaluations
Purchasing cooperatives

MARKETING SUPPORT
Co-op advertising
Ad slicks
Regional marketing

FIVE GUYS BURGERS & FRIES

Financial rating: $$$

4403 Kirchner Ct., #200
Alexandria, VA 22304
Ph: (703)751-6844, Fax: (703)751-5021
www.fiveguys.com
Hamburgers
Began: 1986, Franchising since: 2002
Headquarters size: Info not provided
Franchise department: Info not provided

U.S. franchises: 0
Canadian franchises: 0
Other foreign franchises: 0
Company-owned: 5
Units concentrated in DC, MD, VA

Seeking: All U.S.
Focusing on: East Coast
Seeking in Canada? No
Exclusive territories? Yes
Homebased option? No
Kiosk option? No
Employees needed to run franchise:
    Info not provided
Absentee ownership? Info not provided

COSTS
Total cost: $152.6K-360.3K
Franchise fee: $25K
Royalty fee: 6%
Term of agreement: 20 years renewable
    at no charge
Franchisees required to buy multiple
    units? Yes

FINANCING
In-house: None
3rd-party: Equipment, franchise fee,
    inventory, start-up costs

QUALIFICATIONS
Net worth: $500K
Cash liquidity: $250K
Experience:
    Industry experience
    General business experience

TRAINING
At franchisee's location: 2 weeks

BUSINESS SUPPORT
Newsletter
Grand opening
Internet
Lease negotiations
Security/safety procedures
Field operations/evaluations
Purchasing cooperatives

MARKETING SUPPORT
Regional marketing

FLAMERS CHARBURGERS

Current financial data not available

500 S. 3rd St.
Jacksonville Beach, FL 32250
Ph: (904)322-1781
Fax: (904)302-4335
www.flamersgrill.com
Hamburgers & chicken
Began: 1986, Franchising since: 1987
Headquarters size: 9 employees
Franchise department: 3 employees

U.S. franchises: 50
Canadian franchises: 0
Other foreign franchises: 12
Company-owned: 0
Units concentrated in DC, FL, MD, VA

Seeking: All U.S.
Focusing on: Northeast
Seeking in Canada? Yes
Exclusive territories? Yes
Homebased option? No
Kiosk option? Info not provided
Employees needed to run franchise: 15
Absentee ownership? Yes

COSTS
Total cost: $164.5K-268.5K
Franchise fee: $30K
Royalty fee: 5%
Term of agreement: 10 years renewable
    for 50% of current franchise fee
Franchisees required to buy multiple
    units? Outside the U.S. only

FINANCING
In-house: None
Equipment, start-up costs

QUALIFICATIONS
Net worth: $350K+
Cash liquidity: $60K-80K
Experience:
    General business experience
    Restaurant experience

TRAINING
At headquarters: 2-3 weeks
At franchisee's location: 2-4 weeks
In Boston, MA: 2 weeks

BUSINESS SUPPORT
Newsletter
Toll-free phone line
Grand opening
Internet
Security/safety procedures
Field operations/evaluations
Purchasing cooperatives

MARKETING SUPPORT
Co-op advertising
Ad slicks
National media campaign
Regional marketing

HARDEE'S

Ranked #51 in Entrepreneur Magazine's 2004 Franchise 500   *Financial rating: $$$*

3916 State St., #100
Santa Barbara, CA 93105
Ph: (866)253-7655, Fax: (805)898-4206
www.ckr.com
Hamburgers, chicken & biscuits
Began: 1961, Franchising since: 1962
Headquarters size: 230 employees
Franchise department: 4 employees

U.S. franchises: 1,281
Canadian franchises: 0
Other foreign franchises: 144
Company-owned: 729
Units concentrated in states east of the
    Mississippi River

Seeking: Midwest, Northeast,
    Northwest, South, Southeast
Focusing on: States east of the
    Mississippi River except AL, AR,
    KY, MD, MI, MN, NH, NJ, NY,
    OH, PA, VT
Seeking in Canada? Yes
Exclusive territories? Yes
Homebased option? No
Kiosk option? No

Employees needed to run franchise:
    Info not provided
Absentee ownership? No

COSTS
Total cost: $770.8K-1.1M
Franchise fee: $35K
Royalty fee: 4%
Term of agreement: 20 years renewable
Franchisees required to buy multiple
    units? Yes

FINANCING
No financing available

QUALIFICATIONS
Experience:
    Industry experience
    General business experience
    Experience in restaurant opera-
    tions
    Business ownership experience

TRAINING
At headquarters
At franchisee's location

BUSINESS SUPPORT
Newsletter
Meetings
Toll-free phone line
Grand opening
Internet
Lease negotiations
Field operations/evaluations
Purchasing cooperatives

MARKETING SUPPORT
Co-op advertising
Ad slicks
National media campaign
Regional marketing

KRYSTAL RESTAURANTS

Ranked #164 in Entrepreneur Magazine's 2004 Franchise 500   *Financial rating: $$$$*

1 Union Sq.
Chattanooga, TN 37402
Ph: (800)458-5912
Fax: (423)757-1588
www.krystal.com
Hamburgers
Began: 1932, Franchising since: 1990
Headquarters size: 115 employees
Franchise department: 6 employees

U.S. franchises: 185
Canadian franchises: 0
Other foreign franchises: 0
Company-owned: 246
Units concentrated in AL, AR, FL, GA,
    KY, LA, MS, NC, SC, TN, TX, VA

Seeking: Midwest, Northeast, South,
    Southeast, Southwest
Focusing on: AL, AR, FL, GA, KS, KY,
    LA, MO, MS, NC, OK, SC, TN, TX,
    VA, WV
Seeking in Canada? No
Exclusive territories? Yes
Homebased option? No

Kiosk option? No
Employees needed to run franchise: 30
Absentee ownership? No

COSTS
Total cost: $900K-1M
Franchise fee: $32.5K
Royalty fee: 4.5%
Term of agreement: 20 years renewable
    for $8.1K
Franchisees required to buy multiple
    units? Yes

FINANCING
No financing available

QUALIFICATIONS
Net worth: $400K
Cash liquidity: $200K
Experience:
    Industry experience
    General business experience

TRAINING
At headquarters: 5 weeks
At franchisee's location: 5 weeks

BUSINESS SUPPORT
Newsletter
Meetings
Toll-free phone line
Grand opening
Internet
Lease negotiations
Security/safety procedures
Field operations/evaluations
Purchasing cooperatives

MARKETING SUPPORT
Co-op advertising
Ad slicks
Regional marketing

MCDONALD'S

Ranked #7 in Entrepreneur Magazine's 2004 Franchise 500   *Financial rating: $$$$*

Kroc Dr.
Oak Brook, IL 60523
Ph: (630)623-6196
Fax: (630)623-5658
www.mcdonalds.com
Hamburgers, chicken, salads
Began: 1955, Franchising since: 1955
Headquarters size: 885 employees
Franchise department: 15 employees

U.S. franchises: 11,533
Canadian franchises: 843
Other foreign franchises: 9,740
Company-owned: 8,065
Units concentrated in all U.S.

Seeking: All U.S.
Seeking in Canada? Yes
Exclusive territories? No
Homebased option? No
Kiosk option? Yes
Employees needed to run franchise:
    Info not provided
Absentee ownership? No

COSTS
Total cost: $506K-1.6M
Franchise fee: $45K
Royalty fee: 12.5%+
Term of agreement: 20 years renewable
    for $45K
Franchisees required to buy multiple
    units? No

FINANCING
No financing available

QUALIFICATIONS
Cash liquidity: $100K
Experience:
    Industry experience
    General business experience
    Marketing skills

TRAINING
At headquarters: 1 week
At local restaurant: 12-24 months

BUSINESS SUPPORT
Newsletter
Meetings
Toll-free phone line
Grand opening
Internet
Lease negotiations
Security/safety procedures
Field operations/evaluations
Purchasing cooperatives

MARKETING SUPPORT
Co-op advertising
Ad slicks
National media campaign
Regional marketing
Restaurant-specific support

SONIC DRIVE IN RESTAURANTS

Ranked #13 in Entrepreneur Magazine's 2004 Franchise 500   *Financial rating: $$$$*

300 Johnny Bench Wy.
Oklahoma City, OK 73104
Ph: (800)569-6656/(405)225-5000
Fax: (405)225-5963
www.sonicdrivein.com
Drive-in restaurant
Began: 1954, Franchising since: 1959
Headquarters size: 200 employees
Franchise department: Info not provided

U.S. franchises: 2,207
Canadian franchises: 0
Other foreign franchises: 5
Company-owned: 497
Units concentrated in AL, AR, AZ, CO,
    FL, GA, KS, KY, LA, MO, MS, NC,
    NM, OK, SC, TN, TX

Seeking: Midwest, South, Southeast,
    Southwest, West
Focusing on: All U.S.
Seeking in Canada? No
Exclusive territories? Yes
Homebased option? No
Kiosk option? No
Employees needed to run franchise: 25
Absentee ownership? No

COSTS
Total cost: $710K-2.3M
Franchise fee: $30K
Royalty fee: 1-5%
Term of agreement: 20 years renewable
    at $6K for 10 years
Franchisees required to buy multiple
    units? Outside the U.S. only

FINANCING
No financing available

QUALIFICATIONS
Net worth: $1M
Cash liquidity: $500K
Experience:
    Industry experience
    General business experience
    If no industry experience, must
    have an operating equity partner

TRAINING
At headquarters: 1 week
At franchisee's location: 11 weeks
Additional training: 1 day to 1 week

BUSINESS SUPPORT
Newsletter
Meetings
Grand opening
Internet
Security/safety procedures
Field operations/evaluations
Purchasing cooperatives

MARKETING SUPPORT
Co-op advertising
Ad slicks
National media campaign
Regional marketing

TOPZ RESTAURANT

Current financial data not available

6345 Balboa Blvd., Bldg. 3, #170
Encino, CA 91316
Ph: (800)996-8679/(818)345-0600
Fax: (818)345-4919
www.topz.com
Quick-service restaurant specializing in lean burgers, hot dogs & fruit shakes
Began: 1998, Franchising since: 2002
Headquarters size: 5 employees
Franchise department: 3 employees

U.S. franchises: 4
Canadian franchises: 0
Other foreign franchises: 0
Company-owned: 3
Units concentrated in CA

Seeking: All U.S.
Seeking in Canada? Yes
Exclusive territories? Yes
Homebased option? No
Kiosk option? Yes
Employees needed to run franchise: 7-15
Absentee ownership? No

COSTS
Total cost: $242.5K-313K
Kiosk cost: $150K
Franchise fee: $20K
Royalty fee: 6%
Term of agreement: 10 years renewable for 50% of current fee
Franchisees required to buy multiple units? Outside the U.S. only

FINANCING
In-house: None
3rd-party: Accounts receivable, equipment, inventory, start-up costs

QUALIFICATIONS
Net worth: $400K
Cash liquidity: $100K
Experience:
    Industry experience
    General business experience
    Marketing skills
    Multi-unit restaurant-operating experience

TRAINING
At franchisee's location: 3 weeks
At company units & regional training centers: 120 hours

BUSINESS SUPPORT
Newsletter
Meetings
Grand opening
Internet
Lease negotiations
Security/safety procedures
Field operations/evaluations
Purchasing cooperatives

MARKETING SUPPORT
Ad slicks

QUICK SERVICE ◢ *Hot Dogs*

JODY MARONI'S SAUSAGE KINGDOM

Financial rating: $$$

5441 W. 104th St.
Los Angeles, CA 90045
Ph: (310)348-1500, Fax: (310)348-1510
www.jodymaroni.com
Gourmet sausages & hot dogs
Began: 1979, Franchising since: 1998
Headquarters size: 12 employees
Franchise department: 6 employees

U.S. franchises: 19
Canadian franchises: 0
Other foreign franchises: 0
Company-owned: 2
Units concentrated in CA

Seeking: All U.S.
Focusing on: CA, IL, NY
Seeking in Canada? No
Exclusive territories? Yes
Homebased option? No
Kiosk option? Yes
Employees needed to run franchise: 7
Absentee ownership? Yes

COSTS
Total cost: $50K-425K
Kiosk cost: $50K-100K
Franchise fee: $30K
Royalty fee: 7%
Term of agreement: 10 years renewable for 25% of franchise fee
Franchisees required to buy multiple units? No

FINANCING
No financing available

QUALIFICATIONS
Net worth: $400K
Cash liquidity: $100K
Experience:
    General business experience
    Marketing skills

TRAINING
At headquarters: 7 days

BUSINESS SUPPORT
Newsletter
Meetings
Toll-free phone line
Grand opening
Internet
Security/safety procedures
Field operations/evaluations
Purchasing cooperatives

MARKETING SUPPORT
Co-op advertising
Ad slicks
National media campaign
Regional marketing

NATHAN'S FAMOUS INC.

Current financial data not available

1400 Old Country Rd., #400
Westbury, NY 11590
Ph: (516)338-8500
Fax: (516)338-7220
www.nathansfamous.com
Hot dogs, hamburgers, seafood, chicken
Began: 1916, Franchising since: 1988
Headquarters size: Info not provided
Franchise department: Info not provided

U.S. franchises: 158
Canadian franchises: 0
Other foreign franchises: 7
Company-owned: 10
Units concentrated in Most of the U.S.

Seeking: All U.S.
Seeking in Canada? Yes
Exclusive territories? Yes
Homebased option? No
Kiosk option? Yes
Employees needed to run franchise: 14
Absentee ownership? Info not provided

COSTS
Total cost: $250K-450K
Kiosk cost: $30K-75K
Franchise fee: $30K
Royalty fee: 5%
Term of agreement: 20 years renewable
Franchisees required to buy multiple
    units? No

FINANCING
In-house: Franchise fee, equipment,
    inventory
3rd-party: None

QUALIFICATIONS
Net worth: $500K
Cash liquidity: $200K
Experience:
    Industry experience
    General business experience

TRAINING
At headquarters: 3 weeks
At franchisee's location: 3 days

BUSINESS SUPPORT
Newsletter
Meetings
Toll-free phone line
Grand opening
Internet
Lease negotiations
Field operations/evaluations
Purchasing cooperatives

MARKETING SUPPORT
Co-op advertising
Ad slicks

WIENERSCHNITZEL

Ranked #114 in Entrepreneur Magazine's 2004 Franchise 500   *Financial rating: $$$$*

4440 Von Karman
Newport Beach, CA 92660
Ph: (800)764-9353/(949)851-2609
Fax: (949)851-2618
www.wienerschnitzel.com
Hot dogs & hamburgers
Began: 1961, Franchising since: 1965
Headquarters size: 55 employees
Franchise department: 6 employees

U.S. franchises: 343
Canadian franchises: 0
Other foreign franchises: 0
Company-owned: 0
Units concentrated in CA, Southwest,
    Northwest

Seeking: Southwest, West
Focusing on: AZ, CA, CO, NM, NV,
    OK, OR, UT, WA
Seeking in Canada? No
Exclusive territories? No
Homebased option? No
Kiosk option? No
Employees needed to run franchise: 25
Absentee ownership? Yes

COSTS
Total cost: $136K-1M
Franchise fee: $20K
Royalty fee: 5%
Term of agreement: 20 years renewable
    for $1K
Franchisees required to buy multiple
    units? No

FINANCING
In-house: None
3rd-party: Equipment, inventory,
    start-up costs

QUALIFICATIONS
Net worth: $100K-250K
Cash liquidity: $100K-250K
Experience:
    Industry experience
    General business experience
    Restaurant experience

TRAINING
At headquarters: 7 days
At franchisee's location: 5 weeks
Management development training:
    6-8 weeks

BUSINESS SUPPORT
Newsletter
Meetings
Toll-free phone line
Grand opening
Internet
Security/safety procedures
Field operations/evaluations
Purchasing cooperatives

MARKETING SUPPORT
Co-op advertising
Ad slicks
National media campaign
Regional marketing
Field marketing support

WOODY'S HOT DOGS

Ranked #419 in Entrepreneur Magazine's 2004 Franchise 500

Financial rating: $$

23254 Valley High Rd.
Morrison, CO 80465
Ph: (877)469-6639/(303)697-3962
Fax: (303)697-3965
www.woodyshotdogs.com
Hot dog, beverage & coffee carts/in-
line outlets
Began: 1990, Franchising since: 1991
Headquarters size: 6 employees
Franchise department: 2 employees

U.S. franchises: 75
Canadian franchises: 0
Other foreign franchises: 0
Company-owned: 0

Seeking: Midwest, Southwest, West
Focusing on: IA, KS, NM, OK, SD
Seeking in Canada? No
Exclusive territories? Yes
Homebased option? No
Kiosk option? Yes
Employees needed to run franchise: 1-2
Absentee ownership? No

COSTS
Total cost: $48.6K-394K
Kiosk cost: $45K
Franchise fee: Varies
Royalty fee: 6%
Term of agreement: 5 years renewable
for $2K
Franchisees required to buy multiple
units? No

FINANCING
No financing available

QUALIFICATIONS
Experience:
General business experience

TRAINING
At franchisee's location: 1 week

BUSINESS SUPPORT
Newsletter
Meetings
Toll-free phone line
Grand opening
Internet
Security/safety procedures
Field operations/evaluations

MARKETING SUPPORT
Grass roots marketing program

QUICK SERVICE | *Ice Cream, Shaved Ice, Frozen Custard*

ALL AMERICAN SPECIALTY RESTAURANTS INC.

Current financial data not available

812 S.W. Washington St., #1110
Portland, OR 97205
Ph: (800)311-3930/(503)224-6199
Fax: (503)224-5042
www.allamericanicecream.com
Ice cream, frozen yogurt, deli sand-
wiches
Began: 1986, Franchising since: 1988
Headquarters size: 5 employees
Franchise department: 2 employees

U.S. franchises: 29
Canadian franchises: 0
Other foreign franchises: 0
Company-owned: 0

Seeking: All U.S.
Focusing on: AZ, CA, CO, HI, ID, NM,
NV, OR, TX, UT, WA
Seeking in Canada? No
Exclusive territories? No
Homebased option? No
Kiosk option? Yes
Employees needed to run franchise: 6-7
Absentee ownership? Yes

COSTS
Total cost: $91K-224K
Kiosk cost: $90.5K
Franchise fee: $6K-25K
Royalty fee: 5%
Term of agreement: 10 years renewable
for $6K
Franchisees required to buy multiple
units? Yes

FINANCING
In-house: Franchise fee
3rd-party: Accounts receivable, equip-
ment, inventory, start-up costs

QUALIFICATIONS
Net worth: $250K
Cash liquidity: $45K
Experience:
General business experience

TRAINING
At headquarters: 2 weeks
At franchisee's location: 2 weeks

BUSINESS SUPPORT
Newsletter
Meetings
Toll-free phone line
Grand opening
Security/safety procedures
Field operations/evaluations

MARKETING SUPPORT
Ad slicks
Regional marketing

BAHAMA BUCK'S ORIGINAL SHAVED ICE CO.

Financial rating: 0

465 E. Chilton Dr., #5
Chandler, AZ 85225
Ph: (480)539-6952
Fax: (480)539-6953
www.bahamabucks.com
Shaved ice & fruit smoothies
Began: 1989, Franchising since: 1993
Headquarters size: 10 employees
Franchise department: 3 employees

U.S. franchises: 13
Canadian franchises: 0
Other foreign franchises: 0
Company-owned: 4
Units concentrated in AZ, NM, TX

Seeking: South, Southeast, Southwest,
   West
Focusing on: AZ, NM, TX
Seeking in Canada? No
Exclusive territories? Yes
Homebased option? No
Kiosk option? Yes
Employees needed to run franchise: 12
Absentee ownership? Yes

COSTS
Total cost: $95K-275K
Kiosk cost: $95K
Franchise fee: $20K
Royalty fee: 6%
Term of agreement: 10 years renewable
   for $5K
Franchisees required to buy multiple
   units? No

FINANCING
In-house: None
3rd-party: Accounts receivable, equipment, franchise fee, inventory, payroll, start-up costs

QUALIFICATIONS
Net worth: $150K
Cash liquidity: $45K
Experience:
   General business experience

TRAINING
At headquarters: 5 days
At franchisee's location: 5 days

BUSINESS SUPPORT
Newsletter
Meetings
Toll-free phone line
Grand opening
Internet
Lease negotiations
Security/safety procedures
Field operations/evaluations
Purchasing cooperatives

MARKETING SUPPORT
Co-op advertising
Ad slicks
Regional marketing

BASKIN-ROBBINS USA CO.

Ranked #10 in Entrepreneur Magazine's 2004 Franchise 500

Financial rating: $$$$

14 Pacella Park Dr.
Randolph, MA 02368
Ph: (800)777-9983
www.baskinrobbins.com
Ice cream & yogurt
Began: 1945, Franchising since: 1948
Headquarters size: Info not provided
Franchise department: Info not pro-
   vided

U.S. franchises: 2,753
Canadian franchises: 150
Other foreign franchises: 2,202
Company-owned: 0

Seeking: All U.S.
Focusing on: Northeast
Seeking in Canada? Yes
Exclusive territories? No
Homebased option? No
Kiosk option? Yes
Employees needed to run franchise:
   Info not provided
Absentee ownership? No

COSTS
Total cost: $145.7K-527.8K
Kiosk cost: Varies
Franchise fee: $40K
Royalty fee: 5.9%
Term of agreement: Info not provided
Franchisees required to buy multiple
   units? No

FINANCING
No financing available

QUALIFICATIONS
Net worth: $300K
Cash liquidity: $200K
Experience:
   Industry experience
   General business experience
   Marketing skills

TRAINING
At headquarters: Varies

BUSINESS SUPPORT
Newsletter
Meetings
Toll-free phone line
Grand opening
Security/safety procedures
Field operations/evaluations

MARKETING SUPPORT
Regional marketing

BEN & JERRY'S

Ranked #135 in Entrepreneur Magazine's 2004 Franchise 500   *Financial rating: $$$$*

30 Community Dr.
South Burlington, VT 05403
Ph: (802)846-1500, Fax: (802)846-1538
www.benjerry.com
Ice cream parlor
Began: 1978, Franchising since: 1981
Headquarters size: 200 employees
Franchise department: 27 employees

U.S. franchises: 259
Canadian franchises: 7
Other foreign franchises: 100
Company-owned: 9

Seeking: All U.S.
Focusing on: All U.S. except AR, IA,
    ID, KS, MS, MT, ND, NE, NY, OK,
    SD, WI, WV, WY
Seeking in Canada? Yes
Exclusive territories? Yes
Homebased option? No
Kiosk option? Yes
Employees needed to run franchise:
    Info not provided
Absentee ownership? No

COSTS
Total cost: $129.5K-316K
    Kiosk cost: Same as total cost
Franchise fee: $9K-30K
Royalty fee: 1.5%
Term of agreement: 10 years renewable
    for 50% of then-current fee
Franchisees required to buy multiple
    units? Yes

FINANCING
No financing available

QUALIFICATIONS
Net worth: $200K
Cash liquidity: $80K
Experience:
    Industry experience
    General business experience
    Marketing skills

TRAINING
At headquarters: 6 days
At franchisee's location: 3-5 days

BUSINESS SUPPORT
Newsletter
Meetings
Toll-free phone line
Grand opening
Internet
Security/safety procedures
Field operations/evaluations

MARKETING SUPPORT
Co-op advertising
Ad slicks
National media campaign
Regional marketing

BRUSTER'S OLD-FASHIONED ICE CREAM & YOGURT

Ranked #105 in Entrepreneur Magazine's 2004 Franchise 500   *Financial rating: $$$$*

730 Mulberry St.
Bridgewater, PA 15009
Ph: (724)774-4250, Fax: (724)774-0666
www.brusters.com
Homemade ice cream
Began: 1989, Franchising since: 1993
Headquarters size: 20 employees
Franchise department: 2 employees

U.S. franchises: 139
Canadian franchises: 0
Other foreign franchises: 0
Company-owned: 8
Units concentrated in AL, FL, GA, IN,
    MD, NC, NH, NY, OH, PA, SC, TN,
    VA, WV

Seeking: Northeast, South, Southeast
Focusing on: AK, DE, KY, LA, MS
Seeking in Canada? No
Exclusive territories? Yes
Homebased option? No
Kiosk option? No
Employees needed to run franchise:
    15-30
Absentee ownership? Yes

COSTS
Total cost: $165K-968K
Franchise fee: $30K
Royalty fee: 5%
Term of agreement: 10 years renewable
    at no charge
Franchisees required to buy multiple
    units? No

FINANCING
In-house: None
3rd-party: Equipment, franchise fee,
    inventory, start-up costs

QUALIFICATIONS
Cash liquidity: $200K

TRAINING
At headquarters: 13 days

BUSINESS SUPPORT
Newsletter
Meetings
Internet
Security/safety procedures
Field operations/evaluations
Purchasing cooperatives

MARKETING SUPPORT
Co-op advertising
Ad slicks
Regional marketing

CARVEL

Ranked #79 in Entrepreneur Magazine's 2004 Franchise 500   *Financial rating: $$$$*

200 Glenridge Point Pkwy., #200
Atlanta, GA 30342
Ph: (404)255-3250
Fax: (404)255-4978
www.carvel.com
Ice cream & ice cream cakes
Began: 1934, Franchising since: 1947
Headquarters size: 18 employees
Franchise department: 17 employees

U.S. franchises: 427
Canadian franchises: 3
Other foreign franchises: 0
Company-owned: 0
Units concentrated in CT, FL, GA,
    MA, MD, NC, NJ, NY, RI, SC, TN,
    TX, VA

Seeking: All U.S.
Seeking in Canada? No
Exclusive territories? No
Homebased option? No
Kiosk option? Yes
Employees needed to run franchise: 6
Absentee ownership? Yes

COSTS
Total cost: $177.5K-260.9K
Kiosk cost: $30K-199.6K
Franchise fee: $15K-25K
Royalty fee: $1.74/gal.
Term of agreement: 20 years renewable
    at then-current fee
Franchisees required to buy multiple
    units? No

FINANCING
In-house: None
3rd-party: Equipment, franchise fee,
    inventory, start-up costs

QUALIFICATIONS
Net worth: $250K+
Cash liquidity: $100K
Experience:
    General business experience

TRAINING
At headquarters: 10 days
At franchisee's location: 5 days
Additional training annually

BUSINESS SUPPORT
Newsletter
Meetings
Toll-free phone line
Grand opening
Internet
Security/safety procedures
Field operations/evaluations
Purchasing cooperatives

MARKETING SUPPORT
Co-op advertising
Ad slicks
Regional marketing
Broadcast media

COLD STONE CREAMERY

Ranked #112 in Entrepreneur Magazine's 2004 Franchise 500   *Financial rating: $$*

16101 N. 82nd St., #A4
Scottsdale, AZ 85260
Ph: (888)218-3349
Fax: (480)348-1718
www.coldstonecreamery.com
Ice cream, frozen yogurt, Italian sorbet
Began: 1988, Franchising since: 1994
Headquarters size: 106 employees
Franchise department: 6 employees

U.S. franchises: 423
Canadian franchises: 0
Other foreign franchises: 0
Company-owned: 4
Units concentrated in all U.S.

Seeking: All U.S.
Seeking in Canada? Yes
Exclusive territories? No
Homebased option? No
Kiosk option? No
Employees needed to run franchise: 15
Absentee ownership? No

COSTS
Total cost: $245K-353K
Franchise fee: $31K-35K
Royalty fee: 6%
Term of agreement: 10 years renewable
    at no charge
Franchisees required to buy multiple
    units? No

FINANCING
In-house: None
3rd-party: Equipment, franchise fee,
    inventory, start-up costs

QUALIFICATIONS
Cash liquidity: $50K-70K+

TRAINING
At headquarters: 11 days
At franchisee's location: 3 days

BUSINESS SUPPORT
Newsletter
Meetings
Toll-free phone line
Grand opening
Internet
Lease negotiations
Security/safety procedures
Field operations/evaluations
Purchasing cooperatives

MARKETING SUPPORT
Co-op advertising
Ad slicks
National media campaign
Regional marketing
In-house creative services group
Local store marketing support

CULVER FRANCHISING SYSTEM INC.

Ranked #82 in Entrepreneur Magazine's 2004 Franchise 500   *Financial rating: $$$$*

540 Water St.
Prairie du Sac, WI 53578
Ph: (608)643-7980, Fax: (608)643-7982
www.culvers.com
Frozen custard & butter burgers
Began: 1984, Franchising since: 1988
Headquarters size: 67 employees
Franchise department: 4 employees

U.S. franchises: 218
Canadian franchises: 0
Other foreign franchises: 0
Company-owned: 5
Units concentrated in IA, IL, IN, KS, MI, MN, MS, ND, NE, SD, TX, WI

Seeking: Midwest
Focusing on: CO, IA, IL, IN, KS, KY, MI, MN, MS, ND, NE, OH, SD, TX, WI
Seeking in Canada? No
Exclusive territories? No
Homebased option? No
Kiosk option? No
Employees needed to run franchise: 40-50
Absentee ownership? No

COSTS
Total cost: $340.4K-2.9M
Franchise fee: $50K
Royalty fee: 4%
Term of agreement: 15 years renewable for $50K
Franchisees required to buy multiple units? No

FINANCING
In-house: None
3rd-party: Accounts receivable, equipment, franchise fee, inventory, payroll, start-up costs

QUALIFICATIONS
Net worth: $500K
Cash liquidity: $200K

TRAINING
At headquarters: 16 weeks

BUSINESS SUPPORT
Newsletter
Meetings
Grand opening
Internet
Security/safety procedures
Field operations/evaluations
Purchasing cooperatives

MARKETING SUPPORT
Ad slicks
National media campaign
Regional marketing

DAIRY QUEEN

Ranked #30 in Entrepreneur Magazine's 2004 Franchise 500   *Financial rating: $$$$*

P.O. Box 39286
Minneapolis, MN 55439-0286
Ph: (800)679-6556/(952)830-0200
Fax: (952)830-0450
www.dairyqueen.com
Soft-serve dairy products & sandwiches
Began: 1940, Franchising since: 1944
Headquarters size: 320 employees
Franchise department: 33 employees

U.S. franchises: 4,839
Canadian franchises: 564
Other foreign franchises: 326
Company-owned: 66

Seeking: All U.S.
Seeking in Canada? Yes
Exclusive territories? No
Homebased option? No
Kiosk option? No
Employees needed to run franchise: 20-40
Absentee ownership? Yes

COSTS
Total cost: $655K-1.3M
Franchise fee: $20K/35K
Royalty fee: 4-5%
Term of agreement: Renewable term
Franchisees required to buy multiple units? Outside the U.S. only

FINANCING
No financing available

QUALIFICATIONS
Net worth: $500K
Cash liquidity: $300K
Experience:
    Industry experience
    General business experience

TRAINING
At headquarters: 3 weeks
At franchisee's location: Pre- & post-opening
At existing store: 2 weeks

BUSINESS SUPPORT
Newsletter
Meetings
Toll-free phone line
Grand opening
Field operations/evaluations
Purchasing cooperatives

MARKETING SUPPORT
Co-op advertising
Ad slicks
National media campaign
Regional marketing
Local promotions

DIPPIN' DOTS FRANCHISING INC.

Ranked #101 in Entrepreneur Magazine's 2004 Franchise 500　　　　*Financial rating: $$$$*

5110 Charter Oak Dr.
Paducah, KY 42001
Ph: (270)575-6990
Fax: (270)575-6997
www.dippindots.com
Specialty ice cream, frozen yogurt, ices
Began: 1988, Franchising since: 2000
Headquarters size: 22 employees
Franchise department: 12 employees

U.S. franchises: 598
Canadian franchises: 0
Other foreign franchises: 0
Company-owned: 2
Units concentrated in all U.S.

Seeking: All U.S.
Seeking in Canada? No
Exclusive territories? No
Homebased option? No
Kiosk option? Yes
Employees needed to run franchise: 3
Absentee ownership? Yes

COSTS
Total cost: $45.6K-189.8K
Kiosk cost: $55K-110K
Franchise fee: $12.5K
Royalty fee: 4%
Term of agreement: 5 years renewable
Franchisees required to buy multiple
　　units? No

FINANCING
No financing available

QUALIFICATIONS
Net worth: $250K
Cash liquidity: $75K
Experience:
　　General business experience

TRAINING
At headquarters: 2 days
At franchisee's location: 2 days

BUSINESS SUPPORT
Newsletter
Meetings
Grand opening
Internet
Field operations/evaluations
Purchasing cooperatives

MARKETING SUPPORT
Ad slicks
POP customization

THE HAAGEN-DAZS SHOPPE CO. INC.

Ranked #174 in Entrepreneur Magazine's 2004 Franchise 500　　　　*Financial rating: $$$$*

200 S. 6th St., Mail Stop 29R1
Minneapolis, MN 55402
Ph: (612)330-8877
Fax: (612)330-7074
www.haagendazs.com
Ice cream & frozen yogurt
Began: 1961, Franchising since: 1977
Headquarters size: 22 employees
Franchise department: 3 employees

U.S. franchises: 231
Canadian franchises: 0
Other foreign franchises: 438
Company-owned: 103
Units concentrated in CA, FL, NY

Seeking: All U.S.
Seeking in Canada? No
Exclusive territories? No
Homebased option? No
Kiosk option? Yes
Employees needed to run franchise: 8
Absentee ownership? Yes

COSTS
Total cost: $54.6K-390.6K
Kiosk cost: $225K
Franchise fee: $10K-20K
Royalty fee: 3%
Term of agreement: 10 years renewable
　　at current franchise fee
Franchisees required to buy multiple
　　units? No

FINANCING
No financing available

QUALIFICATIONS
Net worth: $200K
Cash liquidity: $80K
Experience:
　　General business experience

TRAINING
At headquarters: 2 weeks

BUSINESS SUPPORT
Newsletter
Meetings
Grand opening
Field operations/evaluations

MARKETING SUPPORT
Info not provided

MAGGIEMOO'S ICE CREAM & TREATERY

Ranked #169 in Entrepreneur Magazine's 2004 Franchise 500   *Financial rating: $$$$*

10025 Governor Warfield Pkwy., #301
Columbia, MD 21044
Ph: (800)949-8114
Fax: (410)740-1500
www.maggiemoos.com
Ice cream, smoothies, cakes
Began: 1996, Franchising since: 1997
Headquarters size: 19 employees
Franchise department: 3 employees

U.S. franchises: 95
Canadian franchises: 0
Other foreign franchises: 0
Company-owned: 2
Units concentrated in DC, MD, OH,
    TX, VA

Seeking: All U.S.
Seeking in Canada? Yes
Exclusive territories? Yes
Homebased option? No
Kiosk option? Yes
Employees needed to run franchise: 12
Absentee ownership? Yes

COSTS
Total cost: $198.9K-296.9K
Kiosk cost: Same as total cost
Franchise fee: $28K
Royalty fee: 6%
Term of agreement: 10 years renewable
    for $5K
Franchisees required to buy multiple
    units? Outside the U.S. only

FINANCING
In-house: None
Equipment, start-up costs

QUALIFICATIONS
Net worth: $400K
Cash liquidity: $100K
Experience:
    Industry experience
    General business experience

TRAINING
At headquarters: 14 days
At franchisee's location: 7 days

BUSINESS SUPPORT
Newsletter
Meetings
Grand opening
Internet
Lease negotiations
Security/safety procedures
Field operations/evaluations

MARKETING SUPPORT
Co-op advertising
Ad slicks

MARBLE SLAB CREAMERY INC.

Ranked #304 in Entrepreneur Magazine's 2004 Franchise 500   *Financial rating: $*

3100 S. Gessner, #305
Houston, TX 77063
Ph: (713)780-3601
Fax: (713)780-0264
www.marbleslab.com
Ice cream, frozen yogurt, baked goods
Began: 1983, Franchising since: 1984
Headquarters size: 25 employees
Franchise department: 8 employees

U.S. franchises: 209
Canadian franchises: 0
Other foreign franchises: 0
Company-owned: 1
Units concentrated in all U.S.

Seeking: All U.S.
Seeking in Canada? Yes
Exclusive territories? Yes
Homebased option? No
Kiosk option? Yes
Employees needed to run franchise:
    8-10
Absentee ownership? Yes

COSTS
Total cost: $187.4K-251.98K
Kiosk cost: Same as total cost
Franchise fee: $25K
Royalty fee: 6%
Term of agreement: 10 years renewable
    for 20% of current franchise fee
Franchisees required to buy multiple
    units? No

FINANCING
In-house: None
3rd-party: Equipment, franchise fee,
    inventory, start-up costs

QUALIFICATIONS
Net worth: $250K
Cash liquidity: $50K
Experience:
    General business experience

TRAINING
At headquarters: 10 days
At franchisee's location: 6 days

BUSINESS SUPPORT
Newsletter
Meetings
Toll-free phone line
Grand opening
Internet
Lease negotiations
Security/safety procedures
Field operations/evaluations

MARKETING SUPPORT
Co-op advertising
Ad slicks
Regional marketing
Market-specific advertising

RITA'S

Ranked #102 in Entrepreneur Magazine's 2004 Franchise 500   *Financial rating: $$$$*

1525 Ford Rd.
Bensalem, PA 19020
Ph: (800)677-7482/(215)633-9899
Fax: (215)633-9922
www.ritasice.com
Italian ice, frozen custard, gelati, soft
   pretzels
Began: 1984, Franchising since: 1989
Headquarters size: 37 employees
Franchise department: 8 employees

U.S. franchises: 277
Canadian franchises: 0
Other foreign franchises: 0
Company-owned: 1
Units concentrated in DE, FL, MD, NJ,
   NY, OH, PA, SC, VA

Seeking: Midwest, Northeast,
   Southeast
Focusing on: CT, DE, FL, MD, NJ, NY,
   OH, PA, SC, VA
Seeking in Canada? No
Exclusive territories? Yes
Homebased option? No

Kiosk option? No
Employees needed to run franchise:
   10-15
Absentee ownership? No

COSTS
Total cost: $137.2K-247.4K
Franchise fee: $25K
Royalty fee: 6.5%
Term of agreement: 10 years renewable
   for 50% of current franchise fee
Franchisees required to buy multiple
   units? No

FINANCING
In-house: None
3rd-party: Equipment, inventory,
   start-up costs

QUALIFICATIONS
Net worth: $250K
Cash liquidity: $75K

TRAINING
At headquarters: 6 days
At franchisee's location: 2-4 days

BUSINESS SUPPORT
Newsletter
Meetings
Toll-free phone line
Grand opening
Lease negotiations
Security/safety procedures
Field operations/evaluations

MARKETING SUPPORT
Ad slicks
National media campaign
Regional marketing

RITTER'S FROZEN CUSTARD

Ranked #384 in Entrepreneur Magazine's 2004 Franchise 500   *Financial rating: $$$*

12400 N. Meridian St., #190
Carmel, IN 46032
Ph: (317)819-0700
Fax: (317)819-0261
www.ritters.com
Frozen custard
Began: 1990, Franchising since: 1994
Headquarters size: 10 employees
Franchise department: 9 employees

U.S. franchises: 42
Canadian franchises: 0
Other foreign franchises: 0
Company-owned: 2
Units concentrated in FL, IN, MI, OH,
   PA, SC, TN, TX

Seeking: Midwest, South, Southeast
Focusing on: GA, IL, KY
Seeking in Canada? No
Exclusive territories? Yes
Homebased option? No
Kiosk option? No
Employees needed to run franchise: 20
Absentee ownership? No

COSTS
Total cost: $225K-1.2M
Franchise fee: $25K
Royalty fee: 5%
Term of agreement: 10 years renewable
   for $5K
Franchisees required to buy multiple
   units? No

FINANCING
No financing available

QUALIFICATIONS
Experience:
   General business experience
   Marketing skills

TRAINING
At headquarters: 15 days
During store opening: 10 days

BUSINESS SUPPORT
Meetings
Grand opening
Internet
Lease negotiations
Security/safety procedures
Field operations/evaluations

MARKETING SUPPORT
Co-op advertising
Ad slicks
Regional marketing
Intranet

SHAKE'S FROZEN CUSTARD

Ranked #433 in Entrepreneur Magazine's 2004 Franchise 500   *Financial rating: 0*

244 W. Dickson St.
Fayetteville, AR 72701
Ph: (479)587-9115, Fax: (479)587-0780
www.shakesfrozencustard.com
Frozen custard
Began: 1991, Franchising since: 1998
Headquarters size: 15 employees
Franchise department: 13 employees

U.S. franchises: 43
Canadian franchises: 0
Other foreign franchises: 0
Company-owned: 2
Units concentrated in AL, AR, FL, KS, MO, OK, TN, TX

Seeking: Midwest, South, Southeast, Southwest
Focusing on: AL, AZ, FL, IL, LA, MO, MS, NV, OK, TX
Seeking in Canada? No
Exclusive territories? Yes
Homebased option? No
Kiosk option? No
Employees needed to run franchise: 20
Absentee ownership? Yes

COSTS
Total cost: $168K-800K
Franchise fee: $30K
Royalty fee: 5%
Term of agreement: 15 years renewable for 50% of initial franchise fee
Franchisees required to buy multiple units? No

FINANCING
In-house: None
3rd-party: Equipment, inventory, start-up costs

QUALIFICATIONS
Experience:
    General business experience

TRAINING
At headquarters: 2 weeks
At franchisee's location: 1 week
Additional training available

BUSINESS SUPPORT
Newsletter
Meetings
Toll-free phone line
Grand opening
Internet
Security/safety procedures
Field operations/evaluations

MARKETING SUPPORT
Co-op advertising
Ad slicks

TCBY SYSTEMS LLC

Current financial data not available

2855 E. Cottonwood Pkwy., #400
Salt Lake City, UT 84121
Ph: (800)348-6311/(801)736-5936
Fax: (801)736-5936
www.tcby.com
Frozen yogurt, ice cream, sorbet, smoothies
Began: 1981, Franchising since: 1982
Headquarters size: 150 employees
Franchise department: 25 employees

U.S. franchises: 0
Canadian franchises: 0
Other foreign franchises: 0
Company-owned: 72
Units concentrated in all U.S.

Seeking: All U.S.
Seeking in Canada? Yes
Exclusive territories? No
Homebased option? No
Kiosk option? Info not provided
Employees needed to run franchise: Info not provided
Absentee ownership? Info not provided

COSTS
Total cost: $180K-247K
Franchise fee: $25K
Royalty fee: 4%
Term of agreement: 10 years renewable
Franchisees required to buy multiple units? Outside the U.S. only

FINANCING
No financing available

QUALIFICATIONS
Net worth: $150K
Cash liquidity: $75K

TRAINING
At headquarters: 6 days

BUSINESS SUPPORT
Newsletter
Meetings
Toll-free phone line
Internet
Field operations/evaluations

MARKETING SUPPORT
Ad slicks
National media campaign

2 SCOOPS CAFE

Current financial data not available

4651 36th St., #600
Orlando, FL 32811
Ph: (407)381-0378
Fax: (407)996-1214
www.2scoopscafe.com
Ice cream parlor/cafe
Began: 2002, Franchising since: 2002
Headquarters size: 1 employee
Franchise department: 1 employee

U.S. franchises: 1
Canadian franchises: 0
Other foreign franchises: 0
Company-owned: 0
Units concentrated in FL

Seeking: All U.S.
Seeking in Canada? No
Exclusive territories? Yes
Homebased option? No
Kiosk option? Yes
Employees needed to run franchise:
2-4
Absentee ownership? Yes

COSTS
Total cost: $50K-75K
Kiosk cost: $40K-50K
Franchise fee: $15K
Royalty fee: 5%
Term of agreement: 5 years renewable
for 25% of then-current fee
Franchisees required to buy multiple
units? No

FINANCING
No financing available

QUALIFICATIONS
Net worth: $150K
Cash liquidity: $40K-50K
Experience:
General business experience
People skills

TRAINING
At headquarters: 5-10 days
At franchisee's location: 5-10 days

BUSINESS SUPPORT
Newsletter
Meetings
Toll-free phone line
Grand opening
Internet
Lease negotiations
Security/safety procedures
Field operations/evaluations
Purchasing cooperatives

MARKETING SUPPORT
Co-op advertising
Ad slicks
Regional marketing

YOGEN FRUZ WORLDWIDE

Current financial data not available

8300 Woodbine Ave., 5th Fl.
Markham, ON Canada L3R 9Y7
Ph: (905)479-8762
Fax: (905)479-5235
www.coolbrandsinternational.com
Frozen yogurt & ice cream
Began: 1986, Franchising since: 1987
Headquarters size: 20 employees
Franchise department: Info not pro-
vided

U.S. franchises: 1,706
Canadian franchises: 805
Other foreign franchises: 2,806
Company-owned: 10

Seeking: All U.S.
Seeking in Canada? Yes
Exclusive territories? Yes
Homebased option? No
Kiosk option? Yes
Employees needed to run franchise: 4-7
Absentee ownership? No

COSTS
Total cost: $150K-200K
Kiosk cost: $50K-100K
Franchise fee: $25K
Royalty fee: 6%
Term of agreement: 7-10 years renew-
able for 50% of current fee
Franchisees required to buy multiple
units? Outside the U.S. only

FINANCING
No financing available

QUALIFICATIONS
Net worth: $400K+
Cash liquidity: $75K+

TRAINING
At headquarters: 1 week
At franchisee's location: 1 week

BUSINESS SUPPORT
Meetings
Grand opening
Internet
Security/safety procedures
Field operations/evaluations
Purchasing cooperatives

MARKETING SUPPORT
Co-op advertising
Ad slicks
National media campaign
Regional marketing

QUICK SERVICE · *Italian*

FAZOLI'S SYSTEMS INC.

Current financial data not available

2470 Palumbo Dr.
Lexington, KY 40509
Ph: (859)268-1668. Fax: (859)268-2263
www.fazolis.com
Fast-casual Italian food
Began: 1988, Franchising since: 1991
Headquarters size: Info not provided
Franchise department: 3 employees

U.S. franchises: 221
Canadian franchises: 0
Other foreign franchises: 3
Company-owned: 175
Units concentrated in GA, IL, KY, MI, OH, SC, TN, TX, VA

Focusing on: AL, CA, ID, IL, LA, MI, MN, NV, OK, SC, TN, TX, UT, VA, WY
Seeking in Canada? No
Exclusive territories? No
Homebased option? No
Kiosk option? No
Employees needed to run franchise: Info not provided
Absentee ownership? Yes

COSTS
Total cost: $431K-1.1M
Franchise fee: $30K
Royalty fee: 4%
Term of agreement: 15 years renewable for 30% of current franchise fee
Franchisees required to buy multiple units? No

FINANCING
No financing available

QUALIFICATIONS
Net worth: $1M
Cash liquidity: $350K
Experience:
    Industry experience
    General business experience

TRAINING
At headquarters: 6 weeks
At franchisee's location: 3 weeks
Additional training: 5 days

BUSINESS SUPPORT
Newsletter
Meetings
Toll-free phone line
Grand opening
Internet
Security/safety procedures
Field operations/evaluations

MARKETING SUPPORT
Co-op advertising
Ad slicks

MRS. VANELLI'S FRESH ITALIAN FOODS

Financial rating: $$$$

700 Kerr St.
Oakville, ON Canada L6K 3W5
Ph: (905)337-7777, Fax: (905)337-0331
www.donatogroup.com
Italian fast food
Began: 1981, Franchising since: 1984
Headquarters size: 25 employees
Franchise department: Info not provided

U.S. franchises: 0
Canadian franchises: 92
Other foreign franchises: 15
Company-owned: 5
Units concentrated in Canada

Not available in the U.S.
Seeking in Canada? Yes
Exclusive territories? Yes
Homebased option? No
Kiosk option? No

Employees needed to run franchise: Info not provided
Absentee ownership? Yes

COSTS
Total cost: $168.8K-226.6K
Franchise fee: $25K
Royalty fee: 6%
Term of agreement: 10 years renewable for $1K per year
Franchisees required to buy multiple units? No

FINANCING
No financing available

QUALIFICATIONS
Cash liquidity: $80K

TRAINING
At headquarters: 18 days
At franchisee's location: 1 week

BUSINESS SUPPORT
Newsletter
Meetings
Toll-free phone line
Grand opening
Internet
Security/safety procedures
Field operations/evaluations
Purchasing cooperatives

MARKETING SUPPORT
Co-op advertising
Ad slicks
National media campaign
Regional marketing

QUICK SERVICE   *Juice Bars*

BOOSTER JUICE

Financial rating: 0

131 N. State St., #D
Lake Oswego, OR 97034
Ph: (877)577-7511
Fax: (503)296-5877
www.boosterjuice.com
Juice & smoothie bar
Began: 1999, Franchising since: 2000
Headquarters size: 18 employees
Franchise department: 4 employees

U.S. franchises: 0
Canadian franchises: 75
Other foreign franchises: 0
Company-owned: 10

Seeking: All U.S.
Seeking in Canada? Yes
Exclusive territories? Yes
Homebased option? No
Kiosk option? Yes
Employees needed to run franchise:
   8-10
Absentee ownership? Yes

COSTS
Total cost: $153K-240K
Kiosk cost: $75K-150K
Franchise fee: $20K
Royalty fee: 6%
Term of agreement: 5-10 years renew-
   able for $5K
Franchisees required to buy multiple
   units? Outside the U.S. only

FINANCING
No financing available

QUALIFICATIONS
Net worth: $100K
Cash liquidity: $50K

TRAINING
At headquarters: 5-10 days
At franchisee's location: 1-3 days
At local training store: 5 days (optional)

BUSINESS SUPPORT
Newsletter
Meetings
Toll-free phone line
Grand opening
Internet
Security/safety procedures
Field operations/evaluations
Purchasing cooperatives

MARKETING SUPPORT
Co-op advertising
Ad slicks
Regional marketing
Local marketing

HAPPY & HEALTHY PRODUCTS INC.

Financial rating: $$$$

1600 S. Dixie Hwy., #200
Boca Raton, FL 33432
Ph: (800)764-6114
Fax: (561)368-5267
www.fruitfull.com
Frozen fruit bars & smoothies
Began: 1991, Franchising since: 1993
Headquarters size: 10 employees
Franchise department: 4 employees

U.S. franchises: 76
Canadian franchises: 0
Other foreign franchises: 0
Company-owned: 0
Units concentrated in all U.S. except
   HI, LA, ME, ND, WA

Seeking: All U.S.
Seeking in Canada? No
Exclusive territories? No
Homebased option? Yes
Kiosk option? No
Employees needed to run franchise: 0
Absentee ownership? No

COSTS
Total cost: $23K-55K
Franchise fee: $17K-24K
Royalty fee: 0
Term of agreement: 10 years renewable
   at up to $500
Franchisees required to buy multiple
   units? No

FINANCING
No financing available

QUALIFICATIONS
Net worth: $25K+
Cash liquidity: $25K+
Experience:
   General business experience
   Marketing skills

TRAINING
At franchisee's location: 1-2 weeks

BUSINESS SUPPORT
Newsletter
Meetings
Internet

MARKETING SUPPORT
Ad slicks
National media campaign

JUICE IT UP!

Ranked #251 in Entrepreneur Magazine's 2004 Franchise 500   *Financial rating: $$$*

17915 Sky Park Cir., #J
Irvine, CA 92614
Ph: (949)475-0146
Fax: (949)475-0137
www.juiceitup.com
Juice bar
Began: 1995, Franchising since: 1998
Headquarters size: 8 employees
Franchise department: 8 employees

U.S. franchises: 44
Canadian franchises: 0
Other foreign franchises: 0
Company-owned: 2
Units concentrated in CA

Seeking: All U.S.
Seeking in Canada? Yes
Exclusive territories? Yes
Homebased option? No
Kiosk option? Yes
Employees needed to run franchise: 10
Absentee ownership? No

COSTS
Total cost: $173.8K-277.7K
Kiosk cost: $100K-180K
Franchise fee: $25K
Royalty fee: 6%
Term of agreement: 10 years renewable
  at no charge
Franchisees required to buy multiple
  units? Outside the U.S. only

FINANCING
In-house: None
3rd-party: Equipment, franchise fee,
  inventory, start-up costs

QUALIFICATIONS
Net worth: $250K
Cash liquidity: $50K
Experience:
  General business experience
  Marketing skills

TRAINING
At headquarters: 2 weeks
At franchisee's location: 1 week

BUSINESS SUPPORT
Newsletter
Meetings
Toll-free phone line
Grand opening
Internet
Lease negotiations
Security/safety procedures
Field operations/evaluations
Purchasing cooperatives

MARKETING SUPPORT
Co-op advertising
Ad slicks
Regional marketing

MAUI WOWI

Ranked #178 in Entrepreneur Magazine's 2004 Franchise 500   *Financial rating: $*

5601 S. Broadway, #200
Littleton, CO 80121
Ph: (888)862-8555
Fax: (303)781-2438
www.mauiwowi.com
Smoothie & espresso kiosks
Began: 1983, Franchising since: 1997
Headquarters size: 20 employees
Franchise department: 5 employees

U.S. franchises: 286
Canadian franchises: 0
Other foreign franchises: 0
Company-owned: 0
Units concentrated in all U.S.

Seeking: All U.S.
Seeking in Canada? Yes
Exclusive territories? Yes
Homebased option? Yes
Kiosk option? Yes
Employees needed to run franchise:
  2-3
Absentee ownership? Yes

COSTS
Total cost: $55K-200K
Kiosk cost: Same as total cost
Franchise fee: $27.5K
Royalty fee: 0
Term of agreement: 10 years renewable
  for $5K
Franchisees required to buy multiple
  units? Yes

FINANCING
In-house: None
3rd-party: Equipment, inventory,
  start-up costs

QUALIFICATIONS
Net worth: $250K
Cash liquidity: $70K
Experience:
  General business experience
  Sales & marketing experience

TRAINING
At headquarters: 4 days

BUSINESS SUPPORT
Newsletter
Meetings
Toll-free phone line
Grand opening
Internet
Lease negotiations
Security/safety procedures
Field operations/evaluations
Purchasing cooperatives

MARKETING SUPPORT
Co-op advertising
Ad slicks
National media campaign
Regional marketing
PR support
Location acquisition assistance

PLANET SMOOTHIE

Financial rating: 0

2800 Hessmer Ave., #C
Metarie, LA 70002
Ph: (504)454-9459, Fax: (504)454-9460
www.planetsmoothie.com
Smoothies & sandwiches
Began: 1995, Franchising since: 1998
Headquarters size: 10 employees
Franchise department: 4 employees

U.S. franchises: 130
Canadian franchises: 0
Other foreign franchises: 1
Company-owned: 0
Units concentrated in AK, AL, CA,
    CO, FL, GA, IL, KY, LA, MA, MD,
    MI, NC, NJ, OH, OK, PA, RI, SC,
    SD, TX, VA

Seeking: Midwest, Northeast, South,
    Southeast, Southwest, West
Focusing on: AK, AL, CA, CO, FL, GA,
    HI, IL, KY, LA, MA, MD, MI, NC,
    NJ, OH, OK, PA, RI, SC, SD, TX, VA
Seeking in Canada? No
Exclusive territories? No
Homebased option? No

Kiosk option? Yes
Employees needed to run franchise: 10
Absentee ownership? Yes

COSTS
Total cost: $90.3K-182.7K
Franchise fee: $22.5K-45K
Royalty fee: 5%
Term of agreement: 10 years renewable
    for 50% of then-current fee
Franchisees required to buy multiple
    units? No

FINANCING
No financing available

QUALIFICATIONS
Net worth: $150K
Cash liquidity: $50K
Experience:
    General business experience
    Marketing skills
    Retail experience
    Management experience

TRAINING
At headquarters: 4 days
At franchisee's location: 4 days

BUSINESS SUPPORT
Newsletter
Meetings
Toll-free phone line
Grand opening
Internet
Lease negotiations
Security/safety procedures
Field operations/evaluations
Purchasing cooperatives

MARKETING SUPPORT
Co-op advertising
Ad slicks
Regional marketing

RUBYJUICE FRUIT AND SMOOTHIES

Current financial data not available

55 E. 8th St.
Holland, MI 49423
Ph: (616)546-9412
Fax: (616)396-0219
www.rubyjuice.com
Smoothies, juices, sandwiches
Began: 2000, Franchising since: 2003
Headquarters size: 20 employees
Franchise department: 5 employees

U.S. franchises: 1
Canadian franchises: 0
Other foreign franchises: 0
Company-owned: 1
Units concentrated in FL, MI

Seeking: All U.S.
Seeking in Canada? No
Exclusive territories? Yes
Homebased option? No
Kiosk option? Yes
Employees needed to run franchise:
    10-20
Absentee ownership? Yes

COSTS
Total cost: $106K-223K
Kiosk cost: $106K-188K
Franchise fee: $20K
Royalty fee: 5.5%
Term of agreement: 10 years renewable
    for 10% of current franchise fee
Franchisees required to buy multiple
    units? No

FINANCING
No financing available

QUALIFICATIONS
Net worth: $100K
Cash liquidity: $30K-50K

TRAINING
At headquarters: 1 week
At franchisee's location: 5 days

BUSINESS SUPPORT
Meetings
Toll-free phone line
Grand opening
Internet
Security/safety procedures

MARKETING SUPPORT
Ad slicks
Marketing concepts

SMOOTHIE KING

Ranked #125 in Entrepreneur Magazine's 2004 Franchise 500　　　*Financial rating: $$$*

2400 Veterans Blvd., #110
Kenner, LA 70062
Ph: (800)577-4200/(504)467-4006
Fax: (504)469-1274
www.smoothieking.com
Smoothies & healthy products
Began: 1987, Franchising since: 1988
Headquarters size: 40 employees
Franchise department: 3 employees

U.S. franchises: 318
Canadian franchises: 0
Other foreign franchises: 1
Company-owned: 1
Units concentrated in AL, AZ, CA,
　　DC, FL, GA, IL, IN, KS, KY, LA,
　　MD, MO, MS, NC, OH, TN, TX, VA

Seeking: All U.S.
Seeking in Canada? Yes
Exclusive territories? No
Homebased option? No
Kiosk option? Yes
Employees needed to run franchise:
　　Info not provided
Absentee ownership? Yes

COSTS
Total cost: $126.5K-204.5K
Kiosk cost: $60K-120K
Franchise fee: $25K
Royalty fee: 6%
Term of agreement: 10 years renewable
　　at no charge
Franchisees required to buy multiple
　　units? No

FINANCING
No financing available

QUALIFICATIONS
Net worth: $100K+
Cash liquidity: $50K
Experience:
　　General business experience
　　Marketing skills

TRAINING
At headquarters: 1 day
At franchisee's location: 7 days

BUSINESS SUPPORT
Newsletter
Meetings
Toll-free phone line
Grand opening
Internet
Lease negotiations
Security/safety procedures
Field operations/evaluations
Purchasing cooperatives

MARKETING SUPPORT
Co-op advertising
Ad slicks
National media campaign

SURF CITY SQUEEZE

Current financial data not available

7730 E. Greenway Rd., #104
Scottsdale, AZ 85260-1706
Ph: (480)443-0200
Fax: (480)443-1972
www.kahalacorp.com
Smoothies, juices, healthy consum-
　　ables
Began: 1989, Franchising since: 1995
Headquarters size: 30 employees
Franchise department: 30 employees

U.S. franchises: 88
Canadian franchises: 19
Other foreign franchises: 5
Company-owned: 1
Units concentrated in AZ, CA, IL, MI,
　　NV, WA

Seeking: All U.S.
Seeking in Canada? Yes
Exclusive territories? Yes
Homebased option? No
Kiosk option? Yes
Employees needed to run franchise: 5
Absentee ownership? Yes

COSTS
Total cost: $142.3K-345.2K
Kiosk cost: $7.5K
Franchise fee: $30K
Royalty fee: 6%
Term of agreement: 10 years renewable
　　for 75% of then-current fee
Franchisees required to buy multiple
　　units? No

FINANCING
No financing available

QUALIFICATIONS
Experience:
　　Industry experience
　　General business experience

TRAINING
At headquarters: 1 week
At franchisee's location: 2 weeks

BUSINESS SUPPORT
Newsletter
Meetings
Toll-free phone line
Grand opening
Internet
Security/safety procedures
Field operations/evaluations
Purchasing cooperatives

MARKETING SUPPORT
Co-op advertising
Ad slicks
Regional marketing

TROPICAL SMOOTHIE CAFE
Ranked #192 in Entrepreneur Magazine's 2004 Franchise 500

Financial rating: $$$

1190 Eglin Pkwy.
Shalimar, FL 32579
Ph: (888)292-2522
Fax: (850)609-6023
www.tropicalsmoothie.com
Smoothies, sandwiches, wraps, coffee
Began: 1997, Franchising since: 1997
Headquarters size: 11 employees
Franchise department: 2 employees

U.S. franchises: 90
Canadian franchises: 0
Other foreign franchises: 1
Company-owned: 0

Seeking: All U.S.
Seeking in Canada? Yes
Exclusive territories? No
Homebased option? No
Kiosk option? Yes
Employees needed to run franchise: 10-20
Absentee ownership? Yes

COSTS
Total cost: $130K-200K
Kiosk cost: Varies
Franchise fee: $15K
Royalty fee: 6%
Term of agreement: 20 years renewable at no charge
Franchisees required to buy multiple units? No

FINANCING
In-house: None
3rd-party: Accounts receivable, equipment, franchise fee, inventory, payroll, start-up costs

QUALIFICATIONS
Net worth: $100K
Cash liquidity: $50K

TRAINING
At headquarters: 1 week
At franchisee's location: 1 week

BUSINESS SUPPORT
Newsletter
Meetings
Toll-free phone line
Grand opening
Internet
Lease negotiations
Security/safety procedures
Field operations/evaluations
Purchasing cooperatives

MARKETING SUPPORT
Co-op advertising
Ad slicks
National media campaign
Regional marketing

QUICK SERVICE ◀ *Mexican*

BAJA SOL TORTILLA GRILL

Financial rating: $$

7173 Oak Pointe Curve
Bloomington, MN 55438
Ph: (612)280-1467
Fax: (952)944-2001
www.bajasol.us
Fresh-Mex food
Began: 1995, Franchising since: 1995
Headquarters size: 2 employees
Franchise department: 1 employee

U.S. franchises: 4
Canadian franchises: 0
Other foreign franchises: 0
Company-owned: 5
Units concentrated in MN

Seeking: Midwest
Focusing on: All U.S.
Seeking in Canada? No
Exclusive territories? Yes
Homebased option? No
Kiosk option? No
Employees needed to run franchise: 15
Absentee ownership? Info not provided

COSTS
Total cost: $166K-400K
Franchise fee: $25K
Royalty fee: 4.5%
Term of agreement: 10 years renewable at no charge
Franchisees required to buy multiple units? No

FINANCING
No financing available

QUALIFICATIONS
Net worth: $300K
Cash liquidity: $100K

TRAINING
At headquarters: 2 weeks
At franchisee's location: 5 days

BUSINESS SUPPORT
Grand opening
Lease negotiations
Field operations/evaluations
Purchasing cooperatives

MARKETING SUPPORT
Co-op advertising
Ad slicks

DEL TACO INC.

Ranked #100 in Entrepreneur Magazine's 2004 Franchise 500

Financial rating: $$$$

25521 Commercentre Dr.
Lake Forest, CA 92630
Ph: (949)462-7319, Fax: (949)462-7311
www.deltaco.com
Mexican/American food
Began: 1964, Franchising since: 1967
Headquarters size: 100 employees
Franchise department: 3 employees

U.S. franchises: 159
Canadian franchises: 0
Other foreign franchises: 0
Company-owned: 258
Units concentrated in AZ, CA, CO, NV, UT

Seeking: Midwest, Southwest, West
Focusing on: CA, CO, ID, IL, IN, MO, ND, NM, OR, SD, WA, WY
Seeking in Canada? No
Exclusive territories? Yes
Homebased option? No
Kiosk option? No
Employees needed to run franchise: 50
Absentee ownership? No

COSTS

Total cost: $1M
Franchise fee: $25K
Royalty fee: 5%
Term of agreement: 20 years renewable for $25K
Franchisees required to buy multiple units? Yes

FINANCING

In-house: None
3rd-party: Accounts receivable, equipment, franchise fee, inventory, payroll, start-up costs

QUALIFICATIONS

Net worth: $750K
Cash liquidity: $250K
Experience:
    Industry experience
    General business experience

TRAINING

At headquarters: 4 days
At training store: 4 weeks

BUSINESS SUPPORT

Newsletter
Meetings
Grand opening
Security/safety procedures
Field operations/evaluations

MARKETING SUPPORT

Ad slicks
Regional marketing

DESERT MOON-FRESH MEXICAN GRILLE

Ranked #360 in Entrepreneur Magazine's 2004 Franchise 500

Financial rating: $$$

612 Corporate Way, #1M
Valley Cottage, NY 10989
Ph: (845)267-3300
Fax: (845)267-2548
www.desertmooncafe.com
Fresh-Mex/Southwestern food
Began: 1992, Franchising since: 1999
Headquarters size: 6 employees
Franchise department: 1 employee

U.S. franchises: 12
Canadian franchises: 0
Other foreign franchises: 0
Company-owned: 5

Seeking: Midwest, Northeast, Southeast
Seeking in Canada? Yes
Exclusive territories? Yes
Homebased option? No
Kiosk option? Yes
Employees needed to run franchise: 10
Absentee ownership? Yes

COSTS

Total cost: $186.5K-356.4K
Kiosk cost: $200K
Franchise fee: $25K
Royalty fee: 5%
Term of agreement: 15 years not renewable
Franchisees required to buy multiple units? No

FINANCING

In-house: None
3rd-party: Equipment, inventory, start-up costs

QUALIFICATIONS

Net worth: $250K
Cash liquidity: $75K
Experience:
    Industry experience

TRAINING

At headquarters: 4 weeks
At franchisee's location: 2 weeks

BUSINESS SUPPORT

Newsletter
Meetings
Toll-free phone line
Grand opening
Internet
Field operations/evaluations
Purchasing cooperatives

MARKETING SUPPORT

Co-op advertising
Ad slicks
Regional marketing

LA SALSA FRESH MEXICAN GRILL

Financial rating: $$$

3916 State St., #100
Santa Barbara, CA 93105
Ph: (800)527-2572
Fax: (805)898-4206
www.lasalsa.com
Fresh-Mex grill
Began: 1979, Franchising since: 1988
Headquarters size: 25 employees
Franchise department: 5 employees

U.S. franchises: 40
Canadian franchises: 0
Other foreign franchises: 0
Company-owned: 57

Seeking: All U.S.
Seeking in Canada? No
Exclusive territories? Yes
Homebased option? No
Kiosk option? No
Employees needed to run franchise: 12
Absentee ownership? Yes

COSTS
Total cost: $431K-612K
Franchise fee: $20K-30K
Royalty fee: 5%
Term of agreement: 10 years renewable
Franchisees required to buy multiple
    units? Yes

FINANCING
No financing available

QUALIFICATIONS
Net worth: $1.2M
Experience:
    Industry experience

TRAINING
At corporate store: 5 weeks

BUSINESS SUPPORT
Meetings
Toll-free phone line
Field operations/evaluations
Purchasing cooperatives

MARKETING SUPPORT
Co-op advertising
Ad slicks

MOE'S SOUTHWEST GRILL

Financial rating: $$

2915 Peachtree Rd.
Atlanta, GA 30305
Ph: (404)844-8335
Fax: (404)442-8320
www.moes.com
Fresh-Mex food
Began: 2000, Franchising since: 2001
Headquarters size: 20 employees
Franchise department: 8 employees

U.S. franchises: 60
Canadian franchises: 0
Other foreign franchises: 0
Company-owned: 1
Units concentrated in South, Mid-
    Atlantic

Seeking: All U.S.
Seeking in Canada? No
Exclusive territories? No
Homebased option? No
Kiosk option? Yes
Employees needed to run franchise: 15
Absentee ownership? Yes

COSTS
Total cost: $300K
Kiosk cost: $250K
Franchise fee: $20K
Royalty fee: 5%
Term of agreement: 20 years renewable
    at no charge
Franchisees required to buy multiple
    units? No

FINANCING
In-house: None
3rd-party: Equipment, franchise fee,
    inventory, start-up costs

QUALIFICATIONS
Experience:
    Industry experience
    General business experience
    Marketing skills
    Attention to detail

TRAINING
At headquarters: 2 weeks
At franchisee's location: 1 week

BUSINESS SUPPORT
Newsletter
Meetings
Grand opening
Internet
Security/safety procedures
Field operations/evaluations
Purchasing cooperatives

MARKETING SUPPORT
Co-op advertising
Ad slicks
National media campaign
Regional marketing
Web site & promo tools

QDOBA MEXICAN GRILL

Ranked #197 in Entrepreneur Magazine's 2004 Franchise 500

Financial rating: $$$

4865 Ward Rd., #500
Wheat Ridge, CO 80033
Ph: (720)898-2300, Fax: (720)898-2396
www.qdoba.com
Mexican food
Began: 1995, Franchising since: 1997
Headquarters size: 35 employees
Franchise department: 6 employees

U.S. franchises: 70
Canadian franchises: 0
Other foreign franchises: 0
Company-owned: 31
Units concentrated in all U.S.

Seeking: All U.S.
Seeking in Canada? No
Exclusive territories? Yes
Homebased option? No
Kiosk option? No
Employees needed to run franchise: 15
Absentee ownership? Yes

COSTS

Total cost: $300K-450K
Franchise fee: $25K
Royalty fee: 5%
Term of agreement: 10 years renewable
    for $5K
Franchisees required to buy multiple
    units? Yes

FINANCING

In-house: None
3rd-party: Available

QUALIFICATIONS

Net worth: $2M
Cash liquidity: $500K
Experience:
    Industry experience
    General business experience
    Marketing skills

TRAINING

At headquarters: 4 weeks

BUSINESS SUPPORT

Newsletter
Meetings
Toll-free phone line
Grand opening
Internet
Security/safety procedures
Field operations/evaluations
Purchasing cooperatives

MARKETING SUPPORT

Co-op advertising
Ad slicks
Local marketing

TACO BELL CORP.

Ranked #42 in Entrepreneur Magazine's 2004 Franchise 500

Financial rating: $$$

17901 Von Karman
Irvine, CA 92614
Ph: (949)863-4500
Fax: (949)863-2252
www.tacobell.com
Mexican food
Began: 1962, Franchising since: 1964
Headquarters size: 500 employees
Franchise department: Info not pro-
    vided

U.S. franchises: 4,881
Canadian franchises: 138
Other foreign franchises: 63
Company-owned: 1,350
Units concentrated in CA, TX

Seeking: All U.S.
Seeking in Canada? Yes
Exclusive territories? No
Homebased option? No
Kiosk option? No
Employees needed to run franchise: 25
Absentee ownership? Yes

COSTS

Total cost: $3M
Franchise fee: $45K
Royalty fee: 5.5%
Term of agreement: 20 years
Franchisees required to buy multiple
    units? No

FINANCING

No financing available

QUALIFICATIONS

Net worth: $600K
Cash liquidity: $360K
Experience:
    Industry experience
    General business experience
    Marketing skills

TRAINING

At headquarters
Additional training available

BUSINESS SUPPORT

Newsletter
Meetings
Grand opening
Internet
Security/safety procedures
Field operations/evaluations

MARKETING SUPPORT

Co-op advertising
National media campaign
Regional marketing

TACO JOHN'S INT'L. INC.

Ranked #175 in Entrepreneur Magazine's 2004 Franchise 500

Financial rating: $$$$

808 W. 20th
Cheyenne, WY 82001
Ph: (307)635-0101, Fax: (307)638-0603
www.tacojohns.com
Mexican food
Began: 1968, Franchising since: 1969
Headquarters size: 60 employees
Franchise department: 4 employees

U.S. franchises: 395
Canadian franchises: 0
Other foreign franchises: 0
Company-owned: 6
Units concentrated in CO, IA, ID, IL,
   IN, KS, KY, MN, MO, MT, ND, NE,
   OH, SD, TN, WA, WY

Seeking: Midwest, West
Focusing on: CO, IA, ID, IL, IN, KS,
   KY, MN, MO, MT, ND, NE, OH,
   SD, TN, WA, WY
Seeking in Canada? No
Exclusive territories? Yes
Homebased option? No
Kiosk option? No
Employees needed to run franchise: 15
Absentee ownership? Yes

COSTS
Total cost: $453K-706.5K
Franchise fee: $15K-22.5K
Royalty fee: 4%
Term of agreement: 20 years renewable
   at no charge
Franchisees required to buy multiple
   units? No

FINANCING
In-house: None
Equipment, start-up costs

QUALIFICATIONS
Net worth: $250K
Cash liquidity: $100K
Experience:
   Industry experience
   General business experience

TRAINING
At headquarters: 4 weeks
At franchisee's location: 1 week

BUSINESS SUPPORT
Newsletter
Meetings
Toll-free phone line
Grand opening
Internet
Security/safety procedures
Field operations/evaluations
Purchasing cooperatives

MARKETING SUPPORT
Co-op advertising
Ad slicks

THE TACO MAKER

Ranked #237 in Entrepreneur Magazine's 2004 Franchise 500

Financial rating: $$$$

P.O. Box 150650
Ogden, UT 84415
Ph: (801)476-9780
Fax: (801)476-9788
www.tacomaker.com
Mexican food
Began: 1978, Franchising since: 1978
Headquarters size: 25 employees
Franchise department: 4 employees

U.S. franchises: 128
Canadian franchises: 0
Other foreign franchises: 3
Company-owned: 2
Units concentrated in ID, UT

Seeking: All U.S.
Seeking in Canada? Yes
Exclusive territories? Yes
Homebased option? No
Kiosk option? No
Employees needed to run franchise: 35
Absentee ownership? No

COSTS
Total cost: $221K-325.2K
Franchise fee: $19K
Royalty fee: 5%
Term of agreement: 15 years renewable
   for $5K
Franchisees required to buy multiple
   units? Outside the U.S. only

FINANCING
In-house: None
3rd-party: Equipment, franchise fee,
   inventory, start-up costs

QUALIFICATIONS
Net worth: $500K
Cash liquidity: $100K
Experience:
   Industry experience
   General business experience

TRAINING
At headquarters: 1 month

BUSINESS SUPPORT
Newsletter
Toll-free phone line
Grand opening
Field operations/evaluations
Purchasing cooperatives

MARKETING SUPPORT
Co-op advertising
National media campaign

TACO PALACE FRANCHISING CORP.

Current financial data not available

P.O. Box 87, 814 E. Hwy. 60
Monett, MO 65708
Ph: (417)235-1150/(417)235-6595
Fax: (417)235-1150
www.tacopalace.com
Mexican food
Began: 1985, Franchising since: 1996
Headquarters size: 4 employees
Franchise department: 3 employees

U.S. franchises: 6
Canadian franchises: 1
Other foreign franchises: 0
Company-owned: 2
Units concentrated in MO

Seeking: All U.S.
Seeking in Canada? Yes
Exclusive territories? Yes
Homebased option? No
Kiosk option? Yes
Employees needed to run franchise: 8
Absentee ownership? Yes

COSTS
Total cost: $75K-99K
Kiosk cost: $69.5K-80K
Franchise fee: 0
Royalty fee: 0
Term of agreement: 1 year renewable
at no charge
Franchisees required to buy multiple
units? No

FINANCING
No financing available

QUALIFICATIONS
Net worth: $75K
Cash liquidity: $75K
Experience:
General business experience

TRAINING
At headquarters: As needed
At franchisee's location: 3 weeks

BUSINESS SUPPORT
Internet
Lease negotiations
Purchasing cooperatives

MARKETING SUPPORT
Ad slicks

TACO TIME INT'L. INC.

Current financial data not available

3880 W. 11th Ave.
Eugene, OR 97402
Ph: (800)547-8907/(541)687-8222
Fax: (541)343-5208
www.tacotime.com
Mexican food
Began: 1959, Franchising since: 1961
Headquarters size: 25 employees
Franchise department: 3 employees

U.S. franchises: 164
Canadian franchises: 115
Other foreign franchises: 5
Company-owned: 6
Units concentrated in ID, MT, OR, UT,
WA, WY

Seeking: All U.S.
Seeking in Canada? Yes
Exclusive territories? Yes
Homebased option? No
Kiosk option? Yes
Employees needed to run franchise: 15
Absentee ownership? No

COSTS
Total cost: $43K-355.5K
Franchise fee: $12.5K-50K
Royalty fee: 5%
Term of agreement: 15 years renewable
at no charge
Franchisees required to buy multiple
units? No

FINANCING
In-house: None
3rd-party: Equipment, franchise fee,
start-up costs

QUALIFICATIONS
Net worth: $300K
Cash liquidity: $100K
Experience:
General business experience

TRAINING
At headquarters: 2-4 weeks

BUSINESS SUPPORT
Newsletter
Meetings
Toll-free phone line
Grand opening
Security/safety procedures
Field operations/evaluations

MARKETING SUPPORT
Co-op advertising
National media campaign
Regional marketing

TIJUANA FLATS BURRITO COMPANY INC.

Financial rating: $$$

150 N. Swoope Ave.
Maitland, FL 32751
Ph: (800)460-9000, Fax: (972)716-9913
www.tijuanaflats.com
Tex-Mex restaurant; hot sauces
Began: 1995, Franchising since: 2002
Headquarters size: 7 employees
Franchise department: 2 employees

U.S. franchises: 0
Canadian franchises: 0
Other foreign franchises: 0
Company-owned: 14

Seeking: All U.S.
Focusing on: Southeast
Seeking in Canada? No
Exclusive territories? Yes
Homebased option? No
Kiosk option? No
Employees needed to run franchise:
    Info not provided
Absentee ownership? Yes

COSTS

Total cost: $159.5K-245.6K
Franchise fee: $25K
Royalty fee: 5%
Term of agreement: 15 years renewable
    at no charge
Franchisees required to buy multiple
    units? No

FINANCING

In-house: None
3rd-party: Equipment, inventory,
    start-up costs

QUALIFICATIONS

Net worth: $500K
Cash liquidity: $250K
Experience:
    Industry experience
    General business experience

TRAINING

At headquarters: 4-6 weeks
At franchisee's location: 2 weeks

BUSINESS SUPPORT

Meetings
Toll-free phone line
Grand opening
Security/safety procedures
Field operations/evaluations
Purchasing cooperatives

MARKETING SUPPORT

Co-op advertising
Ad slicks
Regional marketing

QUICK SERVICE ▶ *Pizza*

BLACKJACK PIZZA FRANCHISING INC.

Ranked #469 in Entrepreneur Magazine's 2004 Franchise 500

Financial rating: $$$

9088 Marshall Ct.
Westminster, CO 80031
Ph: (303)426-1921, Fax: (303)428-0174
www.blackjackpizza.com
Pizza
Began: 1983, Franchising since: 1988
Headquarters size: 5 employees
Franchise department: 5 employees

U.S. franchises: 44
Canadian franchises: 0
Other foreign franchises: 0
Company-owned: 2
Units concentrated in AZ, CO, OR,
    UT, WY

Seeking: All U.S.
Focusing on: West
Seeking in Canada? No
Exclusive territories? Yes
Homebased option? No
Kiosk option? No
Employees needed to run franchise:
    15-30
Absentee ownership? No

COSTS

Total cost: $140.8K-300.4K
Franchise fee: $10K
Royalty fee: to 4%
Term of agreement: 10 years renewable
    for $1K
Franchisees required to buy multiple
    units? No

FINANCING

In-house: None
3rd-party: Accounts receivable, equip-
    ment, franchise fee, inventory, pay-
    roll, start-up costs

QUALIFICATIONS

Net worth: $200K
Cash liquidity: $50K
Experience:
    Industry experience
    General business experience
    Marketing skills

TRAINING

At headquarters: Up to 20 days
At franchisee's location: Up to 20 days
Ongoing

BUSINESS SUPPORT

Newsletter
Meetings
Grand opening
Internet
Lease negotiations
Security/safety procedures
Field operations/evaluations
Purchasing cooperatives

MARKETING SUPPORT

Co-op advertising
Ad slicks
Regional marketing
TV ads

BREADEAUX PIZZA

Ranked #432 in Entrepreneur Magazine's 2004 Franchise 500   *Financial rating: $$$$*

P.O. Box 6158, Fairleigh Sta.
St. Joseph, MO 64506
Ph: (816)364-1088
Fax: (816)364-3739
www.breadeauxpizza.com
French-crust pizza & cookies
Began: 1985, Franchising since: 1985
Headquarters size: 15 employees
Franchise department: 2 employees

U.S. franchises: 81
Canadian franchises: 4
Other foreign franchises: 0
Company-owned: 3
Units concentrated in IA, MO

Seeking: Midwest
Focusing on: IA, IL, KS, MI, MO, NE
Seeking in Canada? No
Exclusive territories? Yes
Homebased option? No
Kiosk option? Yes
Employees needed to run franchise: 12
Absentee ownership? Yes

COSTS
Total cost: $69.5K-310K
Kiosk cost: $45K-80K
Franchise fee: $15K
Royalty fee: 5%
Term of agreement: 15 years renewable for 25% of then-current fee
Franchisees required to buy multiple units? No

FINANCING
In-house: None
3rd-party: Equipment

QUALIFICATIONS
Net worth: $350K
Cash liquidity: $100K

TRAINING
At headquarters: 2 weeks
At franchisee's location: During first week

BUSINESS SUPPORT
Newsletter
Meetings
Toll-free phone line
Grand opening
Internet
Field operations/evaluations
Purchasing cooperatives

MARKETING SUPPORT
Co-op advertising
Ad slicks
National media campaign
Additional support available

BRU-GO'S TAKE-N-BAKE PIZZA CO.

Current financial data not available

26590 Hwy. 88
Pioneer, CA 95666-9584
Ph: (800)560-3434
Fax: (209)295-2229
Take-&-bake pizza, Mexican food, cinnamon rolls
Began: 1991, Franchising since: 2002
Headquarters size: 6 employees
Franchise department: 3 employees

U.S. franchises: 0
Canadian franchises: 0
Other foreign franchises: 0
Company-owned: 2

Seeking: All U.S.
Seeking in Canada? Yes
Exclusive territories? Yes
Homebased option? No
Kiosk option? Yes
Employees needed to run franchise: 5
Absentee ownership? Yes

COSTS
Total cost: $74.5K-128.8K
Kiosk cost: $60K-80K
Franchise fee: $19.5K-14.5K
Royalty fee: 4-5%
Term of agreement: 10 years renewable for 10% of franchise fee
Franchisees required to buy multiple units? No

FINANCING
In-house: None
3rd-party: Accounts receivable, equipment, franchise fee, inventory, payroll, start-up costs

QUALIFICATIONS
Net worth: $150K
Cash liquidity: $60K
Experience:
   Industry experience
   General business experience
   Marketing skills

TRAINING
At headquarters: 7 days
At franchisee's location: 4 days+
Pre-training available before signing: 3 days

BUSINESS SUPPORT
Newsletter
Meetings
Toll-free phone line
Grand opening
Internet
Lease negotiations
Security/safety procedures
Field operations/evaluations
Purchasing cooperatives

MARKETING SUPPORT
Co-op advertising
Ad slicks
National media campaign
Regional marketing
Online ordering for each store

BUCK'S PIZZA

Ranked #402 in Entrepreneur Magazine's 2004 Franchise 500

Financial rating: $$$$

P.O. Box 405
DuBois, PA 15801
Ph: (800)310-8848, Fax: (814)371-4214
www.buckspizza.com
Pizza
Began: 1994, Franchising since: 1994
Headquarters size: 10 employees
Franchise department: 6 employees

U.S. franchises: 81
Canadian franchises: 0
Other foreign franchises: 0
Company-owned: 0

Seeking: All U.S.
Focusing on: AL, AZ, FL, GA, IN, LA,
    KY, MI, MN, MO, MS, NC, NY, OK,
    PA, SC, TN, TX, WA, WI, WV, WY
Seeking in Canada? Yes
Exclusive territories? Yes
Homebased option? No
Kiosk option? Yes
Employees needed to run franchise: 12
Absentee ownership? Yes

COSTS
Total cost: $111.3K-196.9K
Kiosk cost: Varies
Franchise fee: $10K
Royalty fee: 3%
Term of agreement: 10 years renewable
    at no charge
Franchisees required to buy multiple
    units? No

FINANCING
In-house: None
3rd-party: Equipment, franchise fee,
    inventory, start-up costs

QUALIFICATIONS
Net worth: $30K-40K
Cash liquidity: $30K-40K
Experience:
    Industry experience
    General business experience
    Marketing skills

TRAINING
At headquarters: 1-2 days
At franchisee's location: 10-14 days

BUSINESS SUPPORT
Newsletter
Meetings
Toll-free phone line
Grand opening
Internet
Lease negotiations
Field operations/evaluations
Purchasing cooperatives

MARKETING SUPPORT
Co-op advertising
Ad slicks

CAPTAIN TONY'S PIZZA & PASTA EMPORIUM

Financial rating: $$$

2607 S. Woodland Blvd., PMB 300
Deland, FL 32720
Ph: (800)332-8669/(386)736-9855
Fax: (386)736-7237
www.captaintonys.com
Pizza & pasta
Began: 1972, Franchising since: 1985
Headquarters size: Info not provided
Franchise department: Info not pro-
    vided

U.S. franchises: 9
Canadian franchises: 0
Other foreign franchises: 3
Company-owned: 0
Units concentrated in all U.S.

Seeking: All U.S.
Seeking in Canada? Yes
Exclusive territories? No
Homebased option? No
Kiosk option? Yes
Employees needed to run franchise:
    5-10
Absentee ownership? Info not provided

COSTS
Total cost: $150.8K-282.9K
Kiosk cost: $50K-80K
Franchise fee: $10K-20K
Royalty fee: 4.5%
Term of agreement: 20 years renewable
    at no charge
Franchisees required to buy multiple
    units? Outside the U.S. only

FINANCING
In-house: None
3rd-party: Franchise fee

QUALIFICATIONS
Net worth: $250K
Cash liquidity: $50K

TRAINING
At headquarters: 3 weeks

BUSINESS SUPPORT
Toll-free phone line
Internet
Field operations/evaluations
Purchasing cooperatives

MARKETING SUPPORT
Co-op advertising
Ad slicks

CHICAGO'S PIZZA FRANCHISES

Financial rating: $$$

1111 N. Broadway
Greenfield, IN 46140
Ph: (317)462-9878
Fax: (317)467-1877
Pizza, salad, sandwiches
Began: 1979, Franchising since: 1981
Headquarters size: 2 employees
Franchise department: 2 employees

U.S. franchises: 11
Canadian franchises: 0
Other foreign franchises: 0
Company-owned: 0
Units concentrated in IN, OH

Seeking: Midwest
Focusing on: IL, KY, MI
Seeking in Canada? No
Exclusive territories? Yes
Homebased option? No
Kiosk option? No
Employees needed to run franchise: 15
Absentee ownership? No

COSTS
Total cost: $87.3K-173.1K
Franchise fee: $18K
Royalty fee: 4%
Term of agreement: 5 years renewable
at no charge
Franchisees required to buy multiple
units? No

FINANCING
No financing available

QUALIFICATIONS
Net worth: $100K-200K
Cash liquidity: $43.5K-86.5K
Experience:
Industry experience
General business experience
Marketing skills
People skills

TRAINING
At headquarters: 2 weeks
At franchisee's location: 4 weeks
At existing stores: 2 weeks

BUSINESS SUPPORT
Grand opening
Lease negotiations
Field operations/evaluations
Purchasing cooperatives

MARKETING SUPPORT
Co-op advertising
Ad slicks
Additional support available

DOLLY'S PIZZA FRANCHISING INC.

Current financial data not available

1097-B Union Lake Rd.
White Lake, MI 48386
Ph: (866)336-5597/(248)360-6440
Fax: (248)360-7020
www.dollyspizza.com
Pizza
Began: 1966, Franchising since: 1993
Headquarters size: Info not provided
Franchise department: Info not provided

U.S. franchises: 37
Canadian franchises: 0
Other foreign franchises: 0
Company-owned: 2
Units concentrated in all U.S.

Seeking: All U.S.
Seeking in Canada? No
Exclusive territories? Yes
Homebased option? No
Kiosk option? Yes
Employees needed to run franchise: 10
Absentee ownership? Yes

COSTS
Total cost: $125K-180K
Kiosk cost: $30K-50K
Franchise fee: $17.5K
Royalty fee: 4%
Term of agreement: 10 years renewable
for $5K
Franchisees required to buy multiple
units? No

FINANCING
No financing available

QUALIFICATIONS
Net worth: $200K
Cash liquidity: $50K

TRAINING
At headquarters: 30 days
At franchisee's location: 30 days
Additional training available

BUSINESS SUPPORT
Newsletter
Meetings
Toll-free phone line
Grand opening
Internet
Lease negotiations
Security/safety procedures
Field operations/evaluations
Purchasing cooperatives

MARKETING SUPPORT
Co-op advertising
Ad slicks
Regional marketing

DOMINO'S PIZZA LLC

Ranked #14 in Entrepreneur Magazine's 2004 Franchise 500   *Financial rating: $$$$*

30 Frank Lloyd Wright Dr.
P.O. Box 997
Ann Arbor, MI 48106
Ph: (734)930-3030, Fax: (734)930-4346
www.dominos.com
Pizza, buffalo wings, breadsticks
Began: 1960, Franchising since: 1967
Headquarters size: 350 employees
Franchise department: Info not
    provided

U.S. franchises: 4,283
Canadian/other foreign franchises:
    2,429
Company-owned: 579
Units concentrated in all U.S.

Seeking: All U.S.
Seeking in Canada? Yes
Exclusive territories? Yes
Homebased option? No
Kiosk option? Yes
Employees needed to run franchise:
    15-20
Absentee ownership? No

COSTS
Total cost: $141.4K-415.1K
Kiosk cost: $99.35K-402.1K
Franchise fee: to $3.3K
Royalty fee: 5.5%
Term of agreement: 10 years renewable
    at no charge
Franchisees required to buy multiple
    units? No

FINANCING
In-house: None
3rd-party: Accounts receivable, equip-
    ment, franchise fee, inventory, pay-
    roll, start-up costs

QUALIFICATIONS
Net worth: $200K
Cash liquidity: $50K
Experience:
    Industry experience

TRAINING
At headquarters: 6-10 weeks
At training store: 6-8 weeks

BUSINESS SUPPORT
Newsletter
Meetings
Internet
Security/safety procedures
Field operations/evaluations

MARKETING SUPPORT
Co-op advertising
Ad slicks
National media campaign

EXTREME PIZZA

Ranked #428 in Entrepreneur Magazine's 2004 Franchise 500   *Financial rating: $$$*

1052 Folsom St.
San Francisco, CA 94103
Ph: (866)695-5595, Fax: (415)503-1633
www.extremepizza.com
Gourmet pizzas, take-&-bake pizza,
    subs, salads
Began: 1994, Franchising since: 2000
Headquarters size: Info not provided
Franchise department: Info not
    provided

U.S. franchises: 9
Canadian franchises: 0
Other foreign franchises: 0
Company-owned: 4
Units concentrated in AZ, CA, CO

Seeking: All U.S.
Focusing on: AZ, CA, CO, FL, NJ, TX
Seeking in Canada? No
Exclusive territories? Yes
Homebased option? No
Kiosk option? No
Employees needed to run franchise: 7
Absentee ownership? Yes

COSTS
Total cost: $123.5K-351K
Franchise fee: $25K
Royalty fee: 4%
Term of agreement: 15 years renewable
    at no charge
Franchisees required to buy multiple
    units? No

FINANCING
In-house: None
3rd-party: Equipment, franchise fee,
    inventory, start-up costs

QUALIFICATIONS
Net worth: $250K
Cash liquidity: $100K
Experience:
    Industry experience
    General business experience

TRAINING
At headquarters: 4 weeks
At franchisee's location: 2 weeks

BUSINESS SUPPORT
Newsletter
Toll-free phone line
Grand opening
Internet

MARKETING SUPPORT
Co-op advertising
Ad slicks

FOX'S PIZZA DEN

Ranked #150 in Entrepreneur Magazine's 2004 Franchise 500

3243 Old Frankstown Rd.
Pittsburgh, PA 15239
Ph: (724)733-7888
Fax: (724)325-5479
www.foxspizza.com
Pizza & sandwiches
Began: 1971, Franchising since: 1974
Headquarters size: 12 employees
Franchise department: 3 employees

U.S. franchises: 216
Canadian franchises: 0
Other foreign franchises: 0
Company-owned: 0
Units concentrated in AL, FL, GA, LA,
    IA, MD, MI, MO, NC, NY

Seeking: All U.S.
Seeking in Canada? No
Exclusive territories? Yes
Homebased option? No
Kiosk option? Yes
Employees needed to run franchise: 10
Absentee ownership? No

COSTS

Total cost: $68.3K-79K
Kiosk cost: Varies
Franchise fee: $8K
Royalty fee: $200/mo.
Term of agreement: 5 years renewable
    at no charge
Franchisees required to buy multiple
    units? No

FINANCING

In-house: Franchise fee
3rd-party: Accounts receivable, equip-
    ment, franchise fee, inventory, pay-
    roll, start-up costs

QUALIFICATIONS

Info not provided

TRA...

At headq...
At franchisee...

BUSINESS SUPPORT

Newsletter
Toll-free phone line
Internet
Lease negotiations
Purchasing cooperatives

MARKETING SUPPORT

Co-op advertising
Ad slicks
Regional marketing
National program with mail marketing

GRECO PIZZA-DONAIR

Current financial data not available

P.O. Box 1040
Truro, NS Canada B2N 5G9
Ph: (902)893-4141
Fax: (902)895-7635
www.greco.ca
Pizza, sandwiches & donair delivery
Began: 1977, Franchising since: 1977
Headquarters size: 20 employees
Franchise department: 2 employees

U.S. franchises: 0
Canadian franchises: 154
Other foreign franchises: 0
Company-owned: 2

Not available in the U.S.
Seeking in Canada? Yes
Exclusive territories? Yes
Homebased option? No
Kiosk option? Yes
Employees needed to run franchise:
    10-15
Absentee ownership? Yes

COSTS

Total cost: $150K-170K
Kiosk cost: $100K
Franchise fee: $20K
Royalty fee: 5%
Term of agreement: 10 years renewable
    for $2K-3K
Franchisees required to buy multiple
    units? No

FINANCING

No financing available

QUALIFICATIONS

Cash liquidity: $40K

TRAINING

At headquarters: 2 weeks
At franchisee's location: 2 weeks
At existing restaurant: 2 weeks

BUSINESS SUPPORT

Newsletter
Meetings
Toll-free phone line
Grand opening
Internet
Security/safety procedures
Field operations/evaluations
Purchasing cooperatives

MARKETING SUPPORT

Co-op advertising
Ad slicks
National media campaign
Regional marketing
Local market assistance

GRY HOWIE'S PIZZA & SUBS

ked #73 in Entrepreneur Magazine's 2004 Franchise 500   *Financial rating: $$$$*

300 Stephenson Hwy.
Madison Heights, MI 48071
Ph: (800)624-8122
Fax: (248)414-3301
www.hungryhowies.com
Pizza, subs, salads
Began: 1973, Franchising since: 1982
Headquarters size: 50 employees
Franchise department: 10 employees

U.S. franchises: 472
Canadian franchises: 3
Other foreign franchises: 0
Company-owned: 0
Units concentrated in FL, MI

Seeking: All U.S.
Seeking in Canada? No
Exclusive territories? Yes
Homebased option? No
Kiosk option? No
Employees needed to run franchise: 10
Absentee ownership? No

COSTS
Total cost: $83.1K-220.5K
Franchise fee: $15K/9.5K
Royalty fee: 5%
Term of agreement: 20 years renewable
   at no charge
Franchisees required to buy multiple
   units? No

FINANCING
In-house: None
3rd-party: Equipment, franchise fee,
   start-up costs

QUALIFICATIONS
Net worth: $150K
Cash liquidity: $50K

TRAINING
At headquarters: 5 weeks
Regional seminars

BUSINESS SUPPORT
Newsletter
Meetings
Grand opening
Internet
Lease negotiations
Security/safety procedures
Field operations/evaluations

MARKETING SUPPORT
Co-op advertising
Ad slicks
Regional marketing

JET CITY PIZZA

Ranked #495 in Entrepreneur Magazine's 2004 Franchise 500   *Financial rating: $$$*

13450 N.E. 177th Pl.
Woodinville, WA 98072
Ph: (425)402-9673
Fax: (425)488-8919
www.jetcitypizza.com
Gourmet pizza, grinders, wings, ice
   cream
Began: 1994, Franchising since: 1996
Headquarters size: 6 employees
Franchise department: 2 employees

U.S. franchises: 6
Canadian franchises: 0
Other foreign franchises: 0
Company-owned: 4

Seeking: West
Seeking in Canada? No
Exclusive territories? Yes
Homebased option? No
Kiosk option? No
Employees needed to run franchise: 15
Absentee ownership? Yes

COSTS
Total cost: $59.1K-258.3K
Franchise fee: $15K
Royalty fee: 4.5%
Term of agreement: 10 years renewable
   for $3K
Franchisees required to buy multiple
   units? No

FINANCING
In-house: Inventory
3rd-party: Equipment, franchise fee
Other: Tenant improvements

QUALIFICATIONS
Net worth: $120K
Cash liquidity: $60K

TRAINING
At headquarters: 80 hours
At franchisee's location: 220 hours

BUSINESS SUPPORT
Newsletter
Meetings
Grand opening
Internet
Security/safety procedures
Field operations/evaluations
Purchasing cooperatives

MARKETING SUPPORT
Co-op advertising
Ad slicks
Regional marketing

JET'S PIZZA

Current financial data not available

37177 Mound Rd.
Sterling Heights, MI 48310
Ph: (586)268-5870
Fax: (586)268-6762
www.jetspizza.com
Pizza, subs, salads
Began: 1978, Franchising since: 1990
Headquarters size: 8 employees
Franchise department: 5 employees

U.S. franchises: 87
Canadian franchises: 0
Other foreign franchises: 0
Company-owned: 10
Units concentrated in FL, MI

Seeking: All U.S.
Focusing on: FL, GA, OH
Seeking in Canada? No
Exclusive territories? Yes
Homebased option? No
Kiosk option? No
Employees needed to run franchise: 15
Absentee ownership? No

COSTS
Total cost: $201.8K-269.5K
Franchise fee: $15K
Royalty fee: 8-10%
Term of agreement: 10 years renewable
   for $2K
Franchisees required to buy multiple
   units? Outside the U.S. only

FINANCING
No financing available

QUALIFICATIONS
Net worth: $240K
Cash liquidity: $100K
Experience:
   General business experience
   Customer service skills
   Management skills

TRAINING
At headquarters: 4 weeks

BUSINESS SUPPORT
Grand opening
Field operations/evaluations
Purchasing cooperatives

MARKETING SUPPORT
Co-op advertising

LEDO PIZZA SYSTEM INC.

Ranked #353 in Entrepreneur Magazine's 2004 Franchise 500   *Financial rating: $$$$*

2568-A Riva Rd., #202
Annapolis, MD 21401
Ph: (410)721-6887
Fax: (410)266-6888
www.ledopizza.com
Pizza, subs, pasta
Began: 1986, Franchising since: 1989
Headquarters size: 12 employees
Franchise department: 12 employees

U.S. franchises: 57
Canadian franchises: 0
Other foreign franchises: 0
Company-owned: 0
Units concentrated in DE, FL, MD,
   NC, PA, VA

Seeking: All U.S.
Focusing on: FL, GA, NC
Seeking in Canada? No
Exclusive territories? Yes
Homebased option? No
Kiosk option? No
Employees needed to run franchise: 40
Absentee ownership? No

COSTS
Total cost: $115.3K-419K
Franchise fee: $20K
Royalty fee: 5%
Term of agreement: 5 years renewable
   at no charge
Franchisees required to buy multiple
   units? No

FINANCING
No financing available

QUALIFICATIONS
Experience:
   Industry experience
   General business experience
   Marketing skills

TRAINING
At headquarters: 2-3 days
At franchisee's location: 30 days

BUSINESS SUPPORT
Newsletter
Meetings
Internet
Security/safety procedures
Field operations/evaluations
Purchasing cooperatives

MARKETING SUPPORT
Co-op advertising
Ad slicks
Regional marketing

MANNY & OLGA'S PIZZA

Current financial data not available

13707 Northgate Dr.
Silver Spring, MD 20906
Ph: (301)588-2500
Fax: (301)924-1151
www.mannyandolgas.com
Pizza
Began: 1983, Franchising since: 1998
Headquarters size: 4 employees
Franchise department: 4 employees

U.S. franchises: 1
Canadian franchises: 0
Other foreign franchises: 0
Company-owned: 4
Units concentrated in DC, MD,

Focusing on: DC, DE, MD, VA
Seeking in Canada? No
Exclusive territories? Yes
Homebased option? No
Kiosk option? Info not provided
Employees needed to run franchise: 5
Absentee ownership? No

COSTS
Total cost: $125K-220K
Franchise fee: $25K
Royalty fee: 5%
Term of agreement: 5 years renewable
    for $5K
Franchisees required to buy multiple
    units? Info not provided

FINANCING
In-house: Accounts receivable, inventory, start-up costs
3rd-party: Equipment, franchise fee

QUALIFICATIONS
Net worth: $95K
Cash liquidity: $50K
Experience:
    General business experience

TRAINING
At headquarters: 6 weeks
After opening: 2 weeks

BUSINESS SUPPORT
Toll-free phone line
Grand opening
Lease negotiations
Field operations/evaluations
Purchasing cooperatives

MARKETING SUPPORT
Co-op advertising
Ad slicks

MARCO'S INC.

Ranked #390 in Entrepreneur Magazine's 2004 Franchise 500   *Financial rating: $$$$*

5252 Monroe St.
Toledo, OH 43623
Ph: (800)262-7267/(419)885-7000
Fax: (419)885-5215
www.marcos.com
Pizza & subs
Began: 1978, Franchising since: 1979
Headquarters size: 34 employees
Franchise department: 6 employees

U.S. franchises: 82
Canadian franchises: 0
Other foreign franchises: 0
Company-owned: 39
Units concentrated in IN, MI, OH

Seeking: Midwest, Southeast
Focusing on: Midwest
Seeking in Canada? No
Exclusive territories? Yes
Homebased option? No
Kiosk option? No
Employees needed to run franchise: 20
Absentee ownership? No

COSTS
Total cost: $119K-250K
Franchise fee: $15K
Royalty fee: 3-5%
Term of agreement: 10 years renewable
    for $3K or 25% of franchise fee
Franchisees required to buy multiple
    units? No

FINANCING
In-house: None
Equipment, start-up costs

QUALIFICATIONS
Net worth: $100K
Cash liquidity: $70K
Experience:
    Industry experience
    General business experience
    Marketing skills

TRAINING
At headquarters: 6-8 weeks
At franchisee's location: 1-2 weeks

BUSINESS SUPPORT
Newsletter
Meetings
Toll-free phone line
Grand opening
Internet
Security/safety procedures
Field operations/evaluations
Purchasing cooperatives

MARKETING SUPPORT
Co-op advertising
Ad slicks
Regional marketing

ME-N-ED'S PIZZERIAS

Ranked #411 in Entrepreneur Magazine's 2004 Franchise 500   *Financial rating: $$$$*

5701 N. West Ave.
Fresno, CA 93711
Ph: (559)432-0399
Fax: (559)432-0398
Brick-oven-baked pizza
Began: 1958, Franchising since: 1958
Headquarters size: 18 employees
Franchise department: 2 employees

U.S. franchises: 12
Canadian franchises: 0
Other foreign franchises: 0
Company-owned: 46
Units concentrated in CA

Seeking: All U.S.
Focusing on: CA
Seeking in Canada? No
Exclusive territories? Yes
Homebased option? No
Kiosk option? No
Employees needed to run franchise:
    10-25
Absentee ownership? Yes

COSTS
Total cost: $175K-486K
Franchise fee: $25K
Royalty fee: 5%
Term of agreement: Renewable term at
    $1.5K
Franchisees required to buy multiple
    units? No

FINANCING
In-house: None
3rd-party: Equipment, franchise fee,
    inventory, start-up costs

QUALIFICATIONS
Net worth: $150K
Cash liquidity: $100K

TRAINING
At headquarters
At franchisee's location
Opening support

BUSINESS SUPPORT
Newsletter
Toll-free phone line
Grand opening
Security/safety procedures
Field operations/evaluations
Purchasing cooperatives

MARKETING SUPPORT
Ad slicks
Regional marketing
Menus
POP

MOM'S BAKE AT HOME PIZZA

Financial rating: $$$$

4457 Main St.
Philadelphia, PA 19127
Ph: (215)482-1044
Fax: (215)482-0402
www.momsbakeathomepizza.com
Bake-at-home pizza
Began: 1961, Franchising since: 1979
Headquarters size: 12 employees
Franchise department: 1 employee

U.S. franchises: 12
Canadian franchises: 0
Other foreign franchises: 0
Company-owned: 0
Units concentrated in NJ, PA

Seeking: All U.S.
Focusing on: NJ, PA
Seeking in Canada? No
Exclusive territories? Yes
Homebased option? No
Kiosk option? No
Employees needed to run franchise: 3
Absentee ownership? No

COSTS
Total cost: $46.8K-52.9K
Franchise fee: $15K
Royalty fee: 0
Term of agreement: 10 years renewable
    at no charge
Franchisees required to buy multiple
    units? No

FINANCING
No financing available

QUALIFICATIONS
Experience:
    General business experience

TRAINING
At franchisee's location: 1 day
At existing location: 4 days

BUSINESS SUPPORT
Meetings
Toll-free phone line
Grand opening

MARKETING SUPPORT
Co-op advertising
Ad slicks
Regional marketing
Direct mail

PAPA MURPHY'S

Ranked #50 in Entrepreneur Magazine's 2004 Franchise 500   *Financial rating: $$$*

8000 N.E. Parkway Dr., #350
Vancouver, WA 98662
Ph: (360)260-7272, Fax: (360)260-0500
www.papamurphys.com
Take-&-bake pizza
Began: 1981, Franchising since: 1982
Headquarters size: 106 employees
Franchise department: 4 employees

U.S. franchises: 749
Canadian franchises: 0
Other foreign franchises: 0
Company-owned: 11
Units concentrated in AK, CA, CO, IA,
    ID, IL, KS, MN, MT, ND, NE, OR,
    SD, VT, WA, WI

Seeking: Midwest, Southwest
Focusing on: IL, IN, MI, MO, OH
Seeking in Canada? No
Exclusive territories? No
Homebased option? No
Kiosk option? No
Employees needed to run franchise:
    11-12
Absentee ownership? No

COSTS
Total cost: $140.6K-203K
Franchise fee: $25K/15K
Royalty fee: 5%
Term of agreement: 10 years renewable
    for $5K
Franchisees required to buy multiple
    units? No

FINANCING
In-house: None
3rd-party: Equipment, inventory,
    start-up costs

QUALIFICATIONS
Net worth: $250K
Cash liquidity: $80K

TRAINING
At headquarters: 1 week
At franchisee's location: 5 weeks

BUSINESS SUPPORT
Newsletter
Meetings
Toll-free phone line
Grand opening
Internet
Lease negotiations
Security/safety procedures
Field operations/evaluations
Purchasing cooperatives

MARKETING SUPPORT
Co-op advertising
Ad slicks
National media campaign
Regional marketing
In-house graphics
Local marketing

PAPA'S PIZZA TO-GO INC.

Ranked #401 in Entrepreneur Magazine's 2004 Franchise 500   *Financial rating: $$$$*

4465 Commerce Dr., #101
Buford, GA 30518
Ph: (770)614-6676
Fax: (770)614-9095
www.papapizzatogo.com
Pizza, subs, salads, wings & pasta
Began: 1987, Franchising since: 1990
Headquarters size: 13 employees
Franchise department: 1 employee

U.S. franchises: 74
Canadian franchises: 0
Other foreign franchises: 0
Company-owned: 13
Units concentrated in AL, FL, GA, IL,
    MS, NC, SC, TN, VA

Seeking: All U.S.
Seeking in Canada? No
Exclusive territories? Yes
Homebased option? No
Kiosk option? No
Employees needed to run franchise: 15
Absentee ownership? Yes

COSTS
Total cost: $139.5K-175.7K
Franchise fee: $9.5K
Royalty fee: 5%
Term of agreement: 10 years renewable
    for 20% of franchise fee
Franchisees required to buy multiple
    units? No

FINANCING
In-house: None
Equipment, start-up costs

QUALIFICATIONS
Cash liquidity: $30K-35K
Experience:
    Industry experience
    General business experience
    Marketing skills

TRAINING
At headquarters: 1 day
At franchisee's location: 1 week
Owner/manager training at company
    store: 2 weeks

BUSINESS SUPPORT
Newsletter
Meetings
Grand opening
Lease negotiations
Security/safety procedures
Field operations/evaluations

MARKETING SUPPORT
Co-op advertising
Ad slicks
Regional marketing
Monthly coupon program

PIZZA FACTORY INC.

Ranked #254 in Entrepreneur Magazine's 2004 Franchise 500　　*Financial rating: $$$$*

49430 Rd. 426, P.O. Box 989
Oakhurst, CA 93644
Ph: (800)654-4840/(559)683-3377
Fax: (559)683-6879
www.pizzafactory.com
Pizza, pasta, sandwiches
Began: 1979, Franchising since: 1985
Headquarters size: 7 employees
Franchise department: 7 employees

U.S. franchises: 110
Canadian franchises: 0
Other foreign franchises: 4
Company-owned: 0
Units concentrated in AZ, CA, ID,
　MN, NV, WA

Seeking: All U.S.
Seeking in Canada? Yes
Exclusive territories? No
Homebased option? No
Kiosk option? Yes
Employees needed to run franchise:
　8-10
Absentee ownership? Yes

COSTS
Total cost: $69.2K-261.9K
Kiosk cost: $70K-120K
Franchise fee: $5K-20K
Royalty fee: 5%
Term of agreement: 20 years renewable
　for $5K
Franchisees required to buy multiple
　units? No

FINANCING
In-house: None
3rd-party: Equipment

QUALIFICATIONS
Net worth: $175K
Cash liquidity: $50K-80K
Experience:
　General business experience

TRAINING
At training store: 325 hours

BUSINESS SUPPORT
Newsletter
Meetings
Toll-free phone line
Grand opening
Internet
Lease negotiations
Security/safety procedures
Field operations/evaluations

MARKETING SUPPORT
Ad slicks
National media campaign
Regional marketing

PIZZA HUT INC.

Financial rating: $$$

14841 N. Dallas Pkwy.
Dallas, TX 75240-2100
Ph: (972)338-7992
Fax: (972)338-7689
www.pizzahut.com
Pizza
Began: 1957, Franchising since: 1959
Headquarters size: Info not provided
Franchise department: Info not
　provided

U.S. franchises: 4,725
Canadian/other foreign franchises:
　2,562
Company-owned: 2,544
Units concentrated in all U.S.

Seeking: All U.S.
Seeking in Canada? Yes
Exclusive territories? No
Homebased option? No
Kiosk option? Info not provided
Employees needed to run franchise:
　Info not provided
Absentee ownership? No

COSTS
Total cost: $268K-1.4M
Franchise fee: $25K
Royalty fee: 6.5%
Term of agreement: Info not provided
Franchisees required to buy multiple
　units? Yes

FINANCING
No financing available

QUALIFICATIONS
Experience:
　Industry experience
　General business experience
　Marketing skills

TRAINING
Info not provided

BUSINESS SUPPORT
Info not provided

MARKETING SUPPORT
Info not provided

PIZZA INN INC.

Ranked #325 in Entrepreneur Magazine's 2004 Franchise 500

Financial rating: $$$$

3551 Plano Pkwy.
The Colony, TX 75056
Ph: (469)384-5000, Fax: (469)384-5059
www.pizzainn.com
Pizza, pasta, salads
Began: 1960, Franchising since: 1963
Headquarters size: 75 employees
Franchise department: 5 employees

U.S. franchises: 350
Canadian franchises: 0
Other foreign franchises: 59
Company-owned: 3
Units concentrated in AR, MS, NC,
    TN, TX

Seeking: South, Southeast, Southwest
Focusing on: Southeast & Southwest
Seeking in Canada? Yes
Exclusive territories? Yes
Homebased option? No
Kiosk option? Yes
Employees needed to run franchise:
    Info not provided
Absentee ownership? Yes

COSTS
Total cost: $56.6K-871.7K
Kiosk cost: $56K-89K
Franchise fee: $5K-20K
Royalty fee: 4-6%
Term of agreement: 10 years renewable
Franchisees required to buy multiple
    units? Outside the U.S. only

FINANCING
No financing available

QUALIFICATIONS
Net worth: $100K-200K
Cash liquidity: $50K-125K
Experience:
    General business experience

TRAINING
At headquarters: 24 days

BUSINESS SUPPORT
Newsletter
Meetings
Toll-free phone line
Grand opening
Field operations/evaluations

MARKETING SUPPORT
Co-op advertising
Ad slicks
Regional marketing

PIZZA MAN - HE DELIVERS

Current financial data not available

6930 1/2 Tujunga Ave.
North Hollywood, CA 91605
Ph: (818)766-4395
Fax: (818)766-1496
Pizza, chicken, ribs
Began: 1964, Franchising since: 1971
Headquarters size: 8 employees
Franchise department: 3 employees

U.S. franchises: 50
Canadian franchises: 0
Other foreign franchises: 0
Company-owned: 0
Units concentrated in CA

Seeking: All U.S.
Seeking in Canada? Yes
Exclusive territories? Yes
Homebased option? No
Kiosk option? No
Employees needed to run franchise:
    0-3
Absentee ownership? Yes

COSTS
Total cost: $162.9K-178.5K
Franchise fee: $25K
Royalty fee: 4%
Term of agreement: 1 year renewable
    at no charge
Franchisees required to buy multiple
    units? No

FINANCING
In-house: Franchise fee, inventory,
    start-up costs
3rd-party: Accounts receivable, equip-
    ment, franchise fee, payroll, start-
    up costs

QUALIFICATIONS
Net worth: $160K
Cash liquidity: $20K
Experience:
    Industry experience
    General business experience
    Marketing skills

TRAINING
At headquarters: 2 weeks
At franchisee's location: 2 weeks

BUSINESS SUPPORT
Meetings
Grand opening
Internet
Lease negotiations
Field operations/evaluations

MARKETING SUPPORT
Co-op advertising
Regional marketing

THE PIZZA RANCH
Ranked #346 in Entrepreneur Magazine's 2004 Franchise 500   *Financial rating: $$$*

1121 Main, Box 823
Hull, IA 51239
Ph: (800)321-3401/(712)439-1150
Fax: (712)439-1125
www.pizza-ranch.com
Pizza & chicken
Began: 1981, Franchising since: 1984
Headquarters size: 17 employees
Franchise department: 2 employees

U.S. franchises: 100
Canadian franchises: 0
Other foreign franchises: 0
Company-owned: 0
Units concentrated in IA, MN, ND, NE, SD

Seeking: Midwest
Focusing on: IA, IL, MN, ND, NE, SD, WI
Seeking in Canada? No
Exclusive territories? Yes
Homebased option? No
Kiosk option? No
Employees needed to run franchise: 30-40
Absentee ownership? No

COSTS
Total cost: $209.6K-496.6K
Franchise fee: $15K
Royalty fee: 4%
Term of agreement: 10 years renewable for $2.5K
Franchisees required to buy multiple units? No

FINANCING
No financing available

QUALIFICATIONS
Cash liquidity: $25K-75K
Experience:
    General business experience
    Marketing skills

TRAINING
At headquarters: 3 weeks
At franchisee's location: 2 weeks

BUSINESS SUPPORT
Newsletter
Meetings
Toll-free phone line
Grand opening
Lease negotiations
Security/safety procedures
Field operations/evaluations
Purchasing cooperatives

MARKETING SUPPORT
Co-op advertising
Ad slicks
Regional marketing

RONZIO PIZZA
Financial rating: $$

111 John St.
Lincoln, RI 02865
Ph: (401)334-9750, Fax: (401)334-0030
www.ronziopizza.com
Pizza & subs
Began: 1986, Franchising since: 1992
Headquarters size: 3 employees
Franchise department: 2 employees

U.S. franchises: 16
Canadian franchises: 0
Other foreign franchises: 0
Company-owned: 0
Units concentrated in MA, RI

Seeking: Northeast
Focusing on: MA, RI
Seeking in Canada? No
Exclusive territories? Yes
Homebased option? No
Kiosk option? Yes
Employees needed to run franchise: 12-15
Absentee ownership? Yes

COSTS
Total cost: $119K-168K
Kiosk cost: $75K-100K
Franchise fee: $10K
Royalty fee: 4%
Term of agreement: 10 years renewable at no charge
Franchisees required to buy multiple units? No

FINANCING
No financing available

QUALIFICATIONS
Net worth: $150K
Cash liquidity: $40K
Experience:
    General business experience

TRAINING
At headquarters: 2 weeks
At franchisee's location: 2 weeks

BUSINESS SUPPORT
Newsletter
Meetings
Grand opening
Internet
Security/safety procedures
Field operations/evaluations
Purchasing cooperatives

MARKETING SUPPORT
Co-op advertising
Ad slicks
Regional marketing

SAN FRANCISCO OVEN

Financial rating: $$$

34601 Ridge Rd.
Willoughby, OH 44094
Ph: (440)860-0130
Fax: (440)860-0129
www.sanfranciscooven.com
Brick-oven pizza, soups, salads, sandwiches
Began: 2001, Franchising since: 2003
Headquarters size: 3 employees
Franchise department: 1 employee

U.S. franchises: 0
Canadian franchises: 0
Other foreign franchises: 0
Company-owned: 1

Seeking: All U.S.
Seeking in Canada? No
Exclusive territories? Yes
Homebased option? No
Kiosk option? No
Employees needed to run franchise:
    20-30
Absentee ownership? No

COSTS
Total cost: $225.5K-477.8K
Franchise fee: $25K
Royalty fee: 5%
Term of agreement: 10 years renewable
    at no charge
Franchisees required to buy multiple
    units? Yes

FINANCING
No financing available

QUALIFICATIONS
Net worth: $500K
Cash liquidity: $250K
Experience:
    Industry experience
    General business experience
    Marketing skills

TRAINING
At headquarters: 4 weeks
At franchisee's location: 2 weeks

BUSINESS SUPPORT
Newsletter
Meetings
Toll-free phone line
Grand opening
Internet
Lease negotiations
Security/safety procedures
Field operations/evaluations
Purchasing cooperatives

MARKETING SUPPORT
Co-op advertising
Ad slicks
National media campaign
Regional marketing
Local marketing

SARPINO'S PIZZERIA

Financial rating: 0

3690 Shelbourne St., #202
Victoria, BC Canada V8P 4H2
Ph: (250)881-8733, Fax: (250)881-7573
www.sarpinos.com
Pizza, pasta, salads, wings
Began: 2000, Franchising since: 2001
Headquarters size: 5 employees
Franchise department: 4 employees

U.S. franchises: 11
Canadian franchises: 5
Other foreign franchises: 5
Company-owned: 2
Units concentrated in AZ, CA, CO,
    GA, IA, IL, MI, MN, MO, OH, SD,
    TN, TX

Seeking: All U.S.
Seeking in Canada? Yes
Exclusive territories? Yes
Homebased option? No
Kiosk option? Yes
Employees needed to run franchise:
    6-10
Absentee ownership? No

COSTS
Total cost: $165K-207K
Kiosk cost: Varies
Franchise fee: $15K
Royalty fee: 6%
Term of agreement: 5 years renewable
    at no charge
Franchisees required to buy multiple
    units? No

FINANCING
In-house: None
3rd-party: Equipment, franchise fee,
    start-up costs

QUALIFICATIONS
Net worth: $85K
Cash liquidity: $85K
Experience:
    Industry experience
    General business experience

TRAINING
At headquarters: 2-3 weeks
At franchisee's location: 7-10 days

BUSINESS SUPPORT
Meetings
Grand opening
Internet
Field operations/evaluations

MARKETING SUPPORT
Ad slicks
Regional marketing
Franchise shows

SIMPLE SIMON'S PIZZA

Current financial data not available

6650 S. Lewis
Tulsa, OK 74136
Ph: (918)496-1272, Fax: (918)493-6516
www.simple-simon.com
Pizza & pizza-related items
Began: 1982, Franchising since: 1986
Headquarters size: Info not provided
Franchise department: Info not provided

U.S. franchises: 226
Canadian franchises: 0
Other foreign franchises: 0
Company-owned: 6
Units concentrated in AL, AR, GA, IA, KS, LA, MO, NM, OK, TX

Seeking: Midwest, South
Focusing on: AL, AR, GA, IA, KS, LA, MO, NM, OK, TX
Seeking in Canada? No
Exclusive territories? Yes
Homebased option? No
Kiosk option? Yes
Employees needed to run franchise: 10-12
Absentee ownership? Info not provided

COSTS
Total cost: $125K/78.7K
Kiosk cost: $25K-50K
Franchise fee: $15K/5K
Royalty fee: 3%/5%
Term of agreement: Info not provided
Franchisees required to buy multiple units? No

FINANCING
In-house: Equipment
3rd-party: Accounts receivable, equipment, franchise fee, inventory, payroll, start-up costs

QUALIFICATIONS
Experience:
    Industry experience
    General business experience
    Marketing skills

TRAINING
At headquarters: 3 days/6 days

BUSINESS SUPPORT
Newsletter
Meetings
Toll-free phone line
Grand opening
Internet
Lease negotiations
Security/safety procedures
Field operations/evaluations
Purchasing cooperatives

MARKETING SUPPORT
Ad slicks
National media campaign

SNAPPY TOMATO PIZZA

Current financial data not available

7230 Turfway Rd., P.O Box 336
Florence, KY 41042
Ph: (888)463-7627/(859)525-4680
Fax: (859)525-4686
www.snappytomato.com
Pizza
Began: 1978, Franchising since: 1981
Headquarters size: Info not provided
Franchise department: Info not provided

U.S. franchises: 58
Canadian franchises: 0
Other foreign franchises: 0
Company-owned: 3
Units concentrated in FL, IN, KY, OH,TN

Seeking: Midwest, South, Southeast, Southwest
Seeking in Canada? Yes
Exclusive territories? Yes
Homebased option? No
Kiosk option? Yes
Employees needed to run franchise: 20
Absentee ownership? Yes

COSTS
Total cost: $70K-160K
Kiosk cost: $60K-70K
Franchise fee: $15K
Royalty fee: 5%
Term of agreement: 15 years renewable for $2.5K
Franchisees required to buy multiple units? Outside the U.S. only

FINANCING
No financing available

QUALIFICATIONS
Experience:
    Industry experience
    General business experience
    Marketing skills

TRAINING
At headquarters: As needed
At franchisee's location: As needed
Additional training available

BUSINESS SUPPORT
Newsletter
Meetings
Grand opening
Lease negotiations
Security/safety procedures
Field operations/evaluations
Purchasing cooperatives

MARKETING SUPPORT
Co-op advertising
Ad slicks
Regional marketing

STRAW HAT PIZZA

Current financial data not available

18 Crow Canyon Court, #150
San Ramon, CA 94583
Ph: (925)837-3400
Fax: (925)820-1080
www.strawhatpizza.com
Pizza, salads & sandwiches
Began: 1969, Franchising since: 1969
Headquarters size: 5 employees
Franchise department: Info not provided

U.S. franchises: 42
Canadian franchises: 0
Other foreign franchises: 0
Company-owned: 0
Units concentrated in CA, NY

Seeking: All U.S.
Focusing on: CA, NV, OR, WA
Seeking in Canada? No
Exclusive territories? Yes
Homebased option? No
Kiosk option? Info not provided
Employees needed to run franchise: 20
Absentee ownership? Info not provided

COSTS
Total cost: $172.5K-993K
Franchise fee: $10K
Royalty fee: 2%
Term of agreement: 10 years renewable
    at no charge
Franchisees required to buy multiple
    units? No

FINANCING
In-house: None
Equipment, start-up costs

QUALIFICATIONS
Net worth: $250K
Cash liquidity: $100K

TRAINING
At operating restaurant: 4 weeks

BUSINESS SUPPORT
Newsletter
Meetings
Grand opening
Internet
Security/safety procedures
Field operations/evaluations
Purchasing cooperatives

MARKETING SUPPORT
Co-op advertising
Ad slicks
Regional marketing

STUFT PIZZA

Current financial data not available

1040 Calle Cordillera, #103
San Clemente, CA 92673
Ph: (949)361-2522, Fax: (949)361-2501
www.stuftpizza.com
Pizza, pasta, sandwiches, salads, micro-
    brewery
Began: 1976, Franchising since: 1985
Headquarters size: 3 employees
Franchise department: Info not pro-
    vided

U.S. franchises: 23
Canadian franchises: 0
Other foreign franchises: 0
Company-owned: 1
Units concentrated in CA

Seeking: West
Focusing on: CA
Seeking in Canada? No
Exclusive territories? Yes
Homebased option? No
Kiosk option? No
Employees needed to run franchise:
    10-20
Absentee ownership? Info not provided

COSTS
Total cost: $350K-650K
Franchise fee: $25K
Royalty fee: 4%
Term of agreement: Info not provided
Franchisees required to buy multiple
    units? No

FINANCING
No financing available

QUALIFICATIONS
Net worth: $500K
Cash liquidity: $200K

TRAINING
At headquarters: 2 weeks
At franchisee's location: 1 week

BUSINESS SUPPORT
Newsletter
Grand opening
Internet
Lease negotiations
Field operations/evaluations
Purchasing cooperatives

MARKETING SUPPORT
Info not provided

VILLA PIZZA/COZZOLI'S PIZZERIA
Ranked #396 in Entrepreneur Magazine's 2004 Franchise 500   *Financial rating: $$$*

17 Elm St.
Morristown, NJ 07960
Ph: (973)285-4800
Fax: (973)285-5252
www.villapizza.com
Quick-service pizza & Italian restaurant
Began: 1964, Franchising since: 1994
Headquarters size: Info not provided
Franchise department: Info not provided

U.S. franchises: 67
Canadian franchises: 0
Other foreign franchises: 14
Company-owned: 114
Units concentrated in all U.S.

Seeking: All U.S.
Seeking in Canada? Yes
Exclusive territories? No
Homebased option? No
Kiosk option? Yes
Employees needed to run franchise: 8
Absentee ownership? No

COSTS
Total cost: $190K-350K
Franchise fee: $25K
Royalty fee: 6%
Term of agreement: 12 years renewable at no charge
Franchisees required to buy multiple units? No

FINANCING
In-house: None
3rd-party: Accounts receivable, equipment, franchise fee, inventory, payroll, start-up costs

QUALIFICATIONS
Net worth: $250K-300K
Cash liquidity: $100K-250K
Experience:
    Industry experience
    General business experience

TRAINING
At headquarters: 3 weeks
Ongoing

BUSINESS SUPPORT
Newsletter
Meetings
Grand opening
Internet
Lease negotiations
Field operations/evaluations
Purchasing cooperatives

MARKETING SUPPORT
Co-op advertising
Ad slicks
National media campaign
Regional marketing

VOCELLI PIZZA
Financial rating: 0

2101 Greentree Rd., #A-202
Pittsburgh, PA 15220
Ph: (412)279-9100
Fax: (412)279-9781
www.vocellipizza.com
Pizza, subs, wings
Began: 1988, Franchising since: 1989
Headquarters size: 30 employees
Franchise department: 1 employee

U.S. franchises: 72
Canadian franchises: 0
Other foreign franchises: 0
Company-owned: 33
Units concentrated in OH, PA, VA, WV

Seeking: Midwest, Northeast, Southeast
Focusing on: FL, MD, OH, PA, VA, WV
Seeking in Canada? No
Exclusive territories? Yes
Homebased option? No
Kiosk option? No
Employees needed to run franchise: 11
Absentee ownership? Info not provided

COSTS
Total cost: $95K-185K
Franchise fee: $15K
Royalty fee: 4%
Term of agreement: 10 years renewable for 20% of then-current fee
Franchisees required to buy multiple units? No

FINANCING
In-house: None
3rd-party: Equipment, franchise fee, inventory, start-up costs

QUALIFICATIONS
Info not provided

TRAINING
At headquarters: 3-7 weeks

BUSINESS SUPPORT
Newsletter
Meetings
Toll-free phone line
Grand opening
Internet
Lease negotiations
Security/safety procedures
Field operations/evaluations
Purchasing cooperatives

MARKETING SUPPORT
Co-op advertising
Ad slicks
National media campaign
Regional marketing
Promotional materials

Z PIZZA

Current financial data not available

619 Spring Tide Dr.
Newport Beach, CA 92660
Ph: (714)552-3079
Fax: (949)706-2746
www.zpizza.com
Pizza & pasta
Began: 1986, Franchising since: 1999
Headquarters size: 8 employees
Franchise department: 6 employees

U.S. franchises: 18
Canadian franchises: 0
Other foreign franchises: 0
Company-owned: 9
Units concentrated in all U.S.

Seeking: Northwest, Southwest, West
Focusing on: All U.S.
Seeking in Canada? No
Exclusive territories? Yes
Homebased option? No
Kiosk option? No
Employees needed to run franchise: 15
Absentee ownership? No

COSTS
Total cost: $100K-150K
Franchise fee: $20K
Royalty fee: 5%
Term of agreement: 10 years renewable at no charge
Franchisees required to buy multiple units? Yes

FINANCING
In-house: None
3rd-party: Accounts receivable, equipment, franchise fee, inventory, payroll, start-up costs

QUALIFICATIONS
Net worth: $100K
Cash liquidity: $50K
Experience:
    General business experience

TRAINING
At headquarters: 4 weeks
At franchisee's location: 2 weeks
Additional training available

BUSINESS SUPPORT
Newsletter
Meetings
Grand opening
Internet
Lease negotiations
Security/safety procedures
Field operations/evaluations
Purchasing cooperatives

MARKETING SUPPORT
Co-op advertising
Ad slicks
National media campaign
Regional marketing

QUICK SERVICE   *Pretzels*

AUNTIE ANNE'S HAND-ROLLED SOFT PRETZELS
Ranked #61 in Entrepreneur Magazine's 2004 Franchise 500

Financial rating: $$$$

P.O. Box 529
Gap, PA 17527
Ph: (717)442-4766
Fax: (717)442-4139
www.auntieannes.com
Hand-rolled soft pretzels
Began: 1988, Franchising since: 1989
Headquarters size: 125 employees
Franchise department: 9 employees

U.S. franchises: 651
Canadian franchises: 6
Other foreign franchises: 99
Company-owned: 27
Units concentrated in CA, FL, IL, PA

Seeking: All U.S.
Seeking in Canada? No
Exclusive territories? No
Homebased option? No
Kiosk option? Yes
Employees needed to run franchise: 10
Absentee ownership? Yes

COSTS
Total cost: $192.5K-326K
Kiosk cost: Same as total cost
Franchise fee: $30K
Royalty fee: 6%
Term of agreement: 5 years renewable at no charge
Franchisees required to buy multiple units? Outside the U.S. only

FINANCING
No financing available

QUALIFICATIONS
Net worth: $300K
Experience:
    General business experience

TRAINING
At headquarters: 6-9 days
At franchisee's location: Up to 7 days
Ongoing on-site store support

BUSINESS SUPPORT
Newsletter
Meetings
Grand opening
Lease negotiations
Security/safety procedures
Field operations/evaluations

MARKETING SUPPORT
Regional marketing
Individual marketing plans

PRETZEL TIME

Current financial data not available

2855 E. Cottonwood Pkwy., #400
Salt Lake City, UT 84121
Ph: (800)348-6311/(801)736-5600
Fax: (801)763-5936
www.pretzeltime.com
Hand-rolled soft pretzels
Began: 1991, Franchising since: 1992
Headquarters size: 150 employees
Franchise department: 25 employees

U.S. franchises: 167
Canadian franchises: 0
Other foreign franchises: 5
Company-owned: 21
Units concentrated in all U.S.

Seeking: All U.S.
Seeking in Canada? Yes
Exclusive territories? No
Homebased option? No
Kiosk option? Info not provided
Employees needed to run franchise:
    Info not provided
Absentee ownership? Info not provided

COSTS
Total cost: $107K-238.5K
Franchise fee: $25K
Royalty fee: 7%
Term of agreement: 7 years renewable
Franchisees required to buy multiple
    units? Outside the U.S. only

FINANCING
No financing available

QUALIFICATIONS
Net worth: $150K
Cash liquidity: $75K

TRAINING
At headquarters: 5 days

BUSINESS SUPPORT
Meetings
Toll-free phone line
Internet

MARKETING SUPPORT
Ad slicks
Regional marketing

THE PRETZEL TWISTER

Ranked #471 in Entrepreneur Magazine's 2004 Franchise 500   *Financial rating: $$$*

2706 S. Horseshoe Dr., #112
Naples, FL 34104
Ph: (888)638-8806/(941)643-2075
Fax: (941)353-6479
www.pretzeltwister.com
Hand-twisted soft pretzels & fruit
    shakes
Began: 1992, Franchising since: 1993
Headquarters size: 2 employees
Franchise department: 1 employee

U.S. franchises: 43
Canadian franchises: 0
Other foreign franchises: 0
Company-owned: 0
Units concentrated in all U.S.

Seeking: All U.S.
Seeking in Canada? Yes
Exclusive territories? No
Homebased option? No
Kiosk option? Yes
Employees needed to run franchise: 8
Absentee ownership? Yes

COSTS
Total cost: $114.5K-175.2K
Kiosk cost: $100K
Franchise fee: $22.5K
Royalty fee: 5%
Term of agreement: Info not provided
Franchisees required to buy multiple
    units? Outside the U.S. only

FINANCING
In-house: None
3rd-party: Accounts receivable, equip-
    ment, franchise fee, inventory, pay-
    roll, start-up costs

QUALIFICATIONS
Cash liquidity: $40K

TRAINING
At headquarters: 5 days
At franchisee's location: 2 days

BUSINESS SUPPORT
Newsletter
Meetings
Toll-free phone line
Grand opening
Internet
Security/safety procedures
Field operations/evaluations

MARKETING SUPPORT
Ad slicks
Posters, mobiles & other signage

PRETZELMAKER INC.

Current financial data not available

2855 E. Cottonwood Pkwy., #400
Salt Lake City, UT 84121
Ph: (800)348-6311/(801)736-5600
Fax: (801)736-5936
www.mrsfields.com
Gourmet pretzels
Began: 1991, Franchising since: 1992
Headquarters size: 150 employees
Franchise department: 25 employees

U.S. franchises: 167
Canadian franchises: 0
Other foreign franchises: 25
Company-owned: 72
Units concentrated in all U.S.

Seeking: All U.S.
Seeking in Canada? Yes
Exclusive territories? No
Homebased option? No
Kiosk option? Info not provided
Employees needed to run franchise:
   Info not provided
Absentee ownership? Info not provided

COSTS
Total cost: $107K-238.5K
Franchise fee: $25K
Royalty fee: 6%
Term of agreement: 7 years renewable
Franchisees required to buy multiple
   units? Outside the U.S. only

FINANCING
No financing available

QUALIFICATIONS
Net worth: $150K
Cash liquidity: $75K

TRAINING
At headquarters: 5 days

BUSINESS SUPPORT
Meetings
Toll-free phone line
Internet
Field operations/evaluations

MARKETING SUPPORT
Ad slicks
Regional marketing

PRETZELS PLUS INC.

Current financial data not available

639 Frederick St.
Hanover, PA 17331
Ph: (800)559-7927
Fax: (717)633-5078
www.pretzelsplus.com
Hand-rolled soft pretzels, sandwiches,
   hand-dipped ice cream
Began: 1991, Franchising since: 1991
Headquarters size: 10 employees
Franchise department: 5 employees

U.S. franchises: 25
Canadian franchises: 0
Other foreign franchises: 0
Company-owned: 0
Units concentrated in all U.S.

Seeking: All U.S.
Seeking in Canada? No
Exclusive territories? No
Homebased option? No
Kiosk option? No
Employees needed to run franchise:
   5-15
Absentee ownership? Yes

COSTS
Total cost: $80K
Franchise fee: $12K
Royalty fee: 4%
Term of agreement: Renewable term at
   50% of franchise fee
Franchisees required to buy multiple
   units? No

FINANCING
No financing available

QUALIFICATIONS
Net worth: $100K
Cash liquidity: $25K

TRAINING
At franchisee's location: 3 days+

BUSINESS SUPPORT
Newsletter
Toll-free phone line
Lease negotiations
Field operations/evaluations

MARKETING SUPPORT
Info not provided

WE'RE ROLLING PRETZEL CO.

Ranked #329 in Entrepreneur Magazine's 2004 Franchise 500　　　*Financial rating: $$*

2500 W. State St.
Alliance, OH 44601
Ph: (888)549-7655/(330)823-0575
Fax: (330)821-8908
www.wererolling.com
Homemade soft pretzels
Began: 1996, Franchising since: 1998
Headquarters size: 11 employees
Franchise department: 3 employees

U.S. franchises: 23
Canadian franchises: 0
Other foreign franchises: 0
Company-owned: 2
Units concentrated in IN, KY, OH,
　PA, WV

Seeking: Midwest
Focusing on: IN, KY, MI, OH, PA, TN,
　VA, WV
Seeking in Canada? No
Exclusive territories? Yes
Homebased option? No
Kiosk option? Yes
Employees needed to run franchise: 6-8
Absentee ownership? Yes

COSTS
Total cost: $65K-149K
Kiosk cost: Same as total cost
Franchise fee: $15K
Royalty fee: 5%
Term of agreement: 5 years renewable
　for $1K
Franchisees required to buy multiple
　units? No

FINANCING
No financing available

QUALIFICATIONS
Net worth: $100K
Cash liquidity: $50K
Experience:
　General business experience

TRAINING
At headquarters: 7 days
At franchisee's location: 7 days

BUSINESS SUPPORT
Newsletter
Meetings
Toll-free phone line
Grand opening
Security/safety procedures
Field operations/evaluations

MARKETING SUPPORT
Ad slicks
Regional marketing

WETZEL'S PRETZELS

Ranked #142 in Entrepreneur Magazine's 2004 Franchise 500　　　*Financial rating: $$$$*

35 Hugus Alley, #300
Pasadena, CA 91103
Ph: (626)432-6900
Fax: (626)432-6904
www.wetzels.com
Soft pretzels, lemonade, hot dogs
Began: 1994, Franchising since: 1996
Headquarters size: 12 employees
Franchise department: 3 employees

U.S. franchises: 148
Canadian franchises: 30
Other foreign franchises: 19
Company-owned: 7
Units concentrated in all U.S.

Seeking: All U.S.
Seeking in Canada? Yes
Exclusive territories? Yes
Homebased option? No
Kiosk option? Yes
Employees needed to run franchise: 8
Absentee ownership? No

COSTS
Total cost: $128.9K-352.5K
Kiosk cost: $150K
Franchise fee: $30K
Royalty fee: 6%
Term of agreement: 10 years renewable
Franchisees required to buy multiple
　units? No

FINANCING
In-house: None
3rd-party: Equipment, franchise fee,
　inventory, start-up costs

QUALIFICATIONS
Net worth: $200K
Cash liquidity: $50K
Experience:
　General business experience

TRAINING
At headquarters: 2 weeks
At franchisee's location: 4 days

BUSINESS SUPPORT
Newsletter
Meetings
Grand opening
Internet
Security/safety procedures
Field operations/evaluations
Purchasing cooperatives

MARKETING SUPPORT
Co-op advertising
Ad slicks

QUICK SERVICE *Sandwiches*

ARBY'S

Ranked #62 in Entrepreneur Magazine's 2004 Franchise 500   *Financial rating: $$*

1000 Corporate Dr.
Ft. Lauderdale, FL 33334
Ph: (800)487-2729/(954)351-5100
Fax: (954)351-5222
www.arbys.com
Roast beef sandwiches, chicken, subs
Began: 1964, Franchising since: 1965
Headquarters size: 120 employees
Franchise department: 59 employees

U.S. franchises: 3,030
Canadian franchises: 130
Other foreign franchises: 20
Company-owned: 239
Units concentrated in all U.S.

Seeking: All U.S.
Seeking in Canada? No
Exclusive territories? Yes
Homebased option? No
Kiosk option? No
Employees needed to run franchise:
    Info not provided
Absentee ownership? Yes

COSTS

Total cost: $333.7K-2.3M
Franchise fee: $37.5K/25K
Royalty fee: 4%
Term of agreement: 20 years renewable
    for 10% of current franchise fee
Franchisees required to buy multiple
    units? No

FINANCING

In-house: None
3rd-party: Accounts receivable, equip-
    ment, franchise fee, inventory, pay-
    roll, start-up costs

QUALIFICATIONS

Net worth: $1M
Cash liquidity: $500K
Experience:
    Industry experience
    General business experience
    Marketing skills

TRAINING

At headquarters: Several visits
At franchisee's location: Ongoing
At training restaurant: 5 weeks

BUSINESS SUPPORT

Newsletter
Meetings
Toll-free phone line
Grand opening
Security/safety procedures
Field operations/evaluations
Purchasing cooperatives

MARKETING SUPPORT

Supplied by franchisee association

BAKER BROS. AMERICAN DELI

                    Financial rating: $$$

5500 Greenville Ave., #1102
Dallas, TX 75206
Ph: (214)696-8780, Fax: (214)696-8809
www.bakerbrosdeli.com
Specialty sandwiches, gourmet pizzas,
    salads
Began: 1998, Franchising since: 2000
Headquarters size: 4 employees
Franchise department: 1 employee

U.S. franchises: 1
Canadian franchises: 0
Other foreign franchises: 1
Company-owned: 4
Units concentrated in TX

Seeking: All U.S.
Seeking in Canada? No
Exclusive territories? Yes
Homebased option? No
Kiosk option? No
Employees needed to run franchise: 18
Absentee ownership? Yes

COSTS

Total cost: $353K-641K
Franchise fee: $20K-30K
Royalty fee: 4-5%
Term of agreement: 10 years renewable
    for 50% of current franchise fee
Franchisees required to buy multiple
    units? Outside the U.S. only

FINANCING

In-house: None
3rd-party: Accounts receivable, equip-
    ment, franchise fee, inventory, pay-
    roll, start-up costs

QUALIFICATIONS

Net worth: $800K
Cash liquidity: $400K
Experience:
    Industry experience
    General business experience

TRAINING

At headquarters: 6-8 weeks
At franchisee's location: 5-10 days

BUSINESS SUPPORT

Lease negotiations
Security/safety procedures
Field operations/evaluations
Purchasing cooperatives

MARKETING SUPPORT

Ad slicks

BLIMPIE INT'L. INC.

Ranked #332 in Entrepreneur Magazine's 2004 Franchise 500   *Financial rating: $$$*

180 Interstate North Pkwy., #500
Atlanta, GA 30339
Ph: (800)447-6256/(770)984-2707
Fax: (770)980-9176
www.blimpie.com
Submarine sandwiches & salads
Began: 1964, Franchising since: 1970
Headquarters size: 75 employees
Franchise department: 5 employees

U.S. franchises: 1,575
Canadian franchises: 5
Other foreign franchises: 16
Company-owned: 0
Units concentrated in all U.S.

Seeking: All U.S.
Seeking in Canada? Yes
Exclusive territories? No
Homebased option? No
Kiosk option? Yes
Employees needed to run franchise: 4-6
Absentee ownership? Yes

COSTS
Total cost: $72.8K-338.2K
Kiosk cost: $10K-30K
Franchise fee: $18K
Royalty fee: 6%
Term of agreement: 20 years renewable
    at no charge
Franchisees required to buy multiple
    units? No

FINANCING
In-house: None
3rd-party: Accounts receivable, equipment, franchise fee, inventory, payroll, start-up costs

QUALIFICATIONS
Cash liquidity: $75K
Experience:
    General business experience

TRAINING
At headquarters: 2 weeks
At franchisee's location: 40 hours

BUSINESS SUPPORT
Newsletter
Meetings
Toll-free phone line
Grand opening
Internet
Lease negotiations
Security/safety procedures
Field operations/evaluations
Purchasing cooperatives

MARKETING SUPPORT
Co-op advertising
Ad slicks
National media campaign
Regional marketing

CAMILLE'S SIDEWALK CAFE

Ranked #358 in Entrepreneur Magazine's 2004 Franchise 500   *Financial rating: $$$*

8801 S. Yale, #110
Tulsa, OK 74137
Ph: (918)488-9727
Fax: (918)497-1916
www.camillescafe.com
Wraps, sandwiches, salads, smoothies,
    coffee
Began: 1996, Franchising since: 1999
Headquarters size: 20 employees
Franchise department: 20 employees

U.S. franchises: 17
Canadian franchises: 0
Other foreign franchises: 0
Company-owned: 1
Units concentrated in OK

Seeking: All U.S.
Seeking in Canada? No
Exclusive territories? Yes
Homebased option? No
Kiosk option? No
Employees needed to run franchise: 30
Absentee ownership? Yes

COSTS
Total cost: $210K-470K
Franchise fee: $25K
Royalty fee: 5%
Term of agreement: 20 years renewable
    for 50% of current franchise fee
Franchisees required to buy multiple
    units? No

FINANCING
In-house: None
3rd-party: Equipment, franchise fee,
    inventory, start-up costs

QUALIFICATIONS
Net worth: $300K
Cash liquidity: $50K
Experience:
    Industry experience
    General business experience
    Marketing skills

TRAINING
At headquarters: 2-3 weeks
At franchisee's location: 2-3 days

BUSINESS SUPPORT
Newsletter
Toll-free phone line
Grand opening
Internet
Field operations/evaluations
Purchasing cooperatives

MARKETING SUPPORT
Co-op advertising
Ad slicks

CHARLEY'S GRILLED SUBS

Ranked #120 in Entrepreneur Magazine's 2004 Franchise 500   *Financial rating: $$$$*

6610 Busch Blvd., #100
Columbus, OH 43229
Ph: (614)847-8100
Fax: (614)847-8110
www.cgsubs.com
Grilled subs, fries, salads
Began: 1986, Franchising since: 1991
Headquarters size: 35 employees
Franchise department: 8 employees

U.S. franchises: 155
Canadian franchises: 4
Other foreign franchises: 12
Company-owned: 7
Units concentrated in all U.S.

Seeking: All U.S.
Seeking in Canada? No
Exclusive territories? No
Homebased option? No
Kiosk option? No
Employees needed to run franchise: 20
Absentee ownership? No

COSTS
Total cost: $122.5K-294.5K
Franchise fee: $19.5K
Royalty fee: 5%
Term of agreement: 10 years renewable
    for $5K
Franchisees required to buy multiple
    units? No

FINANCING
In-house: None
3rd-party: Equipment, inventory,
    start-up costs

QUALIFICATIONS
Net worth: $200K
Cash liquidity: $70K
Experience:
    General business experience

TRAINING
At headquarters: 3 weeks
At franchisee's location: 7 days

BUSINESS SUPPORT
Newsletter
Meetings
Toll-free phone line
Grand opening
Security/safety procedures
Purchasing cooperatives

MARKETING SUPPORT
Co-op advertising
Ad slicks

COUSINS SUBS

Ranked #253 in Entrepreneur Magazine's 2004 Franchise 500   *Financial rating: $$$*

N83 W13400 Leon Rd.
Menomonee Falls, WI 53051
Ph: (800)238-9736/(262)253-7700
Fax: (262)253-7710
www.cousinssubs.com
Hot/cold subs, salads, soups & desserts
Began: 1972, Franchising since: 1985
Headquarters size: 50 employees
Franchise department: 16 employees

U.S. franchises: 135
Canadian franchises: 0
Other foreign franchises: 0
Company-owned: 40
Units concentrated in AZ, CA, CO, IL,
    IN, MI, MN, ND, TX, WI

Seeking: All U.S.
Focusing on: AZ, CA, CO, IL, IN, MI,
    MN, ND, TX, WI
Seeking in Canada? No
Exclusive territories? Yes
Homebased option? No
Kiosk option? No
Employees needed to run franchise: 20
Absentee ownership? No

COSTS
Total cost: $200K-275K
Franchise fee: $20K
Royalty fee: 6%
Term of agreement: 10 years renewable
    at no charge
Franchisees required to buy multiple
    units? No

FINANCING
In-house: None
3rd-party: Equipment, franchise fee,
    start-up costs

QUALIFICATIONS
Net worth: $300K
Cash liquidity: $60K-100K
Experience:
    Industry experience
    General business experience
    Marketing skills
    People skills

TRAINING
At headquarters: 3 days
At franchisee's location: 10 days
At training store: 5 weeks

BUSINESS SUPPORT
Newsletter
Meetings
Toll-free phone line
Grand opening
Internet
Security/safety procedures
Field operations/evaluations
Purchasing cooperatives

MARKETING SUPPORT
Co-op advertising
Ad slicks
National media campaign
Regional marketing

D'ANGELO SANDWICH SHOPS

Ranked #266 in Entrepreneur Magazine's 2004 Franchise 500   *Financial rating: $$$*

600 Providence Hwy.
Dedham, MA 02026
Ph: (781)467-1663, Fax: (781)329-8796
www.dangelos.com
Sandwiches, soups, salads
Began: 1967, Franchising since: 1988
Headquarters size: 200 employees
Franchise department: 7 employees

U.S. franchises: 56
Canadian franchises: 0
Other foreign franchises: 0
Company-owned: 160
Units concentrated in Northeast

Seeking: Mid-Atlantic, Florida
Seeking in Canada? No
Exclusive territories? Yes
Homebased option? No
Kiosk option? No
Employees needed to run franchise: 12
Absentee ownership? Yes

COSTS
Total cost: $200.1K-342.4K
Franchise fee: $15K
Royalty fee: 5.5%
Term of agreement: 20 years renewable
    for $7.5K
Franchisees required to buy multiple
    units? No

FINANCING
In-house: None
3rd-party: Accounts receivable, equipment, franchise fee, inventory, payroll, start-up costs

QUALIFICATIONS
Net worth: $400K
Cash liquidity: $80K
Experience:
    General business experience
    Marketing skills

TRAINING
At headquarters: 5 weeks

BUSINESS SUPPORT
Newsletter
Meetings
Toll-free phone line
Grand opening
Internet
Lease negotiations
Security/safety procedures
Field operations/evaluations
Purchasing cooperatives

MARKETING SUPPORT
Co-op advertising
Ad slicks
Regional marketing

ERBERT & GERBERT'S SUBS & CLUBS

Current financial data not available

205 E. Grand Ave.
Eau Claire, WI 54701
Ph: (800)283-5241
Fax: (715)833-8523
www.erbertandgerberts.com
Submarine sandwiches
Began: 1987, Franchising since: 1992
Headquarters size: 10 employees
Franchise department: 10 employees

U.S. franchises: 25
Canadian franchises: 0
Other foreign franchises: 0
Company-owned: 1
Units concentrated in MN, ND, WI

Seeking: All U.S.
Seeking in Canada? No
Exclusive territories? Yes
Homebased option? No
Kiosk option? Info not provided
Employees needed to run franchise: 15
Absentee ownership? No

COSTS
Total cost: $194K-356K
Franchise fee: $25K
Royalty fee: 6.5%
Term of agreement: 15 years renewable
    at no charge
Franchisees required to buy multiple
    units? No

FINANCING
No financing available

QUALIFICATIONS
Net worth: $250K
Cash liquidity: $25K
Experience:
    Industry experience
    General business experience

TRAINING
At headquarters: 1 month
At franchisee's location: 1 week

BUSINESS SUPPORT
Newsletter
Meetings
Toll-free phone line
Grand opening
Internet
Lease negotiations
Field operations/evaluations

MARKETING SUPPORT
Co-op advertising
Ad slicks
Regional marketing

GREAT OUTDOORS SUB SHOPS

Current financial data not available

900 E. Parker Rd.
Plano, TX 75074
Ph: (972)423-2693
Fax: (972)424-8244
Submarine sandwiches, salads,
    ice cream
Began: 1973, Franchising since: 1994
Headquarters size: 5 employees
Franchise department: 3 employees

U.S. franchises: 3
Canadian franchises: 0
Other foreign franchises: 0
Company-owned: 0
Units concentrated in TX

Focusing on: TX
Seeking in Canada? No
Exclusive territories? Yes
Homebased option? No
Kiosk option? Info not provided
Employees needed to run franchise: 10
Absentee ownership? No

COSTS
Total cost: $220.9K-275K
Franchise fee: $25K
Royalty fee: 4%
Term of agreement: 10 years renewable
    for $5K
Franchisees required to buy multiple
    units? No

FINANCING
In-house: Inventory
3rd-party: None

QUALIFICATIONS
Net worth: $275K
Cash liquidity: $75K
Experience:
    General business experience

TRAINING
At headquarters: 8 weeks
At franchisee's location: 1 week at
    opening

BUSINESS SUPPORT
Toll-free phone line
Grand opening
Internet
Lease negotiations
Field operations/evaluations

MARKETING SUPPORT
Ad slicks
Regional marketing

THE GREAT STEAK & POTATO CO.

Ranked #365 in Entrepreneur Magazine's 2004 Franchise 500   *Current financial data not available*

188 N. Brookwood Ave., #100
Hamilton, OH 45013
Ph: (513)896-9695
Fax: (513)896-3750
www.thegreatsteak.com
Cheesesteaks/grilled sandwiches &
    salads
Began: 1983, Franchising since: 1986
Headquarters size: 18 employees
Franchise department: 11 employees

U.S. franchises: 224
Canadian franchises: 10
Other foreign franchises: 5
Company-owned: 10
Units concentrated in Midwest, West
    Coast

Seeking: All U.S.
Seeking in Canada? No
Exclusive territories? Yes
Homebased option? No
Kiosk option? Yes
Employees needed to run franchise: 10
Absentee ownership? Yes

COSTS
Total cost: $153K-280K
Kiosk cost: $150K-160K
Franchise fee: $25K
Royalty fee: 5%
Term of agreement: 10 years renewable
    for $5K
Franchisees required to buy multiple
    units? Outside the U.S. only

FINANCING
In-house: None
3rd-party: Accounts receivable, equip-
    ment, franchise fee, inventory, pay-
    roll, start-up costs

QUALIFICATIONS
Net worth: $250K
Cash liquidity: $100K
Experience:
    Industry experience
    General business experience

TRAINING
At headquarters: 2 weeks
At franchisee's location: 2 weeks
At existing locations: As needed

BUSINESS SUPPORT
Newsletter
Meetings
Grand opening
Internet
Lease negotiations
Security/safety procedures
Field operations/evaluations
Purchasing cooperatives

MARKETING SUPPORT
Ad slicks
National media campaign
Regional marketing

GROUCHO'S DELI

Financial rating: $$$

611 Harden St.
Columbia, SC 29205
Ph: (803)799-5708
Fax: (803)799-2297
www.grouchosdeli.com
Sandwiches & salads
Began: 1941, Franchising since: 2001
Headquarters size: 4 employees
Franchise department: 4 employees

U.S. franchises: 7
Canadian franchises: 0
Other foreign franchises: 0
Company-owned: 1
Units concentrated in NC, SC

Seeking: South, Southeast
Focusing on: GA, NC, SC
Seeking in Canada? No
Exclusive territories? Yes
Homebased option? No
Kiosk option? Yes
Employees needed to run franchise:
    12-13
Absentee ownership? Yes

COSTS
Total cost: $115.7K-163.2K
Kiosk cost: $25K
Franchise fee: $15K
Royalty fee: 4%
Term of agreement: 10 years renewable
    at no charge
Franchisees required to buy multiple
    units? No

FINANCING
No financing available

QUALIFICATIONS
Net worth: $150K
Cash liquidity: $60K
Experience:
    Industry experience
    General business experience

TRAINING
At headquarters: 7 days
At franchisee's location: 10 days
Additional training: 30 days

BUSINESS SUPPORT
Newsletter
Meetings
Toll-free phone line
Grand opening
Internet
Lease negotiations
Security/safety procedures
Field operations/evaluations
Purchasing cooperatives

MARKETING SUPPORT
Co-op advertising
Regional marketing

JERRY'S SUBS & PIZZA

Ranked #300 in Entrepreneur Magazine's 2004 Franchise 500

Financial rating: $$$

15942 Shady Grove Rd.
Gaithersburg, MD 20877
Ph: (301)921-8777, Fax: (301)948-3508
www.jerrys-subs.com
Submarine sandwiches & pizza
Began: 1954, Franchising since: 1980
Headquarters size: Info not provided
Franchise department: Info not pro-
    vided

U.S. franchises: 92
Canadian franchises: 0
Other foreign franchises: 15
Company-owned: 2
Units concentrated in DC, DE, MD,
    PA, VA

Seeking: All U.S.
Focusing on: DC, DE, MD, PA, VA
Seeking in Canada? No
Exclusive territories? Yes
Homebased option? No
Kiosk option? Info not provided
Employees needed to run franchise: 20
Absentee ownership? Yes

COSTS
Total cost: $250K-350K
Franchise fee: $25K
Royalty fee: 6%
Term of agreement: 20 years renewable
    for $25K
Franchisees required to buy multiple
    units? No

FINANCING
In-house: None
3rd-party: Accounts receivable, equip-
    ment, franchise fee, inventory, pay-
    roll, start-up costs

QUALIFICATIONS
Cash liquidity: $75K
Experience:
    Good interpersonal skills

TRAINING
At headquarters: 5 weeks

BUSINESS SUPPORT
Newsletter
Meetings
Toll-free phone line
Grand opening
Lease negotiations
Security/safety procedures
Field operations/evaluations
Purchasing cooperatives

MARKETING SUPPORT
Co-op advertising

JERSEY MIKE'S SUBMARINES & SALADS

Ranked #280 in Entrepreneur Magazine's 2004 Franchise 500

Financial rating: $$

1973 Hwy. #34, #E-21
Wall, NJ 07719
Ph: (732)282-2323
Fax: (732)282-2233
www.jerseymikes.com
Submarine sandwiches & salads
Began: 1956, Franchising since: 1987
Headquarters size: 25 employees
Franchise department: 25 employees

U.S. franchises: 252
Canadian franchises: 0
Other foreign franchises: 0
Company-owned: 1
Units concentrated in all U.S.

Seeking: All U.S.
Seeking in Canada? Yes
Exclusive territories? Yes
Homebased option? No
Kiosk option? No
Employees needed to run franchise:
    10-15
Absentee ownership? Yes

COSTS
Total cost: $71K-185K
Franchise fee: $18.5K
Royalty fee: 6.5%
Term of agreement: 10 years renewable
    at no charge
Franchisees required to buy multiple
    units? No

FINANCING
In-house: None
3rd-party: Equipment, franchise fee,
    start-up costs

QUALIFICATIONS
Net worth: $100K
Cash liquidity: $50K
Experience:
    Restaurant experience

TRAINING
At headquarters: 14 days
At training location: 1-3 months

BUSINESS SUPPORT
Newsletter
Meetings
Toll-free phone line
Grand opening
Internet
Field operations/evaluations

MARKETING SUPPORT
Co-op advertising
Ad slicks
Regional marketing

JIMMY JOHN'S GOURMET SANDWICH SHOPS

Ranked #151 in Entrepreneur Magazine's 2004 Franchise 500

Financial rating: $$

600 Tollgate Rd.
Elgin, IL 60123
Ph: (800)546-6904
Fax: (847)888-7070
www.jimmyjohns.com
Gourmet sandwiches
Began: 1983, Franchising since: 1993
Headquarters size: 18 employees
Franchise department: 15 employees

U.S. franchises: 184
Canadian franchises: 0
Other foreign franchises: 6
Company-owned: 18
Units concentrated in all U.S.

Seeking: All U.S.
Seeking in Canada? No
Exclusive territories? Yes
Homebased option? No
Kiosk option? Yes
Employees needed to run franchise: 6-8
Absentee ownership? No

COSTS
Total cost: $199.4K-353K
Kiosk cost: $50K-75K
Franchise fee: $20K-30K
Royalty fee: 6%
Term of agreement: 10 years renewable
    for $2.5K
Franchisees required to buy multiple
    units? Outside the U.S. only

FINANCING
In-house: None
3rd-party: Accounts receivable, equip-
    ment, franchise fee, inventory, pay-
    roll, start-up costs

QUALIFICATIONS
Net worth: $300K
Cash liquidity: $80K
Experience:
    General business experience

TRAINING
At headquarters: 3-7 weeks

BUSINESS SUPPORT
Newsletter
Meetings
Toll-free phone line
Grand opening
Internet
Field operations/evaluations

MARKETING SUPPORT
Co-op advertising
Ad slicks
National media campaign
Regional marketing

LARRY'S GIANT SUBS

Current financial data not available

8616 Bay Meadows Rd.
Jacksonville, FL 32256
Ph: (904)739-2498
Fax: (904)739-1218
www.larryssubs.com
New York-style subs, sandwiches, salads
Began: 1982, Franchising since: 1986
Headquarters size: 15 employees
Franchise department: 3 employees

U.S. franchises: 81
Canadian franchises: 0
Other foreign franchises: 0
Company-owned: 2

Seeking: All U.S.
Seeking in Canada? No
Exclusive territories? Yes
Homebased option? No
Kiosk option? No
Employees needed to run franchise: 12
Absentee ownership? Yes

COSTS
Total cost: $131K-195.6K
Franchise fee: $20K
Royalty fee: 6%
Term of agreement: 10 years renewable
    for $1K
Franchisees required to buy multiple
    units? No

FINANCING
In-house: None
3rd-party: Accounts receivable, equip-
    ment, franchise fee, inventory, pay-
    roll, start-up costs

QUALIFICATIONS
Net worth: $100K
Experience:
    Industry experience
    General business experience

TRAINING
At headquarters: 3 days
At franchisee's location: 7 days
At existing locations: As needed

BUSINESS SUPPORT
Newsletter
Meetings
Toll-free phone line
Grand opening
Field operations/evaluations
Purchasing cooperatives

MARKETING SUPPORT
Co-op advertising
Ad slicks
Regional marketing

MAID-RITE CORP.

Current financial data not available

2951 86th St.
Des Moines, IA 50322
Ph: (515)276-5448, Fax: (515)276-5449
www.maid-rite.com
Loose-meat sandwiches
Began: 1926, Franchising since: 1926
Headquarters size: 15 employees
Franchise department: 10 employees

U.S. franchises: 70
Canadian franchises: 0
Other foreign franchises: 0
Company-owned: 2
Units concentrated in IA, IL, MN, MO,
    NE, WI

Seeking: All U.S.
Focusing on: AZ, CO, IA, IL, IN, KS,
    MI, MN, MO, NE, OH, SD, TX, WI
Seeking in Canada? Yes
Exclusive territories? Yes
Homebased option? No
Kiosk option? No
Employees needed to run franchise: 8 -14
Absentee ownership? Yes

COSTS
Total cost: $129K-336K+
Franchise fee: $15K
Royalty fee: 4%
Term of agreement: 10 years renewable
    for $1K
Franchisees required to buy multiple
    units? No

FINANCING
In-house: None
3rd-party: Equipment, franchise fee

QUALIFICATIONS
Net worth: $350K
Cash liquidity: $100K
Experience:
    General business experience

TRAINING
At headquarters: 1 week to 10 days
At franchisee's location: 1 week
Ongoing online training

BUSINESS SUPPORT
Newsletter
Meetings
Toll-free phone line
Grand opening
Internet
Lease negotiations
Security/safety procedures
Field operations/evaluations
Purchasing cooperatives

MARKETING SUPPORT
Co-op advertising
Ad slicks

MCALISTER'S DELI

Ranked #155 in Entrepreneur Magazine's 2004 Franchise 500

Financial rating: $$$$

731 S. Pear Orchard Rd., #51
Ridgeland, MS 39157
Ph: (888)855-3354
Fax: (601)952-1138
www.mcalistersdeli.com
Southern-style upscale deli
Began: 1989, Franchising since: 1994
Headquarters size: 35 employees
Franchise department: 7 employees

U.S. franchises: 92
Canadian franchises: 0
Other foreign franchises: 0
Company-owned: 23
Units concentrated in AL, AR, FL, GA,
   IN, LA, KY, MI, MO, MS, NC, OH,
   OK, SC, TN, TX, VA

Seeking: All U.S.
Seeking in Canada? No
Exclusive territories? Yes
Homebased option? No
Kiosk option? No
Employees needed to run franchise: 40
Absentee ownership? Yes

COSTS
Total cost: $329.5K-1.4M
Franchise fee: $20K-30K
Royalty fee: 5%
Term of agreement: 10 years renewable
   at no charge
Franchisees required to buy multiple
   units? No

FINANCING
In-house: None
3rd-party: Equipment, franchise fee,
   inventory, start-up costs

QUALIFICATIONS
Net worth: $500K
Cash liquidity: $200K
Experience:
   General business experience

TRAINING
At headquarters: 10 weeks
At franchisee's location: 10 days

BUSINESS SUPPORT
Newsletter
Meetings
Toll-free phone line
Grand opening
Internet
Lease negotiations
Security/safety procedures
Field operations/evaluations
Purchasing cooperatives

MARKETING SUPPORT
Ad slicks
Regional marketing

MR. GOODCENTS FRANCHISE SYSTEMS INC.

Ranked #113 in Entrepreneur Magazine's 2004 Franchise 500

Financial rating: $$$$

8997 Commerce Dr.
De Soto, KS 66018
Ph: (800)648-2368/(913)583-8400
Fax: (913)583-3500
www.mrgoodcents.com
Submarine sandwiches & pastas
Began: 1988, Franchising since: 1990
Headquarters size: 28 employees
Franchise department: 3 employees

U.S. franchises: 161
Canadian franchises: 0
Other foreign franchises: 0
Company-owned: 4
Units concentrated in AZ, KS, MO,
   NE, OK

Seeking: All U.S.
Seeking in Canada? No
Exclusive territories? Yes
Homebased option? No
Kiosk option? No
Employees needed to run franchise: 10
Absentee ownership? Yes

COSTS
Total cost: $77K-242.8K
Franchise fee: $12.5K
Royalty fee: 5%
Term of agreement: 10 years renewable
   for 60% of current franchise fee
Franchisees required to buy multiple
   units? No

FINANCING
In-house: None
3rd-party: Accounts receivable, equipment, franchise fee, inventory, payroll, start-up costs

QUALIFICATIONS
Net worth: $150K+
Cash liquidity: $35K-50K
Experience:
   Industry experience
   General business experience
   Marketing skills

TRAINING
At headquarters: 5 days
At franchisee's location: 20 days
Training workbook

BUSINESS SUPPORT
Newsletter
Meetings
Toll-free phone line
Grand opening
Internet
Lease negotiations
Security/safety procedures
Field operations/evaluations
Purchasing cooperatives

MARKETING SUPPORT
Co-op advertising
Ad slicks
National media campaign

MR. HERO RESTAURANTS

Financial rating: $$$$

5755 Granger Rd., #200
Independence, OH 44131
Ph: (800)837-9599, Fax: (216)398-0707
www.mrhero.com
Specialty sandwiches
Began: 1965, Franchising since: 1970
Headquarters size: 50 employees
Franchise department: 5 employees

U.S. franchises: 110
Canadian franchises: 0
Other foreign franchises: 0
Company-owned: 10
Units concentrated in DC, IL, MI, NC, OH, VA

Seeking: All U.S.
Focusing on: DE, GA, IL, MI, NC, OH, TN, VA
Seeking in Canada? Yes
Exclusive territories? Yes
Homebased option? No
Kiosk option? Yes
Employees needed to run franchise: 10
Absentee ownership? No

COSTS
Total cost: $113K-305K
Kiosk cost: $54.8K-124.8K
Franchise fee: $18K
Royalty fee: 5.5%
Term of agreement: 10 years renewable at no charge
Franchisees required to buy multiple units? No

FINANCING
In-house: Equipment, start-up costs
3rd-party: None

QUALIFICATIONS
Net worth: $150K-250K
Cash liquidity: $30K-75K
Experience:
    Industry experience
    General business experience
    Marketing skills

TRAINING
At headquarters: 4 weeks
At franchisee's location: 1 week

BUSINESS SUPPORT
Newsletter
Meetings
Toll-free phone line
Grand opening
Internet
Lease negotiations
Security/safety procedures
Field operations/evaluations
Purchasing cooperatives

MARKETING SUPPORT
Co-op advertising
Ad slicks
National media campaign
Regional marketing

MR. PITA/PITA DEPOT

Financial rating: $$

48238 Lake Valley Cir.
Shelby, MI 48317
Ph: (866)738-7482
Fax: (586)323-3625
www.mrpita.net
Rolled pita sandwiches, soups, salads
Began: 1993, Franchising since: 1994
Headquarters size: 6 employees
Franchise department: 1 employee

U.S. franchises: 37
Canadian franchises: 0
Other foreign franchises: 0
Company-owned: 0
Units concentrated in all U.S.

Seeking: Midwest
Focusing on: IL, IN, OH
Seeking in Canada? No
Exclusive territories? Yes
Homebased option? No
Kiosk option? Yes
Employees needed to run franchise: 12
Absentee ownership? Yes

COSTS
Total cost: $192K-304K
Kiosk cost: $125K
Franchise fee: $15K
Royalty fee: 3%
Term of agreement: 10 years renewable for $1K
Franchisees required to buy multiple units? No

FINANCING
No financing available

QUALIFICATIONS
Net worth: $200K
Cash liquidity: $75K
Experience:
    Industry experience
    General business experience
    Marketing skills

TRAINING
At headquarters: 6 weeks
At franchisee's location: 4 weeks

BUSINESS SUPPORT
Newsletter
Meetings
Grand opening
Field operations/evaluations
Purchasing cooperatives

MARKETING SUPPORT
Co-op advertising
Ad slicks
Local ads

MY FRIEND'S PLACE

Current financial data not available

106 Hammond Dr.
Atlanta, GA 30328
Ph: (404)843-2803
Fax: (404)843-0371
Sandwiches
Began: 1980, Franchising since: 1990
Headquarters size: 4 employees
Franchise department: 4 employees

U.S. franchises: 28
Canadian franchises: 0
Other foreign franchises: 0
Company-owned: 2
Units concentrated in GA

Seeking: Midwest, South, Southeast
Focusing on: FL, GA, IL, KS, NC, OH,
   SC, TN, TX
Seeking in Canada? No
Exclusive territories? Yes
Homebased option? No
Kiosk option? Info not provided
Employees needed to run franchise: 5
Absentee ownership? Yes

COSTS
Total cost: $97.2K-192.3K
Franchise fee: $20K
Royalty fee: $200-325/wk.
Term of agreement: 15 years renewable
   at no charge
Franchisees required to buy multiple
   units? No

FINANCING
In-house: None
3rd-party: Accounts receivable, equipment, franchise fee, inventory,
   start-up costs

QUALIFICATIONS
Net worth: $100K+
Cash liquidity: $40K
Experience:
   General business experience
   Marketing skills

TRAINING
At headquarters: 2 weeks
At franchisee's location: 2 weeks

BUSINESS SUPPORT
Meetings
Grand opening
Lease negotiations
Field operations/evaluations
Purchasing cooperatives

MARKETING SUPPORT
Info not provided

NEW YORK BURRITO-GOURMET WRAPS

Current financial data not available

300 International Pkwy., #100
Heathrow, FL 32746
Ph: (407)333-8998
Fax: (407)333-8852
www.newyorkburrito.com
Quick-service gourmet wraps &
   smoothies
Began: 1995, Franchising since: 1996
Headquarters size: 9 employees
Franchise department: 6 employees

U.S. franchises: 55
Canadian franchises: 0
Other foreign franchises: 0
Company-owned: 0
Units concentrated in ID, MO, NE,
   OR, UT

Focusing on: MO, NE, UT, WA
Seeking in Canada? Yes
Exclusive territories? Yes
Homebased option? No
Kiosk option? Info not provided
Employees needed to run franchise: 6 -15
Absentee ownership? Yes

COSTS
Total cost: $85K-150K
Franchise fee: $15K
Royalty fee: 7%
Term of agreement: 10 years renewable
   for $1K
Franchisees required to buy multiple
   units? Outside the U.S. only

FINANCING
No financing available

QUALIFICATIONS
Cash liquidity: $30K
Experience:
   General business experience
   Marketing skills

TRAINING
At headquarters: 2 weeks
At franchisee's location: 2 weeks

BUSINESS SUPPORT
Newsletter
Meetings
Toll-free phone line
Grand opening
Internet
Security/safety procedures
Field operations/evaluations
Purchasing cooperatives

MARKETING SUPPORT
Co-op advertising
Ad slicks
Regional marketing

NEW YORK SUBS FRESH DELI

Current financial data not available

100 W. Hoover Ave., #12-14
Mesa, AZ 85210
Ph: (480)632-9884
Fax: (480)503-1850
www.newyorksubs.com
Submarine sandwiches
Began: 2001, Franchising since: 2002
Headquarters size: 8 employees
Franchise department: 4 employees

U.S. franchises: 18
Canadian franchises: 0
Other foreign franchises: 0
Company-owned: 1
Units concentrated in AZ, CO, FL, GA,
    IN, NC, SC, TX, UT

Seeking: All U.S.
Seeking in Canada? Yes
Exclusive territories? Yes
Homebased option? No
Kiosk option? No
Employees needed to run franchise:
    10-20
Absentee ownership? Yes

COSTS
Total cost: $125K-250K
Franchise fee: $15K
Royalty fee: 6%
Term of agreement: 10 years renewable
    at no charge
Franchisees required to buy multiple
    units? No

FINANCING
In-house: None
Equipment, start-up costs

QUALIFICATIONS
Net worth: $150K+
Cash liquidity: $25K-40K
Experience:
    General business experience

TRAINING
At headquarters: 1 week
At franchisee's location: 5 days

BUSINESS SUPPORT
Newsletter
Meetings
Toll-free phone line
Grand opening
Internet
Lease negotiations
Security/safety procedures
Field operations/evaluations
Purchasing cooperatives

MARKETING SUPPORT
Co-op advertising
Ad slicks

OBEE'S FRANCHISE SYSTEMS INC.

Current financial data not available

1777 Tamiami Tr.
Port Charlotte, FL 33948
Ph: (866)623-3462
Fax: (941)625-0052
www.obees.com
Submarine sandwiches, soups, salads
Began: 1995, Franchising since: 2000
Headquarters size: 22 employees
Franchise department: 5 employees

U.S. franchises: 45
Canadian franchises: 0
Other foreign franchises: 1
Company-owned: 0
Units concentrated in all U.S.

Seeking: All U.S.
Seeking in Canada? Yes
Exclusive territories? Yes
Homebased option? No
Kiosk option? No
Employees needed to run franchise: 2-8
Absentee ownership? No

COSTS
Total cost: $135K-168K
Franchise fee: $20K
Royalty fee: 5-6%
Term of agreement: 10 years renewable
    at no charge
Franchisees required to buy multiple
    units? No

FINANCING
In-house: None
3rd-party: Equipment, franchise fee,
    inventory, start-up costs

QUALIFICATIONS
Net worth: $50K
Cash liquidity: $30K-40K
Experience:
    General business experience

TRAINING
At headquarters: 3 weeks
At franchisee's location: 2 weeks
Ongoing training: 2 days per year

BUSINESS SUPPORT
Newsletter
Meetings
Toll-free phone line
Grand opening
Lease negotiations
Purchasing cooperatives

MARKETING SUPPORT
Co-op advertising
Ad slicks

PENN STATION EAST COAST SUBS

Ranked #217 in Entrepreneur Magazine's 2004 Franchise 500   *Financial rating: $$$$*

8276 Beechmont Ave.
Cincinnati, OH 45255
Ph: (513)474-5957, Fax: (513)474-7116
www.penn-station.com
Specialty sandwiches
Began: 1985, Franchising since: 1988
Headquarters size: 9 employees
Franchise department: 2 employees

U.S. franchises: 113
Canadian franchises: 0
Other foreign franchises: 0
Company-owned: 4
Units concentrated in IL, IN, KY, MI,
    MO, NC, OH, SC, TN

Seeking: Midwest, Northeast, South,
    Southeast
Focusing on: IL, IN, KY, MI, MO, NC,
    OH, SC, TN
Seeking in Canada? No
Exclusive territories? Yes
Homebased option? No
Kiosk option? No
Employees needed to run franchise: 12
Absentee ownership? Yes

COSTS
Total cost: $221.9K-383.3K
Franchise fee: $22.5K
Royalty fee: 4-8%
Term of agreement: 5 years renewable
    for $2.5K
Franchisees required to buy multiple
    units? No

FINANCING
No financing available

QUALIFICATIONS
Cash liquidity: $70K-80K+
Experience:
    Industry experience
    General business experience

TRAINING
At headquarters: 3 weeks
At franchisee's location: 1 week

BUSINESS SUPPORT
Newsletter
Meetings
Grand opening
Internet
Lease negotiations
Field operations/evaluations

MARKETING SUPPORT
Ad slicks
National media campaign
Regional marketing

PHILLY CONNECTION

Ranked #426 in Entrepreneur Magazine's 2004 Franchise 500   *Financial rating: $*

120 Interstate N. Pkwy. East, #112
Atlanta, GA 30339-2103
Ph: (800)886-8826/(770)952-6152
Fax: (770)952-3168
www.phillyconnection.com
Cheesesteak sandwiches, hoagies,
    salads, ice cream
Began: 1980, Franchising since: 1987
Headquarters size: 17 employees
Franchise department: 3 employees

U.S. franchises: 107
Canadian franchises: 0
Other foreign franchises: 0
Company-owned: 1
Units concentrated in AL, FL, GA, NC,
    NJ, TN, TX

Seeking: South, Southeast, Southwest
Focusing on: IL, VA
Seeking in Canada? No
Exclusive territories? Yes
Homebased option? No
Kiosk option? No
Employees needed to run franchise: 5
Absentee ownership? Yes

COSTS
Total cost: $130K-198.5K
Franchise fee: $20K
Royalty fee: 6%
Term of agreement: 10 years renewable
    for $5K
Franchisees required to buy multiple
    units? No

FINANCING
In-house: None
3rd-party: Equipment, franchise fee,
    inventory, start-up costs

QUALIFICATIONS
Net worth: $150K
Cash liquidity: $50K
Experience:
    General business experience

TRAINING
At training facility: 80 hours

BUSINESS SUPPORT
Toll-free phone line
Grand opening
Lease negotiations
Field operations/evaluations

MARKETING SUPPORT
Co-op advertising
Ad slicks
Regional marketing

PICKERMAN'S SOUP & SANDWICH SHOP

Current financial data not available

5714 Nordic Dr., #400
Cedar Falls, IA 50613
Ph: (800)273-2172/(319)266-7141
Fax: (319)277-1201
www.pickermans.com
Soups, sandwiches, salads
Began: 1975, Franchising since: 1998
Headquarters size: 9 employees
Franchise department: 4 employees

U.S. franchises: 42
Canadian franchises: 0
Other foreign franchises: 0
Company-owned: 0
Units concentrated in IA, ID, IL, IN,
     KS, MI, MN, MO, OK, TN, WI

Seeking: All U.S.
Focusing on: MI, NE, OH, SD, WI
Seeking in Canada? No
Exclusive territories? Yes
Homebased option? No
Kiosk option? Info not provided
Employees needed to run franchise: 12
Absentee ownership? No

COSTS
Total cost: $174.6K-218.8K
Franchise fee: $15K
Royalty fee: 5%
Term of agreement: 10 years renewable
     at no charge
Franchisees required to buy multiple
     units? No

FINANCING
No financing available

QUALIFICATIONS
Net worth: $250K
Cash liquidity: $50K
Experience:
     Industry experience
     General business experience

TRAINING
At headquarters: 1 week
At franchisee's location: 1 week
At existing location: 2 weeks

BUSINESS SUPPORT
Newsletter
Toll-free phone line
Grand opening
Internet
Security/safety procedures
Field operations/evaluations

MARKETING SUPPORT
Direct marketing program
Internet support

PORT OF SUBS

Ranked #244 in Entrepreneur Magazine's 2004 Franchise 500

Financial rating: $$$$

5365 Mae Anne Ave., #A29
Reno, NV 89523
Ph: (800)245-0245/(775)747-0555
Fax: (775)747-1510
www.portofsubs.com
Submarine sandwiches, salads, catering
Began: 1972, Franchising since: 1985
Headquarters size: 25 employees
Franchise department: 3 employees

U.S. franchises: 123
Canadian franchises: 0
Other foreign franchises: 0
Company-owned: 16
Units concentrated in AZ, CA, ID, NV,
     UT, WA

Seeking: Northwest, Southwest, West
Focusing on: AZ, CA, ID, NV, UT, WA
Seeking in Canada? No
Exclusive territories? Yes
Homebased option? No
Kiosk option? No
Employees needed to run franchise: 6
Absentee ownership? Yes

COSTS
Total cost: $52.5K-219.6K
Franchise fee: $2.5K+/16K
Royalty fee: 5.5%
Term of agreement: 10 years renewable
     at no charge
Franchisees required to buy multiple
     units? No

FINANCING
No financing available

QUALIFICATIONS
Net worth: $200K
Cash liquidity: $50K-60K
Experience:
     People skills
     Good credit history

TRAINING
At headquarters: 16 days
At franchisee's location: 10 days

BUSINESS SUPPORT
Newsletter
Meetings
Toll-free phone line
Grand opening
Internet
Security/safety procedures
Field operations/evaluations
Purchasing cooperatives

MARKETING SUPPORT
Co-op advertising
Ad slicks
National media campaign
Regional marketing

THE QUIZNO'S FRANCHISE CO.

Ranked #3 in Entrepreneur Magazine's 2004 Franchise 500   *Financial rating: $$$$*

1415 Larimer
Denver, CO 80202
Ph: (720)359-3300
Fax: (720)359-3399
www.quiznos.com
Submarine sandwiches, soups, salads
Began: 1981, Franchising since: 1983
Headquarters size: 300 employees
Franchise department: 15 employees

U.S. franchises: 2,179
Canadian franchises: 213
Other foreign franchises: 31
Company-owned: 5
Units concentrated in CA, CO, IL, TX

Seeking: All U.S.
Seeking in Canada? Yes
Exclusive territories? No
Homebased option? No
Kiosk option? No
Employees needed to run franchise:
    10-15
Absentee ownership? Yes

COSTS
Total cost: $208.4K-243.8K
Franchise fee: $25K
Royalty fee: 7%
Term of agreement: 15 years renewable
    for $1K
Franchisees required to buy multiple
    units? No

FINANCING
In-house: None
3rd-party: Equipment, franchise fee,
    inventory, start-up costs

QUALIFICATIONS
Net worth: $125K
Cash liquidity: $60K
Experience:
    Industry experience
    General business experience

TRAINING
At headquarters: 1 week
At regional location: 3 weeks

BUSINESS SUPPORT
Newsletter
Meetings
Toll-free phone line
Grand opening
Internet
Security/safety procedures
Field operations/evaluations
Purchasing cooperatives

MARKETING SUPPORT
Ad slicks
National media campaign
Regional marketing

ROLLERZ

Current financial data not available

7730 E. Greenway Rd., #104
Scottsdale, AZ 85260
Ph: (480)443-0200
Fax: (480)443-1972
www.kahalacorp.com
Rolled sandwiches, salads, soups,
    baked goods, smoothies
Began: 1999, Franchising since: 2000
Headquarters size: 30 employees
Franchise department: 30 employees

U.S. franchises: 8
Canadian franchises: 0
Other foreign franchises: 0
Company-owned: 1

Seeking: All U.S.
Seeking in Canada? Yes
Exclusive territories? Yes
Homebased option? No
Kiosk option? Yes
Employees needed to run franchise: 6
Absentee ownership? Yes

COSTS
Total cost: $162.3K-385.2K
Kiosk cost: $7.5K
Franchise fee: $30K
Royalty fee: 6%
Term of agreement: 10 years renewable
    for 75% of then-current fee
Franchisees required to buy multiple
    units? No

FINANCING
No financing available

QUALIFICATIONS
Experience:
    Industry experience
    General business experience

TRAINING
At headquarters: 1 week
At franchisee's location: 2 weeks

BUSINESS SUPPORT
Newsletter
Meetings
Toll-free phone line
Grand opening
Internet
Security/safety procedures
Field operations/evaluations
Purchasing cooperatives

MARKETING SUPPORT
Co-op advertising
Ad slicks
Regional marketing

ROLY POLY FRANCHISE SYSTEMS LLC

Current financial data not available

13245 Atlantic Ave., #4-399
Jacksonville, FL 32225
Ph: (954)525-4506, Fax: (954)525-9017
www.rolypolyusa.com
Rolled sandwiches
Began: 1992, Franchising since: 1997
Headquarters size: 26 employees
Franchise department: 8 employees

U.S. franchises: 171
Canadian franchises: 0
Other foreign franchises: 0
Company-owned: 0
Units concentrated in AL, CT, FL, GA,
    IL, IN, KS, MO

Seeking: All U.S.
Focusing on: IL, IN, KS, MI, MN, MO,
    NE, OH, PA, TN, WI
Seeking in Canada? No
Exclusive territories? Yes
Homebased option? No
Kiosk option? Info not provided
Employees needed to run franchise:
    12-15
Absentee ownership? Yes

COSTS
Total cost: $55K-120K
Franchise fee: $20K
Royalty fee: 4-6%
Term of agreement: 10 years renewable
    for 50% of current franchise fee
Franchisees required to buy multiple
    units? No

FINANCING
No financing available

QUALIFICATIONS
Net worth: $125K
Cash liquidity: $75K

TRAINING
At headquarters: 1 week
At franchisee's location: 2 weeks
Additional training available

BUSINESS SUPPORT
Newsletter
Meetings
Toll-free phone line
Grand opening
Lease negotiations
Security/safety procedures
Field operations/evaluations

MARKETING SUPPORT
Co-op advertising

SCHLOTZSKY'S

Ranked #124 in Entrepreneur Magazine's 2004 Franchise 500

Financial rating: $$$$

203 Colorado St., #300
Austin, TX 78701
Ph: (800)846-2867
Fax: (512)236-3655
www.schlotzskys.com
Sandwiches, soups, salads, pizza
Began: 1971, Franchising since: 1977
Headquarters size: 240 employees
Franchise department: 4 employees

U.S. franchises: 535
Canadian franchises: 1
Other foreign franchises: 20
Company-owned: 38

Seeking: All U.S.
Seeking in Canada? Yes
Exclusive territories? Yes
Homebased option? No
Kiosk option? No
Employees needed to run franchise:
    20-40
Absentee ownership? No

COSTS
Total cost: $400K-825K
Franchise fee: $25K/30K
Royalty fee: 6%
Term of agreement: 20 years renewable
    for $15K
Franchisees required to buy multiple
    units? No

FINANCING
In-house: None
3rd-party: Accounts receivable, equip-
    ment, franchise fee, inventory, pay-
    roll, start-up costs

QUALIFICATIONS
Net worth: $200K
Cash liquidity: $200K
Experience:
    Industry experience
    General business experience

TRAINING
At franchisee's location: As needed
At corporate training school: 4 weeks

BUSINESS SUPPORT
Newsletter
Meetings
Toll-free phone line
Grand opening
Internet
Security/safety procedures
Field operations/evaluations
Purchasing cooperatives

MARKETING SUPPORT
Co-op advertising
Ad slicks
National media campaign
Regional marketing

THE STEAK ESCAPE
Ranked #403 in Entrepreneur Magazine's 2004 Franchise 500

Financial rating: $$$$

222 Neilston St.
Columbus, OH 43215
Ph: (614)224-0300, Fax: (614)224-6460
www.steakescape.com
Grilled sandwiches, baked potatoes,
    salads
Began: 1982, Franchising since: 1983
Headquarters size: 35 employees
Franchise department: 3 employees

U.S. franchises: 162
Canadian franchises: 0
Other foreign franchises: 0
Company-owned: 4
Units concentrated in AZ, CA, CO,
    OH, TN, TX, WV

Seeking: All U.S.
Seeking in Canada? No
Exclusive territories? Yes
Homebased option? No
Kiosk option? No
Employees needed to run franchise:
    20-25
Absentee ownership? Yes

COSTS
Total cost: $190.2K-1.3M
Franchise fee: $25K
Royalty fee: 5-6%
Term of agreement: 20 years renewable
Franchisees required to buy multiple
    units? No

FINANCING
No financing available

QUALIFICATIONS
Net worth: $350K
Cash liquidity: $100K
Experience:
    General business experience

TRAINING
At headquarters: 3 weeks
At franchisee's location: 1 week

BUSINESS SUPPORT
Newsletter
Toll-free phone line
Grand opening
Internet
Lease negotiations
Field operations/evaluations

MARKETING SUPPORT
Info not provided

SUB STATION II

Current financial data not available

P.O. Drawer 2260
Sumter, SC 29150
Ph: (803)773-4711
Fax: (803)775-2220
www.substationii.com
Submarine & deli-style sandwiches
Began: 1975, Franchising since: 1976
Headquarters size: 7 employees
Franchise department: 2 employees

U.S. franchises: 79
Canadian franchises: 0
Other foreign franchises: 0
Company-owned: 1
Units concentrated in GA, NC, SC

Focusing on: FL, GA, NC, SC
Seeking in Canada? No
Exclusive territories? Yes
Homebased option? No
Kiosk option? No
Employees needed to run franchise: 8
Absentee ownership? Yes

COSTS
Total cost: $75K-150K
Franchise fee: $10.5K
Royalty fee: 4%
Term of agreement: 10 years renewable
    at no charge
Franchisees required to buy multiple
    units? No

FINANCING
In-house: None
3rd-party: Equipment, franchise fee,
    start-up costs

QUALIFICATIONS
Net worth: $150K-175K
Cash liquidity: $55K
Experience:
    General business experience

TRAINING
At headquarters: 7-10 days
At franchisee's location: 7-10 days

BUSINESS SUPPORT
Newsletter
Meetings
Grand opening
Internet
Lease negotiations
Security/safety procedures
Field operations/evaluations

MARKETING SUPPORT
Co-op advertising
Ad slicks
Regional marketing

SUBWAY

Ranked #1 in Entrepreneur Magazine's 2004 Franchise 500   *Financial rating: $$$$*

325 Bic Dr.
Milford, CT 06460
Ph: (800)888-4848/(203)877-4281
Fax: (203)783-7329
www.subway.com
Submarine sandwiches & salads
Began: 1965, Franchising since: 1974
Headquarters size: 600 employees
Franchise department: 20 employees

U.S. franchises: 15,784
Canadian franchises: 1,803
Other foreign franchises: 1,651
Company-owned: 1
Units concentrated in all U.S.

Seeking: All U.S.
Seeking in Canada? Yes
Exclusive territories? No
Homebased option? No
Kiosk option? Yes
Employees needed to run franchise: 6-8
Absentee ownership? No

COSTS
Total cost: $86K-213K
Kiosk cost: $69K-174K
Franchise fee: $12.5K
Royalty fee: 8%
Term of agreement: 20 years renewable
    at no charge
Franchisees required to buy multiple
    units? No

FINANCING
In-house: Franchise fee, equipment
3rd-party: Equipment, franchise fee,
    start-up costs

QUALIFICATIONS
Net worth: $30K-90K
Cash liquidity: $30K-90K

TRAINING
At headquarters: 2 weeks
Training available in Australia, China,
    Germany & Miami, FL

BUSINESS SUPPORT
Newsletter
Meetings
Toll-free phone line
Grand opening
Internet
Lease negotiations
Security/safety procedures
Field operations/evaluations
Purchasing cooperatives

MARKETING SUPPORT
Co-op advertising
Ad slicks
National media campaign
Regional marketing
Local store marketing

TOGO'S EATERY

Ranked #103 in Entrepreneur Magazine's 2004 Franchise 500   *Financial rating: $$$*

14 Pacella Park Dr.
Randolph, MA 02368
Ph: (800)777-9983, Fax: (781)961-4207
www.togos.com
Specialty sandwiches, soups, salads,
    catering
Began: 1972, Franchising since: 1977
Headquarters size: 600 employees
Franchise department: Info not pro-
    vided

U.S. franchises: 442
Canadian franchises: 0
Other foreign franchises: 1
Company-owned: 0
Units concentrated in AZ, CA, CO,
    FL, GA, IL, MA, NJ, NV, PA, UT,
    VA, WA

Seeking: All U.S.
Seeking in Canada? No
Exclusive territories? No
Homebased option? No
Kiosk option? No
Employees needed to run franchise:
    Info not provided
Absentee ownership? No

COSTS
Total cost: $194.2K-559.8K
Franchise fee: $50K
Royalty fee: 5.9%
Term of agreement: 20 years renewable
Franchisees required to buy multiple
    units? No

FINANCING
No financing available

QUALIFICATIONS
Net worth: $300K
Cash liquidity: $200K
Experience:
    Industry experience
    General business experience
    Marketing skills

TRAINING
At headquarters: Varies
At franchisee's location: Varies

BUSINESS SUPPORT
Newsletter
Meetings
Toll-free phone line
Grand opening
Internet
Security/safety procedures
Field operations/evaluations
Purchasing cooperatives

MARKETING SUPPORT
Co-op advertising
Ad slicks
National media campaign
Regional marketing

TUBBY'S SUB SHOPS

Financial rating: $$

35807 Moravian
Clinton Township, MI 48035
Ph: (586)792-2369
Fax: (586)792-4250
www.tubby.com
Submarine & pita sandwiches, salads,
soups, desserts
Began: 1968, Franchising since: 1978
Headquarters size: 15 employees
Franchise department: 2 employees

U.S. franchises: 85
Canadian franchises: 0
Other foreign franchises: 0
Company-owned: 1
Units concentrated in MI

Seeking: All U.S.
Focusing on: MI
Seeking in Canada? No
Exclusive territories? Yes
Homebased option? No
Kiosk option? No
Employees needed to run franchise: 3-4
Absentee ownership? Yes

COSTS
Total cost: $72.9K-243.5K
Franchise fee: $8K/15K
Royalty fee: 6%
Term of agreement: 10 years renewable
Franchisees required to buy multiple
    units? No

FINANCING
In-house: None
3rd-party: Accounts receivable, equip-
    ment, franchise fee, inventory, pay-
    roll, start-up costs

QUALIFICATIONS
Net worth: $250K
Cash liquidity: $50K

TRAINING
Company store: 120 hours+

BUSINESS SUPPORT
Newsletter
Grand opening
Field operations/evaluations
Purchasing cooperatives

MARKETING SUPPORT
Co-op advertising
Ad slicks

WALL STREET DELI

Current financial data not available

5 Dakota Dr., #302
Lake Success, NY 11042
Ph: (516)358-0600
Fax: (516)358-5076
Deli sandwiches, wraps, soups, salads
Began: 1966, Franchising since: 1997
Headquarters size: 50 employees
Franchise department: 3 employees

U.S. franchises: 33
Canadian franchises: 0
Other foreign franchises: 0
Company-owned: 14
Units concentrated in AL, CA, CO, FL,
    GA, IN, KY, MD, NC, TX, UT

Seeking: All U.S.
Seeking in Canada? Yes
Exclusive territories? Yes
Homebased option? No
Kiosk option? Yes
Employees needed to run franchise:
    8-12
Absentee ownership? Yes

COSTS
Total cost: $75.2K-467.4K
Kiosk cost: $75.2K
Franchise fee: $30K
Royalty fee: 5%
Term of agreement: 10 years renewable
    for $5K
Franchisees required to buy multiple
    units? Outside the U.S. only

FINANCING
No financing available

QUALIFICATIONS
Net worth: $250K
Cash liquidity: $75K
Experience:
    General business experience

TRAINING
At headquarters: 2 weeks
At franchisee's location

BUSINESS SUPPORT
Meetings
Grand opening
Internet
Security/safety procedures
Field operations/evaluations
Purchasing cooperatives

MARKETING SUPPORT
Ad slicks
Regional marketing

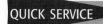

QUICK SERVICE   *Miscellaneous*

CABOTO'S ASSOCIATED FOOD SERVICES INC.

Financial rating: $$

389 N. Industrial, #8
St. George, UT 84770
Ph: (818)845-3339
Fax: (818)688-3979
www.cabotos.com
Food & beverage kiosks/mobile cafes
Began: 1998, Franchising since: 1998
Headquarters size: 6 employees
Franchise department: 2 employees

U.S. franchises: 5
Canadian franchises: 0
Other foreign franchises: 0
Company-owned: 10

Seeking: All U.S.
Seeking in Canada? Yes
Exclusive territories? No
Homebased option? Yes
Kiosk option? Yes
Employees needed to run franchise: 2
Absentee ownership? Yes

COSTS
Total cost: $45K-90K
Kiosk cost: $19.5K-35K
Franchise fee: $15K
Royalty fee: 0
Term of agreement: 10 years renewable
Franchisees required to buy multiple
    units? No

FINANCING
No financing available

QUALIFICATIONS
Net worth: $200K
Cash liquidity: $50K

TRAINING
At headquarters: 3-4 days

BUSINESS SUPPORT
Newsletter
Toll-free phone line
Internet
Field operations/evaluations

MARKETING SUPPORT
Co-op advertising
Ad slicks
Brochures
Booking support

CREPEMAKER

Current financial data not available

14363 S.W. 142nd St.
Miami, FL 33156
Ph: (305)233-1113
Fax: (305)233-2441
www.crepemaker.com
Crepes
Began: 1992, Franchising since: 2001
Headquarters size: 10 employees
Franchise department: 3 employees

U.S. franchises: 4
Canadian franchises: 0
Other foreign franchises: 0
Company-owned: 1

Seeking: All U.S.
Seeking in Canada? No
Exclusive territories? Yes
Homebased option? No
Kiosk option? Yes
Employees needed to run franchise: 4
Absentee ownership? Yes

COSTS
Total cost: $44.3K-61.1K
Franchise fee: $8.6K
Royalty fee: 6%
Term of agreement: 5 years renewable
    for 25% of fee
Franchisees required to buy multiple
    units? Yes

FINANCING
No financing available

QUALIFICATIONS
Net worth: $50K
Cash liquidity: $25K

TRAINING
At headquarters
At franchisee's location

BUSINESS SUPPORT
Field operations/evaluations
Purchasing cooperatives

MARKETING SUPPORT
Co-op advertising

FRESH CITY FRANCHISING

Financial rating: $$$$

145 Rosemary St., #C
Needham, MA 02494
Ph: (781)453-0200
Fax: (781)453-8686
www.freshcity.com
Fresh food restaurants
Began: 1997, Franchising since: 2003
Headquarters size: 14 employees
Franchise department: 1 employee

U.S. franchises: 0
Canadian franchises: 0
Other foreign franchises: 0
Company-owned: 5

Seeking: Northeast, Southeast
Seeking in Canada? No
Exclusive territories? Yes
Homebased option? No
Kiosk option? No
Employees needed to run franchise: 25
Absentee ownership? No

COSTS
Total cost: $696K-1.1M
Franchise fee: $35K
Royalty fee: 5%
Term of agreement: 10 years renewable
    for 25% of then-current fee
Franchisees required to buy multiple
    units? Yes

FINANCING
No financing available

QUALIFICATIONS
Cash liquidity: $2.5M
Experience:
    Industry experience
    General business experience
    Multi-unit development

TRAINING
At headquarters: 9 weeks
At franchisee's location: 1-2 weeks

BUSINESS SUPPORT
Newsletter
Toll-free phone line
Grand opening
Internet
Security/safety procedures
Field operations/evaluations

MARKETING SUPPORT
Ad slicks
Community marketing program

FRULLATI CAFE & BAKERY

Current financial data not available

7730 E. Greenway Rd., #104
Scottsdale, AZ 85260
Ph: (480)443-0200
Fax: (480)443-0972
www.kahalacorp.com
Sandwiches, salads, smoothies, baked
    goods
Began: 1985, Franchising since: 1994
Headquarters size: 30 employees
Franchise department: 30 employees

U.S. franchises: 91
Canadian franchises: 0
Other foreign franchises: 0
Company-owned: 0

Seeking: All U.S.
Seeking in Canada? Yes
Exclusive territories? Yes
Homebased option? No
Kiosk option? Yes
Employees needed to run franchise: 6
Absentee ownership? Yes

COSTS
Total cost: $151K-298K
Kiosk cost: $7.5K
Franchise fee: $20K
Royalty fee: 6%
Term of agreement: 10 years renewable
    for 75% of then-current fee
Franchisees required to buy multiple
    units? Yes

FINANCING
No financing available

QUALIFICATIONS
Experience:
    Industry experience
    General business experience

TRAINING
At headquarters: 1 week
At franchisee's location: 2 weeks

BUSINESS SUPPORT
Newsletter
Meetings
Toll-free phone line
Grand opening
Internet
Security/safety procedures
Field operations/evaluations
Purchasing cooperatives

MARKETING SUPPORT
Co-op advertising
Ad slicks
Regional marketing

GOLDEN KRUST FRANCHISING INC.

Current financial data not available

3958 Park Ave.
Bronx, NY 10457
Ph: (718)583-0360
Fax: (718)583-1883
www.goldenkrustbakery.com
Caribbean-style bakery & restaurant
Began: 1988, Franchising since: 1996
Headquarters size: Info not provided
Franchise department: Info not provided

U.S. franchises: 58
Canadian franchises: 0
Other foreign franchises: 0
Company-owned: 2
Units concentrated in CT, NJ, NY, PA

Focusing on: CT, GA, MA, MD, NC, NJ, NY, PA, VA
Seeking in Canada? No
Exclusive territories? Yes
Homebased option? No
Kiosk option? No
Employees needed to run franchise: 8
Absentee ownership? Info not provided

COSTS
Total cost: $135.2K-325.9K
Franchise fee: $25K
Royalty fee: 3%
Term of agreement: 10 years renewable
Franchisees required to buy multiple units? No

FINANCING
No financing available

QUALIFICATIONS
Net worth: $444K
Cash liquidity: $90K
Experience:
  Industry experience
  General business experience
  Marketing skills

TRAINING
At headquarters: 2 weeks
At franchisee's location: 1 week
Ongoing

BUSINESS SUPPORT
Newsletter
Meetings
Grand opening
Lease negotiations
Field operations/evaluations

MARKETING SUPPORT
Co-op advertising
Ad slicks
National media campaign
Regional marketing

HAPPY JOE'S

Ranked #417 in Entrepreneur Magazine's 2004 Franchise 500

Financial rating: $$$$

2705 Happy Joe Dr.
Bettendorf, IA 52722
Ph: (563)332-8811, Fax: (563)332-5822
www.happyjoes.com
Pizza, pasta, ice cream
Began: 1972, Franchising since: 1973
Headquarters size: 22 employees
Franchise department: 20 employees

U.S. franchises: 56
Canadian franchises: 0
Other foreign franchises: 0
Company-owned: 7
Units concentrated in IA, IL, MN, MO, ND, WI

Seeking: Midwest
Focusing on: FL, IA, KS, MN, MO, ND, NE
Seeking in Canada? No
Exclusive territories? Yes
Homebased option? No
Kiosk option? Yes
Employees needed to run franchise: 15-60
Absentee ownership? Yes

COSTS
Total cost: $79.7K-1.1M
Kiosk cost: $20K-100K
Franchise fee: $1.5K-20K
Royalty fee: 4.5%
Term of agreement: 15 years renewable for 10% of franchise fee
Franchisees required to buy multiple units? No

FINANCING
In-house: None
3rd-party: Accounts receivable, equipment, franchise fee, inventory, payroll, start-up costs

QUALIFICATIONS
Net worth: $250K
Cash liquidity: $100K
Experience:
  Industry experience
  General business experience
  Marketing skills

TRAINING
At headquarters: 1-5 weeks
At franchisee's location: 1-2 weeks
Annual franchise meeting

BUSINESS SUPPORT
Newsletter
Meetings
Grand opening
Internet
Lease negotiations
Security/safety procedures
Field operations/evaluations

MARKETING SUPPORT
Co-op advertising
Ad slicks
Regional marketing

HEALTHY BITES GRILL

Current financial data not available

1761 W. Hillsboro Blvd., #203
Deerfield Beach, FL 33442
Ph: (954)570-5900
Fax: (954)570-5917
www.hexs.com
Quick-service healthy food restaurants
Began: 2001, Franchising since: 2003
Headquarters size: 7 employees
Franchise department: 2 employees

U.S. franchises: 1
Canadian franchises: 0
Other foreign franchises: 0
Company-owned: 1

Seeking: Southeast
Seeking in Canada? No
Exclusive territories? Yes
Homebased option? No
Kiosk option? No
Employees needed to run franchise: 20
Absentee ownership? No

COSTS
Total cost: $258.8K-637K
Franchise fee: $30K
Royalty fee: 4%
Term of agreement: 10 years renewable
   at no charge
Franchisees required to buy multiple
   units? No

FINANCING
No financing available

QUALIFICATIONS
Net worth: $500K
Cash liquidity: $150K
Experience:
   General business experience
   Service-oriented
   Communication skills
   Planning skills

TRAINING
At headquarters: 1 week
At franchisee's location: 10 days
At corporate store: 4 weeks

BUSINESS SUPPORT
Newsletter
Meetings
Toll-free phone line
Grand opening
Internet
Lease negotiations
Field operations/evaluations

MARKETING SUPPORT
Ad slicks
Regional marketing
TV & print ads

ICEBOX/SOUPBOX

Current financial data not available

2943 N. Broadway
Chicago, IL 60657
Ph: (773)935-9800/(773)665-7000
Fax: (773)665-7776
www.jetboxinc.com
Combination soup & frozen dessert
   restaurant
Began: 1995, Franchising since: 1998
Headquarters size: 4 employees
Franchise department: 2 employees

U.S. franchises: 1
Canadian franchises: 0
Other foreign franchises: 0
Company-owned: 1
Units concentrated in IL

Seeking: All U.S.
Focusing on: IL
Seeking in Canada? Yes
Exclusive territories? Yes
Homebased option? No
Kiosk option? No
Employees needed to run franchise: 10
Absentee ownership? Yes

COSTS
Total cost: $69.5K-174.5K
Franchise fee: $14K-20K
Royalty fee: 4%
Term of agreement: 10 years renewable
Franchisees required to buy multiple
   units? No

FINANCING
No financing available

QUALIFICATIONS
Net worth: $250K
Experience:
   General business experience

TRAINING
At headquarters: 1 week
At franchisee's location: 1 week

BUSINESS SUPPORT
Newsletter
Meetings
Toll-free phone line
Grand opening
Internet
Lease negotiations
Security/safety procedures
Field operations/evaluations
Purchasing cooperatives

MARKETING SUPPORT
Co-op advertising
Ad slicks
Regional marketing

MR. GOODBURGER'S

Current financial data not available

1300 Bristol St. N.
Newport Beach, CA 92660
Ph: (866)778-5019/(949)752-7770
Fax: (949)752-7773
www.mrgoodburgers.com
All-meatless burger restaurant
Began: 2001, Franchising since: 2003
Headquarters size: 16 employees
Franchise department: 10 employees

U.S. franchises: 0
Canadian franchises: 0
Other foreign franchises: 0
Company-owned: 1

Seeking: All U.S.
Seeking in Canada? Yes
Exclusive territories? Yes
Homebased option? No
Kiosk option? Yes
Employees needed to run franchise: 4
Absentee ownership? Info not provided

COSTS
Total cost: $155K-210K
Kiosk cost: Varies
Franchise fee: $25K
Royalty fee: 6-8%
Term of agreement: 5 years renewable
    at no charge
Franchisees required to buy multiple
    units? No

FINANCING
No financing available

QUALIFICATIONS
Net worth: $40K
Cash liquidity: $95K-155K
Experience:
    Industry experience
    General business experience

TRAINING
At franchisee's location: 80 hours
Internet refresher courses

BUSINESS SUPPORT
Newsletter
Meetings
Toll-free phone line
Grand opening
Internet
Security/safety procedures
Field operations/evaluations
Purchasing cooperatives

MARKETING SUPPORT
Ad slicks
National media campaign
Regional marketing
Local store media kit

OFF THE GRILL FRANCHISING INC.

Current financial data not available

7110 Crossroads Blvd., #500
Brentwood, TN 37027
Ph: (877)684-2100
Fax: (615)371-1405
www.offthegrill.com
Food take-out & delivery
Began: 1998, Franchising since: 1999
Headquarters size: 12 employees
Franchise department: 8 employees

U.S. franchises: 17
Canadian franchises: 0
Other foreign franchises: 0
Company-owned: 3
Units concentrated in AL, AZ, CA, KS,
    MI, MO, NC, OK, OR, TN

Seeking: All U.S.
Seeking in Canada? No
Exclusive territories? Yes
Homebased option? No
Kiosk option? No
Employees needed to run franchise: 15
Absentee ownership? No

COSTS
Total cost: $275K
Franchise fee: $25K
Royalty fee: 4%
Term of agreement: 10 years renewable
Franchisees required to buy multiple
    units? No

FINANCING
In-house: None
3rd-party: Equipment, inventory

QUALIFICATIONS
Cash liquidity: $50K
Experience:
    General business experience
    Marketing skills

TRAINING
At headquarters: 4-6 weeks

BUSINESS SUPPORT
Newsletter
Meetings
Toll-free phone line
Grand opening
Internet
Security/safety procedures
Field operations/evaluations
Purchasing cooperatives

MARKETING SUPPORT
Co-op advertising
Ad slicks
Regional marketing

ORANGE JULIUS OF AMERICA

Ranked #351 in Entrepreneur Magazine's 2004 Franchise 500

Financial rating: $$$$

P.O. Box 39286
Minneapolis, MN 55439-0286
Ph: (952)830-0200
Fax: (952)830-0450
www.orangejulius.com
Fast food
Began: 1926, Franchising since: 1948
Headquarters size: 320 employees
Franchise department: 33 employees

U.S. franchises: 193
Canadian franchises: 80
Other foreign franchises: 21
Company-owned: 0
Units concentrated in all U.S.

Seeking: All U.S.
Seeking in Canada? Yes
Exclusive territories? No
Homebased option? No
Kiosk option? Yes
Employees needed to run franchise:
    10-20
Absentee ownership? Yes

COSTS

Total cost: $194.2K-380.6K
Kiosk cost: Same as total cost
Franchise fee: $20K-35K
Royalty fee: 6%
Term of agreement: 15 years (or for
    duration of lease) renewable for
    $2.5K
Franchisees required to buy multiple
    units? Outside the U.S. only

FINANCING

No financing available

QUALIFICATIONS

Net worth: $200K
Cash liquidity: $175K
Experience:
    General business experience

TRAINING

At headquarters: 1-1/2 weeks
At franchisee's location: Pre- & post-
    opening
At existing location: 4 days+

BUSINESS SUPPORT

Newsletter
Meetings
Toll-free phone line
Grand opening
Internet
Lease negotiations
Field operations/evaluations
Purchasing cooperatives

MARKETING SUPPORT

Co-op advertising
Ad slicks
Local promotions

ORION FOOD SYSTEMS LLC

Ranked #41 in Entrepreneur Magazine's 2004 Franchise 500

Financial rating: $$$$

2930 W. Maple, P.O. Box 780
Sioux Falls, SD 57101
Ph: (605)336-6961
Fax: (605)336-0141
www.orionfoodsys.com
Fast-food systems for non-traditional
    markets
Began: 1982, Franchising since: 1993
Headquarters size: 300 employees
Franchise department: 40 employees

U.S. franchises: 1,094
Canadian franchises: 17
Other foreign franchises: 0
Company-owned: 1
Units concentrated in all U.S.

Seeking: All U.S.
Seeking in Canada? Yes
Exclusive territories? Yes
Homebased option? No
Kiosk option? Yes
Employees needed to run franchise:
    Info not provided
Absentee ownership? Yes

COSTS

Total cost: $16K-680K
Kiosk cost: Same as total cost
Franchise fee: $2.99K
Royalty fee: 0
Term of agreement: 10 years renewable
    for $1K
Franchisees required to buy multiple
    units? No

FINANCING

In-house: None
Equipment, start-up costs

QUALIFICATIONS

Net worth: $100K
Experience:
    Industry experience
    General business experience
    Marketing skills

TRAINING

At franchisee's location: 5 days

BUSINESS SUPPORT

Newsletter
Meetings
Toll-free phone line
Grand opening
Internet
Security/safety procedures
Field operations/evaluations

MARKETING SUPPORT

Ad slicks
National media campaign
Regional marketing

OZON

Current financial data not available

81 W. Allendale Ave.
Allendale, NJ 07401
Ph: (212)695-0961
Fax: (212)563-9334
www.ozononline.com
Quick-service restaurant
Began: 2002, Franchising since: 2003
Headquarters size: 4 employees
Franchise department: 1 employee

U.S. franchises: 0
Canadian franchises: 0
Other foreign franchises: 0
Company-owned: 1

Seeking: All U.S.
Seeking in Canada? Yes
Exclusive territories? No
Homebased option? No
Kiosk option? Yes
Employees needed to run franchise:
    Info not provided
Absentee ownership? Yes

COSTS
Total cost: $238.5K-629.5K
Kiosk cost: $47.2K-90.5K
Franchise fee: $30K
Royalty fee: 7%
Term of agreement: 10 years renewable
    for $5K
Franchisees required to buy multiple
    units? No

FINANCING
No financing available

QUALIFICATIONS
Net worth: $250K
Cash liquidity: $50K-75K
Experience:
    Industry experience
    General business experience

TRAINING
At headquarters: 2 weeks
At franchisee's location: 1 week

BUSINESS SUPPORT
Newsletter
Meetings
Grand opening
Internet
Lease negotiations
Security/safety procedures
Field operations/evaluations

MARKETING SUPPORT
Co-op advertising
Ad slicks
National media campaign
Regional marketing

STEAK-OUT FRANCHISING INC.

Ranked #459 in Entrepreneur Magazine's 2004 Franchise 500

Financial rating: $$$

6801 Governors Lake Pkwy., #100
Norcross, GA 30071-1130
Ph: (678)533-6000, Fax: (678)291-0222
www.steakout.com
Charbroiled steaks, burgers & chicken
    delivery
Began: 1986, Franchising since: 1988
Headquarters size: 21 employees
Franchise department: 9 employees

U.S. franchises: 62
Canadian franchises: 0
Other foreign franchises: 0
Company-owned: 4
Units concentrated in AL, FL, GA, MS,
    NC, SC, TN

Seeking: Midwest, South, Southeast
Focusing on: AL, AR, CO, FL, GA, IL,
    IN, LA, MD, MO, NC, PA, SC, TN,
    TX, UT, VA
Seeking in Canada? No
Exclusive territories? Yes
Homebased option? No
Kiosk option? No
Employees needed to run franchise: 30
Absentee ownership? Yes

COSTS
Total cost: $221.4K-342.2K
Franchise fee: $25K
Royalty fee: 5%
Term of agreement: 10 years renewable
    for $12.5K
Franchisees required to buy multiple
    units? No

FINANCING
3rd-party: Equipment, franchise fee,
    inventory
Other: Leasehold improvements

QUALIFICATIONS
Net worth: $350K+
Cash liquidity: $75K-100K
Experience:
    General business experience
    Marketing skills
    Industry experience required for
    multi-unit operation

TRAINING
At headquarters: 4 weeks
At franchisee's location: 1-2 weeks

BUSINESS SUPPORT
Newsletter
Meetings
Toll-free phone line
Grand opening
Internet
Security/safety procedures
Field operations/evaluations
Purchasing cooperatives

MARKETING SUPPORT
Ad slicks
National media campaign
Local store marketing

STEAKS TO GO

Current financial data not available

352 W. Northfield Blvd., #4-B
Murfreesboro, TN 37129
Ph: (615)895-8646
Fax: (615)895-8647
www.steaks-to-go.com
Steaks, chicken & sandwich delivery
Began: 1990, Franchising since: 1995
Headquarters size: 3 employees
Franchise department: 2 employees

U.S. franchises: 12
Canadian franchises: 0
Other foreign franchises: 0
Company-owned: 0
Units concentrated in all U.S.

Seeking: All U.S.
Seeking in Canada? Yes
Exclusive territories? Yes
Homebased option? No
Kiosk option? No
Employees needed to run franchise: 10
Absentee ownership? Yes

COSTS
Total cost: $72K-110K
Franchise fee: $24.5K
Royalty fee: $250/wk. or 3%
Term of agreement: 5 years renewable
    at no charge
Franchisees required to buy multiple
    units? No

FINANCING
Area development financing

QUALIFICATIONS
Net worth: $160K
Cash liquidity: $60K

TRAINING
At headquarters: 3 weeks

BUSINESS SUPPORT
Grand opening
Internet
Field operations/evaluations

MARKETING SUPPORT
Info not provided

TAPIOCA EXPRESS INC.

Current financial data not available

1908 Central Ave.
South El Monte, CA 91733
Ph: (888)887-1616/(626)453-0777
Fax: (626)453-0778
www.tapiocaexpress.ws
Tapioca & milk tea beverages
Began: 1999, Franchising since: 2000
Headquarters size: 16 employees
Franchise department: Info not pro-
    vided

U.S. franchises: 43
Canadian franchises: 0
Other foreign franchises: 0
Company-owned: 3

Seeking: All U.S.
Seeking in Canada? Yes
Exclusive territories? Yes
Homebased option? No
Kiosk option? No
Employees needed to run franchise: 5
Absentee ownership? Info not provided

COSTS
Total cost: $62.7K-195.4K
Franchise fee: $7K
Royalty fee: $0.045/cup
Term of agreement: Renewable term at
    $1.2K for two years
Franchisees required to buy multiple
    units? No

FINANCING
No financing available

QUALIFICATIONS
Net worth: $200K
Cash liquidity: $150K
Experience:
    Industry experience
    General business experience
    Marketing skills

TRAINING
At headquarters: 2 days
At company store: 8 days

BUSINESS SUPPORT
Newsletter
Meetings
Grand opening
Internet
Field operations/evaluations
Purchasing cooperatives

MARKETING SUPPORT
Co-op advertising
Ad slicks
National media campaign
Regional marketing

WILD NOODLES

Current financial data not available

8700 E. Via De Ventura, #305
Scottsdale, AZ 85258
Ph: (480)778-9090
Fax: (480)778-1960
www.wildnoodles.com
Noodles, salads, desserts
Began: 2001, Franchising since: 2003
Headquarters size: 10 employees
Franchise department: 10 employees

U.S. franchises: 0
Canadian franchises: 0
Other foreign franchises: 0
Company-owned: 2
Units concentrated in AZ

Seeking: All U.S.
Seeking in Canada? No
Exclusive territories? Yes
Homebased option? No
Kiosk option? No
Employees needed to run franchise:
    12-15
Absentee ownership? Yes

COSTS
Total cost: $273.5K-350K
Franchise fee: $25K
Royalty fee: 5%
Term of agreement: 20 years renewable
    for 50% of current franchise fee
Franchisees required to buy multiple
    units? Yes

FINANCING
In-house: None
3rd-party: Accounts receivable, equipment, franchise fee, inventory, payroll, start-up costs

QUALIFICATIONS
Net worth: $300K
Cash liquidity: $75K-100K
Experience:
    Management experience

TRAINING
At headquarters: 4 weeks
At franchisee's location: 2 weeks

BUSINESS SUPPORT
Meetings
Toll-free phone line
Grand opening
Internet
Lease negotiations
Security/safety procedures
Field operations/evaluations
Purchasing cooperatives

MARKETING SUPPORT
Co-op advertising
Ad slicks
Regional marketing
Menu rollouts

QUICK SERVICE ▸ *Other Franchises*

BEAR ROCK CAFE
*Ranked #440 in Entrepreneur
    Magazine's 2004 Franchise 500*
1225 Crescent Green Dr., #115
Cary, NC 27511
Ph: (919)859-6610
www.bearrockfoods.com
Sandwiches, salads, soups, baked
    goods

DOMINIC'S OF NEW YORK
4101 Cox Rd., #120
Glen Allen, VA 23060
Ph: (888)366-6369
www.domofny.com
Italian sausages, hot dogs, sandwiches

EAST OF CHICAGO PIZZA COMPANY
318 W. Walton
Willard, OH 44890
Ph: (419)935-3033
www.eastofchicago.com
Pizza, subs, pasta

ERIK'S DELICAFE FRANCHISES INC.
365 Coral St.
Santa Cruz, CA 95060
Ph: (831)458-1818
www.eriksdelicafe.com
Soups, sandwiches, salads, baked
    goods

FRANK & STEIN
P.O. Box 20608
Salem, VA 24018
Ph: (540)774-0300
Gourmet hot dogs & draft beers
business experience

GREAT WRAPS INC.
4 Executive Park E., #315
Atlanta, GA 30329
Ph: (888)489-7277/(404)248-9900
www.greatwraps.net
Hot-wrapped sandwiches, cheesesteaks, smoothies

HOGI YOGI
4833 N. Edgewood Dr.
Provo, UT 84604
Ph: (800)653-4581/(801)222-9004
www.hogiyogi.com
Sandwiches, frozen yogurt, smoothies

HOT 'N NOW HAMBURGERS
4205 Charlar Dr.
Holt, MI 48842
Ph: (517)694-4240
Hamburgers, chicken, wraps, fries

LAMAR'S DONUTS
385 Inverness Dr. S., #440
Englewood, CO 80112-5849
Ph: (800)533-7489
www.lamars.com
Donuts, baked goods, specialty coffees

MAMA FU'S NOODLE HOUSE INC.

1935 Peachtree Rd.
Atlanta, GA 30309
Ph: (404)367-5443
www.mamafus.com
Pan-Asian food

MOE'S ITALIAN SANDWICHES

15 Constitution Dr., #140
Bedford, NH 03110
Ph: (603)472-8008
www.moesitaliansandwiches.com
Italian sandwiches

MR. JIMS PIZZA

4276 Kellway Cir.
Addison, TX 75001
Ph: (972)267-5467
www.mrjimspizza.net
Pizza, subs, pasta

MR. SUB

4576 Yonge St., #600
Toronto, ON Canada M2N 6P1
Ph: (416)225-5545
www.mrsub.ca
Subs, sandwiches, wraps, salads, soups,
   specialty drinks

PAPA JOHN'S INT'L. INC.

*Ranked #24 in Entrepreneur Magazine's
   2004 Franchise 500*
2002 Papa John's Blvd.
Louisville, KY 40299
Ph: (888)255-7272/(502)261-4143
www.papajohns.com
Pizza

PIZZA PIZZA LTD.

580 Jarvis St.
Toronto, ON Canada M4Y 2H9
Ph: (800)263-5556/(416)967-1010
www.pizzapizza.ca
Pizza, chicken, sandwiches

PIZZA SCHMIZZA

1055 N.E. 25th, #B
Hillsboro, OR 97124
Ph: (503)640-2328
www.schmizza.com
Pizza

RUBIO'S FRESH MEXICAN GRILL

1902 Wright Pl., #300
Carlsbad, CA 92008
Ph: (760)929-8226
www.rubios.com
Mexican food

SALADWORKS

Eight Tower Bridge, 161 Washington
   St., #225
Conshohocken, PA 19428
Ph: (610)825-3080
www.saladworks.com
Salads, pastas, sandwiches

SALSARITA'S FRESH CANTINA

7301 Carmel Executive Park Dr., #101-A
Charlotte, NC 28226
Ph: (704)540-9447
www.salsaritas.com
Fresh Mex-style cantina

SAVOIA T'GO FRANCHISE LLC

85 Independence Wy.
Chicago Heights, IL 60411
Ph: (800)867-2782
www.savoiatgo.com
Italian carry-out food & catering

SBARRO THE ITALIAN EATERY

401 Broadhollow Rd.
Melville, NY 11787
Ph: (631)715-4150
www.sbarro.com
Quick-service Italian restaurant

STALLONE'S

129 N.W. 13th St., #D-33
Boca Raton, FL 33434
Ph: (800)462-3745
www.stallonesfranchise.com
Italian gourmet sandwich shops

U.S. BISTRO

P.O. Box 20608
Roanoke, VA 24018
Ph: (540)389-8435
Soups, salads wrap sandwiches

WENDY'S

4288 Dublin Granville Rd.
Dublin, OH 43017
Ph: (614)764-6859
www.wendys.com
Quick-service restaurant
Not actively franchising

WINCHELL'S DONUT HOUSE

2223 Wellington Ave., #300
Santa Ana, CA 92701
Ph: (714)565-1800
www.winchells.com
Donuts, muffins, croissants, bagels,
   coffee

WORLD WRAPPS

401 Second Ave. S., #150
Seattle, WA 98104
Ph: (206)233-9727
www.worldwrapps.com
Wraps, smoothies & juices

ZERO'S SUBS

2859 Virginia Beach Blvd., #105
Virginia Beach, VA 23452
Ph: (800)588-0782/(757)486-8338
www.zeros.com
Subs, pizza, wraps

 FOOD/RETAIL · *Candy*

CANDY EXPRESS

Current financial data not available

10480 Little Patuxent Pkwy., #400
Columbia, MD 21044
Ph: (410)964-5500
Fax: (410)964-6404
www.candyexpress.com
Candies, chocolates, gifts
Began: 1988, Franchising since: 1989
Headquarters size: 10 employees
Franchise department: 2 employees

U.S. franchises: 50
Canadian franchises: 0
Other foreign franchises: 30
Company-owned: 0
Units concentrated in all U.S.

Seeking: All U.S.
Seeking in Canada? Yes
Exclusive territories? Yes
Homebased option? No
Kiosk option? Yes
Employees needed to run franchise: 4
Absentee ownership? Yes

COSTS
Total cost: $77.3K-225K
Kiosk cost: $100K
Franchise fee: $35K
Royalty fee: 7%
Term of agreement: 10 years renewable
    for $2K
Franchisees required to buy multiple
    units? Outside the U.S. only

FINANCING
In-house: None
3rd-party: Accounts receivable, equip-
    ment, franchise fee, inventory, pay-
    roll, start-up costs

QUALIFICATIONS
Net worth: $200K
Cash liquidity: $50K

TRAINING
At headquarters: 5 days
At franchisee's location: 5 days

BUSINESS SUPPORT
Newsletter
Meetings
Toll-free phone line
Grand opening
Internet
Security/safety procedures
Field operations/evaluations
Purchasing cooperatives

MARKETING SUPPORT
Co-op advertising
Ad slicks
National media campaign
Regional marketing
Buying service

CHOCOLATE CHOCOLATE CHOCOLATE COMPANY

Current financial data not available

112 N. Kirkwood Rd.
St. Louis, MO 63122
Ph: (314)832-2639
Fax: (314)832-2299
www.chocolatechocolate.com
Chocolates & candies
Began: 1981, Franchising since: 2002
Headquarters size: 13 employees
Franchise department: 4 employees

U.S. franchises: 4
Canadian franchises: 0
Other foreign franchises: 0
Company-owned: 0
Units concentrated in MO

Focusing on: IL, KS, MO
Seeking in Canada? No
Exclusive territories? Yes
Homebased option? No
Kiosk option? No
Employees needed to run franchise: 4
Absentee ownership? Yes

COSTS
Total cost: $185K
Franchise fee: $15K
Royalty fee: 5%
Term of agreement: 5 years renewable for $2K
Franchisees required to buy multiple units? No

FINANCING
No financing available

QUALIFICATIONS
Net worth: $300K
Cash liquidity: $100K
Experience:
 General business experience

TRAINING
At headquarters: 3 weeks & as needed
At franchisee's location: 1 week & as needed

BUSINESS SUPPORT
Meetings
Grand opening
Internet
Lease negotiations
Security/safety procedures
Field operations/evaluations

MARKETING SUPPORT
Ad slicks
Regional marketing

THE FUDGE COMPANY

Current financial data not available

103 Belvedere Ave.
Charlevoix, MI 49720
Ph: (231)547-9941
Fax: (231)547-4612
Homemade fudge & candy
Began: 1978, Franchising since: 1981
Headquarters size: 2 employees
Franchise department: Info not provided

U.S. franchises: 3
Canadian franchises: 0
Other foreign franchises: 12
Company-owned: 1
Units concentrated in AK, AZ, VA

Seeking: All U.S.
Seeking in Canada? Yes
Exclusive territories? Yes
Homebased option? No
Kiosk option? Yes
Employees needed to run franchise: 3
Absentee ownership? Info not provided

COSTS
Total cost: $32K-45K
Franchise fee: $12.5K-15K
Royalty fee: 3%
Term of agreement: Renewable term
Franchisees required to buy multiple units? No

FINANCING
No financing available

QUALIFICATIONS
Net worth: $100K
Cash liquidity: $35K
Experience:
 Retail experience

TRAINING
At headquarters: 2 weeks
At franchisee's location: 3-5 days

BUSINESS SUPPORT
Grand opening
Lease negotiations

MARKETING SUPPORT
Info not provided

FUZZIWIG'S CANDY FACTORY INC.

Financial rating: 0

10 Town Plaza, P.O. Box 222
Durango, CO 81301
Ph: (970)247-2770
Fax: (970)247-2735
www.fuzziwigscandyfactory.com
Self-serve bulk candy, ice cream, small
    toys
Began: 1996, Franchising since: 2002
Headquarters size: 6 employees
Franchise department: 6 employees

U.S. franchises: 7
Canadian franchises: 0
Other foreign franchises: 0
Company-owned: 18
Units concentrated in all U.S.

Seeking: All U.S.
Seeking in Canada? No
Exclusive territories? Yes
Homebased option? No
Kiosk option? Yes
Employees needed to run franchise: 4
Absentee ownership? Yes

COSTS
Total cost: $194.8K-315.1K
Kiosk cost: $100K
Franchise fee: $20K-30K
Royalty fee: 7%
Term of agreement: 10 years renewable
    for $100
Franchisees required to buy multiple
    units? No

FINANCING
No financing available

QUALIFICATIONS
Net worth: $300K
Cash liquidity: $50K
Experience:
    General business experience
    Marketing skills

TRAINING
At headquarters: 7 days
At franchisee's location: 5 days

BUSINESS SUPPORT
Newsletter
Meetings
Toll-free phone line
Internet
Field operations/evaluations
Purchasing cooperatives

MARKETING SUPPORT
Info not provided

GUMBALL GOURMET

Ranked #337 in Entrepreneur Magazine's 2004 Franchise 500

Financial rating: $$$

1460 Commerce Wy.
Idaho Falls, ID 83403-3111
Ph: (866)486-2255
Fax: (208)524-0783
www.gumballgourmet.com
Gumball machine kiosks
Began: 2001, Franchising since: 2001
Headquarters size: 6 employees
Franchise department: 2 employees

U.S. franchises: 197
Canadian franchises: 0
Other foreign franchises: 0
Company-owned: 20
Units concentrated in all U.S.

Seeking: All U.S.
Seeking in Canada? Yes
Exclusive territories? Yes
Homebased option? Yes
Kiosk option? Yes
Employees needed to run franchise: 0
Absentee ownership? Yes

COSTS
Total cost: $24.6K-462.1K
Kiosk cost: $1K-500K
Franchise fee: $17.2K
Royalty fee: $100/mo.
Term of agreement: 5 years renewable
    for $2K
Franchisees required to buy multiple
    units? No

FINANCING
No financing available

QUALIFICATIONS
Net worth: $20K+
Cash liquidity: $20K+
Experience:
    General business experience

TRAINING
At headquarters: 1 day

BUSINESS SUPPORT
Newsletter
Meetings
Toll-free phone line
Lease negotiations
Field operations/evaluations

MARKETING SUPPORT
Internet & kiosk signs

KILWIN'S CHOCOLATES FRANCHISE

Financial rating: $

355 N. Division Rd.
Petoskey, MI 49770
Ph: (231)347-3800/(231)439-0972
Fax: (231)439-6829
www.kilwins.com
Chocolate, fudge, ice cream
Began: 1946, Franchising since: 1982
Headquarters size: Info not provided
Franchise department: Info not provided

U.S. franchises: 45
Canadian franchises: 0
Other foreign franchises: 0
Company-owned: 2

Seeking: Northeast, Southeast
Seeking in Canada? No
Exclusive territories? Yes
Homebased option? No
Kiosk option? No
Employees needed to run franchise: 10
Absentee ownership? Yes

COSTS
Total cost: $209.9K-480K
Franchise fee: $25K
Royalty fee: 5%
Term of agreement: 10 years renewable
at no charge
Franchisees required to buy multiple
units? No

FINANCING
No financing available

QUALIFICATIONS
Net worth: $350K
Cash liquidity: $55K

TRAINING
At headquarters: 1 week
At franchisee's location: 1 week

BUSINESS SUPPORT
Newsletter
Toll-free phone line
Grand opening
Internet
Lease negotiations
Security/safety procedures
Field operations/evaluations

MARKETING SUPPORT
Promotions & marketing assistance

POP CULTURE

Current financial data not available

13289 Lakepoint Blvd.
Belleville, MI 48111
Ph: (877)767-2858
Fax: (734)480-9590
www.popcult.com
Gourmet popcorn & popcorn gifts
Began: 1996, Franchising since: 1999
Headquarters size: 5 employees
Franchise department: 3 employees

U.S. franchises: 3
Canadian franchises: 0
Other foreign franchises: 0
Company-owned: 0
Units concentrated in all U.S.

Seeking: All U.S.
Seeking in Canada? Yes
Exclusive territories? Yes
Homebased option? No
Kiosk option? Info not provided
Employees needed to run franchise: 5
Absentee ownership? No

COSTS
Total cost: $107.5K-160K
Franchise fee: $25K
Royalty fee: 5%
Term of agreement: 5 years renewable
for 25% of current franchise fee
Franchisees required to buy multiple
units? Outside the U.S. only

FINANCING
No financing available

QUALIFICATIONS
Net worth: $150K
Cash liquidity: $50K

TRAINING
At headquarters: 2 weeks
At franchisee's location: 1 week

BUSINESS SUPPORT
Toll-free phone line
Grand opening
Internet
Security/safety procedures
Field operations/evaluations

MARKETING SUPPORT
Info not provided

ROCKY MOUNTAIN CHOCOLATE FACTORY

Ranked #243 in Entrepreneur Magazine's 2004 Franchise 500　　　　*Financial rating: $$$$*

265 Turner Dr.
Durango, CO 81303
Ph: (800)438-7623/(970)259-0554
Fax: (970)259-5895
www.rmcf.com
Chocolate & confections
Began: 1981, Franchising since: 1982
Headquarters size: 130 employees
Franchise department: 5 employees

U.S. franchises: 200
Canadian franchises: 25
Other foreign franchises: 2
Company-owned: 8

Seeking: All U.S.
Seeking in Canada? No
Exclusive territories? No
Homebased option? No
Kiosk option? Yes
Employees needed to run franchise: 7
Absentee ownership? Yes

COSTS
Total cost: $88.5K-430.5K
Franchise fee: $19.5K
Royalty fee: 5%
Term of agreement: 10 years renewable
　　for $100
Franchisees required to buy multiple
　　units? No

FINANCING
No financing available

QUALIFICATIONS
Net worth: $250K
Cash liquidity: $50K

TRAINING
At headquarters: 7 days

BUSINESS SUPPORT
Meetings
Grand opening
Field operations/evaluations

MARKETING SUPPORT
Info not provided

SCHAKOLAD CHOCOLATE FACTORY

Ranked #283 in Entrepreneur Magazine's 2004 Franchise 500　　　　*Financial rating: $$$*

5966 Lake Hurst Dr.
Orlando, FL 32819
Ph: (407)248-6400, Fax: (407)248-1466
www.schakolad.com
Freshly-made European-style choco-
　　lates
Began: 1995, Franchising since: 1999
Headquarters size: 4 employees
Franchise department: 4 employees

U.S. franchises: 15
Canadian franchises: 0
Other foreign franchises: 2
Company-owned: 2
Units concentrated in East Coast,
　　Midwest, South

Seeking: Northeast, South, Southeast
Focusing on: East Coast, Midwest,
　　South
Seeking in Canada? No
Exclusive territories? No
Homebased option? No
Kiosk option? Yes
Employees needed to run franchise: 2-5
Absentee ownership? No

COSTS
Total cost: $93.2K-127.5K
Kiosk cost: $25K-50K
Franchise fee: $30K
Royalty fee: 4%
Term of agreement: 10 years renewable
　　for 20% of current franchise fee
Franchisees required to buy multiple
　　units? No

FINANCING
In-house: None
3rd-party: Equipment, inventory,
　　start-up costs

QUALIFICATIONS
Net worth: $250K
Cash liquidity: $75K
Experience:
　　General business experience
　　Marketing skills

TRAINING
At headquarters: 1-2 weeks
At franchisee's location: 1-2 weeks

BUSINESS SUPPORT
Newsletter
Grand opening
Internet
Field operations/evaluations
Purchasing cooperatives

MARKETING SUPPORT
Co-op advertising
Regional marketing

SOUTH BEND CHOCOLATE CO.

Financial rating: $$$$

3300 W. Sample St.
South Bend, IN 46619
Ph: (574)233-2577, Fax: (574)233-3150
www.sbchocolate.com
Chocolates
Began: 1991, Franchising since: 1997
Headquarters size: 60 employees
Franchise department: 2 employees

U.S. franchises: 11
Canadian franchises: 0
Other foreign franchises: 0
Company-owned: 10
Units concentrated in IN, MI

Seeking: All U.S.
Focusing on: IL, MI, OH
Seeking in Canada? No
Exclusive territories? Yes
Homebased option? No
Kiosk option? Yes
Employees needed to run franchise:
    6-20
Absentee ownership? No

COSTS
Total cost: $74.95K-295.5K
Kiosk cost: $64K-269K
Franchise fee: $35K
Royalty fee: 4%
Term of agreement: 4 years renewable
    for $150
Franchisees required to buy multiple
    units? No

FINANCING
No financing available

QUALIFICATIONS
Net worth: $500K
Cash liquidity: $50K
Experience:
    Overall qualifications considered;
    no specific experience is necessary

TRAINING
At headquarters: 4 days
At franchisee's location: 80 hours
Monthly visits

BUSINESS SUPPORT
Newsletter
Meetings
Toll-free phone line
Grand opening
Internet
Lease negotiations
Field operations/evaluations

MARKETING SUPPORT
Co-op advertising
Ad slicks
Regional marketing

TROPIK SUN FRUIT & NUT

Ranked #463 in Entrepreneur Magazine's 2004 Franchise 500

Financial rating: $$$$

14052 Petronella Dr., #102
Libertyville, IL 60048
Ph: (847)968-4415
Fax: (847)968-5535
www.tropiksun.com
Candy, nuts, popcorn, chocolates,
    drinks, gifts
Began: 1980, Franchising since: 1980
Headquarters size: 8 employees
Franchise department: 3 employees

U.S. franchises: 57
Canadian franchises: 0
Other foreign franchises: 0
Company-owned: 2
Units concentrated in OH, TX

Seeking: All U.S.
Seeking in Canada? Yes
Exclusive territories? No
Homebased option? No
Kiosk option? Yes
Employees needed to run franchise: 6-8
Absentee ownership? Yes

COSTS
Total cost: $93K-214K
Kiosk cost: 93K-161K
Franchise fee: $20K
Royalty fee: 6%
Term of agreement: Based on lease
    term, renewable
Franchisees required to buy multiple
    units? No

FINANCING
3rd-party: Equipment, franchise fee,
    inventory, start-up costs
Other: Build-out costs

QUALIFICATIONS
Net worth: $100K
Cash liquidity: $35K
Experience:
    General business experience

TRAINING
At headquarters: As necessary
At franchisee's location: Upon opening

BUSINESS SUPPORT
Newsletter
Meetings
Grand opening
Lease negotiations
Field operations/evaluations
Purchasing cooperatives

MARKETING SUPPORT
Info not provided

FOOD/RETAIL *Miscellaneous*

BORVIN BEVERAGE

Current financial data not available

1022 King St.
Alexandria, VA 22314
Ph: (703)683-9463
Fax: (703)836-6654
www.borvinbeverage.com
Wine wholesaling & distribution
Began: 1993, Franchising since: 1994
Headquarters size: 4 employees
Franchise department: 1 employee

U.S. franchises: 0
Canadian franchises: 0
Other foreign franchises: 0
Company-owned: 1
Units concentrated in VA

Seeking: All U.S.
Seeking in Canada? No
Exclusive territories? Yes
Homebased option? No
Kiosk option? No
Employees needed to run franchise: 3
Absentee ownership? No

COSTS
Total cost: $50K-60K
Franchise fee: $20K
Royalty fee: 5%
Term of agreement: 10 years renewable
for $2K
Franchisees required to buy multiple
units? No

FINANCING
In-house: Franchise fee
3rd-party: None

QUALIFICATIONS
Net worth: $250K
Cash liquidity: $50K
Experience:
General business experience
Marketing skills
Sales experience

TRAINING
At headquarters: 10 days

BUSINESS SUPPORT
Meetings
Internet
Field operations/evaluations

MARKETING SUPPORT
Promotional materials

CANDY BOUQUET

Ranked # 89 in Entrepreneur Magazine's 2004 Franchise 500

Financial rating: $$$$

423 E. Third St.
Little Rock, AR 72201
Ph: (877)226-3901, Fax: (501)375-9998
www.candybouquet.com
Floral-like designer gifts & gourmet
confections
Began: 1989, Franchising since: 1993
Headquarters size: 30 employees
Franchise department: 30 employees

U.S. franchises: 542
Canadian franchises: 34
Other foreign franchises: 43
Company-owned: 1
Units concentrated in all U.S.

Seeking: All U.S.
Seeking in Canada? Yes
Exclusive territories? Yes
Homebased option? Yes
Kiosk option? Yes
Employees needed to run franchise: 1
Absentee ownership? Yes

COSTS
Total cost: $7.3K-44.1K
Kiosk cost: Same as total cost
Franchise fee: $2K-27K
Royalty fee: 0
Term of agreement: 5 years renewable
for 25% of original fee
Franchisees required to buy multiple
units? No

FINANCING
No financing available

QUALIFICATIONS
Experience:
Industry experience
General business experience
Marketing skills

TRAINING
At headquarters: 5 days

BUSINESS SUPPORT
Newsletter
Meetings
Toll-free phone line
Internet

MARKETING SUPPORT
Co-op advertising
Ad slicks

THE CONNOISSEUR

Financial rating: $$$

201 Torrance Blvd.
Redondo Beach, CA 90277
Ph: (310)374-9768
Fax: (310)372-9097
www.giftsofwine.com
Personalized fine wine gifts
Began: 1972, Franchising since: 1988
Headquarters size: 5 employees
Franchise department: 2 employees

U.S. franchises: 6
Canadian franchises: 0
Other foreign franchises: 0
Company-owned: 1
Units concentrated in CA, CO, IL,
    MO, TX

Seeking: All U.S.
Seeking in Canada? No
Exclusive territories? No
Homebased option? No
Kiosk option? No
Employees needed to run franchise: 2
Absentee ownership? Yes

COSTS
Total cost: $200K-270K
Franchise fee: $29.5K
Royalty fee: 6%
Term of agreement: 10 years renewable
    at no charge
Franchisees required to buy multiple
    units? No

FINANCING
No financing available

QUALIFICATIONS
Net worth: $450K
Cash liquidity: $225K
Experience:
    Marketing skills

TRAINING
At headquarters: 5 days

BUSINESS SUPPORT
Meetings
Toll-free phone line
Grand opening
Internet
Lease negotiations
Security/safety procedures
Field operations/evaluations
Purchasing cooperatives

MARKETING SUPPORT
Co-op advertising
Ad slicks

COOKIES BY DESIGN/COOKIE BOUQUET
Ranked #184 in Entrepreneur Magazine's 2004 Franchise 500

Financial rating: $$$$

1865 Summit Ave., #605
Plano, TX 75074
Ph: (800)945-2665/(972)398-9536
Fax: (972)398-9542
www.cookiesbydesign.com
Cookie arrangements & cookies
Began: 1983, Franchising since: 1987
Headquarters size: 25 employees
Franchise department: 2 employees

U.S. franchises: 249
Canadian franchises: 0
Other foreign franchises: 0
Company-owned: 0
Units concentrated in all U.S.

Seeking: All U.S.
Seeking in Canada? No
Exclusive territories? Yes
Homebased option? No
Kiosk option? No
Employees needed to run franchise: 5
Absentee ownership? No

COSTS
Total cost: $90K-175K
Franchise fee: $12.5K-35K
Royalty fee: 6%
Term of agreement: 5 years renewable
    for 25% of original fee
Franchisees required to buy multiple
    units? No

FINANCING
No financing available

QUALIFICATIONS
Cash liquidity: $30K
Experience:
    General business experience
    Marketing skills

TRAINING
At headquarters: 2 weeks
At franchisee's location: 2 days

BUSINESS SUPPORT
Newsletter
Meetings
Toll-free phone line
Internet
Lease negotiations
Field operations/evaluations

MARKETING SUPPORT
Ad slicks
National media campaign

COOKIES IN BLOOM

Financial rating: $$$

12700 Hillcrest Rd., #251
Dallas, TX 75230
Ph: (972)490-8644
Fax: (972)490-8646
www.cookiesinbloom.com
Cookie gift baskets
Began: 1988, Franchising since: 1992
Headquarters size: 5 employees
Franchise department: 2 employees

U.S. franchises: 20
Canadian franchises: 0
Other foreign franchises: 0
Company-owned: 0
Units concentrated in CA, FL, TX

Seeking: All U.S.
Seeking in Canada? Yes
Exclusive territories? Yes
Homebased option? No
Kiosk option? Yes
Employees needed to run franchise: 4
Absentee ownership? Yes

COSTS
Total cost: $60K-114K
Kiosk cost: $50K
Franchise fee: $19.5K
Royalty fee: 5%
Term of agreement: 5 years renewable
    for $1K
Franchisees required to buy multiple
    units? Outside the U.S. only

FINANCING
No financing available

QUALIFICATIONS
Net worth: $200K
Cash liquidity: $50K
Experience:
    General business experience
    Marketing skills
    Creativity
    Customer service experience
    People skills

TRAINING
At headquarters: 10 days
At franchisee's location: 5 days
On-the-job training at corporate-
    approved shop

BUSINESS SUPPORT
Newsletter
Meetings
Toll-free phone line
Grand opening
Internet
Lease negotiations
Security/safety procedures
Field operations/evaluations
Purchasing cooperatives

MARKETING SUPPORT
Co-op advertising
Ad slicks
Regional marketing

EDIBLE ARRANGEMENTS
Ranked #446 in Entrepreneur Magazine's 2004 Franchise 500

Financial rating: $$$$

1920 Dixwell Ave.
Hamden, CT 06514
Ph: (888)727-4258
Fax: (203)230-0792
www.ediblearrangements.com
Floral-like designs from sculpted
    fresh fruit
Began: 1998, Franchising since: 2000
Headquarters size: 6 employees
Franchise department: 3 employees

U.S. franchises: 15
Canadian franchises: 1
Other foreign franchises: 0
Company-owned: 0
Units concentrated in CA, GA, MA,
    NJ, NY, OH, RI

Seeking: All U.S.
Seeking in Canada? No
Exclusive territories? No
Homebased option? No
Kiosk option? No
Employees needed to run franchise: 4
Absentee ownership? No

COSTS
Total cost: $80.2K-130K
Franchise fee: $25K
Royalty fee: 5%
Term of agreement: 10 years renewable
    for $2K
Franchisees required to buy multiple
    units? No

FINANCING
No financing available

QUALIFICATIONS
Experience:
    General business experience

TRAINING
At headquarters: 1 week
At franchisee's location: 2 weeks
Follow-up at franchisee's location:
    2 days

BUSINESS SUPPORT
Toll-free phone line
Internet
Field operations/evaluations
Purchasing cooperatives

MARKETING SUPPORT
Ad slicks
Regional marketing

THE HONEYBAKED HAM CO. & CAFE

Ranked #258 in Entrepreneur Magazine's 2004 Franchise 500

Financial rating: $$$$

5445 Triangle Pkwy., #400
Norcross, GA 30092
Ph: (800)968-7424
Fax: (678)966-3133
www.honeybakedonline.com
Specialty hams & turkeys, cafe
Began: 1957, Franchising since: 1998
Headquarters size: 125 employees
Franchise department: 12 employees

U.S. franchises: 38
Canadian franchises: 0
Other foreign franchises: 0
Company-owned: 299

Seeking: Midwest, South, Southeast,
   Southwest, West
Seeking in Canada? No
Exclusive territories? Yes
Homebased option? No
Kiosk option? No
Employees needed to run franchise:
   7-10
Absentee ownership? Yes

COSTS

Total cost: $217.3K-340.5K
Franchise fee: $30K
Royalty fee: 5-6%
Term of agreement: 7 years renewable
Franchisees required to buy multiple
   units? No

FINANCING

No financing available

QUALIFICATIONS

Net worth: $300K
Cash liquidity: $100K
Experience:
   Industry experience
   General business experience
   Marketing skills

TRAINING

At headquarters: 2 weeks
At franchisee's location: 1 week

BUSINESS SUPPORT

Newsletter
Meetings
Toll-free phone line
Grand opening
Internet
Security/safety procedures
Field operations/evaluations
Purchasing cooperatives

MARKETING SUPPORT

Co-op advertising
Ad slicks
National media campaign
Regional marketing

INCREDIBLY EDIBLE DELITES INC.

Current financial data not available

One Summit Ave.
Broomall, PA 19008
Ph: (610)353-8844
Fax: (610)359-9188
www.fruitflowers.com
Floral fruit & vegetable bouquets
Began: 1985, Franchising since: 1993
Headquarters size: 4 employees
Franchise department: 4 employees

U.S. franchises: 12
Canadian franchises: 0
Other foreign franchises: 0
Company-owned: 1
Units concentrated in all U.S.

Seeking: All U.S.
Seeking in Canada? No
Exclusive territories? Yes
Homebased option? No
Kiosk option? No
Employees needed to run franchise: 6-8
Absentee ownership? No

COSTS

Total cost: $100K-150K
Franchise fee: $25K
Royalty fee: 4.5%
Term of agreement: Renewable term at
   $5K
Franchisees required to buy multiple
   units? No

FINANCING

No financing available

QUALIFICATIONS

Net worth: $500K
Cash liquidity: $50K
Experience:
   Marketing skills

TRAINING

At headquarters: 3 weeks

BUSINESS SUPPORT

Newsletter
Meetings
Toll-free phone line
Grand opening
Internet
Security/safety procedures
Field operations/evaluations

MARKETING SUPPORT

Co-op advertising
Ad slicks
National media campaign
Regional marketing

M & M MEAT SHOPS LTD.

Current financial data not available

640 Trillium Dr., P.O. Box 2488
Kitchener, ON Canada N2H 6M3
Ph: (519)895-1075
Fax: (519)895-0762
www.mmmeatshops.com
Specialty frozen foods
Began: 1980, Franchising since: 1981
Headquarters size: 90 employees
Franchise department: 5 employees

U.S. franchises: 0
Canadian franchises: 357
Other foreign franchises: 0
Company-owned: 5

Not available in the U.S.
Seeking in Canada? Yes
Exclusive territories? Yes
Homebased option? No
Kiosk option? No
Employees needed to run franchise:
    Info not provided
Absentee ownership? Info not provided

COSTS
Total cost: $300K
Franchise fee: $30K
Royalty fee: 3%
Term of agreement: Renewable term at
    no charge
Franchisees required to buy multiple
    units? No

FINANCING
No financing available

QUALIFICATIONS
Net worth: $300K
Cash liquidity: $150K

TRAINING
At headquarters: 2 weeks
At franchisee's location: 2 weeks

BUSINESS SUPPORT
Newsletter
Meetings
Toll-free phone line
Grand opening
Internet
Lease negotiations
Security/safety procedures
Field operations/evaluations

MARKETING SUPPORT
Co-op advertising
Ad slicks
National media campaign
Regional marketing

THE NEW YORK BUTCHER SHOPPE

Financial rating: 0

1256 Ben Sawyer Blvd., #F
Mt. Pleasant, SC 29464
Ph: (843)856-9675, Fax: (843)856-9387
www.nybutcher.com
Gourmet food stores
Began: 1999, Franchising since: 2003
Headquarters size: 8 employees
Franchise department: 4 employees

U.S. franchises: 2
Canadian franchises: 0
Other foreign franchises: 0
Company-owned: 1
Units concentrated in SC

Seeking: Southeast
Focusing on: FL, GA, NC
Seeking in Canada? No
Exclusive territories? Yes
Homebased option? No
Kiosk option? No
Employees needed to run franchise: 5
Absentee ownership? Yes

COSTS
Total cost: $173.5K-237.5K
Franchise fee: $25K
Royalty fee: 6%
Term of agreement: 10 years renewable
    for 20% of franchise fee
Franchisees required to buy multiple
    units? No

FINANCING
In-house: None
3rd-party: Equipment

QUALIFICATIONS
Net worth: $300K
Cash liquidity: $150K
Experience:
    General business experience

TRAINING
At headquarters: 2 weeks
At franchisee's location: 10 days

BUSINESS SUPPORT
Newsletter
Meetings
Toll-free phone line
Grand opening
Internet
Lease negotiations
Field operations/evaluations
Purchasing cooperatives

MARKETING SUPPORT
Co-op advertising
Ad slicks
Regional marketing

SEATTLE SUTTON'S HEALTHY EATING

Current financial data not available

611 E. Stevenson Rd.
Ottawa, IL 61350
Ph: (888)442-3438
Fax: (815)434-4494
www.sshe.com
Freshly-prepared packaged meals
Began: 1985, Franchising since: 1998
Headquarters size: 145 employees
Franchise department: 4 employees

U.S. franchises: 1
Canadian franchises: 0
Other foreign franchises: 0
Company-owned: 1
Units concentrated in MN

Seeking: All U.S.
Seeking in Canada? Yes
Exclusive territories? Yes
Homebased option? No
Kiosk option? No
Employees needed to run franchise: 20
Absentee ownership? No

COSTS
Total cost: $400K-675K
Franchise fee: $35K
Royalty fee: 5%
Term of agreement: 10 years renewable
    for $10K
Franchisees required to buy multiple
    units? No

FINANCING
No financing available

QUALIFICATIONS
Net worth: $800K
Experience:
    General business experience
    Marketing skills

TRAINING
At headquarters: 1-6 weeks
At franchisee's location: 2 weeks

BUSINESS SUPPORT
Internet
Security/safety procedures
Field operations/evaluations
Purchasing cooperatives

MARKETING SUPPORT
Ad slicks
Regional marketing

24 SEVEN

Ranked #493 in Entrepreneur Magazine's 2004 Franchise 500

Financial rating: $$$$

1601 Cloverfield Blvd., South Tower,
    #2097
Santa Monica, CA 90404
Ph: (310)460-3675, Fax: (310)460-3667
www.24seven.com
Food & beverage vending machines
Began: 1997, Franchising since: 2001
Headquarters size: 10 employees
Franchise department: 2 employees

U.S. franchises: 3
Canadian franchises: 0
Other foreign franchises: 48
Company-owned: 0
Units concentrated in CA

Seeking: South, West
Focusing on: CA, TX
Seeking in Canada? No
Exclusive territories? No
Homebased option? Yes
Kiosk option? No
Employees needed to run franchise:
    Info not provided
Absentee ownership? No

COSTS
Total cost: $223.3K-244.8K
Franchise fee: $150K-300K
Royalty fee: 10%
Term of agreement: 6 years renewable
    at no charge
Franchisees required to buy multiple
    units? No

FINANCING
In-house: Franchise fee, equipment,
    start-up costs
3rd-party: None

QUALIFICATIONS
Experience:
    Industry experience
    General business experience
    Marketing skills
    Physical work capabilities (to
    service machines)

TRAINING
At headquarters: 3 weeks+

BUSINESS SUPPORT
Toll-free phone line
Field operations/evaluations
Purchasing cooperatives

MARKETING SUPPORT
Marketing & sales support
Business development

FOOD/RETAIL   *Other Franchises*

LOGAN FARMS HONEY GLAZED HAMS
10560 Westheimer
Houston, TX 77042
Ph: (713)781-4335
www.loganfarms.com
Honey-glazed hams

WINESTYLES INC.
3000 N.E. 30th Pl.
Ft. Lauderdale, FL 33308
Ph: (561)477-8300
www.winestyles.net
Wine store

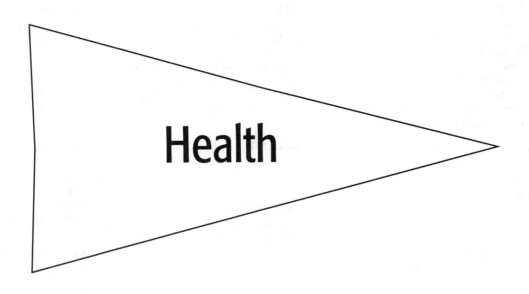

HEALTH | *Nutritional Products*

DISCOUNT SPORT NUTRITION

Financial rating: $$$

1920 Abrams Pkwy., #422
Dallas, TX 75214
Ph: (972)489-7925
Fax: (214)292-8619
www.sportsupplements.com
Sport supplements, vitamins, herbs
Began: 1996, Franchising since: 2000
Headquarters size: 8 employees
Franchise department: 2 employees

U.S. franchises: 4
Canadian franchises: 0
Other foreign franchises: 0
Company-owned: 0
Units concentrated in OK, TX

Seeking: All U.S.
Seeking in Canada? Yes
Exclusive territories? Yes
Homebased option? No
Kiosk option? Yes
Employees needed to run franchise: 2-3
Absentee ownership? Yes

COSTS
Total cost: $82.7K-165.3K
Kiosk cost: Varies
Franchise fee: $25K
Royalty fee: 5%
Term of agreement: 10 years renewable
    for $25K
Franchisees required to buy multiple
    units? No

FINANCING
No financing available

QUALIFICATIONS
Net worth: $62.7K+
Experience:
    General business experience

TRAINING
At headquarters: 2-3 days
At franchisee's location: 3-5 days

BUSINESS SUPPORT
Newsletter
Toll-free phone line
Grand opening
Internet
Lease negotiations
Security/safety procedures
Field operations/evaluations
Purchasing cooperatives

MARKETING SUPPORT
Co-op advertising
Ad slicks
National media campaign
Regional marketing

GNC FRANCHISING INC.

Ranked #58 in Entrepreneur Magazine's 2004 Franchise 500   *Financial rating: $$*

300 6th Ave., 4th Fl.
Pittsburgh, PA 15222
Ph: (800)766-7099/(412)402-7121
Fax: (412)402-7105
www.gncfranchising.com
Vitamin & nutrition stores
Began: 1935, Franchising since: 1988
Headquarters size: 600 employees
Franchise department: 28 employees

U.S. franchises: 1,402
Canadian franchises: 7
Other foreign franchises: 566
Company-owned: 2,531
Units concentrated in all U.S.

Seeking: All U.S.
Seeking in Canada? Yes
Exclusive territories? Yes
Homebased option? No
Kiosk option? No
Employees needed to run franchise: 3-4
Absentee ownership? No

COSTS
Total cost: $132.7K-182K
Franchise fee: $40K/30K
Royalty fee: 6%
Term of agreement: 10 years renewable
   at current franchise fee
Franchisees required to buy multiple
   units? Outside the U.S. only

FINANCING
In-house: Equipment
3rd-party: None

QUALIFICATIONS
Net worth: $100K
Cash liquidity: $65K

TRAINING
At headquarters: 1 week
At franchisee's location: 1 week
At corporate store: 1 week

BUSINESS SUPPORT
Newsletter
Meetings
Toll-free phone line
Grand opening
Internet
Lease negotiations
Security/safety procedures
Field operations/evaluations
Purchasing cooperatives

MARKETING SUPPORT
Co-op advertising
Ad slicks
National media campaign
Regional marketing
Franchise intranet system

MAX MUSCLE

Current financial data not available

1641 S. Sinclair
Anaheim, CA 92806
Ph: (800)530-3539
Fax: (714)978-0273
www.maxmuscle.com
Sports nutrition products &
   fitness gear
Began: 1988, Franchising since: 2001
Headquarters size: 50 employees
Franchise department: 5 employees

U.S. franchises: 91
Canadian franchises: 0
Other foreign franchises: 17
Company-owned: 2
Units concentrated in all U.S.

Seeking: All U.S.
Seeking in Canada? No
Exclusive territories? Yes
Homebased option? No
Kiosk option? No
Employees needed to run franchise:
   2-5
Absentee ownership? Yes

COSTS
Total cost: $58K-112K
Franchise fee: $25K
Royalty fee: 3%
Term of agreement: 5 years renewable
   for $1.5K
Franchisees required to buy multiple
   units? No

FINANCING
No financing available

QUALIFICATIONS
Net worth: $200K
Cash liquidity: $100K
Experience:
   General business experience
   Marketing skills

TRAINING
At headquarters: 2 weeks

BUSINESS SUPPORT
Newsletter
Meetings
Toll-free phone line
Grand opening
Internet
Field operations/evaluations
Purchasing cooperatives

MARKETING SUPPORT
Co-op advertising
Ad slicks
National media campaign
Regional marketing
National advertising

PURIFIED WATER TO GO

Ranked #277 in Entrepreneur Magazine's 2004 Franchise 500　　　　*Financial rating: $$$$*

5160 S. Valley View Blvd., #100
Las Vegas, NV 89118-1778
Ph: (800)976-9283/(702)895-9350
Fax: (702)895-9306
www.watertogo.com
Retail water & nutrition stores
Began: 1992, Franchising since: 1995
Headquarters size: 9 employees
Franchise department: 3 employees

U.S. franchises: 64
Canadian franchises: 0
Other foreign franchises: 0
Company-owned: 0
Units concentrated in all U.S.

Seeking: All U.S.
Seeking in Canada? Yes
Exclusive territories? Yes
Homebased option? No
Kiosk option? Yes
Employees needed to run franchise: 1-2
Absentee ownership? No

COSTS
Total cost: $100K-157K
Kiosk cost: $100K
Franchise fee: $23.5K/29.5K
Royalty fee: 5-6%
Term of agreement: 5 years renewable
　　for $5K
Franchisees required to buy multiple
　　units? Outside the U.S. only

FINANCING
In-house: None
3rd-party: Equipment, inventory,
　　start-up costs

QUALIFICATIONS
Net worth: $150K
Cash liquidity: $25K-40K
Experience:
　　General business experience
　　Customer service skills

TRAINING
At headquarters: 5 days
At franchisee's location: 1-3 days
Annual convention: 4 days

BUSINESS SUPPORT
Newsletter
Meetings
Toll-free phone line
Grand opening
Internet
Purchasing cooperatives

MARKETING SUPPORT
Co-op advertising
Ad slicks
National media campaign

SANGSTER'S HEALTH CENTRES

Current financial data not available

2218 Hanselman Ave.
Saskatoon, SK Canada S7L 6A4
Ph: (306)653-4481
Fax: (306)653-4688
www.sangsters.com
Vitamins, cosmetics, food
Began: 1971, Franchising since: 1978
Headquarters size: 13 employees
Franchise department: 13 employees

U.S. franchises: 0
Canadian franchises: 40
Other foreign franchises: 0
Company-owned: 5
Units concentrated in Canada

Not available in the U.S.
Focusing on: All U.S.
Seeking in Canada? Yes
Exclusive territories? Yes
Homebased option? No
Kiosk option? Yes
Employees needed to run franchise: 2
Absentee ownership? Yes

COSTS
Total cost: $125K-160K
Kiosk cost: $50K
Franchise fee: $25K
Royalty fee: 5%
Term of agreement: 2-5 years renew-
　　able for $5K
Franchisees required to buy multiple
　　units? No

FINANCING
In-house: Franchise fee
3rd-party: Equipment, inventory

QUALIFICATIONS
Net worth: $75K
Cash liquidity: $50K
Experience:
　　General business experience
　　Marketing skills

TRAINING
At headquarters: 2 weeks
At franchisee's location: 1 week

BUSINESS SUPPORT
Newsletter
Meetings
Grand opening
Internet
Field operations/evaluations
Purchasing cooperatives

MARKETING SUPPORT
Co-op advertising
Ad slicks
National media campaign
Regional marketing

HEALTH | *Optical Stores*

MACY'S VISION EXPRESS

Financial rating: $$

16013 S. Desert Foothills Pkwy., #2044
Phoenix, AZ 85048
Ph: (480)460-4676, Fax: (480)460-8225
Optical centers
Began: 1996, Franchising since: 2002
Headquarters size: Info not provided
Franchise department: Info not provided

U.S. franchises: 8
Canadian franchises: 0
Other foreign franchises: 0
Company-owned: 1
Units concentrated in NY, PA & Puerto Rico

Seeking: Northeast, Southeast
Focusing on: FL, GA, MA, NJ, NY
Seeking in Canada? No
Exclusive territories? Yes
Homebased option? No
Kiosk option? Yes
Employees needed to run franchise: 8 -15
Absentee ownership? No

COSTS
Total cost: $350K-685K
Kiosk cost: $250K
Franchise fee: $15K
Royalty fee: 7%
Term of agreement: 10 years renewable
at no charge
Franchisees required to buy multiple
units? No

FINANCING
In-house: None
3rd-party: Accounts receivable, equipment, franchise fee, inventory, payroll, start-up costs

QUALIFICATIONS
Experience:
General business experience

TRAINING
At headquarters: 3 days-2 months
At franchisee's location: 1-2 weeks
Monthly support

BUSINESS SUPPORT
Newsletter
Meetings
Toll-free phone line
Grand opening
Internet
Lease negotiations
Security/safety procedures
Field operations/evaluations
Purchasing cooperatives

MARKETING SUPPORT
Co-op advertising
Ad slicks
Regional marketing

PEARLE VISION INC.
Ranked #47 in Entrepreneur Magazine's 2004 Franchise 500

Financial rating: $$$$

1925 Enterprise Pkwy.
Twinsburg, OH 44087
Ph: (330)486-3365, Fax: (330)486-3425
www.pearlevision.com/franchise
Eye-care centers
Began: 1961, Franchising since: 1980
Headquarters size: 600 employees
Franchise department: 27 employees

U.S. franchises: 499
Canadian franchises: 21
Other foreign franchises: 6
Company-owned: 352
Units concentrated in all U.S. except CA

Seeking: All U.S.
Seeking in Canada? Yes
Exclusive territories? Yes
Homebased option? No
Kiosk option? No
Employees needed to run franchise: 6
Absentee ownership? No

COSTS
Total cost: $115.8K-372.8K
Franchise fee: $10K-30K
Royalty fee: 7%
Term of agreement: 10 years (or for
duration of lease) renewable for
$2.5K
Franchisees required to buy multiple
units? No

FINANCING
In-house: Accounts receivable, equipment, inventory, payroll, start-up
costs
3rd-party: Accounts receivable, equipment, franchise fee, inventory, payroll, start-up costs

QUALIFICATIONS
Net worth: $200K
Cash liquidity: $75K
Experience:
Industry experience
General business experience

TRAINING
At headquarters: 1 week
At franchisee's location: 1 week
At company-owned location: 1 week
(optional)

BUSINESS SUPPORT
Newsletter
Meetings
Toll-free phone line
Grand opening
Internet
Lease negotiations
Security/safety procedures
Field operations/evaluations
Purchasing cooperatives

MARKETING SUPPORT
Co-op advertising
Ad slicks
National media campaign
Regional marketing

HEALTH · *Miscellaneous*

AMERICAN RAMP SYSTEMS

Current financial data not available

202 W. First St.
South Boston, MA 02127-1110
Ph: (800)649-5215, Fax: (617)268-3701
www.americanramp.com
Wheelchair ramps
Began: 1970, Franchising since: 2002
Headquarters size: 25 employees
Franchise department: 4 employees

U.S. franchises: 3
Canadian franchises: 0
Other foreign franchises: 0
Company-owned: 2

Seeking: All U.S.
Focusing on: GA, IL, IN, KY, MD, MI,
    NC, OH, PA, SC, TN, WI, WV
Seeking in Canada? No
Exclusive territories? Yes
Homebased option? Yes
Kiosk option? No
Employees needed to run franchise: 2
Absentee ownership? Yes

COSTS
Total cost: $47K-134K
Franchise fee: $22.5K
Royalty fee: 12%
Term of agreement: 10 years renewable
    for $5K
Franchisees required to buy multiple
    units? No

FINANCING
In-house: Inventory
3rd-party: None

QUALIFICATIONS
Net worth: $200K
Cash liquidity: $150K
Experience:
    Marketing skills

TRAINING
At headquarters: 1 week

BUSINESS SUPPORT
Toll-free phone line
Internet
Field operations/evaluations

MARKETING SUPPORT
Co-op advertising
Ad slicks
National media campaign
Regional marketing

THE DENTIST'S CHOICE

Ranked #321 in Entrepreneur Magazine's 2004 Franchise 500

Financial rating: $$$

774 Mays Blvd., #10-297
Incline Village, NV 89451
Ph: (800)757-1300
www.thedentistschoice.com
Dental handpiece repairs & products
Began: 1992, Franchising since: 1994
Headquarters size: 5 employees
Franchise department: 1 employee

U.S. franchises: 107
Canadian franchises: 3
Other foreign franchises: 0
Company-owned: 0
Units concentrated in all U.S.

Seeking: All U.S.
Seeking in Canada? Yes
Exclusive territories? Yes
Homebased option? Yes
Kiosk option? No
Employees needed to run franchise: 0
Absentee ownership? No

COSTS
Total cost: $25.9K-30.1K
Franchise fee: $17.5K
Royalty fee: 1-5%
Term of agreement: 10 years renewable
    for $1.5K
Franchisees required to buy multiple
    units? No

FINANCING
No financing available

QUALIFICATIONS
Cash liquidity: $25K
Experience:
    Marketing skills

TRAINING
At headquarters: 1 week

BUSINESS SUPPORT
Newsletter
Meetings
Toll-free phone line
Field operations/evaluations
Purchasing cooperatives

MARKETING SUPPORT
Ad slicks
Comprehensive marketing manual

FOOT SOLUTIONS INC.

Ranked #249 in Entrepreneur Magazine's 2004 Franchise 500

Financial rating: $$$$

1730 Cumberland Point Dr., #5
Marietta, GA 30067
Ph: (866)338-2597/(770)955-0099
Fax: (770)951-2666
www.footsolutions.com
Custom insoles & specialty shoes
Began: 2000, Franchising since: 2000
Headquarters size: 10 employees
Franchise department: 10 employees

U.S. franchises: 64
Canadian franchises: 10
Other foreign franchises: 0
Company-owned: 0
Units concentrated in CA, GA

Seeking: All U.S.
Seeking in Canada? Yes
Exclusive territories? Yes
Homebased option? No
Kiosk option? No
Employees needed to run franchise:
    Info not provided
Absentee ownership? Yes

COSTS

Total cost: $171.7K-230.8K
Franchise fee: $25K
Royalty fee: 5%
Term of agreement: 20 years renewable
    for 10% of current franchise fee
Franchisees required to buy multiple
    units? Outside the U.S. only

FINANCING

In-house: None
3rd-party: Accounts receivable, equip-
    ment, inventory, start-up costs

QUALIFICATIONS

Net worth: $200K+
Cash liquidity: $30K-50K
Experience:
    General business experience

TRAINING

At headquarters: 14 days
At franchisee's location: 3-4 days

BUSINESS SUPPORT

Newsletter
Meetings
Toll-free phone line
Grand opening
Internet
Lease negotiations
Security/safety procedures
Field operations/evaluations
Purchasing cooperatives

MARKETING SUPPORT

Co-op advertising
Ad slicks
Regional marketing

HAYES HANDPIECE FRANCHISES INC.

Ranked #291 in Entrepreneur Magazine's 2004 Franchise 500

Financial rating: $$$$

5375 Avenida Encinas
Carlsbad, CA 92008
Ph: (760)602-0521
Fax: (760)602-0505
www.hayeshandpiece.com
Dental handpiece repairs
Began: 1989, Franchising since: 1995
Headquarters size: 20 employees
Franchise department: 3 employees

U.S. franchises: 66
Canadian franchises: 2
Other foreign franchises: 2
Company-owned: 1
Units concentrated in all U.S.

Seeking: All U.S.
Seeking in Canada? Yes
Exclusive territories? Yes
Homebased option? Yes
Kiosk option? No
Employees needed to run franchise: 5
Absentee ownership? No

COSTS

Total cost: $57.2K-59.9K
Franchise fee: $45K
Royalty fee: 3.5-5%
Term of agreement: 10 years renewable
    at no charge
Franchisees required to buy multiple
    units? No

FINANCING

No financing available

QUALIFICATIONS

Experience:
    General business experience
    Marketing skills
    Sales experience

TRAINING

At headquarters: 2 weeks
At franchisee's location: 3 days

BUSINESS SUPPORT

Newsletter
Meetings
Toll-free phone line
Grand opening
Internet
Security/safety procedures
Field operations/evaluations
Purchasing cooperatives

MARKETING SUPPORT

Co-op advertising
Ad slicks
National media campaign
Regional marketing
Call center

MIRACLE EAR INC.

Ranked #44 in Entrepreneur Magazine's 2004 Franchise 500

Financial rating: $$$$

5000 Cheshire Ln. N.
Plymouth, MN 55446
Ph: (800)234-7714/(763)268-4048
Fax: (763)268-4254
www.miracle-ear.com
Hearing aids
Began: 1948, Franchising since: 1983
Headquarters size: 100 employees
Franchise department: 6 employees

U.S. franchises: 952
Canadian franchises: 0
Other foreign franchises: 40
Company-owned: 178
Units concentrated in all U.S.

Seeking: All U.S.
Seeking in Canada? No
Exclusive territories? Yes
Homebased option? No
Kiosk option? No
Employees needed to run franchise: 3
Absentee ownership? No

COSTS
Total cost: $89K-198K
Franchise fee: $30K+
Royalty fee: $49/aid
Term of agreement: 5 years renewable
    for $2K-10K
Franchisees required to buy multiple
    units? Outside the U.S. only

FINANCING
In-house: None
3rd-party: Accounts receivable, equip-
    ment, franchise fee, inventory,
    start-up costs

QUALIFICATIONS
Cash liquidity: $25K
Experience:
    General business experience
    Marketing skills

TRAINING
At headquarters: 2 weeks
At franchisee's location: As needed
Ongoing

BUSINESS SUPPORT
Newsletter
Meetings
Toll-free phone line
Grand opening
Internet
Lease negotiations
Security/safety procedures
Field operations/evaluations
Purchasing cooperatives

MARKETING SUPPORT
Co-op advertising
Ad slicks
National media campaign
Regional marketing

PASSPORT HEALTH INC.

Ranked #316 in Entrepreneur Magazine's 2004 Franchise 500

Financial rating: $$$$

921 E. Fort Ave., #102
Baltimore, MD 21230
Ph: (410)727-0556, Fax: (410)727-0696
www.passporthealthusa.com
Immunization/vaccination service for
    international travelers
Began: 1995, Franchising since: 1997
Headquarters size: 5 employees
Franchise department: 3 employees

U.S. franchises: 39
Canadian franchises: 0
Other foreign franchises: 0
Company-owned: 1
Units concentrated in all U.S.

Seeking: All U.S.
Focusing on: OR, TN, WA
Seeking in Canada? Yes
Exclusive territories? Yes
Homebased option? No
Kiosk option? No
Employees needed to run franchise: 3
Absentee ownership? No

COSTS
Total cost: $52.95K-150K
Franchise fee: $25K-100K
Royalty fee: 7%
Term of agreement: 10 years renewable
    for $3K
Franchisees required to buy multiple
    units? No

FINANCING
No financing available

QUALIFICATIONS
Net worth: $76K-150K
Cash liquidity: $50K
Experience:
    Good business sense

TRAINING
At headquarters: 1 week
At franchisee's location: 3 days

BUSINESS SUPPORT
Newsletter
Meetings
Field operations/evaluations

MARKETING SUPPORT
Web site
National contract negotiations

RELAX THE BACK CORP.

Financial rating: $

17785 Center Court Dr., #250
Cerritos, CA 90703
Ph: (800)290-2225/(562)860-1019
Fax: (562)860-1312
www.relaxtheback.com
Products for back pain relief & pre-
vention
Began: 1984, Franchising since: 1989
Headquarters size: 21 employees
Franchise department: 5 employees

U.S. franchises: 81
Canadian franchises: 2
Other foreign franchises: 0
Company-owned: 8
Units concentrated in CA, FL, MS, NE

Seeking: All U.S.
Seeking in Canada? Yes
Exclusive territories? Yes
Homebased option? No
Kiosk option? No
Employees needed to run franchise: 4-5
Absentee ownership? No

COSTS
Total cost: $192.2K-320.5K
Franchise fee: $25K
Royalty fee: 4%
Term of agreement: 10 years renewable
Franchisees required to buy multiple
units? No

FINANCING
No financing available

QUALIFICATIONS
Net worth: $300K+
Cash liquidity: $120K
Experience:
General business experience

TRAINING
At headquarters: 5 days
At franchisee's location: 2 days
Regional training: 1 day

BUSINESS SUPPORT
Newsletter
Grand opening
Internet
Field operations/evaluations

MARKETING SUPPORT
National media campaign
Regional marketing
CDs

WHEELCHAIR GETAWAYS INC.

Financial rating: $$$$

P.O. Box 605
Versailles, KY 40383
Ph: (800)536-5518/(859)873-4973
Fax: (859)873-8039
www.wheelchairgetaways.com
Wheelchair-accessible van rentals
Began: 1988, Franchising since: 1989
Headquarters size: 5 employees
Franchise department: 2 employees

U.S. franchises: 44
Canadian franchises: 0
Other foreign franchises: 0
Company-owned: 1
Units concentrated in all U.S.

Seeking: All U.S.
Seeking in Canada? Yes
Exclusive territories? Yes
Homebased option? Yes
Kiosk option? No
Employees needed to run franchise: 3
Absentee ownership? Yes

COSTS
Total cost: $40K-108K
Franchise fee: $17.5K
Royalty fee: $550/van/yr.
Term of agreement: 10 years renewable
for $5K
Franchisees required to buy multiple
units? No

FINANCING
No financing available

QUALIFICATIONS
Experience:
Industry experience
General business experience
Marketing skills

TRAINING
At existing location: 2 days

BUSINESS SUPPORT
Newsletter
Meetings
Toll-free phone line
Internet
Field operations/evaluations
Purchasing cooperatives

MARKETING SUPPORT
Co-op advertising
Ad slicks
National media campaign
Regional marketing

WOMEN'S HEALTH BOUTIQUE FRANCHISE SYSTEM INC.

Ranked #460 in Entrepreneur Magazine's 2004 Franchise 500   *Financial rating: $$$$*

12715 Telge Rd.
Cypress, TX 77429
Ph: (888)280-2053/(281)256-4100
Fax: (281)256-4178
www.w-h-b.com
Women's health-care products & services
Began: 1991, Franchising since: 1994
Headquarters size: 155 employees
Franchise department: 100 employees

U.S. franchises: 15
Canadian franchises: 0
Other foreign franchises: 0
Company-owned: 0
Units concentrated in CA, MI, OK, TX

Seeking: All U.S.
Seeking in Canada? No
Exclusive territories? Yes
Homebased option? No
Kiosk option? No
Employees needed to run franchise: 3
Absentee ownership? Yes

COSTS
Total cost: $197.4K-225.4K
Franchise fee: $20.8K
Royalty fee: 4-7%
Term of agreement: 15 years renewable at no charge
Franchisees required to buy multiple units? No

FINANCING
In-house: None
3rd-party: Equipment, franchise fee, inventory, start-up costs

QUALIFICATIONS
Cash liquidity: $49K
Experience:
    General business experience
    Compassionate individual

TRAINING
At headquarters: 3 weeks
At franchisee's location: 1 week

BUSINESS SUPPORT
Newsletter
Meetings
Toll-free phone line
Grand opening
Internet
Field operations/evaluations
Purchasing cooperatives

MARKETING SUPPORT
Mailing & telemarketing services

HEALTH   *Other Franchises*

BEVERLY HILLS WEIGHT LOSS AND WELLNESS
300 International Pkwy., #100
Heathrow, FL 32746
Ph: (407)333-8998
www.beverlyhillsintl.net
Weight-loss clinics & wellness products/services

DGU CENTER FOR ADVANCED HEMORRHOID CARE
1814 Spruce St.
Philadelphia, PA 19103
Ph: (215)545-1300
www.dgucenter.com
Hemorrhoid care centers

DIET CENTER WORLDWIDE INC.
395 Springside Dr.
Akron, OH 44333-2496
Ph: (800)656-3294/(330)665-5861
www.dietcenterworldwide.com
Weight-control programs & products

FORM YOU 3 INT'L. INC.
395 Springside Dr.
Akron, OH 44333
Ph: (800)525-6315
Weight-control programs & products

MEDSONIX
2626 Rainbow Blvd.
Las Vegas, NV 89146
Ph: (800)631-2272
www.medsonix.com
Pain therapy

PHYSICIANS WEIGHT LOSS CENTERS OF AMERICA INC.
395 Springside Dr.
Akron, OH 44333-2496
Ph: (800)205-7887/(330)666-7952
www.pwlc.com
Weight-control programs & products

WATERIA
13120 Barton Rd.
Whittier, CA 90605
Ph: (562)906-1001
www.wateriausa.com
Purified water stores

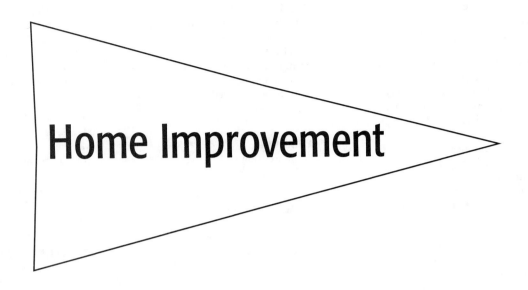

HOME | *Building & Remodeling*

A-1 CONCRETE LEVELING INC.
Ranked #216 in Entrepreneur Magazine's 2004 Franchise 500   *Financial rating: $$$$*

1 Cascade Plaza, #2100
Akron, OH 44308
Ph: (888)675-3835
Fax: (330)253-1261
www.a1concrete.com
Concrete leveling & repair services
Began: 1992, Franchising since: 1993
Headquarters size: 1 employee
Franchise department: 1 employee

U.S. franchises: 48
Canadian franchises: 0
Other foreign franchises: 0
Company-owned: 0
Units concentrated in all U.S.

Seeking: All U.S.
Seeking in Canada? No
Exclusive territories? Yes
Homebased option? Yes
Kiosk option? No
Employees needed to run franchise: 2
Absentee ownership? Yes

COSTS
Total cost: $75K-89K
Franchise fee: $70K
Royalty fee: 6%
Term of agreement: 15 years renewable
Franchisees required to buy multiple
    units? No

FINANCING
In-house: Accounts receivable, franchise
    fee, payroll
3rd-party: Equipment, inventory, start-
    up costs

QUALIFICATIONS
Cash liquidity: $5K
Experience:
    General business experience

TRAINING
At headquarters: 1 week
At franchisee's location: 2 weeks

BUSINESS SUPPORT
Newsletter
Meetings
Toll-free phone line
Internet
Security/safety procedures
Field operations/evaluations

MARKETING SUPPORT
Ad slicks

ABC INC.

Ranked #225 in Entrepreneur Magazine's 2004 Franchise 500

Financial rating: $$$$

3001 Fiechtner Dr.
Fargo, ND 58103
Ph: (800)732-6577/(701)293-5952
Fax: (701)293-3107
www.abcseamless.com
Seamless siding system
Began: 1973, Franchising since: 1978
Headquarters size: 99 employees
Franchise department: 14 employees

U.S. franchises: 127
Canadian franchises: 0
Other foreign franchises: 0
Company-owned: 9
Units concentrated in all U.S.

Seeking: All U.S.
Seeking in Canada? No
Exclusive territories? Yes
Homebased option? Yes
Kiosk option? No
Employees needed to run franchise: 10
Absentee ownership? Info not provided

COSTS
Total cost: $98.1K-212.5K
Franchise fee: $18K
Royalty fee: Varies
Term of agreement: 10 years renewable at no charge
Franchisees required to buy multiple units? No

FINANCING
In-house: None
3rd-party: Equipment

QUALIFICATIONS
Experience:
 Industry experience
 General business experience

TRAINING
At headquarters: Ongoing
At franchisee's location: 3 weeks
Monthly sales training classes at headquarters
Annual & regional meetings: 2-4 days

BUSINESS SUPPORT
Newsletter
Meetings
Toll-free phone line
Internet
Lease negotiations
Security/safety procedures
Field operations/evaluations

MARKETING SUPPORT
Ad slicks
Product development for advertising

ARCHADECK

Ranked #284 in Entrepreneur Magazine's 2004 Franchise 500

Financial rating: $$$$

2112 W. Laburnum Ave., #100
Richmond, VA 23727
Ph: (800)789-3325/(804)353-6999
Fax: (804)358-1878
www.archadeck.com
Wooden decks, screened porches, gazebos
Began: 1980, Franchising since: 1984
Headquarters size: 20 employees
Franchise department: 2 employees

U.S. franchises: 75
Canadian franchises: 2
Other foreign franchises: 2
Company-owned: 1
Units concentrated in Eastern U.S.

Seeking: All U.S.
Seeking in Canada? Yes
Exclusive territories? Yes
Homebased option? Yes
Kiosk option? No
Employees needed to run franchise: 1
Absentee ownership? No

COSTS
Total cost: $29.3K-78.8K
Franchise fee: $28K
Royalty fee: 3.5-5.5%+
Term of agreement: 10 years renewable at no charge
Franchisees required to buy multiple units? Outside the U.S. only

FINANCING
In-house: Franchise fee
3rd-party: Equipment, franchise fee, start-up costs

QUALIFICATIONS
Net worth: $100K
Cash liquidity: $40K-75K
Experience:
 General business experience

TRAINING
At headquarters: 20 days
At franchisee's location: 9 days

BUSINESS SUPPORT
Newsletter
Meetings
Toll-free phone line
Internet
Field operations/evaluations

MARKETING SUPPORT
Ad slicks
National media campaign

COMPAGNIA DEL MOBILE

Current financial data not available

4100 N.E. 2nd Ave., #106
Miami, FL 33137
Ph: (305)573-2500
Fax: (305)573-2555
www.compagniadelmobileusa.com
Kitchen & bathroom cabinets, home
    furnishings
Began: 1939, Franchising since: 2000
Headquarters size: 200 employees
Franchise department: 10 employees

U.S. franchises: 2
Canadian franchises: 0
Other foreign franchises: 60
Company-owned: 3

Seeking: All U.S.
Seeking in Canada? Yes
Exclusive territories? Yes
Homebased option? Yes
Kiosk option? Yes
Employees needed to run franchise: 2
Absentee ownership? Yes

COSTS
Total cost: $60K-130K
Kiosk cost: $30K
Franchise fee: to $5K
Royalty fee: 2%
Term of agreement: 5 years renewable
    for $1K
Franchisees required to buy multiple
    units? Info not provided

FINANCING
In-house: None
3rd-party: Inventory, start-up costs

QUALIFICATIONS
Net worth: $50K
Cash liquidity: $40K
Experience:
    General business experience

TRAINING
At headquarters: 5 days
At franchisee's location: 1 week
At Italian headquarters: 1 week

BUSINESS SUPPORT
Meetings
Grand opening
Internet
Security/safety procedures
Field operations/evaluations

MARKETING SUPPORT
Co-op advertising
Ad slicks
Regional marketing
Catalogs & brochures
POP materials

CONCRETE RAISING OF AMERICA INC.

Current financial data not available

2855 S. 166th St.
New Berlin, WI 53151
Ph: (800)270-0011/(262)827-5000
Fax: (262)827-5005
www.crc1.com
Concrete raising
Began: 1947, Franchising since: 1993
Headquarters size: 10 employees
Franchise department: 2 employees

U.S. franchises: 8
Canadian franchises: 0
Other foreign franchises: 0
Company-owned: 1
Units concentrated in MO, NJ, OK,
    TX, WI

Seeking: All U.S.
Focusing on: AL, AR, AZ, CA, CO, FL,
    GA, ID, MD, MN, MO, MS, NC,
    NM, NV, OR, PA, RI, TN, UT, WA
Seeking in Canada? No
Exclusive territories? Yes
Homebased option? Yes
Kiosk option? No
Employees needed to run franchise: 3-4
Absentee ownership? Yes

COSTS
Total cost: $44.6K-195.6K
Franchise fee: $25K
Royalty fee: 4-8%
Term of agreement: 20 years renewable
    at no charge
Franchisees required to buy multiple
    units? No

FINANCING
In-house: Franchise fee
Equipment, start-up costs

QUALIFICATIONS
Net worth: $50K
Cash liquidity: $4K
Experience:
    General business experience

TRAINING
At headquarters: 10 days
At franchisee's location: As needed
Biannual operator certification by
    franchisor

BUSINESS SUPPORT
Meetings
Toll-free phone line
Security/safety procedures
Field operations/evaluations
Purchasing cooperatives

MARKETING SUPPORT
Co-op advertising

THE CRACK TEAM

Financial rating: 0

11694 Lackland Rd.
St. Louis, MO 63146
Ph: (314)426-0900
Fax: (314)426-0915
www.thecrackteam.com
Foundation crack repair
Began: 1985, Franchising since: 2000
Headquarters size: 20 employees
Franchise department: 5 employees

U.S. franchises: 4
Canadian franchises: 0
Other foreign franchises: 0
Company-owned: 6

Seeking: Midwest, Northeast,
    Northwest, South, Southeast
Focusing on: All U.S.
Seeking in Canada? Yes
Exclusive territories? Yes
Homebased option? Yes
Kiosk option? No
Employees needed to run franchise: 2-4
Absentee ownership? No

COSTS
Total cost: $38.6K-69.1K
Franchise fee: $15K
Royalty fee: 6%
Term of agreement: Info not provided
Franchisees required to buy multiple
    units? No

FINANCING
No financing available

QUALIFICATIONS
Net worth: $100K
Cash liquidity: $60K
Experience:
    General business experience
    Marketing skills

TRAINING
At headquarters: 2 weeks
At franchisee's location: 1 week

BUSINESS SUPPORT
Newsletter
Meetings
Toll-free phone line
Internet
Security/safety procedures
Field operations/evaluations

MARKETING SUPPORT
Ad slicks
Regional marketing

DECKARE SERVICES

Current financial data not available

1501 Raff Rd. S.W.
Canton, OH 44710
Ph: (877)433-2527, Fax: (330)478-0311
www.deckare.com
Exterior wood surface restoration &
    maintenance
Began: 1995, Franchising since: 1997
Headquarters size: 10 employees
Franchise department: 10 employees

U.S. franchises: 27
Canadian franchises: 0
Other foreign franchises: 0
Company-owned: 1
Units concentrated in all U.S.

Seeking: All U.S.
Seeking in Canada? No
Exclusive territories? Yes
Homebased option? Yes
Kiosk option? No
Employees needed to run franchise:
    Info not provided
Absentee ownership? Info not provided

COSTS
Total cost: $25K-40K
Franchise fee: $14.5K
Royalty fee: 5%
Term of agreement: Info not provided
Franchisees required to buy multiple
    units? No

FINANCING
In-house: Franchise fee
3rd-party: None

QUALIFICATIONS
Net worth: $35K
Cash liquidity: $10K
Experience:
    General business experience
    Marketing skills

TRAINING
At headquarters: 4 days
At franchisee's location: 4 days
Ongoing

BUSINESS SUPPORT
Newsletter
Meetings
Toll-free phone line
Grand opening
Internet
Security/safety procedures

MARKETING SUPPORT
Ad slicks
National media campaign

DREAMMAKER BATH & KITCHEN BY WORLDWIDE

Financial rating: 0

1020 N. University Parks Dr.
Waco, TX 76707
Ph: (800)583-9099
Fax: (254)745-2588
www.dreammaker-remodel.com
Bath & kitchen remodeling
Began: 1971, Franchising since: 1972
Headquarters size: 25 employees
Franchise department: 5 employees

U.S. franchises: 99
Canadian franchises: 4
Other foreign franchises: 83
Company-owned: 0
Units concentrated in all U.S.

Seeking: All U.S.
Seeking in Canada? Yes
Exclusive territories? Yes
Homebased option? Yes
Kiosk option? No
Employees needed to run franchise: 5
Absentee ownership? Yes

COSTS
Total cost: $64.1K-113K+
Franchise fee: $27K
Royalty fee: 6-3%
Term of agreement: 10 years renewable
    for $2.5K
Franchisees required to buy multiple
    units? Outside the U.S. only

FINANCING
In-house: Franchise fee
3rd-party: Equipment, inventory,
    start-up costs

QUALIFICATIONS
Net worth: $100K
Cash liquidity: $50K
Experience:
    Industry experience
    General business experience
    Marketing skills
    Remodeling/construction experi-
    ence

TRAINING
At headquarters: 2 weeks
At franchisee's location: As needed
Technical training: 1-2 weeks

BUSINESS SUPPORT
Newsletter
Meetings
Toll-free phone line
Internet
Security/safety procedures
Field operations/evaluations

MARKETING SUPPORT
Co-op advertising
Ad slicks
National media campaign
Regional marketing

DRY-B-LO INT'L. INC.
Ranked #461 in Entrepreneur Magazine's 2004 Franchise 500

Financial rating: $

475 Tribble Gap Rd., #305
Cumming, GA 30040
Ph: (800)437-9256/(770)781-4754
Fax: (770)886-7408
www.dry-b-lo.com
Decorative below-deck aluminum
    rain-carrying ceiling
Began: 1993, Franchising since: 1997
Headquarters size: 5 employees
Franchise department: 2 employees

U.S. franchises: 30
Canadian franchises: 0
Other foreign franchises: 0
Company-owned: 0
Units concentrated in AL, CO, GA, KS,
    MO, NC, PA, SC, TX, VA

Seeking: All U.S.
Seeking in Canada? No
Exclusive territories? Yes
Homebased option? Yes
Kiosk option? No
Employees needed to run franchise: 4-5
Absentee ownership? No

COSTS
Total cost: $44.7K-150.3K
Franchise fee: $15K/25K
Royalty fee: 7.5%
Term of agreement: 5 years renewable
    at no charge
Franchisees required to buy multiple
    units? No

FINANCING
In-house: None
3rd-party: Equipment

QUALIFICATIONS
Net worth: $250K
Cash liquidity: $50K
Experience:
    General business experience

TRAINING
At headquarters: 1 week
At franchisee's location: 3 days
In Denver, CO: 1 week

BUSINESS SUPPORT
Newsletter
Meetings
Toll-free phone line
Grand opening
Internet
Security/safety procedures
Field operations/evaluations
Purchasing cooperatives

MARKETING SUPPORT
Co-op advertising
Ad slicks
National media campaign
Regional marketing
PR campaign

THE GUTTER GUYS

Ranked #416 in Entrepreneur Magazine's 2004 Franchise 500　　　*Financial rating: $$$*

2547 Fire Rd., #E-5
Egg Harbor Township, NJ 08234
Ph: (800)848-8837
www.thegutterguys.com
Seamless gutter manufacturing, instal-
　lation & maintenance
Began: 1988, Franchising since: 2000
Headquarters size: 45 employees
Franchise department: 3 employees

U.S. franchises: 10
Canadian franchises: 0
Other foreign franchises: 0
Company-owned: 4
Units concentrated in DE, MD, NJ, PA

Seeking: Northeast, South, Southeast
Focusing on: CT, FL, GA, MD, PA, VA
Seeking in Canada? No
Exclusive territories? Yes
Homebased option? Yes
Kiosk option? No
Employees needed to run franchise: 7
Absentee ownership? Yes

COSTS
Total cost: $71.6K
Franchise fee: $10K
Royalty fee: 5%
Term of agreement: 10 years renewable
　for 25% of franchise fee
Franchisees required to buy multiple
　units? No

FINANCING
In-house: Equipment, franchise fee
3rd-party: Equipment
Other: Vehicle

QUALIFICATIONS
Cash liquidity: $28K
Experience:
　People skills

TRAINING
At headquarters: 2 weeks
At franchisee's location: 1 week

BUSINESS SUPPORT
Toll-free phone line
Grand opening
Internet
Field operations/evaluations
Purchasing cooperatives

MARKETING SUPPORT
Co-op advertising
Ad slicks
Regional marketing

IDRC FRANCHISING CORP.

Current financial data not available

231 S. Whisman Rd., #C
Mountain View, CA 94041
Ph: (866)315-4372
Fax: (650)965-4326
www.idrcfranchising.com
Interior door replacement services
Began: 1997, Franchising since: 2001
Headquarters size: Info not provided
Franchise department: Info not pro-
　vided

U.S. franchises: 8
Canadian franchises: 0
Other foreign franchises: 0
Company-owned: 1
Units concentrated in CA

Seeking: West
Focusing on: AZ, CA, NV
Seeking in Canada? No
Exclusive territories? Yes
Homebased option? No
Kiosk option? No
Employees needed to run franchise: 4-6
Absentee ownership? No

COSTS
Total cost: $144K-194.5K
Franchise fee: $20K-40K
Royalty fee: 6%
Term of agreement: 10 years renewable
　at no charge
Franchisees required to buy multiple
　units? No

FINANCING
No financing available

QUALIFICATIONS
Net worth: $300K
Cash liquidity: $150K
Experience:
　General business experience
　Marketing skills

TRAINING
At headquarters: Up to 10 days
At franchisee's location: 5 days

BUSINESS SUPPORT
Newsletter
Meetings
Grand opening
Internet
Lease negotiations
Field operations/evaluations
Purchasing cooperatives

MARKETING SUPPORT
Co-op advertising
Regional marketing

KITCHEN SOLVERS INC.

Ranked #224 in Entrepreneur Magazine's 2004 Franchise 500

Financial rating: $$$

401 Jay St.
LaCrosse, WI 54601
Ph: (800)845-6779/(608)791-5516
Fax: (608)784-2917
www.kitchensolvers.com
Kitchen/bath remodeling & cabinet
    refacing, laminate flooring, closet
    organizers
Began: 1982, Franchising since: 1984
Headquarters size: 7 employees
Franchise department: 7 employees

U.S. franchises: 121
Canadian franchises: 8
Other foreign franchises: 0
Company-owned: 0
Units concentrated in all U.S.

Seeking: All U.S.
Seeking in Canada? Yes
Exclusive territories? Yes
Homebased option? Yes
Kiosk option? No
Employees needed to run franchise:
    1-2
Absentee ownership? No

COSTS

Total cost: $35.3K-47.1K
Franchise fee: $19.99K
Royalty fee: 4-6%
Term of agreement: 10 years renewable
    at no charge
Franchisees required to buy multiple
    units? No

FINANCING

In-house: Franchise fee
3rd-party: None

QUALIFICATIONS

Cash liquidity: $35.5K

TRAINING

At headquarters: 6 days

BUSINESS SUPPORT

Newsletter
Meetings
Toll-free phone line
Internet
Field operations/evaluations

MARKETING SUPPORT

Co-op advertising
Ad slicks
National media campaign
Regional marketing

KITCHEN TUNE-UP

Ranked #106 in Entrepreneur Magazine's 2004 Franchise 500

Financial rating: $$$$

813 Circle Dr.
Aberdeen, SD 57401
Ph: (800)333-6385/(605)225-4049
Fax: (605)225-1371
www.kitchentuneup.com
Wood restoration, custom
    cabinets/refacing, floor finishing
Began: 1986, Franchising since: 1988
Headquarters size: 10 employees
Franchise department: 9 employees

U.S. franchises: 297
Canadian franchises: 3
Other foreign franchises: 0
Company-owned: 0
Units concentrated in all U.S.

Seeking: All U.S.
Seeking in Canada? Yes
Exclusive territories? Yes
Homebased option? Yes
Kiosk option? No
Employees needed to run franchise: 3
Absentee ownership? Yes

COSTS

Total cost: $39.6K-46.9K
Franchise fee: $25K/10K
Royalty fee: 4.5-7%
Term of agreement: 10 years renewable
    at no charge
Franchisees required to buy multiple
    units? Outside the U.S. only

FINANCING

In-house: Equipment
3rd-party: Accounts receivable, equip-
    ment, franchise fee, inventory,
    start-up costs

QUALIFICATIONS

Net worth: $50K
Cash liquidity: $15K-25K
Experience:
    General business experience

TRAINING

At headquarters: 8 days
At franchisee's location: Varies
At mentor location: 3-5 days

BUSINESS SUPPORT

Newsletter
Meetings
Toll-free phone line
Grand opening
Internet
Field operations/evaluations
Purchasing cooperatives

MARKETING SUPPORT

Co-op advertising
Ad slicks
National media campaign
Regional marketing
Internet advertising

MARBLELIFE

Current financial data not available

805 W. North Carrier Pkwy., #220
Grand Prairie, TX 75050
Ph: (800)627-4569/(972)623-0500
Fax: (972)623-0220
www.marblelife.com
Marble/stone restoration & preservation services
Began: 1989, Franchising since: 1989
Headquarters size: 14 employees
Franchise department: 12 employees

U.S. franchises: 45
Canadian franchises: 1
Other foreign franchises: 10
Company-owned: 0

Seeking: All U.S.
Seeking in Canada? Yes
Exclusive territories? Yes
Homebased option? Yes
Kiosk option? No
Employees needed to run franchise: 3
Absentee ownership? Yes

COSTS
Total cost: $56K-140K
Franchise fee: $15K+
Royalty fee: 6%
Term of agreement: 10 years renewable
Franchisees required to buy multiple units? No

FINANCING
In-house: None
3rd-party: Equipment, franchise fee, inventory, start-up costs

QUALIFICATIONS
Net worth: $75K
Cash liquidity: $25K
Experience:
    General business experience

TRAINING
At headquarters: 2 weeks

BUSINESS SUPPORT
Newsletter
Meetings
Toll-free phone line
Grand opening
Internet
Security/safety procedures
Field operations/evaluations

MARKETING SUPPORT
Ad slicks

OWENS CORNING BASEMENT FINISHING SYSTEM

Financial rating: $$

One Owens Corning Pkwy.
Toledo, OH 43659
Ph: (419)248-6091, Fax: (419)325-1091
www.owenscorning.com
Basement finishing system
Began: 2000, Franchising since: 2000
Headquarters size: 1,000 employees
Franchise department: Info not provided

U.S. franchises: 51
Canadian franchises: 0
Other foreign franchises: 0
Company-owned: 2
Units concentrated in DE, IN, KY, MA, ME, MI, NH, NY, OH, PA, VA

Seeking: Midwest, Northeast, Northwest, Southeast, West
Focusing on: AL, IA, IL, KS, MN, MO, MT, ND, OR, SD, UT, WA, WI
Seeking in Canada? No
Exclusive territories? Yes
Homebased option? No
Kiosk option? No
Employees needed to run franchise: 20
Absentee ownership? No

COSTS
Total cost: $54K-122K
Franchise fee: $15K+
Royalty fee: 5%
Term of agreement: 5 years renewable for $9K
Franchisees required to buy multiple units? No

FINANCING
No financing available

QUALIFICATIONS
Cash liquidity: $150K
Experience:
    Industry experience
    General business experience
    Sales & marketing skills
    Must have or obtain a general contracting license

TRAINING
At headquarters: 1 week
At franchisee's location: 1-3 days

BUSINESS SUPPORT
Meetings
Internet
Field operations/evaluations
Purchasing cooperatives

MARKETING SUPPORT
Co-op advertising
Ad slicks
National media campaign

PRECISION CONCRETE CUTTING

Financial rating: $$$$

3191 N. Canyon Rd.
Provo, UT 84604
Ph: (801)373-3990, Fax: (801)373-6088
www.pccfranchise.com
Concrete cutting specializing in trip-hazard removal
Began: 1991, Franchising since: 2002
Headquarters size: 15 employees
Franchise department: 4 employees

U.S. franchises: 6
Canadian franchises: 0
Other foreign franchises: 0
Company-owned: 1
Units concentrated in AZ, CA, CO, UT, WA

Seeking: All U.S.
Focusing on: FL, NM, OR, TX, VA
Seeking in Canada? No
Exclusive territories? Yes
Homebased option? Yes
Kiosk option? No
Employees needed to run franchise: 3
Absentee ownership? Yes

COSTS
Total cost: $98K-100K
Franchise fee: $95K
Royalty fee: 4%
Term of agreement: 10 years renewable for $1K
Franchisees required to buy multiple units? No

FINANCING
In-house: None
3rd-party: Accounts receivable, equipment, franchise fee, inventory, payroll, start-up costs

QUALIFICATIONS
Net worth: $70K
Cash liquidity: $40K

TRAINING
At headquarters: 1 week
At franchisee's location: 1 week

BUSINESS SUPPORT
Toll-free phone line
Internet
Security/safety procedures

MARKETING SUPPORT
Regional marketing
Sales leads

RENOVATION PROFESSIONALS

Financial rating: 0

4124 Brookpointe Ct.
Sarasota, FL 34238
Ph: (800)400-6455
www.renovationprofessionals.com
General contracting services for renovation, remodeling & restoration projects
Began: 1997, Franchising since: 2002
Headquarters size: 4 employees
Franchise department: 3 employees

U.S. franchises: 10
Canadian franchises: 0
Other foreign franchises: 0
Company-owned: 1
Units concentrated in Midwest, Southeast

Seeking: Midwest, South, Southeast, Southwest
Focusing on: All U.S.
Seeking in Canada? No
Exclusive territories? Yes
Homebased option? Yes
Kiosk option? No
Employees needed to run franchise: 1
Absentee ownership? Yes

COSTS
Total cost: $28.5K-50.98K
Franchise fee: $24.5K
Royalty fee: 4%
Term of agreement: 5 years renewable at no charge
Franchisees required to buy multiple units? No

FINANCING
No financing available

QUALIFICATIONS
Net worth: $25K
Cash liquidity: $3K

TRAINING
At headquarters: 1 week
At franchisee's location: 1 week
Online training

BUSINESS SUPPORT
Newsletter
Meetings
Toll-free phone line
Grand opening
Internet
Field operations/evaluations
Purchasing cooperatives

MARKETING SUPPORT
Ad slicks
Regional marketing

SYSTEMS PAVING FRANCHISING INC.

Financial rating: $$$$

1600 Dove St., #250
Newport Beach, CA 92660
Ph: (949)263-8300
Fax: (949)263-0452
www.systemspaving.com
Interlocking stone paving system
Began: 1992, Franchising since: 2001
Headquarters size: 15 employees
Franchise department: 8 employees

U.S. franchises: 4
Canadian franchises: 0
Other foreign franchises: 0
Company-owned: 4
Units concentrated in CA, CO, GA,
    IL, MA

Seeking: All U.S.
Seeking in Canada? No
Exclusive territories? Yes
Homebased option? No
Kiosk option? No
Employees needed to run franchise:
    5-15
Absentee ownership? No

COSTS
Total cost: $100K-210.5K
Franchise fee: $39.8K
Royalty fee: 6%
Term of agreement: 10 years renewable
    for $500
Franchisees required to buy multiple
    units? No

FINANCING
No financing available

QUALIFICATIONS
Cash liquidity: $100K-210K
Experience:
    Sales & sales management experi-
    ence

TRAINING
At headquarters: 2 weeks
At franchisee's location: 6 weeks

BUSINESS SUPPORT
Newsletter
Meetings
Toll-free phone line
Internet

MARKETING SUPPORT
Co-op advertising
National media campaign
Regional marketing
Leads

UBUILDIT

Ranked #466 in Entrepreneur Magazine's 2004 Franchise 500

Financial rating: 0

12006 98th Ave. N.E., #200
Kirkland, WA 98034
Ph: (800)992-4357/(425)821-6200
Fax: (425)821-6876
www.ubuildit.com
Construction consulting services
Began: 1988, Franchising since: 1998
Headquarters size: 11 employees
Franchise department: 6 employees

U.S. franchises: 79
Canadian franchises: 0
Other foreign franchises: 0
Company-owned: 0
Units concentrated in all U.S.

Seeking: All U.S.
Seeking in Canada? No
Exclusive territories? No
Homebased option? No
Kiosk option? No
Employees needed to run franchise: 3
Absentee ownership? Yes

COSTS
Total cost: $50K-150K
Franchise fee: $25K
Royalty fee: 5-8%
Term of agreement: 10 years renewable
    for $2K
Franchisees required to buy multiple
    units? No

FINANCING
In-house: None
3rd-party: Accounts receivable, equip-
    ment, franchise fee, payroll, start-
    up costs

QUALIFICATIONS
Net worth: $100K
Cash liquidity: $40K-100K
Experience:
    General business experience
    Marketing skills

TRAINING
At headquarters: 2 weeks
Annual convention: 2 days

BUSINESS SUPPORT
Newsletter
Meetings
Toll-free phone line
Grand opening
Internet
Field operations/evaluations
Purchasing cooperatives

MARKETING SUPPORT
Co-op advertising
Ad slicks
Regional marketing

UNITED STATES SEAMLESS INC.
Ranked #382 in Entrepreneur Magazine's 2004 Franchise 500

Financial rating: $$$$

2001 1st Ave. N.
Fargo, ND 58102
Ph: (701)241-8888, Fax: (701)241-9999
www.usseamless.com
Seamless steel siding, gutters, windows
& doors
Began: 1992, Franchising since: 1992
Headquarters size: 6 employees
Franchise department: 6 employees

U.S. franchises: 88
Canadian franchises: 0
Other foreign franchises: 0
Company-owned: 12
Units concentrated in IA, MN, ND,
NE, SD, WI

Seeking: All U.S.
Seeking in Canada? No
Exclusive territories? Yes
Homebased option? Yes
Kiosk option? No
Employees needed to run franchise: 4
Absentee ownership? Yes

COSTS
Total cost: $49.5K-147K
Franchise fee: $8.5K
Royalty fee: Varies
Term of agreement: 15 years renewable
at no charge
Franchisees required to buy multiple
units? No

FINANCING
In-house: Franchise fee, equipment
3rd-party: Accounts receivable, inventory, payroll, start-up costs

QUALIFICATIONS
Cash liquidity: $4.5K-18.5K
Experience:
Industry experience
General business experience

TRAINING
At headquarters: Ongoing

BUSINESS SUPPORT
Newsletter
Meetings
Toll-free phone line
Internet
Lease negotiations
Security/safety procedures
Field operations/evaluations

MARKETING SUPPORT
Ad slicks
Marketing literature

WOOD RE NEW

Financial rating: $$

220 S. Dysart
Springfield, MO 65802
Ph: (417)833-3303, Fax: (417)833-5479
www.woodrenew.com
Exterior wood restoration system
Began: 1993, Franchising since: 2001
Headquarters size: 11 employees
Franchise department: 3 employees

U.S. franchises: 9
Canadian franchises: 0
Other foreign franchises: 0
Company-owned: 1
Units concentrated in AR, CO, KS,
MO, OK

Seeking: Midwest, South, Southeast
Focusing on: Southeast
Seeking in Canada? No
Exclusive territories? Yes
Homebased option? Yes
Kiosk option? No
Employees needed to run franchise: 1
Absentee ownership? Yes

COSTS
Total cost: $50K
Franchise fee: $25K
Royalty fee: 4%
Term of agreement: 10 years renewable
for $2.5K
Franchisees required to buy multiple
units? No

FINANCING
No financing available

QUALIFICATIONS
Info not provided

TRAINING
At headquarters: 1 week
At franchisee's location: 1 week
Ongoing

BUSINESS SUPPORT
Newsletter
Meetings
Toll-free phone line
Internet

MARKETING SUPPORT
Info not provided

CLOSET & STORAGE CONCEPTS

Financial rating: $$

1000 Laurel Oak Corporate Ctr., #208
Voorhees, NJ 08043
Ph: (856)627-5700, Fax: (856)627-7447
www.closetandstorageconcepts.com
Residential/commercial closet & storage systems
Began: 1987, Franchising since: 2000
Headquarters size: 22 employees
Franchise department: 7 employees

U.S. franchises: 13
Canadian franchises: 0
Other foreign franchises: 0
Company-owned: 1
Units concentrated in all U.S.

Seeking: All U.S.
Seeking in Canada? Yes
Exclusive territories? Yes
Homebased option? No
Kiosk option? No
Employees needed to run franchise: 10-12
Absentee ownership? No

COSTS
Total cost: $145K
Franchise fee: $40K
Royalty fee: 5%
Term of agreement: 10 years renewable at the lesser of current fee
Franchisees required to buy multiple units? No

FINANCING
In-house: None
3rd-party: Accounts receivable, equipment, franchise fee, inventory, payroll, start-up costs

QUALIFICATIONS
Net worth: $100K
Cash liquidity: $50K
Experience:
    Industry experience
    General business experience
    Marketing skills
    Strong sales background

TRAINING
At headquarters: 2 weeks
At franchisee's location: 2 weeks

BUSINESS SUPPORT
Newsletter
Meetings
Toll-free phone line
Grand opening
Internet
Lease negotiations
Security/safety procedures
Field operations/evaluations
Purchasing cooperatives

MARKETING SUPPORT
Co-op advertising
Ad slicks
National media campaign
Regional marketing
In-house graphics department

THE CLOSET FACTORY

Current financial data not available

12800 S. Broadway
Los Angeles, CA 90061
Ph: (310)715-1000
Fax: (310)516-8065
www.closet-factory.com
Custom-closet systems
Began: 1983, Franchising since: 1986
Headquarters size: 120 employees
Franchise department: 20 employees

U.S. franchises: 81
Canadian franchises: 0
Other foreign franchises: 9
Company-owned: 27
Units concentrated in all U.S.

Seeking: All U.S.
Seeking in Canada? Yes
Exclusive territories? Yes
Homebased option? No
Kiosk option? No
Employees needed to run franchise: 6
Absentee ownership? Yes

COSTS
Total cost: $99.5K-196.1K
Franchise fee: $28.5K-39.5K
Royalty fee: 5.75%
Term of agreement: 5 years renewable for $7K
Franchisees required to buy multiple units? Outside the U.S. only

FINANCING
No financing available

QUALIFICATIONS
Cash liquidity: $50K+
Experience:
    General business experience
    Marketing skills
    People skills

TRAINING
At headquarters: 2 weeks
At franchisee's location: 1 month

BUSINESS SUPPORT
Newsletter
Meetings
Toll-free phone line
Grand opening
Internet
Security/safety procedures
Field operations/evaluations
Purchasing cooperatives

MARKETING SUPPORT
Co-op advertising
Ad slicks
National media campaign
Regional marketing
Ad agency
In-house graphics

CLOSETS BY DESIGN FRANCHISING
Ranked #315 in Entrepreneur Magazine's 2004 Franchise 500

Financial rating: $$$$

13151 S. Western Ave.
Gardena, CA 90249
Ph: (310)965-2040
Fax: (310)527-8955
www.closets-by-design.com
Custom closet & home/office organizational system
Began: 1982, Franchising since: 1998
Headquarters size: 120 employees
Franchise department: 12 employees

U.S. franchises: 36
Canadian franchises: 0
Other foreign franchises: 0
Company-owned: 8
Units concentrated in all U.S.

Seeking: All U.S.
Seeking in Canada? Yes
Exclusive territories? Yes
Homebased option? No
Kiosk option? No
Employees needed to run franchise: 5
Absentee ownership? No

COSTS
Total cost: $88.5K-275.9K
Franchise fee: $19.5K-34.9K
Royalty fee: 6%
Term of agreement: 5 years renewable for $5K (waived if meet sales requirement)
Franchisees required to buy multiple units? Yes

FINANCING
In-house: None
3rd-party: Equipment, franchise fee, inventory, start-up costs

QUALIFICATIONS
Cash liquidity: $50K-80K
Experience:
    General business experience
    Marketing skills

TRAINING
At headquarters: 3 weeks
At franchisee's location: 3 weeks

BUSINESS SUPPORT
Newsletter
Meetings
Toll-free phone line
Grand opening
Internet
Security/safety procedures
Field operations/evaluations
Purchasing cooperatives

MARKETING SUPPORT
Co-op advertising
Ad slicks
National media campaign
Regional marketing
In-house art department

HOME ◄ *Decorating Products*

BLIND MAN OF AMERICA

Financial rating: 0

606 Freemont Cir.
Colorado Springs, CO 80919
Ph: (800)547-9889, Fax: (719)272-4105
www.blindmanofamerica.com
Mobile window coverings
Began: 1991, Franchising since: 1996
Headquarters size: 3 employees
Franchise department: 3 employees

U.S. franchises: 7
Canadian franchises: 0
Other foreign franchises: 0
Company-owned: 1
Units concentrated in CO

Seeking: Midwest, Southwest, West
Focusing on: AZ, CA, CO, ID, KS, MT, NE, NM, NV, OK, TX, UT, WA, WY
Seeking in Canada? No
Exclusive territories? Info not provided
Homebased option? Yes
Kiosk option? No
Employees needed to run franchise: 0-1
Absentee ownership? No

COSTS
Total cost: $26.8K-50.4K
Franchise fee: $15K
Royalty fee: 4.3%
Term of agreement: 5 years renewable for $1K
Franchisees required to buy multiple units? No

FINANCING
No financing available

QUALIFICATIONS
Experience:
    General business experience

TRAINING
At headquarters: 2 weeks

BUSINESS SUPPORT
Newsletter
Meetings
Toll-free phone line

MARKETING SUPPORT
Ad slicks

BUDGET BLINDS INC.

Ranked #75 in Entrepreneur Magazine's 2004 Franchise 500

Financial rating: $$

733 W. Taft Ave.
Orange, CA 92865
Ph: (800)420-5374, Fax: (714)637-1400
www.budgetblinds.com
Window coverings
Began: 1992, Franchising since: 1994
Headquarters size: Info not provided
Franchise department: Info not provided

U.S. franchises: 466
Canadian franchises: 0
Other foreign franchises: 0
Company-owned: 0
Units concentrated in all U.S.

Seeking: All U.S.
Seeking in Canada? Yes
Exclusive territories? Yes
Homebased option? Yes
Kiosk option? No
Employees needed to run franchise:
    Info not provided
Absentee ownership? Info not provided

COSTS

Total cost: $54.7K-81.1K
Franchise fee: $24.95K
Royalty fee: Varies
Term of agreement: Info not provided
Franchisees required to buy multiple
    units? No

FINANCING

In-house: Franchise fee
3rd-party: None

QUALIFICATIONS

Cash liquidity: $30K-56K
Experience:
    Industry experience
    Marketing skills

TRAINING

At headquarters: 2 weeks
At franchisee's location: Optional
Ongoing

BUSINESS SUPPORT

Newsletter
Meetings
Toll-free phone line
Internet
Field operations/evaluations

MARKETING SUPPORT

Co-op advertising
Ad slicks
National media campaign
Regional marketing

CARPET NETWORK

Financial rating: 0

109 Gaither Dr., #302
Mt. Laurel, NJ 08054
Ph: (800)428-1067/(856)273-9393
Fax: (856)273-0160
www.carpetnetwork.com
Mobile floor coverings & window
    treatments
Began: 1991, Franchising since: 1992
Headquarters size: 5 employees
Franchise department: 2 employees

U.S. franchises: 34
Canadian franchises: 0
Other foreign franchises: 0
Company-owned: 0
Units concentrated in all U.S.

Seeking: All U.S.
Seeking in Canada? No
Exclusive territories? Yes
Homebased option? Yes
Kiosk option? No
Employees needed to run franchise: 1
Absentee ownership? No

COSTS

Total cost: $25K-35K
Franchise fee: $14.5K
Royalty fee: 2-7%
Term of agreement: 15 years renewable
    at no charge
Franchisees required to buy multiple
    units? No

FINANCING

In-house: Franchise fee
3rd-party: None

QUALIFICATIONS

Net worth: $30K
Experience:
    Must enjoy working with people

TRAINING

At headquarters: 6 days
At franchisee's location: 14 days

BUSINESS SUPPORT

Newsletter
Meetings
Toll-free phone line
Internet
Purchasing cooperatives

MARKETING SUPPORT

Ad slicks
National media campaign

DECOR-AT-YOUR-DOOR INT'L.

Current financial data not available

1319 E. 17th Ave.
Denver, CO 80218
Ph: (800)936-3326
Fax: (720)294-9998
www.decor-at-your-door.com
Mobile window & floor coverings
Began: 1983, Franchising since: 1995
Headquarters size: 1 employee
Franchise department: 1 employee

U.S. franchises: 11
Canadian franchises: 0
Other foreign franchises: 0
Company-owned: 0
Units concentrated in all U.S.

Seeking: All U.S.
Seeking in Canada? No
Exclusive territories? Yes
Homebased option? Yes
Kiosk option? No
Employees needed to run franchise: 1
Absentee ownership? No

COSTS
Total cost: $10.6K-46K
Franchise fee: $6K
Royalty fee: 1%
Term of agreement: 10 years renewable
at no charge
Franchisees required to buy multiple
units? No

FINANCING
In-house: Franchise fee
3rd-party: None

QUALIFICATIONS
Net worth: $20K
Cash liquidity: $10K

TRAINING
At headquarters: 5 days

BUSINESS SUPPORT
Newsletter
Meetings
Internet
Security/safety procedures
Field operations/evaluations
Purchasing cooperatives

MARKETING SUPPORT
Co-op advertising
Ad slicks

FLOOR COVERINGS INT'L.

Financial rating: 0

5182 Old Dixie Hwy., #B
Forest Park, GA 30297
Ph: (800)955-4324/(404)361-5047
Fax: (404)366-4606
www.floorcoveringsintl.com
Mobile floor coverings & window
blinds
Began: 1988, Franchising since: 1989
Headquarters size: 9 employees
Franchise department: 2 employees

U.S. franchises: 108
Canadian franchises: 5
Other foreign franchises: 12
Company-owned: 0
Units concentrated in all U.S.

Seeking: All U.S.
Seeking in Canada? Yes
Exclusive territories? No
Homebased option? Yes
Kiosk option? No
Employees needed to run franchise: 2
Absentee ownership? No

COSTS
Total cost: $36K-79.1K
Franchise fee: $18K-25K
Royalty fee: 6-3%
Term of agreement: 5 years renewable
at no charge
Franchisees required to buy multiple
units? No

FINANCING
In-house: Start-up costs
3rd-party: Equipment, franchise fee,
start-up costs
Other: Opening sample package

QUALIFICATIONS
Net worth: $200K
Cash liquidity: $30K
Experience:
General business experience
Marketing skills
Direct sales experience

TRAINING
At headquarters: 6 days
At franchisee's location: 2 days
Regional meetings & national conven-
tion

BUSINESS SUPPORT
Newsletter
Meetings
Toll-free phone line
Internet
Field operations/evaluations
Purchasing cooperatives

MARKETING SUPPORT
Ad slicks
Regional marketing

GOTCHA COVERED

Ranked #218 in Entrepreneur Magazine's 2004 Franchise 500　　　　*Financial rating: $$$$*

2625 N. Josey Ln., #108
Carrollton, TX 75007
Ph: (972)466-2544
Fax: (972)446-6774
www.gotchacoveredblinds.com
Blinds, shades, shutters, draperies
Began: 1995, Franchising since: 1999
Headquarters size: 7 employees
Franchise department: 4 employees

U.S. franchises: 51
Canadian franchises: 0
Other foreign franchises: 0
Company-owned: 0
Units concentrated in all U.S.

Seeking: All U.S.
Seeking in Canada? No
Exclusive territories? Yes
Homebased option? Yes
Kiosk option? No
Employees needed to run franchise: 1-5
Absentee ownership? Yes

COSTS
Total cost: $50.5K-76.3K
Franchise fee: $44.95K
Royalty fee: $700/mo.
Term of agreement: 5 years renewable
　for $1K
Franchisees required to buy multiple
　units? No

FINANCING
In-house: None
3rd-party: Franchise fee, start-up costs

QUALIFICATIONS
Net worth: $150K
Cash liquidity: $20K
Experience:
　People skills

TRAINING
At headquarters: 3 weeks
At franchisee's location: 16 weeks

BUSINESS SUPPORT
Newsletter
Meetings
Toll-free phone line
Internet
Field operations/evaluations
Purchasing cooperatives

MARKETING SUPPORT
Co-op advertising
Ad slicks
National media campaign
Regional marketing
Radio ads

NATIONWIDE FLOOR & WINDOW COVERINGS

Ranked #236 in Entrepreneur Magazine's 2004 Franchise 500　　　　*Financial rating: $$$$*

111 E. Kilbourn Ave., #2400
Milwaukee, WI 53202
Ph: (800)366-8088
Fax: (414)765-1300
www.floorsandwindows.com
Floor & window coverings
Began: 1992, Franchising since: 1992
Headquarters size: 12 employees
Franchise department: 3 employees

U.S. franchises: 86
Canadian franchises: 7
Other foreign franchises: 0
Company-owned: 1
Units concentrated in all U.S.

Seeking: All U.S.
Seeking in Canada? No
Exclusive territories? Yes
Homebased option? Yes
Kiosk option? No
Employees needed to run franchise: 1-2
Absentee ownership? No

COSTS
Total cost: $42.8K-115.1K
Franchise fee: $24.9K-39.9K
Royalty fee: 5%
Term of agreement: 10 years renewable
　at no charge
Franchisees required to buy multiple
　units? No

FINANCING
In-house: None
3rd-party: Accounts receivable, equip-
　ment, franchise fee, inventory, pay-
　roll, start-up costs

QUALIFICATIONS
Net worth: $200K
Cash liquidity: $50K
Experience:
　General business experience
　Marketing skills

TRAINING
At headquarters: 1 week
At franchisee's location: 8 weeks

BUSINESS SUPPORT
Newsletter
Meetings
Toll-free phone line
Grand opening
Internet
Security/safety procedures
Field operations/evaluations
Purchasing cooperatives

MARKETING SUPPORT
Co-op advertising
Ad slicks
National media campaign
Regional marketing

ONLY DOORS & WINDOWS

Current financial data not available

23881 Via Fabricante, #522
Mission Viejo, CA 92691
Ph: (949)770-1236
Fax: (949)770-0776
www.onlydoorsandwindows.com
Replacement windows & doors
Began: 1999, Franchising since: 2003
Headquarters size: 9 employees
Franchise department: 4 employees

U.S. franchises: 0
Canadian franchises: 0
Other foreign franchises: 0
Company-owned: 1
Units concentrated in CA

Seeking: West
Focusing on: CA
Seeking in Canada? No
Exclusive territories? Yes
Homebased option? Yes
Kiosk option? No
Employees needed to run franchise: 3
Absentee ownership? Yes

COSTS
Total cost: $57.3K-89.3K
Franchise fee: $30K
Royalty fee: 5%
Term of agreement: 10 years renewable
    for $4.9K
Franchisees required to buy multiple
    units? No

FINANCING
In-house: Franchise fee
3rd-party: None

QUALIFICATIONS
Net worth: $100K
Cash liquidity: $50K
Experience:
    General business experience
    Marketing skills

TRAINING
At headquarters: 7 days

BUSINESS SUPPORT
Newsletter
Meetings
Toll-free phone line
Internet
Purchasing cooperatives

MARKETING SUPPORT
Co-op advertising
Ad slicks

THE RUG PLACE

Current financial data not available

6485 Perkins Rd.
Baton Rouge, LA 70808
Ph: (866)666-0784/(225)766-0599
Fax: (225)766-0655
www.rugplace.com
Rugs
Began: 1997, Franchising since: 2000
Headquarters size: 3 employees
Franchise department: 3 employees

U.S. franchises: 1
Canadian franchises: 0
Other foreign franchises: 0
Company-owned: 2
Units concentrated in LA

Seeking: All U.S.
Focusing on: AL, FL, LA, MS, TX
Seeking in Canada? No
Exclusive territories? Yes
Homebased option? No
Kiosk option? No
Employees needed to run franchise: 1-2
Absentee ownership? Yes

COSTS
Total cost: $150K-275K
Franchise fee: $25K
Royalty fee: 5%
Term of agreement: Renewable term at
    to 20% of then-current fee
Franchisees required to buy multiple
    units? No

FINANCING
No financing available

QUALIFICATIONS
Experience:
    People skills
    Good color sense

TRAINING
At headquarters: 1 week
At franchisee's location: 1 week
Additional training available annually

BUSINESS SUPPORT
Newsletter
Toll-free phone line
Grand opening
Internet
Security/safety procedures
Field operations/evaluations

MARKETING SUPPORT
Ad slicks
Advertising plan & support
TV & radio commercials

TODAY'S WINDOW FASHIONS

Financial rating: 0

P.O. Box 549
Frazier Park, CA 93225
Ph: (888)649-1600
Fax: (661)245-2793
www.todaysblinds.com
Custom blinds, shades & shutters
Began: 1993, Franchising since: 1997
Headquarters size: 3 employees
Franchise department: 3 employees

U.S. franchises: 25
Canadian franchises: 0
Other foreign franchises: 0
Company-owned: 1

Seeking: All U.S.
Seeking in Canada? No
Exclusive territories? Yes
Homebased option? Yes
Kiosk option? No
Employees needed to run franchise: 1-2
Absentee ownership? Yes

COSTS
Total cost: $19.6K-26.9K
Franchise fee: $19.5K
Royalty fee: 4%
Term of agreement: 5 years renewable
 for $750
Franchisees required to buy multiple
 units? No

FINANCING
No financing available

QUALIFICATIONS
Net worth: $25K
Cash liquidity: $15K
Experience:
 General business experience

TRAINING
At headquarters: 5 days
At franchisee's location: 3 days

BUSINESS SUPPORT
Newsletter
Meetings
Toll-free phone line
Internet
Purchasing cooperatives

MARKETING SUPPORT
Co-op advertising
Ad slicks
National media campaign
Regional marketing
Direct mail
Internet

V2K, THE VIRTUAL WINDOW FASHION STORE

Ranked #279 in Entrepreneur Magazine's 2004 Franchise 500

Financial rating: $$$

1127 Auraria Pkwy., #204
Denver, CO 80204
Ph: (800)200-0835
Fax: (303)202-5201
www.v2kwf.com
Window treatments/digital design
 services
Began: 1996, Franchising since: 1997
Headquarters size: 13 employees
Franchise department: 13 employees

U.S. franchises: 77
Canadian franchises: 0
Other foreign franchises: 0
Company-owned: 0
Units concentrated in all U.S.

Seeking: All U.S.
Seeking in Canada? No
Exclusive territories? Yes
Homebased option? Yes
Kiosk option? Yes
Employees needed to run franchise: 1
Absentee ownership? Yes

COSTS
Total cost: $45K
Franchise fee: $34.5K
Royalty fee: 6.5-8%
Term of agreement: 10 years renewable
 at no charge
Franchisees required to buy multiple
 units? No

FINANCING
No financing available

QUALIFICATIONS
Cash liquidity: $40K
Experience:
 Sales & marketing skills

TRAINING
At headquarters: 2 weeks
Ongoing field training & support

BUSINESS SUPPORT
Meetings
Toll-free phone line
Internet
Field operations/evaluations
Purchasing cooperatives

MARKETING SUPPORT
Co-op advertising
Ad slicks
Regional marketing
TV, radio & direct-mail advertising

WINDOW WORKS INT'L. INC.

Current financial data not available

3601 Minnesota Dr., #800
Edina, MN 55435
Ph: (952)943-4353
Fax: (952)921-5801
www.windowworks.net
Custom draperies, shutters, blinds
Began: 1978, Franchising since: 1979
Headquarters size: 4 employees
Franchise department: 3 employees

U.S. franchises: 5
Canadian franchises: 0
Other foreign franchises: 0
Company-owned: 0
Units concentrated in MA, MI,
     OH, TX

Seeking: All U.S.
Seeking in Canada? No
Exclusive territories? Yes
Homebased option? No
Kiosk option? No
Employees needed to run franchise: 2-3
Absentee ownership? Info not provided

COSTS
Total cost: $60K-90K
Franchise fee: to $30K
Royalty fee: 4%
Term of agreement: 15 years renewable
     at no charge
Franchisees required to buy multiple
     units? No

FINANCING
No financing available

QUALIFICATIONS
Info not provided

TRAINING
At headquarters: 1 week
At franchisee's location: 1 week
Additional training through vendors

BUSINESS SUPPORT
Newsletter
Toll-free phone line
Grand opening
Internet
Field operations/evaluations

MARKETING SUPPORT
Ad slicks
Marketing materials
Vehicle graphics
Post cards

HOME ▶ *Decorating Services*

CHRISTMAS DECOR INC.

Ranked #319 in Entrepreneur Magazine's 2004 Franchise 500

Financial rating: $$$$

P.O. Box 5946
Lubbock, TX 79408-5946
Ph: (800)687-9551
Fax: (806)722-9627
www.christmasdecor.net
Holiday & event decorating services
Began: 1984, Franchising since: 1996
Headquarters size: 24 employees
Franchise department: 20 employees

U.S. franchises: 325
Canadian franchises: 18
Other foreign franchises: 1
Company-owned: 0
Units concentrated in all U.S.

Seeking: All U.S.
Seeking in Canada? Yes
Exclusive territories? Yes
Homebased option? Yes
Kiosk option? No
Employees needed to run franchise:
     3-10
Absentee ownership? No

COSTS
Total cost: $19.2K-42.4K
Franchise fee: $10.9K-17.5K
Royalty fee: 2-4.5%
Term of agreement: 5 years renewable
     for $2K
Franchisees required to buy multiple
     units? No

FINANCING
In-house: Franchise fee
3rd-party: None

QUALIFICATIONS
Experience:
     General business experience

TRAINING
At headquarters: 4 days
At regional locations: 4 days

BUSINESS SUPPORT
Newsletter
Meetings
Toll-free phone line
Internet
Security/safety procedures
Purchasing cooperatives

MARKETING SUPPORT
Co-op advertising
Ad slicks
National media campaign

DECOR & YOU INC.

Ranked #399 in Entrepreneur Magazine's 2004 Franchise 500

Financial rating: $$$

900 Main St. S., Bldg. 2
Southbury, CT 06488
Ph: (203)264-3500
Fax: (203)264-5095
www.decorandyou.com
Interior decorating services & products
Began: 1994, Franchising since: 1998
Headquarters size: 4 employees
Franchise department: 2 employees

U.S. franchises: 22
Canadian franchises: 0
Other foreign franchises: 0
Company-owned: 0
Units concentrated in CO, CT, FL, IA,
    MI, NC, NJ, NY, TX, VA

Seeking: All U.S.
Seeking in Canada? Yes
Exclusive territories? Yes
Homebased option? Yes
Kiosk option? No
Employees needed to run franchise: 0
Absentee ownership? No

COSTS
Total cost: $29.7K-119.2K
Franchise fee: $14.5K/75K
Royalty fee: 10%
Term of agreement: 10 years renewable
    for 10% of franchise fee
Franchisees required to buy multiple
    units? Outside the U.S. only

FINANCING
No financing available

QUALIFICATIONS
Net worth: $50K/100K
Cash liquidity: $25K/50K
Experience:
    Marketing skills
    Interest in decorating

TRAINING
At headquarters: 11 days
At franchisee's location: As needed
By phone
Seminars & conferences

BUSINESS SUPPORT
Meetings
Grand opening
Field operations/evaluations
Purchasing cooperatives

MARKETING SUPPORT
Ad slicks
Regional marketing
Local marketing events

EARTH GRAPHICS

Current financial data not available

P.O. Box 18945
Greensboro, NC 27419
Ph: (877)327-8441
Fax: (336)854-8060
www.earthg.com
Landscape design, digital imaging
    services
Began: 1994, Franchising since: 1999
Headquarters size: 7 employees
Franchise department: 3 employees

U.S. franchises: 4
Canadian franchises: 0
Other foreign franchises: 0
Company-owned: 3
Units concentrated in NC, SC

Seeking: South, Southeast
Focusing on: GA, NC, SC
Seeking in Canada? No
Exclusive territories? Yes
Homebased option? No
Kiosk option? No
Employees needed to run franchise: 2
Absentee ownership? Yes

COSTS
Total cost: $34.1K-40.3K
Franchise fee: $23K
Royalty fee: 8%
Term of agreement: 5 years renewable
Franchisees required to buy multiple
    units? No

FINANCING
No financing available

QUALIFICATIONS
Net worth: $40K
Cash liquidity: $8K
Experience:
    Industry experience
    General business experience
    Marketing skills

TRAINING
At headquarters: 2 weeks
At franchisee's location: 2 weeks
Additional training: 1-2 weeks

BUSINESS SUPPORT
Newsletter
Meetings
Toll-free phone line
Grand opening
Internet
Field operations/evaluations

MARKETING SUPPORT
Regional marketing

INTERIORS BY DECORATING DEN

Ranked #85 in Entrepreneur Magazine's 2004 Franchise 500   *Financial rating: $$$$*

19100 Montgomery Ave.
Montgomery Village, MD 20866
Ph: (800)686-6393/(301)272-1500
Fax: (301)272-1520
www.decoratingden.com
Interior decorating services & products
Began: 1969, Franchising since: 1970
Headquarters size: 38 employees
Franchise department: 6 employees

U.S. franchises: 407
Canadian franchises: 42
Other foreign franchises: 17
Company-owned: 0
Units concentrated in all U.S.

Seeking: All U.S.
Seeking in Canada? Yes
Exclusive territories? Yes
Homebased option? Yes
Kiosk option? No
Employees needed to run franchise: 0
Absentee ownership? No

COSTS
Total cost: $40K
Franchise fee: $24.9K
Royalty fee: 7-9%
Term of agreement: 10 years renewable
   at no charge
Franchisees required to buy multiple
   units? No

FINANCING
In-house: Franchise fee
3rd-party: None

QUALIFICATIONS
Net worth: $50K
Cash liquidity: $40K
Experience:
   Decorating skills
   People skills

TRAINING
At headquarters: 2 weeks
At franchisee's location: Ongoing

BUSINESS SUPPORT
Newsletter
Meetings
Toll-free phone line
Grand opening
Internet
Purchasing cooperatives

MARKETING SUPPORT
Co-op advertising
Ad slicks
National media campaign
Regional marketing

HOME   *Furniture*

DOTI DESIGN STORES

Current financial data not available

18-3 E. Dundee Rd., #208
Barrington, IL 60010
Ph: (888)382-7488
Fax: (847)713-2636
www.doti.com
Upscale home furnishings & design
   stores
Began: 1983, Franchising since: 1998
Headquarters size: 10 employees
Franchise department: 4 employees

U.S. franchises: 7
Canadian franchises: 0
Other foreign franchises: 0
Company-owned: 2
Units concentrated in all U.S.

Seeking: All U.S.
Seeking in Canada? Yes
Exclusive territories? Yes
Homebased option? No
Kiosk option? No
Employees needed to run franchise: 9
Absentee ownership? No

COSTS
Total cost: $266K-326K
Franchise fee: $36K
Royalty fee: 6%
Term of agreement: 5 years renewable
   at no charge
Franchisees required to buy multiple
   units? No

FINANCING
In-house: None
3rd-party: Inventory, start-up costs

QUALIFICATIONS
Net worth: $450K
Cash liquidity: $100K
Experience:
   General business experience
   Marketing skills
   Management experience

TRAINING
At headquarters: 1 week
At franchisee's location: 2 weeks
At various locations: 2 weeks

BUSINESS SUPPORT
Newsletter
Meetings
Toll-free phone line
Grand opening
Internet
Lease negotiations
Security/safety procedures
Field operations/evaluations
Purchasing cooperatives

MARKETING SUPPORT
Co-op advertising
Ad slicks
National media campaign
Marketing & ad agency

MORE SPACE PLACE

Financial rating: $

12555 Enterprise Blvd., #101
Largo, FL 33763
Ph: (888)731-3051
Fax: (727)524-6382
www.morespaceplace.com
Space-saving furniture system
Began: 1985, Franchising since: 1993
Headquarters size: 35 employees
Franchise department: 4 employees

U.S. franchises: 22
Canadian franchises: 0
Other foreign franchises: 0
Company-owned: 3
Units concentrated in FL, MI, NC

Seeking: All U.S.
Seeking in Canada? No
Exclusive territories? Yes
Homebased option? No
Kiosk option? No
Employees needed to run franchise: 3
Absentee ownership? Yes

COSTS
Total cost: $89.5K-166.8K
Franchise fee: $22.5K
Royalty fee: 4.5%
Term of agreement: 10 years renewable
   for 15% of initial franchise fee
Franchisees required to buy multiple
   units? No

FINANCING
In-house: None
3rd-party: Equipment, franchise fee,
   inventory, start-up costs

QUALIFICATIONS
Cash liquidity: $30K-166.8K
Experience:
   General business experience
   Customer interaction skills

TRAINING
At headquarters: 1 week+
At franchisee's location: 1 week
Additional training available

BUSINESS SUPPORT
Newsletter
Meetings
Toll-free phone line
Grand opening
Internet
Lease negotiations
Security/safety procedures
Field operations/evaluations

MARKETING SUPPORT
Ad slicks
National media campaign
Ready-to-use materials

NORWALK - THE FURNITURE IDEA
Ranked #434 in Entrepreneur Magazine's 2004 Franchise 500

Financial rating: $$$$

100 Furniture Pkwy.
Norwalk, OH 44857
Ph: (888)667-9255/(419)668-4461
Fax: (419)744-3212
www.norwalkfurnitureidea.com
Custom furniture & accessories
Began: 1902, Franchising since: 1987
Headquarters size: 750 employees
Franchise department: 15 employees

U.S. franchises: 46
Canadian franchises: 8
Other foreign franchises: 0
Company-owned: 16
Units concentrated in AL, AR, AZ, CA,
   CO, FL, GA, ID, IN, IL, KS, KY, LA,
   MO, MS, NC, NV, OH, OK, OR,
   PA, SC, TN, TX, UT, VA, WA

Seeking: All U.S.
Focusing on: AL, AZ, CA, FL, GA,
   PA, WA
Seeking in Canada? No
Exclusive territories? Yes
Homebased option? No
Kiosk option? No
Employees needed to run franchise: 14
Absentee ownership? Yes

COSTS
Total cost: $380K-400K
Franchise fee: $35K
Royalty fee: 0
Term of agreement: 5 years renewable
   at no charge
Franchisees required to buy multiple
   units? No

FINANCING
In-house: None
3rd-party: Equipment, inventory,
   start-up costs

QUALIFICATIONS
Net worth: $350K+
Cash liquidity: $100K
Experience:
   Industry experience
   General business experience

TRAINING
At headquarters: 5 days
At franchisee's location: 10 days
Additional training: 10 days

BUSINESS SUPPORT
Newsletter
Meetings
Toll-free phone line
Grand opening
Internet
Lease negotiations
Field operations/evaluations

MARKETING SUPPORT
Ad slicks
National media campaign
Regional marketing

SLUMBERLAND INT'L. CO.

Current financial data not available

3060 Centerville Rd.
Little Canada, MN 55117
Ph: (651)482-7500, Fax: (651)490-0479
www.slumberland.com
Home & home office furnishings
Began: 1967, Franchising since: 1977
Headquarters size: Info not provided
Franchise department: Info not provided

U.S. franchises: 52
Canadian franchises: 0
Other foreign franchises: 0
Company-owned: 30
Units concentrated in IA, IL, MN, MO,
ND, NE, SD, WI

Seeking: Midwest
Focusing on: IA, IL, MI, MN, MO,
MT, ND, NE, SD, WI, WY
Seeking in Canada? No
Exclusive territories? No
Homebased option? No
Kiosk option? No
Employees needed to run franchise:
Info not provided
Absentee ownership? Yes

COSTS
Total cost: $416K-1M
Franchise fee: $25K
Royalty fee: 3%
Term of agreement: 10 years renewable
at no charge
Franchisees required to buy multiple
units? No

FINANCING
No financing available

QUALIFICATIONS
Net worth: $200K+
Cash liquidity: $100K+
Experience:
Industry experience
General business experience
Marketing skills

TRAINING
At headquarters: 2-3 days
At franchisee's location: 2 weeks
Ongoing

BUSINESS SUPPORT
Newsletter
Meetings
Grand opening
Internet
Field operations/evaluations
Purchasing cooperatives

MARKETING SUPPORT
Co-op advertising
Ad slicks
National media campaign
Regional marketing

VERLO MATTRESS FACTORY STORES

Financial rating: $$

P.O. Box 298
Whitewater, WI 53190
Ph: (262)473-8957
Fax: (262)473-4623
www.verlofranchise.com
Mattresses, futons, sofa sleepers, head-
boards
Began: 1958, Franchising since: 1989
Headquarters size: 9 employees
Franchise department: 2 employees

U.S. franchises: 59
Canadian franchises: 0
Other foreign franchises: 0
Company-owned: 9
Units concentrated in IL, WI

Seeking: All U.S.
Seeking in Canada? Yes
Exclusive territories? No
Homebased option? No
Kiosk option? No
Employees needed to run franchise: 7
Absentee ownership? Yes

COSTS
Total cost: $192.2K
Franchise fee: $30K
Royalty fee: 5%
Term of agreement: 5 years renewable
at no charge
Franchisees required to buy multiple
units? No

FINANCING
No financing available

QUALIFICATIONS
Net worth: $200K
Cash liquidity: $50K-70K
Experience:
General business experience

TRAINING
At headquarters: 7-10 days
At franchisee's location: 1 week
Field support: Ongoing

BUSINESS SUPPORT
Newsletter
Meetings
Toll-free phone line
Grand opening
Internet
Lease negotiations
Security/safety procedures
Field operations/evaluations
Purchasing cooperatives

MARKETING SUPPORT
Co-op advertising
Ad slicks
National media campaign
Regional marketing
In-house media agency

HOME | *Handyman Services*

ANDY ONCALL

Ranked #292 in Entrepreneur Magazine's 2004 Franchise 500　　　　*Financial rating: $$$$*

921 E. Main St.
Chattanooga, TN 37408
Ph: (877)263-9662
Fax: (423)622-0580
www.andyoncall.com
Handyman services
Began: 1993, Franchising since: 1999
Headquarters size: 7 employees
Franchise department: 2 employees

U.S. franchises: 28
Canadian franchises: 0
Other foreign franchises: 0
Company-owned: 0
Units concentrated in GA, NC, SC, TN

Seeking: All U.S.
Seeking in Canada? Yes
Exclusive territories? Yes
Homebased option? No
Kiosk option? No
Employees needed to run franchise: 2
Absentee ownership? No

COSTS
Total cost: $30.6K-49.2K
Franchise fee: $23K
Royalty fee: 5%
Term of agreement: 10 years renewable
　at no charge
Franchisees required to buy multiple
　units? No

FINANCING
In-house: Franchise fee
3rd-party: None

QUALIFICATIONS
Net worth: $100K
Cash liquidity: $40K
Experience:
　General business experience
　Sales & people skills

TRAINING
At headquarters: 9 days
At franchisee's location: 5 days

BUSINESS SUPPORT
Newsletter
Toll-free phone line
Grand opening
Internet

MARKETING SUPPORT
Ad slicks
Direct mail

CASE HANDYMAN SERVICES

Financial rating: $$$

4701 Sangamore Rd., No. Plaza, #40
Bethesda, MD 20816
Ph: (800)426-9434, Fax: (301)229-8992
www.casehandyman.com
Handyman services
Began: 1961, Franchising since: 1997
Headquarters size: 250 employees
Franchise department: 20 employees

U.S. franchises: 43
Canadian franchises: 0
Other foreign franchises: 0
Company-owned: 0
Units concentrated in all U.S.

Seeking: All U.S.
Seeking in Canada? No
Exclusive territories? Yes
Homebased option? No
Kiosk option? No
Employees needed to run franchise: 5
Absentee ownership? Info not provided

COSTS
Total cost: $125K-175K
Franchise fee: $40K
Royalty fee: 4-6%
Term of agreement: 10 years
Franchisees required to buy multiple
　units? No

FINANCING
No financing available

QUALIFICATIONS
Net worth: $100K
Cash liquidity: $50K
Experience:
　General business experience

TRAINING
At headquarters: Ongoing
At franchisee's location: Ongoing

BUSINESS SUPPORT
Meetings
Grand opening

MARKETING SUPPORT
Ad slicks

HANDYMAN CONNECTION

Current financial data not available

10250 Alliance Rd., #100
Cincinnati, OH 45242
Ph: (800)466-5530
Fax: (513)771-6439
www.handymanconnection.com
Home repairs & remodeling services
Began: 1990, Franchising since: 1991
Headquarters size: 14 employees
Franchise department: 3 employees

U.S. franchises: 111
Canadian franchises: 24
Other foreign franchises: 0
Company-owned: 2
Units concentrated in all U.S.

Seeking: All U.S.
Seeking in Canada? Yes
Exclusive territories? Yes
Homebased option? No
Kiosk option? No
Employees needed to run franchise: 3
Absentee ownership? Yes

COSTS
Total cost: $80K-180K
Franchise fee: $35K-90K
Royalty fee: 5%
Term of agreement: 10 years renewable
for 10% of franchise fee
Franchisees required to buy multiple
units? No

FINANCING
In-house: Franchise fee
3rd-party: Franchise fee, payroll, start-
up costs

QUALIFICATIONS
Net worth: $175K
Cash liquidity: $70K
Experience:
General business experience
Marketing skills

TRAINING
At headquarters: 2 weeks
At franchisee's location: 1 week
Biannual training: 2 days

BUSINESS SUPPORT
Newsletter
Meetings
Toll-free phone line
Grand opening
Internet
Field operations/evaluations
Purchasing cooperatives

MARKETING SUPPORT
Ad slicks
National media campaign
Regional marketing

HANDYMAN NETWORK

Financial rating: $$$

1165 San Antonio Dr., #G
Long Beach, CA 90807
Ph: (877)942-6396
Fax: (562)984-4370
www.handyman-network.com
Handyman services
Began: 2000, Franchising since: 2002
Headquarters size: 9 employees
Franchise department: 3 employees

U.S. franchises: 6
Canadian franchises: 0
Other foreign franchises: 0
Company-owned: 1
Units concentrated in all U.S.

Seeking: All U.S.
Seeking in Canada? No
Exclusive territories? Yes
Homebased option? No
Kiosk option? No
Employees needed to run franchise: 2-3
Absentee ownership? No

COSTS
Total cost: $46.9K-95.6K
Franchise fee: $28.5K
Royalty fee: 5%
Term of agreement: 5 years renewable
at no charge
Franchisees required to buy multiple
units? No

FINANCING
No financing available

QUALIFICATIONS
Net worth: $150K
Cash liquidity: $60K
Experience:
General business experience
Marketing skills

TRAINING
At headquarters: 2 weeks
At franchisee's location: 4 days

BUSINESS SUPPORT
Newsletter
Meetings
Toll-free phone line
Grand opening
Internet
Field operations/evaluations

MARKETING SUPPORT
Ad slicks

HANDYPRO HANDYMAN SERVICES INC.

Financial rating: $$$

995 S. Main
Plymouth, MI 48170
Ph: (800)942-6394
Fax: (734)254-9171
www.handypro.com
Handyman services
Began: 1996, Franchising since: 2000
Headquarters size: 13 employees
Franchise department: 3 employees

U.S. franchises: 4
Canadian franchises: 0
Other foreign franchises: 0
Company-owned: 1
Units concentrated in MI

Seeking: All U.S.
Focusing on: IL, OH, TX, WI
Seeking in Canada? No
Exclusive territories? Yes
Homebased option? Yes
Kiosk option? No
Employees needed to run franchise:
     1-10
Absentee ownership? Yes

COSTS
Total cost: $36.4K-61.9K
Franchise fee: $25K
Royalty fee: $600-1.5K/mo.
Term of agreement: 7 years renewable
     for 25% of initial franchise fee
Franchisees required to buy multiple
     units? No

FINANCING
No financing available

QUALIFICATIONS
Net worth: $50K
Cash liquidity: $30K
Experience:
     General business experience
     Management experience

TRAINING
At headquarters: 1 week
At franchisee's location: 1 week quar-
     terly

BUSINESS SUPPORT
Newsletter
Meetings
Toll-free phone line
Grand opening
Internet
Security/safety procedures
Field operations/evaluations
Purchasing cooperatives

MARKETING SUPPORT
Co-op advertising
Ad slicks

HOMEPROS

Financial rating: 0

2102 Kotter Ave., #A
Evansville, IN 47715
Ph: (812)473-1776
Fax: (812)473-1781
www.homepros.net
Home repair & renovation services
Began: 2001, Franchising since: 2002
Headquarters size: 12 employees
Franchise department: 4 employees

U.S. franchises: 7
Canadian franchises: 0
Other foreign franchises: 0
Company-owned: 1
Units concentrated in FL, IL, IN, KY

Seeking: All U.S. except CA, NY, VA
Focusing on: IL, IN, KY
Seeking in Canada? No
Exclusive territories? Yes
Homebased option? Yes
Kiosk option? No
Employees needed to run franchise: 2
Absentee ownership? No

COSTS
Total cost: $50.8K-89K
Franchise fee: $26K
Royalty fee: 6%
Term of agreement: 5 years renewable
     at no charge
Franchisees required to buy multiple
     units? No

FINANCING
In-house: Franchise fee
3rd-party: None

QUALIFICATIONS
Net worth: $50K
Cash liquidity: $20K
Experience:
     Industry experience
     General business experience
     Basic home repair skills

TRAINING
At headquarters: 1 week
At franchisee's location: Quarterly

BUSINESS SUPPORT
Newsletter
Meetings
Grand opening
Internet
Field operations/evaluations

MARKETING SUPPORT
Ad slicks
Ad campaigns
Ongoing marketing support

HOUSE DOCTORS

Ranked #199 in Entrepreneur Magazine's 2004 Franchise 500　　　　*Financial rating: $$$$*

575 Chamber Dr.
Milford, OH 45150
Ph: (800)319-3359
Fax: (513)469-2226
www.housedoctors.com
Handyman services & home repairs
Began: 1994, Franchising since: 1995
Headquarters size: 23 employees
Franchise department: 12 employees

U.S. franchises: 200
Canadian franchises: 0
Other foreign franchises: 2
Company-owned: 0
Units concentrated in all U.S. except HI

Seeking: All U.S.
Seeking in Canada? No
Exclusive territories? Yes
Homebased option? Yes
Kiosk option? No
Employees needed to run franchise:
　　Info not provided
Absentee ownership? No

COSTS
Total cost: $24K-51.6K
Franchise fee: $13.9K-32.9K
Royalty fee: 6%
Term of agreement: 10 years renewable
　　at no charge
Franchisees required to buy multiple
　　units? No

FINANCING
In-house: Franchise fee
3rd-party: None

QUALIFICATIONS
Experience:
　　General business experience

TRAINING
At headquarters: 1 week

BUSINESS SUPPORT
Newsletter
Meetings
Toll-free phone line
Internet
Field operations/evaluations

MARKETING SUPPORT
Ad slicks

MAINTENANCE MADE SIMPLE

Current financial data not available

9820 E. Dreyfus Ave.
Scottsdale, AZ 85260
Ph: (866)778-6283
www.m2simple.com
Handyman & home maintenance serv-
　　ices
Began: 2003, Franchising since: 2003
Headquarters size: 2 employees
Franchise department: Info not pro-
　　vided

U.S. franchises: 1
Canadian franchises: 0
Other foreign franchises: 0
Company-owned: 0

Seeking: All U.S.
Seeking in Canada? No
Exclusive territories? Yes
Homebased option? Yes
Kiosk option? No
Employees needed to run franchise: 1
Absentee ownership? Yes

COSTS
Total cost: $35.3K-64.8K
Franchise fee: $30K
Royalty fee: 7%
Term of agreement: 15 years renewable
　　at no charge
Franchisees required to buy multiple
　　units? No

FINANCING
No financing available

QUALIFICATIONS
Info not provided

TRAINING
At headquarters: 7 days

BUSINESS SUPPORT
Newsletter
Meetings
Toll-free phone line
Grand opening
Internet
Security/safety procedures
Field operations/evaluations
Purchasing cooperatives

MARKETING SUPPORT
Co-op advertising
Ad slicks
National media campaign
Regional marketing
Inbound & outbound call center

MR. HANDYMAN INT'L. LLC

Ranked #344 in Entrepreneur Magazine's 2004 Franchise 500   *Financial rating: $$$$*

3948 Ranchero Dr.
Ann Arbor, MI 48108
Ph: (800)289-4600
Fax: (734)822-6888
www.mrhandyman.com
Home maintenance & repairs
Began: 2000, Franchising since: 2000
Headquarters size: 65 employees
Franchise department: 12 employees

U.S. franchises: 96
Canadian franchises: 5
Other foreign franchises: 0
Company-owned: 6
Units concentrated in CA, CO, GA, IL,
   MI, MN, OH

Seeking: All U.S.
Seeking in Canada? Yes
Exclusive territories? Yes
Homebased option? Yes
Kiosk option? No
Employees needed to run franchise: 8
Absentee ownership? No

COSTS
Total cost: $92K-110K
Franchise fee: $6.9K
Royalty fee: 7%
Term of agreement: 10 years renewable
   for 20% of current franchise fee
Franchisees required to buy multiple
   units? No

FINANCING
No financing available

QUALIFICATIONS
Net worth: $100K
Cash liquidity: $30K
Experience:
   General business experience
   Marketing skills

TRAINING
At headquarters: 1 week
At franchisee's location: 6-9 weeks

BUSINESS SUPPORT
Newsletter
Meetings
Toll-free phone line
Grand opening
Internet
Security/safety procedures
Field operations/evaluations
Purchasing cooperatives

MARKETING SUPPORT
Co-op advertising
Ad slicks
Press releases
Vehicle decals

HOME ◀ *Surface Refinishing*

MIRACLE METHOD SURFACE RESTORATION

Ranked #467 in Entrepreneur Magazine's 2004 Franchise 500   *Financial rating: $$$$*

4239 N. Nevada, #115
Colorado Springs, CO 80907
Ph: (800)444-8827/(719)594-9196
Fax: (719)594-9282
www.miraclemethod.com
Bathtub, sink, countertop & tile
   repair/refinishing
Began: 1977, Franchising since: 1980
Headquarters size: 4 employees
Franchise department: 4 employees

U.S. franchises: 78
Canadian franchises: 0
Other foreign franchises: 19
Company-owned: 0
Units concentrated in all U.S.

Seeking: All U.S.
Seeking in Canada? Yes
Exclusive territories? Yes
Homebased option? Yes
Kiosk option? No
Employees needed to run franchise: 3
Absentee ownership? Yes

COSTS
Total cost: $12.5K-40K
Franchise fee: $15K
Royalty fee: 5-5.5%
Term of agreement: 5 years renewable
   for 5% of franchise fee
Franchisees required to buy multiple
   units? Outside the U.S. only

FINANCING
In-house: Franchise fee
3rd-party: None

QUALIFICATIONS
Net worth: $20K
Cash liquidity: $13K
Experience:
   Marketing skills

TRAINING
At headquarters: 2 weeks
At franchisee's location: 1 week

BUSINESS SUPPORT
Newsletter
Meetings
Toll-free phone line
Internet
Security/safety procedures
Field operations/evaluations
Purchasing cooperatives

MARKETING SUPPORT
Co-op advertising
Ad slicks
National media campaign
Regional marketing

PERMA-GLAZE

Current financial data not available

1638 S. Research Loop Rd., #160
Tucson, AZ 85710
Ph: (800)332-7397/(520)722-9718
Fax: (520)296-4393
www.permaglaze.com
Bathroom & kitchen fixture restoration/refinishing
Began: 1978, Franchising since: 1981
Headquarters size: 10 employees
Franchise department: 2 employees

U.S. franchises: 144
Canadian franchises: 3
Other foreign franchises: 16
Company-owned: 2
Units concentrated in all U.S.

Seeking: All U.S.
Seeking in Canada? Yes
Exclusive territories? Yes
Homebased option? Yes
Kiosk option? No
Employees needed to run franchise: 1
Absentee ownership? Yes

COSTS
Total cost: $26.5K-47.5K
Franchise fee: $21.5K+
Royalty fee: Varies
Term of agreement: 10 years renewable
    at no charge
Franchisees required to buy multiple
    units? Outside the U.S. only

FINANCING
In-house: None
3rd-party: Franchise fee, start-up costs

QUALIFICATIONS
Cash liquidity: $2.5K-5K

TRAINING
At headquarters: 1 week-10 days
At franchisee's location: Upon request
Additional training available

BUSINESS SUPPORT
Newsletter
Meetings
Toll-free phone line

MARKETING SUPPORT
Ad slicks
National media campaign
Internet advertising

RE-BATH LLC

Ranked #211 in Entrepreneur Magazine's 2004 Franchise 500

Financial rating: $$$$

1055 S. Country Club Dr., Bldg. 2
Mesa, AZ 85210-4613
Ph: (800)426-4573/(480)844-1575
Fax: (480)833-7199
www.re-bath.com
Acrylic liners for bathtubs, showers &
    walls
Began: 1979, Franchising since: 1991
Headquarters size: 13 employees
Franchise department: 3 employees

U.S. franchises: 147
Canadian franchises: 2
Other foreign franchises: 1
Company-owned: 0

Seeking: All U.S.
Seeking in Canada? Yes
Exclusive territories? Yes
Homebased option? No
Kiosk option? No
Employees needed to run franchise: 3-5
Absentee ownership? No

COSTS
Total cost: $33.9K-200K
Franchise fee: $3.5K-40K
Royalty fee: $25/liner
Term of agreement: 5 years renewable
    for $1K
Franchisees required to buy multiple
    units? No

FINANCING
No financing available

QUALIFICATIONS
Net worth: $250K
Cash liquidity: $100K
Experience:
    Industry experience
    General business experience
    Marketing skills

TRAINING
At headquarters: 9 days
At franchisee's location: As needed
Sales training: 3 days

BUSINESS SUPPORT
Newsletter
Meetings
Toll-free phone line
Internet

MARKETING SUPPORT
Co-op advertising
Ad slicks
National media campaign

SURFACE SPECIALISTS SYSTEMS INC.

Financial rating: 0

621-B Stallings Rd.
Matthews, NC 28105
Ph: (866)239-8707, Fax: (704)821-2097
www.surfacespecialists.com
Kitchen & bath repair, refinishing &
  resurfacing
Began: 1981, Franchising since: 1982
Headquarters size: 3 employees
Franchise department: 1 employee

U.S. franchises: 34
Canadian franchises: 0
Other foreign franchises: 0
Company-owned: 0
Units concentrated in all U.S.

Seeking: All U.S.
Seeking in Canada? No
Exclusive territories? Yes
Homebased option? Yes
Kiosk option? No
Employees needed to run franchise: 2-3
Absentee ownership? No

COSTS
Total cost: $25.3K-34.9K
Franchise fee: $19.5K
Royalty fee: 5%
Term of agreement: 10 years renewable
  at no charge
Franchisees required to buy multiple
  units? No

FINANCING
In-house: Franchise fee
3rd-party: None

QUALIFICATIONS
Net worth: $75K
Cash liquidity: $25K
Experience:
    Industry experience
    General business experience
    Marketing skills

TRAINING
At headquarters: 3 weeks
Follow-up training at franchisee's
  location

BUSINESS SUPPORT
Newsletter
Meetings
Toll-free phone line
Internet
Security/safety procedures
Purchasing cooperatives

MARKETING SUPPORT
Ad slicks
Marketing manual

HOME ▶ *Miscellaneous*

CERTA PROPAINTERS LTD.
Ranked #157 in Entrepreneur Magazine's 2004 Franchise 500

Financial rating: $$$$

P.O. Box 836
Oaks, PA 19456
Ph: (800)611-3782/(770)455-4300
Fax: (770)455-4422
www.gocerta.com
Residential & commercial painting
Began: 1992, Franchising since: 1992
Headquarters size: 24 employees
Franchise department: 9 employees

U.S. franchises: 230
Canadian franchises: 25
Other foreign franchises: 7
Company-owned: 0
Units concentrated in all U.S.

Seeking: All U.S.
Seeking in Canada? Yes
Exclusive territories? Yes
Homebased option? Yes
Kiosk option? No
Employees needed to run franchise:
    Info not provided
Absentee ownership? No

COSTS
Total cost: $66.2K-84.3K
Franchise fee: $30K
Royalty fee: 2-5%
Term of agreement: 10 years renewable
  for 10% of current franchise fee
Franchisees required to buy multiple
  units? No

FINANCING
In-house: None
3rd-party: Equipment, franchise fee,
  start-up costs

QUALIFICATIONS
Experience:
    General business experience

TRAINING
At headquarters: 3 weeks
At franchisee's location: Varies
Additional training available

BUSINESS SUPPORT
Meetings
Toll-free phone line
Field operations/evaluations

MARKETING SUPPORT
Ad slicks
National media campaign
Regional marketing
Local marketing materials & support

GROUT DOCTOR GLOBAL FRANCHISE CORP.

Financial rating: $

6017 E. McKellips Rd., #104
Mesa, AZ 85215
Ph: (877)476-8800, Fax: (877)615-2173
www.groutdoctor.com
Ceramic tile grout repair & maintenance
Began: 1994, Franchising since: 2001
Headquarters size: 6 employees
Franchise department: 5 employees

U.S. franchises: 38
Canadian franchises: 0
Other foreign franchises: 0
Company-owned: 8
Units concentrated in AZ, CA, GA, IL, KY, MO, OH, TX, UT, WA

Seeking: All U.S.
Seeking in Canada? Yes
Exclusive territories? Yes
Homebased option? Yes
Kiosk option? No
Employees needed to run franchise: 0
Absentee ownership? Yes

COSTS
Total cost: $15.7K-28.6K
Franchise fee: $12.5K
Royalty fee: $750/mo.
Term of agreement: 7 years renewable for $1K
Franchisees required to buy multiple units? No

FINANCING
In-house: Franchise fee
3rd-party: None

QUALIFICATIONS
Cash liquidity: $9.4K

TRAINING
At headquarters: 5 days
At franchisee's location: 2 days
In AZ, CA, IL, TX or WA: 5 days

BUSINESS SUPPORT
Newsletter
Meetings
Toll-free phone line
Grand opening
Internet
Security/safety procedures
Field operations/evaluations
Purchasing cooperatives

MARKETING SUPPORT
Co-op advertising
Ad slicks
Adminstrative support
Regional marketing
Media package
Promotional products
Vendor discounts
Signage

GROUT WIZARD

Financial rating: 0

1056 El Capitan Dr.
Danville, CA 94526
Ph: (925)314-0369
Fax: (925)314-0579
www.groutwizard.com
Grout cleaning & restoration
Began: 1997, Franchising since: 2001
Headquarters size: 2 employees
Franchise department: 1 employee

U.S. franchises: 7
Canadian franchises: 0
Other foreign franchises: 0
Company-owned: 0
Units concentrated in CA, CO

Seeking: All U.S.
Seeking in Canada? Yes
Exclusive territories? Yes
Homebased option? Yes
Kiosk option? No
Employees needed to run franchise: 0
Absentee ownership? No

COSTS
Total cost: $15.6K-25.2K
Franchise fee: $12.5K
Royalty fee: Varies
Term of agreement: 5 years renewable for $2K
Franchisees required to buy multiple units? No

FINANCING
In-house: Franchise fee
3rd-party: None

QUALIFICATIONS
Experience:
    Basic business skills

TRAINING
At headquarters: 1 week+

BUSINESS SUPPORT
Newsletter
Meetings
Toll-free phone line
Internet
Security/safety procedures
Purchasing cooperatives

MARKETING SUPPORT
Co-op advertising
Ad slicks

HUMITECH FRANCHISE CORP.

Current financial data not available

15851 Dallas Pkwy., #410
Addison, TX 75001
Ph: (972)490-9393
Fax: (972)490-9220
www.humitechgroup.com
Humidity control products
Began: 2001, Franchising since: 2002
Headquarters size: 14 employees
Franchise department: 4 employees

U.S. franchises: 65
Canadian franchises: 0
Other foreign franchises: 8
Company-owned: 1
Units concentrated in all U.S.

Seeking: All U.S.
Seeking in Canada? Yes
Exclusive territories? Yes
Homebased option? Yes
Kiosk option? No
Employees needed to run franchise:
    1-10
Absentee ownership? Yes

COSTS

Total cost: $10K+
Franchise fee: 0
Royalty fee: 0
Term of agreement: 10 years renewable
    for $1K
Franchisees required to buy multiple
    units? No

FINANCING

In-house: None
3rd-party: Accounts receivable, equipment, franchise fee, inventory, payroll, start-up costs

QUALIFICATIONS

Experience:
    General business experience
    Marketing skills
    Sales experience

TRAINING

At franchisee's location: 1 week
Additional training: 1 week

BUSINESS SUPPORT

Newsletter
Meetings
Toll-free phone line
Internet
Security/safety procedures
Field operations/evaluations

MARKETING SUPPORT

Co-op advertising
Ad slicks
National media campaign
Regional marketing

LIFESTYLE TECHNOLOGIES

Current financial data not available

8809 Lenox Pointe Dr., #G
Charlotte, NC 28273
Ph: (704)552-1000, Fax: (704)644-1428
www.lifestech.com
Home networking technology, security
    & entertainment systems
Began: 2000, Franchising since: 2001
Headquarters size: 9 employees
Franchise department: Info not provided

U.S. franchises: 14
Canadian franchises: 0
Other foreign franchises: 0
Company-owned: 2
Units concentrated in TX

Seeking: All U.S.
Focusing on: AR, CA, FL, IL, IN, MN,
    MO, NJ, NV, VA, WA
Seeking in Canada? No
Exclusive territories? Info not provided
Homebased option? No
Kiosk option? No
Employees needed to run franchise:
    Info not provided
Absentee ownership? Yes

COSTS

Total cost: $154K-195K
Franchise fee: $40K
Royalty fee: 6%
Term of agreement: 10 years renewable
    for $5K
Franchisees required to buy multiple
    units? No

FINANCING

No financing available

QUALIFICATIONS

Net worth: $500K
Cash liquidity: $250K

TRAINING

At headquarters: 2-3 weeks

BUSINESS SUPPORT

Newsletter
Meetings
Internet
Field operations/evaluations
Purchasing cooperatives

MARKETING SUPPORT

Co-op advertising
Ad slicks

NITE TIME DECOR INC.
Ranked #407 in Entrepreneur Magazine's 2004 Franchise 500　　　　*Financial rating: $$$*

P.O. Box 5183
Lubbock, TX 79408-5183
Ph: (877)552-4242
Fax: (806)722-9627
www.nitetimedecor.com
Landscape & architectural lighting
　service
Began: 1989, Franchising since: 1999
Headquarters size: 20 employees
Franchise department: 6 employees

U.S. franchises: 48
Canadian franchises: 0
Other foreign franchises: 0
Company-owned: 0

Seeking: All U.S.
Seeking in Canada? No
Exclusive territories? Yes
Homebased option? Yes
Kiosk option? No
Employees needed to run franchise: 3-4
Absentee ownership? No

COSTS
Total cost: $58K-87.8K
Franchise fee: $17.9K
Royalty fee: 2-4.5%
Term of agreement: 10 years renewable
　for $2K
Franchisees required to buy multiple
　units? No

FINANCING
No financing available

QUALIFICATIONS
Experience:
　　General business experience

TRAINING
At headquarters: 3 days

BUSINESS SUPPORT
Newsletter
Meetings
Toll-free phone line
Internet
Security/safety procedures
Field operations/evaluations
Purchasing cooperatives

MARKETING SUPPORT
Ad slicks
National media campaign

OUTDOOR LIGHTING PERSPECTIVES
Ranked #357 in Entrepreneur Magazine's 2004 Franchise 500　　　　*Financial rating: $$$$*

1122 Industrial Dr.
Matthews, NC 28105
Ph: (704)845-1675, Fax: (704)845-1677
www.outdoorlights.com
Outdoor lighting systems & mainte-
　nance
Began: 1995, Franchising since: 1998
Headquarters size: 7 employees
Franchise department: 7 employees

U.S. franchises: 44
Canadian franchises: 0
Other foreign franchises: 0
Company-owned: 1
Units concentrated in all U.S.

Seeking: All U.S.
Seeking in Canada? No
Exclusive territories? Yes
Homebased option? Yes
Kiosk option? No
Employees needed to run franchise:
　　Info not provided
Absentee ownership? No

COSTS
Total cost: $71.5K-211.5K
Franchise fee: $45K-130K
Royalty fee: 7%
Term of agreement: 5 years renewable
　for $500
Franchisees required to buy multiple
　units? Yes

FINANCING
No financing available

QUALIFICATIONS
Net worth: $500K
Cash liquidity: $100K
Experience:
　　General business experience
　　Marketing skills

TRAINING
At headquarters: 1 week
At franchisee's location: 1 week
Online training

BUSINESS SUPPORT
Newsletter
Meetings
Toll-free phone line
Internet
Field operations/evaluations
Purchasing cooperatives

MARKETING SUPPORT
Co-op advertising
Ad slicks
Regional marketing

SIGNATURE LANDSCAPE LIGHTING

Current financial data not available

P.O. Box 355
Novi, MI 48376
Ph: (248)347-1117
Fax: (248)344-1761
www.signaturelights.com
Exterior residential lighting systems
Began: 1995, Franchising since: 2001
Headquarters size: 3 employees
Franchise department: 1 employee

U.S. franchises: 0
Canadian franchises: 0
Other foreign franchises: 0
Company-owned: 1

Seeking: All U.S.
Seeking in Canada? Yes
Exclusive territories? Yes
Homebased option? Yes
Kiosk option? No
Employees needed to run franchise: 2-4
Absentee ownership? Info not provided

COSTS
Total cost: $59.5K
Franchise fee: $40K
Royalty fee: 5%
Term of agreement: 5 years renewable
    at no charge
Franchisees required to buy multiple
    units? No

FINANCING
In-house: Inventory
3rd-party: None

QUALIFICATIONS
Net worth: $125K
Cash liquidity: $50K
Experience:
    Contracting experience
    Corporate sales experience
    Organizational experience

TRAINING
At headquarters: 1 week
At franchisee's location: 1 week

BUSINESS SUPPORT
Newsletter
Meetings
Toll-free phone line
Internet
Security/safety procedures
Field operations/evaluations
Purchasing cooperatives

MARKETING SUPPORT
Ad slicks
Regional marketing
Marketing promotional kit

STAINED GLASS OVERLAY

Current financial data not available

1827 N. Case St.
Orange, CA 92865
Ph: (800)944-4746/(714)974-6124
Fax: (714)974-6529
www.stainedglassoverlay.com
Patented overlay process for creating
    art glass
Began: 1974, Franchising since: 1981
Headquarters size: 15 employees
Franchise department: 4 employees

U.S. franchises: 170
Canadian franchises: 15
Other foreign franchises: 144
Company-owned: 0
Units concentrated in all U.S.

Seeking: All U.S.
Seeking in Canada? Yes
Exclusive territories? Yes
Homebased option? No
Kiosk option? No
Employees needed to run franchise: 2
Absentee ownership? No

COSTS
Total cost: $66K-90K
Franchise fee: $45K+
Royalty fee: 5%
Term of agreement: 10 years renewable
    for $1K
Franchisees required to buy multiple
    units? Outside the U.S. only

FINANCING
No financing available

QUALIFICATIONS
Net worth: $150K
Cash liquidity: $68K
Experience:
    General business experience

TRAINING
At headquarters: 2 weeks

BUSINESS SUPPORT
Newsletter
Meetings
Toll-free phone line
Internet
Security/safety procedures
Field operations/evaluations
Purchasing cooperatives

MARKETING SUPPORT
Co-op advertising
Ad slicks
Regional marketing

HOME *Other Franchises*

AFFORDABLE WINDOW COVERINGS
41655 Reagan St., #J
Murrieta, CA 92562
Ph: (909)698-1391
www.affordablewindow.com
Window fashions

CALIFORNIA CLOSET COMPANY
*Ranked #320 in Entrepreneur
    Magazine's 2004 Franchise 500*
1000 4th St., #800
San Rafael, CA 94901
Ph: (800)241-3222/(415)256-8500
www.calclosets.com
Custom closet, garage & office organ-
    izing system

ESSENTIALS PROTECTIVE COATINGS
5209 Capital Blvd.
Raleigh, NC 27616
Ph: (919)785-3015
www.epc-tubs.com
Protective plastic-coating system

FOUR SEASONS SUNROOMS
5005 Veterans Memorial Hwy.
Holbrook, NY 11741
Ph: (800)368-7732/(631)563-4000
www.four-seasons-sunrooms.com
Conservatories, solariums, sunrooms

GARAGETEK INC.
*Ranked #363 in Entrepreneur
    Magazine's 2004 Franchise 500*
5 Aerial Wy., #200
Syosset, NY 11710
Ph: (516)621-4300
www.garagetek.com
Garage organization systems

GCO CARPET OUTLET
4301 Earth City Expwy.
Earth City, MO 63045
Ph: (314)291-0000
www.gcocarpet.com
Retail & wholesale floor coverings

KOTT KOATINGS
27161 Burbank St.
Foothill Ranch, CA 92610
Ph: (949)770-5055
www.thebathtubpeople.com
Bathtub refinishing

LUXURY BATH SYSTEMS
1958 Brandon Ct.
Glendale Heights, IL 60139
Ph: (800)354-2284
www.luxurybath.com
Bathtub liners

MOUNTAIN COMFORT FURNISHINGS
507 Summit Blvd.
Frisco, CO 80443
Ph: (970)668-3661
www.mountaincomfort.net
Home furnishings

WINDOW-OLOGY
P.O. Box 1737
Pleasanton, CA 94566
Ph: (925)462-1207
www.window-ology.com
Mobile window coverings

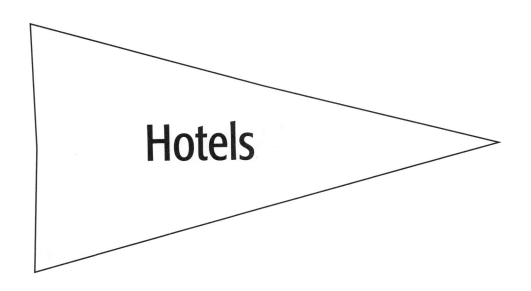

HOTELS

AMERIHOST FRANCHISE SYSTEMS INC.
Ranked #203 in Entrepreneur Magazine's 2004 Franchise 500

Financial rating: $$$$

1 Sylvan Way
Parsippany, NJ 07054
Ph: (800)758-8999
Fax: (800)643-2107
www.amerihostinn.com
Hotels
Began: 1989, Franchising since: 1998
Headquarters size: 600 employees
Franchise department: 173 employees

U.S. franchises: 99
Canadian franchises: 1
Other foreign franchises: 0
Company-owned: 0
Units concentrated in all U.S.

Seeking: All U.S.
Seeking in Canada? Yes
Exclusive territories? Yes
Homebased option? No
Kiosk option? No
Employees needed to run franchise:
    Info not provided
Absentee ownership? Yes

COSTS
Total cost: $3.2M-4.5M
Franchise fee: Varies
Royalty fee: 4-5%
Term of agreement: 20 years not renewable
Franchisees required to buy multiple units? Outside the U.S. only

FINANCING
3rd-party: Equipment, franchise fee, inventory, payroll, start-up costs
Other: Development incentives

QUALIFICATIONS
Experience:
    General business experience

TRAINING
At headquarters: 2-8 days
At franchisee's location: 4-5 days
Regional workshops

BUSINESS SUPPORT
Newsletter
Meetings
Toll-free phone line
Grand opening
Internet
Field operations/evaluations
Purchasing cooperatives

MARKETING SUPPORT
Ad slicks
National media campaign

AMERISUITES FRANCHISING INC.

Current financial data not available

700 Rte. 46 E.
Fairfield, NJ 07007-2700
Ph: (973)882-1010
Fax: (973)882-1991
www.amerisuites.com
Hotels
Began: 1985, Franchising since: 1998
Headquarters size: 120 employees
Franchise department: Info not provided

U.S. franchises: 50
Canadian franchises: 0
Other foreign franchises: 0
Company-owned: 100
Units concentrated in all U.S.

Seeking: All U.S.
Seeking in Canada? No
Exclusive territories? Yes
Homebased option? No
Kiosk option? No
Employees needed to run franchise:
    20-25
Absentee ownership? Yes

COSTS
Total cost: $5.9M-9.7M
Franchise fee: Varies
Royalty fee: 5%
Term of agreement: 20 years renewable
Franchisees required to buy multiple
    units? No

FINANCING
In-house: None
3rd-party: Accounts receivable, equipment, franchise fee, inventory, payroll, start-up costs

QUALIFICATIONS
Experience:
    General business experience

TRAINING
At headquarters: 1 week
At franchisee's location: 1 week
Additional training: 2 weeks

BUSINESS SUPPORT
Newsletter
Meetings
Toll-free phone line
Grand opening
Internet
Lease negotiations
Security/safety procedures
Field operations/evaluations
Purchasing cooperatives

MARKETING SUPPORT
National media campaign
Regional marketing

BAYMONT FRANCHISES INT'L. INC.

Ranked #429 in Entrepreneur Magazine's 2004 Franchise 500

Financial rating: $$$$

100 E. Wisconsin Ave.
Milwaukee, WI 53202
Ph: (414)905-1376, Fax: (414)905-2496
www.baymontinns.com
Mid-priced lodging
Began: 1973, Franchising since: 1986
Headquarters size: 60 employees
Franchise department: 10 employees

U.S. franchises: 89
Canadian franchises: 0
Other foreign franchises: 0
Company-owned: 92
Units concentrated in AL, AR, AZ, CT,
    FL, GA, IA, IL, IN, LA, MA, MI,
    MN, MO, MS, NC, NE, NM, NY,
    OH, PA, SC, TN, TX, UT, WI

Seeking: All U.S.
Seeking in Canada? Yes
Exclusive territories? Yes
Homebased option? No
Kiosk option? No
Employees needed to run franchise: 15
Absentee ownership? Yes

COSTS
Total cost: $4.1M-4.9M
Franchise fee: $35K
Royalty fee: 5%
Term of agreement: 10-20 years not
    renewable
Franchisees required to buy multiple
    units? No

FINANCING
No financing available

QUALIFICATIONS
Net worth: $1M
Cash liquidity: $500K
Experience:
    Industry experience
    General business experience
    Marketing skills

TRAINING
At headquarters: 1 week

BUSINESS SUPPORT
Newsletter
Meetings
Grand opening
Internet
Security/safety procedures
Field operations/evaluations
Purchasing cooperatives

MARKETING SUPPORT
National media campaign

CHOICE HOTELS INT'L.

Ranked #40 in Entrepreneur Magazine's 2004 Franchise 500   *Financial rating: $$*

10750 Columbia Pike
Silver Spring, MD 20901
Ph: (800)547-0007
Fax: (301)592-6205
www.choicehotels.com
Hotels, inns, suites, resorts
Began: 1939, Franchising since: 1962
Headquarters size: 450 employees
Franchise department: 90 employees

U.S. franchises: 3,562
Canadian franchises: 254
Other foreign franchises: 924
Company-owned: 3
Units concentrated in all U.S.

Seeking: All U.S.
Seeking in Canada? Yes
Exclusive territories? Yes
Homebased option? No
Kiosk option? No
Employees needed to run franchise:
     Info not provided
Absentee ownership? Yes

COSTS
Total cost: $4M-6M
Franchise fee: $25K-50K
Royalty fee: 3.5-5.3%
Term of agreement: 20 years not
     renewable
Franchisees required to buy multiple
     units? Outside the U.S. only

FINANCING
In-house: None
3rd-party: Equipment, franchise fee,
     inventory, start-up costs

QUALIFICATIONS
Net worth: $750K
Cash liquidity: $200K
Experience:
     Industry experience
     General business experience

TRAINING
At headquarters: 1 week

BUSINESS SUPPORT
Newsletter
Meetings
Toll-free phone line
Grand opening
Internet
Field operations/evaluations

MARKETING SUPPORT
Co-op advertising
Ad slicks
National media campaign
Regional marketing
PR support

COUNTRY INNS & SUITES BY CARLSON

Ranked #93 in Entrepreneur Magazine's 2004 Franchise 500   *Financial rating: $$$$*

P.O. Box 59159
Minneapolis, MN 55459-8203
Ph: (763)212-2525
Fax: (763)212-1338
www.countryinns.com
Mid-tier hotels
Began: 1986, Franchising since: 1987
Headquarters size: 40 employees
Franchise department: Info not pro-
     vided

U.S. franchises: 293
Canadian franchises: 12
Other foreign franchises: 16
Company-owned: 5

Seeking: All U.S.
Seeking in Canada? Yes
Exclusive territories? Yes
Homebased option? No
Kiosk option? No
Employees needed to run franchise: 25
Absentee ownership? Yes

COSTS
Total cost: $3M-5.5M
Franchise fee: Varies
Royalty fee: 4.5%
Term of agreement: 15 years not
     renewable
Franchisees required to buy multiple
     units? No

FINANCING
In-house: None
3rd-party: Equipment, franchise fee,
     inventory, start-up costs

QUALIFICATIONS
Experience:
     Industry experience
     General business experience
     Marketing skills

TRAINING
At headquarters: Varies
At franchisee's location: Varies
Additional training available

BUSINESS SUPPORT
Newsletter
Meetings
Toll-free phone line
Grand opening
Internet
Security/safety procedures
Field operations/evaluations
Purchasing cooperatives

MARKETING SUPPORT
Co-op advertising
Ad slicks
National media campaign
Regional marketing

DAYS INNS WORLDWIDE INC.

Ranked #27 in Entrepreneur Magazine's 2004 Franchise 500   *Financial rating: $$$$*

1 Sylvan Way
Parsippany, NJ 07054
Ph: (800)758-8999
Fax: (800)643-2107
www.daysinn.com
Hotels & inns
Began: 1970, Franchising since: 1972
Headquarters size: 600 employees
Franchise department: 175 employees

U.S. franchises: 1,766
Canadian franchises: 76
Other foreign franchises: 61
Company-owned: 0
Units concentrated in all U.S.

Seeking: All U.S.
Seeking in Canada? Yes
Exclusive territories? Yes
Homebased option? No
Kiosk option? No
Employees needed to run franchise:
    Info not provided
Absentee ownership? Yes

COSTS
Total cost: $400K-5.4M
Franchise fee: Varies
Royalty fee: 5%
Term of agreement: 15-20 years not
    renewable
Franchisees required to buy multiple
    units? Outside the U.S. only

FINANCING
In-house: None
3rd-party: Equipment, franchise fee,
    inventory, payroll, start-up costs

QUALIFICATIONS
Experience:
    General business experience

TRAINING
At headquarters: 2-8 days
At franchisee's location: 4-5 days
Regional workshops

BUSINESS SUPPORT
Newsletter
Meetings
Toll-free phone line
Internet
Field operations/evaluations
Purchasing cooperatives

MARKETING SUPPORT
Co-op advertising
Ad slicks
National media campaign
Regional marketing

DOUBLETREE HOTELS, SUITES, RESORTS, CLUBS

Ranked #309 in Entrepreneur Magazine's 2004 Franchise 500   *Financial rating: $$$$*

9336 Civic Center Dr.
Beverly Hills, CA 90210
Ph: (800)286-0645/(310)205-7696
Fax: (310)205-7655
www.doubletreefranchise.com
Hotels
Began: 1969, Franchising since: 1989
Headquarters size: 2,332 employees
Franchise department: 67 employees

U.S. franchises: 64
Canadian franchises: 0
Other foreign franchises: 2
Company-owned: 90
Units concentrated in CA, FL, TX

Seeking: All U.S.
Seeking in Canada? Yes
Exclusive territories? Yes
Homebased option? No
Kiosk option? No
Employees needed to run franchise:
    100
Absentee ownership? Yes

COSTS
Total cost: $7M-40.4M
Franchise fee: $50K+
Royalty fee: 4%
Term of agreement: 10 years renewable
    at initial franchise fee
Franchisees required to buy multiple
    units? No

FINANCING
No financing available

QUALIFICATIONS
Net worth: $15M
Experience:
    Industry experience
    General business experience

TRAINING
General manager training prior to
    certification for opening

BUSINESS SUPPORT
Newsletter
Meetings
Grand opening
Field operations/evaluations
Purchasing cooperatives

MARKETING SUPPORT
Co-op advertising
Ad slicks
National media campaign
Regional marketing

EMBASSY SUITES HOTELS

Ranked #299 in Entrepreneur Magazine's 2004 Franchise 500   *Financial rating: $$$$*

9336 Civic Center Dr.
Beverly Hills, CA 90210
Ph: (800)286-0645/(310)205-7696
Fax: (310)205-7655
www.embassyfranchise.com
All-suite hotels
Began: 1983, Franchising since: 1984
Headquarters size: 2,332 employees
Franchise department: 67 employees

U.S. franchises: 82
Canadian franchises: 1
Other foreign franchises: 3
Company-owned: 91
Units concentrated in CA, CO, FL, TX

Seeking: All U.S.
Seeking in Canada? Yes
Exclusive territories? No
Homebased option? No
Kiosk option? No
Employees needed to run franchise: 75
Absentee ownership? Yes

COSTS
Total cost: $17M-23M
Franchise fee: $100K+
Royalty fee: 4%
Term of agreement: 20 years renewable
Franchisees required to buy multiple
   units? No

FINANCING
No financing available

QUALIFICATIONS
Net worth: $15M
Experience:
   Industry experience
   General business experience

TRAINING
At Memphis, TN, corporate office:
   2 weeks

BUSINESS SUPPORT
Newsletter
Grand opening
Lease negotiations
Field operations/evaluations

MARKETING SUPPORT
Co-op advertising
Ad slicks
National media campaign
Regional marketing

HAMPTON INN/HAMPTON INN & SUITES

Ranked #39 in Entrepreneur Magazine's 2004 Franchise 500   *Financial rating: $$$$*

9336 Civic Ctr. Dr.
Beverly Hills, CA 90210
Ph: (800)286-0645/(310)205-7696
Fax: (310)205-7655
www.hamptonfranchise.com
Mid-priced hotels
Began: 1983, Franchising since: 1984
Headquarters size: 2,332 employees
Franchise department: 67 employees

U.S. franchises: 1,190
Canadian franchises: 13
Other foreign franchises: 11
Company-owned: 25
Units concentrated in FL, GA, NC, TX

Seeking: All U.S.
Seeking in Canada? Yes
Exclusive territories? No
Homebased option? No
Kiosk option? No
Employees needed to run franchise: 25
Absentee ownership? Yes

COSTS
Total cost: $4.9M-8.7M
Franchise fee: $45K+
Royalty fee: 4%
Term of agreement: 20 years renewable
Franchisees required to buy multiple
   units? No

FINANCING
No financing available

QUALIFICATIONS
Net worth: $2M
Experience:
   Industry experience
   General business experience

TRAINING
At Memphis, TN, corporate office:
   2 weeks

BUSINESS SUPPORT
Newsletter
Meetings
Grand opening
Lease negotiations
Field operations/evaluations

MARKETING SUPPORT
Co-op advertising
Ad slicks
National media campaign
Regional marketing

HAWTHORN SUITES

Ranked #481 in Entrepreneur Magazine's 2004 Franchise 500

Financial rating: $$$$

13 Corporate Sq., #250
Atlanta, GA 30329
Ph: (404)321-4045
Fax: (404)321-4482
www.hawthorn.com
Extended-stay suite hotels
Began: 1986, Franchising since: 1986
Headquarters size: 180 employees
Franchise department: 130 employees

U.S. franchises: 111
Canadian franchises: 1
Other foreign franchises: 1
Company-owned: 0
Units concentrated in all U.S.

Seeking: All U.S.
Seeking in Canada? Yes
Exclusive territories? Yes
Homebased option? No
Kiosk option? No
Employees needed to run franchise:
   20-30
Absentee ownership? Yes

COSTS
Total cost: $4.4M-7.4M
Franchise fee: $40K
Royalty fee: 5%
Term of agreement: 20 years renewable
   for 50% of current franchise fee
Franchisees required to buy multiple
   units? No

FINANCING
No financing available

QUALIFICATIONS
Experience:
   Industry experience
   General business experience
   Marketing skills

TRAINING
At headquarters
At franchisee's location
At regional location

BUSINESS SUPPORT
Newsletter
Meetings
Toll-free phone line
Grand opening
Internet
Security/safety procedures
Field operations/evaluations
Purchasing cooperatives

MARKETING SUPPORT
Co-op advertising
Ad slicks
National media campaign

HILTON GARDEN INN

Ranked #139 in Entrepreneur Magazine's 2004 Franchise 500

Financial rating: $$$$

9336 Civic Center Dr.
Beverly Hills, CA 90210
Ph: (800)286-0645/(310)205-7696
Fax: (310)205-7655
www.hiltongardeninnfranchise.com
Upscale mid-priced hotel
Began: 1996, Franchising since: 1996
Headquarters size: 2,332 employees
Franchise department: 67 employees

U.S. franchises: 158
Canadian franchises: 4
Other foreign franchises: 3
Company-owned: 3
Units concentrated in CA, FL, PA, TX

Seeking: All U.S.
Seeking in Canada? Yes
Exclusive territories? No
Homebased option? No
Kiosk option? No
Employees needed to run franchise:
   35-50+
Absentee ownership? Yes

COSTS
Total cost: $8.8M-11.4M
Franchise fee: $60K+
Royalty fee: 5%
Term of agreement: 22 years renewable
Franchisees required to buy multiple
   units? No

FINANCING
No financing available

QUALIFICATIONS
Net worth: $4M
Experience:
   Industry experience
   General business experience

TRAINING
At headquarters: 3 days
Orientation in Beverly Hills, CA

BUSINESS SUPPORT
Meetings
Grand opening
Field operations/evaluations
Purchasing cooperatives

MARKETING SUPPORT
Co-op advertising
Ad slicks
National media campaign
Regional marketing

HILTON HOTELS, SUITES, RESORTS
Ranked #273 in Entrepreneur Magazine's 2004 Franchise 500

Financial rating: $$$$

9336 Civic Center Dr.
Beverly Hills, CA 90210
Ph: (800)286-0645/(310)205-7696
Fax: (310)205-7655
www.hiltonfranchise.com
Upscale hotels & resorts
Began: 1919, Franchising since: 1965
Headquarters size: 2,332 employees
Franchise department: 67 employees

U.S. franchises: 152
Canadian franchises: 9
Other foreign franchises: 2
Company-owned: 68
Units concentrated in CA, FL, TX

Seeking: All U.S.
Seeking in Canada? Yes
Exclusive territories? No
Homebased option? No
Kiosk option? No
Employees needed to run franchise:
    150
Absentee ownership? Yes

COSTS
Total cost: $2M-44.8M
Franchise fee: $75K+
Royalty fee: 5%
Term of agreement: 10 years renewable
Franchisees required to buy multiple
    units? No

FINANCING
No financing available

QUALIFICATIONS
Net worth: $15M
Experience:
    Industry experience
    General business experience

TRAINING
At headquarters: 3 days
At regional office: 3 days
In Dallas, TX: 4 days
At existing hotels

BUSINESS SUPPORT
Newsletter
Meetings
Toll-free phone line
Grand opening
Internet
Security/safety procedures
Field operations/evaluations
Purchasing cooperatives

MARKETING SUPPORT
Co-op advertising
Ad slicks
National media campaign
Regional marketing

HOMEWOOD SUITES BY HILTON
Ranked #239 in Entrepreneur Magazine's 2004 Franchise 500

Financial rating: $$$$

9336 Civic Center Dr.
Beverly Hills, CA 90210
Ph: (800)286-0645/(310)205-7696
Fax: (310)205-7655
www.homewoodfranchise.com
Extended-stay hotels
Began: 1988, Franchising since: 1988
Headquarters size: 2,332 employees
Franchise department: 67 employees

U.S. franchises: 86
Canadian franchises: 1
Other foreign franchises: 0
Company-owned: 37
Units concentrated in FL, OH, TX

Seeking: All U.S.
Seeking in Canada? Yes
Exclusive territories? No
Homebased option? No
Kiosk option? No
Employees needed to run franchise: 25
Absentee ownership? Yes

COSTS
Total cost: $9M-12.2M
Franchise fee: $50K+
Royalty fee: 4%
Term of agreement: 20 years renewable
Franchisees required to buy multiple
    units? No

FINANCING
No financing available

QUALIFICATIONS
Net worth: $4M
Experience:
    Industry experience
    General business experience

TRAINING
At Memphis, TN, corporate office:
    2 weeks

BUSINESS SUPPORT
Newsletter
Meetings
Grand opening
Lease negotiations
Field operations/evaluations

MARKETING SUPPORT
Co-op advertising
Ad slicks
National media campaign
Regional marketing

HOSPITALITY INT'L. INC.

Current financial data not available

1726 Montreal Cir.
Tucker, GA 30084
Ph: (800)247-4677/(770)270-1180
Fax: (770)270-1077
www.bookroomsnow.com
Hotels & motels
Began: 1971, Franchising since: 1977
Headquarters size: 20 employees
Franchise department: 7 employees

U.S. franchises: 240
Canadian franchises: 1
Other foreign franchises: 1
Company-owned: 0
Units concentrated in all U.S. except
    HI, WA

Seeking: All U.S.
Seeking in Canada? Yes
Exclusive territories? No
Homebased option? No
Kiosk option? No
Employees needed to run franchise: 10
Absentee ownership? Yes

COSTS
Total cost: Varies
Franchise fee: $2.5K-5K
Royalty fee: 3-4%
Term of agreement: 5 years renewable
    at no charge
Franchisees required to buy multiple
    units? No

FINANCING
3rd-party: Equipment, franchise fee
Other: Purchase, construction

QUALIFICATIONS
Net worth: 20% of total cost
Cash liquidity: 15% of total cost

TRAINING
At headquarters: 3 days
At franchisee's location: As needed

BUSINESS SUPPORT
Newsletter
Meetings
Toll-free phone line
Grand opening
Internet
Security/safety procedures
Field operations/evaluations

MARKETING SUPPORT
Co-op advertising
Ad slicks
National media campaign

HOWARD JOHNSON INT'L. INC.

Ranked #159 in Entrepreneur Magazine's 2004 Franchise 500

Financial rating: $$$$

1 Sylvan Way
Parsippany, NJ 07054
Ph: (800)758-8999
Fax: (800)643-2107
www.howardjohnson.com
Hotels
Began: 1925, Franchising since: 1954
Headquarters size: 600 employees
Franchise department: 176 employees

U.S. franchises: 388
Canadian franchises: 48
Other foreign franchises: 39
Company-owned: 0
Units concentrated in all U.S.

Seeking: All U.S.
Seeking in Canada? Yes
Exclusive territories? Yes
Homebased option? No
Kiosk option? No
Employees needed to run franchise:
    Info not provided
Absentee ownership? Yes

COSTS
Total cost: $365K-6.2M
Franchise fee: Varies
Royalty fee: 4%
Term of agreement: 15-20 years not
    renewable
Franchisees required to buy multiple
    units? Outside the U.S. only

FINANCING
3rd-party: Equipment, franchise fee,
    inventory, payroll, start-up costs
Other: Development incentives

QUALIFICATIONS
Experience:
    General business experience

TRAINING
At headquarters: 2-8 days
At franchisee's location: 4-5 days
Regional workshops

BUSINESS SUPPORT
Newsletter
Meetings
Toll-free phone line
Grand opening
Internet
Field operations/evaluations
Purchasing cooperatives

MARKETING SUPPORT
Co-op advertising
Ad slicks
National media campaign
Regional marketing
Customer loyalty club & kids' pro-
    grams

INTERCONTINENTAL HOTELS GROUP

Ranked #12 in Entrepreneur Magazine's 2004 Franchise 500   *Financial rating: $$$$*

3 Ravinia Dr., #1000
Atlanta, GA 30346
Ph: (770)604-2000
Fax: (770)604-8639
www.ichotelsgroup.com
Hotels
Began: 1952, Franchising since: 1954
Headquarters size: 1,800 employees
Franchise department: 100 employees

U.S. franchises: 2,361
Canadian franchises: 104
Other foreign franchises: 728
Company-owned: 177
Units concentrated in all U.S.

Seeking: All U.S.
Seeking in Canada? Yes
Exclusive territories? Yes
Homebased option? No
Kiosk option? No
Employees needed to run franchise:
    Info not provided
Absentee ownership? Yes

COSTS
Total cost: Varies
Franchise fee: Varies
Royalty fee: 5%
Term of agreement: Renewable term
    (avg. 10 years)
Franchisees required to buy multiple
    units? No

FINANCING
In-house: None
3rd-party: Accounts receivable, equip-
    ment, franchise fee, inventory, pay-
    roll, start-up costs

QUALIFICATIONS
Experience:
    Industry experience
    General business experience
    Marketing skills

TRAINING
At headquarters: Varies
At franchisee's location: Varies

BUSINESS SUPPORT
Newsletter
Meetings
Toll-free phone line
Grand opening
Internet
Lease negotiations
Security/safety procedures
Field operations/evaluations

MARKETING SUPPORT
Co-op advertising
Ad slicks
National media campaign
Regional marketing

KNIGHTS FRANCHISE SYSTEMS INC.

Ranked #305 in Entrepreneur Magazine's 2004 Franchise 500   *Financial rating: $$$$*

1 Sylvan Way
Parsippany, NJ 07054
Ph: (800)758-8999
Fax: (800)643-2107
www.knightsinn.com
Hotels
Began: 1972, Franchising since: 1991
Headquarters size: 600 employees
Franchise department: 173 employees

U.S. franchises: 195
Canadian franchises: 9
Other foreign franchises: 0
Company-owned: 0
Units concentrated in all U.S.

Seeking: All U.S.
Seeking in Canada? Yes
Exclusive territories? Yes
Homebased option? No
Kiosk option? No
Employees needed to run franchise:
    Info not provided
Absentee ownership? Yes

COSTS
Total cost: $225K-4.4M
Franchise fee: Varies
Royalty fee: 5%
Term of agreement: 15-20 years not
    renewable
Franchisees required to buy multiple
    units? Outside the U.S. only

FINANCING
3rd-party: Equipment, franchise fee,
    inventory, payroll, start-up costs
Other: Development incentives

QUALIFICATIONS
Experience:
    General business experience

TRAINING
At headquarters: 2-8 days
At franchisee's location: 4-5 days
Regional workshops

BUSINESS SUPPORT
Newsletter
Meetings
Toll-free phone line
Grand opening
Internet
Field operations/evaluations
Purchasing cooperatives

MARKETING SUPPORT
National media campaign

MICROTEL INNS & SUITES

Ranked #187 in Entrepreneur Magazine's 2004 Franchise 500   *Financial rating: $$$$*

13 Corporate Sq., #250
Atlanta, GA 30329
Ph: (404)321-4045
Fax: (404)321-4482 E
www.microtelinn.com
Economy hotels
Began: 1987, Franchising since: 1988
Headquarters size: 180 employees
Franchise department: 130 employees

U.S. franchises: 251
Canadian franchises: 0
Other foreign franchises: 7
Company-owned: 0
Units concentrated in all U.S.

Seeking: All U.S.
Seeking in Canada? Yes
Exclusive territories? Yes
Homebased option? No
Kiosk option? No
Employees needed to run franchise:
    12-20
Absentee ownership? Yes

COSTS
Total cost: $2.8M-5.6M
Franchise fee: Varies
Royalty fee: 4-6%
Term of agreement: 20 years renewable
    for 50% of current franchise fee
Franchisees required to buy multiple
    units? No

FINANCING
No financing available

QUALIFICATIONS
Experience:
    General business experience

TRAINING
At headquarters: Varies
At franchisee's location: Varies
At regional locations: 2-3 days

BUSINESS SUPPORT
Newsletter
Meetings
Toll-free phone line
Grand opening
Internet
Security/safety procedures
Field operations/evaluations
Purchasing cooperatives

MARKETING SUPPORT
Co-op advertising
Ad slicks
National media campaign
Regional marketing

MOTEL 6

Ranked #87 in Entrepreneur Magazine's 2004 Franchise 500   *Financial rating: $$$$*

4001 International Pkwy.
Carrollton, TX 75007
Ph: (888)842-2942
Fax: (972)360-5567
www.motel6.com
Economy lodging
Began: 1962, Franchising since: 1996
Headquarters size: 500 employees
Franchise department: 29 employees

U.S. franchises: 142
Canadian franchises: 0
Other foreign franchises: 0
Company-owned: 688
Units concentrated in AZ, CA, TX

Seeking: All U.S.
Seeking in Canada? Yes
Exclusive territories? Yes
Homebased option? No
Kiosk option? No
Employees needed to run franchise:
    2-10
Absentee ownership? Yes

COSTS
Total cost: $1.8M-2.2M
Franchise fee: $25K
Royalty fee: 4%
Term of agreement: 10-15 years
    renewable for 50% of current fran-
    chise fee
Franchisees required to buy multiple
    units? No

FINANCING
In-house: None
3rd-party: Equipment, franchise fee,
    inventory, start-up costs

QUALIFICATIONS
Net worth: $1.5M
Cash liquidity: $300K
Experience:
    General business experience

TRAINING
At headquarters: 1 week
At franchisee's location
Annual convention

BUSINESS SUPPORT
Newsletter
Meetings
Internet
Security/safety procedures
Field operations/evaluations
Purchasing cooperatives

MARKETING SUPPORT
Ad slicks
National media campaign

RADISSON HOTELS & RESORTS

Ranked #336 in Entrepreneur Magazine's 2004 Franchise 500　　　*Financial rating: $$$$*

P.O. Box 59159
Minneapolis, MN 55459-8204
Ph: (763)212-1000
Fax: (763)212-3400
www.radisson.com
Hotels, resorts, cruise ships
Began: 1962, Franchising since: 1983
Headquarters size: 115 employees
Franchise department: Info not provided

U.S. franchises: 225
Canadian franchises: 20
Other foreign franchises: 162
Company-owned: 5

Seeking: All U.S.
Seeking in Canada? Yes
Exclusive territories? Yes
Homebased option? No
Kiosk option? No
Employees needed to run franchise:
　　Info not provided
Absentee ownership? Yes

COSTS
Total cost: $33M-50M
Franchise fee: Varies
Royalty fee: Varies
Term of agreement: 20 years not renewable
Franchisees required to buy multiple units? No

FINANCING
No financing available

QUALIFICATIONS
Experience:
　　Industry experience
　　General business experience
　　Marketing skills

TRAINING
At headquarters: 1 day
At franchisee's location
At Reservation Center in Omaha, NE:
　　2 days

BUSINESS SUPPORT
Newsletter
Meetings
Toll-free phone line
Internet
Field operations/evaluations
Purchasing cooperatives

MARKETING SUPPORT
National media campaign
Regional marketing

RAMADA FRANCHISE SYSTEMS INC.

Ranked #57 in Entrepreneur Magazine's 2004 Franchise 500　　　*Financial rating: $$$$*

1 Sylvan Way
Parsippany, NJ 07054
Ph: (800)758-8999
Fax: (800)643-2107
www.ramada.com
Limiteds, inns, plaza hotels
Began: 1954, Franchising since: 1990
Headquarters size: 600 employees
Franchise department: 182 employees

U.S. franchises: 871
Canadian franchises: 71
Other foreign franchises: 0
Company-owned: 0
Units concentrated in all U.S.

Seeking: All U.S.
Seeking in Canada? No
Exclusive territories? Yes
Homebased option? No
Kiosk option? No
Employees needed to run franchise: 45
Absentee ownership? Yes

COSTS
Total cost: $380K-6.2M
Franchise fee: Varies
Royalty fee: 4%
Term of agreement: 15-20 years not renewable
Franchisees required to buy multiple units? No

FINANCING
3rd-party: Equipment, franchise fee, inventory, payroll, start-up costs
Other: Development incentives

QUALIFICATIONS
Experience:
　　General business experience

TRAINING
At headquarters: 2-8 days
At franchisee's location: 4-5 days
Regional workshops

BUSINESS SUPPORT
Newsletter
Meetings
Toll-free phone line
Grand opening
Field operations/evaluations
Purchasing cooperatives

MARKETING SUPPORT
Ad slicks
National media campaign
Regional marketing

RED ROOF INNS INC.

Ranked #354 in Entrepreneur Magazine's 2004 Franchise 500　　　*Financial rating: $$$*

4001 International Pkwy.
Carrollton, TX 75007
Ph: (888)842-2942, Fax: (972)360-5567
www.redroof.com
Economy business lodging
Began: 1967, Franchising since: 1996
Headquarters size: 500 employees
Franchise department: 29 employees

U.S. franchises: 95
Canadian franchises: 0
Other foreign franchises: 0
Company-owned: 254
Units concentrated in CA, OH, TX

Seeking: All U.S.
Seeking in Canada? Yes
Exclusive territories? Yes
Homebased option? No
Kiosk option? No
Employees needed to run franchise:
　　Info not provided
Absentee ownership? Yes

COSTS
Total cost: $2.6M-3M
Franchise fee: $30K
Royalty fee: 4.5%
Term of agreement: 20 years renewable
　　for 50% of current franchise fee
Franchisees required to buy multiple
　　units? No

FINANCING
In-house: None
3rd-party: Equipment, franchise fee,
　　inventory, start-up costs

QUALIFICATIONS
Net worth: $1.5M
Cash liquidity: $300K
Experience:
　　General business experience

TRAINING
At headquarters: 2 weeks
At franchisee's location: 1 week
At convention: 3 days per year

BUSINESS SUPPORT
Newsletter
Meetings
Grand opening
Internet
Security/safety procedures
Field operations/evaluations
Purchasing cooperatives

MARKETING SUPPORT
Ad slicks
National media campaign

STUDIO 6

Ranked #355 in Entrepreneur Magazine's 2004 Franchise 500　　　*Financial rating: $$$$*

4001 International Pkwy.
Carrollton, TX 75007
Ph: (888)842-2942
Fax: (972)360-5567
www.staystudio6.com
Extended-stay lodging
Began: 1998, Franchising since: 1999
Headquarters size: 500 employees
Franchise department: 29 employees

U.S. franchises: 3
Canadian franchises: 0
Other foreign franchises: 0
Company-owned: 37
Units concentrated in GA, TX

Seeking: All U.S.
Seeking in Canada? Yes
Exclusive territories? Yes
Homebased option? No
Kiosk option? No
Employees needed to run franchise:
　　Info not provided
Absentee ownership? Yes

COSTS
Total cost: $2.7M-3.4M
Franchise fee: $25K
Royalty fee: 5%
Term of agreement: 10-15 years
　　renewable for 50% of current fran-
　　chise fee
Franchisees required to buy multiple
　　units? No

FINANCING
In-house: None
3rd-party: Equipment, franchise fee,
　　inventory, start-up costs

QUALIFICATIONS
Net worth: $1.5M
Cash liquidity: $300K
Experience:
　　General business experience

TRAINING
At headquarters: 1 week
At franchisee's location
Annual convention

BUSINESS SUPPORT
Newsletter
Meetings
Internet
Field operations/evaluations
Purchasing cooperatives

MARKETING SUPPORT
Ad slicks

SUBURBAN FRANCHISE SYSTEMS INC.

Current financial data not available

1000 Circle 75 Pkwy., #700
Atlanta, GA 30339
Ph: (678)742-3300
Fax: (678)742-3301
www.suburbanhotels.com
Extended-stay hotels
Began: 1986, Franchising since: 1989
Headquarters size: 17 employees
Franchise department: 17 employees

U.S. franchises: 62
Canadian franchises: 0
Other foreign franchises: 0
Company-owned: 0
Units concentrated in Eastern U.S.

Seeking: All U.S.
Seeking in Canada? No
Exclusive territories? No
Homebased option? No
Kiosk option? No
Employees needed to run franchise:
    6-10
Absentee ownership? Yes

COSTS
Total cost: $3.5M-6.7M
Franchise fee: Varies
Royalty fee: 4%
Term of agreement: 10 years renewable
    for $30K or $225/room
Franchisees required to buy multiple
    units? No

FINANCING
No financing available

QUALIFICATIONS
Net worth: $1.5M
Cash liquidity: $1M-1.2M
Experience:
    General business experience

TRAINING
At headquarters: Upon request
At franchisee's location: 2 weeks

BUSINESS SUPPORT
Newsletter
Meetings
Toll-free phone line
Grand opening
Internet
Security/safety procedures
Field operations/evaluations
Purchasing cooperatives

MARKETING SUPPORT
Co-op advertising
Ad slicks
Regional marketing

SUPER 8 MOTELS INC.

Ranked #15 in Entrepreneur Magazine's 2004 Franchise 500

Financial rating: $$$$

1 Sylvan Way
Parsippany, NJ 07054
Ph: (800)758-8999
Fax: (800)643-2107
www.super8.com
Economy motels
Began: 1974, Franchising since: 1976
Headquarters size: 600 employees
Franchise department: 173 employees

U.S. franchises: 1,988
Canadian franchises: 99
Other foreign franchises: 0
Company-owned: 0
Units concentrated in all U.S.

Seeking: All U.S.
Seeking in Canada? Yes
Exclusive territories? Yes
Homebased option? No
Kiosk option? No
Employees needed to run franchise:
    Info not provided
Absentee ownership? Yes

COSTS
Total cost: $291K-2.3M
Franchise fee: Varies
Royalty fee: 5%
Term of agreement: 15-20 years not
    renewable
Franchisees required to buy multiple
    units? Outside the U.S. only

FINANCING
3rd-party: Equipment, franchise fee,
    inventory, payroll, start-up costs
Other: Signage credit, development
    incentives

QUALIFICATIONS
Experience:
    General business experience

TRAINING
At headquarters: 2-8 days
At franchisee's location: 4-5 days
Regional workshops

BUSINESS SUPPORT
Newsletter
Meetings
Toll-free phone line
Internet
Field operations/evaluations

MARKETING SUPPORT
National media campaign

TRAVELODGE HOTELS INC.

Ranked #122 in Entrepreneur Magazine's 2004 Franchise 500   *Financial rating: $$$$*

1 Sylvan Way
Parsippany, NJ 07054
Ph: (800)758-8999
Fax: (800)643-2107
www.travelodge.com
Hotels & motels
Began: 1939, Franchising since: 1966
Headquarters size: 600 employees
Franchise department: 173 employees

U.S. franchises: 427
Canadian franchises: 115
Other foreign franchises: 2
Company-owned: 0
Units concentrated in all U.S.

Seeking: All U.S.
Seeking in Canada? Yes
Exclusive territories? Yes
Homebased option? No
Kiosk option? No
Employees needed to run franchise:
   Info not provided
Absentee ownership? Yes

COSTS
Total cost: $366K-5.4M
Franchise fee: Varies
Royalty fee: 4.5%
Term of agreement: 15-20 years not
   renewable
Franchisees required to buy multiple
   units? Outside the U.S. only

FINANCING
3rd-party: Equipment, franchise fee,
   inventory, payroll, start-up costs
Other: Development incentives

QUALIFICATIONS
Experience:
   General business experience

TRAINING
At headquarters: 2-8 days
At franchisee's location: 4-5 days
Regional workshops

BUSINESS SUPPORT
Newsletter
Meetings
Toll-free phone line
Grand opening
Internet
Field operations/evaluations
Purchasing cooperatives

MARKETING SUPPORT
Co-op advertising
Ad slicks
National media campaign
Regional marketing

VILLAGER FRANCHISE SYSTEMS INC.

Ranked #420 in Entrepreneur Magazine's 2004 Franchise 500   *Financial rating: $$$$*

1 Sylvan Way
Parsippany, NJ 07054
Ph: (800)758-8999
Fax: (800)643-2107
www.villager.com
Extended-stay hotels
Began: 1989, Franchising since: 1992
Headquarters size: 600 employees
Franchise department: 173 employees

U.S. franchises: 74
Canadian franchises: 2
Other foreign franchises: 1
Company-owned: 0
Units concentrated in all U.S.

Seeking: All U.S.
Seeking in Canada? Yes
Exclusive territories? Yes
Homebased option? No
Kiosk option? No
Employees needed to run franchise:
   Info not provided
Absentee ownership? Yes

COSTS
Total cost: $234K-6.2M
Franchise fee: Varies
Royalty fee: 5%
Term of agreement: 15-20 years not
   renewable
Franchisees required to buy multiple
   units? Outside the U.S. only

FINANCING
3rd-party: Equipment, franchise fee,
   inventory, payroll, start-up costs
Other: Development incentives

QUALIFICATIONS
Experience:
   General business experience

TRAINING
At headquarters: 2-8 days
At franchisee's location: 4-5 days
Regional workshops

BUSINESS SUPPORT
Newsletter
Meetings
Toll-free phone line
Grand opening
Internet
Field operations/evaluations
Purchasing cooperatives

MARKETING SUPPORT
National media campaign

WELLESLEY INN & SUITES FRANCHISING INC.

Current financial data not available

700 Rte. 46 E.
Fairfield, NJ 07004
Ph: (888)778-3111
Fax: (973)882-1991
www.wellesleyonline.com
Hotels
Began: 1985, Franchising since: 1998
Headquarters size: 120 employees
Franchise department: Info not
    provided

U.S. franchises: 78
Canadian franchises: 0
Other foreign franchises: 0
Company-owned: 54
Units concentrated in all U.S.

Seeking: All U.S.
Seeking in Canada? No
Exclusive territories? Yes
Homebased option? No
Kiosk option? No
Employees needed to run franchise:
    20-25
Absentee ownership? Yes

COSTS
Total cost: $338.9K-7.8M
Franchise fee: Varies
Royalty fee: 4.5%
Term of agreement: Info not provided
Franchisees required to buy multiple
    units? No

FINANCING
In-house: None
3rd-party: Accounts receivable, equip-
    ment, franchise fee, inventory, pay-
    roll, start-up costs

QUALIFICATIONS
Experience:
    General business experience

TRAINING
At headquarters: 1 week
At franchisee's location: 1 week
Additional training: 2 weeks

BUSINESS SUPPORT
Newsletter
Meetings
Toll-free phone line
Grand opening
Internet
Lease negotiations
Security/safety procedures
Field operations/evaluations
Purchasing cooperatives

MARKETING SUPPORT
National media campaign
Regional marketing

WINGATE INNS INT'L.

Ranked #200 in Entrepreneur Magazine's 2004 Franchise 500

Financial rating: $$$$

1 Sylvan Way
Parsippany, NJ 07054
Ph: (800)758-8999
Fax: (800)643-2107
www.wingateinns.com
Hotels
Began: 1995, Franchising since: 1995
Headquarters size: 600 employees
Franchise department: 97 employees

U.S. franchises: 126
Canadian franchises: 2
Other foreign franchises: 0
Company-owned: 0
Units concentrated in all U.S.

Seeking: All U.S.
Seeking in Canada? Yes
Exclusive territories? Yes
Homebased option? No
Kiosk option? No
Employees needed to run franchise:
    15-25
Absentee ownership? Yes

COSTS
Total cost: $5.7M-5.9M
Franchise fee: Varies
Royalty fee: 4.5%
Term of agreement: 20 years not
    renewable
Franchisees required to buy multiple
    units? Outside the U.S. only

FINANCING
3rd-party: Equipment, franchise fee,
    inventory, payroll, start-up costs
Other: Development incentives

QUALIFICATIONS
Experience:
    General business experience

TRAINING
At headquarters: 2-8 days
At franchisee's location: 4-5 days
Regional workshops

BUSINESS SUPPORT
Newsletter
Meetings
Toll-free phone line
Grand opening
Internet
Field operations/evaluations
Purchasing cooperatives

MARKETING SUPPORT
Co-op advertising
Ad slicks
National media campaign
Regional marketing

HOTELS — Other Franchises

ASHBURY SUITES & INNS
14545 Eastex Fwy.
Humble, TX 77396
Ph: (281)441-1528
Hotels, suites & inns

BEST INNS/BEST SUITES
Ranked #491 in Entrepreneur
Magazine's 2004 Franchise 500
13 Corporate Sq., #250
Atlanta, GA 30329
Ph: (404)321-4045
www.bestinn.com
Mid-level economy hotels

CANDLEWOOD SUITES
Ranked #473 in Entrepreneur
Magazine's 2004 Franchise 500
8621 E. 21st St. N., #200
Wichita, KS 67206
Ph: (316)631-1300
www.candlewoodsuites.com
Suite hotels

PARK INNS
Ranked #397 in Entrepreneur
Magazine's 2004 Franchise 500
P.O. Box 59159
Minneapolis, MN 55459-8203
Ph: (763)212-1000
www.parkinns.com
Hotels

PARK PLAZA HOTELS AND RESORTS
Ranked #406 in Entrepreneur
Magazine's 2004 Franchise 500
P.O. Box 59159
Minneapolis, MN 55459-8203
Ph: (763)212-1000
www.parkplaza.com
Hotels

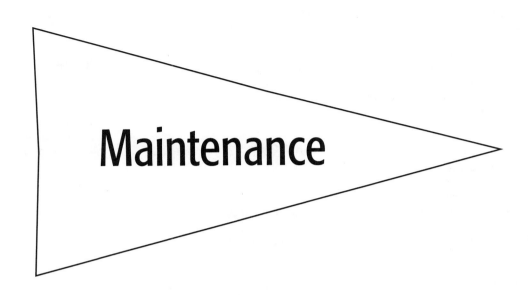

Maintenance

MAINTENANCE ▶ *Carpet Cleaning*

CHEM-DRY CARPET DRAPERY & UPHOLSTERY CLEANING
Ranked #17 in Entrepreneur Magazine's 2004 Franchise 500

Financial rating: $$$$

1530 N. 1000 West
Logan, UT 84321
Ph: (877)307-8233
Fax: (435)755-0021
www.chemdry.com
Carpet, drapery & upholstery cleaning
Began: 1977, Franchising since: 1978
Headquarters size: 75 employees
Franchise department: Info not provided

U.S. franchises: 2,458
Canadian franchises: 112
Other foreign franchises: 1,305
Company-owned: 0
Units concentrated in all U.S.

Seeking: All U.S.
Focusing on: Midwest, Northeast, South
Seeking in Canada? No
Exclusive territories? No
Homebased option? Yes
Kiosk option? No
Employees needed to run franchise: 3
Absentee ownership? Yes

COSTS
Total cost: $23.6K-82.8K
Franchise fee: $9.95K
Royalty fee: $213/mo.
Term of agreement: 5 years renewable
    for $750
Franchisees required to buy multiple
    units? No

FINANCING
In-house: Accounts receivable, franchise
    fee, equipment, inventory, start-up
    costs
3rd-party: None

QUALIFICATIONS
Info not provided

TRAINING
At headquarters: 5 days
Video training

BUSINESS SUPPORT
Newsletter
Meetings
Toll-free phone line
Internet
Security/safety procedures
Field operations/evaluations

MARKETING SUPPORT
Co-op advertising
Ad slicks
National media campaign
Regional marketing
Video & radio commercials

HEAVEN'S BEST CARPET & UPHOLSTERY CLEANING

Ranked #53 in Entrepreneur Magazine's 2004 Franchise 500

Financial rating: $$

247 N. First East, P.O. Box 607
Rexburg, ID 83440
Ph: (800)359-2095
Fax: (208)359-1236
www.heavensbest.com
Carpet & upholstery cleaning
Began: 1983, Franchising since: 1983
Headquarters size: 6 employees
Franchise department: 3 employees

U.S. franchises: 741
Canadian franchises: 4
Other foreign franchises: 10
Company-owned: 0
Units concentrated in all U.S.

Seeking: All U.S.
Seeking in Canada? Yes
Exclusive territories? Yes
Homebased option? Yes
Kiosk option? No
Employees needed to run franchise:
    0-1
Absentee ownership? Yes

COSTS
Total cost: $15.9K-55.6K
Franchise fee: $2.9K
Royalty fee: $80/mo.
Term of agreement: 5 years renewable
    at no charge
Franchisees required to buy multiple
    units? No

FINANCING
In-house: Franchise fee, inventory
3rd-party: None

QUALIFICATIONS
Net worth: $20K
Cash liquidity: $9K
Experience:
    Industry experience
    General business experience
    Marketing skills

TRAINING
At headquarters: 4 days

BUSINESS SUPPORT
Newsletter
Meetings
Toll-free phone line
Internet
Security/safety procedures
Field operations/evaluations

MARKETING SUPPORT
Ad slicks
Regional marketing

MILLICARE COMMERCIAL CARPET CARE

Ranked #476 in Entrepreneur Magazine's 2004 Franchise 500

Financial rating: $$$$

201 Lukken Industrial Dr. W.
LaGrange, GA 30240
Ph: (877)812-8803
Fax: (706)880-3279
www.millicare.com
Commercial carpet maintenance
Began: 1982, Franchising since: 1996
Headquarters size: 19 employees
Franchise department: 14 employees

U.S. franchises: 68
Canadian franchises: 7
Other foreign franchises: 3
Company-owned: 0
Units concentrated in all U.S.

Seeking: All U.S.
Seeking in Canada? No
Exclusive territories? No
Homebased option? No
Kiosk option? No
Employees needed to run franchise: 3
Absentee ownership? Yes

COSTS
Total cost: $94K-128K
Franchise fee: $20K
Royalty fee: 6%
Term of agreement: 5 years renewable
    at no charge
Franchisees required to buy multiple
    units? Yes

FINANCING
No financing available

QUALIFICATIONS
Net worth: $150K
Cash liquidity: $50K
Experience:
    General business experience

TRAINING
At headquarters: 2 weeks
At franchisee's location: 1 week
Additional training: 1-2 weeks

BUSINESS SUPPORT
Newsletter
Meetings
Toll-free phone line
Grand opening
Internet
Field operations/evaluations
Purchasing cooperatives

MARKETING SUPPORT
Co-op advertising
Ad slicks
National media campaign

MODERNISTIC CLEANING SERVICES

Current financial data not available

1460 Rankin St.
Troy, MI 48083
Ph: (866)917-1700
Fax: (248)589-2660
www.modernistic.com
Carpet & upholstery cleaning
Began: 1972, Franchising since: 2000
Headquarters size: 65 employees
Franchise department: 2 employees

U.S. franchises: 4
Canadian franchises: 0
Other foreign franchises: 0
Company-owned: 0
Units concentrated in MI

Seeking: All U.S.
Focusing on: MI, OH
Seeking in Canada? No
Exclusive territories? Yes
Homebased option? Yes
Kiosk option? No
Employees needed to run franchise: 2
Absentee ownership? Yes

COSTS
Total cost: $50K
Franchise fee: $12K-42K
Royalty fee: 6%
Term of agreement: 5 years renewable
at no charge
Franchisees required to buy multiple
units? No

FINANCING
In-house: None
Equipment, start-up costs

QUALIFICATIONS
Net worth: $50K
Cash liquidity: $30K
Experience:
General business experience
Marketing skills

TRAINING
At headquarters: 2 weeks

BUSINESS SUPPORT
Newsletter
Meetings
Toll-free phone line
Grand opening
Field operations/evaluations
Purchasing cooperatives

MARKETING SUPPORT
Co-op advertising
Ad slicks
Ad copy

PROFESSIONAL CARPET SYSTEMS

Current financial data not available

4211 Atlantic Ave.
Raleigh, NC 27604
Ph: (800)925-5055
Fax: (919)875-9855
www.procarpetsys.com
Carpet restoration & replacement
Began: 1978, Franchising since: 1981
Headquarters size: 18 employees
Franchise department: 4 employees

U.S. franchises: 52
Canadian franchises: 4
Other foreign franchises: 3
Company-owned: 0
Units concentrated in South, East

Seeking: All U.S.
Seeking in Canada? Yes
Exclusive territories? Yes
Homebased option? Yes
Kiosk option? No
Employees needed to run franchise: 1
Absentee ownership? Yes

COSTS
Total cost: $18.4K-47.8K
Franchise fee: $59.95K
Royalty fee: 2-6%
Term of agreement: 5 years renewable
for $500
Franchisees required to buy multiple
units? Outside the U.S. only

FINANCING
In-house: Franchise fee
3rd-party: Equipment, inventory

QUALIFICATIONS
Net worth: $20K
Cash liquidity: $20K
Experience:
Computer skills helpful

TRAINING
At headquarters: 2 weeks
At franchisee's location: 2 days
By mail: 1 week

BUSINESS SUPPORT
Newsletter
Meetings
Toll-free phone line
Internet
Security/safety procedures

MARKETING SUPPORT
Ad slicks
Fax
Internet
Direct mail

ROTO-STATIC INT'L.

Current financial data not available

90 Delta Park Blvd., #A
Brampton, ON Canada L6T 5E7
Ph: (877)586-4469/(905)458-7002
Fax: (905)458-8650
www.rotostatic.com
Carpet, upholstery & floor mainte-
nance, ceiling & wall cleaning
Began: 1977, Franchising since: 1977
Headquarters size: 26 employees
Franchise department: 6 employees

U.S. franchises: 0
Canadian franchises: 120
Other foreign franchises: 0
Company-owned: 0
Units concentrated in Canada

Focusing on: Canada; seeking qualified
master franchises in U.S. & inter-
nationally
Exclusive territories? Yes
Homebased option? Yes
Kiosk option? No
Employees needed to run franchise: 0
Absentee ownership? Yes

COSTS
Total cost: $40K
Franchise fee: $15K
Royalty fee: 5%
Term of agreement: 10 years renewable
for $10K
Franchisees required to buy multiple
units? Outside the U.S. only

FINANCING
No financing available

QUALIFICATIONS
Info not provided

TRAINING
At headquarters: 1 week
At franchisee's location: 2 days
Ongoing seminars

BUSINESS SUPPORT
Newsletter
Meetings
Toll-free phone line
Internet
Field operations/evaluations

MARKETING SUPPORT
Co-op advertising
Ad slicks
Marketing campaign

SEARS CARPET & UPHOLSTERY CARE INC.

Current financial data not available

8101 N. High St., #260
Columbus, OH 43235
Ph: (614)847-1603
Fax: (614)847-4055
www.sears.com
Carpet, upholstery & floor care
Began: 1992, Franchising since: 1999
Headquarters size: 20 employees
Franchise department: 3 employees

U.S. franchises: 114
Canadian franchises: 0
Other foreign franchises: 0
Company-owned: 6
Units concentrated in all U.S.

Seeking: All U.S.
Seeking in Canada? No
Exclusive territories? Yes
Homebased option? Yes
Kiosk option? No
Employees needed to run franchise:
3 -10
Absentee ownership? Yes

COSTS
Total cost: $71.5K-368K
Franchise fee: $5K-95K
Royalty fee: 8%
Term of agreement: 10 years renewable
for $2.5K
Franchisees required to buy multiple
units? No

FINANCING
In-house: Franchise fee
3rd-party: Equipment

QUALIFICATIONS
Net worth: $100K-750K
Cash liquidity: $50K-350K
Experience:
General business experience
Marketing skills
Sales experience

TRAINING
At headquarters: 1 week
At franchisee's location: As needed
At regional location: 1 day

BUSINESS SUPPORT
Newsletter
Meetings
Toll-free phone line
Internet
Security/safety procedures
Field operations/evaluations
Purchasing cooperatives

MARKETING SUPPORT
Co-op advertising
Ad slicks
Discounted print advertising

STANLEY STEEMER CARPET CLEANER
Ranked #141 in Entrepreneur Magazine's 2004 Franchise 500

Financial rating: $$$$

5500 Stanley Steemer Pkwy.
Dublin, OH 43016
Ph: (800)848-7496/(614)764-2007
Fax: (614)764-2394
www.stanleysteemer.com
Carpet & upholstery cleaning
Began: 1947, Franchising since: 1972
Headquarters size: 80 employees
Franchise department: 15 employees

U.S. franchises: 239
Canadian franchises: 0
Other foreign franchises: 0
Company-owned: 40
Units concentrated in all U.S.

Seeking: All U.S.
Seeking in Canada? Yes
Exclusive territories? Yes
Homebased option? Yes
Kiosk option? No
Employees needed to run franchise: 16
Absentee ownership? Yes

COSTS
Total cost: $81.1K-343.1K
Franchise fee: $20K+
Royalty fee: 7%
Term of agreement: 20 years renewable
Franchisees required to buy multiple
    units? No

FINANCING
In-house: Franchise fee, inventory
3rd-party: Equipment, franchise fee

QUALIFICATIONS
Experience:
    General business experience
    Marketing skills

TRAINING
At headquarters: 2 weeks
Ongoing

BUSINESS SUPPORT
Newsletter
Meetings
Toll-free phone line
Internet
Security/safety procedures

MARKETING SUPPORT
Co-op advertising
Ad slicks
National media campaign

STEAM BROTHERS INC.

Current financial data not available

2124 E. Sweet Ave.
Bismarck, ND 58504-6023
Ph: (800)767-5064, Fax: (701)222-1372
www.steambrothers.com
Carpet, upholstery, drapery & air-duct
    cleaning & restoration
Began: 1977, Franchising since: 1984
Headquarters size: 2 employees
Franchise department: 1 employee

U.S. franchises: 24
Canadian franchises: 0
Other foreign franchises: 0
Company-owned: 0
Units concentrated in Upper Midwest

Seeking: Midwest
Focusing on: CO, IA, KS, MN, MT,
    NE, SD, WY
Seeking in Canada? No
Exclusive territories? Yes
Homebased option? Yes
Kiosk option? No
Employees needed to run franchise: 1-2
Absentee ownership? No

COSTS
Total cost: $22K-53.5K
Franchise fee: $16K
Royalty fee: 5-6.5%
Term of agreement: 10 years renewable
    for $1K
Franchisees required to buy multiple
    units? No

FINANCING
In-house: None
3rd-party: Equipment

QUALIFICATIONS
Cash liquidity: $22K
Experience:
    General business experience

TRAINING
At headquarters: 2 weeks
At franchisee's location: As needed

BUSINESS SUPPORT
Newsletter
Meetings
Toll-free phone line
Grand opening
Internet
Field operations/evaluations

MARKETING SUPPORT
Ad slicks

AEROWEST/WESTAIR DEODORIZING SERVICES

Ranked #306 in Entrepreneur Magazine's 2004 Franchise 500

Financial rating: $$$$

3882 Del Amo Blvd., #3602
Torrance, CA 90503
Ph: (310)793-4242, Fax: (310)793-4250
www.westsanitation.com
Restroom deodorizing system
Began: 1943, Franchising since: 1978
Headquarters size: 20 employees
Franchise department: 10 employees

U.S. franchises: 58
Canadian franchises: 0
Other foreign franchises: 0
Company-owned: 19
Units concentrated in AL, CA, FL, IL,
LA, NY, TX

Seeking: All U.S.
Focusing on: CA, MD, MN, NC, VA
Seeking in Canada? No
Exclusive territories? No
Homebased option? Yes
Kiosk option? No
Employees needed to run franchise: 1
Absentee ownership? No

COSTS
Total cost: $10.3K-36.7K
Franchise fee: $4K
Royalty fee: 8%
Term of agreement: 5 years renewable
at no charge
Franchisees required to buy multiple
units? No

FINANCING
In-house: Equipment, inventory, start-
up costs
3rd-party: None

QUALIFICATIONS
Net worth: $10K+
Cash liquidity: $5K
Experience:
General business experience
Marketing skills
Sales & service skills

TRAINING
At franchisee's location: 2 weeks
In-field training

BUSINESS SUPPORT
Newsletter
Toll-free phone line
Field operations/evaluations
Purchasing cooperatives

MARKETING SUPPORT
Regional marketing

AIRE-MASTER OF AMERICA INC.

Ranked #409 in Entrepreneur Magazine's 2004 Franchise 500

Financial rating: $$$$

1821 N. Hwy. CC, P.O. Box 2310
Nixa, MO 65714
Ph: (800)525-0957/(417)725-2691
Fax: (417)725-8227
www.airemaster.com
Restroom deodorizing & maintenance
services
Began: 1958, Franchising since: 1976
Headquarters size: 66 employees
Franchise department: 2 employees

U.S. franchises: 54
Canadian franchises: 2
Other foreign franchises: 0
Company-owned: 5
Units concentrated in all U.S.

Seeking: All U.S.
Seeking in Canada? Yes
Exclusive territories? Yes
Homebased option? Yes
Kiosk option? No
Employees needed to run franchise: 2
Absentee ownership? No

COSTS
Total cost: $40.6K-110.9K
Franchise fee: $22K-50.5K
Royalty fee: 5%
Term of agreement: 20 years renewable
at no charge
Franchisees required to buy multiple
units? No

FINANCING
In-house: Equipment
3rd-party: Franchise fee

QUALIFICATIONS
Experience:
Marketing skills

TRAINING
At headquarters: 5 days
At franchisee's location: 5 days
Quarterly training available at head-
quarters

BUSINESS SUPPORT
Newsletter
Meetings
Toll-free phone line
Internet
Field operations/evaluations

MARKETING SUPPORT
Customer analysis & literature

AMERICARE FRANCHISE LTD.

Current financial data not available

225 Laura Dr.
Addison, IL 60101
Ph: (800)745-6191
Fax: (630)458-1994
www.americarehygiene.com
Restroom sanitation & air-freshening
services
Began: 1964, Franchising since: 1968
Headquarters size: 10 employees
Franchise department: 5 employees

U.S. franchises: 21
Canadian franchises: 0
Other foreign franchises: 0
Company-owned: 20
Units concentrated in IL

Seeking: All U.S.
Focusing on: IL, IN, MI, WI
Seeking in Canada? Yes
Exclusive territories? Yes
Homebased option? Yes
Kiosk option? No
Employees needed to run franchise: 2
Absentee ownership? No

COSTS
Total cost: $9.5K-35K
Franchise fee: $9.5K/35K
Royalty fee: 15%
Term of agreement: 10 years renewable
Franchisees required to buy multiple
units? Info not provided

FINANCING
In-house: Accounts receivable, franchise fee, equipment, inventory,
start-up costs
3rd-party: None

QUALIFICATIONS
Net worth: $100K
Cash liquidity: $10K
Experience:
General business experience

TRAINING
At headquarters: 2 weeks
At franchisee's location: 1 week+

BUSINESS SUPPORT
Meetings
Toll-free phone line
Grand opening
Internet
Security/safety procedures
Field operations/evaluations

MARKETING SUPPORT
Co-op advertising
Regional marketing
Yellow Pages

ANAGO FRANCHISING INC.

Ranked #146 in Entrepreneur Magazine's 2004 Franchise 500

Financial rating: $$$

1515 University Dr., #203
Coral Springs, FL 33071
Ph: (800)213-5857, Fax: (954)656-1014
www.goanago.com
Commercial cleaning
Began: 1989, Franchising since: 1991
Headquarters size: 10 employees
Franchise department: 10 employees

U.S. franchises: 279
Canadian franchises: 0
Other foreign franchises: 0
Company-owned: 0
Units concentrated in FL, GA, IL, OH

Seeking: All U.S.
Seeking in Canada? Yes
Exclusive territories? Yes
Homebased option? Yes
Kiosk option? No
Employees needed to run franchise:
4-10
Absentee ownership? No

COSTS
Total cost: $7.8K-457K
Franchise fee: $5.4K-500K
Royalty fee: 10%/5%
Term of agreement: 10 years renewable
at no charge
Franchisees required to buy multiple
units? No

FINANCING
In-house: Accounts receivable, fran-
chise fee
3rd-party: Equipment, payroll

QUALIFICATIONS
Net worth: $80K-100K
Cash liquidity: $6K-125K
Experience:
General business experience
Marketing skills

TRAINING
At headquarters: 4 weeks
At franchisee's location: Ongoing

BUSINESS SUPPORT
Newsletter
Meetings
Toll-free phone line
Grand opening
Internet
Security/safety procedures
Field operations/evaluations

MARKETING SUPPORT
Regional marketing

AWC COMMERCIAL WINDOW COVERINGS

Financial rating: $$$

825 W. Williamson Wy.
Fullerton, CA 92832
Ph: (800)252-2280/(714)879-3880
Fax: (714)879-8419
www.awc-cwc.com
Mobile commercial window-covering
    dry cleaning & sales
Began: 1963, Franchising since: 1992
Headquarters size: 18 employees
Franchise department: 3 employees

U.S. franchises: 5
Canadian franchises: 0
Other foreign franchises: 0
Company-owned: 4

Seeking: All U.S.
Seeking in Canada? Yes
Exclusive territories? Yes
Homebased option? Yes
Kiosk option? No
Employees needed to run franchise: 1-2
Absentee ownership? No

COSTS
Total cost: $110K-120K
Franchise fee: $25K
Royalty fee: 5-12.5%
Term of agreement: 10 years renewable
    at no charge
Franchisees required to buy multiple
    units? Outside the U.S. only

FINANCING
In-house: None
3rd-party: Accounts receivable, equip-
    ment, franchise fee, inventory,
    start-up costs

QUALIFICATIONS
Cash liquidity: $25K-50K
Experience:
    Industry experience
    General business experience
    Marketing skills
    Hospitality/health-care experience
    helpful

TRAINING
At headquarters: 7-10 days
At franchisee's location: 5 days
Ongoing

BUSINESS SUPPORT
Toll-free phone line
Grand opening
Internet
Purchasing cooperatives

MARKETING SUPPORT
Regional marketing
Contracts with national chain
    accounts

BEARCOM BUILDING SERVICES

Ranked #313 in Entrepreneur Magazine's 2004 Franchise 500

Financial rating: $$$

Formerly known as Laser Chem
7022 S. 400 West
Midvale, UT 84047
Ph: (888)569-9533/(801)569-9500
Fax: (801)569-8400
www.bearcomservices.com
Commercial cleaning
Began: 1979, Franchising since: 1990
Headquarters size: 9 employees
Franchise department: 2 employees

U.S. franchises: 58
Canadian franchises: 0
Other foreign franchises: 0
Company-owned: 0
Units concentrated in UT

Seeking: West
Focusing on: All U.S.
Seeking in Canada? No
Exclusive territories? No
Homebased option? Yes
Kiosk option? No
Employees needed to run franchise: 0-2
Absentee ownership? No

COSTS
Total cost: $12.1K-34.5K+
Franchise fee: $9.3K-13K+
Royalty fee: 8%
Term of agreement: 10 years renewable
    at no charge
Franchisees required to buy multiple
    units? No

FINANCING
In-house: Accounts receivable, equip-
    ment, franchise fee
3rd-party: None

QUALIFICATIONS
Experience:
    Industry experience
    General business experience
    Marketing skills

TRAINING
At headquarters: 24 hours

BUSINESS SUPPORT
Newsletter
Toll-free phone line
Internet
Field operations/evaluations

MARKETING SUPPORT
Marketing training

BONUS BUILDING CARE

Ranked #248 in Entrepreneur Magazine's 2004 Franchise 500

Financial rating: 0

P.O. Box 300
Indianola, OK 74442
Ph: (918)823-4990
Fax: (918)823-4994
www.bonusbuildingcare.com
Commercial cleaning
Began: 1996, Franchising since: 1996
Headquarters size: 30 employees
Franchise department: Info not provided

U.S. franchises: 494
Canadian franchises: 0
Other foreign franchises: 0
Company-owned: 3
Units concentrated in MO, TN, TX

Seeking: All U.S.
Seeking in Canada? Yes
Exclusive territories? Yes
Homebased option? Yes
Kiosk option? No
Employees needed to run franchise: 1-5
Absentee ownership? No

COSTS
Total cost: $7.6K-13.3K
Franchise fee: $6.5K
Royalty fee: 10%
Term of agreement: 20 years renewable for $2K
Franchisees required to buy multiple units? Outside the U.S. only

FINANCING
In-house: Accounts receivable, equipment, franchise fee
3rd-party: Accounts receivable, equipment, payroll, start-up costs
Other: Growth financing

QUALIFICATIONS
Info not provided

TRAINING
At headquarters: As needed
At franchisee's location: As needed

BUSINESS SUPPORT
Newsletter
Meetings
Toll-free phone line
Grand opening
Internet
Lease negotiations
Security/safety procedures
Field operations/evaluations
Purchasing cooperatives

MARKETING SUPPORT
Ad slicks
National media campaign
Regional marketing
Direct marketing in local areas
Newspaper ads
Referrals
Trade shows

BUILDINGSTARS INC.

Ranked #373 in Entrepreneur Magazine's 2004 Franchise 500

Financial rating: $$$$

11489 Page Service Dr.
St. Louis, MO 63146
Ph: (314)991-3356
Fax: (314)991-3198
www.buildingstars.com
Commercial cleaning
Began: 1994, Franchising since: 2000
Headquarters size: 18 employees
Franchise department: 3 employees

U.S. franchises: 135
Canadian franchises: 0
Other foreign franchises: 0
Company-owned: 0
Units concentrated in IL, MO

Seeking: All U.S.
Focusing on: IL, MO
Seeking in Canada? No
Exclusive territories? No
Homebased option? Yes
Kiosk option? No
Employees needed to run franchise: 5
Absentee ownership? No

COSTS
Total cost: $1.9K-42.2K
Franchise fee: $995-3.99K
Royalty fee: 10%
Term of agreement: 5 years renewable at no charge
Franchisees required to buy multiple units? No

FINANCING
In-house: Accounts receivable, equipment, franchise fee, start-up costs
3rd-party: None

QUALIFICATIONS
Info not provided

TRAINING
At headquarters: 1 week

BUSINESS SUPPORT
Newsletter
Meetings
Internet

MARKETING SUPPORT
Info not provided

CITY WIDE FRANCHISE CO. INC.

Current financial data not available

8460 Nieman Rd.
Lenexa, KS 66214
Ph: (866)887-4029
Fax: (913)888-5151
citywidefranchise.com
Commercial building maintenance
    services
Began: 1959, Franchising since: 2001
Headquarters size: 50 employees
Franchise department: 4 employees

U.S. franchises: 4
Canadian franchises: 0
Other foreign franchises: 0
Company-owned: 2
Units concentrated in CA, CO, MO,
    OH, TX

Seeking: All U.S.
Seeking in Canada? No
Exclusive territories? Yes
Homebased option? No
Kiosk option? No
Employees needed to run franchise: 3
Absentee ownership? No

COSTS
Total cost: $225K-287K
Franchise fee: $100K
Royalty fee: 5%
Term of agreement: 15 years renewable
    for 10% of franchise fee
Franchisees required to buy multiple
    units? No

FINANCING
In-house: Franchise fee
3rd-party: None

QUALIFICATIONS
Net worth: $250K
Cash liquidity: $150K
Experience:
    General business experience
    Marketing skills

TRAINING
At headquarters: 2 weeks
At franchisee's location: 2 weeks
Annual training meeting

BUSINESS SUPPORT
Newsletter
Meetings
Toll-free phone line
Grand opening
Internet
Security/safety procedures
Field operations/evaluations

MARKETING SUPPORT
Ad slicks
Marketing materials

THE CLEANING AUTHORITY

Ranked #149 in Entrepreneur Magazine's 2004 Franchise 500

Financial rating: $$$$

6994 Columbia Gateway Dr., #100
Columbia, MD 21046
Ph: (800)783-6243/(410)740-1900
Fax: (410)740-1906
www.thecleaningauthority.com
Residential cleaning
Began: 1978, Franchising since: 1996
Headquarters size: 35 employees
Franchise department: 12 employees

U.S. franchises: 115
Canadian franchises: 0
Other foreign franchises: 0
Company-owned: 1
Units concentrated in FL, GA, IL, MD,
    MI, MN, OH, VA

Seeking: All U.S.
Seeking in Canada? No
Exclusive territories? Yes
Homebased option? No
Kiosk option? No
Employees needed to run franchise:
    2-30
Absentee ownership? No

COSTS
Total cost: $67.2K-96.5K
Franchise fee: $22.5K-36K
Royalty fee: 4-6%
Term of agreement: Renewable term at
    no charge
Franchisees required to buy multiple
    units? No

FINANCING
In-house: None
3rd-party: Equipment, franchise fee,
    inventory, start-up costs

QUALIFICATIONS
Net worth: $100K
Cash liquidity: $20K
Experience:
    General business experience
    People skills

TRAINING
At headquarters: 2 weeks

BUSINESS SUPPORT
Newsletter
Meetings
Toll-free phone line
Internet
Field operations/evaluations

MARKETING SUPPORT
Co-op advertising
Ad slicks
Direct mail marketing

CLEANNET USA INC.

Ranked #34 in Entrepreneur Magazine's 2004 Franchise 500

Financial rating: $$$$

9861 Broken Land Pkwy., #208
Columbia, MD 21046
Ph: (800)735-8838/(410)720-6444
Fax: (410)720-5307
www.cleannetusa.com
Commercial office cleaning
Began: 1988, Franchising since: 1988
Headquarters size: 45 employees
Franchise department: 32 employees

U.S. franchises: 2,591
Canadian franchises: 0
Other foreign franchises: 0
Company-owned: 6
Units concentrated in CA, DE, FL, GA,
   IL, MA, MD, MI, NJ, PA, TX, VA

Seeking: All U.S.
Seeking in Canada? Yes
Exclusive territories? Yes
Homebased option? Yes
Kiosk option? No
Employees needed to run franchise:
   3-10
Absentee ownership? Yes

COSTS
Total cost: $3.9K-35.5K
Franchise fee: $2.95K-32K
Royalty fee: 3%
Term of agreement: 20 years renewable
   for $5K
Franchisees required to buy multiple
   units? Yes

FINANCING
In-house: Franchise fee, equipment,
   inventory, start-up costs
3rd-party: None

QUALIFICATIONS
Net worth: $10K-300K
Cash liquidity: $5K-100K
Experience:
   General business experience

TRAINING
At headquarters: 1-4 weeks
At franchisee's location: 1-4 weeks

BUSINESS SUPPORT
Newsletter
Meetings
Toll-free phone line
Grand opening
Internet
Lease negotiations
Security/safety procedures
Field operations/evaluations
Purchasing cooperatives

MARKETING SUPPORT
Regional marketing

COTTAGECARE INC.

Financial rating: $$$

6323 W. 110th St.
Overland Park, KS 66211
Ph: (913)469-8778, Fax: (913)469-0822
www.cottagecare.com
Residential cleaning
Began: 1988, Franchising since: 1989
Headquarters size: 14 employees
Franchise department: 2 employees

U.S. franchises: 40
Canadian franchises: 6
Other foreign franchises: 0
Company-owned: 3
Units concentrated in CA, CO, KS,
   MO, NC, NY, OH, OK, TX, VA

Seeking: All U.S.
Focusing on: All except HI, ND, SD
Seeking in Canada? Yes
Exclusive territories? Yes
Homebased option? No
Kiosk option? No
Employees needed to run franchise:
   1-16
Absentee ownership? Yes

COSTS
Total cost: $49.5K-75.5K
Franchise fee: $9.5K-17K
Royalty fee: 5.5%
Term of agreement: 10 years renewable
   at up to $3K
Franchisees required to buy multiple
   units? No

FINANCING
No financing available

QUALIFICATIONS
Cash liquidity: $46K-72.5K
Experience:
   General business experience

TRAINING
At headquarters: 2 weeks
Additional training available

BUSINESS SUPPORT
Newsletter
Meetings
Internet
Lease negotiations
Security/safety procedures
Field operations/evaluations
Purchasing cooperatives

MARKETING SUPPORT
Co-op advertising
National media campaign
Ongoing direct-mail program

COVERALL CLEANING CONCEPTS
Ranked #35 in Entrepreneur Magazine's 2004 Franchise 500   *Financial rating: $*

500 W. Cypress Creek Rd., #580
Ft. Lauderdale, FL 33309
Ph: (800)537-3371/(954)351-1110
Fax: (954)492-5044
www.coverall.com
Commercial cleaning
Began: 1985, Franchising since: 1985
Headquarters size: 73 employees
Franchise department: 182 employees

U.S. franchises: 7,123
Canadian franchises: 155
Other foreign franchises: 202
Company-owned: 0
Units concentrated in all U.S.

Seeking: All U.S.
Seeking in Canada? Yes
Exclusive territories? Yes
Homebased option? Yes
Kiosk option? No
Employees needed to run franchise: 2
Absentee ownership? Yes

COSTS
Total cost: $6.3K-35.9K
Franchise fee: $6K-32.2K
Royalty fee: 5%
Term of agreement: 20 years renewable
    at no charge
Franchisees required to buy multiple
    units? No

FINANCING
In-house: Franchise fee, equipment,
    inventory, start-up costs
3rd-party: None

QUALIFICATIONS
Net worth: $6K-32K
Cash liquidity: $1.5K

TRAINING
At headquarters: 80 hours
At franchisee's location: 40+ hours &
    ongoing
At international master office:
    10 weeks

BUSINESS SUPPORT
Newsletter
Meetings
Toll-free phone line
Grand opening
Internet
Field operations/evaluations

MARKETING SUPPORT
Co-op advertising
Ad slicks
National media campaign
Regional marketing

E.P.I.C. SYSTEMS INC.

Financial rating: $$$

402 E. Maryland St.
Evansville, IN 47711
Ph: (800)230-3742
Fax: (812)428-4162
Commercial cleaning
Began: 1994, Franchising since: 1994
Headquarters size: 3 employees
Franchise department: 3 employees

U.S. franchises: 7
Canadian franchises: 0
Other foreign franchises: 0
Company-owned: 0
Units concentrated in IN, KY

Seeking: All U.S.
Focusing on: IN, KY, OH, TN
Seeking in Canada? No
Exclusive territories? Yes
Homebased option? Yes
Kiosk option? No
Employees needed to run franchise: 4
Absentee ownership? No

COSTS
Total cost: $10.2K-28.5K
Franchise fee: $6.5K/25K
Royalty fee: 4-10%
Term of agreement: 10 years renewable
    for 10% of initial franchise fee
Franchisees required to buy multiple
    units? No

FINANCING
In-house: Franchise fee
3rd-party: None

QUALIFICATIONS
Net worth: $25K
Cash liquidity: $5K
Experience:
    Industry experience
    General business experience

TRAINING
At headquarters: 2 weeks

BUSINESS SUPPORT
Meetings
Toll-free phone line
Internet
Security/safety procedures
Field operations/evaluations
Purchasing cooperatives

MARKETING SUPPORT
Ad slicks

HOME CLEANING CENTERS OF AMERICA
Ranked #391 in Entrepreneur Magazine's 2004 Franchise 500

Financial rating: $$$

10851 Mastin Blvd., #130
Overland Park, KS 66210
Ph: (800)767-1118
Fax: (913)327-5272
www.homecleaningcenters.com
Home, office, carpet & window cleaning
Began: 1981, Franchising since: 1984
Headquarters size: 2 employees
Franchise department: 2 employees

U.S. franchises: 34
Canadian franchises: 0
Other foreign franchises: 0
Company-owned: 0
Units concentrated in all U.S.

Seeking: All U.S.
Seeking in Canada? No
Exclusive territories? Yes
Homebased option? No
Kiosk option? No
Employees needed to run franchise: 12
Absentee ownership? No

COSTS
Total cost: $23.8K-25.8K
Franchise fee: $9.5K
Royalty fee: 3-5%
Term of agreement: 10 years renewable at no charge
Franchisees required to buy multiple units? No

FINANCING
No financing available

QUALIFICATIONS
Experience:
　　Management skills

TRAINING
At franchisee's location: 1 week

BUSINESS SUPPORT
Newsletter
Meetings
Toll-free phone line
Grand opening
Internet
Lease negotiations
Security/safety procedures
Field operations/evaluations
Purchasing cooperatives

MARKETING SUPPORT
Ad slicks

JAN-PRO FRANCHISING INT'L. INC.
Ranked #22 in Entrepreneur Magazine's 2004 Franchise 500

Financial rating: $$$

383 Strand Industrial Dr.
Little River, SC 29566
Ph: (800)668-1001/(843)399-9895
Fax: (843)399-9890
www.jan-pro.com
Commercial cleaning
Began: 1991, Franchising since: 1992
Headquarters size: 10 employees
Franchise department: 6 employees

U.S. franchises: 2,085
Canadian franchises: 141
Other foreign franchises: 0
Company-owned: 0
Units concentrated in all U.S.

Seeking: All U.S.
Seeking in Canada? Yes
Exclusive territories? Yes
Homebased option? Yes
Kiosk option? No
Employees needed to run franchise: 1
Absentee ownership? No

COSTS
Total cost: $1K-14K+
Franchise fee: $1K-14K+
Royalty fee: 8%
Term of agreement: 10 years renewable at no charge
Franchisees required to buy multiple units? No

FINANCING
In-house: Accounts receivable, equipment, franchise fee
3rd-party: None

QUALIFICATIONS
Net worth: $1K-14K+
Cash liquidity: $1K+
Experience:
　　Management skills

TRAINING
At headquarters: 1 week
At franchisee's location: 4 weeks

BUSINESS SUPPORT
Newsletter
Meetings
Toll-free phone line
Grand opening
Internet
Security/safety procedures
Field operations/evaluations
Purchasing cooperatives

MARKETING SUPPORT
National media campaign
Regional marketing

JANI-KING

Ranked #8 in Entrepreneur Magazine's 2004 Franchise 500

Financial rating: $$$$

16885 Dallas Pkwy.
Addison, TX 75001
Ph: (800)552-5264
Fax: (972)991-5723/(972)239-7706
www.janiking.com
Commercial cleaning
Began: 1969, Franchising since: 1974
Headquarters size: 100 employees
Franchise department: 100 employees

U.S. franchises: 8,506
Canadian franchises: 524
Other foreign franchises: 1,319
Company-owned: 25
Units concentrated in Most of the U.S.

Seeking: All U.S.
Focusing on: Most of the U.S.
Seeking in Canada? Yes
Exclusive territories? Yes
Homebased option? Yes
Kiosk option? No
Employees needed to run franchise:
    Info not provided
Absentee ownership? No

COSTS
Total cost: $11.3K-34.1K+
Franchise fee: $8.6K-16.3K+
Royalty fee: 10%
Term of agreement: 20 years renewable
    at no charge
Franchisees required to buy multiple
    units? No

FINANCING
In-house: Accounts receivable, equipment
3rd-party: Equipment, franchise fee,
    start-up costs

QUALIFICATIONS
Info not provided

TRAINING
At local office: 40-1/2+ hours

BUSINESS SUPPORT
Newsletter
Meetings
Toll-free phone line
Internet
Security/safety procedures
Field operations/evaluations
Purchasing cooperatives

MARKETING SUPPORT
Co-op advertising
Ad slicks
National media campaign
Regional marketing
Sponsorship of car racing program
PR assistance

JANTIZE AMERICA

Current financial data not available

15449 Middlebelt
Livonia, MI 48154
Ph: (800)968-9182
Fax: (734)421-4936
www.jantize.com
Commercial cleaning
Began: 1988, Franchising since: 1988
Headquarters size: 4 employees
Franchise department: 4 employees

U.S. franchises: 23
Canadian franchises: 0
Other foreign franchises: 0
Company-owned: 1
Units concentrated in MI, NC

Seeking: All U.S.
Seeking in Canada? No
Exclusive territories? Yes
Homebased option? Yes
Kiosk option? No
Employees needed to run franchise: 4
Absentee ownership? No

COSTS
Total cost: $9.8K-16.8K
Franchise fee: $3.5K-8.5K
Royalty fee: 6-9%
Term of agreement: 10 years renewable
    at no charge
Franchisees required to buy multiple
    units? No

FINANCING
In-house: Franchise fee, equipment
3rd-party: None

QUALIFICATIONS
Net worth: $25K
Cash liquidity: $10K

TRAINING
At headquarters: 3 days
At franchisee's location: 2 days

BUSINESS SUPPORT
Toll-free phone line
Internet
Lease negotiations
Field operations/evaluations

MARKETING SUPPORT
National media campaign
Regional marketing

MAID BRIGADE USA/MINIMAID CANADA

Ranked #109 in Entrepreneur Magazine's 2004 Franchise 500 *Financial rating: $$$*

4 Concourse Pkwy., #200
Atlanta, GA 30328
Ph: (800)722-6243
Fax: (770)391-9092
www.maidbrigade.com
Residential cleaning
Began: 1979, Franchising since: 1980
Headquarters size: Info not provided
Franchise department: Info not provided

U.S. franchises: 261
Canadian franchises: 76
Other foreign franchises: 1
Company-owned: 4
Units concentrated in all U.S.

Seeking: All U.S.
Seeking in Canada? Yes
Exclusive territories? Yes
Homebased option? No
Kiosk option? No
Employees needed to run franchise:
    Info not provided
Absentee ownership? No

COSTS
Total cost: $46.4K-232.5K
Franchise fee: $18.5K+
Royalty fee: 3.5-6.9%
Term of agreement: 10 years renewable
    at no charge
Franchisees required to buy multiple
    units? No

FINANCING
In-house: None
3rd-party: Equipment, franchise fee,
    start-up costs

QUALIFICATIONS
Net worth: $100K
Cash liquidity: $50K
Experience:
    General business experience
    Marketing skills

TRAINING
At headquarters: 5 days
At franchisee's location: 5 days
Ongoing

BUSINESS SUPPORT
Newsletter
Meetings
Toll-free phone line
Grand opening
Internet
Security/safety procedures
Field operations/evaluations

MARKETING SUPPORT
Co-op advertising
Ad slicks
National media campaign
Regional marketing

MAID TO PERFECTION

Ranked #171 in Entrepreneur Magazine's 2004 Franchise 500 *Financial rating: $$$$*

1101 Opal Ct., 2nd Fl.
Hagerstown, MD 21740
Ph: (800)648-6243/(301)790-7900
Fax: (301)790-3949
www.maidtoperfectioncorp.com
Residential & light commercial cleaning
Began: 1980, Franchising since: 1990
Headquarters size: 8 employees
Franchise department: 8 employees

U.S. franchises: 220
Canadian franchises: 20
Other foreign franchises: 0
Company-owned: 0
Units concentrated in CA, FL, MD, PA

Seeking: All U.S.
Seeking in Canada? Yes
Exclusive territories? Yes
Homebased option? No
Kiosk option? No
Employees needed to run franchise:
    2+
Absentee ownership? No

COSTS
Total cost: $36.3K-43.6K
Franchise fee: $9.95K
Royalty fee: 4-7%
Term of agreement: 5-10 years renew-
    able at no charge
Franchisees required to buy multiple
    units? No

FINANCING
In-house: None
3rd-party: Equipment, franchise fee,
    inventory, start-up costs

QUALIFICATIONS
Net worth: $80K
Cash liquidity: $45K
Experience:
    General business experience
    Marketing skills

TRAINING
At headquarters: 5-7 days
At franchisee's location: 1-21 days
After start-up: 5-7 days

BUSINESS SUPPORT
Newsletter
Meetings
Toll-free phone line
Grand opening
Internet
Field operations/evaluations
Purchasing cooperatives

MARKETING SUPPORT
Co-op advertising
Ad slicks
Regional marketing
Phone routing

MAIDPRO

Ranked #369 in Entrepreneur Magazine's 2004 Franchise 500   *Financial rating: $$$*

180 Canal St.
Boston, MA 02114
Ph: (888)624-3776/(617)742-8787
Fax: (617)720-0700
www.maidpro.com
Professional home & office cleaning
Began: 1991, Franchising since: 1997
Headquarters size: 9 employees
Franchise department: 5 employees

U.S. franchises: 32
Canadian franchises: 0
Other foreign franchises: 0
Company-owned: 1
Units concentrated in CA, CO, CT, FL,
    IA, MA, MD, NH, NJ, NV, NY, OH,
    TX, WA

Seeking: All U.S.
Seeking in Canada? No
Exclusive territories? Yes
Homebased option? No
Kiosk option? No
Employees needed to run franchise:
    6-25
Absentee ownership? No

COSTS
Total cost: $27.9K-75.9K
Franchise fee: $7.9K
Royalty fee: 3-6%
Term of agreement: 10 years renewable
    for $500
Franchisees required to buy multiple
    units? No

FINANCING
In-house: None
3rd-party: Equipment, franchise fee,
    inventory, start-up costs

QUALIFICATIONS
Net worth: $100K
Cash liquidity: $50K
Experience:
    General business experience
    Computer literacy

TRAINING
At headquarters: 2 weeks
At franchisee's location: As needed

BUSINESS SUPPORT
Newsletter
Meetings
Toll-free phone line
Grand opening
Internet
Security/safety procedures
Field operations/evaluations
Purchasing cooperatives

MARKETING SUPPORT
Co-op advertising
Ad slicks
Regional marketing
Design & direct-mail services

THE MAIDS HOME SERVICE

Ranked #193 in Entrepreneur Magazine's 2004 Franchise 500   *Financial rating: 0*

4820 Dodge St.
Omaha, NE 68132
Ph: (800)843-6243
Fax: (402)558-4112
www.maids.com
Residential cleaning
Began: 1979, Franchising since: 1981
Headquarters size: 29 employees
Franchise department: 10 employees

U.S. franchises: 561
Canadian franchises: 14
Other foreign franchises: 0
Company-owned: 31

Seeking: All U.S.
Seeking in Canada? Yes
Exclusive territories? Yes
Homebased option? No
Kiosk option? No
Employees needed to run franchise: 20
Absentee ownership? Yes

COSTS
Total cost: $69.7K-216.6K
Franchise fee: $10K
Royalty fee: 3.9-6.9%
Term of agreement: 20 years renewable
    at no charge
Franchisees required to buy multiple
    units? No

FINANCING
In-house: None
3rd-party: Equipment, franchise fee,
    inventory, start-up costs

QUALIFICATIONS
Net worth: $250K
Cash liquidity: $50K
Experience:
    General business experience
    Marketing skills
    Management & people skills

TRAINING
At headquarters: 10 days
At franchisee's location: 5 days
Phone consultation: 6-8 weeks

BUSINESS SUPPORT
Newsletter
Meetings
Toll-free phone line
Internet
Security/safety procedures
Field operations/evaluations
Purchasing cooperatives

MARKETING SUPPORT
Co-op advertising
Ad slicks
National media campaign
Regional marketing
Intranet
PR support
Customized collateral pieces
Proprietary software

MAIDS TO ORDER

Ranked #484 in Entrepreneur Magazine's 2004 Franchise 500

Financial rating: 0

919 E. Cherry St., #B
Canal Fulton, OH 44614
Ph: (800)701-6243
Fax: (330)854-9382
www.maidstoorder.com
Residential & commercial cleaning
Began: 1988, Franchising since: 1992
Headquarters size: 6 employees
Franchise department: 5 employees

U.S. franchises: 31
Canadian franchises: 0
Other foreign franchises: 4
Company-owned: 0

Seeking: All U.S.
Seeking in Canada? Yes
Exclusive territories? Yes
Homebased option? No
Kiosk option? No
Employees needed to run franchise:
    Info not provided
Absentee ownership? Yes

COSTS
Total cost: $47.6K-95K
Franchise fee: $25K-50K
Royalty fee: 3-5%
Term of agreement: 15 years renewable
    at no charge
Franchisees required to buy multiple
    units? Outside the U.S. only

FINANCING
In-house: Franchise fee
3rd-party: None

QUALIFICATIONS
Cash liquidity: $5K-15K

TRAINING
At headquarters: 1 week
At franchisee's location: 1-2 days

BUSINESS SUPPORT
Newsletter
Meetings
Toll-free phone line
Grand opening
Internet

MARKETING SUPPORT
Co-op advertising
Ad slicks

MERRY MAIDS

Ranked #55 in Entrepreneur Magazine's 2004 Franchise 500

Financial rating: $$$$

860 Ridge Lake Blvd.
Memphis, TN 38120
Ph: (800)798-8000
Fax: (901)537-8140
www.merrymaids.com
Residential cleaning
Began: 1979, Franchising since: 1980
Headquarters size: 52 employees
Franchise department: 23 employees

U.S. franchises: 753
Canadian franchises: 67
Other foreign franchises: 427
Company-owned: 143
Units concentrated in all U.S.

Seeking: All U.S.
Seeking in Canada? Yes
Exclusive territories? Yes
Homebased option? No
Kiosk option? No
Employees needed to run franchise: 12
Absentee ownership? Yes

COSTS
Total cost: $20.95K-50.5K
Franchise fee: $17K-25K
Royalty fee: 5-7%
Term of agreement: 5 years renewable
    at no charge
Franchisees required to buy multiple
    units? No

FINANCING
In-house: Franchise fee, inventory
3rd-party: Equipment

QUALIFICATIONS
Net worth: $32.5K-50.5K
Cash liquidity: $28.7K-43.3K
Experience:
    General business experience

TRAINING
At headquarters: 8 days
At franchisee's location: As needed
Additional training in Memphis, TN &
    regional locations

BUSINESS SUPPORT
Newsletter
Meetings
Toll-free phone line
Internet
Security/safety procedures
Field operations/evaluations

MARKETING SUPPORT
Ad slicks
National media campaign
Yellow Pages

MOLLY MAID

Ranked #204 in Entrepreneur Magazine's 2004 Franchise 500   *Financial rating: $$$$*

3948 Ranchero Dr.
Ann Arbor, MI 48108
Ph: (800)665-5962
Fax: (734)822-6888
www.mollymaid.com
Residential cleaning
Began: 1979, Franchising since: 1979
Headquarters size: 40 employees
Franchise department: 6 employees

U.S. franchises: 272
Canadian franchises: 172
Other foreign franchises: 106
Company-owned: 0
Units concentrated in all U.S.

Seeking: All U.S.
Seeking in Canada? Yes
Exclusive territories? Yes
Homebased option? No
Kiosk option? No
Employees needed to run franchise: 14
Absentee ownership? Yes

COSTS
Total cost: $62.6K-92.1K
Franchise fee: $6.9K
Royalty fee: 6.5-3%
Term of agreement: 10 years renewable
    for $500
Franchisees required to buy multiple
    units? No

FINANCING
No financing available

QUALIFICATIONS
Net worth: $250K
Cash liquidity: $30K
Experience:
    General business experience
    Marketing skills

TRAINING
At headquarters: 1 week
At franchisee's location: 2 days
Regional training center: 1 week

BUSINESS SUPPORT
Newsletter
Meetings
Toll-free phone line
Grand opening
Internet
Security/safety procedures
Field operations/evaluations
Purchasing cooperatives

MARKETING SUPPORT
Co-op advertising
Ad slicks
National media campaign

OMEX - OFFICE MAINTENANCE EXPERTS

Financial rating: $$$

3905 Hartzdale Dr., #506
Camp Hill, PA 17011
Ph: (800)827-6639/(717)737-7311
Fax: (717)737-9271
www.omexcorp.com
Office cleaning management
Began: 1979, Franchising since: 1991
Headquarters size: 200 employees
Franchise department: 8 employees

U.S. franchises: 15
Canadian franchises: 0
Other foreign franchises: 0
Company-owned: 1
Units concentrated in all U.S.

Seeking: All U.S.
Seeking in Canada? Yes
Exclusive territories? Yes
Homebased option? No
Kiosk option? No
Employees needed to run franchise:
    Info not provided
Absentee ownership? No

COSTS
Total cost: $40.4K-70.6K
Franchise fee: $15K-25K
Royalty fee: 4%
Term of agreement: 10 years renewable
    at no charge
Franchisees required to buy multiple
    units? No

FINANCING
No financing available

QUALIFICATIONS
Net worth: $150K
Cash liquidity: $40K
Experience:
    General business experience
    Marketing skills
    Management experience

TRAINING
At headquarters: 1 week
At franchisee's location: 1 week

BUSINESS SUPPORT
Newsletter
Toll-free phone line
Grand opening
Internet
Security/safety procedures
Field operations/evaluations
Purchasing cooperatives

MARKETING SUPPORT
Co-op advertising
Ad slicks
Regional marketing
Grand opening mailer

OPENWORKS

Ranked #161 in Entrepreneur Magazine's 2004 Franchise 500   *Financial rating: $$$$*

4742 N. 24th St., #300
Phoenix, AZ 85016
Ph: (800)777-6736
Fax: (602)468-3788
www.openworksweb.com
Commercial cleaning
Began: 1983, Franchising since: 1983
Headquarters size: 31 employees
Franchise department: 11 employees

U.S. franchises: 392
Canadian franchises: 0
Other foreign franchises: 0
Company-owned: 0
Units concentrated in AZ, CA, WA

Seeking: All U.S.
Focusing on: Master franchises
    throughout the U.S.
Seeking in Canada? No
Exclusive territories? Yes
Homebased option? Yes
Kiosk option? No
Employees needed to run franchise: 5
Absentee ownership? No

COSTS
Total cost: $15K+
Franchise fee: $14K-67.5K
Royalty fee: 10%
Term of agreement: 10 years renewable
    at no charge
Franchisees required to buy multiple
    units? No

FINANCING
In-house: Accounts receivable, fran-
    chise fee, equipment, inventory,
    start-up costs
3rd-party: None

QUALIFICATIONS
Cash liquidity: $7K
Experience:
    General business experience

TRAINING
At headquarters: 2 weeks
At franchisee's location: Ongoing
At regional locations: 2+ weeks &
    ongoing

BUSINESS SUPPORT
Newsletter
Meetings
Toll-free phone line
Security/safety procedures
Field operations/evaluations
Purchasing cooperatives

MARKETING SUPPORT
Regional marketing
Bid preparation & presentation

SERVICE ONE JANITORIAL

Current financial data not available

5104 N. Orange Blossom Tr., #114
Orlando, FL 32810
Ph: (800)522-7111/(407)293-7645
Fax: (407)299-4306
www.serviceonejanitorial.net
Janitorial services
Began: 1967, Franchising since: 1985
Headquarters size: 6 employees
Franchise department: 4 employees

U.S. franchises: 185
Canadian franchises: 0
Other foreign franchises: 0
Company-owned: 0
Units concentrated in all U.S.

Seeking: All U.S.
Seeking in Canada? No
Exclusive territories? No
Homebased option? Yes
Kiosk option? No
Employees needed to run franchise: 2
Absentee ownership? Yes

COSTS
Total cost: $6.8K-19.3K
Franchise fee: Incl. in start-up
Royalty fee: $175/mo.
Term of agreement: 10 years renewable
    at no charge
Franchisees required to buy multiple
    units? No

FINANCING
In-house: Accounts receivable, equip-
    ment, franchise fee, inventory
3rd-party: None

QUALIFICATIONS
Net worth: $10K
Cash liquidity: $2K
Experience:
    General business experience

TRAINING
At headquarters: 3 days
At franchisee's location: 3 days

BUSINESS SUPPORT
Newsletter
Meetings
Toll-free phone line
Grand opening
Internet
Security/safety procedures

MARKETING SUPPORT
Ad slicks

SERVICEMASTER CLEAN

Ranked #18 in Entrepreneur Magazine's 2004 Franchise 500   *Financial rating: $$$$*

860 Ridge Lake Blvd.
Memphis, TN 38120
Ph: (800)255-9687/(901)684-7500
Fax: (901)684-7580
www.ownafranchise.com
Commercial & residential cleaning, disaster restoration
Began: 1947, Franchising since: 1952
Headquarters size: 134 employees
Franchise department: 8 employees

U.S. franchises: 2,722
Canadian franchises: 176
Other foreign franchises: 1,398
Company-owned: 0
Units concentrated in all U.S.

Seeking: All U.S.
Seeking in Canada? Yes
Exclusive territories? No
Homebased option? Yes
Kiosk option? No
Employees needed to run franchise: 3
Absentee ownership? No

COSTS
Total cost: $26.6K-90.5K
Franchise fee: $16.9K-33.5K
Royalty fee: 4-10%
Term of agreement: 5 years renewable at no charge
Franchisees required to buy multiple units? Outside the U.S. only

FINANCING
In-house: Accounts receivable, equipment, franchise fee, inventory, payroll, start-up costs
Other: Vehicles, line-of-credit

QUALIFICATIONS
Net worth: $50K-75K
Cash liquidity: $15K-25K
Experience:
     General business experience

TRAINING
At headquarters: 2 weeks
At franchisee's location: 1-2 days
Annual convention & regional seminars

BUSINESS SUPPORT
Newsletter
Meetings
Toll-free phone line
Internet
Security/safety procedures
Field operations/evaluations

MARKETING SUPPORT
Co-op advertising
Ad slicks
National media campaign
Regional marketing
Intranet
Web design templates

SPARKLE WASH

Ranked #418 in Entrepreneur Magazine's 2004 Franchise 500   *Financial rating: $$$$*

26851 Richmond Rd.
Cleveland, OH 44146
Ph: (800)321-0770/(216)464-4212
Fax: (216)464-8869
www.sparklewash.com
On-site cleaning & restoration
Began: 1965, Franchising since: 1967
Headquarters size: 10 employees
Franchise department: 2 employees

U.S. franchises: 74
Canadian franchises: 1
Other foreign franchises: 36
Company-owned: 1
Units concentrated in IA, MI, MN, NC, NY, OH, PA, WI, WV

Seeking: All U.S.
Seeking in Canada? Yes
Exclusive territories? Yes
Homebased option? Yes
Kiosk option? No
Employees needed to run franchise: 2
Absentee ownership? Yes

COSTS
Total cost: $18.8K-85.3K
Franchise fee: $15K-40K
Royalty fee: 3-5%
Term of agreement: 20 years renewable at no charge
Franchisees required to buy multiple units? No

FINANCING
In-house: Franchise fee
3rd-party: Equipment

QUALIFICATIONS
Net worth: $100K
Cash liquidity: $35K
Experience:
     General business experience

TRAINING
At headquarters: 1 week
At franchisee's location: 1 week
Additional training available

BUSINESS SUPPORT
Newsletter
Meetings
Toll-free phone line
Internet
Security/safety procedures
Field operations/evaluations

MARKETING SUPPORT
Co-op advertising
Ad slicks

SWISHER HYGIENE FRANCHISE CORP.
Ranked #230 in Entrepreneur Magazine's 2004 Franchise 500   *Financial rating: $$$$*

6849 Fairview Rd.
Charlotte, NC 28210
Ph: (800)444-4138/(704)364-7707
Fax: (800)444-4565
www.swisheronline.com
Restroom-hygiene/commercial pest-control services
Began: 1983, Franchising since: 1989
Headquarters size: 70 employees
Franchise department: 70 employees

U.S. franchises: 99
Canadian franchises: 8
Other foreign franchises: 37
Company-owned: 1
Units concentrated in all U.S.

Seeking: All U.S.
Seeking in Canada? Yes
Exclusive territories? Yes
Homebased option? Yes
Kiosk option? No
Employees needed to run franchise:
    Info not provided
Absentee ownership? No

COSTS
Total cost: $44.2K-170.1K
Franchise fee: $35K-85K
Royalty fee: 6%
Term of agreement: 5 years renewable
Franchisees required to buy multiple
    units? Outside the U.S. only

FINANCING
In-house: Franchise fee, start-up costs
3rd-party: Equipment, franchise fee,
    inventory, start-up costs

QUALIFICATIONS
Net worth: $50K-150K
Cash liquidity: $15K-50K
Experience:
    General business experience

TRAINING
At headquarters: 1 week
At franchisee's location: 1 week
As needed

BUSINESS SUPPORT
Newsletter
Meetings
Toll-free phone line
Grand opening
Internet

MARKETING SUPPORT
National media campaign

TOWER CLEANING SYSTEMS
Ranked #350 in Entrepreneur Magazine's 2004 Franchise 500   *Financial rating: $$$*

P.O. Box 2468
Southeastern, PA 19399
Ph: (610)278-9000, Fax: (610)275-8025
www.toweronline.com
Office cleaning
Began: 1988, Franchising since: 1990
Headquarters size: 175 employees
Franchise department: 18 employees

U.S. franchises: 496
Canadian franchises: 0
Other foreign franchises: 0
Company-owned: 0
Units concentrated in MI, MN, NJ, PA

Seeking: Midwest, Northeast,
    Southeast, West
Focusing on: GA, HI, MI, MN, NJ,
    OH, PA
Seeking in Canada? No
Exclusive territories? No
Homebased option? Yes
Kiosk option? No
Employees needed to run franchise: 1
Absentee ownership? No

COSTS
Total cost: $1.9K-23.8K
Franchise fee: $1.5K-13.5K
Royalty fee: 3%
Term of agreement: 10 years renewable
    at no charge
Franchisees required to buy multiple
    units? No

FINANCING
In-house: Franchise fee, equipment
3rd-party: None

QUALIFICATIONS
Info not provided

TRAINING
At headquarters: 2 weeks

BUSINESS SUPPORT
Newsletter
Toll-free phone line
Security/safety procedures
Field operations/evaluations

MARKETING SUPPORT
Regional marketing

VANGUARD CLEANING SYSTEMS

Ranked #205 in Entrepreneur Magazine's 2004 Franchise 500   *Financial rating: $$$$*

655 Mariners Island Blvd., #303
San Mateo, CA 94404
Ph: (800)564-6422/(650)594-1500
Fax: (650)591-1545
www.vanguardcleaning.com
Commercial cleaning
Began: 1984, Franchising since: 1984
Headquarters size: 20 employees
Franchise department: 3 employees

U.S. franchises: 270
Canadian franchises: 0
Other foreign franchises: 0
Company-owned: 3
Units concentrated in CA, FL, PA, UT

Seeking: All U.S.
Seeking in Canada? Yes
Exclusive territories? No
Homebased option? Yes
Kiosk option? No
Employees needed to run franchise: 1-2
Absentee ownership? No

COSTS
Total cost: $2.2K-33.7K
Franchise fee: $1.9K-32.8K
Royalty fee: 5%
Term of agreement: 10 years renewable
     at no charge
Franchisees required to buy multiple
     units? No

FINANCING
In-house: Franchise fee
3rd-party: None

QUALIFICATIONS
Cash liquidity: $2.8K-9K
Experience:
     General business experience

TRAINING
At headquarters: 2 weeks
At regional offices: 2 weeks

BUSINESS SUPPORT
Newsletter
Toll-free phone line
Field operations/evaluations

MARKETING SUPPORT
Regional marketing
Initial customer base

MAINTENANCE   *Home Repairs*

AIRE SERV HEATING & AIR CONDITIONING INC.

Ranked #311 in Entrepreneur Magazine's 2004 Franchise 500   *Financial rating: $$$$*

1020 N. University Parks Dr.
Waco, TX 76707
Ph: (800)583-2662, Fax: (254)745-5098

www.aireserv.com
Heating & air conditioning services
Began: 1993, Franchising since: 1993
Headquarters size: 110 employees
Franchise department: 30 employees

U.S. franchises: 63
Canadian franchises: 0
Other foreign franchises: 9
Company-owned: 0
Units concentrated in all U.S.

Seeking: All U.S.
Seeking in Canada? Yes
Exclusive territories? Yes
Homebased option? Yes
Kiosk option? No
Employees needed to run franchise: 5-6
Absentee ownership? No

COSTS
Total cost: $31.6K-119.5K
Franchise fee: $17.5K
Royalty fee: 2.5-4.5%
Term of agreement: 10 years renewable
     for $2.5K
Franchisees required to buy multiple
     units? Outside the U.S. only

FINANCING
In-house: Franchise fee
3rd-party: None

QUALIFICATIONS
Net worth: $150K+
Cash liquidity: $35K
Experience:
     Industry experience

TRAINING
At headquarters: 7 days
At franchisee's location: 3 days
Regional training meetings: 3 days

BUSINESS SUPPORT
Newsletter
Meetings
Toll-free phone line
Grand opening
Internet
Field operations/evaluations
Purchasing cooperatives

MARKETING SUPPORT
Co-op advertising
Ad slicks
National media campaign
Local ad plan

FURNITURE MEDIC

Ranked #97 in Entrepreneur Magazine's 2004 Franchise 500   *Financial rating: $$$$*

860 Ridge Lake Blvd.
Memphis, TN 38120
Ph: (800)877-9933/(901)820-8600
Fax: (901)820-8660
www.furnituremedicfranchise.com
Furniture restoration & repair services
Began: 1992, Franchising since: 1992
Headquarters size: 24 employees
Franchise department: 8 employees

U.S. franchises: 410
Canadian franchises: 70
Other foreign franchises: 108
Company-owned: 0
Units concentrated in all U.S.

Seeking: All U.S.
Seeking in Canada? Yes
Exclusive territories? No
Homebased option? Yes
Kiosk option? No
Employees needed to run franchise: 1
Absentee ownership? No

COSTS
Total cost: $35.5K-78.9K
Franchise fee: $22K
Royalty fee: 7%
Term of agreement: 5 years renewable
at no charge
Franchisees required to buy multiple
units? Outside the U.S. only

FINANCING
In-house: Accounts receivable, equipment, franchise fee, inventory, payroll, start-up costs
Other: Vehicle, line-of-credit

QUALIFICATIONS
Net worth: $60K-80K
Cash liquidity: $15K-25K
Experience:
Industry experience
General business experience
Marketing skills

TRAINING
At headquarters: 2 weeks
Home study/mentor program:
2 weeks+

BUSINESS SUPPORT
Newsletter
Meetings
Toll-free phone line
Internet
Security/safety procedures
Field operations/evaluations

MARKETING SUPPORT
Ad slicks
National media campaign
Web site template

GLASS DOCTOR

Ranked #134 in Entrepreneur Magazine's 2004 Franchise 500   *Financial rating: $$$$*

1020 N. University Parks Dr.
Waco, TX 76707
Ph: (800)280-9858
Fax: (800)209-7621
www.glassdoctor.com
Glass replacement services
Began: 1962, Franchising since: 1981
Headquarters size: 110 employees
Franchise department: 30 employees

U.S. franchises: 100
Canadian franchises: 1
Other foreign franchises: 0
Company-owned: 0
Units concentrated in all U.S.

Seeking: All U.S.
Seeking in Canada? Yes
Exclusive territories? Yes
Homebased option? No
Kiosk option? No
Employees needed to run franchise: 5-6
Absentee ownership? No

COSTS
Total cost: $107.2K-259.2K
Franchise fee: $19.9K
Royalty fee: 4-7%
Term of agreement: 10 years renewable
for $2.5K
Franchisees required to buy multiple
units? Outside the U.S. only

FINANCING
In-house: Franchise fee
3rd-party: None

QUALIFICATIONS
Net worth: $100K
Cash liquidity: $50K
Experience:
Industry experience

TRAINING
At headquarters: 10 days
At franchisee's location: 3 days
Regional training meetings: Twice a
year

BUSINESS SUPPORT
Newsletter
Meetings
Toll-free phone line
Grand opening
Internet
Field operations/evaluations

MARKETING SUPPORT
Co-op advertising
Ad slicks
National media campaign

GUARDSMAN FURNITUREPRO

Current financial data not available

4999 36th St. S.E.
Grand Rapids, MI 49512
Ph: (800)496-6377
Fax: (616)285-7882
www.guardsmanfurniturepro.com
Mobile furniture repair & refinishing
Began: 1865, Franchising since: 1994
Headquarters size: 70 employees
Franchise department: 8 employees

U.S. franchises: 118
Canadian franchises: 2
Other foreign franchises: 0
Company-owned: 0
Units concentrated in all U.S.

Seeking: All U.S.
Seeking in Canada? Yes
Exclusive territories? Yes
Homebased option? Yes
Kiosk option? No
Employees needed to run franchise: 1-2
Absentee ownership? Info not provided

COSTS
Total cost: $10K-25K
Franchise fee: $7K
Royalty fee: Varies
Term of agreement: 5 years renewable
at no charge
Franchisees required to buy multiple
units? No

FINANCING
In-house: Territory fee
3rd-party: None

QUALIFICATIONS
Net worth: $100K
Cash liquidity: $20K

TRAINING
At headquarters: 2 weeks

BUSINESS SUPPORT
Newsletter
Meetings
Toll-free phone line
Internet
Security/safety procedures
Field operations/evaluations

MARKETING SUPPORT
Ad slicks
National media campaign

MR. APPLIANCE CORP.

Ranked #285 in Entrepreneur Magazine's 2004 Franchise 500　　　*Financial rating: $$$$*

1020 N. University Parks Dr.
Waco, TX 76707
Ph: (800)290-1422
Fax: (800)209-7621
www.mrappliance.com
Household appliance services &
repairs
Began: 1996, Franchising since: 1996
Headquarters size: 110 employees
Franchise department: 30 employees

U.S. franchises: 60
Canadian franchises: 1
Other foreign franchises: 2
Company-owned: 0
Units concentrated in all U.S.

Seeking: All U.S.
Seeking in Canada? Yes
Exclusive territories? Yes
Homebased option? Yes
Kiosk option? No
Employees needed to run franchise: 1-3
Absentee ownership? No

COSTS
Total cost: $32.2K-68.9K
Franchise fee: $15.9K
Royalty fee: 3-7%
Term of agreement: 10 years renewable
for $2.5K
Franchisees required to buy multiple
units? Outside the U.S. only

FINANCING
In-house: Franchise fee
3rd-party: None

QUALIFICATIONS
Net worth: $100K
Cash liquidity: $25K
Experience:
Industry experience

TRAINING
At headquarters: 1 week
At franchisee's location: Varies
Regional meetings

BUSINESS SUPPORT
Newsletter
Meetings
Toll-free phone line
Internet
Field operations/evaluations

MARKETING SUPPORT
Co-op advertising
Ad slicks
National media campaign

MR. ELECTRIC
Ranked #212 in Entrepreneur Magazine's 2004 Franchise 500   *Financial rating: $$$$*

1020 N. University Parks Dr.
Waco, TX 76707
Ph: (800)805-0575
Fax: (800)209-7621
www.mrelectric.com
Electrical services/repairs contracting
Began: 1994, Franchising since: 1994
Headquarters size: 110 employees
Franchise department: 30 employees

U.S. franchises: 110
Canadian franchises: 4
Other foreign franchises: 25
Company-owned: 0
Units concentrated in all U.S.

Seeking: All U.S.
Seeking in Canada? Yes
Exclusive territories? Yes
Homebased option? Yes
Kiosk option? No
Employees needed to run franchise: 2-3
Absentee ownership? No

COSTS
Total cost: $64.1K-156.5K
Franchise fee: $19.5K
Royalty fee: 3-6%
Term of agreement: 10 years renewable
    for $2.5K
Franchisees required to buy multiple
    units? Outside the U.S. only

FINANCING
In-house: Franchise fee
3rd-party: None

QUALIFICATIONS
Net worth: $100K
Cash liquidity: $25K-50K
Experience:
    Industry experience

TRAINING
At headquarters: 10 days
At franchisee's location: 2-3 days
At regional locations: 2 days

BUSINESS SUPPORT
Newsletter
Meetings
Toll-free phone line
Internet
Field operations/evaluations

MARKETING SUPPORT
Co-op advertising
Ad slicks
National media campaign

PRECISION DOOR SERVICE INC.
Ranked #227 in Entrepreneur Magazine's 2004 Franchise 500   *Financial rating: $$$*

571 Haverty Ct., #W
Rockledge, FL 32955
Ph: (888)833-3494/(321)433-3494
Fax: (321)433-3062
www.precisiondoor.net
Garage door repair & installation
    service
Began: 1997, Franchising since: 1999
Headquarters size: 20 employees
Franchise department: 4 employees

U.S. franchises: 54
Canadian franchises: 0
Other foreign franchises: 0
Company-owned: 3
Units concentrated in CA, FL, NC, NJ,
    NY, SC, TX

Seeking: All U.S.
Seeking in Canada? No
Exclusive territories? Yes
Homebased option? No
Kiosk option? No
Employees needed to run franchise: 3
Absentee ownership? Yes

COSTS
Total cost: $73.5K+
Franchise fee: $25K+
Royalty fee: $250/wk.+
Term of agreement: 10 years renewable
    at no charge
Franchisees required to buy multiple
    units? No

FINANCING
In-house: Franchise fee
3rd-party: Franchise fee

QUALIFICATIONS
Net worth: $75K-200K
Cash liquidity: $60K+

TRAINING
At headquarters: 14 days

BUSINESS SUPPORT
Newsletter
Meetings
Security/safety procedures
Field operations/evaluations

MARKETING SUPPORT
Ad slicks
National media campaign

SCREEN MACHINE

Ranked #498 in Entrepreneur Magazine's 2004 Franchise 500　　　　*Financial rating: $$$*

4173 First St.
Livermore, CA 94557
Ph: (877)505-1985
Fax: (925)443-9983
www.screen-machine.com
Mobile window screen repair & fabrication services
Began: 1986, Franchising since: 1988
Headquarters size: 3 employees
Franchise department: 3 employees

U.S. franchises: 26
Canadian franchises: 0
Other foreign franchises: 0
Company-owned: 1
Units concentrated in CA

Seeking: All U.S.
Seeking in Canada? No
Exclusive territories? Yes
Homebased option? Yes
Kiosk option? No
Employees needed to run franchise: 1
Absentee ownership? No

COSTS
Total cost: $47K-72.1K
Franchise fee: $25K
Royalty fee: 5%
Term of agreement: 10 years renewable for $2K
Franchisees required to buy multiple units? No

FINANCING
In-house: None
3rd-party: Equipment, franchise fee, inventory, start-up costs

QUALIFICATIONS
Net worth: $50K
Cash liquidity: $25K
Experience:
　General business experience
　Marketing skills

TRAINING
At headquarters: 1 week
Annual meeting: 2 days

BUSINESS SUPPORT
Meetings
Toll-free phone line
Internet
Purchasing cooperatives

MARKETING SUPPORT
Co-op advertising
Ad slicks

THE SCREENMOBILE

Ranked #377 in Entrepreneur Magazine's 2004 Franchise 500　　　　*Financial rating: $$$$*

72050-A Corporate Wy.
Thousand Palms, CA 92276
Ph: (866)540-5800
Fax: (760)343-3500
www.screenmobile.com
Mobile window & door screening
Began: 1982, Franchising since: 1984
Headquarters size: 8 employees
Franchise department: 3 employees

U.S. franchises: 66
Canadian franchises: 0
Other foreign franchises: 0
Company-owned: 1

Seeking: All U.S.
Seeking in Canada? No
Exclusive territories? Yes
Homebased option? Yes
Kiosk option? No
Employees needed to run franchise: 1
Absentee ownership? Yes

COSTS
Total cost: $72.7K-76.9K
Franchise fee: $69.3K
Royalty fee: 5%
Term of agreement: 5 years renewable at no charge
Franchisees required to buy multiple units? No

FINANCING
No financing available

QUALIFICATIONS
Net worth: $70K
Cash liquidity: $54.3K

TRAINING
At headquarters: 6 days
At franchisee's location: 2 days

BUSINESS SUPPORT
Newsletter
Meetings
Internet
Security/safety procedures
Field operations/evaluations

MARKETING SUPPORT
Ad slicks
Web site

MAINTENANCE ▶ *Lawn Care*

CLINTAR GROUNDSKEEPING SERVICES

Current financial data not available

70 Esna Park Dr., #1
Markham, ON Canada L3R 1E3
Ph: (800)361-3542/(905)943-9530
Fax: (905)943-9529
www.clintar.com
Commercial groundskeeping & snow
clearing
Began: 1973, Franchising since: 1983
Headquarters size: 15 employees
Franchise department: 15 employees

U.S. franchises: 0
Canadian franchises: 12
Other foreign franchises: 0
Company-owned: 1

Seeking: Midwest, Northeast
Focusing on: Northeast & Great Lakes
area
Seeking in Canada? Yes
Exclusive territories? Yes
Homebased option? No
Kiosk option? No
Employees needed to run franchise: 15
Absentee ownership? No

COSTS
Total cost: $125K
Franchise fee: $30K
Royalty fee: 8%
Term of agreement: 10 years renewable
at no charge
Franchisees required to buy multiple
units? No

FINANCING
In-house: Franchise fee
Equipment, start-up costs

QUALIFICATIONS
Net worth: $250K
Cash liquidity: $50K
Experience:
General business experience
Marketing skills

TRAINING
At headquarters: 1 week
At franchisee's location: Ongoing
Ongoing

BUSINESS SUPPORT
Newsletter
Meetings
Toll-free phone line
Grand opening
Internet
Lease negotiations
Security/safety procedures
Field operations/evaluations
Purchasing cooperatives

MARKETING SUPPORT
Co-op advertising
Ad slicks
Regional marketing

ENVIRO MASTERS LAWN CARE

Current financial data not available

Box 178
Caledon East, ON L0N 1E0 Canada
Ph: (905)584-9592
Fax: (905)584-0402
www.enviromasters.com
Organic lawn care
Began: 1987, Franchising since: 1991
Headquarters size: 6 employees
Franchise department: 6 employees

U.S. franchises: 0
Canadian franchises: 34
Other foreign franchises: 0
Company-owned: 3
Units concentrated in Canada

Seeking in Canada? Yes
Exclusive territories? Yes
Homebased option? Yes
Kiosk option? No
Employees needed to run franchise: 2
Absentee ownership? No

COSTS
Total cost: $30K-40K
Franchise fee: $25K
Royalty fee: 5%
Term of agreement: 10 years renewable
for 50% of franchise fee
Franchisees required to buy multiple
units? No

FINANCING
In-house: None
3rd-party: Accounts receivable, equipment, franchise fee, inventory, payroll, start-up costs

QUALIFICATIONS
Net worth: $40K
Cash liquidity: $25K
Experience:
General business experience
Marketing skills

TRAINING
At headquarters: 2 weeks
At franchisee's location: 2 days
Ongoing

BUSINESS SUPPORT
Newsletter
Meetings
Toll-free phone line
Grand opening
Internet
Security/safety procedures
Field operations/evaluations
Purchasing cooperatives

MARKETING SUPPORT
Co-op advertising
Ad slicks
National media campaign
Regional marketing

GREENLAND IRRIGATION

Current financial data not available

150 Ambleside Dr.
London, ON Canada N6G 4R1
Ph: (519)439-0220
Fax: (519)433-9780
www.greenlandirrigation.com
Lawn sprinkler system
Began: 1986, Franchising since: 1995
Headquarters size: 12 employees
Franchise department: 1 employee

U.S. franchises: 0
Canadian franchises: 6
Other foreign franchises: 0
Company-owned: 0

Seeking in Canada? Yes
Exclusive territories? Yes
Homebased option? Yes
Kiosk option? No
Employees needed to run franchise: 3
Absentee ownership? No

COSTS
Total cost: $30K
Franchise fee: $15K
Royalty fee: 3-10%
Term of agreement: 10 years renewable
    at no charge
Franchisees required to buy multiple
    units? No

FINANCING
No financing available

QUALIFICATIONS
Net worth: $100K
Cash liquidity: $50K
Experience:
    General business experience

TRAINING
At headquarters: 3 days
At franchisee's location: 2 days
At local supplier: 2 days

BUSINESS SUPPORT
Meetings
Toll-free phone line
Internet
Field operations/evaluations
Purchasing cooperatives

MARKETING SUPPORT
Co-op advertising
Home shows

LAWN DOCTOR

Ranked #84 in Entrepreneur Magazine's 2004 Franchise 500

Financial rating: $$$$

142 Hwy. 34
Holmdel, NJ 07733-0401
Ph: (800)452-9637
Fax: (732)946-9089
www.lawndoctor.com
Lawn, tree & shrub care
Began: 1967, Franchising since: 1967
Headquarters size: 70 employees
Franchise department: 3 employees

U.S. franchises: 435
Canadian franchises: 0
Other foreign franchises: 0
Company-owned: 0

Seeking: All U.S.
Seeking in Canada? No
Exclusive territories? Yes
Homebased option? Yes
Kiosk option? No
Employees needed to run franchise:
    Info not provided
Absentee ownership? Info not provided

COSTS
Total cost: $82.9K-83.3K
Franchise fee: $74.9K
Royalty fee: 10%
Term of agreement: 20 years renewable
    at no charge
Franchisees required to buy multiple
    units? No

FINANCING
In-house: Franchise fee, equipment,
    start-up costs
3rd-party: Equipment, franchise fee,
    start-up costs

QUALIFICATIONS
Net worth: $150K
Cash liquidity: $40.7K

TRAINING
At headquarters: 2 weeks

BUSINESS SUPPORT
Newsletter
Meetings
Toll-free phone line
Internet
Security/safety procedures
Field operations/evaluations

MARKETING SUPPORT
Co-op advertising
Ad slicks
Regional marketing

NATURALAWN OF AMERICA INC.
Ranked #308 in Entrepreneur Magazine's 2004 Franchise 500 *Financial rating: $$$$*

1 E. Church St.
Frederick, MD 21701
Ph: (800)989-5444, Fax: (301)846-0320
www.nl-amer.com
Organic/biological-based lawn care
  system
Began: 1987, Franchising since: 1989
Headquarters size: 14 employees
Franchise department: 2 employees

U.S. franchises: 58
Canadian franchises: 0
Other foreign franchises: 0
Company-owned: 3
Units concentrated in CA, CO, CT, IL,
  MA, MD, ME, MN, NC, NJ, PA, WI

Seeking: Midwest, Northeast, South,
  Southeast, Southwest
Focusing on: All except AL, HI,
  ND, SD
Seeking in Canada? Yes
Exclusive territories? Yes
Homebased option? No
Kiosk option? No
Employees needed to run franchise: 2-6
Absentee ownership? Yes

COSTS
Total cost: $55K-60K
Franchise fee: $29.5K
Royalty fee: 7-9%
Term of agreement: 5 years renewable
  at no charge
Franchisees required to buy multiple
  units? Outside the U.S. only

FINANCING
In-house: None
3rd-party: Equipment, franchise fee,
  inventory, start-up costs

QUALIFICATIONS
Net worth: $250K
Cash liquidity: $50K
Experience:
    General business experience
    Sales experience
    Management experience

TRAINING
At headquarters
At franchisee's location
At regional location

BUSINESS SUPPORT
Newsletter
Meetings
Toll-free phone line
Grand opening
Internet
Security/safety procedures
Field operations/evaluations
Purchasing cooperatives

MARKETING SUPPORT
Co-op advertising
Ad slicks
Regional marketing
Internet marketing

NATURE'S PRO
Current financial data not available

382 S. Franklin St.
Hempstead, NY 11550
Ph: (800)645-6464, Fax: (516)538-2042
www.naturespro.com
Organic-based lawn, tree & shrub care
Began: 1975, Franchising since: 1999
Headquarters size: 11 employees
Franchise department: 3 employees

U.S. franchises: 10
Canadian franchises: 0
Other foreign franchises: 0
Company-owned: 1
Units concentrated in all U.S.

Seeking: Midwest, Northeast, South,
  Southeast
Focusing on: All U.S.
Seeking in Canada? No
Exclusive territories? Yes
Homebased option? Yes
Kiosk option? No
Employees needed to run franchise:
    Info not provided
Absentee ownership? Yes

COSTS
Total cost: $57.2K-103K
Franchise fee: $17.5K-40K
Royalty fee: 5%
Term of agreement: 10 years renewable
  for $5K
Franchisees required to buy multiple
  units? Info not provided

FINANCING
In-house: Franchise fee, inventory
3rd-party: Equipment, start-up costs

QUALIFICATIONS
Net worth: $250K
Cash liquidity: $50K
Experience:
    General business experience
    Marketing skills

TRAINING
At headquarters: 3-5 days
At franchisee's location: 9-12 days
At a resort location: 3-5 days

BUSINESS SUPPORT
Newsletter
Meetings
Grand opening
Internet
Field operations/evaluations
Purchasing cooperatives

MARKETING SUPPORT
Ad slicks
Press releases
Trade shows
House shows

NUTRI-LAWN

Current financial data not available

5397 Eglinton Ave. W., #110
Toronto, ON Canada M9C 5K6
Ph: (416)620-7100
Fax: (416)620-7771
www.nutri-lawn.com
Lawn care
Began: 1983, Franchising since: 1985
Headquarters size: 4 employees
Franchise department: 1 employee

U.S. franchises: 5
Canadian franchises: 30
Other foreign franchises: 1
Company-owned: 0
Units concentrated in NJ, PA, UT, WA

Seeking: Midwest, Northeast,
    Northwest, West
Focusing on: IL, MA, NJ, OH, PA
Seeking in Canada? No
Exclusive territories? Yes
Homebased option? Yes
Kiosk option? No
Employees needed to run franchise: 5
Absentee ownership? No

COSTS
Total cost: $75K
Franchise fee: $25K
Royalty fee: 6%
Term of agreement: 5 years renewable
    at no charge
Franchisees required to buy multiple
    units? Outside the U.S. only

FINANCING
No financing available

QUALIFICATIONS
Net worth: $100K
Cash liquidity: $40K
Experience:
    Marketing skills
    Management experience

TRAINING
At headquarters: 6 days
At franchisee's location: 12 days

BUSINESS SUPPORT
Newsletter
Meetings
Toll-free phone line
Internet
Field operations/evaluations
Purchasing cooperatives

MARKETING SUPPORT
Co-op advertising
National media campaign

SCOTTS LAWN SERVICE

Ranked #158 in Entrepreneur Magazine's 2004 Franchise 500

Financial rating: $$$$

14111 Scottslawn Rd.
Marysville, OH 43041
Ph: (800)264-8973, Fax: (847)934-4760
www.scottslawnservice.com
Lawn care
Began: 1984, Franchising since: 1985
Headquarters size: 21 employees
Franchise department: 7 employees

U.S. franchises: 67
Canadian franchises: 0
Other foreign franchises: 0
Company-owned: 47
Units concentrated in IL, IN, MI,
    SC, TN

Seeking: All U.S.
Focusing on: CA, FL, IA, LA, NV, NJ,
    NY, PA
Seeking in Canada? Yes
Exclusive territories? Yes
Homebased option? Yes
Kiosk option? No
Employees needed to run franchise:
    3-10
Absentee ownership? Yes

COSTS
Total cost: $86.7K-406.9K
Franchise fee: $30K-250K
Royalty fee: 6-10%
Term of agreement: 10 years renewable
Franchisees required to buy multiple
    units? Outside the U.S. only

FINANCING
In-house: Franchise fee, inventory
3rd-party: None

QUALIFICATIONS
Net worth: $100K
Cash liquidity: $40K-60K
Experience:
    General business experience

TRAINING
At headquarters: 1 week
At franchisee's location: 1 week
Annual business & operations training

BUSINESS SUPPORT
Meetings
Toll-free phone line
Internet
Security/safety procedures
Field operations/evaluations
Purchasing cooperatives

MARKETING SUPPORT
Co-op advertising
National media campaign
Regional marketing
National direct-mail campaign

SPRING-GREEN LAWN CARE

Financial rating: $$$$

11909 Spaulding School Dr.
Plainfield, IL 60544
Ph: (800)435-4051/(815)436-8777
Fax: (815)436-9056
www.spring-green.com
Lawn & tree care
Began: 1977, Franchising since: 1977
Headquarters size: 12 employees
Franchise department: 7 employees

U.S. franchises: 76
Canadian franchises: 0
Other foreign franchises: 0
Company-owned: 21
Units concentrated in IL, MN, NC, PA,
SC, VA, WA, WI

Seeking: Midwest, South, Southeast
Focusing on: AL, GA, NC, OH, OR,
SC, TX, VA, WA
Seeking in Canada? No
Exclusive territories? Yes
Homebased option? Yes
Kiosk option? No
Employees needed to run franchise: 0
Absentee ownership? No

COSTS
Total cost: $76.9K-87.2K
Franchise fee: $21.9K
Royalty fee: 6-9%
Term of agreement: 10 years renewable
at no charge
Franchisees required to buy multiple
units? No

FINANCING
In-house: Equipment
3rd-party: Equipment

QUALIFICATIONS
Net worth: $150K
Cash liquidity: $30K
Experience:
General business experience
Marketing skills

TRAINING
At headquarters: 1 week
At franchisee's location: Ongoing

BUSINESS SUPPORT
Newsletter
Meetings
Toll-free phone line
Internet
Security/safety procedures
Field operations/evaluations

MARKETING SUPPORT
Co-op advertising
Ad slicks
National media campaign
Regional marketing

U.S. LAWNS

Ranked #232 in Entrepreneur Magazine's 2004 Franchise 500

Financial rating: $$$

4407 Vineland Rd., #D-13
Orlando, FL 32811
Ph: (800)875-2967
Fax: (407)246-1623
www.uslawns.com
Landscape maintenance services
Began: 1986, Franchising since: 1987
Headquarters size: 9 employees
Franchise department: 3 employees

U.S. franchises: 107
Canadian franchises: 0
Other foreign franchises: 0
Company-owned: 0
Units concentrated in all U.S.

Seeking: All U.S.
Seeking in Canada? No
Exclusive territories? No
Homebased option? Yes
Kiosk option? No
Employees needed to run franchise:
10-15
Absentee ownership? No

COSTS
Total cost: $48.5K-56K
Franchise fee: $29K
Royalty fee: 3-4%
Term of agreement: 10 years renewable
at no charge
Franchisees required to buy multiple
units? No

FINANCING
In-house: Franchise fee
3rd-party: Equipment, inventory,
start-up costs

QUALIFICATIONS
Cash liquidity: $15K+
Experience:
General business experience
Marketing skills

TRAINING
At headquarters: 1 week
At franchisee's location: Ongoing

BUSINESS SUPPORT
Newsletter
Meetings
Toll-free phone line
Internet
Security/safety procedures
Field operations/evaluations
Purchasing cooperatives

MARKETING SUPPORT
Co-op advertising
Ad slicks
National media campaign
Regional marketing
Internet support
National sales team

WEED MAN

Ranked #214 in Entrepreneur Magazine's 2004 Franchise 500

Financial rating: $$$$

11 Grand Marshall Dr.
Scarborough, ON Canada M1B 5N6
Ph: (416)269-5754
Fax: (416)269-8233
www.weed-man.com
Lawn care
Began: 1970, Franchising since: 1976
Headquarters size: 8 employees
Franchise department: 4 employees

U.S. franchises: 62
Canadian franchises: 125
Other foreign franchises: 1
Company-owned: 0
Units concentrated in all U.S.

Seeking: All U.S.
Seeking in Canada? Yes
Exclusive territories? Yes
Homebased option? Yes
Kiosk option? No
Employees needed to run franchise:
    4-6
Absentee ownership? Yes

COSTS
Total cost: $48.6K-70.3K
Franchise fee: $20K-33.8K
Royalty fee: 6%
Term of agreement: 10 years renewable
    for 50% of original fee
Franchisees required to buy multiple
    units? No

FINANCING
No financing available

QUALIFICATIONS
Net worth: $60K
Cash liquidity: $30K
Experience:
    General business experience

TRAINING
At headquarters: 2 weeks
At franchisee's location: 2-4 days
At various locations: 3 days

BUSINESS SUPPORT
Newsletter
Meetings
Internet
Security/safety procedures
Field operations/evaluations
Purchasing cooperatives

MARKETING SUPPORT
National media campaign

MAINTENANCE *Pest Control*

CRITTER CONTROL INC.

Ranked #347 in Entrepreneur Magazine's 2004 Franchise 500

Financial rating: $$$

9435 E. Cherry Bend Rd.
Traverse City, MI 49684
Ph: (231)947-2400
Fax: (231)947-9440
www.crittercontrol.com
Urban & rural wildlife management
Began: 1983, Franchising since: 1987
Headquarters size: 8 employees
Franchise department: 3 employees

U.S. franchises: 87
Canadian franchises: 2
Other foreign franchises: 0
Company-owned: 9
Units concentrated in FL, MI

Seeking: All U.S.
Seeking in Canada? Yes
Exclusive territories? Yes
Homebased option? Yes
Kiosk option? No
Employees needed to run franchise: 2
Absentee ownership? No

COSTS
Total cost: $9.8K-66K
Franchise fee: $2.5K-33K
Royalty fee: 6-16%
Term of agreement: 10 years renewable
    at no charge
Franchisees required to buy multiple
    units? No

FINANCING
In-house: Equipment, inventory
3rd-party: Franchise fee

QUALIFICATIONS
Experience:
    Industry experience
    General business experience
    Marketing skills
    Animal/wildlife-control experience

TRAINING
In Columbus, OH: 1 week

BUSINESS SUPPORT
Newsletter
Meetings
Toll-free phone line
Grand opening
Internet
Security/safety procedures
Field operations/evaluations
Purchasing cooperatives

MARKETING SUPPORT
Co-op advertising
Ad slicks
National media campaign

NATURZONE PEST CONTROL INC.

Financial rating: $$$

1899 Porter Lake Dr., #103
Sarasota, FL 34240
Ph: (941)378-3334
Fax: (941)378-8584
www.naturzone.com
Pest control
Began: 1982, Franchising since: 1998
Headquarters size: 10 employees
Franchise department: 2 employees

U.S. franchises: 5
Canadian franchises: 0
Other foreign franchises: 4
Company-owned: 1
Units concentrated in all U.S.

Seeking: All U.S.
Seeking in Canada? Yes
Exclusive territories? Yes
Homebased option? Yes
Kiosk option? No
Employees needed to run franchise: 2
Absentee ownership? No

COSTS
Total cost: $19K-25K
Franchise fee: $20K
Royalty fee: 5%
Term of agreement: Perpetual
Franchisees required to buy multiple
    units? No

FINANCING
No financing available

QUALIFICATIONS
Net worth: $50K
Cash liquidity: $10K

TRAINING
At headquarters: 3 weeks

BUSINESS SUPPORT
Newsletter
Meetings
Internet
Security/safety procedures
Field operations/evaluations
Purchasing cooperatives

MARKETING SUPPORT
Co-op advertising
Ad slicks

PESTMASTER SERVICES

Financial rating: $$

137 E. South St.
Bishop, CA 93514
Ph: (760)873-8100
Fax: (760)873-3268
www.pestmaster.com
Pest control
Began: 1979, Franchising since: 1991
Headquarters size: 12 employees
Franchise department: 1 employee

U.S. franchises: 13
Canadian franchises: 0
Other foreign franchises: 0
Company-owned: 11
Units concentrated in CA, FL, NY,
    OK, TX

Seeking: All U.S.
Seeking in Canada? No
Exclusive territories? Yes
Homebased option? Yes
Kiosk option? No
Employees needed to run franchise: 2
Absentee ownership? No

COSTS
Total cost: $30K-79.3K
Franchise fee: $15K-30K
Royalty fee: 5-7%
Term of agreement: 10 years renewable
    at no charge
Franchisees required to buy multiple
    units? No

FINANCING
No financing available

QUALIFICATIONS
Cash liquidity: $50K
Experience:
    Industry experience
    General business experience

TRAINING
At headquarters: 1 week
At franchisee's location: 2 weeks
At Pestmaster University: 1 week

BUSINESS SUPPORT
Newsletter
Meetings
Toll-free phone line
Grand opening
Internet
Field operations/evaluations
Purchasing cooperatives

MARKETING SUPPORT
Co-op advertising
Ad slicks

TERMINIX TERMITE & PEST CONTROL

Financial rating: $$$$

860 Ridge Lake Blvd.
Memphis, TN 38120
Ph: (800)654-7848/(901)766-1356
Fax: (901)766-1208
www.terminix.com
Termite & pest control
Began: 1927, Franchising since: 1927
Headquarters size: 450 employees
Franchise department: 7 employees

U.S. franchises: 136
Canadian franchises: 0
Other foreign franchises: 0
Company-owned: 297

Seeking: All U.S.
Focusing on: AZ, MT, NM, NV, SD
Seeking in Canada? Yes
Exclusive territories? Yes
Homebased option? Yes
Kiosk option? No
Employees needed to run franchise:
    Info not provided
Absentee ownership? Yes

COSTS
Total cost: $24.7K-85.3K
Franchise fee: $25K-50K
Royalty fee: 7-10%
Term of agreement: 5 years renewable
    at no charge
Franchisees required to buy multiple
    units? Outside the U.S. only

FINANCING
In-house: None
3rd-party: Accounts receivable, fran-
    chise fee

QUALIFICATIONS
Experience:
    General business experience

TRAINING
At headquarters: 1 week
In-field training & ongoing self-
    tutorial

BUSINESS SUPPORT
Newsletter
Meetings
Toll-free phone line
Internet
Security/safety procedures
Field operations/evaluations
Purchasing cooperatives

MARKETING SUPPORT
Co-op advertising
National media campaign
Additional support

TRULY NOLEN

Financial rating: $$$$

3636 E. Speedway
Tucson, AZ 85716
Ph: (800)458-3664/(520)977-5817
Fax: (520)322-4010
www.trulynolen.com
Pest & termite control, lawn care
Began: 1938, Franchising since: 1996
Headquarters size: 35 employees
Franchise department: 2 employees

U.S. franchises: 8
Canadian franchises: 0
Other foreign franchises: 69
Company-owned: 68
Units concentrated in all U.S.

Seeking: All U.S.
Seeking in Canada? No
Exclusive territories? Yes
Homebased option? Yes
Kiosk option? No
Employees needed to run franchise: 2
Absentee ownership? Yes

COSTS
Total cost: $3.6K-300.5K
Franchise fee: $1.5K-45K
Royalty fee: 7%
Term of agreement: 5 years renewable
    for $1.5K
Franchisees required to buy multiple
    units? No

FINANCING
No financing available

QUALIFICATIONS
Net worth: $50K
Cash liquidity: $10K
Experience:
    Industry experience
    General business experience
    Marketing skills

TRAINING
At headquarters: 1 week
At franchisee's location: 1 week
At training centers

BUSINESS SUPPORT
Newsletter
Meetings
Toll-free phone line
Grand opening
Internet
Security/safety procedures
Field operations/evaluations
Purchasing cooperatives

MARKETING SUPPORT
Co-op advertising
Ad slicks
National media campaign
Regional marketing

 *Plumbing*

ACE DURAFLO SYSTEMS LLC

Financial rating: $

711 W. Kimberly Ave., #100
Placentia, CA 92870
Ph: (714)256-0220, Fax: (714)854-1833
www.fixmypipes.com
Pipe restoration services
Began: 1997, Franchising since: 2001
Headquarters size: 14 employees
Franchise department: 8 employees

U.S. franchises: 12
Canadian franchises: 0
Other foreign franchises: 0
Company-owned: 3
Units concentrated in all U.S.

Seeking: All U.S.
Seeking in Canada? Yes
Exclusive territories? No
Homebased option? No
Kiosk option? No
Employees needed to run franchise: 5
Absentee ownership? Yes

COSTS
Total cost: $125.7K-420.1K
Franchise fee: $24.9K
Royalty fee: 6-8%
Term of agreement: 10 years renewable
    for $1K
Franchisees required to buy multiple
    units? No

FINANCING
In-house: None
3rd-party: Equipment, inventory,
    start-up costs

QUALIFICATIONS
Net worth: $420.1K
Cash liquidity: $206.1K
Experience:
    Industry experience
    General business experience
    Marketing skills

TRAINING
At headquarters: 1 week

BUSINESS SUPPORT
Newsletter
Meetings
Toll-free phone line
Internet
Security/safety procedures
Field operations/evaluations

MARKETING SUPPORT
Co-op advertising
Ad slicks
National media campaign
Regional marketing

BENJAMIN FRANKLIN PLUMBING
Ranked #453 in Entrepreneur Magazine's 2004 Franchise 500

Financial rating: $$$

1 Sarasota Tower, #506
Sarasota, FL 34236
Ph: (866)423-6669
www.benfranklinplumbing.com
Plumbing services
Began: 2000, Franchising since: 2001
Headquarters size: 25 employees
Franchise department: 3 employees

U.S. franchises: 78
Canadian franchises: 0
Other foreign franchises: 0
Company-owned: 0
Units concentrated in all U.S.

Seeking: All U.S.
Seeking in Canada? Yes
Exclusive territories? Yes
Homebased option? Yes
Kiosk option? No
Employees needed to run franchise:
    4-12
Absentee ownership? Yes

COSTS
Total cost: $41.5K-279.5K
Franchise fee: $10K
Royalty fee: 3-5%
Term of agreement: 10 years renewable
    for 50% of franchise fee
Franchisees required to buy multiple
    units? No

FINANCING
No financing available

QUALIFICATIONS
Experience:
    Industry experience
    General business experience
    Marketing skills

TRAINING
At headquarters: 4 days
At franchisee's location: 3 days &
    as needed
At hotel/meeting space: 1-1/2 days

BUSINESS SUPPORT
Meetings
Internet
Field operations/evaluations
Purchasing cooperatives

MARKETING SUPPORT
Ad slicks

MR. ROOTER

Ranked #307 in Entrepreneur Magazine's 2004 Franchise 500

Financial rating: $$$$

1020 N. University Parks Dr.
Waco, TX 76707
Ph: (800)298-6855, Fax: (800)209-7621
www.mrrooter.com
Plumbing, sewer & drain cleaning
    services
Began: 1968, Franchising since: 1972
Headquarters size: 110 employees
Franchise department: 30 employees

U.S. franchises: 178
Canadian franchises: 17
Other foreign franchises: 65
Company-owned: 0
Units concentrated in all U.S.

Seeking: All U.S.
Seeking in Canada? Yes
Exclusive territories? Yes
Homebased option? Yes
Kiosk option? No
Employees needed to run franchise: 5-6
Absentee ownership? No

COSTS
Total cost: $46.8K-120.5K
Franchise fee: $22.5K
Royalty fee: 4-7%
Term of agreement: 10 years renewable
    for $2.5K
Franchisees required to buy multiple
    units? Outside the U.S. only

FINANCING
In-house: Franchise fee
3rd-party: Equipment

QUALIFICATIONS
Net worth: $100K
Cash liquidity: $25K
Experience:
    Industry experience

TRAINING
At headquarters: 10 days
At franchisee's location: 2 days
At regional location: 2 days

BUSINESS SUPPORT
Newsletter
Meetings
Toll-free phone line
Internet
Field operations/evaluations

MARKETING SUPPORT
Co-op advertising
Ad slicks
National media campaign

ROOTER-MAN

Ranked #255 in Entrepreneur Magazine's 2004 Franchise 500

Financial rating: $$$

268 Rangeway Rd.
North Billerica, MA 01862
Ph: (800)700-8062
Fax: (978)663-0061
www.rooterman.com
Plumbing, drain & sewer cleaning
Began: 1970, Franchising since: 1981
Headquarters size: 28 employees
Franchise department: 5 employees

U.S. franchises: 57
Canadian franchises: 3
Other foreign franchises: 1
Company-owned: 0
Units concentrated in New England

Seeking: All U.S.
Focusing on: CA, FL, NV, TX
Seeking in Canada? Yes
Exclusive territories? Yes
Homebased option? Yes
Kiosk option? No
Employees needed to run franchise: 3-5
Absentee ownership? Yes

COSTS
Total cost: $46.8K-137.6K
Franchise fee: $3.98K
Royalty fee: Varies
Term of agreement: 5 years renewable
    for $2.5K
Franchisees required to buy multiple
    units? No

FINANCING
In-house: Franchise fee
3rd-party: Equipment, inventory,
    start-up costs

QUALIFICATIONS
Net worth: $25K
Cash liquidity: $10K
Experience:
    Mechanical skills

TRAINING
At headquarters: 6 weeks
At franchisee's location: 2 days
At training seminar: 2 days

BUSINESS SUPPORT
Newsletter
Meetings
Grand opening
Internet
Lease negotiations
Security/safety procedures
Field operations/evaluations
Purchasing cooperatives

MARKETING SUPPORT
Co-op advertising
Ad slicks
National media campaign
Regional marketing

ROTO-ROOTER CORP.

Financial rating: $$$$

300 Ashworth Rd.
West Des Moines, IA 50265
Ph: (515)223-1343
Fax: (515)223-6109
www.rotorooter.com
Sewer, drain-cleaning & plumbing
　services
Began: 1935, Franchising since: 1935
Headquarters size: 160 employees
Franchise department: 45 employees

U.S. franchises: 483
Canadian franchises: 15
Other foreign franchises: 23
Company-owned: 124

Sold out in the U.S.
Focusing on: International master
　franchise licenses available in select
　countries
Seeking in Canada? Yes
Exclusive territories? Yes
Homebased option? Yes
Kiosk option? No
Employees needed to run franchise: 3
Absentee ownership? No

COSTS
Total cost: $40K-65K
Franchise fee: $15K
Royalty fee: Varies
Term of agreement: 10 years renewable
　at no charge
Franchisees required to buy multiple
　units? Outside the U.S. only

FINANCING
No financing available

QUALIFICATIONS
Experience:
　Industry experience
　General business experience
　Marketing skills
　Leadership experience
　Franchising experience

TRAINING
At headquarters: 3 weeks
At franchisee's location: Ongoing
Company-wide meetings

BUSINESS SUPPORT
Newsletter
Meetings
Security/safety procedures
Field operations/evaluations

MARKETING SUPPORT
Info not provided

MAINTENANCE ▶ *Restoration Services*

DISASTER KLEENUP INT'L.

Current financial data not available

P.O. Box 661368
Chicago, IL 60666-1368
Ph: (630)350-3000, Fax: (630)350-9354
www.disasterkleenup.com
Insurance restoration services
Began: 1974, Franchising since: 1994
Headquarters size: 10 employees
Franchise department: 10 employees

U.S. franchises: 98
Canadian franchises: 53
Other foreign franchises: 0
Company-owned: 0
Units concentrated in all U.S.

Seeking: All U.S.
Seeking in Canada? No
Exclusive territories? Yes
Homebased option? No
Kiosk option? No
Employees needed to run franchise:
　10-100
Absentee ownership? No

COSTS
Total cost: $15K-30K
Franchise fee: $15K
Royalty fee: $600-1.95K/mo.
Term of agreement: 2 years renewable
　for $250
Franchisees required to buy multiple
　units? No

FINANCING
No financing available

QUALIFICATIONS
Experience:
　Industry experience
　Must own a restoration/remodel-
　ing/construction company with at
　least $1 million in revenue from
　insurance restoration

TRAINING
At headquarters: 1 day & ongoing
Ongoing national/regional conferences
　& meetings

BUSINESS SUPPORT
Newsletter
Meetings
Toll-free phone line
Internet
Purchasing cooperatives

MARKETING SUPPORT
Co-op advertising
National media campaign
Regional marketing

DURACLEAN INT'L.

Ranked #176 in Entrepreneur Magazine's 2004 Franchise 500   *Financial rating: $$$*

220 Campus Dr.
Arlington Heights, IL 60004
Ph: (800)251-7070/(847)704-7100
Fax: (847)704-7101
www.duraclean.com
Water & fire damage restoration, mold
    remediation, carpet & upholstery
    cleaning
Began: 1930, Franchising since: 1945
Headquarters size: 20 employees
Franchise department: 3 employees

U.S. franchises: 245
Canadian franchises: 12
Other foreign franchises: 116
Company-owned: 2
Units concentrated in all U.S.

Seeking: All U.S.
Seeking in Canada? Yes
Exclusive territories? Yes
Homebased option? Yes
Kiosk option? No
Employees needed to run franchise:
    Info not provided
Absentee ownership? Yes

COSTS
Total cost: $25.1K-81.5K
Franchise fee: $10K
Royalty fee: 2-8%
Term of agreement: 5 years renewable
    at no charge
Franchisees required to buy multiple
    units? No

FINANCING
In-house: Franchise fee
3rd-party: None

QUALIFICATIONS
Cash liquidity: $50K

TRAINING
At headquarters: 5 days
In-field training: 2 days

BUSINESS SUPPORT
Newsletter
Meetings
Toll-free phone line
Internet
Field operations/evaluations

MARKETING SUPPORT
Co-op advertising
Ad slicks

PAUL DAVIS RESTORATION INC.

Ranked #250 in Entrepreneur Magazine's 2004 Franchise 500   *Financial rating: $$$$*

1 Independent Dr., #2300
Jacksonville, FL 32202
Ph: (904)737-2779
Fax: (904)737-4204
www.pdrestoration.com
Insurance restoration services
Began: 1966, Franchising since: 1970
Headquarters size: 30 employees
Franchise department: 30 employees

U.S. franchises: 213
Canadian franchises: 0
Other foreign franchises: 0
Company-owned: 0
Units concentrated in all U.S.

Seeking: All U.S.
Seeking in Canada? No
Exclusive territories? Yes
Homebased option? No
Kiosk option? No
Employees needed to run franchise:
    5-10
Absentee ownership? No

COSTS
Total cost: $114.9K-162.97K
Franchise fee: $52.5K
Royalty fee: 3.5%
Term of agreement: 10 years renewable
    at no charge
Franchisees required to buy multiple
    units? No

FINANCING
No financing available

QUALIFICATIONS
Net worth: $150K
Cash liquidity: $100K
Experience:
    General business experience
    Marketing skills

TRAINING
At headquarters: 4 weeks
At franchisee's location: 2 weeks
Follow-up training at 6-month
    anniversary: 3 days

BUSINESS SUPPORT
Newsletter
Meetings
Toll-free phone line
Internet
Field operations/evaluations
Purchasing cooperatives

MARKETING SUPPORT
Co-op advertising
Ad slicks
National media campaign
Regional marketing

PUROSYSTEMS INC.

Ranked #242 in Entrepreneur Magazine's 2004 Franchise 500   *Financial rating: $$$$*

5350 N.W. 35th Ave.
Ft. Lauderdale, FL 33309
Ph: (800)247-9047
Fax: (954)731-1915
www.puroclean.com
Insurance restoration services
Began: 1986, Franchising since: 1991
Headquarters size: 14 employees
Franchise department: 8 employees

U.S. franchises: 84
Canadian franchises: 0
Other foreign franchises: 0
Company-owned: 0
Units concentrated in AZ, CA, KY,
NJ, PA

Seeking: All U.S.
Seeking in Canada? No
Exclusive territories? Yes
Homebased option? Yes
Kiosk option? No
Employees needed to run franchise: 4
Absentee ownership? No

COSTS
Total cost: $79.3K-122.2K
Franchise fee: $25K
Royalty fee: 8-10%
Term of agreement: 20 years renewable
at no charge
Franchisees required to buy multiple
units? No

FINANCING
In-house: None
3rd-party: Equipment

QUALIFICATIONS
Cash liquidity: $15K

TRAINING
At headquarters: 10 days
At franchisee's location: 3 days

BUSINESS SUPPORT
Newsletter
Meetings
Toll-free phone line
Internet
Field operations/evaluations

MARKETING SUPPORT
Regional marketing

RAINBOW INT'L. CARPET CARE & RESTORATION

Ranked #262 in Entrepreneur Magazine's 2004 Franchise 500   *Financial rating: $$$$*

1020 N. University Parks Dr.
Waco, TX 76707
Ph: (800)280-9963
Fax: (800)209-7621
www.rainbowintl.com
Indoor restoration & cleaning
Began: 1981, Franchising since: 1981
Headquarters size: 110 employees
Franchise department: 30 employees

U.S. franchises: 240
Canadian franchises: 15
Other foreign franchises: 150
Company-owned: 0
Units concentrated in all U.S.

Seeking: All U.S.
Seeking in Canada? Yes
Exclusive territories? Yes
Homebased option? Yes
Kiosk option? No
Employees needed to run franchise: 1-3
Absentee ownership? No

COSTS
Total cost: $64.6K-117.4K
Franchise fee: $15.9K
Royalty fee: 4-7%
Term of agreement: 10 years renewable
for $2.5K
Franchisees required to buy multiple
units? Outside the U.S. only

FINANCING
In-house: Franchise fee
3rd-party: Equipment

QUALIFICATIONS
Net worth: $100K
Cash liquidity: $25K
Experience:
Industry experience
General business experience
Marketing skills

TRAINING
At headquarters: 14 days
At franchisee's location: 2 days
Regional training: 2-5 days

BUSINESS SUPPORT
Newsletter
Meetings
Toll-free phone line
Internet
Field operations/evaluations

MARKETING SUPPORT
Co-op advertising
Ad slicks
National media campaign

SERVICE TEAM OF PROFESSIONALS INC.

Financial rating: $$$$

10036 N.W. Ambassador Dr.
Kansas City, MO 64153-1362
Ph: (800)452-8326/(816)880-4746
Fax: (816)880-9395
www.stoprestoration.com
Disaster restoration, carpet cleaning,
   mold remediation
Began: 1971, Franchising since: 1996
Headquarters size: 3 employees
Franchise department: 3 employees

U.S. franchises: 36
Canadian franchises: 0
Other foreign franchises: 0
Company-owned: 0
Units concentrated in CA, MN, MO,
   OH, WI

Seeking: All U.S.
Seeking in Canada? No
Exclusive territories? Yes
Homebased option? Yes
Kiosk option? No
Employees needed to run franchise: 30
Absentee ownership? Yes

COSTS
Total cost: $10K-104K
Franchise fee: $8K-34K
Royalty fee: 5-9%
Term of agreement: 10 years renewable
   at no charge
Franchisees required to buy multiple
   units? No

FINANCING
No financing available

QUALIFICATIONS
Net worth: $10K
Cash liquidity: $10K+
Experience:
   Management skills

TRAINING
At headquarters: 1 week
Training conventions: 3 per year

BUSINESS SUPPORT
Meetings
Toll-free phone line
Internet
Purchasing cooperatives

MARKETING SUPPORT
Co-op advertising
Ad slicks
National marketing support

SERVPRO

Ranked #33 in Entrepreneur Magazine's 2004 Franchise 500

Financial rating: $$$$

575 Airport Blvd.
Gallatin, TN 37066
Ph: (800)826-9586/(615)451-0600
Fax: (615)451-1602
www.servpro.com
Insurance/disaster restoration &
   cleaning
Began: 1967, Franchising since: 1969
Headquarters size: 105 employees
Franchise department: 6 employees

U.S. franchises: 1,165
Canadian franchises: 0
Other foreign franchises: 0
Company-owned: 0
Units concentrated in all U.S.

Seeking: All U.S.
Seeking in Canada? No
Exclusive territories? No
Homebased option? Yes
Kiosk option? No
Employees needed to run franchise:
   5-10
Absentee ownership? No

COSTS
Total cost: $89.5K-138.1K
Franchise fee: $33K
Royalty fee: 3-10%
Term of agreement: 5 years renewable
   at no charge
Franchisees required to buy multiple
   units? No

FINANCING
In-house: Equipment, inventory, payroll
3rd-party: None

QUALIFICATIONS
Net worth: $100K
Cash liquidity: $50K
Experience:
   General business experience
   Marketing skills

TRAINING
At headquarters: 2 weeks
At franchisee's location: 1 week

BUSINESS SUPPORT
Newsletter
Meetings
Toll-free phone line
Grand opening
Internet
Security/safety procedures
Field operations/evaluations
Purchasing cooperatives

MARKETING SUPPORT
Co-op advertising
Ad slicks
National media campaign
Regional marketing
National accounts

MAINTENANCE ▶ *Vinyl Repair*

CARTEX LIMITED

Ranked #489 in Entrepreneur Magazine's 2004 Franchise 500　　　　*Financial rating: $$$*

42816 Mound Rd.
Sterling Heights, MI 48314
Ph: (586)739-4330, Fax: (586)739-4331
www.fabrion.net
Leather, vinyl, plastic & cloth repair
Began: 1987, Franchising since: 1988
Headquarters size: 10 employees
Franchise department: 3 employees

U.S. franchises: 104
Canadian franchises: 1
Other foreign franchises: 0
Company-owned: 0
Units concentrated in CA, FL

Seeking: All U.S.
Seeking in Canada? No
Exclusive territories? Yes
Homebased option? Yes
Kiosk option? No
Employees needed to run franchise: 1-3
Absentee ownership? No

COSTS
Total cost: $34.5K-95.2K
Franchise fee: $23.5K-36.5K
Royalty fee: 7%
Term of agreement: 5 years renewable
　　at no charge
Franchisees required to buy multiple
　　units? No

FINANCING
No financing available

QUALIFICATIONS
Net worth: $50K
Cash liquidity: $35K

TRAINING
At franchisee's location: 1 week
In-field training: 2 weeks

BUSINESS SUPPORT
Newsletter
Meetings
Toll-free phone line
Internet
Field operations/evaluations

MARKETING SUPPORT
Info not provided

COLOR-GLO INT'L. INC.

Ranked #437 in Entrepreneur Magazine's 2004 Franchise 500　　　　*Financial rating: $$$*

7111 Ohms Ln.
Minneapolis, MN 55439
Ph: (800)328-6347/(952)835-1338
Fax: (952)835-1395
www.color-glo.com
Fabric dyeing & restoration
Began: 1979, Franchising since: 1983
Headquarters size: 15 employees
Franchise department: 3 employees

U.S. franchises: 114
Canadian franchises: 8
Other foreign franchises: 84
Company-owned: 1
Units concentrated in all U.S.

Seeking: All U.S.
Seeking in Canada? Yes
Exclusive territories? Yes
Homebased option? Yes
Kiosk option? No
Employees needed to run franchise: 2
Absentee ownership? Yes

COSTS
Total cost: $26.5K-30.3K
Franchise fee: $25K
Royalty fee: 4%
Term of agreement: 10 years
Franchisees required to buy multiple
　　units? Yes

FINANCING
In-house: Available
3rd-party: None

QUALIFICATIONS
Net worth: $50K
Cash liquidity: $25K

TRAINING
At headquarters: 2 weeks
At franchisee's location: 1 week
Ongoing

BUSINESS SUPPORT
Newsletter
Meetings
Toll-free phone line
Grand opening
Internet
Lease negotiations
Security/safety procedures
Field operations/evaluations
Purchasing cooperatives

MARKETING SUPPORT
Co-op advertising
Ad slicks
National media campaign
Regional marketing

CREATIVE COLORS INT'L. INC.

Financial rating: $$

5550 W. 175th St.
Tinley Park, IL 60477
Ph: (800)933-2656/(708)614-7786
Fax: (708)614-9685
www.creativecolorsintl.com
Mobile plastic, vinyl, leather restoration/repair
Began: 1980, Franchising since: 1991
Headquarters size: 10 employees
Franchise department: Info not provided

U.S. franchises: 48
Canadian franchises: 1
Other foreign franchises: 0
Company-owned: 5
Units concentrated in FL, Midwest

Seeking: All U.S.
Focusing on: TX
Seeking in Canada? No
Exclusive territories? Yes
Homebased option? Yes
Kiosk option? No
Employees needed to run franchise: 1-4
Absentee ownership? Yes

COSTS
Total cost: $53.6K-70.4K
Franchise fee: $19.5K+
Royalty fee: 6%
Term of agreement: 10 years renewable at to 20% of current fee
Franchisees required to buy multiple units? No

FINANCING
In-house: Start-up costs
3rd-party: None

QUALIFICATIONS
Net worth: $50K+
Cash liquidity: $20K+
Experience:
    General business experience
    Marketing skills

TRAINING
At headquarters: 3 weeks
At franchisee's location: 1 week

BUSINESS SUPPORT
Newsletter
Meetings
Toll-free phone line
Grand opening
Internet
Security/safety procedures
Field operations/evaluations

MARKETING SUPPORT
Regional marketing

DR. VINYL & ASSOCIATES LTD.

Ranked #148 in Entrepreneur Magazine's 2004 Franchise 500

Financial rating: $$$

821 N.W. Commerce
Lee's Summit, MO 64086
Ph: (800)531-6600
Fax: (816)525-6333
www.drvinyl.com
Mobile vinyl & leather repair/windshield repair
Began: 1972, Franchising since: 1981
Headquarters size: 14 employees
Franchise department: 9 employees

U.S. franchises: 202
Canadian franchises: 1
Other foreign franchises: 39
Company-owned: 2
Units concentrated in all U.S.

Seeking: All U.S.
Seeking in Canada? Yes
Exclusive territories? Yes
Homebased option? Yes
Kiosk option? No
Employees needed to run franchise: 1
Absentee ownership? No

COSTS
Total cost: $41K-66.5K
Franchise fee: $29.5K
Royalty fee: 7%
Term of agreement: 10 years renewable at no charge
Franchisees required to buy multiple units? Outside the U.S. only

FINANCING
In-house: Franchise fee, equipment, inventory
3rd-party: Equipment, franchise fee, inventory, start-up costs

QUALIFICATIONS
Net worth: $50K
Cash liquidity: $15K
Experience:
    General business experience
    Marketing skills

TRAINING
At headquarters: 2 weeks
At franchisee's location: 2 weeks
At corporate location & in-field

BUSINESS SUPPORT
Newsletter
Meetings
Toll-free phone line
Grand opening
Internet
Field operations/evaluations
Purchasing cooperatives

MARKETING SUPPORT
Co-op advertising
Ad slicks
National media campaign

FIBRENEW

Ranked #477 in Entrepreneur Magazine's 2004 Franchise 500

Financial rating: $$

Box 33, Site 16, RR8
Calgary, AB Canada T2J 2T9
Ph: (403)278-7818
Fax: (403)278-1434
www.fibrenew.com
Leather, plastic & vinyl restoration
Began: 1985, Franchising since: 1987
Headquarters size: 5 employees
Franchise department: 2 employees

U.S. franchises: 19
Canadian franchises: 73
Other foreign franchises: 44
Company-owned: 4
Units concentrated in Central U.S. &
    East Coast

Seeking: All U.S.
Seeking in Canada? Yes
Exclusive territories? Yes
Homebased option? Yes
Kiosk option? No
Employees needed to run franchise: 1
Absentee ownership? Yes

COSTS
Total cost: $30K-50K
Franchise fee: $30K-50K
Royalty fee: $300/mo.
Term of agreement: 5 years renewable
    at no charge
Franchisees required to buy multiple
    units? No

FINANCING
In-house: Franchise fee
3rd-party: None

QUALIFICATIONS
Net worth: $30K
Cash liquidity: $15K

TRAINING
At headquarters: 2 weeks

BUSINESS SUPPORT
Newsletter
Meetings
Toll-free phone line
Internet
Field operations/evaluations

MARKETING SUPPORT
Info not provided

MAINTENANCE   *Window Cleaning*

CLEAN & HAPPY WINDOWS

Current financial data not available

10019 Des Moines Memorial Dr.
Seattle, WA 98168
Ph: (866)762-7617, Fax: (206)762-7637
www.cleanhappy.com
Window & gutter cleaning, pressure
    washing, roof cleaning
Began: 1991, Franchising since: 2000
Headquarters size: 10 employees
Franchise department: 3 employees

U.S. franchises: 2
Canadian franchises: 0
Other foreign franchises: 0
Company-owned: 1
Units concentrated in FL, TX

Seeking: All U.S.
Seeking in Canada? No
Exclusive territories? Yes
Homebased option? Yes
Kiosk option? No
Employees needed to run franchise: 1-2
Absentee ownership? No

COSTS
Total cost: $100-2K
Franchise fee: 0
Royalty fee: 7%
Term of agreement: 5 years renewable
    at no charge
Franchisees required to buy multiple
    units? No

FINANCING
No financing available

QUALIFICATIONS
Net worth: $4K
Cash liquidity: $4K
Experience:
    General business experience
    Marketing skills
    Able to work at high heights

TRAINING
At headquarters: 5 days

BUSINESS SUPPORT
Toll-free phone line
Grand opening
Internet
Security/safety procedures
Field operations/evaluations

MARKETING SUPPORT
Ad slicks

DR. GLASS WINDOW WASHING

Current financial data not available

3573 Nyland Wy.
Lafayette, CO 80026
Ph: (888)282-0052
Fax: (303)499-0855
www.docglass.com
Window cleaning
Began: 1978, Franchising since: 2001
Headquarters size: 2 employees
Franchise department: 2 employees

U.S. franchises: 5
Canadian franchises: 0
Other foreign franchises: 0
Company-owned: 5
Units concentrated in all U.S.

Seeking: All U.S.
Seeking in Canada? Yes
Exclusive territories? Yes
Homebased option? Yes
Kiosk option? No
Employees needed to run franchise: 2
Absentee ownership? No

COSTS
Total cost: $4.6K
Franchise fee: $3K
Royalty fee: 10%
Term of agreement: Info not provided
Franchisees required to buy multiple
    units? No

FINANCING
In-house: Franchise fee
3rd-party: None

QUALIFICATIONS
Experience:
    General business experience

TRAINING
At headquarters: 1 week

BUSINESS SUPPORT
Newsletter
Toll-free phone line
Internet
Purchasing cooperatives

MARKETING SUPPORT
Info not provided

FISH WINDOW CLEANING SERVICES INC.

Ranked #388 in Entrepreneur Magazine's 2004 Franchise 500

Financial rating: 0

148-G Chesterfield Industrial Blvd.
Chesterfield, MO 63005
Ph: (877)707-3474
Fax: (636)530-7856
www.fishwindowcleaning.com
Window cleaning
Began: 1978, Franchising since: 1998
Headquarters size: 23 employees
Franchise department: 15 employees

U.S. franchises: 103
Canadian franchises: 0
Other foreign franchises: 0
Company-owned: 0
Units concentrated in Eastern half of
    the U.S.

Seeking: All U.S.
Seeking in Canada? No
Exclusive territories? Yes
Homebased option? No
Kiosk option? No
Employees needed to run franchise: 5
Absentee ownership? No

COSTS
Total cost: $55.7K-115.8K
Franchise fee: $24.5K-49.5K
Royalty fee: 6-8%
Term of agreement: 10 years renewable
    for $3K
Franchisees required to buy multiple
    units? No

FINANCING
In-house: None
3rd-party: Equipment, franchise fee,
    inventory, start-up costs

QUALIFICATIONS
Net worth: $250K
Cash liquidity: $60K-120K
Experience:
    Marketing skills
    Management skills

TRAINING
At headquarters: 10 days
At franchisee's location: 3 days

BUSINESS SUPPORT
Newsletter
Meetings
Toll-free phone line
Grand opening
Internet
Security/safety procedures
Field operations/evaluations
Purchasing cooperatives

MARKETING SUPPORT
Co-op advertising
Ad slicks
National media campaign
Regional marketing
Sales brochures
Training videos
National account referrals

WINDOW BUTLER

Financial rating: $$

P.O. Box 22
O'Fallon, IL 62269
Ph: (800)808-6470
www.windowbutler.com
Residential & commercial window
    cleaning, gutter cleaning, pressure
    washing
Began: 1997, Franchising since: 1997
Headquarters size: 4 employees
Franchise department: 2 employees

U.S. franchises: 8
Canadian franchises: 0
Other foreign franchises: 0
Company-owned: 1
Units concentrated in East of the
    Mississippi River

Seeking: All U.S.
Seeking in Canada? No
Exclusive territories? Yes
Homebased option? Yes
Kiosk option? No
Employees needed to run franchise: 3
Absentee ownership? Yes

COSTS
Total cost: $17.3K-28.5K
Franchise fee: $7K+
Royalty fee: 6%
Term of agreement: 10 years renewable
    at no charge
Franchisees required to buy multiple
    units? No

FINANCING
In-house: Franchise fee
3rd-party: None

QUALIFICATIONS
Net worth: $50K
Cash liquidity: $10K
Experience:
    Marketing skills

TRAINING
At headquarters: 1 week
At franchisee's location: 3 days

BUSINESS SUPPORT
Newsletter
Meetings
Toll-free phone line
Grand opening
Internet
Security/safety procedures
Field operations/evaluations
Purchasing cooperatives

MARKETING SUPPORT
Co-op advertising
Ad slicks
Regional marketing

WINDOW GANG
Ranked #222 in Entrepreneur Magazine's 2004 Franchise 500

Financial rating: $$$$

1509 Ann St.
Beaufort, NC 28516
Ph: (252)726-4314
Fax: (252)726-2837
www.windowgang.com
Window & pressure cleaning
Began: 1986, Franchising since: 1996
Headquarters size: 6 employees
Franchise department: 3 employees

U.S. franchises: 101
Canadian franchises: 20
Other foreign franchises: 0
Company-owned: 0
Units concentrated in AL, FL, GA,
    MO, NC, SC, TN, TX, VA

Seeking: All U.S.
Seeking in Canada? Yes
Exclusive territories? Yes
Homebased option? Yes
Kiosk option? No
Employees needed to run franchise: 5
Absentee ownership? Yes

COSTS
Total cost: $14.4K-78.1K
Franchise fee: $5K-75K
Royalty fee: 6%
Term of agreement: 10 years renewable
    for $2.5K
Franchisees required to buy multiple
    units? No

FINANCING
In-house: Franchise fee
3rd-party: Accounts receivable, equip-
    ment, inventory, start-up costs

QUALIFICATIONS
Net worth: $50K
Cash liquidity: $10K
Experience:
    Marketing skills

TRAINING
At headquarters: 7-14 days
At franchisee's location: 7 days

BUSINESS SUPPORT
Newsletter
Meetings
Toll-free phone line
Internet
Security/safety procedures
Field operations/evaluations
Purchasing cooperatives

MARKETING SUPPORT
Ad slicks

WINDOW GENIE

Ranked #343 in Entrepreneur Magazine's 2004 Franchise 500   *Financial rating: $$$*

350 Gest St.
Cincinnati, OH 45203
Ph: (800)700-0022
Fax: (513)412-7760
www.windowgenie.com
Residential window cleaning, window tinting, pressure washing
Began: 1994, Franchising since: 1998
Headquarters size: 9 employees
Franchise department: 3 employees

U.S. franchises: 55
Canadian franchises: 0
Other foreign franchises: 0
Company-owned: 0
Units concentrated in all U.S.

Seeking: All U.S.
Seeking in Canada? Yes
Exclusive territories? Yes
Homebased option? Yes
Kiosk option? No
Employees needed to run franchise: 3
Absentee ownership? No

COSTS
Total cost: $38.9K-48.8K
Franchise fee: $19.5K
Royalty fee: 6%
Term of agreement: 10 years renewable at no charge
Franchisees required to buy multiple units? No

FINANCING
No financing available

QUALIFICATIONS
Net worth: $75K
Cash liquidity: $30K
Experience:
    General business experience

TRAINING
At headquarters: 5 days
At franchisee's location: 5 days

BUSINESS SUPPORT
Meetings
Toll-free phone line
Grand opening
Internet
Security/safety procedures
Field operations/evaluations
Purchasing cooperatives

MARKETING SUPPORT
Ad slicks
Regional marketing

MAINTENANCE   *Miscellaneous*

AMERICAN ASPHALT SEALCOATING

Current financial data not available

P.O. Box 600
Chesterland, OH 44026
Ph: (888)603-7325/(440)729-8080
Fax: (440)729-2231
www.american-sealcoating.com
Asphalt maintenence services/protective coatings
Began: 1988, Franchising since: 1998
Headquarters size: 11 employees
Franchise department: 6 employees

U.S. franchises: 8
Canadian franchises: 0
Other foreign franchises: 0
Company-owned: 1
Units concentrated in all U.S.

Seeking: All U.S.
Seeking in Canada? Yes
Exclusive territories? Yes
Homebased option? Yes
Kiosk option? No
Employees needed to run franchise: 1-2
Absentee ownership? Yes

COSTS
Total cost: $35K-45K
Franchise fee: $15K
Royalty fee: 5-7%
Term of agreement: 15 years renewable
Franchisees required to buy multiple units? Yes

FINANCING
In-house: Inventory
3rd-party: Accounts receivable, equipment, franchise fee, payroll, start-up costs

QUALIFICATIONS
Experience:
    Aggressive & outgoing personality

TRAINING
At headquarters: 7-10 days
At franchisee's location: 3 days
Additional training available

BUSINESS SUPPORT
Newsletter
Meetings
Toll-free phone line
Grand opening
Internet
Security/safety procedures
Field operations/evaluations
Purchasing cooperatives

MARKETING SUPPORT
Co-op advertising
Ad slicks
Ad designs
Rate negotiations

AMERICAN LEAK DETECTION
Ranked #131 in Entrepreneur Magazine's 2004 Franchise 500   *Financial rating: $$$$*

888 Research Dr., #100
Palm Springs, CA 92262
Ph: (800)755-6697/(760)320-9991
Fax: (760)320-1288
www.americanleakdetection.com
Concealed water & gas leak-detection
    services
Began: 1974, Franchising since: 1984
Headquarters size: 40 employees
Franchise department: 2 employees

U.S. franchises: 233
Canadian franchises: 8
Other foreign franchises: 70
Company-owned: 6
Units concentrated in AZ, CA, CO,
    FL, NC, OH, OK, OR, SC, TN,
    TX, VA, WA

Seeking: Midwest, Northeast
Focusing on: CT, IL, NY
Seeking in Canada? Yes
Exclusive territories? Yes
Homebased option? Yes
Kiosk option? No
Employees needed to run franchise: 2-3
Absentee ownership? No

COSTS
Total cost: $71.3K-155.1K
Franchise fee: $57.5K+
Royalty fee: 6-10%
Term of agreement: 10 years renewable
    at no charge
Franchisees required to buy multiple
    units? Outside the U.S. only

FINANCING
In-house: Franchise fee, equipment
3rd-party: Equipment, franchise fee,
    start-up costs

QUALIFICATIONS
Net worth: $200K
Cash liquidity: $65K
Experience:
    General business experience
    Marketing skills

TRAINING
At headquarters: 6-12 weeks
At franchisee's location: 1 week
Annual convention: 4 days

BUSINESS SUPPORT
Newsletter
Meetings
Toll-free phone line
Internet
Security/safety procedures
Field operations/evaluations

MARKETING SUPPORT
Ad slicks
Regional marketing
Regional advertising matching funds
    program

CHEMSTATION
Ranked #282 in Entrepreneur Magazine's 2004 Franchise 500   *Financial rating: $$$$*

3400 Encrete Ln.
Dayton, OH 45439
Ph: (937)294-8265
Fax: (937)294-5360
www.chemstation.com
Industrial cleanser manufacturing &
    distribution
Began: 1965, Franchising since: 1983
Headquarters size: 40 employees
Franchise department: 2 employees

U.S. franchises: 43
Canadian franchises: 0
Other foreign franchises: 0
Company-owned: 2
Units concentrated in all U.S.

Seeking: Midwest, Northeast, West
Focusing on: CA, MA, MN, NJ, NY
Seeking in Canada? Yes
Exclusive territories? Yes
Homebased option? No
Kiosk option? No
Employees needed to run franchise: 6
Absentee ownership? No

COSTS
Total cost: $500K-700K
Franchise fee: $45K
Royalty fee: 4%
Term of agreement: 10 years renewable
    at no charge
Franchisees required to buy multiple
    units? No

FINANCING
In-house: Franchise fee, equipment
3rd-party: None

QUALIFICATIONS
Net worth: $1M
Cash liquidity: $300K-500K
Experience:
    Marketing skills

TRAINING
At headquarters: As needed
At franchisee's location: As needed

BUSINESS SUPPORT
Newsletter
Meetings
Toll-free phone line
Internet
Security/safety procedures
Field operations/evaluations
Purchasing cooperatives

MARKETING SUPPORT
Co-op advertising
Ad slicks
National media campaign
Regional marketing

DUCT DOCTOR USA INC.

Ranked #427 in Entrepreneur Magazine's 2004 Franchise 500

Financial rating: $$$

5555 Oakbrook Pkwy., #660
Atlanta, GA 30093
Ph: (770)446-1764
Fax: (770)447-4486
www.ductdoctorusa.com
Residential & commercial air-duct
    cleaning
Began: 1985, Franchising since: 2000
Headquarters size: 12 employees
Franchise department: 2 employees

U.S. franchises: 6
Canadian franchises: 0
Other foreign franchises: 0
Company-owned: 8
Units concentrated in all U.S.

Seeking: All U.S.
Seeking in Canada? No
Exclusive territories? Yes
Homebased option? Yes
Kiosk option? No
Employees needed to run franchise: 2
Absentee ownership? No

COSTS
Total cost: $41K-64K
Franchise fee: $25K
Royalty fee: 5-8%
Term of agreement: 10 years renewable
    for 10% of initial franchise fee
Franchisees required to buy multiple
    units? No

FINANCING
In-house: Franchise fee
3rd-party: None

QUALIFICATIONS
Net worth: $100K
Cash liquidity: $50K
Experience:
    General business experience

TRAINING
At headquarters: 3 weeks
At franchisee's location: 1 week

BUSINESS SUPPORT
Newsletter
Meetings
Toll-free phone line
Grand opening
Internet
Security/safety procedures
Field operations/evaluations
Purchasing cooperatives

MARKETING SUPPORT
Ad slicks
Regional marketing
In-market business development

FILTAFRY

Ranked #334 in Entrepreneur Magazine's 2004 Franchise 500

Financial rating: $$$

5401 S. Kirkman Rd., #310
Orlando, FL 32819
Ph: (407)926-0255
Fax: (407)926-0256
www.filtafry.com
Fryer management & filtration servic-
    es to food outlets
Began: 1996, Franchising since: 1997
Headquarters size: 12 employees
Franchise department: 12 employees

U.S. franchises: 28
Canadian franchises: 0
Other foreign franchises: 89
Company-owned: 0
Units concentrated in all U.S.

Seeking: All U.S.
Seeking in Canada? Yes
Exclusive territories? Yes
Homebased option? Yes
Kiosk option? No
Employees needed to run franchise: 0
Absentee ownership? No

COSTS
Total cost: $46.3K-47.5K
Franchise fee: $15K
Royalty fee: to $450/mo.
Term of agreement: 5 years renewable
Franchisees required to buy multiple
    units? Outside the U.S. only

FINANCING
In-house: Equipment, inventory, start-
    up costs
3rd-party: None

QUALIFICATIONS
Experience:
    General business experience
    required for multi-unit developers

TRAINING
At headquarters: 2 weeks
At franchisee's location: 2-3 weeks

BUSINESS SUPPORT
Newsletter
Meetings
Toll-free phone line
Internet
Lease negotiations
Security/safety procedures
Field operations/evaluations

MARKETING SUPPORT
National media campaign

JET-BLACK INT'L. INC.
Ranked #271 in Entrepreneur Magazine's 2004 Franchise 500

Financial rating: $$$

25 W. Cliff Rd., #103
Burnsville, MN 55337
Ph: (888)538-2525/(952)890-8343
Fax: (952)890-7022
www.jet-black.com
Asphalt maintenance services
Began: 1988, Franchising since: 1993
Headquarters size: 10 employees
Franchise department: 4 employees

U.S. franchises: 146
Canadian franchises: 0
Other foreign franchises: 0
Company-owned: 2
Units concentrated in all U.S.

Seeking: All U.S.
Seeking in Canada? Yes
Exclusive territories? Yes
Homebased option? Yes
Kiosk option? No
Employees needed to run franchise: 2
Absentee ownership? Yes

COSTS
Total cost: $39.7K-106.7K
Franchise fee: $15K
Royalty fee: 8%
Term of agreement: 15 years renewable
    at no charge
Franchisees required to buy multiple
    units? No

FINANCING
No financing available

QUALIFICATIONS
Net worth: $50K
Cash liquidity: $20K
Experience:
    Industry experience
    General business experience
    Marketing skills

TRAINING
At headquarters: 1 week
At franchisee's location: 2 days

BUSINESS SUPPORT
Newsletter
Meetings
Toll-free phone line
Grand opening
Internet
Security/safety procedures
Field operations/evaluations
Purchasing cooperatives

MARKETING SUPPORT
Co-op advertising
Ad slicks
Regional marketing

KCS APPLICATIONS INC.

Financial rating: $

4955 Creaser Rd.
Westmoreland, NY 13490
Ph: (315)853-4805
Fax: (315)853-4805
www.kcs1.com
Acrylic asphalt sealcoating
Began: 1992, Franchising since: 1994
Headquarters size: 2 employees
Franchise department: 2 employees

U.S. franchises: 26
Canadian franchises: 0
Other foreign franchises: 0
Company-owned: 0
Units concentrated in CT, NY, PA

Seeking: Midwest, Northeast
Focusing on: CT, MA, NJ, NY, PA, VT
Seeking in Canada? No
Exclusive territories? No
Homebased option? Yes
Kiosk option? No
Employees needed to run franchise: 0
Absentee ownership? No

COSTS
Total cost: $15.5K
Franchise fee: $15K
Royalty fee: to $350/yr.
Term of agreement: 3 years renewable
    at no charge
Franchisees required to buy multiple
    units? No

FINANCING
No financing available

QUALIFICATIONS
Cash liquidity: $15K

TRAINING
At headquarters: 2 days
At franchisee's location: 1 day

BUSINESS SUPPORT
Meetings
Internet
Field operations/evaluations
Purchasing cooperatives

MARKETING SUPPORT
Local marketing support

RECEIL IT CEILING RESTORATION

Financial rating: $

175-B Liberty St.
Copiague, NY 11726
Ph: (800)234-5464
Fax: (631)980-7668
www.receilit.com
Ceiling restoration services
Began: 1992, Franchising since: 2002
Headquarters size: 5 employees
Franchise department: 4 employees

U.S. franchises: 0
Canadian franchises: 0
Other foreign franchises: 0
Company-owned: 1
Units concentrated in NY

Seeking: All U.S.
Focusing on: CA, CT, DE, MA, MD,
    NJ, NY, PA
Seeking in Canada? Yes
Exclusive territories? Yes
Homebased option? Yes
Kiosk option? No
Employees needed to run franchise: 2
Absentee ownership? No

COSTS
Total cost: $38.9K
Franchise fee: $35K
Royalty fee: 7%
Term of agreement: 10 years renewable
    for $10K
Franchisees required to buy multiple
    units? No

FINANCING
No financing available

QUALIFICATIONS
Net worth: $200K
Cash liquidity: $53.9K
Experience:
    Sales skills

TRAINING
At headquarters: 6 days

BUSINESS SUPPORT
Newsletter
Meetings
Toll-free phone line
Internet
Security/safety procedures
Field operations/evaluations

MARKETING SUPPORT
Regional marketing

SERVICE-TECH CORP.

Current financial data not available

7589 First Pl.
Cleveland, OH 44146-6711
Ph: (800)992-9302
Fax: (440)735-1433
www.service-techcorp.com
Air-duct & exhaust cleaning
Began: 1960, Franchising since: 1987
Headquarters size: 35 employees
Franchise department: 3 employees

U.S. franchises: 2
Canadian franchises: 0
Other foreign franchises: 0
Company-owned: 4
Units concentrated in FL, OH

Seeking: All U.S.
Seeking in Canada? Yes
Exclusive territories? Yes
Homebased option? Yes
Kiosk option? No
Employees needed to run franchise: 4
Absentee ownership? No

COSTS
Total cost: $50K
Franchise fee: $19K
Royalty fee: 4-6%
Term of agreement: 10 years renewable
Franchisees required to buy multiple
    units? No

FINANCING
No financing available

QUALIFICATIONS
Info not provided

TRAINING
At headquarters: 2 weeks
At franchisee's location

BUSINESS SUPPORT
Toll-free phone line
Internet
Security/safety procedures
Field operations/evaluations
Purchasing cooperatives

MARKETING SUPPORT
Co-op advertising
Ad slicks
National media campaign
Regional marketing

MAINTENANCE *Other Franchises*

COIT DRAPERY & CARPET CLEANERS
897 Hinckley Rd.
Burlingame, CA 94010
Ph: (800)243-8797/(650)697-5471
www.coit.com
Carpet, upholstery, drapery & air-duct
   cleaning

SEALMASTER
2520 S. Campbell St.
Sandusky, OH 44870
Ph: (800)395-7325
www.sealmaster.net
Pavement maintenance system

SUPERIOR CARPET CARE
1183 S. Huron St.
Denver, CO 80223
Ph: (800)260-8075/(303)933-3000
www.superiorclean.net
Carpet & upholstery care

WINDOW KING
3578 E. Hartsel St., #137
Colorado Springs, CO 80920
Ph: (719)522-0100
www.windowking.net
Residential & commercial window
   cleaning

PERSONAL CARE ▸ *Cosmetics*

ELIZABETH GRADY

Current financial data not available

222 Boston Ave.
Medford, MA 02155
Ph: (800)322-4257
Fax: (781)391-7828
www.elizabethgrady.com
Skin-care salons
Began: 1975, Franchising since: 1981
Headquarters size: 30 employees
Franchise department: 20 employees

U.S. franchises: 20
Canadian franchises: 0
Other foreign franchises: 0
Company-owned: 10
Units concentrated in New England

Seeking: All U.S.
Focusing on: New England
Seeking in Canada? Yes
Exclusive territories? Yes
Homebased option? No
Kiosk option? No
Employees needed to run franchise: 6
Absentee ownership? Yes

COSTS
Total cost: $300K
Franchise fee: $35K
Royalty fee: 6%
Term of agreement: 10 years renewable
at no charge
Franchisees required to buy multiple
units? No

FINANCING
No financing available

QUALIFICATIONS
Net worth: $300K
Cash liquidity: $100K

TRAINING
At headquarters: 2 weeks
At franchisee's location: 2 weeks

BUSINESS SUPPORT
Meetings
Toll-free phone line
Grand opening
Internet
Security/safety procedures
Field operations/evaluations

MARKETING SUPPORT
Ad slicks

THE EXCLUSIVES BEAUTY BAR

Current financial data not available

347 W. Berry St., #700
Fort Wayne, IN 46802
Ph: (260)437-5405
Fax: (260)426-1152
www.theexclusivesbeautybar.com
Custom skin-care, hair & cosmetic
  products
Began: 2002, Franchising since: 2003
Headquarters size: 3 employees
Franchise department: 3 employees

U.S. franchises: 0
Canadian franchises: 0
Other foreign franchises: 0
Company-owned: 1
Units concentrated in IN

Seeking: All U.S.
Seeking in Canada? Yes
Exclusive territories? Yes
Homebased option? No
Kiosk option? No
Employees needed to run franchise: 3-4
Absentee ownership? Yes

COSTS
Total cost: $29.5K-109K
Franchise fee: $15K
Royalty fee: 9%
Term of agreement: 10 years renewable
  for $1K
Franchisees required to buy multiple
  units? No

FINANCING
In-house: None
3rd-party: Franchise fee, start-up costs

QUALIFICATIONS
Net worth: $25K
Cash liquidity: $15K
Experience:
  General business experience
  Marketing skills
  Retail experience

TRAINING
At headquarters: 5 days

BUSINESS SUPPORT
Grand opening
Internet

MARKETING SUPPORT
Ad slicks

MERLE NORMAN COSMETICS

Ranked #23 in Entrepreneur Magazine's 2004 Franchise 500

Financial rating: $$$$

9130 Bellanca Ave.
Los Angeles, CA 90045
Ph: (800)421-6648/(310)641-3000
Fax: (310)337-2370
www.merlenorman.com
Cosmetics studios
Began: 1931, Franchising since: 1989
Headquarters size: 464 employees
Franchise department: 10 employees

U.S. franchises: 1,787
Canadian franchises: 89
Other foreign franchises: 0
Company-owned: 6
Units concentrated in all U.S.

Seeking: All U.S.
Seeking in Canada? Yes
Exclusive territories? No
Homebased option? No
Kiosk option? No
Employees needed to run franchise: 1-6
Absentee ownership? Yes

COSTS
Total cost: $33.1K-162K
Franchise fee: $0
Royalty fee: 0
Term of agreement: Renewable term
Franchisees required to buy multiple
  units? No

FINANCING
In-house: Accounts receivable, equipment
3rd-party: None

QUALIFICATIONS
Experience:
  Industry experience
  General business experience
  Retail experience
  Customer service skills

TRAINING
At headquarters: 7 days
Field training classes, field visits,
  advanced home office training,
  POS software training

BUSINESS SUPPORT
Newsletter
Meetings
Toll-free phone line
Grand opening
Internet
Lease negotiations
Security/safety procedures
Field operations/evaluations

MARKETING SUPPORT
Co-op advertising
Ad slicks
National media campaign
Regional marketing

SONA LASER CENTERS INC.

Financial rating: 0

1025 Executive Blvd., #112
Chesapeake, VA 23320
Ph: (757)436-0333
Fax: (757)436-7444
www.sonalasercenters.com
Laser hair removal services
Began: 1997, Franchising since: 2002
Headquarters size: 15 employees
Franchise department: 12 employees

U.S. franchises: 9
Canadian franchises: 0
Other foreign franchises: 0
Company-owned: 2
Units concentrated in CA, MN, MS,
    NC, OR, TX, VA

Seeking: All U.S.
Seeking in Canada? No
Exclusive territories? Yes
Homebased option? No
Kiosk option? No
Employees needed to run franchise: 4
Absentee ownership? No

COSTS
Total cost: $330K
Franchise fee: $49.5K
Royalty fee: Varies
Term of agreement: 10 years renewable
    for 25% of franchise fee
Franchisees required to buy multiple
    units? Yes

FINANCING
No financing available

QUALIFICATIONS
Net worth: $500K
Cash liquidity: $150K
Experience:
    Industry experience
    General business experience
    Marketing skills

TRAINING
At headquarters: 3 days
At franchisee's location: 7 days
At corporate-owned center: 7 days

BUSINESS SUPPORT
Meetings
Grand opening
Internet
Security/safety procedures
Field operations/evaluations

MARKETING SUPPORT
Ad slicks
Marketing planning
Infomercial, radio & TV ads

TOP OF THE LINE FRAGRANCES

Financial rating: $$$

515 Bath Ave.
Long Branch, NJ 07740
Ph: (732)229-0014
Fax: (732)222-1762
www.tolfranchise.com
Retail discount cosmetics & fragrances
Began: 1983, Franchising since: 1987
Headquarters size: 9 employees
Franchise department: 6 employees

U.S. franchises: 3
Canadian franchises: 0
Other foreign franchises: 0
Company-owned: 1
Units concentrated in all U.S.

Seeking: All U.S.
Focusing on: FL, NJ, PA
Seeking in Canada? No
Exclusive territories? Yes
Homebased option? No
Kiosk option? No
Employees needed to run franchise: 5
Absentee ownership? Yes

COSTS
Total cost: $164.8K-237.8K
Franchise fee: $20K
Royalty fee: 5%
Term of agreement: 10 years renewable
    at no charge
Franchisees required to buy multiple
    units? No

FINANCING
In-house: None
3rd-party: Equipment, franchise fee,
    inventory, start-up costs

QUALIFICATIONS
Net worth: $250K
Cash liquidity: $150K
Experience:
    General business experience

TRAINING
At franchisee's location: 10 days

BUSINESS SUPPORT
Toll-free phone line
Grand opening
Lease negotiations
Field operations/evaluations

MARKETING SUPPORT
Ad slicks

THE WOODHOUSE DAY SPA

Financial rating: $$$

203 E. Stayton Ave.
Victoria, TX 77901
Ph: (877)570-7772
Fax: (361)578-7116
www.woodhousespas.com
Day spa services, bath & body retail
    products
Began: 2001, Franchising since: 2003
Headquarters size: 28 employees
Franchise department: 5 employees

U.S. franchises: 1
Canadian franchises: 0
Other foreign franchises: 0
Company-owned: 1

Focusing on: All U.S. except CA, CT, HI,
    IA, IL, IN, MD, MI, MN, ND, NE,
    NY, OR, RI, SD, UT, VA, WA, WI
Seeking in Canada? No
Exclusive territories? Yes
Homebased option? No
Kiosk option? No
Employees needed to run franchise: 10
Absentee ownership? No

COSTS
Total cost: $153.7K-226.9K
Franchise fee: $10K
Royalty fee: 6%
Term of agreement: 10 years renewable
    for 50% of then-current fee
Franchisees required to buy multiple
    units? No

FINANCING
No financing available

QUALIFICATIONS
Net worth: $30K-90K
Cash liquidity: $30K-90K
Experience:
    General business experience

TRAINING
At headquarters: 3 weeks

BUSINESS SUPPORT
Newsletter
Meetings
Toll-free phone line
Grand opening
Internet
Security/safety procedures
Field operations/evaluations
Purchasing cooperatives

MARKETING SUPPORT
Co-op advertising
Ad slicks

PERSONAL CARE   *Hair Salons*

CARTOON CUTS

Financial rating: 0

5501 Backlick Rd., #118
Springfield, VA 22151
Ph: (800)701-2887
Fax: (703)354-4431
www.cartooncuts.com
Children's hair salon
Began: 1991, Franchising since: 2000
Headquarters size: 200 employees
Franchise department: 10 employees

U.S. franchises: 4
Canadian franchises: 0
Other foreign franchises: 0
Company-owned: 20
Units concentrated in Puerto Rico

Seeking: All U.S.
Seeking in Canada? No
Exclusive territories? Yes
Homebased option? No
Kiosk option? No
Employees needed to run franchise: 6-8
Absentee ownership? Yes

COSTS
Total cost: $97K-216K
Franchise fee: $25K
Royalty fee: 5%
Term of agreement: 10 years renewable
Franchisees required to buy multiple
    units? No

FINANCING
No financing available

QUALIFICATIONS
Net worth: $250K
Cash liquidity: $40K
Experience:
    General business experience
    Marketing skills
    Customer service skills

TRAINING
At headquarters: 2 weeks
At franchisee's location: 1 week

BUSINESS SUPPORT
Newsletter
Meetings
Toll-free phone line
Grand opening
Internet
Lease negotiations
Security/safety procedures
Field operations/evaluations
Purchasing cooperatives

MARKETING SUPPORT
Ad slicks
Regional marketing

COST CUTTERS FAMILY HAIR CARE
Ranked #66 in Entrepreneur Magazine's 2004 Franchise 500　　　*Financial rating: $$$$*

7201 Metro Blvd.
Minneapolis, MN 55439
Ph: (888)888-7008/(952)947-7777
Fax: (952)947-7301
www.costcutters.com
Family hair-care salons
Began: 1982, Franchising since: 1982
Headquarters size: 650 employees
Franchise department: 100 employees

U.S. franchises: 669
Canadian franchises: 0
Other foreign franchises: 0
Company-owned: 170
Units concentrated in all U.S.

Seeking: All U.S.
Seeking in Canada? No
Exclusive territories? Yes
Homebased option? No
Kiosk option? No
Employees needed to run franchise: 6-8
Absentee ownership? Yes

COSTS
Total cost: $69K-148K
Franchise fee: $12.5K-22.5K
Royalty fee: 6%
Term of agreement: 15 years renewable
　　at no charge
Franchisees required to buy multiple
　　units? Yes

FINANCING
In-house: None
3rd-party: Equipment, franchise fee,
　　inventory, start-up costs

QUALIFICATIONS
Net worth: $300K
Cash liquidity: $100K
Experience:
　　General business experience
　　Marketing skills
　　Retail/service industry experience

TRAINING
At headquarters: 4 days
At franchisee's location: 5 days
Additional training available

BUSINESS SUPPORT
Meetings
Toll-free phone line
Grand opening
Internet
Lease negotiations
Security/safety procedures
Field operations/evaluations

MARKETING SUPPORT
Ad slicks
Regional marketing

FANTASTIC SAMS
Ranked #38 in Entrepreneur Magazine's 2004 Franchise 500　　　*Financial rating: $$$*

10517 Garden Grove Blvd.
Garden Grove, CA 92843
Ph: (714)554-8811
Fax: (714)554-3130
www.fantasticsams.com
Hair salons
Began: 1974, Franchising since: 1976
Headquarters size: 40 employees
Franchise department: 4 employees

U.S. franchises: 1,285
Canadian franchises: 16
Other foreign franchises: 19
Company-owned: 0
Units concentrated in all U.S.

Seeking: All U.S.
Seeking in Canada? Yes
Exclusive territories? Yes
Homebased option? No
Kiosk option? No
Employees needed to run franchise: 8
Absentee ownership? Yes

COSTS
Total cost: $75K-164K
Franchise fee: $25K
Royalty fee: $236/wk.
Term of agreement: 10 years renewable
　　for $6.3K
Franchisees required to buy multiple
　　units? Outside the U.S. only

FINANCING
In-house: None
3rd-party: Equipment, inventory,
　　start-up costs

QUALIFICATIONS
Net worth: $100K
Cash liquidity: $25K
Experience:
　　General business experience

TRAINING
At headquarters: 1 week
At franchisee's location: 1 month
At regional office: 1 week

BUSINESS SUPPORT
Newsletter
Meetings
Grand opening
Internet
Security/safety procedures
Field operations/evaluations

MARKETING SUPPORT
Co-op advertising
Ad slicks
National media campaign
Regional marketing
Turnkey marketing by target groups
In-salon graphics & promotional
　　pieces

FIRST CHOICE HAIRCUTTERS

Ranked #177 in Entrepreneur Magazine's 2004 Franchise 500   *Financial rating: $$$$*

6465 Millcreek Dr., #210
Mississauga, ON Canada L5N 5R6
Ph: (800)617-3961/(905)821-8555
Fax: (905)567-7000
www.firstchoice.com
Full-service family hair care
Began: 1980, Franchising since: 1982
Headquarters size: 40 employees
Franchise department: 20 employees

U.S. franchises: 13
Canadian franchises: 194
Other foreign franchises: 0
Company-owned: 150

Not available in the U.S.
Seeking in Canada? Yes
Exclusive territories? Yes
Homebased option? No
Kiosk option? No
Employees needed to run franchise: 4-6
Absentee ownership? No

COSTS
Total cost: $118K-205K
Franchise fee: $10K-25K
Royalty fee: 5-7%
Term of agreement: 10 years renewable
Franchisees required to buy multiple
    units? No

FINANCING
No financing available

QUALIFICATIONS
Net worth: $100K
Cash liquidity: $40K
Experience:
    General business experience
    Customer-service oriented
    Management skills

TRAINING
At headquarters: 1 week
At franchisee's location: 2 weeks
At annual convention: 2 days

BUSINESS SUPPORT
Newsletter
Meetings
Grand opening
Internet
Lease negotiations
Security/safety procedures
Field operations/evaluations
Purchasing cooperatives

MARKETING SUPPORT
Ad slicks
National media campaign
Regional marketing

FUN CUTS 4 KIDS

Current financial data not available

1026 Germantown Pkwy.
Cordova, TN 38018
Ph: (800)431-8258
Fax: (901)758-0816
www.funcuts4kids.com
Children's & family hair care
Began: 1998, Franchising since: 1999
Headquarters size: 10 employees
Franchise department: 3 employees

U.S. franchises: 2
Canadian franchises: 0
Other foreign franchises: 0
Company-owned: 1
Units concentrated in TN

Seeking: All U.S.
Seeking in Canada? Yes
Exclusive territories? Yes
Homebased option? No
Kiosk option? No
Employees needed to run franchise: 3-6
Absentee ownership? Yes

COSTS
Total cost: $75.1K-161K
Franchise fee: $25K
Royalty fee: $50-125/wk.
Term of agreement: Info not provided
Franchisees required to buy multiple
    units? No

FINANCING
No financing available

QUALIFICATIONS
Experience:
    General business experience

TRAINING
At franchisee's location: Varies

BUSINESS SUPPORT
Meetings
Grand opening
Internet
Lease negotiations
Field operations/evaluations
Purchasing cooperatives

MARKETING SUPPORT
Ad slicks
Marketing materials

GREAT CLIPS INC.

Ranked #36 in Entrepreneur Magazine's 2004 Franchise 500　　　　*Financial rating: $$*

7700 France Ave., #425
Minneapolis, MN 55435
Ph: (800)947-1143/(952)893-9088
Fax: (952)844-3443
www.greatclipsfranchise.com
Family hair salons
Began: 1982, Franchising since: 1983
Headquarters size: 210 employees
Franchise department: 11 employees

U.S. franchises: 1,877
Canadian franchises: 58
Other foreign franchises: 0
Company-owned: 0
Units concentrated in all U.S.

Seeking: Midwest, South, Southeast,
　　Southwest, West
Focusing on: All U.S.
Seeking in Canada? Yes
Exclusive territories? Yes
Homebased option? No
Kiosk option? No
Employees needed to run franchise:
　　8-10
Absentee ownership? Yes

COSTS
Total cost: $94.6K-180.1K
Franchise fee: $25K
Royalty fee: 6%
Term of agreement: 10 years renewable
　　for $1.8K
Franchisees required to buy multiple
　　units? No

FINANCING
In-house: None
3rd-party: Accounts receivable, equip-
　　ment, franchise fee, inventory, pay-
　　roll, start-up costs

QUALIFICATIONS
Net worth: $250K
Cash liquidity: $150K
Experience:
　　General business experience
　　Marketing skills

TRAINING
At headquarters: 5 days
At local training center: 7 days &
　　ongoing

BUSINESS SUPPORT
Newsletter
Meetings
Toll-free phone line
Grand opening
Internet
Security/safety procedures
Field operations/evaluations
Purchasing cooperatives

MARKETING SUPPORT
Co-op advertising
Ad slicks
Regional marketing

THE LEMON TREE

Ranked #455 in Entrepreneur Magazine's 2004 Franchise 500　　　　*Financial rating: $$$*

3301 Hempstead Tpke.
Levittown, NY 11756
Ph: (800)345-9156/(516)735-2828
Fax: (516)735-1851
www.lemontree.com
Family hair care
Began: 1974, Franchising since: 1976
Headquarters size: 5 employees
Franchise department: 3 employees

U.S. franchises: 58
Canadian franchises: 0
Other foreign franchises: 0
Company-owned: 0
Units concentrated in CT, NJ, NY, PA

Seeking: Northeast, South, Southeast
Focusing on: CT, NJ, NY, PA
Seeking in Canada? No
Exclusive territories? Yes
Homebased option? No
Kiosk option? No
Employees needed to run franchise:
　　5-10
Absentee ownership? No

COSTS
Total cost: $44.9K-78K
Franchise fee: $15K
Royalty fee: 6%
Term of agreement: 15 years renewable
　　at no charge
Franchisees required to buy multiple
　　units? No

FINANCING
In-house: Franchise fee, equipment
3rd-party: None

QUALIFICATIONS
Net worth: $100K-200K
Cash liquidity: $50K-75K

TRAINING
At headquarters: 1 week
At franchisee's location: 1 week
Additional training available

BUSINESS SUPPORT
Meetings
Toll-free phone line
Grand opening
Field operations/evaluations
Purchasing cooperatives

MARKETING SUPPORT
Co-op advertising
Ad slicks
National media campaign
Regional marketing

MALE CARE

Current financial data not available

3116 Wrightsboro Rd.
Augusta, GA 30909
Ph: (706)736-9155
Fax: (706)736-1038
www.male-care.com
Combination barber shop, car wash &
dry cleaners
Began: 1998, Franchising since: 2003
Headquarters size: 4 employees
Franchise department: 4 employees

U.S. franchises: 0
Canadian franchises: 0
Other foreign franchises: 0
Company-owned: 1

Seeking: All U.S.
Seeking in Canada? No
Exclusive territories? No
Homebased option? No
Kiosk option? No
Employees needed to run franchise:
8-10
Absentee ownership? Yes

COSTS
Total cost: $61.8K-71.3K
Franchise fee: $35K
Royalty fee: 6%
Term of agreement: 5 years renewable
Franchisees required to buy multiple
units? No

FINANCING
No financing available

QUALIFICATIONS
Net worth: $50K
Cash liquidity: $35K
Experience:
Basic business skills

TRAINING
At headquarters: 2 weeks
At franchisee's location: 3 days

BUSINESS SUPPORT
Toll-free phone line
Grand opening
Internet
Lease negotiations
Field operations/evaluations

MARKETING SUPPORT
Ad slicks
Review of local ads, radio & TV scripts

PRO-CUTS

Ranked #202 in Entrepreneur Magazine's 2004 Franchise 500   *Financial rating: $$$$*

7201 Metro Blvd.
Minneapolis, MN 55439
Ph: (952)947-7777
Fax: (952)947-7300
www.pro-cuts.com
Hair salons
Began: 1982, Franchising since: 1984
Headquarters size: 650 employees
Franchise department: 100 employees

U.S. franchises: 198
Canadian franchises: 0
Other foreign franchises: 0
Company-owned: 9
Units concentrated in TX

Seeking: All U.S.
Seeking in Canada? No
Exclusive territories? Yes
Homebased option? No
Kiosk option? No
Employees needed to run franchise: 6-8
Absentee ownership? Yes

COSTS
Total cost: $111K-207K
Franchise fee: $22.5K
Royalty fee: to 6%
Term of agreement: 10 years renewable
for $2.5K
Franchisees required to buy multiple
units? Yes

FINANCING
In-house: None
3rd-party: Equipment, franchise fee,
inventory, start-up costs

QUALIFICATIONS
Net worth: $150K
Cash liquidity: $30K-60K
Experience:
General business experience

TRAINING
At headquarters: 3-5 days
At franchisee's location: 5 days
Additional training available

BUSINESS SUPPORT
Meetings
Toll-free phone line
Grand opening
Lease negotiations
Field operations/evaluations

MARKETING SUPPORT
Co-op advertising
Ad slicks

SPORT CLIPS
Ranked #138 in Entrepreneur Magazine's 2004 Franchise 500   *Financial rating: $$$$*

P.O. Box 3000-266
Georgetown, TX 78627-3000
Ph: (512)869-1201, Fax: (512)869-0366
www.sportclips.com
Men's sports-themed hair salons
Began: 1993, Franchising since: 1995
Headquarters size: 25 employees
Franchise department: 3 employees

U.S. franchises: 108
Canadian franchises: 0
Other foreign franchises: 0
Company-owned: 9
Units concentrated in all U.S. except
     West coast, Northeast

Seeking: Midwest, South, Southeast,
     Southwest
Focusing on: All U.S. except West
     coast, Northeast
Seeking in Canada? No
Exclusive territories? Yes
Homebased option? No
Kiosk option? No
Employees needed to run franchise:
     6-12
Absentee ownership? Yes

COSTS
Total cost: $98K-197K
Franchise fee: $10K-25K
Royalty fee: 6%
Term of agreement: 5 years renewable
     for $3.5K
Franchisees required to buy multiple
     units? Yes

FINANCING
In-house: None
3rd-party: Equipment, franchise fee,
     inventory, start-up costs

QUALIFICATIONS
Net worth: $250K
Cash liquidity: $50K
Experience:
     General business experience
     Marketing skills
     People skills

TRAINING
At headquarters: 5 days
At franchisee's location: 5 days
At existing locations: 5 days

BUSINESS SUPPORT
Newsletter
Meetings
Toll-free phone line
Grand opening
Internet
Lease negotiations
Security/safety procedures
Field operations/evaluations
Purchasing cooperatives

MARKETING SUPPORT
Co-op advertising
Ad slicks
Ad fund
Local radio & TV
Celebrity fees

SUPERCUTS
Ranked #31 in Entrepreneur Magazine's 2004 Franchise 500   *Financial rating: $$$$*

7201 Metro Blvd.
Minneapolis, MN 55439
Ph: (888)888-7008/(952)947-7777
Fax: (952)947-7300
www.supercuts.com
Family hair care
Began: 1975, Franchising since: 1979
Headquarters size: 650 employees
Franchise department: 100 employees

U.S. franchises: 957
Canadian franchises: 11
Other foreign franchises: 0
Company-owned: 791
Units concentrated in all U.S.

Seeking: All U.S.
Seeking in Canada? Yes
Exclusive territories? Yes
Homebased option? No
Kiosk option? No
Employees needed to run franchise: 6-8
Absentee ownership? Yes

COSTS
Total cost: $90.9K-164.1K
Franchise fee: $10K-22.5K
Royalty fee: 6%
Term of agreement: For duration of
     lease, renewable
Franchisees required to buy multiple
     units? Yes

FINANCING
In-house: None
3rd-party: Equipment, franchise fee,
     inventory, start-up costs

QUALIFICATIONS
Net worth: $300K
Cash liquidity: $100K
Experience:
     General business experience
     Marketing skills
     Retail/service industry experience

TRAINING
At headquarters: 4 days

BUSINESS SUPPORT
Newsletter
Meetings
Toll-free phone line
Grand opening
Internet
Lease negotiations
Security/safety procedures
Field operations/evaluations

MARKETING SUPPORT
Ad slicks

PERSONAL CARE *Seniors*

COMFORCARE SENIOR SERVICES INC.

Financial rating: $$$

42505 Woodward Ave.
Bloomfield Hills, MI 48304
Ph: (800)886-4044, Fax: (248)745-9763
www.comforcare.com/franchise
Non-medical home-care services
Began: 1996, Franchising since: 2001
Headquarters size: 15 employees
Franchise department: 7 employees

U.S. franchises: 28
Canadian franchises: 0
Other foreign franchises: 0
Company-owned: 1
Units concentrated in all U.S.

Seeking: All U.S.
Seeking in Canada? No
Exclusive territories? Yes
Homebased option? No
Kiosk option? No
Employees needed to run franchise: 1
Absentee ownership? Yes

COSTS
Total cost: $19.5K-29.9K
Franchise fee: $12.5K
Royalty fee: 3%
Term of agreement: 10 years renewable
at to $1.5K
Franchisees required to buy multiple
units? No

FINANCING
In-house: None
3rd-party: Accounts receivable, equip-
ment, inventory, start-up costs

QUALIFICATIONS
Net worth: $100K
Cash liquidity: $30K

TRAINING
At headquarters: 1 week
At franchisee's location: Several times
per year
Additional training for key adminis-
trators

BUSINESS SUPPORT
Newsletter
Meetings
Toll-free phone line
Grand opening
Internet
Lease negotiations
Security/safety procedures
Field operations/evaluations
Purchasing cooperatives

MARKETING SUPPORT
Co-op advertising
Ad slicks
Regional marketing
Online ordering
Strategic alliances

COMFORT KEEPERS

Ranked #68 in Entrepreneur Magazine's 2004 Franchise 500

Financial rating: $$$$

6450 Poe Ave., #109
Dayton, OH 45414
Ph: (800)387-2415, Fax: (937)264-3103
www.comfortkeepers.com
Non-medical in-home senior care
Began: 1998, Franchising since: 1999
Headquarters size: 15 employees
Franchise department: 2 employees

U.S. franchises: 373
Canadian franchises: 1
Other foreign franchises: 0
Company-owned: 1
Units concentrated in all U.S.

Seeking: All U.S.
Seeking in Canada? No
Exclusive territories? Yes
Homebased option? Yes
Kiosk option? No
Employees needed to run franchise:
15-20
Absentee ownership? Yes

COSTS
Total cost: $40K-60K
Franchise fee: $18.8K
Royalty fee: 5-3%
Term of agreement: 10 years renewable
at no charge
Franchisees required to buy multiple
units? No

FINANCING
No financing available

QUALIFICATIONS
Net worth: $75K
Cash liquidity: $40K-60K

TRAINING
At headquarters: 1 week
Financial, marketing & operational
training: 6-8 times per year

BUSINESS SUPPORT
Newsletter
Meetings
Toll-free phone line
Grand opening
Internet
Security/safety procedures
Field operations/evaluations
Purchasing cooperatives

MARKETING SUPPORT
Co-op advertising
Ad slicks
Regional marketing

ELDIRECT HOMECARE

Financial rating: $$$

21 W. Mountain, #300
Fayetteville, AR 72701
Ph: (479)443-7173
Fax: (479)443-0183
www.eldirecthomecare.com
Non-medical in-home care
Began: 1996, Franchising since: 2002
Headquarters size: 6 employees
Franchise department: 6 employees

U.S. franchises: 0
Canadian franchises: 0
Other foreign franchises: 0
Company-owned: 1
Units concentrated in all U.S.

Seeking: All U.S.
Seeking in Canada? No
Exclusive territories? Yes
Homebased option? No
Kiosk option? No
Employees needed to run franchise: 2
Absentee ownership? Yes

COSTS
Total cost: $21.9K-29.7K
Franchise fee: $15K
Royalty fee: 5%
Term of agreement: 10 years renewable
    for 10% of current franchise fee
Franchisees required to buy multiple
    units? No

FINANCING
No financing available

QUALIFICATIONS
Info not provided

TRAINING
At headquarters: Up to 5 days
At franchisee's location: Up to 5 days

BUSINESS SUPPORT
Newsletter
Meetings
Toll-free phone line
Grand opening
Internet
Security/safety procedures
Field operations/evaluations
Purchasing cooperatives

MARKETING SUPPORT
Co-op advertising
Ad slicks
National media campaign
Regional marketing

GRISWOLD SPECIAL CARE

Ranked #326 in Entrepreneur Magazine's 2004 Franchise 500

Financial rating: $$$$

717 Bethlehem Pike, #300
Erdenheim, PA 19073
Ph: (215)402-0200, Fax: (215)402-0202
www.home-care.net
Non-medical home-care services
Began: 1982, Franchising since: 1984
Headquarters size: 70 employees
Franchise department: Info not pro-
    vided

U.S. franchises: 70
Canadian franchises: 0
Other foreign franchises: 3
Company-owned: 8
Units concentrated in CT, DE, FL, GA,
    IL, MA, MD, MI, NC, NJ, OH, PA,
    SC, TN, VA, VT

Seeking: Midwest, Northeast, South,
    Southeast, West
Focusing on: TX, East Coast, Midwest
Seeking in Canada? Yes
Exclusive territories? Yes
Homebased option? Yes
Kiosk option? No
Employees needed to run franchise: 1-2
Absentee ownership? No

COSTS
Total cost: $6K-30K
Franchise fee: $0
Royalty fee: Varies
Term of agreement: 7 years renewable
    at no charge
Franchisees required to buy multiple
    units? No

FINANCING
In-house: None
3rd-party: Payroll

QUALIFICATIONS
Experience:
    Industry experience
    General business experience
    Marketing skills

TRAINING
At headquarters: 1 week
At franchisee's location: 2-4 days
In-field
Annual workshops

BUSINESS SUPPORT
Newsletter
Meetings
Toll-free phone line
Internet
Security/safety procedures
Field operations/evaluations
Purchasing cooperatives

MARKETING SUPPORT
Co-op advertising
Ad slicks
National media campaign
Regional marketing
Phone support
Annual workshop series
Customized software
Visits

HOME HELPERS

Ranked #118 in Entrepreneur Magazine's 2004 Franchise 500   *Financial rating: $$$$*

4338 Glendale-Milford Rd.
Cincinnati, OH 45242
Ph: (800)216-4196
Fax: (513)563-2691
www.homehelpers.cc
Non-medical care services
Began: 1997, Franchising since: 1997
Headquarters size: 15 employees
Franchise department: 15 employees

U.S. franchises: 191
Canadian franchises: 0
Other foreign franchises: 0
Company-owned: 0
Units concentrated in all U.S.

Seeking: All U.S.
Seeking in Canada? Yes
Exclusive territories? Yes
Homebased option? Yes
Kiosk option? No
Employees needed to run franchise: 2
Absentee ownership? Yes

COSTS
Total cost: $22.5K-35.9K
Franchise fee: $18.9K-24.9K
Royalty fee: 4-6%
Term of agreement: 10 years renewable
    at no charge
Franchisees required to buy multiple
    units? No

FINANCING
In-house: Franchise fee
3rd-party: None

QUALIFICATIONS
Cash liquidity: $9.5K

TRAINING
At headquarters: 5 business days
At regional & national meeting

BUSINESS SUPPORT
Newsletter
Meetings
Toll-free phone line
Internet
Security/safety procedures
Field operations/evaluations

MARKETING SUPPORT
Ad slicks
National media campaign
Electronic ad templates

HOME INSTEAD SENIOR CARE

Ranked #78 in Entrepreneur Magazine's 2004 Franchise 500   *Financial rating: $$$$*

604 N. 109th Ct.
Omaha, NE 68154
Ph: (888)484-5759/(402)498-4466
Fax: (402)498-5757
www.homeinstead.com
Non-medical senior-care services
Began: 1994, Franchising since: 1995
Headquarters size: 49 employees
Franchise department: 30 employees

U.S. franchises: 417
Canadian franchises: 9
Other foreign franchises: 22
Company-owned: 2
Units concentrated in all U.S.

Seeking: All U.S.
Seeking in Canada? Yes
Exclusive territories? Yes
Homebased option? No
Kiosk option? No
Employees needed to run franchise: 2
Absentee ownership? No

COSTS
Total cost: $30.2K-39.5K
Franchise fee: $21.5K
Royalty fee: 5%
Term of agreement: 10 years renewable
    at no charge
Franchisees required to buy multiple
    units? Outside the U.S. only

FINANCING
In-house: None
3rd-party: Accounts receivable, equip-
    ment, franchise fee, inventory, pay-
    roll, start-up costs

QUALIFICATIONS
Net worth: $75K
Cash liquidity: $50K

TRAINING
At headquarters: 1 week
At franchisee's location: 13 weeks
At existing location: 8 weeks

BUSINESS SUPPORT
Newsletter
Meetings
Toll-free phone line
Internet
Security/safety procedures
Field operations/evaluations
Purchasing cooperatives

MARKETING SUPPORT
Ad slicks
National media campaign
National leads

HOMEWATCH CAREGIVERS

Ranked #323 in Entrepreneur Magazine's 2004 Franchise 500   *Financial rating: $$$*

2865 S. Colorado Blvd.
Denver, CO 80222
Ph: (800)777-9770/(303)758-7290
Fax: (303)758-1724
www.homewatch-intl.com
Home-care services for seniors
Began: 1973, Franchising since: 1986
Headquarters size: 11 employees
Franchise department: 6 employees

U.S. franchises: 40
Canadian franchises: 0
Other foreign franchises: 3
Company-owned: 1
Units concentrated in all U.S.

Seeking: All U.S.
Focusing on: CA, MI, OH, OR, TX, WI
    & East Coast
Seeking in Canada? Yes
Exclusive territories? Yes
Homebased option? No
Kiosk option? No
Employees needed to run franchise:
    3-30
Absentee ownership? Yes

COSTS
Total cost: $23.8K-43.7K
Franchise fee: $12K-17.5K
Royalty fee: 3-5%
Term of agreement: 10 years renewable
    at no charge
Franchisees required to buy multiple
    units? Outside the U.S. only

FINANCING
In-house: None
3rd-party: Franchise fee, start-up costs

QUALIFICATIONS
Net worth: $200K
Cash liquidity: $35K
Experience:
    Industry experience
    General business experience
    Marketing skills
    People skills

TRAINING
At headquarters: 6 days
At franchisee's location: 2-3 days
Ongoing

BUSINESS SUPPORT
Newsletter
Meetings
Grand opening
Internet
Security/safety procedures
Field operations/evaluations
Purchasing cooperatives

MARKETING SUPPORT
Co-op advertising
Ad slicks
Regional marketing

RIGHT AT HOME INC.

Ranked #410 in Entrepreneur Magazine's 2004 Franchise 500   *Financial rating: $$*

2939 S. 120th St.
Omaha, NE 68144
Ph: (402)697-7537
Fax: (402)697-7536
www.rightathome.net
Senior home care & medical staffing
Began: 1995, Franchising since: 2000
Headquarters size: 14 employees
Franchise department: 6 employees

U.S. franchises: 40
Canadian franchises: 0
Other foreign franchises: 0
Company-owned: 1
Units concentrated in all U.S.

Seeking: All U.S.
Seeking in Canada? No
Exclusive territories? Yes
Homebased option? No
Kiosk option? No
Employees needed to run franchise:
    Info not provided
Absentee ownership? No

COSTS
Total cost: $28.5K-64.9K
Franchise fee: $16.5K
Royalty fee: 5%
Term of agreement: 10 years renewable
    at no charge
Franchisees required to buy multiple
    units? No

FINANCING
No financing available

QUALIFICATIONS
Experience:
    General business experience

TRAINING
At headquarters: 2 weeks

BUSINESS SUPPORT
Newsletter
Meetings
Toll-free phone line
Internet
Lease negotiations
Security/safety procedures
Field operations/evaluations

MARKETING SUPPORT
Ad slicks
Web site

SARAH ADULT DAY SERVICES INC.

Financial rating: 0

800 Market Ave. N., #1230
Canton, OH 44702
Ph: (330)454-3200
Fax: (330)454-6807
www.sarahcarefranchises.com
Adult day services
Began: 1985, Franchising since: 2000
Headquarters size: 21 employees
Franchise department: 6 employees

U.S. franchises: 6
Canadian franchises: 0
Other foreign franchises: 0
Company-owned: 2
Units concentrated in all U.S.

Seeking: All U.S.
Seeking in Canada? No
Exclusive territories? Yes
Homebased option? No
Kiosk option? No
Employees needed to run franchise: 15
Absentee ownership? Yes

COSTS
Total cost: $170K
Franchise fee: $19.5K
Royalty fee: 5%
Term of agreement: 10 years renewable
Franchisees required to buy multiple units? No

FINANCING
In-house: None
3rd-party: Equipment, franchise fee, start-up costs

QUALIFICATIONS
Cash liquidity: $70K
Experience:
   General business experience
   Marketing skills

TRAINING
At headquarters: 8 days

BUSINESS SUPPORT
Newsletter
Meetings
Toll-free phone line
Grand opening
Internet
Security/safety procedures
Field operations/evaluations

MARKETING SUPPORT
Regional marketing
Referral system

SUPERIOR SENIOR CARE

Current financial data not available

835 Central Ave.
Hot Springs, AR 71901
Ph: (501)321-1743
Fax: (501)623-7853
www.superiorseniorcare.com
Non-medical in-home senior-care referral services
Began: 1990, Franchising since: 1999
Headquarters size: 4 employees
Franchise department: 2 employees

U.S. franchises: 3
Canadian franchises: 0
Other foreign franchises: 0
Company-owned: 8
Units concentrated in AR, MO

Focusing on: TN, TX
Seeking in Canada? No
Exclusive territories? Yes
Homebased option? No
Kiosk option? No
Employees needed to run franchise: 1-2
Absentee ownership? Yes

COSTS
Total cost: $24K-39K
Franchise fee: $20K
Royalty fee: 5%
Term of agreement: 10 years renewable
Franchisees required to buy multiple units? No

FINANCING
No financing available

QUALIFICATIONS
Experience:
   General business experience
   Marketing skills

TRAINING
At headquarters: 1 week
At franchisee's location: 1 day

BUSINESS SUPPORT
Meetings
Toll-free phone line
Internet
Lease negotiations
Field operations/evaluations
Purchasing cooperatives

MARKETING SUPPORT
Co-op advertising
Ad slicks
Video, audio & print support

VISITING ANGELS
Ranked #404 in Entrepreneur Magazine's 2004 Franchise 500   *Financial rating: $*

28 W. Eagle Rd., #201
Havertown, PA 19083
Ph: (800)365-4189/(610)924-0630
Fax: (610)924-9690
www.livingassistance.com
Non-medical home-care services for
    seniors
Began: 1992, Franchising since: 1998
Headquarters size: 13 employees
Franchise department: 13 employees

U.S. franchises: 142
Canadian franchises: 2
Other foreign franchises: 0
Company-owned: 0
Units concentrated in all U.S.

Seeking: All U.S.
Seeking in Canada? No
Exclusive territories? Yes
Homebased option? Yes
Kiosk option? No
Employees needed to run franchise: 1
Absentee ownership? No

COSTS
Total cost: $19.4K-38.6K
Franchise fee: $9.95K-21.95K
Royalty fee: 2-2.95%
Term of agreement: 10 years renewable
    for $2.5K
Franchisees required to buy multiple
    units? No

FINANCING
No financing available

QUALIFICATIONS
Cash liquidity: $15K

TRAINING
At headquarters: 5 days
Regional meetings: 5 per year

BUSINESS SUPPORT
Newsletter
Meetings
Toll-free phone line
Internet
Purchasing cooperatives

MARKETING SUPPORT
Co-op advertising
National media campaign
PR support

PERSONAL CARE ▶ *Tanning Salons*

CELSIUS TANNERY

Current financial data not available

12142 State Line Rd.
Leawood, KS 66223
Ph: (866)826-7400/(913)451-7000
Fax: (913)451-7001
www.celsiustan.com
Tanning salon
Began: 1995, Franchising since: 2000
Headquarters size: 8 employees
Franchise department: 2 employees

U.S. franchises: 19
Canadian franchises: 0
Other foreign franchises: 0
Company-owned: 3
Units concentrated in KS, MO, NY

Seeking: All U.S.
Seeking in Canada? No
Exclusive territories? Yes
Homebased option? No
Kiosk option? No
Employees needed to run franchise:
    8-15
Absentee ownership? Yes

COSTS
Total cost: $265K-598.5K
Franchise fee: $20K
Royalty fee: 1%
Term of agreement: 5 years renewable
    for $4K
Franchisees required to buy multiple
    units? No

FINANCING
In-house: None
3rd-party: Equipment

QUALIFICATIONS
Net worth: $100K
Cash liquidity: $70K

TRAINING
At headquarters: 2 weeks
At franchisee's location: 1 week
Ongoing by vendors & franchisor

BUSINESS SUPPORT
Meetings
Toll-free phone line
Grand opening
Internet
Lease negotiations
Security/safety procedures
Field operations/evaluations
Purchasing cooperatives

MARKETING SUPPORT
Co-op advertising
Ad slicks
National media campaign
Regional marketing

EXECUTIVE TANS INC.

Ranked #172 in Entrepreneur Magazine's 2004 Franchise 500　　　*Financial rating: $$$*

165 S. Union Blvd., #780
Lakewood, CO 80228
Ph: (877)393-2826/(303)988-9999
Fax: (303)988-5390
www.executivetans.com
Tanning salon
Began: 1991, Franchising since: 1995
Headquarters size: 10 employees
Franchise department: 10 employees

U.S. franchises: 80
Canadian franchises: 0
Other foreign franchises: 0
Company-owned: 2
Units concentrated in CA, CO, FL, IL,
　OH, PA, TX, WI

Seeking: All U.S.
Seeking in Canada? No
Exclusive territories? Yes
Homebased option? No
Kiosk option? Yes
Employees needed to run franchise: 1-2
Absentee ownership? Yes

COSTS
Total cost: $125K-499K
　Kiosk cost: $75K-150K
Franchise fee: to $25K
Royalty fee: $795/mo.
Term of agreement: 5 years renewable
　for $500
Franchisees required to buy multiple
　units? No

FINANCING
In-house: None
3rd-party: Equipment, franchise fee,
　inventory, start-up costs

QUALIFICATIONS
Net worth: $150K
Cash liquidity: $35K
Experience:
　General business experience
　Marketing skills

TRAINING
At headquarters: 1 week
At franchisee's location: 1 week
At off-site locations: As needed

BUSINESS SUPPORT
Newsletter
Meetings
Toll-free phone line
Grand opening
Internet
Lease negotiations
Security/safety procedures
Field operations/evaluations
Purchasing cooperatives

MARKETING SUPPORT
Co-op advertising
Ad slicks
National media campaign
Regional marketing
Radio & TV ads

IMAGE SUN TANNING CENTERS

Ranked #422 in Entrepreneur Magazine's 2004 Franchise 500　　　*Financial rating: $$$*

5514 Metro Pkwy.
Sterling Heights, MI 48310
Ph: (800)837-1388
Fax: (586)303-0050
www.beachbumstanning.com
Indoor tanning center
Began: 1994, Franchising since: 2000
Headquarters size: 6 employees
Franchise department: 5 employees

U.S. franchises: 12
Canadian franchises: 0
Other foreign franchises: 0
Company-owned: 4
Units concentrated in MI, NJ, OH, TX

Seeking: All U.S.
Seeking in Canada? Yes
Exclusive territories? Yes
Homebased option? No
Kiosk option? No
Employees needed to run franchise: 5
Absentee ownership? Yes

COSTS
Total cost: $110K-287K
Franchise fee: $25K
Royalty fee: 5.5%
Term of agreement: 10 years renewable
　for 20% of franchise fee
Franchisees required to buy multiple
　units? No

FINANCING
In-house: None
3rd-party: Equipment, franchise fee,
　inventory, start-up costs

QUALIFICATIONS
Net worth: $100K
Cash liquidity: $40K
Experience:
　General business experience

TRAINING
At headquarters: 1 week+
At franchisee's location: 1 week
Phone support

BUSINESS SUPPORT
Toll-free phone line
Grand opening
Lease negotiations
Field operations/evaluations
Purchasing cooperatives

MARKETING SUPPORT
Co-op advertising
Ad slicks
Regional marketing

PALM BEACH TAN

Financial rating: $

2387 Midway Rd.
Carrollton, TX 75006
Ph: (972)931-6595, Fax: (972)931-6594
www.palmbeachtan.com
Indoor tanning store
Began: 1990, Franchising since: 1998
Headquarters size: 35 employees
Franchise department: 3 employees

U.S. franchises: 11
Canadian franchises: 0
Other foreign franchises: 0
Company-owned: 30
Units concentrated in GA, IL, MD,
    NC, NE, TN, TX, VA

Seeking: All U.S.
Focusing on: AZ, FL, KS, MO, OK
Seeking in Canada? No
Exclusive territories? Yes
Homebased option? No
Kiosk option? No
Employees needed to run franchise:
    10-15
Absentee ownership? Yes

COSTS
Total cost: $345K-612K
Franchise fee: $25K
Royalty fee: 2-6%
Term of agreement: 10 years renewable
Franchisees required to buy multiple
    units? Yes

FINANCING
No financing available

QUALIFICATIONS
Net worth: $1M+
Cash liquidity: $500K
Experience:
    General business experience
    Marketing skills
    Multi-unit retail developer

TRAINING
At headquarters: 4 weeks

BUSINESS SUPPORT
Newsletter
Meetings
Grand opening
Internet
Field operations/evaluations

MARKETING SUPPORT
Ad slicks

PLANET BEACH FRANCHISING CORP.

Ranked #235 in Entrepreneur Magazine's 2004 Franchise 500

Financial rating: $

5161 Taravella Rd.
Marrero, LA 70072
Ph: (888)290-8266/(504)361-5550
Fax: (504)361-5540
www.planetbeach.com
Tanning salon
Began: 1995, Franchising since: 1996
Headquarters size: 40 employees
Franchise department: 15 employees

U.S. franchises: 152
Canadian franchises: 19
Other foreign franchises: 1
Company-owned: 1
Units concentrated in all U.S.

Seeking: All U.S.
Seeking in Canada? No
Exclusive territories? Yes
Homebased option? No
Kiosk option? No
Employees needed to run franchise: 4
Absentee ownership? Yes

COSTS
Total cost: $179.3K-298.6K
Franchise fee: $30K
Royalty fee: 6%
Term of agreement: 10 years renewable
    at no charge
Franchisees required to buy multiple
    units? No

FINANCING
In-house: None
3rd-party: Equipment, franchise fee,
    inventory, start-up costs

QUALIFICATIONS
Net worth: $150K
Cash liquidity: $40K
Experience:
    General business experience
    Marketing skills

TRAINING
At headquarters: 3 days
At franchisee's location: 2 days
During opening
Ongoing online training

BUSINESS SUPPORT
Newsletter
Meetings
Toll-free phone line
Grand opening
Internet
Lease negotiations
Security/safety procedures
Field operations/evaluations
Purchasing cooperatives

MARKETING SUPPORT
Co-op advertising
Ad slicks
National media campaign
Regional marketing
Local ad program

SPRAY TAN OF AMERICA

Financial rating: $$

33505-B Pacific Hwy. S.
Federal Way, WA 98003
Ph: (888)777-2982/(253)835-9594
Fax: (253)835-9595
www.spraytanofamerica.com
Airbrush tanning salon, skin-care
   products
Began: 2002, Franchising since: 2002
Headquarters size: 5 employees
Franchise department: 1 employee

U.S. franchises: 8
Canadian franchises: 0
Other foreign franchises: 0
Company-owned: 2
Units concentrated in all U.S.

Seeking: All U.S.
Seeking in Canada? Yes
Exclusive territories? Yes
Homebased option? No
Kiosk option? No
Employees needed to run franchise: 2
Absentee ownership? Yes

COSTS
Total cost: $31K-52.3K
Franchise fee: $20K
Royalty fee: 8%
Term of agreement: 5 years renewable
   for $2.5K
Franchisees required to buy multiple
   units? No

FINANCING
No financing available

QUALIFICATIONS
Net worth: $60K
Cash liquidity: $30K

TRAINING
At headquarters: 4 days
At franchisee's location: 1 week

BUSINESS SUPPORT
Meetings
Toll-free phone line
Grand opening
Internet
Lease negotiations
Field operations/evaluations

MARKETING SUPPORT
Co-op advertising
Ad slicks
Regional marketing

SUNCHAIN TANNING CENTERS

Current financial data not available

8102 E. McDowell, #2C
Scottsdale, AZ 85257
Ph: (480)421-9630
Fax: (480)421-1505
www.sunchain.com
Tanning salon & products
Began: 1994, Franchising since: 1995
Headquarters size: 3 employees
Franchise department: 3 employees

U.S. franchises: 7
Canadian franchises: 0
Other foreign franchises: 0
Company-owned: 3
Units concentrated in AZ

Seeking: West
Focusing on: NV
Seeking in Canada? No
Exclusive territories? No
Homebased option? No
Kiosk option? No
Employees needed to run franchise: 4
Absentee ownership? Yes

COSTS
Total cost: $98K-233K
Franchise fee: $12.5K
Royalty fee: 4%
Term of agreement: 10 years renewable
   for $250
Franchisees required to buy multiple
   units? No

FINANCING
In-house: None
3rd-party: Equipment

QUALIFICATIONS
Cash liquidity: $50K
Experience:
   General business experience

TRAINING
At headquarters: 1 week
At franchisee's location: 5 days
Manager training: 4 weeks

BUSINESS SUPPORT
Newsletter
Meetings
Toll-free phone line
Grand opening
Internet
Field operations/evaluations
Purchasing cooperatives

MARKETING SUPPORT
Co-op advertising
Ad slicks
Regional marketing
Multi-club membership

PERSONAL CARE *Miscellaneous*

INAARA MEDSPAS

Current financial data not available

9025 Wilshire Blvd., #400
Beverly Hills, CA 90211
Ph: (310)724-8100
Fax: (310)724-8114
www.inaaramedspas.com
Non-invasive cosmetic procedures
    including botox, microdermabra-
    sion & laser hair removal
Began: 2002, Franchising since: 2003
Headquarters size: 14 employees
Franchise department: 10 employees

U.S. franchises: 0
Canadian franchises: 0
Other foreign franchises: 0
Company-owned: 1

Seeking: All U.S.
Seeking in Canada? Yes
Exclusive territories? Yes
Homebased option? No
Kiosk option? No
Employees needed to run franchise: 4
Absentee ownership? Yes

COSTS
Total cost: $157.6K-310K
Franchise fee: $75K
Royalty fee: 5%
Term of agreement: 10 years renewable
    at no charge
Franchisees required to buy multiple
    units? No

FINANCING
No financing available

QUALIFICATIONS
Net worth: $250K
Cash liquidity: $500K
Experience:
    General business experience
    Marketing skills

TRAINING
At headquarters: 1 day
At franchisee's location: 3 days

BUSINESS SUPPORT
Newsletter
Toll-free phone line
Internet
Security/safety procedures
Field operations/evaluations

MARKETING SUPPORT
Ad slicks
National media campaign
Regional marketing

JOHN CASABLANCAS MODELING & CAREER CENTERS

Current financial data not available

111 E. 22nd St., 4th Fl.
New York, NY 10010
Ph: (212)420-0655
Fax: (212)473-2725
www.jc-centers.com
Professional modeling, personal image
    development, acting instruction
Began: 1979, Franchising since: 1979
Headquarters size: 7 employees
Franchise department: 2 employees

U.S. franchises: 42
Canadian franchises: 1
Other foreign franchises: 7
Company-owned: 0
Units concentrated in all U.S.

Seeking: All U.S.
Seeking in Canada? Yes
Exclusive territories? Yes
Homebased option? No
Kiosk option? No
Employees needed to run franchise: 4-7
Absentee ownership? No

COSTS
Total cost: $64.2K-137.4K
Franchise fee: $20K-40K
Royalty fee: 7%
Term of agreement: 10 years renewable
    at no charge
Franchisees required to buy multiple
    units? No

FINANCING
No financing available

QUALIFICATIONS
Net worth: $150K-250K
Cash liquidity: $150K-200K
Experience:
    Industry experience
    General business experience
    Marketing skills
    Sales experience

TRAINING
At headquarters: 7 days
At franchisee's location: 7 days
Ongoing field visits

BUSINESS SUPPORT
Newsletter
Meetings
Grand opening
Lease negotiations
Field operations/evaluations

MARKETING SUPPORT
Co-op advertising
Ad slicks
National media campaign
Regional marketing

POSITIVE CHANGES HYPNOSIS CENTERS

Financial rating: $$$

240 Denn Ln.
Virginia Beach, VA 23462
Ph: (800)880-0436, Fax: (757)499-1029
www.positivechanges.com
Self-improvement products & services
Began: 1987, Franchising since: 2001
Headquarters size: 12 employees
Franchise department: 12 employees

U.S. franchises: 51
Canadian franchises: 0
Other foreign franchises: 0
Company-owned: 0
Units concentrated in all U.S.

Seeking: All U.S.
Seeking in Canada? No
Exclusive territories? Yes
Homebased option? No
Kiosk option? No
Employees needed to run franchise: 8
Absentee ownership? Yes

COSTS
Total cost: $92.8K-329.4K
Franchise fee: $29.5K
Royalty fee: 5%
Term of agreement: 10 years renewable
for 20% of current franchise fee
Franchisees required to buy multiple
units? No

FINANCING
No financing available

QUALIFICATIONS
Net worth: $250K
Cash liquidity: $75K
Experience:
General business experience

TRAINING
At headquarters: 1 week
At franchisee's location: 3 days

BUSINESS SUPPORT
Newsletter
Meetings
Toll-free phone line
Grand opening
Internet
Field operations/evaluations
Purchasing cooperatives

MARKETING SUPPORT
Ad slicks

PROTOCOL LLC

Current financial data not available

1370 Mendota Heights Rd.
Mendota Heights, MN 55120
Ph: (800)227-5336/(651)454-0518 ext.
462
Fax: (651)454-9542
www.protocolvending.com
Personal-care product vending
machines
Began: 1987, Franchising since: 1996
Headquarters size: 60 employees
Franchise department: 10 employees

U.S. franchises: 43
Canadian franchises: 0
Other foreign franchises: 0
Company-owned: 15
Units concentrated in all U.S.

Seeking: All U.S.
Seeking in Canada? Yes
Exclusive territories? Yes
Homebased option? Yes
Kiosk option? No
Employees needed to run franchise: 0-3
Absentee ownership? Yes

COSTS
Total cost: $8.2K-22K
Franchise fee: $500
Royalty fee: 0
Term of agreement: 2 years renewable
at no charge
Franchisees required to buy multiple
units? No

FINANCING
Equipment investment following ini-
tial investment

QUALIFICATIONS
Net worth: $5K
Cash liquidity: $5K
Experience:
General business experience
Marketing skills

TRAINING
At headquarters: 1 day
At franchisee's location: Periodically
At annual convention: 3 days

BUSINESS SUPPORT
Newsletter
Meetings
Toll-free phone line
Internet
Field operations/evaluations
Purchasing cooperatives

MARKETING SUPPORT
Co-op advertising
Ad slicks
National media campaign
Trade shows

PERSONAL CARE — *Other Franchises*

ARISTOCARE
1200 N. El Dorado Pl., #130
Tucson, AZ 85715
Ph: (866)731-2273/(520)577-4825
www.aristocare.net
Private-duty homecare/in-home
  senior care

BERNARD'S SALON & DAY SPA
1018 Laurel Oak Rd., #9
Voorhees, NJ 08043
Ph: (856)354-0034
www.bernardssalon.com
Salon & spa services

FACES COSMETICS INC.
30 Macintosh Blvd., #6
Vaughan, ON Canada L4K 4P1
Ph: (877)773-2237/(905)760-0110
www.faces-cosmetics.com
Cosmetics

HCX
4850 W. Prospect Rd.
Ft. Lauderdale, FL 33309
Ph: (954)315-4900
www.haircolorxpress.com
Salon specializing in hair color & cosmetics

HOLLYWOOD TANS
*Ranked #91 in Entrepreneur Magazine's
  2004 Franchise 500*
CSC Plaza, #400, 1123 Rt. 73 South
Mount Laurel, NJ 08054
Ph: (856)914-9090
www.hollywoodtan.com
Tanning services & lotions

JOHN ROBERT POWERS INT'L.
9220 Sunset Blvd., #100
West Hollywood, CA 90069
Ph: (310)858-3300
www.johnrobertpowers.net
Modeling & personal-development
  schools

THE PALMS TANNING RESORT
8577 E. Arapahoe Rd., #A
Greenwood Village, CO 80112
Ph: (866)725-6748
www.thepalmstanningresort.com
Tanning salon

THE YELLOW BALLOON
12130 Ventura Blvd.
Studio City, CA 91604
Ph: (514)486-4149
www.theyellowballoon.com
Children's hair salon

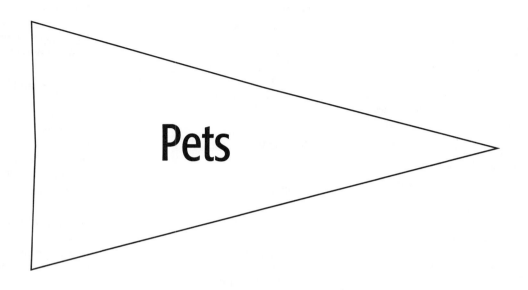

PETS

ANIMAL ADVENTURE

Current financial data not available

5453 S. 76th St.
Greendale, WI 53129
Ph: (414)423-7350
Fax: (414)423-7351
www.petstorefranchise.com
Retail pet store
Began: 1999, Franchising since: 2000
Headquarters size: 12 employees
Franchise department: 4 employees

U.S. franchises: 4
Canadian franchises: 0
Other foreign franchises: 0
Company-owned: 2
Units concentrated in WI

Focusing on: IL, MI, MN, WI
Seeking in Canada? No
Exclusive territories? Yes
Homebased option? No
Kiosk option? No
Employees needed to run franchise: 12
Absentee ownership? No

COSTS
Total cost: $199K-345K
Franchise fee: $25K
Royalty fee: 4%
Term of agreement: 10 years renewable
at no charge
Franchisees required to buy multiple
units? No

FINANCING
No financing available

QUALIFICATIONS
Net worth: $80K

TRAINING
At headquarters: 15 days
At franchisee's location: 5 days

BUSINESS SUPPORT
Newsletter
Meetings
Toll-free phone line
Grand opening
Internet
Lease negotiations
Security/safety procedures
Field operations/evaluations

MARKETING SUPPORT
Co-op advertising
Ad slicks
Regional marketing
Consultation

AUSSIE PET MOBILE
Ranked #72 in Entrepreneur Magazine's 2004 Franchise 500   *Financial rating: $$$$*

34189 Pacific Coast Hwy., #203
Dana Point, CA 92629
Ph: (949)234-0680
Fax: (949)234-0688
www.aussiepetmobile.com
Mobile pet grooming
Began: 1996, Franchising since: 1996
Headquarters size: 12 employees
Franchise department: 12 employees

U.S. franchises: 221
Canadian franchises: 0
Other foreign franchises: 49
Company-owned: 0
Units concentrated in all U.S.

Seeking: All U.S.
Seeking in Canada? No
Exclusive territories? Yes
Homebased option? Yes
Kiosk option? No
Employees needed to run franchise: 1-2
Absentee ownership? Yes

COSTS
Total cost: $60K-352.5K
Franchise fee: $32.5K-112.5K
Royalty fee: 8%
Term of agreement: 10 years renewable
for 33% of original franchise fee
Franchisees required to buy multiple
units? No

FINANCING
In-house: None
3rd-party: Equipment, franchise fee,
inventory, start-up costs

QUALIFICATIONS
Net worth: $150K
Cash liquidity: $55K
Experience:
General business experience
Marketing skills
Outgoing personality

TRAINING
At headquarters: 5-7 days
Additional training for multi-unit
franchisees & groomers: 2-5 days

BUSINESS SUPPORT
Newsletter
Meetings
Grand opening
Internet
Security/safety procedures
Field operations/evaluations
Purchasing cooperatives

MARKETING SUPPORT
Ad slicks
National media campaign
Regional marketing

BARK BUSTERS
Ranked #468 in Entrepreneur Magazine's 2004 Franchise 500   *Financial rating: 0*

5901 S. Vine St.
Greenwood Village, CO 80121
Ph: (877)280-7100
www.barkbusters.com
In-home dog training
Began: 1989, Franchising since: 1994
Headquarters size: 5 employees
Franchise department: 5 employees

U.S. franchises: 31
Canadian franchises: 0
Other foreign franchises: 65
Company-owned: 0
Units concentrated in CO, FL, GA, KS,
NJ, TX, VA

Seeking: All U.S.
Seeking in Canada? Yes
Exclusive territories? Yes
Homebased option? Yes
Kiosk option? No
Employees needed to run franchise: 0
Absentee ownership? No

COSTS
Total cost: $45K-70K
Franchise fee: $22.5K
Royalty fee: 8%
Term of agreement: 5 years renewable
for $1.5K
Franchisees required to buy multiple
units? No

FINANCING
In-house: None
3rd-party: Accounts receivable, equipment, franchise fee, inventory, payroll, start-up costs

QUALIFICATIONS
Net worth: $100K
Cash liquidity: $5K-39K
Experience:
General business experience
Marketing skills
Passion for dogs

TRAINING
At headquarters: 120 hours+

BUSINESS SUPPORT
Newsletter
Meetings
Toll-free phone line
Internet
Security/safety procedures
Field operations/evaluations

MARKETING SUPPORT
Co-op advertising
Ad slicks
National media campaign
PR support

CAMP BOW WOW

Financial rating: $$

17011 Lincoln Ave., #153
Parker, CO 80134
Ph: (866)821-0409
Fax: (303)840-9705
www.campbowwow.tv
Dog day care & boarding services
Began: 2000, Franchising since: 2003
Headquarters size: 15 employees
Franchise department: 5 employees

U.S. franchises: 2
Canadian franchises: 0
Other foreign franchises: 0
Company-owned: 2
Units concentrated in CO, MI

Seeking: All U.S.
Seeking in Canada? Yes
Exclusive territories? Yes
Homebased option? No
Kiosk option? No
Employees needed to run franchise:
    8-12
Absentee ownership? Info not provided

COSTS
Total cost: $108.5K-315.5K
Franchise fee: $25K
Royalty fee: 5%
Term of agreement: Info not provided
Franchisees required to buy multiple
    units? Info not provided

FINANCING
No financing available

QUALIFICATIONS
Net worth: $250K
Cash liquidity: $50K
Experience:
    General business experience

TRAINING
At headquarters: 1 week
At franchisee's location: 1 week
Home study: 1 week

BUSINESS SUPPORT
Newsletter
Meetings
Toll-free phone line
Grand opening
Internet
Security/safety procedures
Field operations/evaluations
Purchasing cooperatives

MARKETING SUPPORT
Co-op advertising
Ad slicks
National media campaign
Regional marketing

FETCH! PET CARE INC.

Current financial data not available

701 Grizzly Peak Blvd.
Berkeley, CA 94708
Ph: (510)527-6420
Fax: (510)525-4054
www.fetchpetcare.com
Pet-sitting & dog walking services
Began: 2002, Franchising since: 2003
Headquarters size: 2 employees
Franchise department: 2 employees

U.S. franchises: 0
Canadian franchises: 0
Other foreign franchises: 0
Company-owned: 1
Units concentrated in CA

Seeking: All U.S.
Seeking in Canada? No
Exclusive territories? Yes
Homebased option? Yes
Kiosk option? No
Employees needed to run franchise: 1
Absentee ownership? Yes

COSTS
Total cost: $13K-30K
Franchise fee: $3K-8K
Royalty fee: 5%
Term of agreement: 10 years renewable
    at no charge
Franchisees required to buy multiple
    units? No

FINANCING
No financing available

QUALIFICATIONS
Net worth: $25K
Cash liquidity: $15K
Experience:
    General business experience

TRAINING
At headquarters: 2 days (optional)
Training manual & video: 1 week or as
    needed

BUSINESS SUPPORT
Newsletter
Toll-free phone line
Internet
Security/safety procedures
Purchasing cooperatives

MARKETING SUPPORT
Ad slicks
National media campaign
Regional marketing
Local marketing materials

HAWKEYE'S HOME SITTERS

Current financial data not available

Box 141
Edmonton, AB Canada T5J 2G9
Ph: (888)247-2787/(780)473-4825
Fax: (780)988-8948
www.homesitter.com
In-home pet care & house-sitting services
Began: 1987, Franchising since: 1997
Headquarters size: 2 employees
Franchise department: 2 employees

U.S. franchises: 0
Canadian franchises: 8
Other foreign franchises: 0
Company-owned: 0

Not available in the U.S.
Seeking in Canada? Yes
Exclusive territories? Yes
Homebased option? Yes
Kiosk option? No
Employees needed to run franchise: 1-2
Absentee ownership? No

COSTS
Total cost: $5K-10K
Franchise fee: $4K-8K
Royalty fee: 4%
Term of agreement: 5 years renewable
for $125
Franchisees required to buy multiple
units? No

FINANCING
No financing available

QUALIFICATIONS
Cash liquidity: $1K

TRAINING
Training manual

BUSINESS SUPPORT
Newsletter
Toll-free phone line
Grand opening
Internet
Security/safety procedures
Purchasing cooperatives

MARKETING SUPPORT
Co-op advertising
National media campaign

LAUND-UR-MUTT

Current financial data not available

8854 S. Edgewood St.
Littleton, CO 80130
Ph: (303)470-1540
Fax: (303)470-8669
www.laundurmutt.com
Self-service dog wash & pet center
Began: 1992, Franchising since: 1994
Headquarters size: 1 employee
Franchise department: 1 employee

U.S. franchises: 5
Canadian franchises: 0
Other foreign franchises: 0
Company-owned: 1
Units concentrated in CO

Seeking: All U.S.
Seeking in Canada? No
Exclusive territories? Yes
Homebased option? No
Kiosk option? No
Employees needed to run franchise: 3-4
Absentee ownership? Yes

COSTS
Total cost: $150K
Franchise fee: $25K
Royalty fee: 5%/mo.
Term of agreement: 10 years renewable
for $12.5K
Franchisees required to buy multiple
units? No

FINANCING
No financing available

QUALIFICATIONS
Net worth: $150K
Cash liquidity: $50K
Experience:
    Love of pets
    Communication skills

TRAINING
At headquarters: 1 week
At franchisee's location: 1 week
Ongoing phone & E-mail training

BUSINESS SUPPORT
Newsletter
Grand opening
Internet
Lease negotiations
Security/safety procedures
Field operations/evaluations

MARKETING SUPPORT
Ad slicks

THE PET PANTRY

Current financial data not available

3719 N. Carson St.
Carson City, NV 89706
Ph: (800)381-7387
Fax: (775)841-9732
www.thepetpantry.com
Pet food
Began: 1994, Franchising since: 1995
Headquarters size: 12 employees
Franchise department: 7 employees

U.S. franchises: 90
Canadian franchises: 0
Other foreign franchises: 2
Company-owned: 0
Units concentrated in all U.S.

Seeking: All U.S.
Seeking in Canada? Yes
Exclusive territories? Yes
Homebased option? Yes
Kiosk option? No
Employees needed to run franchise: 1-2
Absentee ownership? Yes

COSTS
Total cost: $65K-98K
Franchise fee: $8K+
Royalty fee: 0
Term of agreement: 7 years renewable
    for $3K
Franchisees required to buy multiple
    units? Outside the U.S. only

FINANCING
No financing available

QUALIFICATIONS
Net worth: $100K
Cash liquidity: $63K-98K
Experience:
    General business experience
    Marketing skills

TRAINING
At headquarters: 4-1/2 days
Via web & regional seminars

BUSINESS SUPPORT
Newsletter
Meetings
Toll-free phone line
Internet

MARKETING SUPPORT
Custom ads
Media buys
Web site

PET SUPPLIES "PLUS"
Ranked #286 in Entrepreneur Magazine's 2004 Franchise 500

Financial rating: $$$$

22670 Haggerty Rd., #200
Farmington Hills, MI 48335
Ph: (866)477-7748/(248)374-1900
Fax: (248)374-7900
www.petsuppliesplus.com
Pet supplies
Began: 1987, Franchising since: 1990
Headquarters size: 24 employees
Franchise department: 2 employees

U.S. franchises: 181
Canadian franchises: 0
Other foreign franchises: 0
Company-owned: 1
Units concentrated in Eastern U.S.

Seeking: Midwest, Northeast, South,
    Southeast
Focusing on: Eastern U.S.
Seeking in Canada? No
Exclusive territories? Yes
Homebased option? No
Kiosk option? No
Employees needed to run franchise:
    18-20
Absentee ownership? Yes

COSTS
Total cost: $395.5K-611K
Franchise fee: $25K
Royalty fee: Varies
Term of agreement: 5 years renewable
    at no charge
Franchisees required to buy multiple
    units? No

FINANCING
No financing available

QUALIFICATIONS
Net worth: $400K
Cash liquidity: $150K

TRAINING
At headquarters: 4 weeks

BUSINESS SUPPORT
Meetings
Grand opening
Internet
Lease negotiations
Field operations/evaluations
Purchasing cooperatives

MARKETING SUPPORT
Co-op advertising
Ad slicks

PETS ARE INN

Financial rating: $$$

5100 Edina Industrial Blvd., #206
Minneapolis, MN 55439
Ph: (866)343-0086/(952)944-8298
Fax: (952)746-7648
www.petsareinn.com
Pet lodging service in private homes
Began: 1982, Franchising since: 1986
Headquarters size: 7 employees
Franchise department: 5 employees

U.S. franchises: 14
Canadian franchises: 0
Other foreign franchises: 0
Company-owned: 0
Units concentrated in HI, MN, MO,
   PA, TX, VA, WA, WI

Seeking: All U.S.
Seeking in Canada? No
Exclusive territories? Yes
Homebased option? Yes
Kiosk option? No
Employees needed to run franchise: 4
Absentee ownership? No

COSTS
Total cost: $20K-75K
Franchise fee: $12.5K-32.5K
Royalty fee: 5-10%
Term of agreement: 10 years renewable
   for $1K
Franchisees required to buy multiple
   units? No

FINANCING
No financing available

QUALIFICATIONS
Net worth: $100K
Cash liquidity: $25K
Experience:
   General business experience
   Marketing skills
   Must love pets

TRAINING
At headquarters: 5 days
At franchisee's location: 1 day
Weekly, monthly & quarterly "check-
   ups" at owner's location

BUSINESS SUPPORT
Newsletter
Meetings
Toll-free phone line
Grand opening
Internet
Security/safety procedures
Field operations/evaluations
Purchasing cooperatives

MARKETING SUPPORT
Co-op advertising
Ad slicks
PR support

WILD BIRD CENTERS OF AMERICA INC.

Ranked #356 in Entrepreneur Magazine's 2004 Franchise 500

Financial rating: $$$

7370 MacArthur Blvd.
Glen Echo, MD 20812
Ph: (800)945-3247/(301)229-9585
Fax: (301)320-6154
www.wildbirdcenter.com
Bird watching & feeding supplies
Began: 1985, Franchising since: 1990
Headquarters size: 16 employees
Franchise department: 2 employees

U.S. franchises: 88
Canadian franchises: 2
Other foreign franchises: 0
Company-owned: 2
Units concentrated in CA, CO,
   MD, VA

Seeking: All U.S.
Seeking in Canada? Yes
Exclusive territories? Yes
Homebased option? No
Kiosk option? No
Employees needed to run franchise: 3-5
Absentee ownership? Yes

COSTS
Total cost: $102.1K-143.2K
Franchise fee: $20K
Royalty fee: 3-4.5%
Term of agreement: 5 years renewable
   at no charge
Franchisees required to buy multiple
   units? No

FINANCING
No financing available

QUALIFICATIONS
Net worth: $175K
Cash liquidity: $33K-50K
Experience:
   Birding hobby knowledge

TRAINING
At headquarters: 10 days
At franchisee's location: 1-2 days
Annual convention

BUSINESS SUPPORT
Newsletter
Meetings
Toll-free phone line
Grand opening
Internet
Lease negotiations
Security/safety procedures
Field operations/evaluations
Purchasing cooperatives

MARKETING SUPPORT
Co-op advertising
Ad slicks
National media campaign
Regional marketing
Local advertising support

WILD BIRDS UNLIMITED
Ranked #153 in Entrepreneur Magazine's 2004 Franchise 500

Financial rating: $$$$

11711 N. College Ave., #146
Carmel, IN 46032
Ph: (888)730-7108
Fax: (317)571-7110
www.wbu.com
Bird-feeding supplies & nature gift
    items
Began: 1981, Franchising since: 1983
Headquarters size: 45 employees
Franchise department: 2 employees

U.S. franchises: 271
Canadian franchises: 10
Other foreign franchises: 0
Company-owned: 0
Units concentrated in all U.S.

Seeking: All U.S.
Seeking in Canada? Yes
Exclusive territories? Yes
Homebased option? No
Kiosk option? No
Employees needed to run franchise: 4
Absentee ownership? No

COSTS
Total cost: $78K-132K
Franchise fee: $18K
Royalty fee: 4%
Term of agreement: 10 years renewable
    at no charge
Franchisees required to buy multiple
    units? No

FINANCING
In-house: None
3rd-party: Accounts receivable, equip-
    ment, inventory, start-up costs

QUALIFICATIONS
Net worth: $150K
Cash liquidity: $30K
Experience:
    Must love birds & nature
    People skills

TRAINING
At headquarters: 6 days
At franchisee's location: 2 days
Annual meeting: 5 days

BUSINESS SUPPORT
Newsletter
Meetings
Toll-free phone line
Grand opening
Internet
Security/safety procedures
Field operations/evaluations
Purchasing cooperatives

MARKETING SUPPORT
Co-op advertising
Ad slicks
National media campaign

PETS — Other Franchises

JUST DOGS! BARKERY
5101 Cyrus Cir.
Birmingham, AL 35242
Ph: (205)332-0367
www.justdogsbarkery.com
Gourmet dog treats & related
    merchandise

PET HABITAT
6921 Heather St.
Vancouver, BC Canada V6P 3P5
Ph: (604)266-2721
www.pethabitat.com
Pet shop

PETLAND
250 Riverside St.
Chillicothe, OH 45601
Ph: (800)221-5935
www.petland.com
Full-service pet store

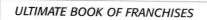

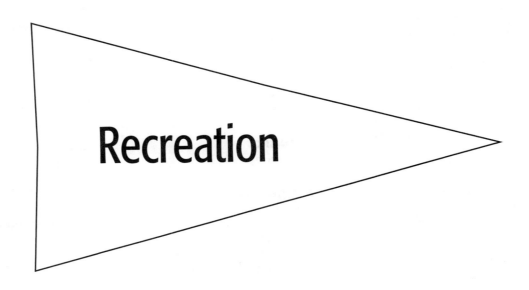

RECREATION   *Athletic Equipment*

THE ATHLETE'S FOOT

Current financial data not available

1950 Vaughn Rd.
Kennesaw, GA 30144
Ph: (800)524-6444/(770)514-4523
Fax: (770)514-4903
www.theathletesfoot.com
Athletic footwear & related sports
    accessories
Began: 1972, Franchising since: 1973
Headquarters size: 150 employees
Franchise department: 50 employees

U.S. franchises: 190
Canadian franchises: 2
Other foreign franchises: 350
Company-owned: 170
Units concentrated in all U.S.

Seeking: All U.S.
Seeking in Canada? Yes
Exclusive territories? Yes
Homebased option? No
Kiosk option? No
Employees needed to run franchise:
    6-10
Absentee ownership? Yes

COSTS
Total cost: $201.6K-640.3K
Franchise fee: $35K
Royalty fee: 5%
Term of agreement: 10 years renewable
    at no charge
Franchisees required to buy multiple
    units? Outside the U.S. only

FINANCING
In-house: None
3rd-party: Accounts receivable, equip-
    ment, franchise fee, inventory, pay-
    roll, start-up costs

QUALIFICATIONS
Net worth: $300K
Cash liquidity: $75K-100K
Experience:
    General business experience

TRAINING
At headquarters: 5 days
At franchisee's location: 5 days at
    opening
Regional meetings: 3 times per year

BUSINESS SUPPORT
Newsletter
Meetings
Toll-free phone line
Grand opening
Internet
Security/safety procedures
Field operations/evaluations

MARKETING SUPPORT
Co-op advertising
Ad slicks
National media campaign
Regional marketing

PLAY IT AGAIN SPORTS

Ranked #223 in Entrepreneur Magazine's 2004 Franchise 500

Financial rating: $$$$

4200 Dahlberg Dr., #100
Minneapolis, MN 55422-4837
Ph: (800)592-8047/(763)520-8480
Fax: (763)520-8501
www.playitagainsports.com
New & used sporting goods/equipment
Began: 1983, Franchising since: 1988
Headquarters size: 100 employees
Franchise department: 5 employees

U.S. franchises: 402
Canadian franchises: 62
Other foreign franchises: 0
Company-owned: 0
Units concentrated in all U.S. except LA, RI, WY

Seeking: All U.S.
Seeking in Canada? Yes
Exclusive territories? Yes
Homebased option? No
Kiosk option? No
Employees needed to run franchise: 7
Absentee ownership? No

COSTS
Total cost: $212.3K-318.9K
Franchise fee: $20K
Royalty fee: 5%
Term of agreement: 10 years renewable for $5K
Franchisees required to buy multiple units? No

FINANCING
No financing available

QUALIFICATIONS
Net worth: $200K
Cash liquidity: $60K-90K
Experience:
    General business experience
    Marketing skills

TRAINING
At headquarters: 2 weeks

BUSINESS SUPPORT
Newsletter
Meetings
Toll-free phone line
Grand opening
Internet
Lease negotiations
Security/safety procedures
Field operations/evaluations
Purchasing cooperatives

MARKETING SUPPORT
Co-op advertising
Ad slicks

PRO IMAGE FRANCHISE LC

Ranked #395 in Entrepreneur Magazine's 2004 Franchise 500

Financial rating: $$$$

233 N. 1250 W., #200
Centerville, UT 84014
Ph: (801)296-9999
Fax: (801)296-1319
www.getproimage.com
Licensed sports apparel & accessories
Began: 1985, Franchising since: 1986
Headquarters size: 9 employees
Franchise department: 3 employees

U.S. franchises: 77
Canadian franchises: 0
Other foreign franchises: 0
Company-owned: 0
Units concentrated in all U.S.

Seeking: All U.S.
Seeking in Canada? Yes
Exclusive territories? No
Homebased option? No
Kiosk option? Yes
Employees needed to run franchise: 2
Absentee ownership? Yes

COSTS
Total cost: $120K-250K
    Kiosk cost: $65K-100K
Franchise fee: $19.5K
Royalty fee: 4%
Term of agreement: 10 years renewable at no charge
Franchisees required to buy multiple units? No

FINANCING
In-house: None
3rd-party: Accounts receivable, equipment, franchise fee, inventory, payroll, start-up costs

QUALIFICATIONS
Net worth: $250K
Cash liquidity: $75K+
Experience:
    Industry experience
    General business experience

TRAINING
At headquarters: 3 days

BUSINESS SUPPORT
Newsletter
Meetings
Toll-free phone line
Grand opening
Internet
Security/safety procedures
Field operations/evaluations
Purchasing cooperatives

MARKETING SUPPORT
Co-op advertising
Ad slicks
POP programs

SOCCER POST

Financial rating: $

2903 Highway 138 E.
Wall, NJ 07719
Ph: (732)578-1377
Fax: (732)578-1399
www.soccerpost.com
Soccer retail store
Began: 1978, Franchising since: 1991
Headquarters size: 75 employees
Franchise department: 5 employees

U.S. franchises: 21
Canadian franchises: 0
Other foreign franchises: 0
Company-owned: 0
Units concentrated in CA, DE, GA, IL,
  MA, NJ, NY, PA, TX

Seeking: All U.S.
Seeking in Canada? No
Exclusive territories? Yes
Homebased option? No
Kiosk option? No
Employees needed to run franchise: 3-4
Absentee ownership? No

COSTS
Total cost: $183.5K-220K
Franchise fee: $29.5K
Royalty fee: 5%
Term of agreement: 10 years renewable
Franchisees required to buy multiple
  units? No

FINANCING
In-house: None
3rd-party: Equipment, franchise fee,
  inventory, start-up costs

QUALIFICATIONS
Net worth: $300K
Cash liquidity: $40K
Experience:
  General business experience

TRAINING
At headquarters: 2 weeks
At franchisee's location: 1 week

BUSINESS SUPPORT
Newsletter
Meetings
Grand opening
Internet
Lease negotiations
Security/safety procedures
Field operations/evaluations

MARKETING SUPPORT
Co-op advertising
Ad slicks
National media campaign
Regional marketing

RECREATION ▶ *Fitness*

ANYTIME FITNESS

Current financial data not available

P.O. Box 18213
West St. Paul, MN 55118
Ph: (800)704-5004
Fax: (651)554-0311
www.anytimefitness.com
Fitness centers
Began: 2002, Franchising since: 2002
Headquarters size: 3 employees
Franchise department: 2 employees

U.S. franchises: 10
Canadian franchises: 0
Other foreign franchises: 0
Company-owned: 1
Units concentrated in CO, MN

Focusing on: CA, FL, GA, PA, TX, VA
Seeking in Canada? No
Exclusive territories? Yes
Homebased option? No
Kiosk option? No
Employees needed to run franchise: 0
Absentee ownership? Yes

COSTS
Total cost: $19.5K-72.6K
Franchise fee: $1.99K
Royalty fee: $359
Term of agreement: 5 years renewable
  for $100
Franchisees required to buy multiple
  units? No

FINANCING
In-house: None
3rd-party: Equipment, franchise fee,
  start-up costs

QUALIFICATIONS
Cash liquidity: $13.5K
Experience:
  General business experience

TRAINING
At headquarters: 3 days+
At franchisee's location: 3 days+
Ongoing

BUSINESS SUPPORT
Newsletter
Toll-free phone line
Grand opening
Lease negotiations
Security/safety procedures
Purchasing cooperatives

MARKETING SUPPORT
Ad slicks

CONTOURS EXPRESS

Ranked #233 in Entrepreneur Magazine's 2004 Franchise 500

Financial rating: $$$$

156 Imperial Wy.
Nicholasville, KY 40356
Ph: (877)227-2282
Fax: (425)920-0534
www.contoursexpress.com
Women's fitness centers
Began: 1998, Franchising since: 1998
Headquarters size: 5 employees
Franchise department: 5 employees

U.S. franchises: 108
Canadian franchises: 3
Other foreign franchises: 0
Company-owned: 0
Units concentrated in all U.S.

Seeking: All U.S.
Seeking in Canada? No
Exclusive territories? Yes
Homebased option? No
Kiosk option? No
Employees needed to run franchise: 2
Absentee ownership? Yes

COSTS
Total cost: $31.2K-45.7K
Franchise fee: $10K
Royalty fee: $395/mo.
Term of agreement: 10 years renewable at no charge
Franchisees required to buy multiple units? No

FINANCING
In-house: None
3rd-party: Equipment, franchise fee, start-up costs

QUALIFICATIONS
Net worth: $50K
Cash liquidity: $15K

TRAINING
At headquarters: 4-5 days
At franchisee's location: 4-5 days

BUSINESS SUPPORT
Newsletter
Meetings
Toll-free phone line
Grand opening
Internet

MARKETING SUPPORT
Ad slicks

CURVES

Ranked #2 in Entrepreneur Magazine's 2004 Franchise 500

Financial rating: $$$$

400 Schroeder
Waco, TX 76710
Ph: (800)848-1096/(254)399-9285
Fax: (254)399-9731
www.buycurves.com
Women's fitness & weight-loss centers
Began: 1992, Franchising since: 1995
Headquarters size: 50 employees
Franchise department: 40 employees

U.S. franchises: 5,205
Canadian franchises: 498
Other foreign franchises: 130
Company-owned: 0
Units concentrated in all U.S.

Seeking: All U.S.
Seeking in Canada? Yes
Exclusive territories? Yes
Homebased option? No
Kiosk option? No
Employees needed to run franchise: 2
Absentee ownership? Yes

COSTS
Total cost: $30.6K-36.1K
Franchise fee: $24.9K
Royalty fee: $395/mo.
Term of agreement: 10 years renewable at no charge
Franchisees required to buy multiple units? No

FINANCING
In-house: Franchise fee, equipment
3rd-party: None

QUALIFICATIONS
Net worth: $60K
Cash liquidity: $30K
Experience:
    Financial stability

TRAINING
At headquarters: 1 week
At franchisee's location: 4 days
At regional meetings: 1 day
Convention: 3 days
Local events: 1 day

BUSINESS SUPPORT
Newsletter
Meetings
Toll-free phone line
Grand opening
Internet
Field operations/evaluations

MARKETING SUPPORT
Co-op advertising
Ad slicks
National media campaign
Regional marketing

CUTS FITNESS FOR MEN

Current financial data not available

109 Lefferts Ln.
Clark, NJ 07066
Ph: (732)574-0999
Fax: (732)574-1130
www.cutsfitnessformen.com
Circuit training for men
Began: 2003, Franchising since: 2003
Headquarters size: 4 employees
Franchise department: 2 employees

U.S. franchises: 1
Canadian franchises: 0
Other foreign franchises: 0
Company-owned: 1

Seeking: All U.S.
Seeking in Canada? Yes
Exclusive territories? Yes
Homebased option? No
Kiosk option? No
Employees needed to run franchise: 1-2
Absentee ownership? No

COSTS
Total cost: $47.1K-70.9K
Franchise fee: $25K
Royalty fee: $400/mo.
Term of agreement: 10 years renewable
    at no charge
Franchisees required to buy multiple
    units? No

FINANCING
No financing available

QUALIFICATIONS
Net worth: $50K
Cash liquidity: $50K
Experience:
    Industry experience
    General business experience
    Marketing skills

TRAINING
At headquarters: 2 days
At franchisee's location: As needed

BUSINESS SUPPORT
Newsletter
Meetings
Grand opening
Internet
Field operations/evaluations
Purchasing cooperatives

MARKETING SUPPORT
Co-op advertising
Regional marketing

FITNESS TOGETHER

Ranked #263 in Entrepreneur Magazine's 2004 Franchise 500

Financial rating: $$$

399 Perry St., #300
Castle Rock, CO 80104
Ph: (303)663-0880
Fax: (303)663-1617
www.fitnesstogetherfranchise.com
Personal fitness training
Began: 1984, Franchising since: 1996
Headquarters size: 6 employees
Franchise department: 6 employees

U.S. franchises: 73
Canadian franchises: 0
Other foreign franchises: 0
Company-owned: 1
Units concentrated in all U.S.

Seeking: All U.S.
Seeking in Canada? Yes
Exclusive territories? Yes
Homebased option? No
Kiosk option? No
Employees needed to run franchise: 3-5
Absentee ownership? Yes

COSTS
Total cost: $130K-175K
Franchise fee: $29K
Royalty fee: 5%
Term of agreement: 10 years renewable
    for 25% of current franchise fee
Franchisees required to buy multiple
    units? No

FINANCING
No financing available

QUALIFICATIONS
Net worth: $250K
Cash liquidity: $100K
Experience:
    Industry experience

TRAINING
At headquarters: 4-5 days
At existing franchise: 1-2 days

BUSINESS SUPPORT
Newsletter
Meetings
Toll-free phone line
Grand opening
Internet
Lease negotiations
Security/safety procedures
Field operations/evaluations
Purchasing cooperatives

MARKETING SUPPORT
Co-op advertising
Ad slicks
National media campaign

GOLD'S GYM FRANCHISING INC.

Ranked #238 in Entrepreneur Magazine's 2004 Franchise 500   *Financial rating: $$*

358 Hampton Dr.
Venice, CA 90291
Ph: (310)392-3005, Fax: (310)392-4680
www.goldsgym.com
Gym & fitness centers
Began: 1979, Franchising since: 1987
Headquarters size: Info not provided
Franchise department: Info not provided

U.S. franchises: 504
Canadian franchises: 14
Other foreign franchises: 49
Company-owned: 30
Units concentrated in CA, FL, GA, NY, VA

Seeking: All U.S.
Seeking in Canada? Yes
Exclusive territories? Yes
Homebased option? No
Kiosk option? No
Employees needed to run franchise: Info not provided
Absentee ownership? Yes

COSTS
Total cost: $300K-2M
Franchise fee: $20K
Royalty fee: $1K/mo.
Term of agreement: Info not provided
Franchisees required to buy multiple units? Outside the U.S. only

FINANCING
In-house: None
3rd-party: Equipment, inventory

QUALIFICATIONS
Net worth: $800K+
Cash liquidity: $300K
Experience:
    Industry experience
    General business experience

TRAINING
At headquarters

BUSINESS SUPPORT
Newsletter
Meetings
Toll-free phone line
Grand opening
Internet
Field operations/evaluations

MARKETING SUPPORT
Marketing campaign

JAZZERCISE INC.

Ranked #25 in Entrepreneur Magazine's 2004 Franchise 500   *Financial rating: $$$$*

2460 Impala Dr.
Carlsbad, CA 92008
Ph: (760)476-1750
Fax: (760)602-7180
www.jazzercise.com
Dance & exercise classes
Began: 1977, Franchising since: 1983
Headquarters size: 125 employees
Franchise department: 3 employees

U.S. franchises: 4,844
Canadian franchises: 94
Other foreign franchises: 888
Company-owned: 1
Units concentrated in CA

Seeking: All U.S.
Seeking in Canada? Yes
Exclusive territories? No
Homebased option? Yes
Kiosk option? No
Employees needed to run franchise: Info not provided
Absentee ownership? No

COSTS
Total cost: $2.6K-32.8K
Franchise fee: $325/$650
Royalty fee: to 20%
Term of agreement: 5 years renewable at no charge
Franchisees required to buy multiple units? No

FINANCING
No financing available

QUALIFICATIONS
Info not provided

TRAINING
At franchisee's location: 2-3 weeks home study
Seminars: 3 days

BUSINESS SUPPORT
Newsletter
Meetings
Toll-free phone line
Internet
Security/safety procedures
Field operations/evaluations

MARKETING SUPPORT
Co-op advertising
Ad slicks
National media campaign
Regional marketing

SHAPE UP SISTERS INC.

Financial rating: 0

425 W. Town Pl., #116
St. Augustine, FL 32092
Ph: (866)774-2738/(904)940-9331
Fax: (904)940-9336
www.shapeupsisters.com
Fitness boutique for women
Began: 2002, Franchising since: 2002
Headquarters size: 4 employees
Franchise department: 2 employees

U.S. franchises: 0
Canadian franchises: 0
Other foreign franchises: 0
Company-owned: 1

Seeking: All U.S.
Seeking in Canada? Yes
Exclusive territories? Yes
Homebased option? No
Kiosk option? No
Employees needed to run franchise: 2
Absentee ownership? No

COSTS
Total cost: $40K-51K
Franchise fee: $24.9K
Royalty fee: $375/mo.
Term of agreement: 10 years renewable
   at no charge
Franchisees required to buy multiple
   units? No

FINANCING
No financing available

QUALIFICATIONS
Net worth: $25K-50K
Cash liquidity: $19.8K
Experience:
   Must enjoy working with & helping
   people

TRAINING
At headquarters: 4 days

BUSINESS SUPPORT
Newsletter
Toll-free phone line
Grand opening
Internet
Lease negotiations
Field operations/evaluations

MARKETING SUPPORT
Ad slicks
Regional marketing

VELOCITY SPORTS PERFORMANCE

Financial rating: 0

2125 Corporate Dr., #101
Marietta, GA 30067
Ph: (770)955-1000
Fax: (770)955-1021
www.velocitysp.com
Sports performance training
Began: 1999, Franchising since: 2002
Headquarters size: 12 employees
Franchise department: 12 employees

U.S. franchises: 5
Canadian franchises: 0
Other foreign franchises: 0
Company-owned: 1
Units concentrated in all U.S.

Seeking: All U.S.
Seeking in Canada? Yes
Exclusive territories? Yes
Homebased option? No
Kiosk option? No
Employees needed to run franchise:
   6-10
Absentee ownership? Yes

COSTS
Total cost: $257K-492K
Franchise fee: $30K
Royalty fee: 4-8%
Term of agreement: 10 years renewable
   at no charge
Franchisees required to buy multiple
   units? No

FINANCING
In-house: None
3rd-party: Equipment, franchise fee,
   inventory, start-up costs

QUALIFICATIONS
Net worth: $300K-500K
Cash liquidity: $100K
Experience:
   General business experience
   Marketing skills

TRAINING
At headquarters: 2 weeks
At franchisee's location: 2 days
Periodic conferences: 2 days each

BUSINESS SUPPORT
Newsletter
Meetings
Toll-free phone line
Grand opening
Internet
Lease negotiations
Security/safety procedures
Field operations/evaluations
Purchasing cooperatives

MARKETING SUPPORT
Co-op advertising
Ad slicks
National media campaign
Regional marketing
Direct-mail pieces
Marketing brochures

RECREATION ▶ *Golf*

ADVANTAGE GOLF TOURNAMENT SERVICES

Financial rating: 0

3790 Arapaho Rd.
Addison, TX 75001
Ph: (800)659-2815/(972)243-6209
Fax: (972)243-4252
www.advantagegolf.com
Golf tournament services
Began: 1996, Franchising since: 1998
Headquarters size: 6 employees
Franchise department: 1 employee

U.S. franchises: 20
Canadian franchises: 0
Other foreign franchises: 0
Company-owned: 0
Units concentrated in CA, FL

Seeking: All U.S.
Seeking in Canada? Yes
Exclusive territories? Yes
Homebased option? No
Kiosk option? No
Employees needed to run franchise:
    3-5
Absentee ownership? Yes

COSTS
Total cost: $79.8K-172.7K
Franchise fee: $25K-65K+
Royalty fee: 5%
Term of agreement: 10 years renewable
    w/5-year options
Franchisees required to buy multiple
    units? No

FINANCING
No financing available

QUALIFICATIONS
Experience:
    General business experience
    Marketing skills
    Sales acumen

TRAINING
At headquarters: 1 week
At franchisee's location: 1 week
Ongoing

BUSINESS SUPPORT
Meetings
Toll-free phone line
Internet
Security/safety procedures

MARKETING SUPPORT
Co-op advertising
Collateral marketing programs

GLOBAL LEADERBOARD

Financial rating: 0

21043-2591 Panorama Dr.
Coquitlam, BC V3E 2Y0 Canada
Ph: (800)411-4448/(604)468-2211
Fax: (604)468-0101
www.globalleaderboard.com
Golf tournament scoring, administra-
    tion & sponsorships
Began: 1995, Franchising since: 2001
Headquarters size: 5 employees
Franchise department: 3 employees

U.S. franchises: 6
Canadian franchises: 1
Other foreign franchises: 0
Company-owned: 0
Units concentrated in CA, FL

Seeking: All U.S.
Seeking in Canada? Yes
Exclusive territories? Yes
Homebased option? Yes
Kiosk option? No
Employees needed to run franchise: 2
Absentee ownership? No

COSTS
Total cost: $36K-138K
Franchise fee: $5K-36K
Royalty fee: Varies
Term of agreement: 5 years renewable
    at no charge
Franchisees required to buy multiple
    units? No

FINANCING
No financing available

QUALIFICATIONS
Net worth: $100K
Cash liquidity: $25K-56K
Experience:
    Industry experience
    General business experience
    Marketing skills

TRAINING
At headquarters: 10 days

BUSINESS SUPPORT
Newsletter
Meetings
Toll-free phone line
Internet
Field operations/evaluations

MARKETING SUPPORT
Co-op advertising
Regional marketing

GOLF ETC.

Ranked #465 in Entrepreneur Magazine's 2004 Franchise 500

Financial rating: $$

2201 Commercial Ln.
Granbury, TX 76048
Ph: (800)806-8633/(817)279-7888
Fax: (817)579-1793
www.golfetc.com
Golf supplies, equipment & services
Began: 1992, Franchising since: 1995
Headquarters size: 20 employees
Franchise department: 3 employees

U.S. franchises: 64
Canadian franchises: 0
Other foreign franchises: 0
Company-owned: 0
Units concentrated in all U.S.

Seeking: All U.S.
Seeking in Canada? Yes
Exclusive territories? Yes
Homebased option? No
Kiosk option? No
Employees needed to run franchise: 3
Absentee ownership? Yes

COSTS
Total cost: $151K-181K
Franchise fee: $15K
Royalty fee: $35/sq. ft.
Term of agreement: 10 years renewable
    at no charge
Franchisees required to buy multiple
    units? No

FINANCING
No financing available

QUALIFICATIONS
Cash liquidity: $50K-60K
Experience:
    General business experience
    Marketing skills

TRAINING
At headquarters: 7 days
At franchisee's location: 10 days
Annual visits

BUSINESS SUPPORT
Newsletter
Meetings
Toll-free phone line
Grand opening
Internet
Security/safety procedures
Field operations/evaluations
Purchasing cooperatives

MARKETING SUPPORT
Ad slicks
National media campaign
Regional marketing

GOLF USA INC.

Ranked #375 in Entrepreneur Magazine's 2004 Franchise 500

Financial rating: $$$$

3705 W. Memorial Rd., #801
Oklahoma City, OK 73134
Ph: (800)488-1107/(405)751-0015
Fax: (405)755-0065
www.golfusa.com
Golf store
Began: 1986, Franchising since: 1989
Headquarters size: 20 employees
Franchise department: 3 employees

U.S. franchises: 89
Canadian franchises: 3
Other foreign franchises: 9
Company-owned: 5
Units concentrated in all U.S.

Seeking: All U.S.
Seeking in Canada? Yes
Exclusive territories? Yes
Homebased option? No
Kiosk option? No
Employees needed to run franchise: 4
Absentee ownership? No

COSTS
Total cost: $189K-286K
Franchise fee: $34K-44K
Royalty fee: 2%
Term of agreement: 15 years renewable
    at no charge
Franchisees required to buy multiple
    units? No

FINANCING
In-house: None
3rd-party: Accounts receivable, equip-
    ment, franchise fee, inventory, pay-
    roll, start-up costs

QUALIFICATIONS
Net worth: $250K
Cash liquidity: $50K
Experience:
    Industry experience
    General business experience
    Marketing skills

TRAINING
At headquarters: 10 days

BUSINESS SUPPORT
Newsletter
Meetings
Toll-free phone line
Grand opening
Internet
Lease negotiations
Security/safety procedures
Field operations/evaluations
Purchasing cooperatives

MARKETING SUPPORT
Co-op advertising
Ad slicks
National media campaign
Regional marketing

NEVADA BOB'S GOLF

Current financial data not available

335 8th Ave. S.W., #2000
Calgary, AB Canada T2P 1C9
Ph: (403)303-8400
Fax: (403)294-9590
www.nevadabobs.com
Golf equipment stores
Began: 1974, Franchising since: 1978
Headquarters size: Info not provided
Franchise department: 9 employees

U.S. franchises: 55
Canadian franchises: 29
Other foreign franchises: 0
Company-owned: 0
Units concentrated in CA, FL, IA, IL,
    IN, KY, LA, MI, MN, MS, NC, SC,
    TN, WI

Seeking: All U.S.
Seeking in Canada? Yes
Exclusive territories? Yes
Homebased option? No
Kiosk option? Yes
Employees needed to run franchise: 5
Absentee ownership? Yes

COSTS
Total cost: $300K-722K
    Kiosk cost: Varies
Franchise fee: $50K
Royalty fee: 3.5%
Term of agreement: 10 years renewable
    for $5K
Franchisees required to buy multiple
    units? Outside the U.S. only

FINANCING
No financing available

QUALIFICATIONS
Net worth: $150K
Cash liquidity: $100K
Experience:
    Industry experience
    General business experience
    Marketing skills

TRAINING
At headquarters: 1 week
At franchisee's location: 1 week

BUSINESS SUPPORT
Newsletter
Meetings
Toll-free phone line
Grand opening
Internet
Lease negotiations
Security/safety procedures
Field operations/evaluations
Purchasing cooperatives

MARKETING SUPPORT
Co-op advertising
Ad slicks
National media campaign

PARMASTERS GOLF TRAINING CENTERS LLC

Current financial data not available

9600 Cameron St., #314
Burnaby, BC Canada V3J 7N3
Ph: (800)663-2331
Fax: (800)416-6325
www.parmastersgolf.com
Indoor golf training centers
Began: 2000, Franchising since: 2001
Headquarters size: 5 employees
Franchise department: 1 employee

U.S. franchises: 0
Canadian franchises: 0
Other foreign franchises: 0
Company-owned: 0

Seeking: All U.S.
Seeking in Canada? Yes
Exclusive territories? Yes
Homebased option? No
Kiosk option? No
Employees needed to run franchise: 15
Absentee ownership? No

COSTS
Total cost: $381.9K-1.1M
Franchise fee: $25K
Royalty fee: 6%
Term of agreement: 10 years renewable
    for $6.2K
Franchisees required to buy multiple
    units? No

FINANCING
In-house: None
Equipment, start-up costs

QUALIFICATIONS
Net worth: $400K
Cash liquidity: $200K
Experience:
    General business experience
    Marketing skills
    Must have a passion for golf

TRAINING
At headquarters: 14 days
At franchisee's location: 7 days
At golf center for pre-opening
    marketing: 2 days

BUSINESS SUPPORT
Newsletter
Meetings
Toll-free phone line
Grand opening
Internet
Lease negotiations
Security/safety procedures
Field operations/evaluations
Purchasing cooperatives

MARKETING SUPPORT
Co-op advertising
Ad slicks
National media campaign
Regional marketing
PR support

PRO GOLF DISCOUNT

Current financial data not available

32751 Middlebelt Rd.
Farmington Hills, MI 48334
Ph: (800)521-6388/(248)737-0553
Fax: (248)737-9077
www.progolfamerica.com
Golf equipment & accessories
Began: 1962, Franchising since: 1972
Headquarters size: 25 employees
Franchise department: 3 employees

U.S. franchises: 113
Canadian franchises: 21
Other foreign franchises: 2
Company-owned: 0
Units concentrated in Midwest, South, Southeast

Seeking: All U.S.
Seeking in Canada? Yes
Exclusive territories? Yes
Homebased option? No
Kiosk option? Yes
Employees needed to run franchise: 4
Absentee ownership? No

COSTS
Total cost: $252.9K-1.1M
Franchise fee: $49.5K
Royalty fee: 2.5%
Term of agreement: 15 years renewable for $2.5K
Franchisees required to buy multiple units? No

FINANCING
In-house: None
3rd-party: Equipment, franchise fee, inventory, start-up costs

QUALIFICATIONS
Net worth: $500K
Cash liquidity: $200K-250K
Experience:
    General business experience
    Marketing skills

TRAINING
At headquarters: 10-14 days
At franchisee's location: 5-7 days
Ongoing

BUSINESS SUPPORT
Newsletter
Meetings
Toll-free phone line
Grand opening
Internet
Lease negotiations
Security/safety procedures
Field operations/evaluations
Purchasing cooperatives

MARKETING SUPPORT
Co-op advertising
Ad slicks
Regional marketing
Web site

RECREATION *Sports Programs*

AMERICAN POOLPLAYERS ASSOCIATION

Ranked #163 in Entrepreneur Magazine's 2004 Franchise 500

Financial rating: $$$$

1000 Lake St. Louis Blvd., #325
Lake St. Louis, MO 63367
Ph: (636)625-8611
Fax: (636)625-2975
www.poolplayers.com
Recreational billiard league
Began: 1981, Franchising since: 1982
Headquarters size: 47 employees
Franchise department: 3 employees

U.S. franchises: 241
Canadian franchises: 15
Other foreign franchises: 0
Company-owned: 0
Units concentrated in all U.S.

Seeking: All U.S.
Seeking in Canada? Yes
Exclusive territories? Yes
Homebased option? Yes
Kiosk option? No
Employees needed to run franchise: 1-3
Absentee ownership? No

COSTS
Total cost: $11.6K-14K
Franchise fee: $5K+
Royalty fee: 20%
Term of agreement: 2 years renewable at no charge
Franchisees required to buy multiple units? No

FINANCING
In-house: Franchise fee
3rd-party: None

QUALIFICATIONS
Experience:
    General business experience
    Marketing skills

TRAINING
At headquarters: 6 days

BUSINESS SUPPORT
Newsletter
Meetings
Toll-free phone line
Internet
Field operations/evaluations

MARKETING SUPPORT
Ad slicks

I9 SPORTS

Financial rating: $$$

1463 Oakfield Dr., #135
Brandon, FL 33511
Ph: (813)662-6773
www.i9sports.com
Amateur sports leagues, tournaments
& events
Began: 2002, Franchising since: 2003
Headquarters size: 6 employees
Franchise department: 6 employees

U.S. franchises: 0
Canadian franchises: 0
Other foreign franchises: 0
Company-owned: 2
Units concentrated in all U.S.

Seeking: All U.S.
Seeking in Canada? No
Exclusive territories? Yes
Homebased option? Yes
Kiosk option? No
Employees needed to run franchise: 2
Absentee ownership? No

COSTS
Total cost: $26.5K-59.7K
Franchise fee: $16K-36K
Royalty fee: 10%
Term of agreement: 10 years renewable
at no charge
Franchisees required to buy multiple
units? No

FINANCING
In-house: Franchise fee
3rd-party: Franchise fee

QUALIFICATIONS
Net worth: $100K
Cash liquidity: $25K
Experience:
    General business experience
    Marketing skills

TRAINING
At headquarters: 1 week
At franchisee's location: 4 days
Optional refresher training available

BUSINESS SUPPORT
Newsletter
Meetings
Toll-free phone line
Internet
Security/safety procedures
Field operations/evaluations
Purchasing cooperatives

MARKETING SUPPORT
Co-op advertising
Ad slicks
National media campaign
Regional marketing
Administrative support
Sales & PR guidance

PERSONAL BEST KARATE

Financial rating: 0

250 E. Main St.
Norton, MA 02766
Ph: (508)285-5425
Fax: (508)285-7064
www.personalbestkarate.com
Karate training
Began: 1991, Franchising since: 2000
Headquarters size: 4 employees
Franchise department: 2 employees

U.S. franchises: 3
Canadian franchises: 0
Other foreign franchises: 0
Company-owned: 2
Units concentrated in MA

Seeking: Northeast
Focusing on: MA
Seeking in Canada? No
Exclusive territories? Yes
Homebased option? No
Kiosk option? No
Employees needed to run franchise: 3
Absentee ownership? No

COSTS
Total cost: $63.5K-113.2K
Franchise fee: $34K
Royalty fee: 10%
Term of agreement: 5 years renewable
at no charge
Franchisees required to buy multiple
units? No

FINANCING
In-house: Franchise fee
3rd-party: None

QUALIFICATIONS
Net worth: $100K
Cash liquidity: $100K
Experience:
    General business experience
    Marketing skills
    Sales experience
    Fitness-related experience

TRAINING
At headquarters: 8 half-day sessions
At franchisee's location: 1 week
Weekly training

BUSINESS SUPPORT
Meetings
Grand opening
Internet
Lease negotiations
Security/safety procedures
Field operations/evaluations
Purchasing cooperatives

MARKETING SUPPORT
Co-op advertising
Ad slicks
Regional marketing

RECRUIT

Current financial data not available

4900 California Ave., #250
Bakersfield, CA 93309
Ph: (661)859-2880
Fax: (661)859-2888
www.mysportsfranchise.com
Athletic recruiting exposure service for high school athletes & college coaches
Began: 1996, Franchising since: 2001
Headquarters size: 7 employees
Franchise department: 1 employee

U.S. franchises: 24
Canadian franchises: 0
Other foreign franchises: 0
Company-owned: 156
Units concentrated in all U.S.

Seeking: All U.S.
Seeking in Canada? Yes
Exclusive territories? Yes
Homebased option? Yes
Kiosk option? No
Employees needed to run franchise: 1
Absentee ownership? Yes

COSTS
Total cost: $12K-45K
Franchise fee: $9.5K
Royalty fee: 0
Term of agreement: 5 years renewable at no charge
Franchisees required to buy multiple units? No

FINANCING
No financing available

QUALIFICATIONS
Net worth: $50K
Experience:
    Athletic coaching or playing experience

TRAINING
At headquarters: 2-3 days
Ongoing

BUSINESS SUPPORT
Newsletter
Meetings
Toll-free phone line
Internet
Field operations/evaluations

MARKETING SUPPORT
Co-op advertising
Regional marketing
Marketing materials

TRIPLE CROWN SPORTS

Current financial data not available

3930 Automation Wy.
Ft. Collins, CO 80525
Ph: (970)223-6644, Fax: (970)223-3636
www.triplecrownsports.com
Amateur sports events
Began: 1982, Franchising since: 1997
Headquarters size: 35 employees
Franchise department: 6 employees

U.S. franchises: 8
Canadian franchises: 0
Other foreign franchises: 0
Company-owned: 1
Units concentrated in AZ, CA, CO, CT, GA, KS, MO, NY, TX, UT

Seeking: All U.S.
Focusing on: AL, LA, MD, MS, NC, NJ, VA, WA
Seeking in Canada? No
Exclusive territories? Yes
Homebased option? Yes
Kiosk option? No
Employees needed to run franchise: 2
Absentee ownership? No

COSTS
Total cost: $19.5K-53K
Franchise fee: $12.5K-22.5K
Royalty fee: 10%
Term of agreement: 5 years renewable at no charge
Franchisees required to buy multiple units? No

FINANCING
No financing available

QUALIFICATIONS
Net worth: $100K
Cash liquidity: $25K
Experience:
    General business experience
    Marketing skills
    Sports lifestyle passion

TRAINING
At headquarters: 1 week
At franchisee's location: 4 days
Ongoing

BUSINESS SUPPORT
Newsletter
Meetings
Toll-free phone line
Internet
Field operations/evaluations
Purchasing cooperatives

MARKETING SUPPORT
Co-op advertising
Ad slicks
National media campaign

WORLD CHAMPIONSHIP ARMWRESTLING

Current financial data not available

303 Sondrol Ave., P.O. Box 882
Ames, IA 50010
Ph: (866)232-5023
Fax: (515)232-5036
www.realitysportsent.com
Arm wrestling tournaments
Began: 2002, Franchising since: 2003
Headquarters size: 6 employees
Franchise department: 6 employees

U.S. franchises: 1
Canadian franchises: 0
Other foreign franchises: 0
Company-owned: 2
Units concentrated in IA, IN

Seeking: All U.S.
Seeking in Canada? Yes
Exclusive territories? Yes
Homebased option? Yes
Kiosk option? No
Employees needed to run franchise: 1
Absentee ownership? Yes

COSTS
Total cost: $41.9K-56.9K
Franchise fee: $35K-50K
Royalty fee: $400/mo.
Term of agreement: 5 years renewable
for $10K
Franchisees required to buy multiple
units? No

FINANCING
In-house: None
3rd-party: Equipment, franchise fee

QUALIFICATIONS
Cash liquidity: $35K
Experience:
Marketing skills

TRAINING
At headquarters: 3 days
At franchisee's location: 1 week

BUSINESS SUPPORT
Newsletter
Meetings
Internet
Field operations/evaluations

MARKETING SUPPORT
National media campaign
PR support

CARLSON WAGONLIT

RECREATION ▸ *Travel*

TRAVEL

Ranked #119 in Entrepreneur Magazine's 2004 Franchise 500   *Financial rating: $$$$*

P.O. Box 59159
Minneapolis, MN 55459-8207
Ph: (800)678-8241/(800)337-2537
Fax: (763)212-2302
www.carlsontravel.com
Travel agency
Began: 1888, Franchising since: 1984
Headquarters size: 611 employees
Franchise department: 137 employees

U.S. franchises: 876
Canadian franchises: 0
Other foreign franchises: 0
Company-owned: 25
Units concentrated in all U.S.

Seeking: All U.S.
Seeking in Canada? No
Exclusive territories? No
Homebased option? No
Kiosk option? No
Employees needed to run franchise: 1+
Absentee ownership? No

COSTS
Total cost: $2.5K-164K
Franchise fee: $1.5K-29.9K
Royalty fee: $480-965/mo.
Term of agreement: 5 years renewable
for $1K
Franchisees required to buy multiple
units? No

FINANCING
In-house: Franchise fee
3rd-party: None

QUALIFICATIONS
Experience:
Industry experience
General business experience
Marketing skills

TRAINING
At headquarters: 3 days
At franchisee's location: Varies
In-field workshops & annual national
meeting: 1-4 days

BUSINESS SUPPORT
Newsletter
Meetings
Toll-free phone line
Internet
Field operations/evaluations

MARKETING SUPPORT
Co-op advertising
Ad slicks
National media campaign
Regional marketing

CRUISE HOLIDAYS INT'L.

Ranked #451 in Entrepreneur Magazine's 2004 Franchise 500   *Financial rating: $$$$*

P.O. Box 59159
Minneapolis, MN 55459
Ph: (800)866-7245
Fax: (763)212-1231
www.cruiseholidays.com
Cruise-only travel agency
Began: 1984, Franchising since: 1984
Headquarters size: 611 employees
Franchise department: 137 employees

U.S. franchises: 96
Canadian franchises: 32
Other foreign franchises: 0
Company-owned: 0
Units concentrated in all U.S. &
    Canada

Seeking: All U.S.
Seeking in Canada? Yes
Exclusive territories? No
Homebased option? No
Kiosk option? No
Employees needed to run franchise:
    Info not provided
Absentee ownership? No

COSTS

Total cost: $70.7K-126.2K
Franchise fee: $5K-19.5K
Royalty fee: $525+/mo.
Term of agreement: 10 years renewable
    for $1K
Franchisees required to buy multiple
    units? No

FINANCING

No financing available

QUALIFICATIONS

Experience:
    General business experience
    Marketing skills

TRAINING

At headquarters: 2 weeks
At franchisee's location: Varies
Annual meeting on a cruise ship:
    4-5 days

BUSINESS SUPPORT

Newsletter
Meetings
Grand opening
Internet
Field operations/evaluations
Purchasing cooperatives

MARKETING SUPPORT

Co-op advertising
Ad slicks
National media campaign
Seminars

CRUISE PLANNERS

Ranked #104 in Entrepreneur Magazine's 2004 Franchise 500   *Financial rating: $$$$*

3300 University Dr., #602
Coral Springs, FL 33065
Ph: (888)582-2150/(954)227-2545
Fax: (954)344-0875
www.cruiseagents.com
Cruise/tour agency
Began: 1994, Franchising since: 1999
Headquarters size: 23 employees
Franchise department: 3 employees

U.S. franchises: 408
Canadian franchises: 0
Other foreign franchises: 0
Company-owned: 0
Units concentrated in all U.S.

Seeking: All U.S.
Seeking in Canada? No
Exclusive territories? No
Homebased option? Yes
Kiosk option? Yes
Employees needed to run franchise: 1-2
Absentee ownership? Yes

COSTS

Total cost: $8.99K-18.6K
    Kiosk cost: Varies
Franchise fee: $8.99K
Royalty fee: 3-0%
Term of agreement: 3 years renewable
    at no charge
Franchisees required to buy multiple
    units? No

FINANCING

No financing available

QUALIFICATIONS

Net worth: $18.6K
Cash liquidity: $8.99K

TRAINING

In Ft. Lauderdale, FL: 5 days

BUSINESS SUPPORT

Newsletter
Meetings
Toll-free phone line
Internet
Purchasing cooperatives

MARKETING SUPPORT

Co-op advertising
Ad slicks
National media campaign
Regional marketing

CRUISEONE INC.

Ranked #137 in Entrepreneur Magazine's 2004 Franchise 500

Financial rating: $$$$

1415 N.W. 62nd St., #205
Ft. Lauderdale, FL 33309
Ph: (800)892-3928
Fax: (954)958-3697
www.cruiseone.com/franchise
Cruise-only travel agency
Began: 1989, Franchising since: 1993
Headquarters size: 50 employees
Franchise department: Info not provided

U.S. franchises: 415
Canadian franchises: 0
Other foreign franchises: 0
Company-owned: 0
Units concentrated in all U.S.

Seeking: All U.S.
Seeking in Canada? No
Exclusive territories? No
Homebased option? Yes
Kiosk option? No
Employees needed to run franchise: 0
Absentee ownership? No

COSTS
Total cost: $9.8K-26.3K
Franchise fee: $9.8K
Royalty fee: 3%
Term of agreement: 5 years renewable at no charge
Franchisees required to buy multiple units? No

FINANCING
In-house: Franchise fee
3rd-party: None

QUALIFICATIONS
Info not provided

TRAINING
At headquarters: 8 days

BUSINESS SUPPORT
Newsletter
Meetings
Toll-free phone line
Internet

MARKETING SUPPORT
Co-op advertising
Ad slicks
Regional marketing

RESULTS! TRAVEL

Ranked #71 in Entrepreneur Magazine's 2004 Franchise 500

Financial rating: $$$$

P.O. Box 59159, Carlson Pkwy
Minneapolis, MN 55459-8207
Ph: (888)523-2200
Fax: (763)212-2302
www.resultstravel.com
Travel services
Began: 2000, Franchising since: 2000
Headquarters size: 611 employees
Franchise department: 137 employees

U.S. franchises: 674
Canadian franchises: 0
Other foreign franchises: 0
Company-owned: 0
Units concentrated in all U.S. except IN

Seeking: All U.S.
Seeking in Canada? No
Exclusive territories? No
Homebased option? No
Kiosk option? No
Employees needed to run franchise:
    Info not provided
Absentee ownership? No

COSTS
Total cost: $25-8.9K
Franchise fee: to $1.5K
Royalty fee: to $600/yr.
Term of agreement: 1 year renewable
Franchisees required to buy multiple units? No

FINANCING
No financing available

QUALIFICATIONS
Experience:
    Industry experience
    General business experience
    Marketing skills

TRAINING
Orientation training: 1-2 days
National conference: 3 days

BUSINESS SUPPORT
Meetings

MARKETING SUPPORT
Co-op advertising
National media campaign

TRAVEL NETWORK
Ranked #389 in Entrepreneur Magazine's 2004 Franchise 500 *Financial rating: $$$$*

560 Sylvan Ave.
Englewood Cliffs, NJ 07632
Ph: (800)669-9000/(201)567-8500
Fax: (201)567-4405
www.travelnetwork.com
Travel agency
Began: 1982, Franchising since: 1983
Headquarters size: 18 employees
Franchise department: 9 employees

U.S. franchises: 267
Canadian franchises: 3
Other foreign franchises: 58
Company-owned: 1
Units concentrated in all U.S.

Seeking: All U.S.
Seeking in Canada? Yes
Exclusive territories? Yes
Homebased option? Yes
Kiosk option? No
Employees needed to run franchise: 2
Absentee ownership? Yes

COSTS
Total cost: $34.2K-99K
Franchise fee: $3.95K-29.9K
Royalty fee: $250-750/mo.
Term of agreement: 15 years renewable for $500
Franchisees required to buy multiple units? No

FINANCING
No financing available

QUALIFICATIONS
Net worth: $15K
Cash liquidity: $15K-30K
Experience:
    General business experience
    Marketing skills

TRAINING
At headquarters: 3 days
At franchisee's location: 4 days per year

BUSINESS SUPPORT
Newsletter
Meetings
Toll-free phone line
Grand opening
Internet
Lease negotiations
Field operations/evaluations
Purchasing cooperatives

MARKETING SUPPORT
Co-op advertising
Ad slicks
National media campaign
Regional marketing

RECREATION ▶ *Miscellaneous*

AMERICAN WILDLIFE ASSOCIATION LLC
Financial rating: $$$$

710 Main
Blue Springs, MO 64015
Ph: (816)220-1000
Fax: (816)224-9595
www.am-wildlife.com
Outdoor sporting clubs
Began: 1989, Franchising since: 2002
Headquarters size: 6 employees
Franchise department: 4 employees

U.S. franchises: 18
Canadian franchises: 0
Other foreign franchises: 0
Company-owned: 3
Units concentrated in all U.S.

Seeking: All U.S.; sold out in AR, KS, MO, NE
Seeking in Canada? No
Exclusive territories? Yes
Homebased option? Yes
Kiosk option? No
Employees needed to run franchise: 2-4
Absentee ownership? No

COSTS
Total cost: $23.1K-76.2K
Franchise fee: $19.8K
Royalty fee: 0
Term of agreement: Perpetual
Franchisees required to buy multiple units? No

FINANCING
No financing available

QUALIFICATIONS
Net worth: $50K
Cash liquidity: $25K
Experience:
    General business experience
    Marketing skills
    Outdoor sports experience

TRAINING
At headquarters: 1 week
At franchisee's location: 1 week

BUSINESS SUPPORT
Newsletter
Meetings
Toll-free phone line
Grand opening
Internet
Lease negotiations
Security/safety procedures
Field operations/evaluations
Purchasing cooperatives

MARKETING SUPPORT
Co-op advertising
Ad slicks
National media campaign
Regional marketing
Web

KAMPGROUNDS OF AMERICA INC.

Ranked #226 in Entrepreneur Magazine's 2004 Franchise 500   *Financial rating: $$$$*

550 N. 31st St., 4th Fl.
Billings, MT 59101
Ph: (406)248-7444
Fax: (406)254-7440
www.koa.com
Campgrounds
Began: 1961, Franchising since: 1962
Headquarters size: 70 employees
Franchise department: 10 employees

U.S. franchises: 415
Canadian franchises: 32
Other foreign franchises: 8
Company-owned: 14
Units concentrated in all U.S.

Seeking: All U.S.
Seeking in Canada? Yes
Exclusive territories? Yes
Homebased option? No
Kiosk option? No
Employees needed to run franchise: 5
Absentee ownership? Yes

COSTS
Total cost: $716K-1.6M
Franchise fee: $25K
Royalty fee: 8%
Term of agreement: 10 years renewable
    at no charge
Franchisees required to buy multiple
    units? No

FINANCING
No financing available

QUALIFICATIONS
Net worth: $300K
Cash liquidity: $100K
Experience:
    People skills

TRAINING
At headquarters: 1 week
At franchisee's location

BUSINESS SUPPORT
Newsletter
Meetings
Toll-free phone line
Grand opening
Internet
Security/safety procedures
Field operations/evaluations

MARKETING SUPPORT
Co-op advertising
Ad slicks
National media campaign

OUTDOOR CONNECTION

Current financial data not available

424 Neosho
Burlington, KS 66839
Ph: (620)364-5500
Fax: (620)364-5563
www.outdoor-connection.com
Fishing & hunting trips
Began: 1988, Franchising since: 1990
Headquarters size: 5 employees
Franchise department: 2 employees

U.S. franchises: 74
Canadian franchises: 0
Other foreign franchises: 0
Company-owned: 3
Units concentrated in all U.S.

Seeking: All U.S.
Seeking in Canada? Yes
Exclusive territories? Yes
Homebased option? Yes
Kiosk option? No
Employees needed to run franchise: 0
Absentee ownership? Yes

COSTS
Total cost: $10.4K-15.1K
Franchise fee: $9.5K
Royalty fee: 3-5%
Term of agreement: 5 years renewable
    for $500
Franchisees required to buy multiple
    units? No

FINANCING
In-house: Franchise fee
3rd-party: None

QUALIFICATIONS
Info not provided

TRAINING
At headquarters: 2 days
At franchisee's location: 2 days

BUSINESS SUPPORT
Newsletter
Meetings
Internet
Field operations/evaluations
Purchasing cooperatives

MARKETING SUPPORT
Co-op advertising
National media campaign

PUCKMASTERS HOCKEY TRAINING CENTERS

Current financial data not available

1260 Hornby St., #102
Vancouver, BC Canada V6Z 1W2
Ph: (888)775-7825
Fax: (604)683-7841
www.puckmasters.com
Hockey training centers
Began: 1993, Franchising since: 1996
Headquarters size: 21 employees
Franchise department: 1 employee

U.S. franchises: 12
Canadian franchises: 8
Other foreign franchises: 0
Company-owned: 1
Units concentrated in all U.S.

Seeking: All U.S.
Seeking in Canada? Yes
Exclusive territories? Yes
Homebased option? No
Kiosk option? No
Employees needed to run franchise: 6
Absentee ownership? Yes

COSTS
Total cost: $30K-300K
Franchise fee: $20K
Royalty fee: 6%
Term of agreement: 10 years renewable
    for $5K
Franchisees required to buy multiple
    units? No

FINANCING
In-house: Franchise fee
3rd-party: None

QUALIFICATIONS
Net worth: $80K
Cash liquidity: $40K
Experience:
    General business experience
    Marketing skills
    Must love hockey & children

TRAINING
At headquarters: 14 days
At franchisee's location: 7 days

BUSINESS SUPPORT
Newsletter
Meetings
Toll-free phone line
Grand opening
Internet
Lease negotiations
Security/safety procedures
Field operations/evaluations
Purchasing cooperatives

MARKETING SUPPORT
Co-op advertising
Ad slicks
National media campaign
Regional marketing
PR support

WHEEL FUN RENTALS

Current financial data not available

4526 Telephone Rd., #202
Ventura, CA 93003
Ph: (805)650-7770
Fax: (805)650-7771
www.wheelfunrentals.com
Recreational rentals
Began: 1987, Franchising since: 2000
Headquarters size: 8 employees
Franchise department: 4 employees

U.S. franchises: 33
Canadian franchises: 0
Other foreign franchises: 0
Company-owned: 18
Units concentrated in CA, OR

Seeking: All U.S.
Seeking in Canada? No
Exclusive territories? Yes
Homebased option? No
Kiosk option? Yes
Employees needed to run franchise:
    3-12
Absentee ownership? No

COSTS
Total cost: $103K-260K
    Kiosk cost: Same as total cost
Franchise fee: $20K
Royalty fee: 6%
Term of agreement: 10 years renewable
    for $1K
Franchisees required to buy multiple
    units? No

FINANCING
In-house: None
3rd-party: Equipment, franchise fee,
    inventory, start-up costs

QUALIFICATIONS
Net worth: $150K
Cash liquidity: $75K
Experience:
    General business experience

TRAINING
At headquarters: 7 days
At franchisee's location: Varies
Additional training available

BUSINESS SUPPORT
Newsletter
Meetings
Toll-free phone line
Grand opening
Internet
Lease negotiations
Field operations/evaluations

MARKETING SUPPORT
Co-op advertising
Ad slicks

YOGI BEAR'S JELLYSTONE CAMP-RESORTS

Current financial data not available

50 W. Techne Center Dr., #G
Milford, OH 45150-9798
Ph: (800)626-3720/(513)831-2100
Fax: (513)579-8670
www.campjellystone.com
Family camping resorts
Began: 1969, Franchising since: 1969
Headquarters size: 8 employees
Franchise department: 3 employees

U.S. franchises: 60
Canadian franchises: 5
Other foreign franchises: 0
Company-owned: 0
Units concentrated in IN, MI, NY, WI

Seeking: All U.S.
Seeking in Canada? Yes
Exclusive territories? Yes
Homebased option? No
Kiosk option? No
Employees needed to run franchise: 15
Absentee ownership? Yes

COSTS
Total cost: $70K+
Franchise fee: $20K
Royalty fee: 6%
Term of agreement: 5 years renewable
at no charge
Franchisees required to buy multiple
units? No

FINANCING
In-house: Franchise fee, inventory,
start-up costs
3rd-party: None

QUALIFICATIONS
Net worth: $250K+
Cash liquidity: $100K+
Experience:
General business experience
Marketing skills

TRAINING
At headquarters: 5 days
At franchisee's location: 2-3 days
In Cincinnati, OH: 2-3 days

BUSINESS SUPPORT
Newsletter
Meetings
Toll-free phone line
Grand opening
Internet
Security/safety procedures
Field operations/evaluations

MARKETING SUPPORT
Co-op advertising
Ad slicks
National media campaign
Regional marketing

RECREATION   *Other Franchises*

BUTTERFLY LIFE
2404 San Ramon Valley Blvd., #200
San Ramon, CA 94583
Ph: (800)288-8373
www.butterflylife.com
Women's healthy living & fitness
center

COLLEGIATE SPORTS OF AMERICA
22900 Ventura Blvd., #100
Woodland Hills, CA 91364
Ph: (800)600-7518
www.csaprepstar.com
Athletic recruiting services

LADY OF AMERICA
500 E. Broward Blvd., #1650
Ft. Lauderdale, FL 33394
Ph: (954)527-5373
www.ladyofamerica.com
Fitness centers

THE UNIGLOBE GROUP
5 Park Plaza, #800
Irvine, CA 92614
Ph: (800)863-1606
www.uniglobefranchise.com
Travel agency

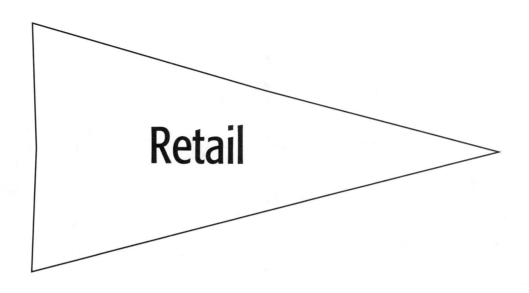

RETAIL   *Apparel*

HANNOUSH JEWELERS

Ranked #412 in Entrepreneur Magazine's 2004 Franchise 500   *Financial rating: $$$$*

134 Capital Dr.
West Springfield, MA 01089
Ph: (413)846-4640
Fax: (413)788-7588
www.hannoush.com
Jewelry stores
Began: 1980, Franchising since: 1995
Headquarters size: 25 employees
Franchise department: 7 employees

U.S. franchises: 20
Canadian franchises: 0
Other foreign franchises: 0
Company-owned: 43
Units concentrated in AZ, CT, MA, ME,
    NC, NJ, NY, VT

Seeking: All U.S.
Seeking in Canada? No
Exclusive territories? Yes
Homebased option? No
Kiosk option? No
Employees needed to run franchise: 6
Absentee ownership? Yes

COSTS
Total cost: $291K-717K
Franchise fee: $20K
Royalty fee: 4%
Term of agreement: 10 years renewable
Franchisees required to buy multiple
    units? No

FINANCING
In-house: Inventory
3rd-party: None

QUALIFICATIONS
Net worth: $100K
Cash liquidity: $100K

TRAINING
At headquarters: 2 weeks
At franchisee's location: 1-3 days at
    opening
Additional training available

BUSINESS SUPPORT
Newsletter
Meetings
Toll-free phone line
Internet
Lease negotiations
Security/safety procedures
Field operations/evaluations

MARKETING SUPPORT
Regional marketing
Radio & print ads

PLATO'S CLOSET
Ranked #198 in Entrepreneur Magazine's 2004 Franchise 500

Financial rating: $$$$

4200 Dahlberg Dr., #100
Minneapolis, MN 55422-4837
Ph: (800)269-4081/(763)520-8581
Fax: (763)520-8501
www.platoscloset.com
Clothing & accessories for teenagers &
young adults
Began: 1998, Franchising since: 1999
Headquarters size: 100 employees
Franchise department: 5 employees

U.S. franchises: 89
Canadian franchises: 0
Other foreign franchises: 0
Company-owned: 1

Seeking: All U.S.
Seeking in Canada? No
Exclusive territories? Yes
Homebased option? No
Kiosk option? No
Employees needed to run franchise: 3-5
Absentee ownership? No

COSTS
Total cost: $139.8K-243.2K
Franchise fee: $20K
Royalty fee: 4%
Term of agreement: 10 years renewable
for $5K
Franchisees required to buy multiple
units? No

FINANCING
No financing available

QUALIFICATIONS
Net worth: $200K
Cash liquidity: $40K-60K
Experience:
General business experience
Marketing skills

TRAINING
At headquarters: 2 weeks

BUSINESS SUPPORT
Newsletter
Meetings
Toll-free phone line
Grand opening
Internet
Lease negotiations
Security/safety procedures
Field operations/evaluations
Purchasing cooperatives

MARKETING SUPPORT
Co-op advertising
Ad slicks

RETAIL — *Convenience Stores*

EXPRESS MART FRANCHISING CORP.

Current financial data not available

6567 Kinne Rd., P.O. Box 46
Dewitt, NY 13214
Ph: (315)446-0125, Fax: (315)446-1355
www.expressmart.com
Gas station & convenience store
Began: 1975, Franchising since: 1990
Headquarters size: Info not provided
Franchise department: Info not pro-
vided

U.S. franchises: 22
Canadian franchises: 0
Other foreign franchises: 0
Company-owned: 48
Units concentrated in CT, MA, NY, PA

Seeking: All U.S.
Seeking in Canada? Yes
Exclusive territories? No
Homebased option? No
Kiosk option? No
Employees needed to run franchise:
Info not provided
Absentee ownership? Yes

COSTS
Total cost: $86.2K-361K
Franchise fee: $15K
Royalty fee: 4%
Term of agreement: 10 years renewable
Franchisees required to buy multiple
units? No

FINANCING
In-house: None
3rd-party: Equipment, inventory,
start-up costs

QUALIFICATIONS
Info not provided

TRAINING
At headquarters
At franchisee's location: 1-2 weeks

BUSINESS SUPPORT
Meetings
Grand opening
Security/safety procedures
Field operations/evaluations
Purchasing cooperatives

MARKETING SUPPORT
Co-op advertising
Ad slicks
Regional marketing

7-ELEVEN INC.

Ranked #4 in Entrepreneur Magazine's 2004 Franchise 500

Financial rating: $$$

2711 N. Haskell Ave., Box 711
Dallas, TX 75221
Ph: (800)255-0711, Fax: (214)841-6776
www.7-eleven.com
Convenience store
Began: 1927, Franchising since: 1964
Headquarters size: 1,000 employees
Franchise department: 18 employees

U.S. franchises: 3,761
Canadian franchises: 0
Other foreign franchises: 18,126
Company-owned: 2,547

Seeking: Midwest, Northeast,
    Southwest, West
Focusing on: AZ, CA, CT, DC, ID, IL,
    IN, KS, MA, ME, MI, MO, NH, NJ,
    NV, NY, OH, OR, PA, RI, VA, WA
Seeking in Canada? No
Exclusive territories? No
Homebased option? No
Kiosk option? No
Employees needed to run franchise:
    7-10
Absentee ownership? No

COSTS
Total cost: Varies
Franchise fee: Varies
Royalty fee: Varies
Term of agreement: 10 years renewable
    at no charge
Franchisees required to buy multiple
    units? No

FINANCING
In-house: Accounts receivable, inven-
    tory, payroll
3rd-party: None

QUALIFICATIONS
Experience:
    Industry experience
    General business experience
    Customer service skills

TRAINING
At local training centers: 6 weeks

BUSINESS SUPPORT
Newsletter
Meetings
Toll-free phone line
Grand opening
Internet
Security/safety procedures
Field operations/evaluations
Purchasing cooperatives

MARKETING SUPPORT
National media campaign
Regional marketing
In-house marketing team

WHITE HEN PANTRY

Ranked #387 in Entrepreneur Magazine's 2004 Franchise 500

Financial rating: $$$

3003 Butterfield Rd.
Oak Brook, IL 60526
Ph: (800)726-8791/(630)366-3000
Fax: (630)366-3447
www.whitehen.com
Convenience store
Began: 1965, Franchising since: 1965
Headquarters size: 225 employees
Franchise department: 6 employees

U.S. franchises: 218
Canadian franchises: 0
Other foreign franchises: 0
Company-owned: 16
Units concentrated in IA, IL, MA, NH

Seeking: Midwest
Focusing on: Midwest, Northeast
Seeking in Canada? No
Exclusive territories? No
Homebased option? No
Kiosk option? No
Employees needed to run franchise:
    10-15
Absentee ownership? No

COSTS
Total cost: $52.4K-225.2K
Franchise fee: to $30K
Royalty fee: Varies
Term of agreement: 10 years renewable
Franchisees required to buy multiple
    units? No

FINANCING
In-house: Franchise fee, inventory,
    start-up costs
3rd-party: None

QUALIFICATIONS
Net worth: $200K
Cash liquidity: $60K
Experience:
    Industry experience
    General business experience

TRAINING
At headquarters: 2 days
At franchisee's location: 13 days

BUSINESS SUPPORT
Newsletter
Meetings
Grand opening
Security/safety procedures
Field operations/evaluations
Purchasing cooperatives

MARKETING SUPPORT
Info not provided

RETAIL ▸ *Flowers*

FLOWERAMA OF AMERICA
Ranked #289 in Entrepreneur Magazine's 2004 Franchise 500   *Financial rating: $$$$*

3165 W. Airline Hwy.
Waterloo, IA 50703
Ph: (319)291-6004, Fax: (319)291-8676
www.flowerama.com
Flowers, plants, gifts, silk items
Began: 1966, Franchising since: 1972
Headquarters size: 40 employees
Franchise department: 4 employees

U.S. franchises: 80
Canadian franchises: 0
Other foreign franchises: 0
Company-owned: 11
Units concentrated in all U.S.

Seeking: All U.S.
Seeking in Canada? No
Exclusive territories? No
Homebased option? No
Kiosk option? No
Employees needed to run franchise:
   8-10
Absentee ownership? Yes

COSTS
Total cost: $180K
Franchise fee: $35K
Royalty fee: 5%
Term of agreement: 20 years renewable
   at no charge
Franchisees required to buy multiple
   units? No

FINANCING
3rd-party: Equipment, inventory
Other: Operating capital, leasehold
   expenses

QUALIFICATIONS
Cash liquidity: $50K

TRAINING
At headquarters: 4-6 weeks
At franchisee's location: 1-2 weeks
Ongoing field training & support

BUSINESS SUPPORT
Newsletter
Toll-free phone line
Grand opening
Internet
Lease negotiations
Security/safety procedures
Field operations/evaluations
Purchasing cooperatives

MARKETING SUPPORT
Co-op advertising
Ad slicks

KABLOOM
Ranked #394 in Entrepreneur Magazine's 2004 Franchise 500   *Financial rating: $$$$*

200 Wildwood Ave.
Woburn, MA 01801
Ph: (781)935-6500
Fax: (781)935-9410
www.kabloom.com
Full-service floral retailer
Began: 1998, Franchising since: 2001
Headquarters size: 30 employees
Franchise department: 7 employees

U.S. franchises: 31
Canadian franchises: 0
Other foreign franchises: 0
Company-owned: 9
Units concentrated in all U.S.

Seeking: All U.S.
Seeking in Canada? No
Exclusive territories? Yes
Homebased option? No
Kiosk option? Yes
Employees needed to run franchise: 3-6
Absentee ownership? Yes

COSTS
Total cost: $143K-212K
Kiosk cost: $70K-100K
Franchise fee: $30K
Royalty fee: 4.5-5.5%
Term of agreement: 10 years renewable
   at no charge
Franchisees required to buy multiple
   units? No

FINANCING
In-house: None
3rd-party: Equipment, franchise fee,
   inventory, start-up costs

QUALIFICATIONS
Net worth: $150K
Cash liquidity: $50K

TRAINING
At headquarters: 4 weeks

BUSINESS SUPPORT
Newsletter
Meetings
Toll-free phone line
Grand opening
Internet
Lease negotiations
Security/safety procedures
Field operations/evaluations

MARKETING SUPPORT
Co-op advertising
Ad slicks
National media campaign
Regional marketing

BIG PICTURE FRAMING

Current financial data not available

855 Highland Ave.
Needham, MA 02494
Ph: (800)315-0024, Fax: (781)444-4291
www.bigpictureframing.com
Custom picture framing & ready-
   made frames
Began: 2000, Franchising since: 2003
Headquarters size: 20 employees
Franchise department: Info not pro-
   vided

U.S. franchises: 0
Canadian franchises: 0
Other foreign franchises: 0
Company-owned: 4

Seeking: All U.S.
Seeking in Canada? No
Exclusive territories? Y
Homebased option? No
Kiosk option? No
Employees needed to run franchise: 3-4
Absentee ownership? Info not provided

COSTS
Total cost: $120K-150K
Franchise fee: $25K
Royalty fee: 5.5%
Term of agreement: 10 years renewable
Franchisees required to buy multiple
   units? No

FINANCING
In-house: None
3rd-party: Equipment, inventory,
   start-up costs

QUALIFICATIONS
Info not provided

TRAINING
At headquarters: 2 weeks
At franchisee's location: 1/2 week

BUSINESS SUPPORT
Meetings
Toll-free phone line
Grand opening
Internet
Security/safety procedures
Field operations/evaluations
Purchasing cooperatives

MARKETING SUPPORT
Ad slicks
Regional marketing

DECK THE WALLS

Ranked #383 in Entrepreneur Magazine's 2004 Franchise 500

Financial rating: $$$$

P.O. Box 1187
Houston, TX 77251-1187
Ph: (800)543-3325/(281)775-5206
Fax: (281)775-5250
www.dtwfraninfo.com
Art, custom framing, wall decor
Began: 1979, Franchising since: 1979
Headquarters size: 29 employees
Franchise department: 6 employees

U.S. franchises: 129
Canadian franchises: 0
Other foreign franchises: 0
Company-owned: 0
Units concentrated in all U.S.

Seeking: All U.S.
Seeking in Canada? No
Exclusive territories? No
Homebased option? No
Kiosk option? No
Employees needed to run franchise: 2-4
Absentee ownership? Yes

COSTS
Total cost: $147.1K-267.4K
Franchise fee: $30K
Royalty fee: 6%
Term of agreement: 10 years renewable
   at no charge
Franchisees required to buy multiple
   units? No

FINANCING
In-house: None
3rd-party: Equipment, franchise fee,
   inventory, payroll, start-up costs

QUALIFICATIONS
Net worth: $250K
Cash liquidity: $75K
Experience:
   General business experience
   People skills

TRAINING
At headquarters: 2 weeks
At franchisee's location: 1 week
Convention & trade shows: 3-5 days

BUSINESS SUPPORT
Newsletter
Meetings
Toll-free phone line
Grand opening
Internet
Lease negotiations
Security/safety procedures
Field operations/evaluations
Purchasing cooperatives

MARKETING SUPPORT
Co-op advertising
Ad slicks
National media campaign
Regional marketing
Local marketing support
Direct mail

FASTFRAME USA INC.
Ranked #86 in Entrepreneur Magazine's 2004 Franchise 500

Financial rating: $$$$

1200 Lawrence Dr., #300
Newbury Park, CA 91320
Ph: (800)333-3225
Fax: (805)498-8983
www.fastframe.com
Custom picture framing & art sales
Began: 1986, Franchising since: 1987
Headquarters size: 17 employees
Franchise department: 3 employees

U.S. franchises: 247
Canadian franchises: 0
Other foreign franchises: 8
Company-owned: 9
Units concentrated in all U.S.

Seeking: All U.S.
Seeking in Canada? No
Exclusive territories? Yes
Homebased option? No
Kiosk option? No
Employees needed to run franchise: 2
Absentee ownership? Yes

COSTS
Total cost: $94.8K-139.3K
Franchise fee: $25K
Royalty fee: 7.5%
Term of agreement: 10 years renewable
for 25% of current franchise fee
Franchisees required to buy multiple
units? No

FINANCING
In-house: Franchise fee
3rd-party: Equipment, franchise fee,
inventory, start-up costs

QUALIFICATIONS
Net worth: $150K
Cash liquidity: $40K
Experience:
General business experience

TRAINING
At headquarters: 2 weeks
At franchisee's location: 1 week
At regional locations: 1-2 days

BUSINESS SUPPORT
Newsletter
Meetings
Toll-free phone line
Grand opening
Internet
Lease negotiations
Security/safety procedures
Field operations/evaluations
Purchasing cooperatives

MARKETING SUPPORT
Co-op advertising
Ad slicks
National media campaign
Regional marketing
Consumer Web site

THE GREAT FRAME UP
Ranked #173 in Entrepreneur Magazine's 2004 Franchise 500

Financial rating: $$$$

P.O. Box 1187
Houston, TX 77251-1187
Ph: (800)543-3325/(281)775-5200
Fax: (281)872-1646
www.tgfufraninfo.com
Art & custom framing services
Began: 1971, Franchising since: 1975
Headquarters size: 29 employees
Franchise department: 6 employees

U.S. franchises: 135
Canadian franchises: 0
Other foreign franchises: 0
Company-owned: 0
Units concentrated in CO, GA, IL

Seeking: All U.S.
Seeking in Canada? No
Exclusive territories? Yes
Homebased option? No
Kiosk option? No
Employees needed to run franchise: 2-4
Absentee ownership? Yes

COSTS
Total cost: $126.1K-162K
Franchise fee: $30K
Royalty fee: 6%
Term of agreement: 10 years renewable
at no charge
Franchisees required to buy multiple
units? No

FINANCING
3rd-party: Equipment, franchise fee,
inventory, payroll, start-up costs
Other: Working capital

QUALIFICATIONS
Net worth: $200K
Cash liquidity: $30K
Experience:
General business experience
Marketing skills
People skills

TRAINING
At headquarters: 2 weeks
At franchisee's location: 1 week
Convention & trade shows: 3-5 days

BUSINESS SUPPORT
Newsletter
Meetings
Toll-free phone line
Grand opening
Internet
Lease negotiations
Security/safety procedures
Field operations/evaluations
Purchasing cooperatives

MARKETING SUPPORT
Co-op advertising
Ad slicks
National media campaign
Regional marketing
Direct-mail program for local markets

ASHLEY AVERY'S HOME COLLECTION

Financial rating: $$$

333 N. Sam Houston Pkwy. E., #690
Houston, TX 77060
Ph: (281)820-0789
Fax: (281)820-2025
www.ashleyaverys.com
Gifts, collectibles, home decor
Began: 1983, Franchising since: 1990
Headquarters size: 10 employees
Franchise department: 3 employees

U.S. franchises: 23
Canadian franchises: 0
Other foreign franchises: 0
Company-owned: 2
Units concentrated in CA, FL, GA, TX

Seeking: All U.S.
Seeking in Canada? No
Exclusive territories? Yes
Homebased option? No
Kiosk option? Yes
Employees needed to run franchise: 2-5
Absentee ownership? Yes

COSTS
Total cost: $272K-403K
Kiosk cost: $95K
Franchise fee: $30K
Royalty fee: 6%
Term of agreement: 10 years renewable
    at no charge
Franchisees required to buy multiple
    units? No

FINANCING
No financing available

QUALIFICATIONS
Net worth: $400K
Cash liquidity: $150K
Experience:
    General business experience
    Marketing skills
    People skills
    Customer service experience

TRAINING
At headquarters: 6 days
At franchisee's location: 1-2 weeks
Conventions: 2-3 days

BUSINESS SUPPORT
Newsletter
Meetings
Toll-free phone line
Grand opening
Internet
Security/safety procedures
Field operations/evaluations
Purchasing cooperatives

MARKETING SUPPORT
Co-op advertising
Ad slicks
National media campaign
Regional marketing

CANDLEMAN CORP.

Current financial data not available

1120 Industrial Park Rd., P.O. Box 731
Brainerd, MN 56401
Ph: (800)328-3453/(218)829-0592
Fax: (218)825-2449
www.candleman.com
Candles, candleholders, accessories
Began: 1992, Franchising since: 1992
Headquarters size: 10 employees
Franchise department: 10 employees

U.S. franchises: 30
Canadian franchises: 2
Other foreign franchises: 8
Company-owned: 1
Units concentrated in all U.S.

Seeking: All U.S.
Seeking in Canada? Yes
Exclusive territories? Yes
Homebased option? No
Kiosk option? No
Employees needed to run franchise: 4
Absentee ownership? No

COSTS
Total cost: $155.9K-329.5K
Franchise fee: $35K
Royalty fee: 6%
Term of agreement: 10 years renewable
    at no charge
Franchisees required to buy multiple
    units? No

FINANCING
In-house: None
3rd-party: Equipment, inventory,
    start-up costs

QUALIFICATIONS
Cash liquidity: $50K-70K
Experience:
    General business experience

TRAINING
At headquarters: 7 days
At franchisee's location: 7 days

BUSINESS SUPPORT
Newsletter
Meetings
Toll-free phone line
Grand opening
Internet
Security/safety procedures
Field operations/evaluations

MARKETING SUPPORT
Co-op advertising
Ad slicks
National media campaign
Regional marketing
Posters
Special buys

COUNTRY CLUTTER

Ranked #414 in Entrepreneur Magazine's 2004 Franchise 500

Financial rating: $$$$

3333 Vaca Valley Pkwy., #900
Vacaville, CA 95688
Ph: (800)425-8883/(707)451-6890
Fax: (707)451-0410
www.countryclutterfranchise.com
Country gifts, collectibles, home decor
Began: 1991, Franchising since: 1992
Headquarters size: 20 employees
Franchise department: 3 employees

U.S. franchises: 59
Canadian franchises: 0
Other foreign franchises: 0
Company-owned: 3
Units concentrated in CA, GA, TX

Seeking: All U.S.
Seeking in Canada? No
Exclusive territories? No
Homebased option? No
Kiosk option? No
Employees needed to run franchise: 5
Absentee ownership? No

COSTS

Total cost: $153.9K-348.5K
Franchise fee: $25K
Royalty fee: 5.5%
Term of agreement: 10 years renewable
    at no charge
Franchisees required to buy multiple
    units? No

FINANCING

In-house: None
3rd-party: Equipment, inventory,
    start-up costs

QUALIFICATIONS

Net worth: $200K+
Cash liquidity: $60K+

TRAINING

At headquarters: 4 days
At franchisee's location: 6 days
Internet training: 20-30 hours

BUSINESS SUPPORT

Newsletter
Meetings
Toll-free phone line
Grand opening
Internet
Lease negotiations
Security/safety procedures
Field operations/evaluations
Purchasing cooperatives

MARKETING SUPPORT

Ad slicks
Customized marketing program

SHEFIELD & SONS

Current financial data not available

2265 W. Railway St., P.O. Box 490
Abbotsford, BC Canada V2S 5Z5
Ph: (604)859-1014
Fax: (604)859-1711
www.shefieldgourmet.com
Tobacco products & gifts
Began: 1976, Franchising since: 1976
Headquarters size: 19 employees
Franchise department: 2 employees

U.S. franchises: 0
Canadian franchises: 63
Other foreign franchises: 0
Company-owned: 4
Units concentrated in Canada

Not available in the U.S.
Seeking in Canada? Yes
Exclusive territories? No
Homebased option? No
Kiosk option? Yes
Employees needed to run franchise:
    Info not provided
Absentee ownership? Yes

COSTS

Total cost: $110K-200K
Kiosk cost: $55K
Franchise fee: $10K
Royalty fee: 2%
Term of agreement: 5 years renewable
    for $5K
Franchisees required to buy multiple
    units? No

FINANCING

No financing available

QUALIFICATIONS

Net worth: $150K
Experience:
    General business experience

TRAINING

At franchisee's location: 2 weeks

BUSINESS SUPPORT

Newsletter
Toll-free phone line
Grand opening
Internet
Lease negotiations
Security/safety procedures
Field operations/evaluations
Purchasing cooperatives

MARKETING SUPPORT

Co-op advertising
Ad slicks
National media campaign

ATLANTIC MOWER PARTS & SUPPLIES INC.

Current financial data not available

13421 S.W. 14th Pl.
Ft. Lauderdale, FL 33325
Ph: (954)474-4942
Fax: (954)475-0414
www.ampsdist.com
Lawn-mower replacement parts
Began: 1978, Franchising since: 1988
Headquarters size: 4 employees
Franchise department: Info not provided

U.S. franchises: 10
Canadian franchises: 0
Other foreign franchises: 0
Company-owned: 0
Units concentrated in FL

Seeking: All U.S.
Seeking in Canada? No
Exclusive territories? Yes
Homebased option? Yes
Kiosk option? No
Employees needed to run franchise: 1
Absentee ownership? No

COSTS
Total cost: $50K
Franchise fee: $15.9K
Royalty fee: 5%
Term of agreement: 10 years renewable at no charge
Franchisees required to buy multiple units? No

FINANCING
No financing available

QUALIFICATIONS
Net worth: $250K
Cash liquidity: $75K

TRAINING
At headquarters: 2 weeks

BUSINESS SUPPORT
Grand opening
Internet
Purchasing cooperatives

MARKETING SUPPORT
Regional marketing

1ST PROPANE FRANCHISING INC.

Financial rating: 0

14670 Cantova Wy., #208
Rancho Murieta, CA 95683
Ph: (916)354-4022
Fax: (916)354-1533
www.1st-propane.com
Bulk propane distribution
Began: 1990, Franchising since: 1998
Headquarters size: 4 employees
Franchise department: 4 employees

U.S. franchises: 12
Canadian franchises: 0
Other foreign franchises: 0
Company-owned: 0
Units concentrated in all U.S.

Seeking: All U.S.
Seeking in Canada? No
Exclusive territories? Yes
Homebased option? Yes
Kiosk option? No
Employees needed to run franchise: 1-5
Absentee ownership? Yes

COSTS
Total cost: $176.6K-442.5K
Franchise fee: $30K
Royalty fee: 6%
Term of agreement: 10 years renewable for $20K
Franchisees required to buy multiple units? No

FINANCING
In-house: None
3rd-party: Equipment

QUALIFICATIONS
Net worth: $250K
Cash liquidity: $100K
Experience:
    General business experience
    Marketing skills
    Organizational skills

TRAINING
At headquarters: 1 week
At franchisee's location: 3 weeks

BUSINESS SUPPORT
Newsletter
Meetings
Toll-free phone line
Grand opening
Internet
Lease negotiations
Security/safety procedures
Field operations/evaluations

MARKETING SUPPORT
Ad slicks
Planning & strategy assistance

MATCO TOOLS

Ranked #32 in Entrepreneur Magazine's 2004 Franchise 500   *Financial rating: $$$$*

4403 Allen Rd.
Stow, OH 44224
Ph: (888)696-2826/(330)929-4949
Fax: (330)926-5325
www.matcotools.com
Automotive/professional tools &
    equipment
Began: 1979, Franchising since: 1993
Headquarters size: 150 employees
Franchise department: 4 employees

U.S. franchises: 1,336
Canadian franchises: 0
Other foreign franchises: 0
Company-owned: 18
Units concentrated in all U.S.

Seeking: All U.S.
Seeking in Canada? No
Exclusive territories? No
Homebased option? Yes
Kiosk option? No
Employees needed to run franchise: 0
Absentee ownership? No

COSTS
Total cost: $60K-158K
Franchise fee: $0
Royalty fee: 0
Term of agreement: 10 years renewable
    at no charge
Franchisees required to buy multiple
    units? No

FINANCING
In-house: Accounts receivable, equip-
    ment, inventory
3rd-party: Accounts receivable, equip-
    ment, inventory, start-up costs

QUALIFICATIONS
Net worth: $30K
Cash liquidity: $20K-30K

TRAINING
At headquarters: 2 weeks
At franchisee's location: 2 weeks

BUSINESS SUPPORT
Newsletter
Meetings
Toll-free phone line
Internet
Field operations/evaluations

MARKETING SUPPORT
Ad slicks
National media campaign
Regional marketing
Direct-sales meetings
Online support

METAL SUPERMARKETS INT'L.

Current financial data not available

170 Wilkinson Rd., #17 & 18
Brampton, ON Canada L6T 4Z5
Ph: (800)807-8755
Fax: (905)459-3690
www.metalsupermarkets.com
Wholesale & retail metal supplier
Began: 1985, Franchising since: 1987
Headquarters size: 17 employees
Franchise department: 4 employees

U.S. franchises: 37
Canadian franchises: 18
Other foreign franchises: 13
Company-owned: 21
Units concentrated in all U.S.

Seeking: All U.S.
Seeking in Canada? Yes
Exclusive territories? Yes
Homebased option? No
Kiosk option? No
Employees needed to run franchise: 3
Absentee ownership? No

COSTS
Total cost: $225K-275K
Franchise fee: $39.5K
Royalty fee: 6%
Term of agreement: 10 years renewable
    for $7.5K
Franchisees required to buy multiple
    units? Outside the U.S. only

FINANCING
No financing available

QUALIFICATIONS
Net worth: $250K
Cash liquidity: $100K-125K
Experience:
    General business experience
    Marketing skills

TRAINING
At headquarters: 3 weeks
At franchisee's location: 2 weeks

BUSINESS SUPPORT
Newsletter
Meetings
Toll-free phone line
Grand opening
Internet
Lease negotiations
Security/safety procedures
Field operations/evaluations

MARKETING SUPPORT
Ad slicks

SNAP-ON TOOLS
Ranked #20 in Entrepreneur Magazine's 2004 Franchise 500

Financial rating: $$$$

2801 80th St., P.O. Box 1410
Kenosha, WI 53141-1410
Ph: (800)756-3344
Fax: (262)656-5088
www.snapon.com
Professional tools & equipment
Began: 1920, Franchising since: 1991
Headquarters size: Info not provided
Franchise department: 10 employees

U.S. franchises: 3,438
Canadian franchises: 355
Other foreign franchises: 855
Company-owned: 66
Units concentrated in all U.S.

Seeking: All U.S.
Seeking in Canada? Yes
Exclusive territories? No
Homebased option? Yes
Kiosk option? No
Employees needed to run franchise: 0
Absentee ownership? No

COSTS
Total cost: $17.6K-254.7K
Franchise fee: $5K
Royalty fee: $50/mo.
Term of agreement: 10 years renewable
    for 50% of current license fee
Franchisees required to buy multiple
    units? No

FINANCING
In-house: None
3rd-party: Accounts receivable, franchise fee, inventory

QUALIFICATIONS
Net worth: $30K
Cash liquidity: $37.4K-47.8K

TRAINING
At franchisee's location: 3 weeks
At branch & regional centers:
    1 week each

BUSINESS SUPPORT
Newsletter
Meetings
Toll-free phone line
Grand opening
Internet
Security/safety procedures
Field operations/evaluations

MARKETING SUPPORT
Info not provided

SUPPLY MASTER USA

Financial rating: $$$

6C White Deer Plaza
Sparta, NJ 07871
Ph: (800)582-1947/(973)729-5006
Fax: (973)729-1975
www.supplymasterusa.com
Mobile distribution of commercial &
    industrial products
Began: 1989, Franchising since: 2001
Headquarters size: 3 employees
Franchise department: 1 employee

U.S. franchises: 3
Canadian franchises: 0
Other foreign franchises: 0
Company-owned: 1
Units concentrated in all U.S.

Seeking: All U.S.
Seeking in Canada? No
Exclusive territories? Yes
Homebased option? Yes
Kiosk option? No
Employees needed to run franchise: 0
Absentee ownership? Yes

COSTS
Total cost: $12.95K-22.7K
Franchise fee: $4.5K-10K
Royalty fee: $25-100/wk.
Term of agreement: 5 years renewable
    for 10% of current franchise fee
Franchisees required to buy multiple
    units? No

FINANCING
No financing available

QUALIFICATIONS
Net worth: $25K-35K
Cash liquidity: $15K-20K
Experience:
    Industry experience
    General business experience

TRAINING
At headquarters: 4 days
At franchisee's location: 2 days

BUSINESS SUPPORT
Meetings
Toll-free phone line
Field operations/evaluations

MARKETING SUPPORT
Ad slicks
Regional marketing

GATEWAY CIGAR STORE/NEWSTANDS
Ranked #96 in Entrepreneur Magazine's 2004 Franchise 500

Financial rating: $$$$

9555 Yonge St., #400
Richmond Hill, ON Canada L4C 9M5
Ph: (905)737-7755, Fax: (905)737-7757
www.gatewaynewstands.com
Newsstand & sundry store
Began: 1983, Franchising since: 1983
Headquarters size: 20 employees
Franchise department: 4 employees

U.S. franchises: 135
Canadian franchises: 231
Other foreign franchises: 0
Company-owned: 0
Units concentrated in all U.S.

Seeking: All U.S.
Seeking in Canada? Yes
Exclusive territories? No
Homebased option? No
Kiosk option? No
Employees needed to run franchise: 1-2
Absentee ownership? Yes

COSTS
Total cost: $55.9K-362.8K
Franchise fee: $15K-125K
Royalty fee: 3%
Term of agreement: 5, 7 or 10 years
    renewable
Franchisees required to buy multiple
    units? No

FINANCING
In-house: None
3rd-party: Start-up costs

QUALIFICATIONS
Net worth: $200K
Cash liquidity: $75K
Experience:
    General business experience

TRAINING
At franchisee's location: 2 days to
    1 week

BUSINESS SUPPORT
Newsletter
Toll-free phone line
Grand opening
Internet
Lease negotiations
Security/safety procedures
Field operations/evaluations
Purchasing cooperatives

MARKETING SUPPORT
Head office & field support

STREET CORNER

Current financial data not available

2945 S.W. Wanamaker Dr.
Topeka, KS 66614
Ph: (785)272-8529. Fax: (785)272-2384
www.streetcornernews.com
Mall-based newsstand/convenience
    stores
Began: 1988, Franchising since: 1995
Headquarters size: 7 employees
Franchise department: 4 employees

U.S. franchises: 34
Canadian franchises: 0
Other foreign franchises: 0
Company-owned: 0
Units concentrated in all U.S.

Seeking: All U.S.
Seeking in Canada? No
Exclusive territories? Yes
Homebased option? No
Kiosk option? Yes
Employees needed to run franchise: 2
Absentee ownership? Yes

COSTS
Total cost: $85K-120K
Kiosk cost: $100K
Franchise fee: $19.9K
Royalty fee: 4.5%
Term of agreement: 7 years renewable
    for $2.5K
Franchisees required to buy multiple
    units? No

FINANCING
In-house: None
3rd-party: Accounts receivable, equip-
    ment, franchise fee, inventory, pay-
    roll, start-up costs

QUALIFICATIONS
Net worth: $150K
Cash liquidity: $30K

TRAINING
At headquarters: Upon request
At franchisee's location: 1 week

BUSINESS SUPPORT
Newsletter
Meetings
Toll-free phone line
Grand opening
Internet
Lease negotiations
Security/safety procedures
Field operations/evaluations
Purchasing cooperatives

MARKETING SUPPORT
Ad slicks
National media campaign
Regional marketing
Store marketing reviews

RETAIL   *Pharmacies*

MEDICAP PHARMACIES INC.

Ranked #421 in Entrepreneur Magazine's 2004 Franchise 500   *Financial rating: $$*

1100 N. Lindbergh Blvd.
St. Louis, MO 63132
Ph: (314)993-6000, Fax: (314)872-5500
www.medicap.com
Pharmacy
Began: 1971, Franchising since: 1974
Headquarters size: 60 employees
Franchise department: 55 employees

U.S. franchises: 159
Canadian franchises: 0
Other foreign franchises: 0
Company-owned: 13
Units concentrated in most of the U.S.

Seeking: All U.S.
Seeking in Canada? No
Exclusive territories? Yes
Homebased option? No
Kiosk option? No
Employees needed to run franchise: 2
Absentee ownership? Yes

COSTS
Total cost: $22.1K-447K
Franchise fee: $3K-15K
Royalty fee: 2-3.9%
Term of agreement: 20 years renewable
    at no charge
Franchisees required to buy multiple
    units? No

FINANCING
In-house: Start-up costs
3rd-party: Accounts receivable, equip-
    ment, franchise fee, inventory,
    start-up costs

QUALIFICATIONS
Cash liquidity: $55K

TRAINING
At headquarters: 5 days
At franchisee's location: Ongoing

BUSINESS SUPPORT
Newsletter
Meetings
Toll-free phone line
Grand opening
Internet
Lease negotiations
Field operations/evaluations

MARKETING SUPPORT
Ad slicks
National media campaign
Regional marketing
TV, radio & billboard ads

MEDICINE SHOPPE INT'L. INC.

Ranked #37 in Entrepreneur Magazine's 2004 Franchise 500   *Financial rating: $$$$*

1100 N. Lindbergh Blvd.
St. Louis, MO 63132
Ph: (314)993-6000
Fax: (314)872-5500
www.medicineshoppe.com
Pharmacy
Began: 1970, Franchising since: 1970
Headquarters size: 220 employees
Franchise department: 20 employees

U.S. franchises: 1,075
Canadian franchises: 76
Other foreign franchises: 154
Company-owned: 34
Units concentrated in all U.S.

Seeking: All U.S.
Seeking in Canada? No
Exclusive territories? Yes
Homebased option? No
Kiosk option? No
Employees needed to run franchise: 3-4
Absentee ownership? Yes

COSTS
Total cost: $74.3K-253.4K
Franchise fee: $10K-18K
Royalty fee: 2-5.5%
Term of agreement: 20 years renewable
    at no charge
Franchisees required to buy multiple
    units? Outside the U.S. only

FINANCING
In-house: Accounts receivable, equip-
    ment, inventory, payroll, start-up
    costs
3rd-party: None

QUALIFICATIONS
Experience:
    Must be pharmacist or must hire
    one for store

TRAINING
At headquarters: 6 days
At franchisee's location: Twice a year
Regional meetings & field seminars:
    1-2 days

BUSINESS SUPPORT
Newsletter
Meetings
Toll-free phone line
Grand opening
Internet
Security/safety procedures
Field operations/evaluations
Purchasing cooperatives

MARKETING SUPPORT
Co-op advertising
Ad slicks
National media campaign
Regional marketing

RETAIL   *Wireless*

@WIRELESS

Ranked #296 in Entrepreneur Magazine's 2004 Franchise 500   *Financial rating: $$$$*

50 Methodist Hill Dr., #1500
Rochester, NY 14623
Ph: (800)613-2355, Fax: (585)359-3253
www.shopatwireless.com
Wireless phones, satellite TV, high-tech toys
Began: 1994, Franchising since: 2000
Headquarters size: 20 employees
Franchise department: 2 employees

U.S. franchises: 53
Canadian franchises: 0
Other foreign franchises: 0
Company-owned: 1
Units concentrated in all U.S. except HI, MN, ND, SD, WA, WI

Seeking: All U.S.
Seeking in Canada? No
Exclusive territories? Yes
Homebased option? No
Kiosk option? Yes
Employees needed to run franchise: 2
Absentee ownership? No

COSTS
Total cost: $70.5K-131.9K
Kiosk cost: $31K-75K
Franchise fee: $15K
Royalty fee: 5-10%
Term of agreement: 10 years renewable for $10K
Franchisees required to buy multiple units? No

FINANCING
In-house: Accounts receivable, inventory
3rd-party: Equipment

QUALIFICATIONS
Net worth: $150K
Cash liquidity: $20K-25K
Experience:
    Industry experience
    General business experience

TRAINING
At headquarters: 1 week
At franchisee's location: 1 week
Ongoing

BUSINESS SUPPORT
Newsletter
Meetings
Toll-free phone line
Grand opening
Internet
Lease negotiations
Security/safety procedures
Field operations/evaluations
Purchasing cooperatives

MARKETING SUPPORT
Co-op advertising
Ad slicks
Regional marketing
Web site

RADIOSHACK

Ranked #26 in Entrepreneur Magazine's 2004 Franchise 500   *Financial rating: $$$$*

300 W. 3rd St., #1600
Ft. Worth, TX 76102
Ph: (817)415-3499
Fax: (817)415-8651
www.radioshack.com
Consumer electronics
Began: 1921, Franchising since: 1968
Headquarters size: 2,000 employees
Franchise department: 150 employees

U.S. franchises: 1,898
Canadian franchises: 0
Other foreign franchises: 55
Company-owned: 5,142
Units concentrated in all U.S.

Seeking: All U.S.
Seeking in Canada? Yes
Exclusive territories? No
Homebased option? No
Kiosk option? No
Employees needed to run franchise: 2
Absentee ownership? No

COSTS
Total cost: $60K
Franchise fee: $30K
Royalty fee: 0
Term of agreement: 10 years renewable at no charge
Franchisees required to buy multiple units? No

FINANCING
In-house: Franchise fee, inventory
3rd-party: None

QUALIFICATIONS
Experience:
    Existing retail business

TRAINING
At franchisee's location: 1 week
Local workshop & annual convention

BUSINESS SUPPORT
Newsletter
Meetings
Toll-free phone line
Grand opening
Internet
Field operations/evaluations

MARKETING SUPPORT
Co-op advertising
Ad slicks
National media campaign

WIRELESS DIMENSIONS

Ranked #462 in Entrepreneur Magazine's 2004 Franchise 500   *Financial rating: $$$$*

1591 Robert J. Conlan Blvd. N.E., #128
Palm Bay, FL 32905
Ph: (888)809-4934
Fax: (321)952-5788
www.wireless-dimensions.com
Wireless accessories
Began: 2002, Franchising since: 2002
Headquarters size: 25 employees
Franchise department: 5 employees

U.S. franchises: 139
Canadian franchises: 0
Other foreign franchises: 0
Company-owned: 0
Units concentrated in Midwest,
      Northeast & Southeast

Seeking: All U.S.
Seeking in Canada? Yes
Exclusive territories? Yes
Homebased option? No
Kiosk option? Yes
Employees needed to run franchise: 0-4
Absentee ownership? Yes

COSTS
Total cost: $23K-34K
Kiosk cost: Same as total cost
Franchise fee: $6.9K
Royalty fee: 6%
Term of agreement: 4 years renewable
      at no charge
Franchisees required to buy multiple
      units? No

FINANCING
In-house: Franchise fee
3rd-party: None

QUALIFICATIONS
Info not provided

TRAINING
At headquarters: 1 week
At franchisee's location: 1 week

BUSINESS SUPPORT
Newsletter
Meetings
Toll-free phone line
Grand opening
Internet
Field operations/evaluations
Purchasing cooperatives

MARKETING SUPPORT
Ad slicks
Regional marketing

WIRELESS TOYZ

Ranked #438 in Entrepreneur Magazine's 2004 Franchise 500   *Financial rating: $$$*

23399 Commerce Dr.
Farmington Hills, MI 48335
Ph: (866)237-2624/(248)426-8200
Fax: (801)858-8285
www.wirelesstoyz.com
Cellular phones, satellite systems,
      accessories
Began: 1995, Franchising since: 2001
Headquarters size: 10 employees
Franchise department: 4 employees

U.S. franchises: 24
Canadian franchises: 0
Other foreign franchises: 0
Company-owned: 3

Seeking: All U.S.
Focusing on: AK, AL, AR, AZ, CO, DE,
      FL, GA, IA, ID, IL, IN, KS, LA, MA,
      ME, MI, MO, MS, MT, NE, NH,
      NJ, NM, NV, OH, OK, OR, PA, SC,
      TN, TX, UT, VT, WV, WY
Seeking in Canada? No
Exclusive territories? Yes
Homebased option? No
Kiosk option? No
Employees needed to run franchise: 4
Absentee ownership? No

COSTS
Total cost: $116.3K-231.5K
Franchise fee: $20K
Royalty fee: 0
Term of agreement: 15 years renewable
      for $10K
Franchisees required to buy multiple
      units? No

FINANCING
In-house: None
3rd-party: Accounts receivable, equip-
      ment, franchise fee, inventory, pay-
      roll, start-up costs

QUALIFICATIONS
Net worth: $100K
Cash liquidity: $40K
Experience:
      General business experience

TRAINING
At headquarters: 4 weeks
At franchisee's location: 1 week

BUSINESS SUPPORT
Meetings
Toll-free phone line
Grand opening
Internet
Security/safety procedures
Field operations/evaluations
Purchasing cooperatives

MARKETING SUPPORT
Co-op advertising
Ad slicks
Regional marketing

WIRELESS ZONE

Ranked #165 in Entrepreneur Magazine's 2004 Franchise 500   *Financial rating: $$$$*

34 Industrial Park Pl.
Middletown, CT 06457
Ph: (860)632-9494, Fax: (860)632-9343
www.wirelesszone.com
Wireless communications store
Began: 1988, Franchising since: 1989
Headquarters size: 35 employees
Franchise department: 14 employees

U.S. franchises: 156
Canadian franchises: 0
Other foreign franchises: 0
Company-owned: 1
Units concentrated in CT, DE, MA, MD,
  ME, NH, NJ, NY, PA, RI, VA, VT

Seeking: Northeast, Southeast
Focusing on: CT, FL, IL, MA, MD, ME,
  MO, NH, NJ, NY, PA, RI, VA, VT
Seeking in Canada? No
Exclusive territories? Yes
Homebased option? No
Kiosk option? Yes
Employees needed to run franchise: 4
Absentee ownership? No

COSTS
Total cost: $42.4K-145.8K
Kiosk cost: Same as total cost
Franchise fee: $7.5K-25K
Royalty fee: Varies
Term of agreement: 7 years renewable
  for $7.5K
Franchisees required to buy multiple
  units? No

FINANCING
In-house: Franchise fee, inventory
3rd-party: None

QUALIFICATIONS
Experience:
  Industry experience
  General business experience
  Marketing skills
  2 years franchise experience

TRAINING
At headquarters
At franchisee's location: Ongoing
Biannual seminars

BUSINESS SUPPORT
Newsletter
Meetings
Grand opening
Internet
Field operations/evaluations

MARKETING SUPPORT
Co-op advertising
Ad slicks
Regional marketing
PR support

RETAIL   *Miscellaneous*

AARON'S SALES & LEASE OWNERSHIP

Ranked #65 in Entrepreneur Magazine's 2004 Franchise 500   *Financial rating: $$$$*

309 E. Paces Ferry Rd.
Atlanta, GA 30305-2377
Ph: (800)551-6015, x3385,
Fax: (678)402-3540
www.aaronsfranchise.com
Furniture, electronics, computer &
  appliance leasing & sales
Began: 1955, Franchising since: 1992
Headquarters size: Info not provided
Franchise department: Info not pro-
  vided

U.S. franchises: 217
Canadian franchises: 0
Other foreign franchises: 0
Company-owned: 425

Seeking: All U.S.
Seeking in Canada? No
Exclusive territories? Yes
Homebased option? No
Kiosk option? No
Employees needed to run franchise:
  7-10
Absentee ownership? Yes

COSTS
Total cost: $263K-543K
Franchise fee: $35K
Royalty fee: 6%
Term of agreement: 10 years renewable
  for $2.5K
Franchisees required to buy multiple
  units? No

FINANCING
In-house: None
3rd-party: Inventory

QUALIFICATIONS
Net worth: $450K
Cash liquidity: $250K
Experience:
  General business experience

TRAINING
At headquarters: 3 days
At franchisee's location: Less than 30
  days
At regional locations: 1 week

BUSINESS SUPPORT
Newsletter
Meetings
Toll-free phone line
Grand opening
Internet
Lease negotiations
Security/safety procedures
Field operations/evaluations
Purchasing cooperatives

MARKETING SUPPORT
Co-op advertising
Ad slicks
National media campaign
Regional marketing
NASCAR sponsorship

AIR TRAFFIC RETAIL FRANCHISE SYSTEMS

Financial rating: $$

451 Cliff Rd. E., #106
Burnsville, MN 55337
Ph: (952)895-5555
Fax: (952)707-9900
www.airtrafficinc.com
Specialty retail store selling flying toys,
    kites & juggling equipment
Began: 1993, Franchising since: 2003
Headquarters size: 9 employees
Franchise department: 3 employees

U.S. franchises: 2
Canadian franchises: 0
Other foreign franchises: 0
Company-owned: 2

Seeking: All U.S.
Seeking in Canada? No
Exclusive territories? Yes
Homebased option? No
Kiosk option? No
Employees needed to run franchise:
    5-10
Absentee ownership? Yes

COSTS
Total cost: $161.2K
Franchise fee: $25K
Royalty fee: 5%
Term of agreement: 10 years renewable
    for $5K
Franchisees required to buy multiple
    units? No

FINANCING
No financing available

QUALIFICATIONS
Net worth: $250K
Cash liquidity: $50K
Experience:
    General business experience
    Must enjoy toys/games

TRAINING
At headquarters: 7 days

BUSINESS SUPPORT
Toll-free phone line
Grand opening
Internet
Security/safety procedures
Field operations/evaluations
Purchasing cooperatives

MARKETING SUPPORT
Co-op advertising

BATTERIES PLUS

Ranked #129 in Entrepreneur Magazine's 2004 Franchise 500

Financial rating: $$$$

925 Walnut Ridge Dr.
Hartland, WI 53029
Ph: (800)274-9155, Fax: (262)369-0680
www.batteriesplus.com
Batteries & related products
Began: 1988, Franchising since: 1992
Headquarters size: 80 employees
Franchise department: 2 employees

U.S. franchises: 196
Canadian franchises: 0
Other foreign franchises: 0
Company-owned: 15
Units concentrated in AZ, CO, FL, IL,
    IN, KY, MI, MS, NC, ND, NM, OK,
    SC, SD, TN, TX, WI

Seeking: All U.S.
Focusing on AL, AR, CA, CT, DE, FL,
    GA, ID, KS, LA, MA, MD, ME, NE,
    NJ, NY, OH, PA, RI, TX, UT, VT,
    WA, WI
Seeking in Canada? No
Exclusive territories? Yes
Homebased option? No
Kiosk option? No
Employees needed to run franchise: 3-4
Absentee ownership? No

COSTS
Total cost: $164.5K-255K
Franchise fee: $25K
Royalty fee: 4%
Term of agreement: 10 years renewable
    for $2K
Franchisees required to buy multiple
    units? No

FINANCING
In-house: None
3rd-party: Accounts receivable, equip-
    ment, inventory, start-up costs

QUALIFICATIONS
Net worth: $500K+
Cash liquidity: $150K+
Experience:
    General business experience
    Marketing skills
    People skills

TRAINING
At headquarters: 3 weeks
At franchisee's location: 2 weeks
Periodic store visits & regional
    meetings

BUSINESS SUPPORT
Newsletter
Meetings
Toll-free phone line
Grand opening
Internet
Lease negotiations
Security/safety procedures
Field operations/evaluations
Purchasing cooperatives

MARKETING SUPPORT
Co-op advertising
Ad slicks
TV & radio ads
POP
Catalogs & literature

CD TRADEPOST

Financial rating: $$

826 S. Kansas Ave.
Topeka, KS 66612
Ph: (785)233-0675
Fax: (785)232-4444
www.cdtradepost.com
Used CDs, videos & video games
Began: 1998, Franchising since: 2002
Headquarters size: 4 employees
Franchise department: 4 employees

U.S. franchises: 2
Canadian franchises: 0
Other foreign franchises: 0
Company-owned: 5
Units concentrated in KS

Seeking: Midwest, South, Southeast, Southwest
Focusing on: AR, CO, IA, KS, MO, NE, OK, TX
Seeking in Canada? No
Exclusive territories? Yes
Homebased option? No
Kiosk option? No
Employees needed to run franchise: 3
Absentee ownership? No

COSTS
Total cost: $85.9K-139.9K
Franchise fee: $18K
Royalty fee: 5-6%
Term of agreement: 10 years renewable for 50% of then-current fee
Franchisees required to buy multiple units? No

FINANCING
No financing available

QUALIFICATIONS
Experience:
  Sales experience
  Management experience

TRAINING
At headquarters: 2 weeks+
At franchisee's location: 1 week+

BUSINESS SUPPORT
Newsletter
Meetings
Grand opening
Internet
Lease negotiations
Security/safety procedures
Field operations/evaluations

MARKETING SUPPORT
Co-op advertising
Ad slicks
National media campaign
Regional marketing
Local campaigns

COLOR ME MINE ENTERPRISES INC.

Ranked #485 in Entrepreneur Magazine's 2004 Franchise 500

Financial rating: $$

5140 Lankershim Blvd.
North Hollywood, CA 91601
Ph: (818)505-2100
Fax: (818)509-9442
www.colormemine.com
Paint-your-own-ceramics studios
Began: 1992, Franchising since: 1995
Headquarters size: 18 employees
Franchise department: 3 employees

U.S. franchises: 58
Canadian franchises: 0
Other foreign franchises: 13
Company-owned: 1
Units concentrated in CA, FL, NJ, PA

Seeking: All U.S.
Seeking in Canada? Yes
Exclusive territories? Yes
Homebased option? No
Kiosk option? No
Employees needed to run franchise: 2-8
Absentee ownership? Yes

COSTS
Total cost: $138.6K-181.3K
Franchise fee: $25K
Royalty fee: 5%
Term of agreement: As long as lease term renewable at no charge
Franchisees required to buy multiple units? No

FINANCING
In-house: Accounts receivable
3rd-party: Equipment, franchise fee, inventory, start-up costs

QUALIFICATIONS
Net worth: $200K+
Cash liquidity: $30K-60K
Experience:
  General business experience
  Marketing skills

TRAINING
At headquarters: 10 days
At franchisee's location: 6 days
Semi-annual workshops

BUSINESS SUPPORT
Newsletter
Meetings
Toll-free phone line
Grand opening
Internet
Lease negotiations
Security/safety procedures
Purchasing cooperatives

MARKETING SUPPORT
Ad slicks
Marketing materials

COLORTYME

Financial rating: 0

5700 Tennyson Pkwy., #180
Plano, TX 75024
Ph: (800)411-8963/(972)608-5376
Fax: (972)403-4936
www.colortyme.com
Rent-to-own electronics, furniture &
    appliances
Began: 1979, Franchising since: 1982
Headquarters size: 20 employees
Franchise department: 1 employee

U.S. franchises: 310
Canadian franchises: 0
Other foreign franchises: 0
Company-owned: 0
Units concentrated in AZ, CT, FL, KS,
    ME, OK, TX, WA

Seeking: All U.S.
Seeking in Canada? No
Exclusive territories? Yes
Homebased option? No
Kiosk option? No
Employees needed to run franchise: 5
Absentee ownership? Yes

COSTS
Total cost: $319.1K-560.5K
Franchise fee: $7.5K-35K
Royalty fee: 2-5%
Term of agreement: 5-10 years renew-
    able at no charge
Franchisees required to buy multiple
    units? No

FINANCING
In-house: None
3rd-party: Inventory

QUALIFICATIONS
Net worth: $300K
Cash liquidity: $120K-160K
Experience:
    Industry experience
    General business experience
    Marketing skills

TRAINING
At headquarters: 2 weeks
At franchisee's location: 2-4 weeks

BUSINESS SUPPORT
Newsletter
Meetings
Grand opening
Internet
Lease negotiations
Field operations/evaluations
Purchasing cooperatives

MARKETING SUPPORT
Co-op advertising
Ad slicks
Direct mail
Local radio & TV ads
POS

CROWN TROPHY INC.

Ranked #188 in Entrepreneur Magazine's 2004 Franchise 500

Financial rating: $$$$

9 Skyline Dr.
Hawthorne, NY 10532
Ph: (800)583-8228
Fax: (914)347-0211
www.crownfranchise.com
Award & recognition items
Began: 1978, Franchising since: 1987
Headquarters size: 10 employees
Franchise department: 5 employees

U.S. franchises: 120
Canadian franchises: 0
Other foreign franchises: 0
Company-owned: 1
Units concentrated in all U.S.

Seeking: All U.S.
Seeking in Canada? No
Exclusive territories? Yes
Homebased option? No
Kiosk option? No
Employees needed to run franchise: 2
Absentee ownership? No

COSTS
Total cost: $115K-144K
Franchise fee: $32K
Royalty fee: 5%
Term of agreement: 5 years renewable
    at no charge
Franchisees required to buy multiple
    units? No

FINANCING
In-house: None
3rd-party: Equipment, inventory,
    start-up costs

QUALIFICATIONS
Cash liquidity: $50K-60K
Experience:
    Marketing skills
    People skills
    Leadership skills

TRAINING
At headquarters: 10 days
At franchisee's location: 1 week

BUSINESS SUPPORT
Newsletter
Meetings
Toll-free phone line
Grand opening
Internet
Lease negotiations
Security/safety procedures
Field operations/evaluations
Purchasing cooperatives

MARKETING SUPPORT
Ad slicks
Regional marketing
In-house marketing materials
Catalogs

DOLLAR DISCOUNT STORES

Ranked #182 in Entrepreneur Magazine's 2004 Franchise 500 *Financial rating: $$$$*

1362 Naamans Creek Rd.
Boothwyn, PA 19061
Ph: (800)227-5314/(888)365-5271
Fax: (610)485-6439
www.dollardiscount.com
Dollar stores
Began: 1982, Franchising since: 1987
Headquarters size: 23 employees
Franchise department: 23 employees

U.S. franchises: 160
Canadian franchises: 0
Other foreign franchises: 0
Company-owned: 0
Units concentrated in all U.S.

Seeking: All U.S.
Seeking in Canada? No
Exclusive territories? Yes
Homebased option? No
Kiosk option? No
Employees needed to run franchise: 4-7
Absentee ownership? Yes

COSTS
Total cost: $99K-195K
Franchise fee: $18K
Royalty fee: 3%
Term of agreement: 10 years renewable
    for 33% of current franchise fee
Franchisees required to buy multiple
    units? No

FINANCING
In-house: None
3rd-party: Accounts receivable, equipment, franchise fee, inventory, payroll, start-up costs

QUALIFICATIONS
Net worth: $100K
Cash liquidity: $20K

TRAINING
At headquarters: 5 days
At franchisee's location: 5-7 days

BUSINESS SUPPORT
Newsletter
Meetings
Toll-free phone line
Grand opening
Internet
Lease negotiations
Security/safety procedures
Field operations/evaluations
Purchasing cooperatives

MARKETING SUPPORT
Ad slicks

ELEPHANT HOUSE

Financial rating: 0

1608 Pine Knoll Dr.
Austin, TX 78758
Ph: (800)276-2405/(512)833-0384
Fax: (512)833-0172
www.elephanthouse.com
Greeting cards
Began: 1991, Franchising since: 1991
Headquarters size: 5 employees
Franchise department: 1 employee

U.S. franchises: 51
Canadian franchises: 12
Other foreign franchises: 217
Company-owned: 0
Units concentrated in all U.S.

Seeking: All U.S.
Seeking in Canada? No
Exclusive territories? Yes
Homebased option? Yes
Kiosk option? No
Employees needed to run franchise: 0
Absentee ownership? Info not provided

COSTS
Total cost: $28K-44.5K
Franchise fee: $10.2K
Royalty fee: 0
Term of agreement: 7 years renewable
    at no charge
Franchisees required to buy multiple
    units? No

FINANCING
No financing available

QUALIFICATIONS
Net worth: $50K-100K
Cash liquidity: $25K-50K
Experience:
    Postive attitude

TRAINING
At franchisee's location: 4 days
Additional training available

BUSINESS SUPPORT
Newsletter
Toll-free phone line

MARKETING SUPPORT
Marketing brochures
National/regional accounts support

HOBBYTOWN USA

Ranked #229 in Entrepreneur Magazine's 2004 Franchise 500   *Financial rating: $$$$*

6301 S. 58th St.
Lincoln, NE 68516
Ph: (800)858-7370
Fax: (402)434-5055
www.hobbytown.com
General hobbies & supplies
Began: 1969, Franchising since: 1986
Headquarters size: 35 employees
Franchise department: 35 employees

U.S. franchises: 141
Canadian franchises: 0
Other foreign franchises: 0
Company-owned: 2
Units concentrated in all U.S.

Seeking: All U.S.
Seeking in Canada? Yes
Exclusive territories? Yes
Homebased option? No
Kiosk option? No
Employees needed to run franchise: 4
Absentee ownership? Yes

COSTS
Total cost: $140K-700K
Franchise fee: $10K-19.5K
Royalty fee: 2.5-3.5%
Term of agreement: 10 years renewable
   for $2K
Franchisees required to buy multiple
   units? No

FINANCING
In-house: None
3rd-party: Equipment, franchise fee,
   inventory, start-up costs

QUALIFICATIONS
Net worth: $100K-300K
Cash liquidity: $35K-175K

TRAINING
At headquarters: 1 week
At franchisee's location: 3 weeks

BUSINESS SUPPORT
Newsletter
Meetings
Toll-free phone line
Grand opening
Internet
Lease negotiations
Security/safety procedures
Field operations/evaluations
Purchasing cooperatives

MARKETING SUPPORT
Co-op advertising
Ad slicks
National media campaign

MUSIC GO ROUND

Financial rating: $$$$

4200 Dahlberg Dr., #100
Minneapolis, MN 55422-4837
Ph: (800)269-4076/(763)520-8582
Fax: (763)520-8501
www.musicgoround.com
Used & new musical instruments,
   sound equipment
Began: 1986, Franchising since: 1994
Headquarters size: 100 employees
Franchise department: 5 employees

U.S. franchises: 43
Canadian franchises: 0
Other foreign franchises: 0
Company-owned: 6
Units concentrated in CA, CO, GA, IA,
   IL, IN, KY, MA, MD, MI, MN, MO,
   MS, NC, ND, NE, NJ, NM, NY,
   OH, OK, PA, TX, UT, WI

Seeking: All U.S.
Seeking in Canada? No
Exclusive territories? Yes
Homebased option? No
Kiosk option? No
Employees needed to run franchise: 3
Absentee ownership? No

COSTS
Total cost: $190.3K-274.6K
Franchise fee: $20K
Royalty fee: 3%
Term of agreement: 10 years renewable
   for $5K
Franchisees required to buy multiple
   units? No

FINANCING
No financing available

QUALIFICATIONS
Net worth: $200K
Cash liquidity: $60K-85K
Experience:
   Industry experience
   General business experience

TRAINING
At headquarters: 2 weeks

BUSINESS SUPPORT
Newsletter
Meetings
Toll-free phone line
Grand opening
Internet
Security/safety procedures
Field operations/evaluations
Purchasing cooperatives

MARKETING SUPPORT
Co-op advertising
Ad slicks
Regional marketing

PARTY AMERICA FRANCHISING INC.

Financial rating: $$$$

Formerly known as Paper Warehouse
980 Atlantic Ave., #103
Alameda, CA 94501
Ph: (510)747-1800
Fax: (510)747-1810
www.partyamerica.com
Party supplies, balloons & cards
Began: 1980; Franchising since: 1987
Headquarters size: 45 employees
Franchise department: 4 employees

U.S. franchises: 51
Canadian franchises: 0
Other foreign franchises: 0
Company-owned: 63

Seeking: All U.S.
Seeking in Canada? Yes
Exclusive territories? Yes
Homebased option? No
Kiosk option? No
Employees need to run franchise: 9-12
Absentee ownership: No

COSTS
Total cost: $250K-400K
Franchise fee: $25K
Royalty fee: 4%
Term of agreement: 10 years renewable
  for 10% of current fee
Franchisees required to buy multiple
  units? Outside the U.S. only

FINANCING
No financing available

QUALIFICATIONS
Net worth: $750K-1M
Cash liquidity: $150K
Experience:
  Industry experience
  General business experience
  Marketing skills
  Customer service skills

TRAINING
At headquarters: 3-5 days
At franchisee's location: 1-2 weeks
At company store: 1-2 weeks

BUSINESS SUPPORT
Meetings
Grand opening
Field operations/evaluations
Purchasing cooperatives

MARKETING SUPPORT
Co-op advertising
Ad slicks
Regional marketing
TV & radio ads

PARTY LAND INC.

Financial rating: 0

5215 Militia Hill Rd.
Plymouth Meeting, PA 19462
Ph: (800)778-9563/(610)941-6200
Fax: (610)941-6301
www.partyland.com
Party supplies & balloons
Began: 1986, Franchising since: 1988
Headquarters size: 20 employees
Franchise department: 4 employees

U.S. franchises: 42
Canadian franchises: 5
Other foreign franchises: 172
Company-owned: 0
Units concentrated in all U.S.

Seeking: All U.S.
Seeking in Canada? Yes
Exclusive territories? Yes
Homebased option? No
Kiosk option? No
Employees needed to run franchise:
  4-12
Absentee ownership? Yes

COSTS
Total cost: $299K
Franchise fee: $35K
Royalty fee: 5%
Term of agreement: 10 years renewable
  for $1K
Franchisees required to buy multiple
  units? No

FINANCING
In-house: None
3rd-party: Accounts receivable, equipment, franchise fee, inventory, payroll, start-up costs

QUALIFICATIONS
Net worth: $250K
Cash liquidity: $80K
Experience:
  General business experience

TRAINING
At headquarters: 1 week
POS training in Toronto: 3 days

BUSINESS SUPPORT
Newsletter
Meetings
Toll-free phone line
Grand opening
Internet
Security/safety procedures
Field operations/evaluations
Purchasing cooperatives

MARKETING SUPPORT
Co-op advertising
Ad slicks
National media campaign
Regional marketing

SHEFIELD GOURMET

Current financial data not available

2265 W. Railway St., P.O. Box 490
Abbotsford, BC Canada V2S 5Z5
Ph: (604)852-8771
Fax: (604)859-1711
www.shefieldgourmet.com
Tobacco products, coffee, accessories
Began: 1996, Franchising since: 1996
Headquarters size: 19 employees
Franchise department: 2 employees

U.S. franchises: 0
Canadian franchises: 18
Other foreign franchises: 0
Company-owned: 3
Units concentrated in Canada

Not available in the U.S.
Seeking in Canada? Yes
Exclusive territories? No
Homebased option? No
Kiosk option? Yes
Employees needed to run franchise:
    Info not provided
Absentee ownership? Yes

COSTS
Total cost: $150K-200K
Kiosk cost: $135K
Franchise fee: $25K
Royalty fee: 5-8%
Term of agreement: 5 years renewable
    for $5K
Franchisees required to buy multiple
    units? No

FINANCING
No financing available

QUALIFICATIONS
Net worth: $150K
Experience:
    General business experience

TRAINING
At franchisee's location: 2 weeks

BUSINESS SUPPORT
Newsletter
Toll-free phone line
Grand opening
Internet
Lease negotiations
Security/safety procedures
Field operations/evaluations
Purchasing cooperatives

MARKETING SUPPORT
Co-op advertising
Ad slicks
National media campaign

TALKING BOOK WORLD

Current financial data not available

18955 Ventura Blvd., #A
Tarzana, CA 91356
Ph: (800)403-2933/(818)609-7102
Fax: (818)609-7102
www.talkingbookworld.com
Audiobook rentals & sales
Began: 1993, Franchising since: 1995
Headquarters size: 5 employees
Franchise department: 2 employees

U.S. franchises: 14
Canadian franchises: 0
Other foreign franchises: 0
Company-owned: 18
Units concentrated in CA, MI

Seeking: All U.S.
Seeking in Canada? Yes
Exclusive territories? Yes
Homebased option? No
Kiosk option? No
Employees needed to run franchise: 3
Absentee ownership? Yes

COSTS
Total cost: $150K-225K
Franchise fee: $25K
Royalty fee: 5%
Term of agreement: 15 years renewable
    for $5K
Franchisees required to buy multiple
    units? No

FINANCING
No financing available

QUALIFICATIONS
Net worth: $100K
Cash liquidity: $50K
Experience:
    Must have passion for books &
    selling

TRAINING
At headquarters: 2 weeks
At franchisee's location: 1 week
Ongoing by phone

BUSINESS SUPPORT
Newsletter
Meetings
Toll-free phone line
Grand opening
Internet
Security/safety procedures
Field operations/evaluations
Purchasing cooperatives

MARKETING SUPPORT
Co-op advertising
Ad slicks
Regional marketing

WOODCRAFT FRANCHISE CORP.
Ranked #480 in Entrepreneur Magazine's 2004 Franchise 500　　　*Financial rating: 0*

1177 Rosemar Rd., P.O. Box 245
Parkersburg, WV 26105
Ph: (304)422-5412
Fax: (304)485-1938
www.woodcraft.com
Woodworking supply-specialty store
Began: 1928, Franchising since: 1997
Headquarters size: 80 employees
Franchise department: 2 employees

U.S. franchises: 51
Canadian franchises: 0
Other foreign franchises: 0
Company-owned: 9
Units concentrated in all U.S.

Seeking: All U.S.
Seeking in Canada? No
Exclusive territories? Yes
Homebased option? No
Kiosk option? No
Employees needed to run franchise: 8-9
Absentee ownership? No

COSTS
Total cost: $445K-545K
Franchise fee: $45K
Royalty fee: 5%
Term of agreement: 10 years renewable
　　at no charge
Franchisees required to buy multiple
　　units? No

FINANCING
No financing available

QUALIFICATIONS
Net worth: $425K-525K
Cash liquidity: $150K
Experience:
　　Must love woodworking

TRAINING
At headquarters: 2 weeks
At franchisee's location: 2-3 weeks

BUSINESS SUPPORT
Newsletter
Meetings
Toll-free phone line
Grand opening
Internet
Security/safety procedures
Field operations/evaluations
Purchasing cooperatives

MARKETING SUPPORT
Co-op advertising
Ad slicks
National media campaign
Regional marketing

RETAIL　　*Other Franchises*

CARDSMART RETAIL CORP.
400 Pine St.
Pawtucket, RI 02860
Ph: (877)227-3762
www.cardsmart.com
Card & gift stores

DIRECT CASKET OUTLET
210 W. Maple
Independence, MO 64050
Ph: (816)252-0979
Funeral merchandise sales

FAN-A-MANIA
8385 S. Allen St., #119
Sandy, UT 84094
Ph: (800)313-2675/(801)569-8189
www.fanamania.com
Entertainment & sports stores

JUST-A-BUCK
30 Matthews St.
Goshen, NY 10924
Ph: (800)332-2229/(914)291-7018
www.just-a-buck.com
General merchandise for $1

PICKLES & ICE CREAM FRANCHISING
203 Main St.
Thomson, GA 30824
Ph: (706)595-9779
www.picklesmaternity.com
Maternity apparel stores

TINDER BOX INTERNATIONAL
3 Bala Plaza E., #102
Bala Cynwyd, PA 19004
Ph: (800)846-3372/(610)668-4220
www.tinderbox.com
Cigars, tobacco products & accessories,
　　gifts & collectibles

TOTALLY LOW CARB STORES INC.
520 S. Sixth St.
Las Vegas, NV 89101
Ph: (800)631-2272
www.tlcstores.com
Low-carb grocery stores

WICKS 'N' STICKS
P.O. 1965
Cypress, TX 77410-1965
Ph: (800)873-3714/(713)856-7442
www.wicksnsticks.com
Candles, home-fragrancing products,
　　related accessories

YOUR DOLLAR STORE WITH MORE
102-1626 Richter St.
Kelowna, BC Canada V1Y 2M3
Ph: (250)860-4225
www.dollarstore.ca
Dollar stores

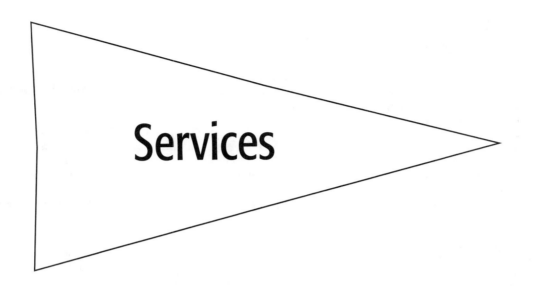

SERVICES · *Dating*

EIGHT AT EIGHT DINNER CLUB

Current financial data not available

P.O. Box 250682
Atlanta, GA 30325
Ph: (404)888-0988
www.8at8.com
Dinner club matchmaking service
Began: 1998, Franchising since: 2003
Headquarters size: 4 employees
Franchise department: 1 employee

U.S. franchises: 1
Canadian franchises: 0
Other foreign franchises: 0
Company-owned: 4

Seeking: All U.S.
Seeking in Canada? No
Exclusive territories? Yes
Homebased option? Yes
Kiosk option? No
Employees needed to run franchise: 1
Absentee ownership? No

COSTS
Total cost: $28.6K-44.6K
Franchise fee: $25.5K
Royalty fee: 10%
Term of agreement: 5 years renewable
   for $5K
Franchisees required to buy multiple
   units? No

FINANCING
No financing available

QUALIFICATIONS
Net worth: $100K
Cash liquidity: $25K
Experience:
   General business experience
   Marketing skills

TRAINING
At headquarters: 30 hours

BUSINESS SUPPORT
Meetings
Grand opening
Internet
Field operations/evaluations

MARKETING SUPPORT
Co-op advertising
Ad slicks
National media campaign
Collateral material
DVDs
Signage

THE RIGHT ONE

Ranked #317 in Entrepreneur Magazine's 2004 Franchise 500   *Financial rating: $$$$*

160 Old Derby St., #339
Hingham, MA 02043
Ph: (800)348-3283
Fax: (781)749-2390
www.therightone.com
Dating service
Began: 1990, Franchising since: 1999
Headquarters size: 25 employees
Franchise department: 6 employees

U.S. franchises: 28
Canadian franchises: 0
Other foreign franchises: 0
Company-owned: 7
Units concentrated in all U.S.

Seeking: All U.S.
Seeking in Canada? Yes
Exclusive territories? Yes
Homebased option? No
Kiosk option? No
Employees needed to run franchise: 6
Absentee ownership? No

COSTS
Total cost: $98.4K-254K
Franchise fee: $50K-150K
Royalty fee: 6%
Term of agreement: 10 years renewable
  for $10K
Franchisees required to buy multiple
  units? No

FINANCING
In-house: Franchise fee
3rd-party: None

QUALIFICATIONS
Net worth: $50K+
Cash liquidity: $25K-50K
Experience:
  Industry experience
  General business experience
  Marketing skills
  People skills

TRAINING
At headquarters: 1 week
At franchisee's location: 1 week
At existing locations: 2 weeks

BUSINESS SUPPORT
Newsletter
Meetings
Toll-free phone line
Grand opening
Internet
Security/safety procedures
Field operations/evaluations
Purchasing cooperatives

MARKETING SUPPORT
Co-op advertising
Ad slicks
National media campaign

TOGETHER DATING SERVICE

Financial rating: 0

5026 Dorsey Hall Dr., #205
Ellicott City, MD 21042
Ph: (410)730-8866
Fax: (410)992-6910
www.togetherdating.com
Dating service
Began: 1974, Franchising since: 1981
Headquarters size: 8 employees
Franchise department: 3 employees

U.S. franchises: 26
Canadian franchises: 0
Other foreign franchises: 0
Company-owned: 4

Seeking: All U.S.
Seeking in Canada? Yes
Exclusive territories? Yes
Homebased option? No
Kiosk option? No
Employees needed to run franchise:
  Info not provided
Absentee ownership? No

COSTS
Total cost: $98.4K-254.9K
Franchise fee: $50K-150K
Royalty fee: 6%
Term of agreement: Info not provided
Franchisees required to buy multiple
  units? No

FINANCING
In-house: Franchise fee
3rd-party: None

QUALIFICATIONS
Net worth: $100K
Cash liquidity: $75K

TRAINING
At headquarters: 1 week
At franchisee's location: 1 week
At existing locations

BUSINESS SUPPORT
Newsletter
Meetings
Toll-free phone line
Grand opening
Internet
Security/safety procedures
Field operations/evaluations
Purchasing cooperatives

MARKETING SUPPORT
Co-op advertising
Ad slicks
National media campaign
Ongoing leadership advice

SERVICES ▶ *Delivery*

DRY CLEANING TO-YOUR-DOOR

Ranked #246 in Entrepreneur Magazine's 2004 Franchise 500   *Financial rating: $$$$*

1121 N.W. Bayshore Dr.
Waldport, OR 97394
Ph: (800)318-1800, Fax: (541)563-6938
www.dctyd.com
Dry cleaning pickup & delivery
Began: 1994, Franchising since: 1997
Headquarters size: Info not provided
Franchise department: Info not provided

U.S. franchises: 87
Canadian franchises: 0
Other foreign franchises: 0
Company-owned: 0
Units concentrated in all U.S.

Seeking: All U.S.
Seeking in Canada? Yes
Exclusive territories? Yes
Homebased option? Yes
Kiosk option? No
Employees needed to run franchise: 0
Absentee ownership? Info not provided

COSTS
Total cost: $39.99K-63.4K
Franchise fee: $24.5K/29.5K
Royalty fee: 4.5%
Term of agreement: 10 years renewable
    at no charge
Franchisees required to buy multiple
    units? No

FINANCING
No financing available

QUALIFICATIONS
Net worth: $75K
Cash liquidity: $24.5K

TRAINING
At headquarters: 5 days
At franchisee's location: 5 days

BUSINESS SUPPORT
Info not provided

MARKETING SUPPORT
Info not provided

1-800-DRYCLEAN

Ranked #359 in Entrepreneur Magazine's 2004 Franchise 500   *Financial rating: $$*

3948 Ranchero Dr.
Ann Arbor, MI 48108
Ph: (866)822-6115
Fax: (734)822-6888
www.1-800-dryclean.com
Dry cleaning pickup & delivery
Began: 1997, Franchising since: 2000
Headquarters size: 15 employees
Franchise department: 4 employees

U.S. franchises: 73
Canadian franchises: 0
Other foreign franchises: 0
Company-owned: 0
Units concentrated in all U.S.

Seeking: All U.S.
Seeking in Canada? No
Exclusive territories? Yes
Homebased option? Yes
Kiosk option? No
Employees needed to run franchise: 3
Absentee ownership? No

COSTS
Total cost: $88K-100K
Franchise fee: $6.9K
Royalty fee: 7%
Term of agreement: 10 years renewable
    for $500
Franchisees required to buy multiple
    units? No

FINANCING
No financing available

QUALIFICATIONS
Net worth: $200K
Cash liquidity: $30K
Experience:
    General business experience
    Marketing skills

TRAINING
At headquarters: 1 week
At franchisee's location: 1 week

BUSINESS SUPPORT
Newsletter
Meetings
Toll-free phone line
Grand opening
Internet
Security/safety procedures
Field operations/evaluations
Purchasing cooperatives

MARKETING SUPPORT
Co-op advertising
Ad slicks
Marketing brochures

PRESSED4TIME INC.

Ranked #252 in Entrepreneur Magazine's 2004 Franchise 500   *Financial rating: $$$*

124 Boston Post Rd.
Sudbury, MA 01776
Ph: (800)423-8711/(978)443-9200
Fax: (978)443-0709
www.pressed4time.com
Dry cleaning pickup & delivery, shoe repair
Began: 1987, Franchising since: 1990
Headquarters size: 5 employees
Franchise department: 2 employees

U.S. franchises: 156
Canadian franchises: 2
Other foreign franchises: 9
Company-owned: 0

Seeking: All U.S.
Seeking in Canada? Yes
Exclusive territories? Yes
Homebased option? Yes
Kiosk option? No
Employees needed to run franchise: 0
Absentee ownership? No

COSTS
Total cost: $19.6K-28.5K
Franchise fee: $17.5K
Royalty fee: 4-6%
Term of agreement: 10 years renewable for 10% of current franchise fee
Franchisees required to buy multiple units? No

FINANCING
No financing available

QUALIFICATIONS
Net worth: $50K
Cash liquidity: $30K
Experience:
    Marketing skills

TRAINING
At headquarters: 3 days
At franchisee's location: 3 days
At franchisee's location: 1-day follow-up

BUSINESS SUPPORT
Newsletter
Meetings
Toll-free phone line
Internet
Security/safety procedures
Field operations/evaluations
Purchasing cooperatives

MARKETING SUPPORT
Ad slicks
Marketing materials
PR program

SERVICES   *Dry Cleaning & Laundry*

COMET CLEANERS

Ranked #213 in Entrepreneur Magazine's 2004 Franchise 500   *Financial rating: $$$$*

406 W. Division St.
Arlington, TX 76011
Ph: (817)461-3555
Fax: (817)861-4779
www.cometcleaners.com
Dry cleaning & laundry services
Began: 1947, Franchising since: 1967
Headquarters size: 7 employees
Franchise department: 5 employees

U.S. franchises: 320
Canadian franchises: 0
Other foreign franchises: 10
Company-owned: 15
Units concentrated in AR, OK, TX

Seeking: All U.S.
Seeking in Canada? No
Exclusive territories? Yes
Homebased option? No
Kiosk option? Yes
Employees needed to run franchise: 10
Absentee ownership? Yes

COSTS
Total cost: $196K-368K
Kiosk cost: $300K
Franchise fee: $25K-50K
Royalty fee: 0
Term of agreement: 5 years renewable
Franchisees required to buy multiple units? No

FINANCING
In-house: None
3rd-party: Equipment, franchise fee, inventory, start-up costs

QUALIFICATIONS
Net worth: $200K
Cash liquidity: $50K
Experience:
    General business experience

TRAINING
At headquarters: 1 week
At franchisee's location: 2 weeks

BUSINESS SUPPORT
Newsletter
Toll-free phone line
Grand opening
Internet
Lease negotiations
Security/safety procedures
Field operations/evaluations
Purchasing cooperatives

MARKETING SUPPORT
Co-op advertising
Ad slicks

DRY CLEANING STATION

Financial rating: $

8301 Golden Valley Rd., #230
Minneapolis, MN 55427
Ph: (800)655-8134
Fax: (763)542-2246
www.drycleaningstation.com
Dry cleaning
Began: 1987, Franchising since: 1992
Headquarters size: 3 employees
Franchise department: 2 employees

U.S. franchises: 25
Canadian franchises: 0
Other foreign franchises: 0
Company-owned: 0
Units concentrated in all U.S.

Seeking: All U.S.
Seeking in Canada? No
Exclusive territories? Yes
Homebased option? No
Kiosk option? No
Employees needed to run franchise: 0
Absentee ownership? No

COSTS
Total cost: $42.5K-485.5K
Franchise fee: $9.5K-25K
Royalty fee: Varies
Term of agreement: 15 years renewable
    at no charge
Franchisees required to buy multiple
    units? No

FINANCING
In-house: None
3rd-party: Accounts receivable, equip-
    ment, franchise fee, inventory, pay-
    roll, start-up costs

QUALIFICATIONS
Net worth: $100K-500K
Cash liquidity: $20K-200K
Experience:
    General business experience
    Marketing skills

TRAINING
At headquarters: 1-3 weeks
At franchisee's location: Up to 1 week

BUSINESS SUPPORT
Newsletter
Meetings
Toll-free phone line
Grand opening
Internet
Lease negotiations
Security/safety procedures
Field operations/evaluations

MARKETING SUPPORT
Co-op advertising
Ad slicks
Regional marketing

DRYCLEAN USA

Ranked #132 in Entrepreneur Magazine's 2004 Franchise 500

Financial rating: $$$$

290 N.E. 68th St.
Miami, FL 33138
Ph: (305)754-9966
Fax: (305)754-8010
www.drycleanusa.com
Dry cleaning
Began: 1976, Franchising since: 1978
Headquarters size: 35 employees
Franchise department: 5 employees

U.S. franchises: 212
Canadian franchises: 0
Other foreign franchises: 267
Company-owned: 0

Seeking: All U.S.
Seeking in Canada? Yes
Exclusive territories? Yes
Homebased option? No
Kiosk option? No
Employees needed to run franchise: 5-7
Absentee ownership? Yes

COSTS
Total cost: $80.7K-518.5K
Franchise fee: $15K/30K
Royalty fee: $5K/yr.
Term of agreement: 10 years renewable
    for $5K
Franchisees required to buy multiple
    units? No

FINANCING
In-house: Franchise fee, inventory
3rd-party: Equipment, start-up costs

QUALIFICATIONS
Net worth: $250K
Cash liquidity: $100K-125K
Experience:
    General business experience

TRAINING
At headquarters
At franchisee's location
At Dryclean USA training plant

BUSINESS SUPPORT
Meetings
Toll-free phone line
Grand opening
Internet
Security/safety procedures
Field operations/evaluations
Purchasing cooperatives

MARKETING SUPPORT
Co-op advertising
Ad slicks
Regional marketing

HANGERS CLEANERS INC.

Ranked #366 in Entrepreneur Magazine's 2004 Franchise 500   *Financial rating: $$$*

3505 County Rd., 42W
Burnsville, MN 55306-3803
Ph: (866)262-9274
Fax: (952)882-5175
www.hangersdrycleaners.com
Dry cleaning & garment-care stores
Began: 1996, Franchising since: 1998
Headquarters size: 13 employees
Franchise department: 5 employees

U.S. franchises: 60
Canadian franchises: 3
Other foreign franchises: 0
Company-owned: 0

Seeking: All U.S.
Seeking in Canada? Yes
Exclusive territories? Yes
Homebased option? No
Kiosk option? No
Employees needed to run franchise: 20
Absentee ownership? Yes

COSTS
Total cost: $750K-1.5M
Franchise fee: $50K
Royalty fee: 4%
Term of agreement: 10 years renewable
    for $5K per territory
Franchisees required to buy multiple
    units? No

FINANCING
No financing available

QUALIFICATIONS
Net worth: $1.5M+
Cash liquidity: $350K-500K
Experience:
    General business experience
    Marketing skills

TRAINING
At franchisee's location: 30 days+

BUSINESS SUPPORT
Meetings
Toll-free phone line
Grand opening
Internet
Security/safety procedures
Field operations/evaluations

MARKETING SUPPORT
Ad slicks

LAPELS

Financial rating: 0

962 Washington St.
Hanover, MA 02339
Ph: (866)695-2735
Fax: (781)829-9546
www.lapelsdrycleaning.com
Dry cleaning stores
Began: 2000, Franchising since: 2001
Headquarters size: 4 employees
Franchise department: 4 employees

U.S. franchises: 11
Canadian franchises: 0
Other foreign franchises: 0
Company-owned: 0
Units concentrated in MA

Seeking: All U.S.
Focusing on: CA, CT, MA, ME, NH,
    NJ, NY, RI, TX, VT
Seeking in Canada? Yes
Exclusive territories? Yes
Homebased option? No
Kiosk option? No
Employees needed to run franchise: 4
Absentee ownership? Yes

COSTS
Total cost: $66.2K-92.1K
Franchise fee: $20K
Royalty fee: 5%
Term of agreement: 10 years renewable
    for $5K
Franchisees required to buy multiple
    units? No

FINANCING
In-house: Equipment
Equipment, start-up costs

QUALIFICATIONS
Net worth: $100K
Cash liquidity: $50K
Experience:
    General business experience
    Customer service skills

TRAINING
At headquarters: 10 days
At franchisee's location: 2 days

BUSINESS SUPPORT
Newsletter
Meetings
Toll-free phone line
Grand opening
Internet
Lease negotiations
Field operations/evaluations
Purchasing cooperatives

MARKETING SUPPORT
Co-op advertising
Ad slicks

MARTINIZING DRY CLEANING
Ranked #147 in Entrepreneur Magazine's 2004 Franchise 500   *Financial rating: $$$$*

422 Wards Corner Rd.
Loveland, OH 45140
Ph: (800)827-0345/(513)351-6211
Fax: (513)731-0818
www.martinizing.com
Dry cleaning & laundry services
Began: 1949, Franchising since: 1949
Headquarters size: 16 employees
Franchise department: 3 employees

U.S. franchises: 430
Canadian franchises: 23
Other foreign franchises: 201
Company-owned: 0
Units concentrated in CA, MI, TX, WI

Seeking: All U.S.
Seeking in Canada? Yes
Exclusive territories? Yes
Homebased option? No
Kiosk option? No
Employees needed to run franchise: 6
Absentee ownership? Yes

COSTS
Total cost: $220K-305K
Franchise fee: $30K
Royalty fee: 4%
Term of agreement: 20 years renewable
for $1K
Franchisees required to buy multiple
units? No

FINANCING
In-house: None
3rd-party: Equipment, franchise fee,
start-up costs

QUALIFICATIONS
Net worth: $225K
Cash liquidity: $110K
Experience:
General business experience

TRAINING
At headquarters: 1 week
At franchisee's location: 2 weeks

BUSINESS SUPPORT
Newsletter
Meetings
Toll-free phone line
Grand opening
Internet
Security/safety procedures
Field operations/evaluations

MARKETING SUPPORT
Co-op advertising
Ad slicks
Regional marketing
Field marketing visits & consultations

NU-LOOK 1 HR. CLEANERS
Current financial data not available

15 S.E. 2nd Ave.
Deerfield Beach, FL 33441-3949
Ph: (800)413-7881, Fax: (954)570-6248
www.nu-look.com
Dry cleaning
Began: 1967, Franchising since: 1967
Headquarters size: 3 employees
Franchise department: 3 employees

U.S. franchises: 48
Canadian franchises: 0
Other foreign franchises: 12
Company-owned: 0
Units concentrated in FL, MD, VA

Seeking: All U.S.
Focusing on: FL, GA, MD, NC, PA
Seeking in Canada? Yes
Exclusive territories? Yes
Homebased option? No
Kiosk option? No
Employees needed to run franchise: 4
Absentee ownership? Yes

COSTS
Total cost: $200K
Franchise fee: $20K
Royalty fee: 2%
Term of agreement: 20 years renewable
at no charge
Franchisees required to buy multiple
units? Outside the U.S. only

FINANCING
In-house: None
3rd-party: Accounts receivable, equipment, franchise fee, inventory, payroll, start-up costs

QUALIFICATIONS
Net worth: $250K
Cash liquidity: $65K
Experience:
General business experience

TRAINING
At headquarters: 2 weeks
At franchisee's location: 2 weeks

BUSINESS SUPPORT
Newsletter
Meetings
Toll-free phone line
Grand opening
Field operations/evaluations
Purchasing cooperatives

MARKETING SUPPORT
Co-op advertising
Ad slicks
Regional marketing

EMBROIDME

Ranked #314 in Entrepreneur Magazine's 2004 Franchise 500   *Financial rating: $$$*

1801 Australian Ave. S.
West Palm Beach, FL 33409
Ph: (561)640-7367, Fax: (561)640-6062
www.embroidme.com
Embroidered items, screen printing &
 ad specialties
Began: 2000, Franchising since: 2001
Headquarters size: 35 employees
Franchise department: Info not pro-
 vided

U.S. franchises: 123
Canadian franchises: 2
Other foreign franchises: 0
Company-owned: 0
Units concentrated in all U.S.

Seeking: All U.S.
Seeking in Canada? Yes
Exclusive territories? Yes
Homebased option? No
Kiosk option? No
Employees needed to run franchise: 2
Absentee ownership? No

COSTS
Total cost: $43.3K-211.1K
Franchise fee: $35.5K
Royalty fee: 5%
Term of agreement: 35 years renewable
 for $1.5K
Franchisees required to buy multiple
 units? No

FINANCING
In-house: None
3rd-party: Equipment, inventory

QUALIFICATIONS
Cash liquidity: $40K+
Experience:
 General business experience

TRAINING
At headquarters: 2 weeks
At franchisee's location: 3 weeks
Ongoing

BUSINESS SUPPORT
Newsletter
Meetings
Toll-free phone line
Grand opening
Internet
Lease negotiations
Security/safety procedures
Field operations/evaluations
Purchasing cooperatives

MARKETING SUPPORT
Co-op advertising
Ad slicks
National media campaign
Regional marketing

HOMETOWN THREADS

Financial rating: 0

200 Wireless Blvd.
Hauppauge, NY 11788
Ph: (631)701-2194, Fax: (631)436-5176
www.hometownthreads.com
Personalized gift & retail embroidery
 service
Began: 1998, Franchising since: 2001
Headquarters size: 10 employees
Franchise department: 10 employees

U.S. franchises: 25
Canadian franchises: 0
Other foreign franchises: 0
Company-owned: 0
Units concentrated in all U.S.

Seeking: All U.S.
Seeking in Canada? No
Exclusive territories? Yes
Homebased option? No
Kiosk option? Yes
Employees needed to run franchise: 4
Absentee ownership? No

COSTS
Total cost: $150K
Kiosk cost: $65K-90K
Franchise fee: $25K
Royalty fee: 5%
Term of agreement: 10 years renewable
 for $5K
Franchisees required to buy multiple
 units? No

FINANCING
In-house: None
3rd-party: Equipment, franchise fee,
 inventory, start-up costs

QUALIFICATIONS
Net worth: $200K
Cash liquidity: $50K
Experience:
 General business experience

TRAINING
At headquarters: 3 weeks
At franchisee's location: 2 weeks

BUSINESS SUPPORT
Newsletter
Meetings
Toll-free phone line
Grand opening
Internet
Lease negotiations
Security/safety procedures
Field operations/evaluations
Purchasing cooperatives

MARKETING SUPPORT
Co-op advertising
Ad slicks
National media campaign
Regional marketing

INSTANT IMPRINTS

Financial rating: $$$

7642 Clairemont Mesa Blvd.
San Diego, CA 92111
Ph: (800)542-3437
Fax: (858)569-9931
www.instantimprints.com
Imprinted sportswear, promotional
    products & designs
Began: 1992, Franchising since: 2001
Headquarters size: 22 employees
Franchise department: 6 employees

U.S. franchises: 13
Canadian franchises: 0
Other foreign franchises: 0
Company-owned: 1
Units concentrated in AZ, CA, CO, NJ

Seeking: All U.S.
Seeking in Canada? No
Exclusive territories? Yes
Homebased option? No
Kiosk option? Yes
Employees needed to run franchise: 3
Absentee ownership? No

COSTS
Total cost: $50.5K-187.1K
Kiosk cost: $80K
Franchise fee: $25K
Royalty fee: 5%
Term of agreement: 15 years renewable
    for $2.5K
Franchisees required to buy multiple
    units? No

FINANCING
In-house: None
3rd-party: Equipment, franchise fee,
    inventory, start-up costs

QUALIFICATIONS
Net worth: $250K
Cash liquidity: $40K
Experience:
    General business experience
    Marketing skills

TRAINING
At headquarters: 2 weeks
At franchisee's location: 1 week

BUSINESS SUPPORT
Newsletter
Meetings
Toll-free phone line
Grand opening
Internet
Field operations/evaluations
Purchasing cooperatives

MARKETING SUPPORT
Co-op advertising
Ad slicks
National media campaign
Regional marketing

SERVICES   *Home Inspections*

ALLSTATE HOME INSPECTIONS/ENVIRONMENTAL TESTING
Ranked #400 in Entrepreneur Magazine's 2004 Franchise 500   *Financial rating: $$$*

2097 N. Randolph Rd.
Randolph Ctr., VT 05061
Ph: (800)245-9932, Fax: (802)728-5534
www.allstatehomeinspection.com
Home inspection & household
    environmental testing
Began: 1989, Franchising since: 1996
Headquarters size: 5 employees
Franchise department: 5 employees

U.S. franchises: 23
Canadian franchises: 0
Other foreign franchises: 0
Company-owned: 0
Units concentrated in CO, MA, NY,
    UT, VT

Seeking: All U.S.
Seeking in Canada? No
Exclusive territories? Yes
Homebased option? Yes
Kiosk option? No
Employees needed to run franchise: 1-3
Absentee ownership? Yes

COSTS
Total cost: $23.9K-44K
Franchise fee: $23.9K
Royalty fee: 7.5%
Term of agreement: 6 years renewable
    for $2K
Franchisees required to buy multiple
    units? No

FINANCING
No financing available

QUALIFICATIONS
Cash liquidity: $7.9K-24K
Experience:
    Industry experience

TRAINING
At headquarters: 10 days
Additional training available

BUSINESS SUPPORT
Newsletter
Meetings
Toll-free phone line
Internet
Field operations/evaluations

MARKETING SUPPORT
Ad slicks
National media campaign
Regional marketing
Telephone Outreach Project

AMERISPEC HOME INSPECTION SERVICES

Ranked #117 in Entrepreneur Magazine's 2004 Franchise 500   *Financial rating: $$$$*

889 Ridge Lake Blvd.
Memphis, TN 38120
Ph: (800)426-2270/(901)820-8500
Fax: (901)820-8520
www.amerispecfranchise.com
Home inspection service
Began: 1987, Franchising since: 1988
Headquarters size: 45 employees
Franchise department: 4 employees

U.S. franchises: 288
Canadian franchises: 74
Other foreign franchises: 0
Company-owned: 2
Units concentrated in all U.S.

Seeking: All U.S.
Seeking in Canada? Yes
Exclusive territories? Yes
Homebased option? Yes
Kiosk option? No
Employees needed to run franchise: 3
Absentee ownership? No

COSTS
Total cost: $24.6K-63.6K
Franchise fee: $18K/26.9K
Royalty fee: 7%
Term of agreement: 5 years renewable
    at no charge
Franchisees required to buy multiple
    units? No

FINANCING
In-house: Franchise fee
3rd-party: None

QUALIFICATIONS
Net worth: $50K
Cash liquidity: $10K
Experience:
    Industry experience
    General business experience
    Marketing skills

TRAINING
At headquarters: 2 weeks
Training by mail: 27 weeks

BUSINESS SUPPORT
Newsletter
Meetings
Toll-free phone line
Internet
Field operations/evaluations
Purchasing cooperatives

MARKETING SUPPORT
Co-op advertising
Ad slicks
National media campaign
Regional marketing

THE BRICKKICKER HOME INSPECTION

Ranked #301 in Entrepreneur Magazine's 2004 Franchise 500   *Financial rating: $$$*

849 N. Ellsworth St.
Naperville, IL 60583
Ph: (800)821-1820
Fax: (630)420-2270
www.brickkicker.com
Home & property inspection service
Began: 1989, Franchising since: 1994
Headquarters size: 19 employees
Franchise department: 6 employees

U.S. franchises: 126
Canadian franchises: 0
Other foreign franchises: 0
Company-owned: 28
Units concentrated in AZ, CA, CO, FL,
    GA, IA, IL, IN, KY, MI, MO, OH,
    PA, SC, SD, VA, WA, WI

Seeking: All U.S.
Seeking in Canada? No
Exclusive territories? Yes
Homebased option? Yes
Kiosk option? No
Employees needed to run franchise: 1-2
Absentee ownership? No

COSTS
Total cost: $13.6K-52.1K
Franchise fee: $7.5K-25K
Royalty fee: 6%
Term of agreement: 7 years renewable
    at no charge
Franchisees required to buy multiple
    units? No

FINANCING
In-house: Franchise fee
3rd-party: None

QUALIFICATIONS
Net worth: $50K
Cash liquidity: $20K

TRAINING
At headquarters: 5-10 days
At franchisee's location: 2-4 days
Continuing education available

BUSINESS SUPPORT
Newsletter
Meetings
Toll-free phone line
Grand opening
Internet
Field operations/evaluations
Purchasing cooperatives

MARKETING SUPPORT
Co-op advertising
Ad slicks
National media campaign

THE HOMETEAM INSPECTION SERVICE
Ranked #144 in Entrepreneur Magazine's 2004 Franchise 500   *Financial rating: $$$$*

575 Chamber Dr.
Milford, OH 45150
Ph: (800)598-5297
Fax: (513)469-2226
www.hmteam.com
Home inspection service
Began: 1991, Franchising since: 1992
Headquarters size: 25 employees
Franchise department: 13 employees

U.S. franchises: 345
Canadian franchises: 8
Other foreign franchises: 0
Company-owned: 0
Units concentrated in all U.S.

Seeking: All U.S.
Seeking in Canada? Yes
Exclusive territories? Yes
Homebased option? Yes
Kiosk option? No
Employees needed to run franchise: 1
Absentee ownership? No

COSTS
Total cost: $19.5K-46.1K
Franchise fee: $11.9K-29.9K
Royalty fee: 6%
Term of agreement: 10 years renewable
    at no charge
Franchisees required to buy multiple
    units? No

FINANCING
In-house: None
Equipment, start-up costs

QUALIFICATIONS
Cash liquidity: $7.5K
Experience:
    Industry experience
    General business experience
    Marketing skills

TRAINING
At headquarters: 2 weeks
At franchisee's location: As needed
Annual meetings

BUSINESS SUPPORT
Newsletter
Meetings
Grand opening
Internet
Security/safety procedures
Field operations/evaluations

MARKETING SUPPORT
Co-op advertising
Ad slicks
National media campaign
National advertising fund

HOUSEMASTER
Ranked #221 in Entrepreneur Magazine's 2004 Franchise 500   *Financial rating: $$$*

421 W. Union Ave.
Bound Brook, NJ 08805
Ph: (800)526-3939
Fax: (732)469-7405
www.housemaster.com
Home inspection service
Began: 1971, Franchising since: 1979
Headquarters size: 24 employees
Franchise department: 24 employees

U.S. franchises: 342
Canadian franchises: 36
Other foreign franchises: 0
Company-owned: 0
Units concentrated in all U.S.

Seeking: All U.S.
Seeking in Canada? Yes
Exclusive territories? Yes
Homebased option? Yes
Kiosk option? No
Employees needed to run franchise: 1-5
Absentee ownership? Yes

COSTS
Total cost: $23K-61K
Franchise fee: $12K-29K
Royalty fee: 6-7.5%
Term of agreement: 5 years renewable
    at no charge
Franchisees required to buy multiple
    units? No

FINANCING
In-house: Franchise fee
3rd-party: None

QUALIFICATIONS
Net worth: $50K
Cash liquidity: $20K
Experience:
    Marketing skills

TRAINING
At headquarters: 1 week

BUSINESS SUPPORT
Newsletter
Meetings
Toll-free phone line
Grand opening
Internet
Security/safety procedures
Field operations/evaluations
Purchasing cooperatives

MARKETING SUPPORT
Co-op advertising
Ad slicks
National media campaign
Regional marketing

INSPECT-IT 1ST PROPERTY INSPECTION
Ranked #339 in Entrepreneur Magazine's 2004 Franchise 500   *Financial rating: $$$*

3420 E. Shea Blvd., #115
Phoenix, AZ 85028
Ph: (800)510-9100/(602)971-9400
Fax: (602)992-3127
www.inspectit1st.com
Home inspection service
Began: 1991, Franchising since: 1998
Headquarters size: 7 employees
Franchise department: 3 employees

U.S. franchises: 61
Canadian franchises: 0
Other foreign franchises: 0
Company-owned: 0
Units concentrated in AZ, CO, FL, GA,
    IL, NM, NV, OR, PA, TN, TX

Seeking: All U.S.
Focusing on: HI, MD, MN, VA, WA
Seeking in Canada? No
Exclusive territories? Yes
Homebased option? Yes
Kiosk option? No
Employees needed to run franchise: 0
Absentee ownership? Yes

COSTS
Total cost: $28.8K-47.9K
Franchise fee: $19.9K-27.9K
Royalty fee: 6-8%
Term of agreement: Renewable term at
    no charge
Franchisees required to buy multiple
    units? Yes

FINANCING
No financing available

QUALIFICATIONS
Net worth: $15K
Cash liquidity: $15K

TRAINING
At headquarters: 2 weeks

BUSINESS SUPPORT
Newsletter
Meetings
Toll-free phone line
Grand opening
Internet
Security/safety procedures
Field operations/evaluations
Purchasing cooperatives

MARKETING SUPPORT
Co-op advertising
Ad slicks
Regional marketing

NATIONAL PROPERTY INSPECTIONS INC.
Ranked #183 in Entrepreneur Magazine's 2004 Franchise 500   *Financial rating: $$$$*

11620 Arbor St., #100
Omaha, NE 68144-2935
Ph: (800)333-9807, Fax: (800)933-2508
www.npiweb.com
Home & commercial property inspec-
    tions
Began: 1987, Franchising since: 1987
Headquarters size: 15 employees
Franchise department: 7 employees

U.S. franchises: 198
Canadian franchises: 5
Other foreign franchises: 0
Company-owned: 0
Units concentrated in all U.S.

Seeking: All U.S.
Seeking in Canada? Yes
Exclusive territories? Yes
Homebased option? Yes
Kiosk option? No
Employees needed to run franchise: 1
Absentee ownership? No

COSTS
Total cost: $28.5K-31K
Franchise fee: $19.8K
Royalty fee: 8%
Term of agreement: 5 years renewable
    at no charge
Franchisees required to buy multiple
    units? No

FINANCING
In-house: None
3rd-party: Franchise fee

QUALIFICATIONS
Cash liquidity: $23K
Experience:
    Industry experience
    Marketing skills

TRAINING
At headquarters: 2 weeks
Optional field training: 1 week

BUSINESS SUPPORT
Newsletter
Meetings
Toll-free phone line
Internet
Field operations/evaluations
Purchasing cooperatives

MARKETING SUPPORT
Ad slicks
Regional marketing
Corporate relocation referral program

PILLAR TO POST

Ranked #90 in Entrepreneur Magazine's 2004 Franchise 500   *Financial rating: $$$$*

13902 N. Dale Mabry Hwy., #300
Tampa, FL 33618
Ph: (877)963-3129
Fax: (813)963-5301
www.pillartopost.com
Home inspection service
Began: 1994, Franchising since: 1994
Headquarters size: 18 employees
Franchise department: 11 employees

U.S. franchises: 325
Canadian franchises: 79
Other foreign franchises: 0
Company-owned: 0
Units concentrated in all U.S.

Seeking: All U.S.
Seeking in Canada? Yes
Exclusive territories? Yes
Homebased option? Yes
Kiosk option? No
Employees needed to run franchise: 1
Absentee ownership? No

COSTS
Total cost: $23.9K-41.7K
Franchise fee: $13.9K-23.9K
Royalty fee: 7%
Term of agreement: 5 years renewable
    at no charge
Franchisees required to buy multiple
    units? No

FINANCING
In-house: Franchise fee
3rd-party: None

QUALIFICATIONS
Net worth: $100K
Cash liquidity: $50K
Experience:
    General business experience
    Marketing skills

TRAINING
At headquarters: 2 weeks

BUSINESS SUPPORT
Newsletter
Meetings
Toll-free phone line
Internet

MARKETING SUPPORT
Co-op advertising
Ad slicks
National media campaign
Regional marketing

WORLD INSPECTION NETWORK

Ranked #195 in Entrepreneur Magazine's 2004 Franchise 500   *Financial rating: $$$$*

6500 6th Ave. N.W.
Seattle, WA 98117
Ph: (800)967-8127
Fax: (206)441-3655
www.winfranchise.com
Home inspection service
Began: 1993, Franchising since: 1994
Headquarters size: 12 employees
Franchise department: 3 employees

U.S. franchises: 129
Canadian franchises: 0
Other foreign franchises: 0
Company-owned: 0
Units concentrated in all U.S.

Seeking: All U.S.
Seeking in Canada? Yes
Exclusive territories? Yes
Homebased option? Yes
Kiosk option? No
Employees needed to run franchise: 1
Absentee ownership? Yes

COSTS
Total cost: $34.4K-49.3K
Franchise fee: $25K
Royalty fee: 6-7%
Term of agreement: 5 years renewable
    for 5% of franchise fee
Franchisees required to buy multiple
    units? No

FINANCING
In-house: Franchise fee
3rd-party: Accounts receivable, equip-
    ment, inventory, start-up costs

QUALIFICATIONS
Cash liquidity: $13K
Experience:
    Marketing skills
    Working knowledge of Windows-
    based software
    Sales skills
    Construction/remodeling back-
    ground

TRAINING
At headquarters: 2 weeks
Pre-training: 2 weeks

BUSINESS SUPPORT
Newsletter
Meetings
Toll-free phone line
Grand opening
Internet
Security/safety procedures
Purchasing cooperatives

MARKETING SUPPORT
Co-op advertising
Ad slicks
National media campaign
Regional marketing

SERVICES — *Moving*

APARTMENT MOVERS ETC.

Financial rating: $

P.O. Box 1065
Maudlin, SC 29662
Ph: (800)847-2861, Fax: (864)231-7772
www.apartmentmoversetc.com
Local moving services
Began: 1995, Franchising since: 1998
Headquarters size: 4 employees
Franchise department: 2 employees

U.S. franchises: 4
Canadian franchises: 0
Other foreign franchises: 0
Company-owned: 0
Units concentrated in KY, SC

Seeking: All U.S.
Seeking in Canada? Yes
Exclusive territories? Yes
Homebased option? No
Kiosk option? No
Employees needed to run franchise: 10
Absentee ownership? Yes

COSTS
Total cost: $67.3K-95K
Franchise fee: $19.5K
Royalty fee: 5%
Term of agreement: 10 years renewable
Franchisees required to buy multiple
    units? Outside the U.S. only

FINANCING
No financing available

QUALIFICATIONS
Info not provided

TRAINING
At headquarters: 1 week
At franchisee's location: 3 days
Ongoing

BUSINESS SUPPORT
Newsletter
Meetings
Toll-free phone line
Grand opening
Internet
Lease negotiations
Security/safety procedures
Field operations/evaluations
Purchasing cooperatives

MARKETING SUPPORT
Co-op advertising
Ad slicks
Regional marketing

TWO MEN AND A TRUCK INT'L. INC.
Ranked #269 in Entrepreneur Magazine's 2004 Franchise 500

Financial rating: $$$$

3400 Belle Chase Wy.
Lansing, MI 48911
Ph: (800)345-1070/(517)394-7210
Fax: (800)278-6114
www.twomenandatruck.com
Moving services
Began: 1985, Franchising since: 1989
Headquarters size: 32 employees
Franchise department: 3 employees

U.S. franchises: 106
Canadian franchises: 0
Other foreign franchises: 0
Company-owned: 0
Units concentrated in FL, GA, MI, NC,
    OH, WI

Seeking: All U.S.
Seeking in Canada? No
Exclusive territories? Yes
Homebased option? No
Kiosk option? No
Employees needed to run franchise: 7
Absentee ownership? Yes

COSTS
Total cost: $80.4K-246.1K
Franchise fee: $32K
Royalty fee: 6%
Term of agreement: 5 years renewable
    for $2.5K
Franchisees required to buy multiple
    units? No

FINANCING
3rd-party: Equipment, franchise fee,
    inventory, start-up costs
Other: Truck financing

QUALIFICATIONS
Net worth: $100K
Cash liquidity: $100K
Experience:
    General business experience

TRAINING
At headquarters: 15 days
At franchisee's location: As requested
At regional location: 2 days

BUSINESS SUPPORT
Newsletter
Meetings
Toll-free phone line
Grand opening
Internet
Field operations/evaluations

MARKETING SUPPORT
Ad slicks
National media campaign
First Gear program

SERVICES ▸ *Photo*

LIL' ANGELS PHOTOGRAPHY

Ranked #264 in Entrepreneur Magazine's 2004 Franchise 500　　　*Financial rating: $$$$*

6080 Quince Rd.
Memphis, TN 38119
Ph: (800)358-9101, Fax: (901)682-2018
www.lilangelsphoto.com
Preschool & day-care photography
Began: 1996, Franchising since: 1998
Headquarters size: Info not provided
Franchise department: Info not provided

U.S. franchises: 95
Canadian franchises: 1
Other foreign franchises: 0
Company-owned: 0
Units concentrated in all U.S.

Seeking: All U.S.
Seeking in Canada? No
Exclusive territories? Yes
Homebased option? Yes
Kiosk option? No
Employees needed to run franchise: 1
Absentee ownership? Yes

COSTS
Total cost: $27.7K-32.2K
Franchise fee: $17K
Royalty fee: 0
Term of agreement: 10 years renewable at no charge
Franchisees required to buy multiple units? No

FINANCING
No financing available

QUALIFICATIONS
Cash liquidity: $29K
Experience:
　　Sales experience

TRAINING
At headquarters: 6 days
At franchisee's location: 2 days
Regional & annual convention

BUSINESS SUPPORT
Meetings

MARKETING SUPPORT
Networking for securing multi-location accounts

MOTOPHOTO

Ranked #405 in Entrepreneur Magazine's 2004 Franchise 500　　　*Financial rating: $$$$*

4444 Lake Center Dr.
Dayton, OH 45426
Ph: (800)733-6686, Fax: (937)854-0140
www.motophoto.com
Film processing, portrait studios, imaging services
Began: 1981, Franchising since: 1982
Headquarters size: 80 employees
Franchise department: 4 employees

U.S. franchises: 218
Canadian franchises: 32
Other foreign franchises: 0
Company-owned: 2

Seeking: All U.S.
Seeking in Canada? No
Exclusive territories? Yes
Homebased option? No
Kiosk option? No
Employees needed to run franchise: 3-6
Absentee ownership? Yes

COSTS
Total cost: $200K-250K
Franchise fee: $35K/5.3K
Royalty fee: 6%
Term of agreement: 10 years renewable for $1.75K
Franchisees required to buy multiple units? No

FINANCING
No financing available

QUALIFICATIONS
Net worth: $150K
Cash liquidity: $80K
Experience:
　　General business experience
　　Marketing skills
　　Communication skills

TRAINING
At headquarters: 3 weeks
At franchisee's location: 1 week
At regional training center: 2 weeks

BUSINESS SUPPORT
Newsletter
Meetings
Toll-free phone line
Grand opening
Field operations/evaluations
Purchasing cooperatives

MARKETING SUPPORT
Co-op advertising
Ad slicks
National media campaign

THE SPORTS SECTION
Ranked #170 in Entrepreneur Magazine's 2004 Franchise 500   *Financial rating: $$$$*

2150 Boggs Rd., #200
Duluth, GA 30096
Ph: (866)877-4746
Fax: (678)740-0808
www.sports-section.com
Youth & sports photography
Began: 1983, Franchising since: 1984
Headquarters size: 130 employees
Franchise department: 35 employees

U.S. franchises: 181
Canadian franchises: 1
Other foreign franchises: 7
Company-owned: 0
Units concentrated in all U.S.

Seeking: All U.S.
Seeking in Canada? Yes
Exclusive territories? Yes
Homebased option? Yes
Kiosk option? No
Employees needed to run franchise: 2-4
Absentee ownership? No

COSTS
Total cost: $17.2K-52.7K
Franchise fee: $10.9K-30.9K
Royalty fee: 0
Term of agreement: 10 years renewable
for $1K
Franchisees required to buy multiple
units? Outside the U.S. only

FINANCING
In-house: Franchise fee
3rd-party: Equipment

QUALIFICATIONS
Cash liquidity: $16.4K-51K
Experience:
Marketing skills
Sales experience

TRAINING
At headquarters: 3 days
At franchisee's location: 5 days

BUSINESS SUPPORT
Newsletter
Meetings
Toll-free phone line
Grand opening
Internet
Security/safety procedures
Field operations/evaluations

MARKETING SUPPORT
Co-op advertising
Ad slicks
Regional marketing

THE VISUAL IMAGE INC.
Financial rating: $

100 E. Bockman Way
Sparta, TN 38583
Ph: (800)344-0323
Fax: (931)836-6279
www.thevisualimageinc.com
Preschool & pet photography
Began: 1984, Franchising since: 1994
Headquarters size: 3 employees
Franchise department: 3 employees

U.S. franchises: 17
Canadian franchises: 0
Other foreign franchises: 0
Company-owned: 3
Units concentrated in FL

Seeking: All U.S.
Seeking in Canada? Yes
Exclusive territories? Yes
Homebased option? Yes
Kiosk option? No
Employees needed to run franchise: 1-2
Absentee ownership? Yes

COSTS
Total cost: $37.3K-37.5K
Franchise fee: $23.5K
Royalty fee: 0
Term of agreement: 3 years renewable
for $2K
Franchisees required to buy multiple
units? No

FINANCING
In-house: Franchise fee, equipment
3rd-party: None

QUALIFICATIONS
Net worth: $50K
Cash liquidity: $35K
Experience:
General business experience
People & sales skills

TRAINING
At headquarters: 2 weeks
At franchisee's location: 1 week

BUSINESS SUPPORT
Newsletter
Meetings
Toll-free phone line
Internet
Field operations/evaluations
Purchasing cooperatives

MARKETING SUPPORT
Co-op advertising
Ad slicks
Regional marketing
Web site

AIM MAIL CENTERS

Ranked #327 in Entrepreneur Magazine's 2004 Franchise 500   *Financial rating: $$$*

15550-D Rockfield Blvd.
Irvine, CA 92618
Ph: (800)669-4246/(949)837-4151
Fax: (949)837-4537
www.aimmailcenters.com
Postal & business services
Began: 1985, Franchising since: 1989
Headquarters size: 10 employees
Franchise department: 2 employees

U.S. franchises: 63
Canadian franchises: 0
Other foreign franchises: 0
Company-owned: 0
Units concentrated in AZ, CA, CO, FL,
    IA, ID, NV, SC, WA

Seeking: All U.S.
Seeking in Canada? No
Exclusive territories? Yes
Homebased option? No
Kiosk option? No
Employees needed to run franchise: 1-2
Absentee ownership? Yes

COSTS

Total cost: $88.9K-133.9K
Franchise fee: $26.9K
Royalty fee: 5%
Term of agreement: 15 years renewable
    for $5K
Franchisees required to buy multiple
    units? No

FINANCING

In-house: None
3rd-party: Equipment, franchise fee,
    inventory, start-up costs

QUALIFICATIONS

Net worth: $150K
Cash liquidity: $35K
Experience:
    General business experience
    Marketing skills

TRAINING

At headquarters: 10 days
At franchisee's location: 3 days
Regional meeting & annual
    convention

BUSINESS SUPPORT

Newsletter
Meetings
Toll-free phone line
Grand opening
Internet
Lease negotiations
Field operations/evaluations
Purchasing cooperatives

MARKETING SUPPORT

Co-op advertising
Ad slicks
Regional marketing

CRATERS & FREIGHTERS

Ranked #413 in Entrepreneur Magazine's 2004 Franchise 500   *Financial rating: $$$$*

7000 E. 47th Avenue Dr., #100
Denver, CO 80216
Ph: (800)949-9931/(303)399-8190
Fax: (303)399-9964
www.cratersandfreighters.com
Specialty freight-handling service
Began: 1990, Franchising since: 1991
Headquarters size: 9 employees
Franchise department: 5 employees

U.S. franchises: 62
Canadian franchises: 0
Other foreign franchises: 0
Company-owned: 0

Seeking: All U.S.
Focusing on: CA, HI, ID, IN, MA, NE,
    NM, NY, PA
Seeking in Canada? Yes
Exclusive territories? Yes
Homebased option? No
Kiosk option? No
Employees needed to run franchise: 3-4
Absentee ownership? No

COSTS

Total cost: $95K-131K
Franchise fee: $27K
Royalty fee: 5%
Term of agreement: 15 years renewable
    at no charge
Franchisees required to buy multiple
    units? Outside the U.S. only

FINANCING

In-house: None
3rd-party: Equipment, inventory,
    start-up costs

QUALIFICATIONS

Net worth: $150K
Cash liquidity: $100K
Experience:
    General business experience
    Computer skills

TRAINING

At headquarters: 10 days
At franchisee's location: 2-3 days
Annual convention: 2 days

BUSINESS SUPPORT

Newsletter
Meetings
Toll-free phone line
Internet
Security/safety procedures
Field operations/evaluations

MARKETING SUPPORT

Ad slicks
National media campaign
PR program

NAVIS PACK & SHIP CENTERS
Ranked #270 in Entrepreneur Magazine's 2004 Franchise 500   *Financial rating: $$*

5675 DTC Blvd., #280
Greenwood Village, CO 80111
Ph: (866)738-6820/(303)741-6626
Fax: (303)741-6653
www.gonavis.com
Packaging & shipping products &
    services
Began: 1980, Franchising since: 1984
Headquarters size: 30 employees
Franchise department: 10 employees

U.S. franchises: 146
Canadian franchises: 1
Other foreign franchises: 0
Company-owned: 0
Units concentrated in CO, CT, IL

Seeking: All U.S.
Seeking in Canada? Yes
Exclusive territories? No
Homebased option? No
Kiosk option? No
Employees needed to run franchise: 3-5
Absentee ownership? No

COSTS
Total cost: $89K-160K
Franchise fee: $29.8K
Royalty fee: 5%
Term of agreement: 10 years renewable
    for $7.5K
Franchisees required to buy multiple
    units? No

FINANCING
In-house: None
3rd-party: Equipment, inventory,
    start-up costs

QUALIFICATIONS
Cash liquidity: $37.5K-50K
Experience:
    General business experience
    Marketing skills

TRAINING
At headquarters: 3 weeks
At franchisee's location: 1 week
Visits during first year

BUSINESS SUPPORT
Newsletter
Meetings
Toll-free phone line
Grand opening
Internet
Lease negotiations
Security/safety procedures
Field operations/evaluations
Purchasing cooperatives

MARKETING SUPPORT
Co-op advertising
Ad slicks
National media campaign
Regional marketing

PAK MAIL
Ranked #338 in Entrepreneur Magazine's 2004 Franchise 500   *Financial rating: $*

7173 S. Havana St., #600
Englewood, CO 80112
Ph: (800)833-2821
Fax: (303)957-1015
www.pakmail.com
Packaging, shipping, mailboxes, busi-
    ness support
Began: 1983, Franchising since: 1984
Headquarters size: 20 employees
Franchise department: 3 employees

U.S. franchises: 346
Canadian franchises: 13
Other foreign franchises: 34
Company-owned: 0
Units concentrated in all U.S.

Seeking: All U.S.
Seeking in Canada? Yes
Exclusive territories? Yes
Homebased option? No
Kiosk option? No
Employees needed to run franchise: 1-5
Absentee ownership? Yes

COSTS
Total cost: $72.4K-132.3K
Franchise fee: $28.95K
Royalty fee: to 5%
Term of agreement: 10 years renewable
    at to $2.5K
Franchisees required to buy multiple
    units? Outside the U.S. only

FINANCING
In-house: None
3rd-party: Equipment, franchise fee,
    inventory, start-up costs

QUALIFICATIONS
Net worth: $150K
Cash liquidity: $35K

TRAINING
At headquarters: 14 days
At franchisee's location: 3 days
At existing center: 2 days+

BUSINESS SUPPORT
Newsletter
Meetings
Toll-free phone line
Grand opening
Internet
Field operations/evaluations
Purchasing cooperatives

MARKETING SUPPORT
Co-op advertising
Ad slicks
National media campaign
Regional marketing
PR support
Desktop publishing
Marketing materials

PARCEL PLUS

Ranked #259 in Entrepreneur Magazine's 2004 Franchise 500   *Financial rating: $$$$*

12715 Telge Rd.
Cypress, TX 77429
Ph: (888)280-2053/(281)256-4100
Fax: (281)256-4178
www.parcelplus.com
Packing, shipping & cargo services
Began: 1986, Franchising since: 1988
Headquarters size: 155 employees
Franchise department: 100 employees

U.S. franchises: 103
Canadian franchises: 0
Other foreign franchises: 0
Company-owned: 0
Units concentrated in all U.S.

Seeking: All U.S.
Seeking in Canada? Yes
Exclusive territories? Yes
Homebased option? No
Kiosk option? No
Employees needed to run franchise: 3
Absentee ownership? No

COSTS
Total cost: $115K-174K
Franchise fee: $25K
Royalty fee: 6%
Term of agreement: 15 years renewable
    at no charge
Franchisees required to buy multiple
    units? No

FINANCING
In-house: None
3rd-party: Equipment, franchise fee,
    inventory, start-up costs

QUALIFICATIONS
Cash liquidity: $32K
Experience:
    General business experience
    Marketing skills

TRAINING
At headquarters: 2 weeks
At franchisee's location: 1 week

BUSINESS SUPPORT
Newsletter
Meetings
Toll-free phone line
Grand opening
Internet
Field operations/evaluations
Purchasing cooperatives

MARKETING SUPPORT
Ad slicks
National media campaign
Marketing, mailing & telemarketing
    services

POSTAL ANNEX+

Ranked #162 in Entrepreneur Magazine's 2004 Franchise 500   *Financial rating: $$$$*

7580 Metropolitan Dr., #200
San Diego, CA 92108
Ph: (800)456-1525/(619)563-4800
Fax: (619)563-9850
www.postalannex.com
Packaging, shipping, postal & business
    services
Began: 1985, Franchising since: 1986
Headquarters size: 24 employees
Franchise department: 7 employees

U.S. franchises: 277
Canadian franchises: 0
Other foreign franchises: 2
Company-owned: 0
Units concentrated in CA, FL, ID, MI,
    NC, NM, NV, OR, TX, WA

Seeking: All U.S.
Seeking in Canada? Yes
Exclusive territories? Yes
Homebased option? No
Kiosk option? Yes
Employees needed to run franchise: 3
Absentee ownership? Yes

COSTS
Total cost: $58.4K-174.1K
Kiosk cost: $85.5K-137.5K
Franchise fee: $29.95K
Royalty fee: 5%
Term of agreement: 15 years renewable
    for $3.5K
Franchisees required to buy multiple
    units? No

FINANCING
70% of total including working capital

QUALIFICATIONS
Net worth: $200K
Cash liquidity: $50K
Experience:
    Must speak English

TRAINING
At headquarters: 12 days
At franchisee's location: 4 days
At regional conferences: 3 days

BUSINESS SUPPORT
Newsletter
Meetings
Toll-free phone line
Grand opening
Internet
Lease negotiations
Security/safety procedures
Field operations/evaluations
Purchasing cooperatives

MARKETING SUPPORT
Co-op advertising
Ad slicks
National media campaign
Regional marketing
Marketing resource guide

POSTAL CONNECTIONS OF AMERICA

Ranked #335 in Entrepreneur Magazine's 2004 Franchise 500   *Financial rating: $$*

1081 Camino Del Rio S., #109
San Diego, CA 92108
Ph: (800)767-8257/(619)294-7550
Fax: (619)294-4550
www.postalconnections.com
Postal & business centers,
     computer/Internet services
Began: 1985, Franchising since: 1995
Headquarters size: 12 employees
Franchise department: 4 employees

U.S. franchises: 36
Canadian franchises: 0
Other foreign franchises: 0
Company-owned: 6
Units concentrated in AZ, CA, IL, MI,
     MO, NC, NY, OR, TX

Seeking: All U.S.
Seeking in Canada? No
Exclusive territories? Yes
Homebased option? No
Kiosk option? No
Employees needed to run franchise: 2
Absentee ownership? Yes

COSTS
Total cost: $98.5K-138.5K
Franchise fee: $18.9K
Royalty fee: 4%
Term of agreement: 10 years renewable
     at no charge
Franchisees required to buy multiple
     units? Outside the U.S. only

FINANCING
In-house: None
3rd-party: Equipment, franchise fee,
     inventory, start-up costs

QUALIFICATIONS
Net worth: $100K
Cash liquidity: $30K
Experience:
     General business experience
     Marketing skills

TRAINING
At headquarters: 7 days
At franchisee's location: 4 days

BUSINESS SUPPORT
Newsletter
Meetings
Toll-free phone line
Grand opening
Internet
Lease negotiations
Security/safety procedures
Field operations/evaluations
Purchasing cooperatives

MARKETING SUPPORT
Co-op advertising
Ad slicks

POSTNET POSTAL & BUSINESS SERVICES

Ranked #121 in Entrepreneur Magazine's 2004 Franchise 500   *Financial rating: $$$*

181 N. Arroyo Grande, #A-100
Henderson, NV 89074
Ph: (800)841-7171/(702)792-7100
Fax: (702)792-7115
www.postnet.com
Business & communications centers
Began: 1985, Franchising since: 1993
Headquarters size: 35 employees
Franchise department: 30 employees

U.S. franchises: 364
Canadian franchises: 0
Other foreign franchises: 290
Company-owned: 1
Units concentrated in all U.S.

Seeking: All U.S.
Seeking in Canada? Yes
Exclusive territories? Yes
Homebased option? No
Kiosk option? No
Employees needed to run franchise: 2-5
Absentee ownership? No

COSTS
Total cost: $154K-164K
Franchise fee: $28.9K
Royalty fee: 4%
Term of agreement: 15 years renewable
     for 15% of current franchise fee
Franchisees required to buy multiple
     units? Outside the U.S. only

FINANCING
In-house: None
3rd-party: Equipment, franchise fee,
     inventory, start-up costs

QUALIFICATIONS
Net worth: $250K
Cash liquidity: $40K-50K
Experience:
     General business experience
     Marketing skills
     Communications skills

TRAINING
At headquarters: 1 week
At franchisee's location: 1 week
At store location: 2-3 days

BUSINESS SUPPORT
Newsletter
Meetings
Toll-free phone line
Grand opening
Internet
Lease negotiations
Security/safety procedures
Field operations/evaluations
Purchasing cooperatives

MARKETING SUPPORT
Co-op advertising
Ad slicks
National media campaign

SUNSHINE PACK & SHIP EXPRESS & RETAIL CENTERS

Financial rating: $

548 48th St. Ct. E.
Bradenton, FL 34208
Ph: (877)751-1513/(941)746-9825
Fax: (941)746-9897
www.sunshinepackandship.com
Packing, crating, shipping & freight
    management services
Began: 1993, Franchising since: 2000
Headquarters size: 7 employees
Franchise department: 4 employees

U.S. franchises: 6
Canadian franchises: 0
Other foreign franchises: 0
Company-owned: 2
Units concentrated in FL

Seeking: All U.S.
Seeking in Canada? No
Exclusive territories? Yes
Homebased option? No
Kiosk option? Yes
Employees needed to run franchise: 2
Absentee ownership? Yes

COSTS
Total cost: $39K-139K
    Kiosk cost: $39K
Franchise fee: $5K/15K
Royalty fee: 5%
Term of agreement: 10 years renewable
    for $1.5K
Franchisees required to buy multiple
    units? No

FINANCING
In-house: Equipment, inventory
3rd-party: Equipment, franchise fee,
    inventory

QUALIFICATIONS
Net worth: $50K-150K
Cash liquidity: $15K-50K
Experience:
    General business experience
    Marketing skills

TRAINING
At headquarters: 40 hours
At franchisee's location: 40 hours
Additional training available

BUSINESS SUPPORT
Newsletter
Meetings
Toll-free phone line
Grand opening
Internet
Lease negotiations
Security/safety procedures
Field operations/evaluations
Purchasing cooperatives

MARKETING SUPPORT
Co-op advertising
Ad slicks
National media campaign
Regional marketing

SUNSHINE PACK & SHIP LOGISTICS CENTERS

Financial rating: $

548 48th St. Ct. E.
Bradenton, FL 34208
Ph: (877)751-1513/(941)746-9825
Fax: (941)746-9897
www.sunshinepackandship.com
Commercial packing, shipping &
    freight brokering services
Began: 2002, Franchising since: 2002
Headquarters size: 7 employees
Franchise department: 4 employees

U.S. franchises: 0
Canadian franchises: 0
Other foreign franchises: 0
Company-owned: 1
Units concentrated in FL

Seeking: All U.S.
Seeking in Canada? No
Exclusive territories? Yes
Homebased option? No
Kiosk option? No
Employees needed to run franchise: 4
Absentee ownership? No

COSTS
Total cost: $89K-129K
Franchise fee: $35K
Royalty fee: 5%
Term of agreement: 10 years renewable
    for $1.5K
Franchisees required to buy multiple
    units? No

FINANCING
In-house: Equipment, inventory
3rd-party: Equipment, franchise fee,
    inventory

QUALIFICATIONS
Net worth: $50K-150K
Cash liquidity: $35K
Experience:
    Industry experience
    General business experience
    Marketing skills

TRAINING
At headquarters: 40 hours
At franchisee's location: 32 hours
At company-owned unit: As needed

BUSINESS SUPPORT
Newsletter
Meetings
Toll-free phone line
Grand opening
Internet
Lease negotiations
Security/safety procedures
Field operations/evaluations
Purchasing cooperatives

MARKETING SUPPORT
Co-op advertising
Ad slicks
Regional marketing

THE UPS STORE

Ranked #6 in Entrepreneur Magazine's 2004 Franchise 500   *Financial rating: $$$$*

6060 Cornerstone Ct. W.
San Diego, CA 92121-3795
Ph: (877)623-7253
Fax: (858)546-7493
www.theupsstore.com
Postal, business & communications
    services
Began: 1980, Franchising since: 1980
Headquarters size: 300 employees
Franchise department: 84 employees

U.S. franchises: 3,497
Canadian franchises: 263
Other foreign franchises: 871
Company-owned: 0
Units concentrated in all U.S.

Seeking: All U.S.
Seeking in Canada? Yes
Exclusive territories? Yes
Homebased option? No
Kiosk option? No
Employees needed to run franchise: 3-5
Absentee ownership? No

COSTS
Total cost: $131.1K-239.7K
Franchise fee: $29.95K
Royalty fee: 5%
Term of agreement: 10 years renewable
    for 25% of current franchise fee
Franchisees required to buy multiple
    units? No

FINANCING
In-house: Equipment, inventory, start-
    up costs
3rd-party: Accounts receivable, equip-
    ment, franchise fee, inventory, pay-
    roll, start-up costs

QUALIFICATIONS
Net worth: $150K
Cash liquidity: $50K
Experience:
    General business experience
    General computer skills

TRAINING
At headquarters: 2 weeks
At franchisee's location: 2 weeks
Online courses & seminars

BUSINESS SUPPORT
Newsletter
Meetings
Toll-free phone line
Grand opening
Internet
Security/safety procedures
Field operations/evaluations
Purchasing cooperatives

MARKETING SUPPORT
Co-op advertising
National media campaign
Regional marketing
Local store marketing

SERVICES   *Printing*

ALLEGRA NETWORK

Ranked #108 in Entrepreneur Magazine's 2004 Franchise 500   *Financial rating: $$$*

1800 W. Maple Rd.
Troy, MI 48084
Ph: (248)614-3700
Fax: (248)614-3719
www.allegranetwork.com
Printing center
Began: 1976, Franchising since: 1977
Headquarters size: 50 employees
Franchise department: 4 employees

U.S. franchises: 437
Canadian franchises: 31
Other foreign franchises: 11
Company-owned: 0
Units concentrated in all U.S.

Seeking: All U.S.
Seeking in Canada? Yes
Exclusive territories? No
Homebased option? No
Kiosk option? No
Employees needed to run franchise: 4
Absentee ownership? Yes

COSTS
Total cost: $256K-358.5K
Franchise fee: $25K
Royalty fee: 3.6-6%
Term of agreement: 20 years renewable
    at no charge
Franchisees required to buy multiple
    units? No

FINANCING
In-house: None
3rd-party: Accounts receivable, equip-
    ment, franchise fee, inventory, pay-
    roll, start-up costs

QUALIFICATIONS
Net worth: $250K-500K
Cash liquidity: $100K-200K
Experience:
    General business experience
    Sales & marketing experience

TRAINING
At headquarters: 2 weeks
At franchisee's location: 1 week
Ongoing

BUSINESS SUPPORT
Newsletter
Meetings
Toll-free phone line
Grand opening
Internet
Field operations/evaluations

MARKETING SUPPORT
Co-op advertising
Ad slicks
Regional marketing
Direct mail
Lead generation program

ALPHAGRAPHICS PRINTSHOPS OF THE FUTURE

Ranked #297 in Entrepreneur Magazine's 2004 Franchise 500   *Financial rating: $$$$*

268 S. State St., #300
Salt Lake City, UT 84111
Ph: (800)528-4885/(801)595-7270
Fax: (801)595-7271
www.alphagraphics.com
Digital publishing, Internet services,
    printing
Began: 1970, Franchising since: 1980
Headquarters size: 98 employees
Franchise department: 6 employees

U.S. franchises: 242
Canadian franchises: 0
Other foreign franchises: 41
Company-owned: 0
Units concentrated in all U.S.

Seeking: All U.S.
Seeking in Canada? Yes
Exclusive territories? Yes
Homebased option? No
Kiosk option? No
Employees needed to run franchise: 6
Absentee ownership? No

COSTS
Total cost: $352K-545.9K
Franchise fee: $25.9K
Royalty fee: 1.5-8%
Term of agreement: 20 years renewable
    at no charge
Franchisees required to buy multiple
    units? No

FINANCING
In-house: None
3rd-party: Accounts receivable, equip-
    ment, franchise fee, inventory, pay-
    roll, start-up costs

QUALIFICATIONS
Net worth: $350K
Cash liquidity: $100K
Experience:
    General business experience
    Marketing skills

TRAINING
At headquarters: 4 weeks
At franchisee's location: 2 weeks
At regional locations: Varies

BUSINESS SUPPORT
Newsletter
Meetings
Toll-free phone line
Grand opening
Internet
Security/safety procedures
Field operations/evaluations
Purchasing cooperatives

MARKETING SUPPORT
Co-op advertising
Ad slicks
Integrated sales & marketing
Direct mail

AMERICAN WHOLESALE THERMOGRAPHERS INC.

Ranked #456 in Entrepreneur Magazine's 2004 Franchise 500   *Financial rating: $$$$*

12715 Telge Rd.
Cypress, TX 77429
Ph: (888)280-2053/(281)256-4100
Fax: (281)256-4178
www.awt.com
Wholesale thermographic printing
Began: 1980, Franchising since: 1981
Headquarters size: 155 employees
Franchise department: 100 employees

U.S. franchises: 13
Canadian franchises: 3
Other foreign franchises: 0
Company-owned: 0
Units concentrated in AZ, CA, OK, TX

Seeking: All U.S.
Seeking in Canada? Yes
Exclusive territories? Yes
Homebased option? No
Kiosk option? No
Employees needed to run franchise: 3
Absentee ownership? No

COSTS
Total cost: $357.6K-381.1K
Franchise fee: $30K
Royalty fee: 7%
Term of agreement: 25 years renewable
    at no charge
Franchisees required to buy multiple
    units? No

FINANCING
In-house: None
3rd-party: Equipment, franchise fee,
    inventory, start-up costs

QUALIFICATIONS
Cash liquidity: $90K
Experience:
    General business experience
    Marketing skills

TRAINING
At headquarters: 2 weeks
At franchisee's location: 1 week
At field site: 2 weeks

BUSINESS SUPPORT
Newsletter
Meetings
Toll-free phone line
Grand opening
Internet
Field operations/evaluations
Purchasing cooperatives

MARKETING SUPPORT
Marketing, mailing & telemarketing
    services

BUSINESS CARDS TOMORROW INC.

Financial rating: $$$$

3000 N.E. 30th Pl., 5th Fl.
Ft. Lauderdale, FL 33306-1957
Ph: (800)627-9998/(954)563-1224
Fax: (954)565-0742
www.bct-net.com
Wholesale thermography, rubber
    stamps
Began: 1975, Franchising since: 1977
Headquarters size: 34 employees
Franchise department: 2 employees

U.S. franchises: 72
Canadian franchises: 8
Other foreign franchises: 0
Company-owned: 2

Focusing on: CA, FL, OH, TX
Seeking in Canada? No
Exclusive territories? Yes
Homebased option? No
Kiosk option? No
Employees needed to run franchise: 6
Absentee ownership? No

COSTS
Total cost: $161.8K-539.5K
Franchise fee: $35K
Royalty fee: 6%
Term of agreement: 25 years renewable
    at no charge
Franchisees required to buy multiple
    units? No

FINANCING
In-house: None
3rd-party: Accounts receivable, equip-
    ment, franchise fee, inventory, pay-
    roll, start-up costs

QUALIFICATIONS
Experience:
    General business experience
    Marketing skills
    Team-building skills

TRAINING
At headquarters: 2 weeks
At franchisee's location: 2 weeks
Follow-up visit: 3 days

BUSINESS SUPPORT
Newsletter
Meetings
Toll-free phone line
Internet
Lease negotiations
Security/safety procedures
Field operations/evaluations
Purchasing cooperatives

MARKETING SUPPORT
Co-op advertising
Trade shows
Marketing materials

COPY CLUB INC.

Ranked #444 in Entrepreneur Magazine's 2004 Franchise 500

Financial rating: $$$$

12715 Telge Rd.
Cypress, TX 77429
Ph: (888)280-2053/(281)256-4100
Fax: (281)256-4178
www.copyclub.com
Business copying & digital imaging
Began: 1992, Franchising since: 1994
Headquarters size: 155 employees
Franchise department: 100 employees

U.S. franchises: 21
Canadian franchises: 0
Other foreign franchises: 0
Company-owned: 0
Units concentrated in AZ, CA, GA, TX

Seeking: All U.S.
Seeking in Canada? No
Exclusive territories? Yes
Homebased option? No
Kiosk option? No
Employees needed to run franchise: 7
Absentee ownership? No

COSTS
Total cost: $311.3K-421.95K
Franchise fee: $30K
Royalty fee: 7%
Term of agreement: 25 years renewable
    at no charge
Franchisees required to buy multiple
    units? No

FINANCING
In-house: None
3rd-party: Equipment, franchise fee,
    inventory, start-up costs

QUALIFICATIONS
Cash liquidity: $105K
Experience:
    General business experience
    Marketing skills

TRAINING
At headquarters: 3 weeks
At franchisee's location: 1 week

BUSINESS SUPPORT
Newsletter
Meetings
Toll-free phone line
Grand opening
Internet
Field operations/evaluations
Purchasing cooperatives

MARKETING SUPPORT
Marketing, mailing & telemarketing
    services

KWIK KOPY BUSINESS CENTERS INC.
Ranked #500 in Entrepreneur Magazine's 2004 Franchise 500   *Financial rating: $$$$*

12715 Telge Rd.
Cypress, TX 77429
Ph: (800)746-9498/(281)256-4100
Fax: (281)256-4178
www.kkbconline.com
Printing, copying, packing & shipping
    services
Began: 2001, Franchising since: 2001
Headquarters size: 150 employees
Franchise department: 100 employees

U.S. franchises: 10
Canadian franchises: 0
Other foreign franchises: 0
Company-owned: 0
Units concentrated in KY, LA, MD,
    NC, TX

Seeking: All U.S.
Seeking in Canada? No
Exclusive territories? Yes
Homebased option? No
Kiosk option? No
Employees needed to run franchise: 2
Absentee ownership? No

COSTS
Total cost: $187K-277.7K
Franchise fee: $30K
Royalty fee: 7%
Term of agreement: 15 years renewable
    at no charge
Franchisees required to buy multiple
    units? No

FINANCING
In-house: None
3rd-party: Equipment, franchise fee,
    inventory, start-up costs

QUALIFICATIONS
Cash liquidity: $40K
Experience:
    General business experience

TRAINING
At headquarters: 4 weeks
At franchisee's location: 1 week

BUSINESS SUPPORT
Newsletter
Meetings
Toll-free phone line
Grand opening
Internet
Field operations/evaluations
Purchasing cooperatives

MARKETING SUPPORT
Co-op advertising
National media campaign

KWIK KOPY PRINTING
Ranked #185 in Entrepreneur Magazine's 2004 Franchise 500   *Financial rating: $$$$*

12715 Telge Rd.
Cypress, TX 77429
Ph: (888)280-2053/(281)256-4100
Fax: (281)256-4178
www.kwikkopy.com
Printing & copying services
Began: 1967, Franchising since: 1967
Headquarters size: 155 employees
Franchise department: 100 employees

U.S. franchises: 257
Canadian franchises: 72
Other foreign franchises: 294
Company-owned: 0

Seeking: All U.S.
Seeking in Canada? No
Exclusive territories? Yes
Homebased option? No
Kiosk option? No
Employees needed to run franchise: 3
Absentee ownership? No

COSTS
Total cost: $320.2K-404.4K
Franchise fee: $25K
Royalty fee: 4-8%
Term of agreement: 25 years renewable
    at no charge
Franchisees required to buy multiple
    units? Outside the U.S. only

FINANCING
In-house: None
3rd-party: Equipment, franchise fee,
    inventory, start-up costs

QUALIFICATIONS
Experience:
    General business experience
    Marketing skills

TRAINING
At headquarters: 3-1/2 weeks
At franchisee's location: 1 week

BUSINESS SUPPORT
Newsletter
Meetings
Toll-free phone line
Grand opening
Internet
Field operations/evaluations
Purchasing cooperatives

MARKETING SUPPORT
Ad slicks
Marketing, mailing & telemarketing

MINUTEMAN PRESS INT'L. INC.

Ranked #54 in Entrepreneur Magazine's 2004 Franchise 500   *Financial rating: $$$$*

61 Executive Blvd.
Farmingdale, NY 11735
Ph: (800)645-3006/(631)249-1370
Fax: (631)249-5618
www.minutemanpress.com
Full-service printing center
Began: 1973, Franchising since: 1975
Headquarters size: 75 employees
Franchise department: 75 employees

U.S. franchises: 714
Canadian franchises: 60
Other foreign franchises: 110
Company-owned: 0
Units concentrated in CA, NY, PA, TX

Seeking: All U.S.
Seeking in Canada? Yes
Exclusive territories? No
Homebased option? No
Kiosk option? No
Employees needed to run franchise: 3
Absentee ownership? Info not provided

COSTS
Total cost: $119.5K-214.9K
Franchise fee: $44.5K
Royalty fee: 6%
Term of agreement: 35 years renewable
  at no charge
Franchisees required to buy multiple
  units? No

FINANCING
In-house: None
3rd-party: Equipment

QUALIFICATIONS
Cash liquidity: $50K

TRAINING
At headquarters: 2.5 weeks
At franchisee's location: 1-2 weeks
Ongoing

BUSINESS SUPPORT
Newsletter
Meetings
Toll-free phone line
Grand opening
Internet
Lease negotiations
Security/safety procedures
Field operations/evaluations

MARKETING SUPPORT
Ad slicks
Regional marketing
In-field training

PIP PRINTING

Ranked #362 in Entrepreneur Magazine's 2004 Franchise 500   *Financial rating: $$$$*

26722 Plaza Dr., #200
Mission Viejo, CA 92691
Ph: (800)894-7498
Fax: (949)282-3899
www.pip.com
Business printing products & services
Began: 1965, Franchising since: 1968
Headquarters size: 35 employees
Franchise department: Info not pro-
  vided

U.S. franchises: 309
Canadian franchises: 0
Other foreign franchises: 9
Company-owned: 0
Units concentrated in all U.S.

Seeking: All U.S.
Seeking in Canada? No
Exclusive territories? Yes
Homebased option? No
Kiosk option? No
Employees needed to run franchise: 4
Absentee ownership? No

COSTS
Total cost: $201K-442K
Franchise fee: $20K
Royalty fee: 2.5-6.5%
Term of agreement: 10 years renewable
  at no charge
Franchisees required to buy multiple
  units? No

FINANCING
No financing available

QUALIFICATIONS
Net worth: $350K
Cash liquidity: $125K
Experience:
  General business experience
  Marketing skills

TRAINING
At headquarters: 2 weeks
At franchisee's location: Ongoing
Regional training & annual
  convention

BUSINESS SUPPORT
Newsletter
Meetings
Toll-free phone line
Grand opening
Internet
Lease negotiations
Security/safety procedures
Field operations/evaluations
Purchasing cooperatives

MARKETING SUPPORT
Co-op advertising
Ad slicks
National media campaign
Regional marketing
Internet

SIGNAL GRAPHICS BUSINESS CENTER

Financial rating: $$$$

852 Broadway, #300
Denver, CO 80203
Ph: (800)852-6336/(303)779-6789
Fax: (303)779-8445
www.signalgraphics.com
Printing, copying, desktop publishing,
 digital services
Began: 1974, Franchising since: 1982
Headquarters size: 8 employees
Franchise department: 8 employees

U.S. franchises: 35
Canadian franchises: 0
Other foreign franchises: 0
Company-owned: 3
Units concentrated in all U.S.

Seeking: All U.S.
Seeking in Canada? No
Exclusive territories? Yes
Homebased option? No
Kiosk option? No
Employees needed to run franchise: 2-5
Absentee ownership? Yes

COSTS
Total cost: $142K-315.9K
Franchise fee: $27K
Royalty fee: to 5%
Term of agreement: 20 years renewable
 at no charge
Franchisees required to buy multiple
 units? No

FINANCING
No financing available

QUALIFICATIONS
Net worth: $150K
Cash liquidity: $60K

TRAINING
At headquarters: 12 days
At franchisee's location: 5 days

BUSINESS SUPPORT
Newsletter
Meetings
Toll-free phone line
Grand opening
Internet
Field operations/evaluations

MARKETING SUPPORT
Co-op advertising
National media campaign
Regional marketing

SIR SPEEDY INC.

Current financial data not available

26722 Plaza Dr.
Mission Viejo, CA 92691
Ph: (800)854-3321/(949)348-5000
Fax: (949)348-5068
www.sirspeedy.com
Printing, copying, digital network
Began: 1968, Franchising since: 1968
Headquarters size: 55 employees
Franchise department: Info not pro-
 vided

U.S. franchises: 483
Canadian franchises: 5
Other foreign franchises: 32
Company-owned: 0
Units concentrated in all U.S.

Seeking: All U.S.
Seeking in Canada? Yes
Exclusive territories? Yes
Homebased option? No
Kiosk option? No
Employees needed to run franchise: 7
Absentee ownership? No

COSTS
Total cost: $243K
Franchise fee: $25K
Royalty fee: 4-6%
Term of agreement: 20 years renewable
 at no charge
Franchisees required to buy multiple
 units? Outside the U.S. only

FINANCING
No financing available

QUALIFICATIONS
Net worth: $350K
Cash liquidity: $125K-150K
Experience:
 Industry experience
 General business experience

TRAINING
At headquarters: 2 weeks
At franchisee's location: 2 weeks
Sales training: 1 week

BUSINESS SUPPORT
Newsletter
Meetings
Toll-free phone line
Grand opening
Internet
Lease negotiations
Security/safety procedures
Field operations/evaluations

MARKETING SUPPORT
Ad slicks
National media campaign
Direct mail
E-commerce marketing

SERVICES — *Real Estate*

ASSIST-2-SELL

Ranked #145 in Entrepreneur Magazine's 2004 Franchise 500   *Financial rating: $$$$*

1610 Meadow Wood Ln.
Reno, NV 89502
Ph: (800)528-7816/(775)688-6060
Fax: (775)823-8823
www.assist2sell.com
Discount real estate services
Began: 1987, Franchising since: 1993
Headquarters size: 20 employees
Franchise department: 20 employees

U.S. franchises: 245
Canadian franchises: 4
Other foreign franchises: 0
Company-owned: 0
Units concentrated in all U.S.

Seeking: All U.S.
Seeking in Canada? Yes
Exclusive territories? Yes
Homebased option? No
Kiosk option? No
Employees needed to run franchise: 3
Absentee ownership? No

COSTS
Total cost: $30K-57K
Franchise fee: $14.5K
Royalty fee: 5%
Term of agreement: Renewable term at
    $2.99K
Franchisees required to buy multiple
    units? No

FINANCING
No financing available

QUALIFICATIONS
Net worth: $100K+
Cash liquidity: $25K+
Experience:
    Industry experience
    Minimum 2 years real estate sales
    experience

TRAINING
At headquarters: 5 days

BUSINESS SUPPORT
Newsletter
Meetings
Toll-free phone line
Internet

MARKETING SUPPORT
Ad slicks

BETTER HOMES REALTY INC.

Current financial data not available

1777 Botelho Dr., #390
Walnut Creek, CA 94596
Ph: (800)642-4428/(925)937-9001
Fax: (925)988-2770
www.bhr.com
Real estate
Began: 1964, Franchising since: 1975
Headquarters size: 7 employees
Franchise department: 1 employee

U.S. franchises: 40
Canadian franchises: 0
Other foreign franchises: 0
Company-owned: 0
Units concentrated in CA

Seeking: West
Focusing on: CA
Seeking in Canada? No
Exclusive territories? Yes
Homebased option? No
Kiosk option? No
Employees needed to run franchise:
    Info not provided
Absentee ownership? Yes

COSTS
Total cost: to $61.5K
Franchise fee: $9.95K
Royalty fee: 6%
Term of agreement: 5 years renewable
    at no charge
Franchisees required to buy multiple
    units? No

FINANCING
In-house: Franchise fee
3rd-party: None

QUALIFICATIONS
Experience:
    Industry experience
    General business experience

TRAINING
Info not provided

BUSINESS SUPPORT
Newsletter
Meetings
Toll-free phone line
Grand opening
Internet

MARKETING SUPPORT
Co-op advertising
Ad slicks
Regional marketing

CENTURY 21 REAL ESTATE CORP.

Ranked #45 in Entrepreneur Magazine's 2004 Franchise 500   *Financial rating: $$$$*

1 Campus Dr.
Parsippany, NJ 07054
Ph: (800)221-5737
Fax: (973)496-1099
www.century21.com
Real estate
Began: 1971, Franchising since: 1972
Headquarters size: Info not provided
Franchise department: Info not provided

U.S. franchises: 4,069
Canadian franchises: 322
Other foreign franchises: 2,130
Company-owned: 0
Units concentrated in all U.S.

Seeking: All U.S.
Seeking in Canada? Yes
Exclusive territories? No
Homebased option? No
Kiosk option? No
Employees needed to run franchise:
    Info not provided
Absentee ownership? No

COSTS
Total cost: $11.6K-522.4K
Franchise fee: to $25K
Royalty fee: 6%
Term of agreement: 10 years
Franchisees required to buy multiple
    units? Outside the U.S. only

FINANCING
In-house: Franchise fee
3rd-party: Equipment, franchise fee

QUALIFICATIONS
Net worth: $25K
Experience:
    Industry experience
    General business experience
    Marketing skills

TRAINING
At conventions & workshops: Varies

BUSINESS SUPPORT
Newsletter
Meetings
Toll-free phone line
Internet
Field operations/evaluations

MARKETING SUPPORT
Co-op advertising
Ad slicks
National media campaign
Regional marketing

COLDWELL BANKER REAL ESTATE CORP.

Ranked #201 in Entrepreneur Magazine's 2004 Franchise 500   *Financial rating: $$$$*

1 Campus Dr.
Parsippany, NJ 07054
Ph: (973)496-5656, Fax: (973)496-9700
www.coldwellbanker.com
Real estate
Began: 1906, Franchising since: 1982
Headquarters size: 100 employees
Franchise department: 30 employees

U.S. franchises: 2,196
Canadian franchises: 213
Other foreign franchises: 146
Company-owned: 861
Units concentrated in all U.S.

Seeking: All U.S.
Seeking in Canada? Yes
Exclusive territories? No
Homebased option? No
Kiosk option? No
Employees needed to run franchise:
    Info not provided
Absentee ownership? No

COSTS
Total cost: $23.5K-477.3K
Franchise fee: $13K-20.5K
Royalty fee: 6%
Term of agreement: 10 years
Franchisees required to buy multiple
    units? Outside the U.S. only

FINANCING
In-house: Franchise fee
3rd-party: Equipment, franchise fee

QUALIFICATIONS
Net worth: $25K
Experience:
    Industry experience

TRAINING
At headquarters: 4 days
At franchisee's location: 1-2 days
At other locations
Via the Internet

BUSINESS SUPPORT
Newsletter
Meetings
Toll-free phone line
Grand opening
Internet
Field operations/evaluations

MARKETING SUPPORT
Ad slicks
National media campaign
Regional marketing
Web site

CRYE-LEIKE FRANCHISES INC.

Current financial data not available

5111 Maryland Wy.
Brentwood, TN 37027
Ph: (615)221-0449, Fax: (615)221-0445
www.crye-leike.com
Real estate
Began: 1977, Franchising since: 1999
Headquarters size: 500 employees
Franchise department: 6 employees

U.S. franchises: 14
Canadian franchises: 0
Other foreign franchises: 0
Company-owned: 0
Units concentrated in AR, FL, KY, MS, TN

Seeking: Midwest, South, Southeast
Focusing on: AL, GA
Seeking in Canada? No
Exclusive territories? No
Homebased option? No
Kiosk option? No
Employees needed to run franchise:
    Info not provided
Absentee ownership? Yes

COSTS
Total cost: $70.7K-298.5K
Franchise fee: $6.5K-13.5K
Royalty fee: 5-6%
Term of agreement: 5 years renewable
    for 10% of initial franchise fee
Franchisees required to buy multiple
    units? No

FINANCING
No financing available

QUALIFICATIONS
Experience:
    Proven business operator

TRAINING
At headquarters: 3 weeks

BUSINESS SUPPORT
Newsletter
Meetings
Toll-free phone line
Grand opening
Internet

MARKETING SUPPORT
Co-op advertising
Ad slicks
Internet marketing support

ERA FRANCHISE SYSTEMS INC.

Ranked #70 in Entrepreneur Magazine's 2004 Franchise 500

Financial rating: $$$$

1 Campus Dr.
Parsippany, NJ 07054
Ph: (973)428-9700
Fax: (973)496-5904
www.era.com
Real estate
Began: 1971, Franchising since: 1972
Headquarters size: Info not provided
Franchise department: Info not pro-
    vided

U.S. franchises: 909
Canadian franchises: 0
Other foreign franchises: 1,474
Company-owned: 30
Units concentrated in all U.S.

Seeking: All U.S.
Seeking in Canada? Yes
Exclusive territories? No
Homebased option? No
Kiosk option? No
Employees needed to run franchise:
    Info not provided
Absentee ownership? No

COSTS
Total cost: $42.7K-205.9K
Franchise fee: to $20K
Royalty fee: 6%
Term of agreement: 10 yearss
Franchisees required to buy multiple
    units? No

FINANCING
In-house: Franchise fee
3rd-party: Equipment, franchise fee

QUALIFICATIONS
Net worth: $25K
Experience:
    Industry experience
    General business experience

TRAINING
Info not provided

BUSINESS SUPPORT
Newsletter
Meetings
Toll-free phone line
Internet
Field operations/evaluations

MARKETING SUPPORT
Ad slicks
National media campaign
Regional marketing

HELP-U-SELL REAL ESTATE

Ranked #98 in Entrepreneur Magazine's 2004 Franchise 500　　　　*Financial rating: $$$$*

6800 Jericho Tpke., #208E
Syosset, NY 11791
Ph: (800)366-1177
Fax: (516)364-8757
www.helpusell.com
Real estate
Began: 1976, Franchising since: 1978
Headquarters size: 10 employees
Franchise department: 5 employees

U.S. franchises: 400
Canadian franchises: 1
Other foreign franchises: 0
Company-owned: 0
Units concentrated in AZ, CA, FL

Seeking: All U.S.
Seeking in Canada? Yes
Exclusive territories? No
Homebased option? No
Kiosk option? No
Employees needed to run franchise: 2-3
Absentee ownership? Yes

COSTS
Total cost: $64.5K-190.5K
Franchise fee: $16.5K
Royalty fee: 6%
Term of agreement: 5 years renewable
    for $500
Franchisees required to buy multiple
    units? No

FINANCING
In-house: Franchise fee
3rd-party: None

QUALIFICATIONS
Net worth: $50K
Cash liquidity: $50K
Experience:
    Industry experience
    General business experience

TRAINING
At franchisee's location: 8 weeks by
    phone
Retreats, regional meetings,
    convention

BUSINESS SUPPORT
Newsletter
Meetings
Toll-free phone line
Grand opening
Internet
Lease negotiations
Field operations/evaluations

MARKETING SUPPORT
Co-op advertising
Ad slicks
National media campaign
Regional marketing
Marketing instruction/training

HOMEVESTORS OF AMERICA INC.

Ranked #99 in Entrepreneur Magazine's 2004 Franchise 500　　　　*Financial rating: $$$*

11910 Greenville Ave., #300
Dallas, TX 75243
Ph: (888)495-5220, Fax: (404)688-5081
www.homevestors.com
Home buying, repair & selling system
Began: 1989, Franchising since: 1996
Headquarters size: 30 employees
Franchise department: 7 employees

U.S. franchises: 171
Canadian franchises: 0
Other foreign franchises: 0
Company-owned: 0

Seeking: Midwest, South, Southeast,
    Southwest
Focusing on: AL, AZ, CO, FL, GA, IL,
    IN, KS, KY, LA, MI, MN, MO, NC,
    NJ, NM, NV, OH, OK, PA, SC, TN,
    TX, UT, WI
Seeking in Canada? No
Exclusive territories? No
Homebased option? No
Kiosk option? No
Employees needed to run franchise: 2
Absentee ownership? No

COSTS
Total cost: $139.2K-219.5K
Franchise fee: $43K
Royalty fee: Varies
Term of agreement: 5 years renewable
    at no charge
Franchisees required to buy multiple
    units? No

FINANCING
In-house: Inventory
3rd-party: None

QUALIFICATIONS
Net worth: $151K
Cash liquidity: $143K
Experience:
    General business experience

TRAINING
At headquarters: 10 days
Advanced training: 2 days

BUSINESS SUPPORT
Newsletter
Meetings
Internet
Field operations/evaluations
Purchasing cooperatives

MARKETING SUPPORT
Co-op advertising
Ad slicks
Regional marketing

INTERNATIONAL REALTY PLUS

Financial rating: 0

1912 E. Andy Devine Ave.
Kingman, AZ 86401
Ph: (941)954-2658
Fax: (941)966-6434
www.internationalrealtyplus.us
Real estate
Began: 1995, Franchising since: 1996
Headquarters size: 3 employees
Franchise department: 2 employees

U.S. franchises: 50
Canadian franchises: 1
Other foreign franchises: 3
Company-owned: 0

Seeking: All U.S.
Seeking in Canada? Yes
Exclusive territories? Yes
Homebased option? No
Kiosk option? No
Employees needed to run franchise:
    Info not provided
Absentee ownership? Yes

COSTS
Total cost: $7.99K-47K
Franchise fee: $7.9K-25K
Royalty fee: Varies
Term of agreement: 5 years renewable
    for up to $7.9K
Franchisees required to buy multiple
    units? No

FINANCING
No financing available

QUALIFICATIONS
Experience:
    Industry experience
    Real estate broker license

TRAINING
At headquarters: 1 week
At franchisee's location: 3 days
Online training as needed

BUSINESS SUPPORT
Newsletter
Meetings
Toll-free phone line
Grand opening
Internet
Security/safety procedures
Field operations/evaluations
Purchasing cooperatives

MARKETING SUPPORT
National media campaign
Regional marketing
Web portal

KELLER WILLIAMS REALTY

Ranked #128 in Entrepreneur Magazine's 2004 Franchise 500

Financial rating: $$$$

3701 Bee Cave Rd., #200
Austin, TX 78746
Ph: (512)327-3070
Fax: (512)328-1433
www.kellerwilliams.com
Real estate
Began: 1983, Franchising since: 1987
Headquarters size: 65 employees
Franchise department: 9 employees

U.S. franchises: 284
Canadian franchises: 3
Other foreign franchises: 0
Company-owned: 0

Seeking: All U.S.
Seeking in Canada? Yes
Exclusive territories? Yes
Homebased option? No
Kiosk option? No
Employees needed to run franchise: 3-4
Absentee ownership? Info not provided

COSTS
Total cost: $121K-252K
Franchise fee: $25K
Royalty fee: 6%
Term of agreement: 5 years renewable
    for $2.5K
Franchisees required to buy multiple
    units? No

FINANCING
No financing available

QUALIFICATIONS
Net worth: $400K
Cash liquidity: $150K
Experience:
    Industry experience
    General business experience
    Marketing skills

TRAINING
At headquarters: 1 week
At franchisee's location: 3 days-1 week
Additional training: 3 days-1 week

BUSINESS SUPPORT
Newsletter
Meetings
Grand opening
Internet
Security/safety procedures
Field operations/evaluations

MARKETING SUPPORT
Regional marketing
In-house marketing department

RE/MAX INT'L. INC.

Ranked #19 in Entrepreneur Magazine's 2004 Franchise 500

Financial rating: $$$$

P.O. Box 3907
Englewood, CO 80155-3907
Ph: (800)525-7452/(303)770-5531
Fax: (303)796-3599
www.remax.com
Real estate
Began: 1973, Franchising since: 1975
Headquarters size: 350 employees
Franchise department: 10 employees

U.S. franchises: 3,183
Canadian franchises: 561
Other foreign franchises: 857
Company-owned: 21
Units concentrated in all U.S.

Seeking: All U.S.
Seeking in Canada? Yes
Exclusive territories? No
Homebased option? No
Kiosk option? No
Employees needed to run franchise: 2
Absentee ownership? Yes

COSTS
Total cost: $20K-200K
Franchise fee: $10K-25K
Royalty fee: Varies
Term of agreement: 5 years renewable
Franchisees required to buy multiple
    units? No

FINANCING
In-house: Franchise fee
3rd-party: None

QUALIFICATIONS
Experience:
    Industry experience
    General business experience
    Marketing skills

TRAINING
At headquarters: 5 days
Semi-annual convention & conference

BUSINESS SUPPORT
Newsletter
Meetings
Toll-free phone line
Grand opening
Internet
Field operations/evaluations
Purchasing cooperatives

MARKETING SUPPORT
Ad slicks
National media campaign
Regional marketing
Brochures, magazines & videos
Online extranet

REAL LIVING

Current financial data not available

77 E. Nationwide Blvd.
Columbus, OH 43215
Ph: (614)273-6090
Fax: (614)459-4477
www.realliving.com
Real estate
Began: 1976, Franchising since: 1981
Headquarters size: 60 employees
Franchise department: 25 employees

U.S. franchises: 30
Canadian franchises: 0
Other foreign franchises: 0
Company-owned: 80
Units concentrated in FL, IN, KY, OH

Focusing on: IL, MI, VA, WV
Seeking in Canada? No
Exclusive territories? No
Homebased option? No
Kiosk option? No
Employees needed to run franchise:
    Info not provided
Absentee ownership? No

COSTS
Total cost: $3K-80K
Franchise fee: $2.5K-80K
Royalty fee: 5%
Term of agreement: 10 years renewable
    at no charge
Franchisees required to buy multiple
    units? No

FINANCING
No financing available

QUALIFICATIONS
Experience:
    Industry experience
    General business experience
    Marketing skills

TRAINING
At headquarters
At franchisee's location

BUSINESS SUPPORT
Newsletter
Meetings
Toll-free phone line
Internet
Lease negotiations
Security/safety procedures
Field operations/evaluations
Purchasing cooperatives

MARKETING SUPPORT
Ad slicks

REALTY EXECUTIVES INT'L. INC.
Ranked #83 in Entrepreneur Magazine's 2004 Franchise 500

Financial rating: $$$$

4427 N. 36th St., #100
Phoenix, AZ 85018
Ph: (800)252-3366/(602)957-0747
Fax: (602)224-5542
www.realtyexecutives.com
Real estate
Began: 1965, Franchising since: 1973
Headquarters size: 15 employees
Franchise department: 4 employees

U.S. franchises: 531
Canadian franchises: 22
Other foreign franchises: 17
Company-owned: 0
Units concentrated in all U.S.

Seeking: All U.S.
Focusing on: ND, NY, OK, SD, WV
Seeking in Canada? Yes
Exclusive territories? Yes
Homebased option? No
Kiosk option? No
Employees needed to run franchise:
    Info not provided
Absentee ownership? Yes

COSTS
Total cost: $22.6K-83.1K
Franchise fee: $1K-20K
Royalty fee: $50/licensee
Term of agreement: 5 years renewable
    at no charge
Franchisees required to buy multiple
    units? No

FINANCING
In-house: None
3rd-party: Accounts receivable, equip-
    ment, franchise fee, inventory, pay-
    roll, start-up costs

QUALIFICATIONS
Cash liquidity: $20K
Experience:
    Industry experience
    General business experience
    Marketing skills

TRAINING
At headquarters: 3 days
Annual meetings

BUSINESS SUPPORT
Newsletter
Meetings
Toll-free phone line
Grand opening
Internet
Lease negotiations
Security/safety procedures
Field operations/evaluations

MARKETING SUPPORT
Co-op advertising
Ad slicks
National media campaign
Regional marketing

STATE WIDE REAL ESTATE

Current financial data not available

P.O. Box 297
Escanaba, MI 49829
Ph: (906)786-8392
Fax: (906)786-1388
www.statewiderealestate.net
Real estate
Began: 1944, Franchising since: 1979
Headquarters size: 6 employees
Franchise department: 2 employees

U.S. franchises: 33
Canadian franchises: 0
Other foreign franchises: 0
Company-owned: 0
Units concentrated in MI

Focusing on: MI
Seeking in Canada? No
Exclusive territories? Yes
Homebased option? No
Kiosk option? No
Employees needed to run franchise:
    2-10
Absentee ownership? No

COSTS
Total cost: $10K-50K
Franchise fee: $5K
Royalty fee: 5%
Term of agreement: 5 years renewable
    at no charge
Franchisees required to buy multiple
    units? No

FINANCING
In-house: Franchise fee
3rd-party: None

QUALIFICATIONS
Net worth: $50K
Cash liquidity: $10K
Experience:
    Industry experience

TRAINING
At headquarters: 1 day
At franchisee's location: 1 day

BUSINESS SUPPORT
Newsletter
Meetings
Toll-free phone line
Grand opening
Internet

MARKETING SUPPORT
Co-op advertising
Ad slicks
Regional marketing

WEICHERT REAL ESTATE AFFILIATES INC.

Current financial data not available

225 Littleton Rd.
Morris Plains, NJ 07950
Ph: (973)359-8377, Fax: (973)292-1428
www.weichert.com
Real estate
Began: 1969, Franchising since: 2001
Headquarters size: 1,200 employees
Franchise department: 17 employees

U.S. franchises: 80
Canadian franchises: 0
Other foreign franchises: 0
Company-owned: 200
Units concentrated in CT, DE, FL,
    GA, LA, NC, NJ, NY, OH, PA, SC,
    TN, TX

Seeking: All U.S.
Focusing on: AL, IL, IN, KY, MA, ME,
    MI, MO, MS, NH, OK, RI
Seeking in Canada? No
Exclusive territories? Yes
Homebased option? No
Kiosk option? No
Employees needed to run franchise: 15
Absentee ownership? Yes

COSTS
Total cost: $45K-254K
Franchise fee: $25K
Royalty fee: 6%
Term of agreement: 7 years renewable
    for $1K
Franchisees required to buy multiple
    units? Outside the U.S. only

FINANCING
No financing available

QUALIFICATIONS
Cash liquidity: $150K+
Experience:
    Industry experience
    General business experience
    Marketing skills

TRAINING
At headquarters: 4 days
At franchisee's location: Ongoing
Annual conference & local workshops

BUSINESS SUPPORT
Newsletter
Meetings
Toll-free phone line
Grand opening
Internet
Field operations/evaluations
Purchasing cooperatives

MARKETING SUPPORT
Co-op advertising
Ad slicks
National media campaign
Regional marketing
PR program
Custom marketing materials

WHY USA

Ranked #331 in Entrepreneur Magazine's 2004 Franchise 500

Financial rating: $$$$

8301 Creekside Cir., #101
Bloomington, MN 55437
Ph: (952)841-7050
Fax: (952)841-7061
www.whyusa.com
Real estate
Began: 1988, Franchising since: 1989
Headquarters size: 10 employees
Franchise department: 4 employees

U.S. franchises: 74
Canadian franchises: 0
Other foreign franchises: 0
Company-owned: 0
Units concentrated in IA, MN, NE, WI

Seeking: All U.S.
Seeking in Canada? No
Exclusive territories? Yes
Homebased option? No
Kiosk option? Yes
Employees needed to run franchise: 2
Absentee ownership? Yes

COSTS
Total cost: $23.8K-103.4K
    Kiosk cost: $20K
Franchise fee: $19.99K
Royalty fee: Varies
Term of agreement: 3 years renewable
    at no charge
Franchisees required to buy multiple
    units? No

FINANCING
In-house: Franchise fee, equipment,
    start-up costs
3rd-party: Accounts receivable, equip-
    ment, franchise fee, payroll, start-
    up costs

QUALIFICATIONS
Experience:
    General business experience
    Marketing skills

TRAINING
At headquarters: 3 days
At franchisee's location: 2 days
Biannual conferences & monthly tele-
    conferences

BUSINESS SUPPORT
Meetings
Internet
Lease negotiations
Field operations/evaluations

MARKETING SUPPORT
Co-op advertising
Ad slicks
Marketing campaigns

INTERQUEST DETECTION CANINES

Ranked #342 in Entrepreneur Magazine's 2004 Franchise 500 *Financial rating: $$$*

21900 Tomball Pkwy.
Houston, TX 77070-1526
Ph: (281)320-1231, Fax: (281)320-2512
www.interquestfranchise.com
Canine detection services
Began: 1988, Franchising since: 1999
Headquarters size: 12 employees
Franchise department: 9 employees

U.S. franchises: 33
Canadian franchises: 0
Other foreign franchises: 0
Company-owned: 2
Units concentrated in CA, TX

Seeking: All U.S.
Focusing on: New England, Southeast
Seeking in Canada? No
Exclusive territories? Yes
Homebased option? Yes
Kiosk option? No
Employees needed to run franchise: 2
Absentee ownership? No

COSTS

Total cost: $46.5K-85.3K
Franchise fee: $30K
Royalty fee: 6%
Term of agreement: 10 years renewable for $3K
Franchisees required to buy multiple units? No

FINANCING

In-house: Equipment, start-up costs
3rd-party: Equipment

QUALIFICATIONS

Net worth: $250K
Cash liquidity: $50K
Experience:
    General business experience
    Marketing skills

TRAINING

At headquarters: 2 weeks
At franchisee's location: 2 days
Quarterly quality-assurance training

BUSINESS SUPPORT

Newsletter
Meetings
Toll-free phone line
Internet
Field operations/evaluations

MARKETING SUPPORT

Co-op advertising
National media campaign

SHIELD SECURITY SYSTEMS

Current financial data not available

1690 Walden Ave.
Buffalo, NY 14225
Ph: (716)681-6677, Fax: (716)636-8819
www.shieldsecurity.net
Burglar & fire alarm installation & sales
Began: 1976, Franchising since: 1992
Headquarters size: 4 employees
Franchise department: 5 employees

U.S. franchises: 8
Canadian franchises: 0
Other foreign franchises: 0
Company-owned: 1
Units concentrated in all U.S.

Seeking: All U.S.
Seeking in Canada? Yes
Exclusive territories? Yes
Homebased option? Yes
Kiosk option? No
Employees needed to run franchise: 2-4
Absentee ownership? Yes

COSTS

Total cost: $33.8K-60.7K
Franchise fee: $30K
Royalty fee: 5%
Term of agreement: 10 years renewable for $1.5K
Franchisees required to buy multiple units? No

FINANCING

No financing available

QUALIFICATIONS

Net worth: $100K
Cash liquidity: $35K
Experience:
    General business experience
    Marketing skills

TRAINING

At headquarters: 7 days
At franchisee's location: 7 days
Online: 4-6 weeks

BUSINESS SUPPORT

Newsletter
Meetings
Toll-free phone line
Internet
Security/safety procedures
Field operations/evaluations
Purchasing cooperatives

MARKETING SUPPORT

Ad slicks
Corporate marketing plan

SIGNATURE ALERT SECURITY

Financial rating: $$

746 E. Winchester St., #G10
Salt Lake City, UT 84107
Ph: (801)743-0101
Fax: (801)743-0808
www.signaturealert.com
Security systems
Began: 1999, Franchising since: 2003
Headquarters size: Info not provided
Franchise department: Info not
    provided

U.S. franchises: 3
Canadian franchises: 0
Other foreign franchises: 0
Company-owned: 2

Seeking: All U.S.
Seeking in Canada? No
Exclusive territories? Yes
Homebased option? Yes
Kiosk option? No
Employees needed to run franchise:
    Info not provided
Absentee ownership? No

COSTS
Total cost: $41K
Franchise fee: $18K
Royalty fee: 10%
Term of agreement: 10 years renewable
    for $3K
Franchisees required to buy multiple
    units? No

FINANCING
No financing available

QUALIFICATIONS
Net worth: $100K
Cash liquidity: $41K

TRAINING
At headquarters: 5 days
At franchisee's location: 2 days

BUSINESS SUPPORT
Newsletter
Meetings
Toll-free phone line
Grand opening
Internet
Security/safety procedures
Field operations/evaluations
Purchasing cooperatives

MARKETING SUPPORT
Co-op advertising

SONITROL

Ranked #276 in Entrepreneur Magazine's 2004 Franchise 500

Financial rating: $$$$

211 N. Union St., #350
Alexandria, VA 22314
Ph: (703)684-6606
Fax: (703)684-6612
www.sonitrol.com
Electronic security services
Began: 1964, Franchising since: 1965
Headquarters size: 30 employees
Franchise department: 30 employees

U.S. franchises: 124
Canadian franchises: 4
Other foreign franchises: 7
Company-owned: 53
Units concentrated in CA, FL, IN

Seeking: All U.S.
Focusing on: CA, IL, OH, PA
Seeking in Canada? No
Exclusive territories? No
Homebased option? No
Kiosk option? No
Employees needed to run franchise: 20
Absentee ownership? Yes

COSTS
Total cost: $148K-474K
Franchise fee: $20K-50K
Royalty fee: 2.5%
Term of agreement: 10 years renewable
    at no charge
Franchisees required to buy multiple
    units? No

FINANCING
No financing available

QUALIFICATIONS
Cash liquidity: $130K-492K
Experience:
    General business experience
    Marketing skills

TRAINING
At headquarters: Varies
At franchisee's location: Varies

BUSINESS SUPPORT
Newsletter
Meetings
Internet
Field operations/evaluations
Purchasing cooperatives

MARKETING SUPPORT
Ad slicks

BALLOON CAFE

Current financial data not available

P.O. Box 398
Providence, UT 84332-0398
Ph: (435)753-4610, Fax: (435)787-8654
www.ballooncafe.com
Balloon design & delivery services
Began: 1999, Franchising since: 2002
Headquarters size: 3 employees
Franchise department: 2 employees

U.S. franchises: 1
Canadian franchises: 0
Other foreign franchises: 0
Company-owned: 0
Units concentrated in UT

Seeking: All U.S.
Seeking in Canada? No
Exclusive territories? Yes
Homebased option? Yes
Kiosk option? No
Employees needed to run franchise: 1-2
Absentee ownership? No

COSTS
Total cost: $7.5K-32.1K
Franchise fee: $3.95K-17K
Royalty fee: $32-136/mo.
Term of agreement: 3 years renewable
   for $500
Franchisees required to buy multiple
   units? No

FINANCING
No financing available

QUALIFICATIONS
Cash liquidity: $7.5K-32.1K
Experience:
   General business experience

TRAINING
At headquarters: 4-1/2 days

BUSINESS SUPPORT
Newsletter
Meetings
Grand opening
Internet
Security/safety procedures
Field operations/evaluations

MARKETING SUPPORT
Ad slicks
Web site
Sales leads
New product ideas
Sales literature

BLACK DIAMOND GOLF

Financial rating: $

4963 Stahl Rd., #112
San Antonio, TX 78217
Ph: (210)590-2384
Fax: (210)590-2386
www.theclubpolisher.com
Golf club-cleaning system
Began: 2001, Franchising since: 2003
Headquarters size: 6 employees
Franchise department: 6 employees

U.S. franchises: 43
Canadian franchises: 0
Other foreign franchises: 0
Company-owned: 1
Units concentrated in all U.S. except
   CA, CT, IL, MD, RI

Seeking: All U.S.
Seeking in Canada? Yes
Exclusive territories? Yes
Homebased option? Yes
Kiosk option? No
Employees needed to run franchise:
   Info not provided
Absentee ownership? No

COSTS
Total cost: $25K-100K
Franchise fee: $3K-50K
Royalty fee: 0
Term of agreement: 12 years renewable
Franchisees required to buy multiple
   units? No

FINANCING
No financing available

QUALIFICATIONS
Net worth: $100K-500K
Cash liquidity: $50K

TRAINING
At headquarters: 2 days

BUSINESS SUPPORT
Newsletter
Meetings
Toll-free phone line
Grand opening
Internet
Security/safety procedures
Field operations/evaluations

MARKETING SUPPORT
Co-op advertising
Ad slicks
National media campaign
Regional marketing

COMPLETE MUSIC

Ranked #267 in Entrepreneur Magazine's 2004 Franchise 500   *Financial rating: $$$$*

7877 L St.
Omaha, NE 68127
Ph: (800)843-3866/(402)339-0001
Fax: (402)898-1777
www.cmusic.com
Mobile DJ entertainment service
Began: 1974, Franchising since: 1983
Headquarters size: 6 employees
Franchise department: 4 employees

U.S. franchises: 159
Canadian franchises: 2
Other foreign franchises: 0
Company-owned: 1
Units concentrated in all U.S.

Seeking: All U.S.
Seeking in Canada? Yes
Exclusive territories? Yes
Homebased option? Yes
Kiosk option? No
Employees needed to run franchise:
    3-50
Absentee ownership? Yes

COSTS
Total cost: $19.7K-33K
Franchise fee: $12K-20K
Royalty fee: 6.5-8%
Term of agreement: 10 years renewable
    at no charge
Franchisees required to buy multiple
    units? No

FINANCING
In-house: Franchise fee, equipment
3rd-party: None

QUALIFICATIONS
Net worth: $50K
Cash liquidity: $10K
Experience:
    General business experience

TRAINING
At headquarters: 9 days
At franchisee's location: 4 days

BUSINESS SUPPORT
Newsletter
Meetings
Toll-free phone line
Internet
Security/safety procedures
Field operations/evaluations

MARKETING SUPPORT
Ad slicks
National media campaign
Regional marketing

CULLIGAN WATER CONDITIONING

Ranked #64 in Entrepreneur Magazine's 2004 Franchise 500   *Financial rating: $$$$*

1 Culligan Pkwy.
Northbrook, IL 60062-6209
Ph: (847)205-5823
Fax: (847)205-6005
www.culligan.com
Water-related products & services
Began: 1936, Franchising since: 1938
Headquarters size: 500 employees
Franchise department: 5 employees

U.S. franchises: 647
Canadian franchises: 38
Other foreign franchises: 0
Company-owned: 95
Units concentrated in all U.S.

Seeking: All U.S.
Seeking in Canada? Yes
Exclusive territories? Yes
Homebased option? No
Kiosk option? No
Employees needed to run franchise:
    Info not provided
Absentee ownership? Yes

COSTS
Total cost: $104.5K-695K
Franchise fee: $5K
Royalty fee: 0.5-5%
Term of agreement: 10 years renewable
    at no charge
Franchisees required to buy multiple
    units? No

FINANCING
In-house: Accounts receivable,
    inventory
3rd-party: None

QUALIFICATIONS
Net worth: $750K
Cash liquidity: $300K
Experience:
    General business experience
    Marketing skills

TRAINING
At headquarters
At franchisee's location

BUSINESS SUPPORT
Newsletter
Meetings
Toll-free phone line
Grand opening
Internet
Security/safety procedures
Field operations/evaluations
Purchasing cooperatives

MARKETING SUPPORT
Co-op advertising
Ad slicks
National media campaign

FAST-FIX JEWELRY REPAIRS
Ranked #210 in Entrepreneur Magazine's 2004 Franchise 500   *Financial rating: $$$*

1300 N.W. 17th Ave., #170
Delray Beach, FL 33445
Ph: (800)359-0407/(561)330-6060
Fax: (561)330-6062
www.fastfix.com
Jewelry & watch repairs
Began: 1984, Franchising since: 1987
Headquarters size: 8 employees
Franchise department: Info not provided

U.S. franchises: 126
Canadian franchises: 0
Other foreign franchises: 0
Company-owned: 0
Units concentrated in all U.S.

Seeking: All U.S.
Seeking in Canada? Yes
Exclusive territories? Yes
Homebased option? No
Kiosk option? Yes
Employees needed to run franchise: 2
Absentee ownership? No

COSTS
Total cost: $123K-221K
Kiosk cost: $115K
Franchise fee: $30K
Royalty fee: 5%
Term of agreement: 10 years renewable for $15K
Franchisees required to buy multiple units? Outside the U.S. only

FINANCING
In-house: None
3rd-party: Equipment, franchise fee, inventory, start-up costs

QUALIFICATIONS
Cash liquidity: $40K
Experience:
    General business experience

TRAINING
At franchisee's location: 3 days at opening
At national training center: 8 days

BUSINESS SUPPORT
Newsletter
Meetings
Toll-free phone line
Grand opening
Internet
Lease negotiations
Security/safety procedures
Field operations/evaluations
Purchasing cooperatives

MARKETING SUPPORT
Ad slicks
Opening marketing support

HEEL QUIK! INC.
Current financial data not available

1730 Cumberland Point Dr., #5
Marietta, GA 30067
Ph: (800)255-8145/(770)951-9440
Fax: (770)933-8268
www.heelquik.net
Shoe repair, clothing alterations, miscellaneous services
Began: 1984, Franchising since: 1985
Headquarters size: 10 employees
Franchise department: 5 employees

U.S. franchises: 53
Canadian franchises: 0
Other foreign franchises: 663
Company-owned: 0
Units concentrated in FL, GA

Seeking: All U.S.
Seeking in Canada? Yes
Exclusive territories? Yes
Homebased option? No
Kiosk option? Yes
Employees needed to run franchise: 1-4
Absentee ownership? Yes

COSTS
Total cost: $45K-95K
Kiosk cost: $45K-75K
Franchise fee: $15.5K-17.5K
Royalty fee: 4%
Term of agreement: 20 years renewable at no charge
Franchisees required to buy multiple units? No

FINANCING
In-house: None
3rd-party: Equipment, franchise fee, inventory, start-up costs

QUALIFICATIONS
Net worth: $50K-200K
Cash liquidity: $15K-35K
Experience:
    General business experience

TRAINING
At headquarters: 2 weeks
At franchisee's location: 1 week
In California: 1 week

BUSINESS SUPPORT
Newsletter
Meetings
Toll-free phone line
Grand opening
Internet
Lease negotiations
Security/safety procedures
Field operations/evaluations
Purchasing cooperatives

MARKETING SUPPORT
Ad slicks
Regional marketing
Quarterly marketing plan

ICE MAGIC FRANCHISING INC.

Current financial data not available

11124 Satellite Blvd.
Orlando, FL 32837
Ph: (407)816-1905
Fax: (407)816-7150
www.icemagicinc.com
Ice sculptures & specialty-molded ice
    products
Began: 1996, Franchising since: 2001
Headquarters size: 13 employees
Franchise department: 1 employee

U.S. franchises: 6
Canadian franchises: 1
Other foreign franchises: 0
Company-owned: 1

Seeking: All U.S.
Seeking in Canada? Yes
Exclusive territories? Yes
Homebased option? No
Kiosk option? No
Employees needed to run franchise: 6
Absentee ownership? No

COSTS
Total cost: $300K-554.3K
Franchise fee: $30K
Royalty fee: Varies
Term of agreement: 20 years renewable
    at no charge
Franchisees required to buy multiple
    units? No

FINANCING
No financing available

QUALIFICATIONS
Experience:
    Industry experience
    General business experience

TRAINING
At headquarters: 2 weeks
At franchisee's location: 2 weeks

BUSINESS SUPPORT
Field operations/evaluations

MARKETING SUPPORT
Trade shows

LANTIS FIREWORKS & LASERS

Financial rating: 0

9101 W. Sahara Ave., #105
Las Vegas, NV 89117
Ph: (702)384-2595
Fax: (702)869-1434
www.fireworks-lasers.com
Pyrotechnic & laser displays
Began: 1945, Franchising since: 2003
Headquarters size: 8 employees
Franchise department: 2 employees

U.S. franchises: 0
Canadian franchises: 0
Other foreign franchises: 0
Company-owned: 3

Seeking: All U.S.
Seeking in Canada? No
Exclusive territories? Yes
Homebased option? Yes
Kiosk option? No
Employees needed to run franchise: 2
Absentee ownership? Yes

COSTS
Total cost: $172.4K-274K
Franchise fee: $50K
Royalty fee: 6%
Term of agreement: 5 years renewable
    for $5K
Franchisees required to buy multiple
    units? No

FINANCING
No financing available

QUALIFICATIONS
Net worth: $173K
Cash liquidity: $75K
Experience:
    General business experience
    Marketing skills

TRAINING
At headquarters: 4-6 weeks

BUSINESS SUPPORT
Meetings
Toll-free phone line
Internet
Security/safety procedures
Field operations/evaluations
Purchasing cooperatives

MARKETING SUPPORT
Co-op advertising

LYONS & WOLIVAR INVESTIGATIONS

Current financial data not available

23332 Mill Creek Rd., #200
Laguna Hills, CA 92653
Ph: (949)305-7383
Fax: (949)305-7864
www.lyonswolivar.com
Private investigation services
Began: 2002, Franchising since: 2002
Headquarters size: 10 employees
Franchise department: 10 employees

U.S. franchises: 10
Canadian franchises: 0
Other foreign franchises: 0
Company-owned: 1
Units concentrated in all U.S.

Seeking: All U.S.
Seeking in Canada? No
Exclusive territories? No
Homebased option? Yes
Kiosk option? No
Employees needed to run franchise: 2-5
Absentee ownership? Yes

COSTS
Total cost: $105K-210K
Franchise fee: $100K-200K
Royalty fee: 5-7%
Term of agreement: 10 years renewable
    at no charge
Franchisees required to buy multiple
    units? No

FINANCING
No financing available

QUALIFICATIONS
Net worth: $100K
Cash liquidity: $100K
Experience:
    General business experience
    Marketing skills
    Strong business leadership skills

TRAINING
At headquarters: 1 year
Training seminars

BUSINESS SUPPORT
Newsletter
Meetings
Internet
Security/safety procedures
Field operations/evaluations

MARKETING SUPPORT
Ad slicks
National media campaign
Regional marketing

MINI-TANKERS USA INC.

Current financial data not available

4739 University Wy. N.E., #1620
Seattle, WA 98105
Ph: (877)218-3003
Fax: (888)682-2213
www.minitankers.us
On-site diesel refueling
Began: 1997, Franchising since: 1997
Headquarters size: 8 employees
Franchise department: 2 employees

U.S. franchises: 4
Canadian franchises: 55
Other foreign franchises: 70
Company-owned: 51
Units concentrated in IL, OR, WA

Focusing on: FL, IL, OR, WA
Seeking in Canada? Yes
Exclusive territories? Yes
Homebased option? Yes
Kiosk option? No
Employees needed to run franchise: 0
Absentee ownership? No

COSTS
Total cost: $169K
Franchise fee: $1K
Royalty fee: 0
Term of agreement: 5 years renewable
    for $1K
Franchisees required to buy multiple
    units? No

FINANCING
In-house: Vehicle leasing

QUALIFICATIONS
Net worth: $25K
Experience:
    Marketing skills
    Customer service skills

TRAINING
At headquarters: 1 week
At franchisee's location: 1 week

BUSINESS SUPPORT
Newsletter
Meetings
Toll-free phone line
Grand opening
Internet
Security/safety procedures
Field operations/evaluations
Purchasing cooperatives

MARKETING SUPPORT
Regional marketing

NORTHWEST AQUIFER SURVEYING INC.

Financial rating: $$$

P.O. Box 123
Adna, WA 98522
Ph: (866)740-6446
Fax: (866)422-5357
www.findwellwater.com
Usable groundwater locating & mapping system
Began: 2001, Franchising since: 2002
Headquarters size: 4 employees
Franchise department: 3 employees

U.S. franchises: 14
Canadian franchises: 0
Other foreign franchises: 0
Company-owned: 1
Units concentrated in all U.S.

Seeking: All U.S.
Seeking in Canada? Yes
Exclusive territories? Yes
Homebased option? Yes
Kiosk option? No
Employees needed to run franchise: 1
Absentee ownership? No

COSTS
Total cost: $53.6K-85K
Franchise fee: $15K-25K
Royalty fee: 4-6%
Term of agreement: 10 years renewable at no charge
Franchisees required to buy multiple units? No

FINANCING
In-house: None
3rd-party: Equipment

QUALIFICATIONS
Experience:
   Good credit

TRAINING
At headquarters: 2 weeks

BUSINESS SUPPORT
Newsletter
Meetings
Toll-free phone line
Internet
Field operations/evaluations
Purchasing cooperatives

MARKETING SUPPORT
Co-op advertising
National media campaign

1-800-GOT-JUNK?

Ranked #392 in Entrepreneur Magazine's 2004 Franchise 500

Financial rating: $$

1523 W. 3rd Ave., 2nd Fl.
Vancouver, BC Canada V6J 1J8
Ph: (877)408-5865, Fax: (801)751-0634
www.1800gotjunk.com
Junk removal service
Began: 1989, Franchising since: 1998
Headquarters size: Info not provided
Franchise department: Info not provided

U.S. franchises: 47
Canadian franchises: 8
Other foreign franchises: 0
Company-owned: 1
Units concentrated in U.S. & Canada

Seeking: All U.S.
Focusing on: U.S. & Canada
Seeking in Canada? Yes
Exclusive territories? Yes
Homebased option? Yes
Kiosk option? No
Employees needed to run franchise: 3
Absentee ownership? Yes

COSTS
Total cost: $46.7K-58.6K
Franchise fee: $18K+
Royalty fee: 8%
Term of agreement: Renewable term
Franchisees required to buy multiple units? No

FINANCING
In-house: Franchise fee
3rd-party: Equipment, franchise fee, start-up costs

QUALIFICATIONS
Net worth: $100K
Cash liquidity: $50K
Experience:
   Management experience
   Operations experience
   Sales & marketing experience

TRAINING
At headquarters: 1 week
At franchisee's location: 3 days
At conference & franchisee location:
   2-3 days each annually

BUSINESS SUPPORT
Newsletter
Meetings
Toll-free phone line
Internet
Security/safety procedures
Field operations/evaluations
Purchasing cooperatives

MARKETING SUPPORT
Co-op advertising
Ad slicks
National media campaign
Regional marketing

PIRTEK
Ranked #278 in Entrepreneur Magazine's 2004 Franchise 500   *Financial rating: $$$$*

501 Haverty Ct.
Rockledge, FL 32955
Ph: (321)504-4422
Fax: (321)504-4433
www.pirtekusa.com
On-site hydraulic hose replacement
   service
Began: 1980, Franchising since: 1987
Headquarters size: 32 employees
Franchise department: 15 employees

U.S. franchises: 23
Canadian franchises: 0
Other foreign franchises: 224
Company-owned: 1
Units concentrated in all U.S.

Seeking: All U.S.
Seeking in Canada? Yes
Exclusive territories? Yes
Homebased option? No
Kiosk option? No
Employees needed to run franchise: 6
Absentee ownership? Yes

COSTS
Total cost: $202K-504K
Franchise fee: $42K
Royalty fee: 1.5-4%
Term of agreement: 10 years renewable
   for $5K
Franchisees required to buy multiple
   units? No

FINANCING
In-house: None
3rd-party: Accounts receivable, equipment, inventory, start-up costs

QUALIFICATIONS
Net worth: $500K
Cash liquidity: $100K
Experience:
   General business experience
   Marketing skills

TRAINING
At headquarters: 3 weeks
At franchisee's location: As needed

BUSINESS SUPPORT
Newsletter
Meetings
Toll-free phone line
Grand opening
Internet
Lease negotiations
Security/safety procedures
Field operations/evaluations
Purchasing cooperatives

MARKETING SUPPORT
Co-op advertising
Ad slicks
National media campaign
Regional marketing

POP-A-LOCK FRANCHISE SYSTEM
Ranked #490 in Entrepreneur Magazine's 2004 Franchise 500   *Financial rating: $$$*

1018 Harding St., #205
Lafayette, LA 70503
Ph: (337)233-6211, Fax: (337)233-6655
www.pop-a-lock.com
Auto locksmithing/roadside assistance
Began: 1991, Franchising since: 1994
Headquarters size: 6 employees
Franchise department: Info not provided

U.S. franchises: 104
Canadian franchises: 0
Other foreign franchises: 0
Company-owned: 0
Units concentrated in AR, AZ, CO,
   DC, DE, FL, GA, KY, LA, MD, MS,
   NC, NV, OK, OR, PA, SC, TN, TX,
   VA, WA

Seeking: All U.S.
Focusing on: CA, NY
Seeking in Canada? No
Exclusive territories? Yes
Homebased option? Yes
Kiosk option? No
Employees needed to run franchise:
   0-20
Absentee ownership? Yes

COSTS
Total cost: $97.6K-741.5K
Franchise fee: $13K-100K
Royalty fee: 6%
Term of agreement: 10 years renewable
   at no charge
Franchisees required to buy multiple
   units? No

FINANCING
No financing available

QUALIFICATIONS
Net worth: $100K
Cash liquidity: $8K-67K
Experience:
   General business experience
   Marketing skills

TRAINING
At headquarters: 2 days
In Lafayette, LA: 1 week

BUSINESS SUPPORT
Newsletter
Meetings
Toll-free phone line
Internet
Security/safety procedures
Field operations/evaluations

MARKETING SUPPORT
Ad slicks
Free consulting services

PRICE ENERGY

Current financial data not available

198 Green Pond Rd.
Rockaway, NJ 07866
Ph: (973)784-7783, Fax: (973)983-0682
www.priceenergy.com
Fuels distribution service
Began: 1999, Franchising since: 2001
Headquarters size: 30 employees
Franchise department: 2 employees

U.S. franchises: 5
Canadian franchises: 0
Other foreign franchises: 0
Company-owned: 1
Units concentrated in Northeast

Seeking: All U.S.
Focusing on: Northeast
Seeking in Canada? Yes
Exclusive territories? Yes
Homebased option? Yes
Kiosk option? No
Employees needed to run franchise: 3
Absentee ownership? No

COSTS
Total cost: $31K-192.3K
Franchise fee: to $15K-40K
Royalty fee: to 0.5%
Term of agreement: 10 years renewable
   at no charge
Franchisees required to buy multiple
   units? No

FINANCING
In-house: Inventory
3rd-party: None

QUALIFICATIONS
Net worth: $500K
Experience:
   General business experience

TRAINING
At headquarters
Driver & fuel delivery training

BUSINESS SUPPORT
Newsletter
Meetings
Toll-free phone line
Grand opening
Internet
Security/safety procedures
Field operations/evaluations

MARKETING SUPPORT
Regional marketing

PROFESSIONAL HOUSE DOCTORS INC.

Current financial data not available

1406 E. 14th St.
Des Moines, IA 50316
Ph: (515)265-6667
Fax: (515)278-2070
www.prohousedr.com
Environmental & building-science
   services
Began: 1982, Franchising since: 1991
Headquarters size: 3 employees
Franchise department: 2 employees

U.S. franchises: 7
Canadian franchises: 0
Other foreign franchises: 0
Company-owned: 1
Units concentrated in all U.S.

Seeking: All U.S.
Seeking in Canada? No
Exclusive territories? Yes
Homebased option? Yes
Kiosk option? No
Employees needed to run franchise: 1
Absentee ownership? No

COSTS
Total cost: $15K
Franchise fee: $9.8K
Royalty fee: 6%
Term of agreement: 5 years renewable
   at no charge
Franchisees required to buy multiple
   units? No

FINANCING
No financing available

QUALIFICATIONS
Net worth: $50K
Cash liquidity: $10K
Experience:
   Marketing skills
   Communication skills

TRAINING
At headquarters: 2 weeks
At franchisee's location: 2 weeks
Continuing education available

BUSINESS SUPPORT
Newsletter
Meetings
Toll-free phone line
Grand opening
Internet
Security/safety procedures
Field operations/evaluations
Purchasing cooperatives

MARKETING SUPPORT
Co-op advertising
Ad slicks
Regional marketing

UCC TOTALHOME
Ranked #268 in Entrepreneur Magazine's 2004 Franchise 500   *Financial rating: $$$$*

8450 Broadway, P.O. Box 13006
Merrillville, IN 46411-3006
Ph: (800)827-6400 x357/(219)736-1100
Fax: (219)755-6208
www.ucctotalhome.com/franchising
Consumer buying club
Began: 1971, Franchising since: 1972
Headquarters size: 170 employees
Franchise department: 4 employees

U.S. franchises: 65
Canadian franchises: 17
Other foreign franchises: 0
Company-owned: 6
Units concentrated in IL, MI, NJ, NY,
    OH, TX

Seeking: All U.S.
Seeking in Canada? Yes
Exclusive territories? Yes
Homebased option? No
Kiosk option? No
Employees needed to run franchise:
    9-12
Absentee ownership? No

COSTS
Total cost: $115K-252K
Franchise fee: $30K-55K
Royalty fee: 22%
Term of agreement: 12 years renewable
    at no charge
Franchisees required to buy multiple
    units? No

FINANCING
In-house: Franchise fee
3rd-party: Equipment, franchise fee,
    start-up costs

QUALIFICATIONS
Net worth: $150K
Cash liquidity: $100K
Experience:
    Marketing skills

TRAINING
At headquarters: 3 weeks
At franchisee's location: 5 weeks
At regional meetings

BUSINESS SUPPORT
Newsletter
Meetings
Internet
Field operations/evaluations

MARKETING SUPPORT
Co-op advertising
Ad slicks
National media campaign

SERVICES — *Other Franchises*

BIOLOGIX
1561 Fairview Ave.
St. Louis, MO 63132
Ph: (800)747-1885
www.biologix.com
Environmental waste elimination

THE BUYER'S AGENT INC.
5705 Stage Rd., #199
Bartlett, TN 38134
Ph: (800)766-8728
www.forbuyers.com
Real estate

CANDLEWICK HOMES
P.O. Box 1992
Mansfield, TX 76063
Ph: (817)477-4288
www.candlewickhomes.com
Home building, design & development
    services

CW&E FRANCHISE CORP.
11926 S.W. 8th St.
Miami, FL 33184
Ph: (888)776-3837/(305)436-6050
www.commercialwater.com
Utility billing & metering

EPMARK INC.
6277 Riverside Dr.
Dublin, OH 43017
Ph: (800)783-3838/(614)761-1010
www.epmarkinc.com
Condominum community develop-
    ment system

GLAMOUR SHOTS LICENSING INC.
1300 Metropolitan Ave.
Oklahoma City, OK 73108
Ph: (405)947-8747
www.glamourshots.com
Portrait photography

IT'S JUST LUNCH FRANCHISE LLC
*Ranked #361 in Entrepreneur
    Magazine's 2004 Franchise 500*
919 Fourth Ave.
San Diego, CA 92101
Ph: (619)234-7200
www.itsjustlunch.com
Dating service

LAZERQUICK
29900 S.W. Kinsman Rd., #200
Wilsonville, OR 97070
Ph: (800)477-2679/(503)682-1322
www.lazerquick.com
Quick printing, copying, laser imaging

THE RESETTLERS FRANCHISE GROUP
5811 Kennett Pike
Centreville, DE 19807
Ph: (302)658-9110
www.resettlers.com
Custom moving & consignment furni-
    ture sales

SCREEN PRINTING USA
534 W. Shawnee Ave.
Plymouth, PA 18651
Ph: (570)779-5175
www.screenprintingusainc.com
Screen-printed apparel, signs &
    posters

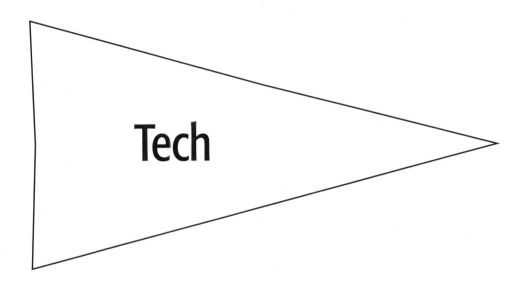

TECH   *Internet*

EASYINTERNETCAFE

Financial rating: $$$

234 W. 42nd St.
New York, NY 10036
Ph: (212)398-6989
Fax: (212)504-3039
www.easyinternetcafe.com
Retail Internet access
Began: 1999, Franchising since: 2001
Headquarters size: 20 employees
Franchise department: 4 employees

U.S. franchises: 1
Canadian franchises: 0
Other foreign franchises: 21
Company-owned: 28
Units concentrated in NY

Seeking: All U.S.
Seeking in Canada? No
Exclusive territories? No
Homebased option? Yes
Kiosk option? Yes
Employees needed to run franchise: 0
Absentee ownership? Yes

COSTS
Total cost: $33.3K-218.9K
    Kiosk cost: $33.3K
Franchise fee: $13.4K-64K
Royalty fee: 5%
Term of agreement: 4 years not renew-
    able
Franchisees required to buy multiple
    units? No

FINANCING
No financing available

QUALIFICATIONS
Experience:
    General business experience

TRAINING
At headquarters: 3 days

BUSINESS SUPPORT
Internet

MARKETING SUPPORT
Info not provided

NETSPACE

Ranked #352 in Entrepreneur Magazine's 2004 Franchise 500   *Financial rating: $$$*

2801 N.E. 208 Terrace, 2nd Fl.
Miami, FL 33180
Ph: (800)638-7722
Fax: (305)931-7772
www.netspace.info
Internet solutions
Began: 1996, Franchising since: 2000
Headquarters size: 25 employees
Franchise department: 4 employees

U.S. franchises: 65
Canadian franchises: 0
Other foreign franchises: 20
Company-owned: 0

Seeking: All U.S.
Seeking in Canada? Yes
Exclusive territories? Yes
Homebased option? No
Kiosk option? No
Employees needed to run franchise: 3-5
Absentee ownership? No

COSTS
Total cost: $51.2K-70.9K
Franchise fee: $39.5K
Royalty fee: 10%
Term of agreement: 10 years renewable
   for $2.5K
Franchisees required to buy multiple
   units? Yes

FINANCING
No financing available

QUALIFICATIONS
Net worth: $250K
Cash liquidity: $50K
Experience:
   General business experience
   Marketing skills

TRAINING
At headquarters: 1 week
At franchisee's location: Ongoing
Quarterly regional meeting: 3 days

BUSINESS SUPPORT
Newsletter
Meetings
Toll-free phone line
Internet
Field operations/evaluations
Purchasing cooperatives

MARKETING SUPPORT
Co-op advertising
Ad slicks
National media campaign
Regional marketing

WSI INTERNET

Ranked #123 in Entrepreneur Magazine's 2004 Franchise 500   *Financial rating: 0*

5915 Airport Rd., #300
Toronto, ON Canada L4V 1T1
Ph: (905)678-7588
Fax: (905)678-7242
www.wsicorporate.com
Internet services
Began: 1995, Franchising since: 1996
Headquarters size: 100 employees
Franchise department: 25 employees

U.S. franchises: 357
Canadian franchises: 107
Other foreign franchises: 772
Company-owned: 1

Seeking: All U.S.
Seeking in Canada? Yes
Exclusive territories? No
Homebased option? Yes
Kiosk option? No
Employees needed to run franchise: 1
Absentee ownership? No

COSTS
Total cost: $40K-50K
Franchise fee: $39.7K
Royalty fee: 10%
Term of agreement: 5 years renewable
   at no charge
Franchisees required to buy multiple
   units? No

FINANCING
No financing available

QUALIFICATIONS
Net worth: $68K-82K
Cash liquidity: $5K
Experience:
   General business experience

TRAINING
At headquarters: 7 days

BUSINESS SUPPORT
Newsletter
Meetings
Toll-free phone line
Internet
Purchasing cooperatives

MARKETING SUPPORT
Co-op advertising
Ad slicks
Marketing materials

DISCOUNT IMAGING FRANCHISE CORP.

Ranked #479 in Entrepreneur Magazine's 2004 Franchise 500

Financial rating: $$$

206 Texas Ave.
Monroe, LA 71201
Ph: (318)324-8977
Fax: (318)324-1211
www.difcorp.com
Ink, toner cartridges & fax
    supplies/services
Began: 1995, Franchising since: 1998
Headquarters size: 15 employees
Franchise department: 15 employees

U.S. franchises: 10
Canadian franchises: 0
Other foreign franchises: 0
Company-owned: 0
Units concentrated in CA

Seeking: All U.S.
Focusing on: CA
Seeking in Canada? No
Exclusive territories? Yes
Homebased option? No
Kiosk option? No
Employees needed to run franchise: 5
Absentee ownership? No

COSTS

Total cost: $90K-115K
Franchise fee: $25K
Royalty fee: 6%
Term of agreement: 10 years renewable
    at no charge
Franchisees required to buy multiple
    units? No

FINANCING

In-house: Accounts receivable, fran-
    chise fee, equipment, inventory,
    payroll, start-up costs
3rd-party: Accounts receivable, equip-
    ment, franchise fee, inventory, pay-
    roll, start-up costs

QUALIFICATIONS

Net worth: $100K
Cash liquidity: $40K
Experience:
    Industry experience
    General business experience
    Marketing skills

TRAINING

At headquarters: 2 weeks
At franchisee's location: 4 weeks

BUSINESS SUPPORT

Newsletter
Meetings
Toll-free phone line
Grand opening
Internet
Lease negotiations
Security/safety procedures
Field operations/evaluations
Purchasing cooperatives

MARKETING SUPPORT

Ad slicks
National media campaign
Regional marketing

INKTONERINC.

Current financial data not available

2550 S. Rainbow, #E-12
Las Vegas, NV 89146
Ph: (888)696-3852/(702)562-3776
Fax: (702)562-3778
www.inktonerinc.com
Printing supplies
Began: 2000, Franchising since: 2002
Headquarters size: 3 employees
Franchise department: 1 employee

U.S. franchises: 0
Canadian franchises: 0
Other foreign franchises: 0
Company-owned: 1

Seeking: All U.S.
Seeking in Canada? Yes
Exclusive territories? Yes
Homebased option? Yes
Kiosk option? No
Employees needed to run franchise: 1-3
Absentee ownership? Yes

COSTS

Total cost: $28K-65K
Franchise fee: $9.5K
Royalty fee: 6%
Term of agreement: 10 years renewable
    for initial franchise fee
Franchisees required to buy multiple
    units? No

FINANCING

No financing available

QUALIFICATIONS

Net worth: $50K
Cash liquidity: $20K
Experience:
    General business experience

TRAINING

At headquarters: 5 days
At franchisee's location: Varies

BUSINESS SUPPORT

Newsletter
Meetings
Toll-free phone line
Grand opening
Internet
Security/safety procedures
Field operations/evaluations
Purchasing cooperatives

MARKETING SUPPORT

Co-op advertising
Ad slicks
National media campaign
Regional marketing
Marketing materials

ISLAND INK-JET SYSTEMS INC.
Ranked #415 in Entrepreneur Magazine's 2004 Franchise 500

Financial rating: 0

1101 Supermall Wy., #T-12
Auburn, WA 98001
Ph: (250)897-0067
Fax: (250)897-0021
www.islandinkjet.com
Ink-jet cartridge replacements & sales
Began: 1995, Franchising since: 2000
Headquarters size: 70 employees
Franchise department: 14 employees

U.S. franchises: 21
Canadian franchises: 96
Other foreign franchises: 3
Company-owned: 3
Units concentrated in MN, UT

Seeking: All U.S.
Seeking in Canada? No
Exclusive territories? Yes
Homebased option? No
Kiosk option? Yes
Employees needed to run franchise: 2
Absentee ownership? Yes

COSTS
Total cost: $80.4K-109.1K
    Kiosk cost: $89.8K
Franchise fee: $22.5K
Royalty fee: 6%
Term of agreement: 10 years renewable
    for $11.3K
Franchisees required to buy multiple
    units? No

FINANCING
In-house: Accounts receivable, fran-
    chise fee
3rd-party: Equipment, franchise fee,
    inventory, payroll, start-up costs

QUALIFICATIONS
Net worth: $150K
Cash liquidity: $150K
Experience:
    General business experience
    Marketing skills

TRAINING
At headquarters: 2-3 weeks
At franchisee's location: 40 hours

BUSINESS SUPPORT
Meetings
Toll-free phone line
Grand opening
Internet
Lease negotiations
Field operations/evaluations

MARKETING SUPPORT
Co-op advertising
Ad slicks
Regional marketing
Grand opening marketing

TECH   *Training*

COMPUCHILD

Financial rating: $

602 Main St., #2
Rochester, IN 46975
Ph: (800)619-5437, Fax: (574)223-4422
www.compuchild.com
Preschool computer education
Began: 1994, Franchising since: 2001
Headquarters size: 2 employees
Franchise department: 2 employees

U.S. franchises: 41
Canadian franchises: 0
Other foreign franchises: 1
Company-owned: 1
Units concentrated in all U.S.

Seeking: All U.S.
Seeking in Canada? Yes
Exclusive territories? Yes
Homebased option? Yes
Kiosk option? No
Employees needed to run franchise: 1
Absentee ownership? Yes

COSTS
Total cost: $13.9K-15K
Franchise fee: $12.5K
Royalty fee: Varies
Term of agreement: 5 years renewable
    at no charge
Franchisees required to buy multiple
    units? Outside the U.S. only

FINANCING
No financing available

QUALIFICATIONS
Net worth: $50K
Cash liquidity: $13.9K-15K
Experience:
    General business experience
    Marketing skills

TRAINING
At headquarters: Varies
At franchisee's location: 3 days
At annual national meeting: 3 days

BUSINESS SUPPORT
Newsletter
Meetings
Toll-free phone line
Internet

MARKETING SUPPORT
National media campaign

COMPUTER MOMS INT'L. CORP.

Financial rating: 0

537 Woodward St., #D
Austin, TX 78704
Ph: (512)477-6667
Fax: (512)692-3711
www.computermoms.com
On-site computer training & support
    services
Began: 1994, Franchising since: 1998
Headquarters size: 9 employees
Franchise department: 2 employees

U.S. franchises: 83
Canadian franchises: 0
Other foreign franchises: 0
Company-owned: 0
Units concentrated in all U.S. except
    HI, MD, ND, RI, SD, VA, WA

Seeking: All U.S.
Seeking in Canada? No
Exclusive territories? Yes
Homebased option? Yes
Kiosk option? No
Employees needed to run franchise: 3-8
Absentee ownership? No

COSTS
Total cost: $46.2K-75.2K
Franchise fee: $9.7K+
Royalty fee: to $800/mo.
Term of agreement: 10 years renewable
    for $500
Franchisees required to buy multiple
    units? No

FINANCING
No financing available

QUALIFICATIONS
Net worth: $150K
Cash liquidity: $40K
Experience:
    General business experience
    Marketing skills

TRAINING
At headquarters: 2 weeks
Additional training via Internet,
    Webcasts, phone & conferences

BUSINESS SUPPORT
Newsletter
Meetings
Toll-free phone line
Internet
Purchasing cooperatives

MARKETING SUPPORT
Info not provided

COMPUTERTOTS/COMPUTER EXPLORERS

Ranked #478 in Entrepreneur Magazine's 2004 Franchise 500

Financial rating: $$$$

12715 Telge Rd.
Cypress, TX 77429
Ph: (888)638-8722/(281)256-4100
Fax: (281)256-4178
www.computertots.com
Educational technology solutions for
    schools, kids & adults
Began: 1983, Franchising since: 1988
Headquarters size: Info not provided
Franchise department: Info not provided

U.S. franchises: 84
Canadian franchises: 0
Other foreign franchises: 5
Company-owned: 2

Seeking: All U.S.
Seeking in Canada? Yes
Exclusive territories? Yes
Homebased option? Yes
Kiosk option? No
Employees needed to run franchise: 6
Absentee ownership? No

COSTS
Total cost: $32.1K-48.5K
Franchise fee: $15K/29.9K
Royalty fee: 8%
Term of agreement: 15 years renewable
    for 5% of franchise fee
Franchisees required to buy multiple
    units? No

FINANCING
In-house: Franchise fee
3rd-party: None

QUALIFICATIONS
Net worth: $100K
Cash liquidity: $40K
Experience:
    General business experience
    Marketing skills

TRAINING
At headquarters: 10 days
At franchisee's location: 2 days

BUSINESS SUPPORT
Newsletter
Meetings
Toll-free phone line
Internet
Security/safety procedures

MARKETING SUPPORT
National media campaign
Regional marketing
Direct mail campaign

NEW HORIZONS COMPUTER LEARNING CENTERS INC.

Ranked #322 in Entrepreneur Magazine's 2004 Franchise 500   *Financial rating: $$$$*

1900 S. State College Blvd., #200
Anaheim, CA 92806
Ph: (714)940-8230
Fax: (714)938-6008
www.newhorizons.com
Computer training & support
Began: 1982, Franchising since: 1992
Headquarters size: 125 employees
Franchise department: 120 employees

U.S. franchises: 129
Canadian franchises: 2
Other foreign franchises: 113
Company-owned: 26
Units concentrated in CA, FL, NY, TX

Seeking: All U.S.
Seeking in Canada? Yes
Exclusive territories? Yes
Homebased option? No
Kiosk option? No
Employees needed to run franchise: 23
Absentee ownership? Yes

COSTS
Total cost: $370K-560K
Franchise fee: $25K-75K
Royalty fee: 6%
Term of agreement: 10 years renewable
Franchisees required to buy multiple
    units? No

FINANCING
In-house: Franchise fee
3rd-party: Accounts receivable, equipment, inventory, start-up costs

QUALIFICATIONS
Net worth: $500K+
Cash liquidity: $300K-500K
Experience:
    General business experience
    Marketing skills

TRAINING
At headquarters

BUSINESS SUPPORT
Newsletter
Meetings
Grand opening
Internet
Lease negotiations
Field operations/evaluations

MARKETING SUPPORT
Ad slicks
National media campaign

TECH   *Miscellaneous*

COMPUTER BUILDERS WAREHOUSE

Current financial data not available

1993 Tobsal Ct.
Warren, MI 48091
Ph: (586)756-2600, Fax: (586)756-8706
www.computerfranchise.com
Custom computers, parts & services
Began: 1990, Franchising since: 1999
Headquarters size: 30 employees
Franchise department: 6 employees

U.S. franchises: 11
Canadian franchises: 0
Other foreign franchises: 0
Company-owned: 3
Units concentrated in AL, AZ, FL, GA,
    MI, NV, TX

Seeking: All U.S.
Seeking in Canada? Yes
Exclusive territories? Yes
Homebased option? No
Kiosk option? No
Employees needed to run franchise: 8
Absentee ownership? No

COSTS
Total cost: $250K+
Franchise fee: $35K
Royalty fee: 2%
Term of agreement: 10 years renewable
    at no charge
Franchisees required to buy multiple
    units? Outside the U.S. only

FINANCING
In-house: None
3rd-party: Accounts receivable, equipment, franchise fee, inventory, payroll, start-up costs

QUALIFICATIONS
Net worth: $200K
Cash liquidity: $100K
Experience:
    General business experience

TRAINING
At headquarters: 2 weeks
At franchisee's location: 2 weeks

BUSINESS SUPPORT
Meetings
Toll-free phone line
Grand opening
Internet
Lease negotiations
Security/safety procedures
Field operations/evaluations
Purchasing cooperatives

MARKETING SUPPORT
Co-op advertising
Ad slicks

COMPUTER PARTS USA

Current financial data not available

7521 Canyon Expwy.
Amarillo, TX 79110
Ph: (806)352-7822
Fax: (806)359-9644
www.computerpartsusa.com
Computer hardware & accessories
Began: 1997, Franchising since: 2002
Headquarters size: 10 employees
Franchise department: 2 employees

U.S. franchises: 1
Canadian franchises: 0
Other foreign franchises: 0
Company-owned: 2
Units concentrated in OK, TX

Seeking: All U.S.
Seeking in Canada? No
Exclusive territories? Yes
Homebased option? No
Kiosk option? No
Employees needed to run franchise: 2
Absentee ownership? No

COSTS
Total cost: $74.3K
Franchise fee: $2K
Royalty fee: 1.5%
Term of agreement: 5 years renewable
　　for $1.5K
Franchisees required to buy multiple
　　units? No

FINANCING
No financing available

QUALIFICATIONS
Experience:
　　General business experience
　　Marketing skills

TRAINING
At headquarters: 2 weeks
At franchisee's location: 2 weeks

BUSINESS SUPPORT
Meetings
Toll-free phone line
Grand opening
Internet
Field operations/evaluations
Purchasing cooperatives

MARKETING SUPPORT
Co-op advertising

COMPUTER TROUBLESHOOTERS

Ranked #231 in Entrepreneur Magazine's 2004 Franchise 500

Financial rating: $$$

3904 N. Druid Hills Rd., #323
Decatur, GA 30033
Ph: (770)454-6382
Fax: (770)234-6162
www.comptroub.com
Computer services & support
Began: 1997, Franchising since: 1997
Headquarters size: 4 employees
Franchise department: 4 employees

U.S. franchises: 112
Canadian franchises: 10
Other foreign franchises: 125
Company-owned: 1
Units concentrated in CA, FL, GA, MI,
　　NC, NJ, OH, TX, WI

Seeking: All U.S.
Seeking in Canada? Yes
Exclusive territories? Yes
Homebased option? Yes
Kiosk option? No
Employees needed to run franchise: 1
Absentee ownership? Yes

COSTS
Total cost: $16.3K-24.4K
Franchise fee: $11K
Royalty fee: $220/mo.
Term of agreement: 10 years renewable
　　at no charge
Franchisees required to buy multiple
　　units? No

FINANCING
No financing available

QUALIFICATIONS
Net worth: $10.5K
Cash liquidity: $7K
Experience:
　　Industry experience

TRAINING
At headquarters: 2 days
At franchisee's location: 2 days
In New York City: 2 days
In Lansing, MI: 2 days

BUSINESS SUPPORT
Newsletter
Meetings
Toll-free phone line
Internet
Field operations/evaluations

MARKETING SUPPORT
Co-op advertising
Ad slicks
National media campaign
Regional marketing

CONCERTO NETWORKS INC.

Financial rating: $$

6440 Lusk Blvd., #D200
San Diego, CA 92121
Ph: (858)366-0122
Fax: (858)366-0124
www.concertonetworks.com
IT professional services
Began: 2002, Franchising since: 2003
Headquarters size: 14
Franchise department: 10

U.S. franchises: 2
Canadian franchises: 0
Other foreign franchises: 0
Company-owned: 0

Seeking: All U.S.
Seeking in Canada? No
Exclusive territories? Info not provided
Homebased option? Yes
Kiosk option? No
Employees needed to run franchise:
    1-2
Absentee ownership? Yes

COSTS
Total cost: $36.5K-47.9K
Franchise fee: $15.8K
Royalty fee: 14%
Term of agreement: 10 years renewable
Franchisees required to buy multiple
    units? Yes

FINANCING
In-house: None
3rd-party: Equipment, start-up costs

QUALIFICATIONS
Net worth: $200K
Cash liquidity: $25K
Experience:
    Industry experience
    General business experience
    Marketing skills

TRAINING
At headquarters: 2 weeks

BUSINESS SUPPORT
Newsletter
Meetings
Toll-free phone line
Grand opening
Internet
Security/safety procedures
Field operations/evaluations
Purchasing cooperatives

MARKETING SUPPORT
Co-op advertising
Ad slicks
National media campaign
Regional marketing

DATA DOCTORS

Current financial data not available

2090 E. University, #101
Tempe, AZ 85281
Ph: (480)921-2444
Fax: (480)921-2975
www.datadoctors.com
Computer sales & services; Web
    services
Began: 1988; Franchising since: 2002
Headquarters size: 37 employees
Franchise department: Info not
    provided

U.S. franchises: 39
Canadian franchises: 0
Other foreign franchises: 0
Company-owned: 4

Seeking: All U.S.
Seeking in Canada? Yes
Exclusive territories? Yes
Homebased option? No
Kiosk option? No
Employees need to run franchise: 2-3
Absentee ownership: No

COSTS
Total cost: $75.4K-105.2K
Franchise fee: $35K
Royalty fee: 5%
Term of agreement: 20 years renewable
    for 5% of then-current fee
Franchisees required to buy multiple
    units? No

FINANCING
In-house: None
3rd-party: Accounts receivable, equip-
    ment, franchise fee, inventory, pay-
    roll, start-up costs

QUALIFICATIONS
Cash liquidity: $75.4K-105.2K
Experience:
    General business experience

TRAINING
At headquarters: Varies
At franchisee's location: Varies

BUSINESS SUPPORT
Newsletter
Meetings
Toll-free phone line
Grand opening
Internet
Security/safety procedures
Field operations/evaluations
Purchasing cooperatives

MARKETING SUPPORT
Co-op advertising
Ad slicks
Regional marketing
Weekly radio show & newspaper
    column

EXPETEC

Financial rating: 0

P.O. Box 487
Aberdeen, SD 57401
Ph: (888)297-2292/(605)225-4122
Fax: (605)225-5176
www.expetec.biz
Computer, printer & telecommunications sales & service
Began: 1992, Franchising since: 1996
Headquarters size: 15 employees
Franchise department: 3 employees

U.S. franchises: 40
Canadian franchises: 0
Other foreign franchises: 0
Company-owned: 0
Units concentrated in CA, FL, TX, WI

Seeking: All U.S.
Seeking in Canada? No
Exclusive territories? Yes
Homebased option? Yes
Kiosk option? No
Employees needed to run franchise: 2-3
Absentee ownership? No

COSTS
Total cost: $57.2K-78.2K
Franchise fee: $20K-28K
Royalty fee: $150-300
Term of agreement: 10 years renewable at no charge
Franchisees required to buy multiple units? No

FINANCING
In-house: Franchise fee, equipment
3rd-party: None

QUALIFICATIONS
Net worth: $100K
Cash liquidity: $35K
Experience:
 General business experience
 Marketing skills

TRAINING
At headquarters: 3 weeks

BUSINESS SUPPORT
Newsletter
Meetings
Toll-free phone line
Internet
Lease negotiations
Field operations/evaluations

MARKETING SUPPORT
Ad slicks
Regional marketing

FRIENDLY COMPUTERS

Ranked #330 in Entrepreneur Magazine's 2004 Franchise 500

Financial rating: $$$

3145 N. Rainbow Blvd.
Las Vegas, NV 89108
Ph: (800)656-3115/(702)656-2780
Fax: (702)656-9487
www.friendlycomputers.com
On-site computer services & sales
Began: 1992, Franchising since: 1999
Headquarters size: 24 employees
Franchise department: 6 employees

U.S. franchises: 25
Canadian franchises: 0
Other foreign franchises: 0
Company-owned: 2
Units concentrated in all U.S.

Seeking: All U.S.
Seeking in Canada? Yes
Exclusive territories? Yes
Homebased option? Yes
Kiosk option? No
Employees needed to run franchise: 4
Absentee ownership? Yes

COSTS
Total cost: $14.5K-180K
Franchise fee: $9.5K/25K
Royalty fee: 3%
Term of agreement: 10 years renewable for $2.5K
Franchisees required to buy multiple units? No

FINANCING
In-house: Franchise fee, equipment, inventory, start-up costs
3rd-party: Equipment, franchise fee, inventory, start-up costs

QUALIFICATIONS
Experience:
 General business experience

TRAINING
At headquarters: 1 week
At franchisee's location: 1 week

BUSINESS SUPPORT
Newsletter
Meetings
Toll-free phone line
Grand opening
Internet
Lease negotiations
Purchasing cooperatives

MARKETING SUPPORT
Co-op advertising
Ad slicks
Regional marketing

GEEKS ON CALL AMERICA

Financial rating: 0

814 Kempsville Rd., #106
Norfolk, VA 23502
Ph: (757)466-3448
Fax: (757)466-3457
www.geeksoncall.com
On-site computer support services
Began: 1999, Franchising since: 2001
Headquarters size: 25 employees
Franchise department: 7 employees

U.S. franchises: 77
Canadian franchises: 0
Other foreign franchises: 0
Company-owned: 0
Units concentrated in all U.S.

Seeking: All U.S.
Seeking in Canada? No
Exclusive territories? Yes
Homebased option? Yes
Kiosk option? No
Employees needed to run franchise: 1-2
Absentee ownership? Yes

COSTS
Total cost: $37.4K-89.2K
Franchise fee: $12K
Royalty fee: Varies
Term of agreement: 10 years renewable
    at no charge
Franchisees required to buy multiple
    units? No

FINANCING
In-house: None
3rd-party: Equipment, franchise fee,
    inventory, start-up costs

QUALIFICATIONS
Cash liquidity: $10K-15K
Experience:
    Industry experience
    General business experience

TRAINING
At headquarters: 1 week
At franchisee's location: 1 week

BUSINESS SUPPORT
Newsletter
Meetings
Toll-free phone line
Grand opening
Internet
Field operations/evaluations
Purchasing cooperatives

MARKETING SUPPORT
Regional marketing

NEXTWAVE COMPUTERS

Current financial data not available

1825 Tamiami Trail, #B-3
Port Charlotte, FL 33948
Ph: (941)764-5800
Fax: (941)764-0094
www.nextwavecomputer.com
Computer hardware, services & repair
Began: 1999, Franchising since: 2003
Headquarters size: 7 employees
Franchise department: 3 employees

U.S. franchises: 0
Canadian franchises: 0
Other foreign franchises: 0
Company-owned: 1

Seeking: All U.S.
Seeking in Canada? No
Exclusive territories? Yes
Homebased option? No
Kiosk option? No
Employees needed to run franchise: 4
Absentee ownership? Yes

COSTS
Total cost: $76K-125K
Franchise fee: $25K
Royalty fee: 5%
Term of agreement: 10 years renewable
    at no charge
Franchisees required to buy multiple
    units? No

FINANCING
In-house: None
3rd-party: Accounts receivable, equip-
    ment, inventory, start-up costs

QUALIFICATIONS
Net worth: $100K
Cash liquidity: $30K
Experience:
    General business experience

TRAINING
At headquarters: 2 weeks+

BUSINESS SUPPORT
Toll-free phone line
Grand opening
Internet
Security/safety procedures
Field operations/evaluations

MARKETING SUPPORT
Ad slicks
Regional marketing

RESCUECOM

Ranked #333 in Entrepreneur Magazine's 2004 Franchise 500   *Financial rating: $$*

2560 Burnet Ave.
Syracuse, NY 13206
Ph: (800)737-2837, Fax: (315)433-5228
www.rescuecom.com
Computer consulting & repair services
Began: 1997, Franchising since: 1998
Headquarters size: 40 employees
Franchise department: Info not provided

U.S. franchises: 51
Canadian franchises: 0
Other foreign franchises: 0
Company-owned: 0
Units concentrated in all U.S.

Seeking: All U.S.
Seeking in Canada? Yes
Exclusive territories? Yes
Homebased option? Yes
Kiosk option? No
Employees needed to run franchise: 1-3
Absentee ownership? No

COSTS
Total cost: $9.8K-80.2K
Franchise fee: $1.5K-18.8K
Royalty fee: 9-24%
Term of agreement: 5 years renewable
    for 50% of current fee
Franchisees required to buy multiple
    units? Outside the U.S. only

FINANCING
In-house: Franchise fee
3rd-party: None

QUALIFICATIONS
Net worth: $1K-5K
Cash liquidity: $20K
Experience:
    Industry experience
    General business experience

TRAINING
At headquarters: 1 week
At franchisee's location: 1 week

BUSINESS SUPPORT
Newsletter
Meetings
Toll-free phone line
Grand opening
Internet
Field operations/evaluations
Purchasing cooperatives

MARKETING SUPPORT
Co-op advertising
Ad slicks

SOFT-TEMPS WORLDWIDE

Financial rating: $$$

1280 N.E. Business Park Pl.
Jensen Beach, FL 34957
Ph: (800)221-2880
Fax: (772)225-3136
www.stfranchise.com
Computer training & consulting
Began: 1999, Franchising since: 2002
Headquarters size: 24 employees
Franchise department: 10 employees

U.S. franchises: 34
Canadian franchises: 0
Other foreign franchises: 0
Company-owned: 0
Units concentrated in all U.S.

Seeking: All U.S.
Seeking in Canada? No
Exclusive territories? No
Homebased option? Yes
Kiosk option? No
Employees needed to run franchise: 0
Absentee ownership? Yes

COSTS
Total cost: $3.99K-4.99K
Franchise fee: $2.99K
Royalty fee: 5%
Term of agreement: 7 years renewable
    for $500
Franchisees required to buy multiple
    units? No

FINANCING
No financing available

QUALIFICATIONS
Cash liquidity: $4.99K
Experience:
    IT experience
    Marketing background

TRAINING
At headquarters: 4 days (optional)
At franchisee's location
Online

BUSINESS SUPPORT
Newsletter
Meetings
Internet
Field operations/evaluations
Purchasing cooperatives

MARKETING SUPPORT
Co-op advertising
Ad slicks
National media campaign
Internet
Direct mail

TECH ▸ *Other Franchises*

ACADEMY OF LEARNING
100 York Blvd., #400
Richmond Hill, ON Canada L4B 1J8
Ph: (905)886-8973
www.academyol.com
Computer & business-skills training

CARTRIDGE WORLD
*Ranked #381 in Entrepreneur
    Magazine's 2004 Franchise 500*
5743-A Horton St.
Emeryville, CA 94608
Ph: (510)594-9900
www.cartridgeworld.com
Printer/fax cartridge replacements &
    sales

COMPUTER RENAISSANCE
124 S. Florida Ave., #202
Lakeland, FL 33801
Ph: (863)669-1155
www.compren.com
Used & new computer sales/services

FULL CIRCLE IMAGE INC.
6256 34th Ave. N.W.
Rochester, MN 55901
Ph: (800)584-7244
www.fullcircleimage.com
Printer ribbons, laser-toner & ink-jet
    cartridges

SHOW ME PCS
12010 Bammel N. Houston, #M
Houston, TX 77088
Ph: (866)600-7672/(281)880-8766
www.showmepcs.com
One-on-one computer training &
    services

SUPPORT ON-SITE COMPUTER SERVICES INC.
18 Technology, #160
Irvine, CA 92618
Ph: (888)497-4319
www.support-onsite.com
On-site business & residential com-
    puter services

Top 10 Franchises
for 2004

1. Subway   www.subway.com   Submarine sandwiches & salads

2. Curves   www.buycurves.com   Women's fitness & weight-loss centers

3. The Quizno's Franchise Co.   www.quiznos.com   Submarine sandwiches, soups, salads

4. 7-Eleven Inc.   www.7-eleven.com   Convenience stores

5. Jackson Hewitt Tax Service   www.jacksonhewitt.com   Tax preparation services

6. The UPS Store   www.theupsstore.com   Postal, business & communications services

7. McDonald's   www.mcdonalds.com   Hamburgers, chicken, salads

8. Jani-King   www.janiking.com   Commercial cleaning

9. Dunkin' Donuts   www.dunkindonuts.com   Donuts & baked goods

10. Baskin-Robbins USA Co.   www.baskinrobbins.com   Ice cream & yogurt

Source: *Entrepreneur* Magazine's 2004 Franchise 500°

Top 10 Homebased Franchises for 2004

(Franchise opportunities that can be run from home)

1. Jani-King — www.janiking.com — Commercial cleaning
2. Chem-Dry — www.chemdry.com — Carpet, drapery & upholstery cleaning
3. ServiceMaster Clean — www.ownafranchise.com — Commercial/residential cleaning & disaster restoration
4. Snap-on Tools — www.snapon.com — Professional tools & equipment
5. Jan-Pro Franchising Int'l. Inc. — www.jan-pro.com — Commercial cleaning
6. Jazzercise Inc. — www.jazzercise.com — Dance/exercise classes
7. Matco Tools — www.matcotools.com — Automotive/professional tools & equipment
8. Servpro — www.servpro.com — Insurance/disaster restoration & cleaning
9. CleanNet USA Inc. — www.cleannetusa.com — Commercial office cleaning
10. Coverall Cleaning Concepts — www.coverall.com — Commercial cleaning

Source: *Entrepreneur's* 2004 Franchise 500°

Top 10 New Franchises for 2004

(Companies that have been franchising since 1999)

1. Fiducial Inc.   www.fiducial.com   Tax, accounting, payroll & financial services

2. Comfort Keepers   www.comfortkeepers.com   Non-medical in-home senior care

3. Results! Travel   www.resultstravel.com   Travel services

4. Dippin' Dots Franchising Inc.   www.dippindots.com   Specialty ice cream, frozen yogurt & ices

5. Cruise Planners   www.cruiseagents.com   Cruise/tour agency

6. Super Wash   www.superwash.com   Coin-operated self-serve & brushless automatic car washes

7. Line-X   www.linexcorp.com   Spray-on truck bed liners & industrial coatings

8. Tutoring Club   www.tutoringclub.com   Individualized instruction for K-12 students

9. Plato's Closet   www.platoscloset.com   New/used clothing for teens & young adults

10. Ident-A-Kid Services of America   www.ident-a-kid.com   Children's identification products & services

Source: *Entrepreneur's* 2004 Franchise 500°

Top 10 Low-Cost Franchises for 2004

(Franchises with minimum total investments of less than $50,000)

1. Curves — www.buycurves.com — Women's fitness & weight-loss centers
2. 7-Eleven Inc. — www.7-eleven.com — Convenience stores
3. Jackson Hewitt Tax Service — www.jacksonhewitt.com — Tax preparation services
4. Jani-King — www.janiking.com — Commercial cleaning
5. Kumon Math & Reading Centers — www.kumon.com — Supplemental education
6. Chem-Dry — www.chemdry.com — Carpet, drapery & upholstery cleaning
7. ServiceMaster Clean — www.ownafranchise.com — Commercial/residential cleaning & disaster restoration
8. RE/MAX Int'l. Inc. — www.remax.com — Real estate
9. Jan-Pro Franchising Int'l. Inc. — www.jan-pro.com — Commercial cleaning
10. Merle Norman Cosmetics — www.merlenorman.com — Cosmetics studios

Source: *Entrepreneur's 2004 Franchise 500*

State Franchise Relationship Laws

THESE STATES HAVE STATUTES WHICH MAY SUPERsede the franchise agreement you have with the franchisor. They typically impose a vaguely defined "good cause" requirement before a franchisor can terminate a relationship during the term of the contract or refuse to renew the contractual term of the franchise.

ARKANSAS [Stat. section 70–807]

CALIFORNIA [Bus. & Prof. Code sections 20000–20043]

CONNECTICUT [Gen. Stat. section 42–133e et seq.]

DELAWARE [Code, tit. 6, ch. 25, Section 2551 et seq.]

DISTRICT OF COLUMBIA [Franchising Act of 1988, DC Code Ann. Sec. 29–1201 to –1208 (1989)]

HAWAII [Rev. Stat. section 482E–1]

ILLINOIS [815 ILCS 705/19 and 705/20]

INDIANA [Stat. section 23–2–2.7]

IOWA [Code sections 523H.1–523H.17]

MICHIGAN [Stat. section 19.854(27)]

MINNESOTA [Stat. section 80C.14]

MISSISSIPPI [Code section 75–24–51]

MISSOURI [Stat. section 407.400]

NEBRASKA [Rev. Stat. section 87–401]

NEW JERSEY [Stat. section 56:10–1]

SOUTH DAKOTA [Codified Laws section 37–5A–51]

VIRGINIA [Code 13.1–557–574–13.1–564]

WASHINGTON [Code section 19.100.180]

WISCONSIN [Stat. section 135.03]

State Franchise Authorities

CALIFORNIA

California Department of Corporations
The Commissioner of Corporations
Department of Corporations
320 West 4th St.
Los Angeles, CA 90013

HAWAII

Business Registration Division
Securities Compliance
Department of Commerce and Consumer
   Affairs
1010 Richards St.
Honolulu, HI 96813

ILLINOIS

Franchise Division Office of the Attorney
   General
Chief, Franchise Division
Office of the Attorney General
500 South Second St.
Springfield, IL 62706

INDIANA

Securities Commissioner
Indiana Securities Division
Room E 111, 302 W. Washington St.
Indianapolis, IN 46204

MARYLAND

Office of the Attorney General
Securities Division
200 St. Paul Pl., 20th Fl.
Baltimore, MD 21202-2020

MICHIGAN

Antitrust and Franchise Unit
Department of the Attorney General
Director, Consumer Protection Division
670 Law Bldg.
Lansing, MI 48913

MINNESOTA

The Commissioner of Commerce
Minnesota Department of Commerce
85 7thplace E., #500
St. Paul, MN 55101-2198

NEW YORK

New York State Department of Law
Bureau of Investor Protection and Securities
120 Broadway, 23rd Fl.
New York, NY 10271

NORTH DAKOTA

The Commissioner of Securities
North Dakota Office of Securities Commissioner
Office of the Securities Commissioner
600 East Blvd., Fifth Fl.
Bismarck, ND 58505

RHODE ISLAND

Rhode Island Division of Securities
Director, Division of Securities
233 Richmond St., #232
Providence, RI 02903

SOUTH DAKOTA

South Dakota Division of Securities
Director, Division of Securities
118 W. Capitol
Pierre, SD 57501

VIRGINIA

State Corporation Commission
Division of Securities and Retail Franchising
1300 East Main St., 9th Fl.
Richmond, VA 23219

WASHINGTON

Department of Financial Institutions
Securities Division
P.O. Box 9033
Olympia, WA 98507-9033

WISCONSIN

The Commissioner of Securities
Wisconsin Securities Commission
P.O. Box 1768
Madison, WI 53701

Other Information Sources

FTC INFORMATION

Contact the Federal Trade Commission (FTC) for general investment information if you are interested in buying a franchise or business opportunity venture. The Web site is well worth a visit, and the FTC encourages investors to contact the agency if they discover an unlawful franchise practice.

Internet: www.ftc.gov

Phone: Consumer Response Center at (877) 382-4357

U.S. Mail: Federal Trade Commission, Attn: Consumer Response Center, Washington, DC 20580

BETTER BUSINESS BUREAU

Look for your local office of the Better Business Bureau in the phone book or on the Web.

State Franchise Laws

State	Franchise Investment Law?	Franchise Relationship Law?
Alabama	No	No
Alaska	No	No
Arizona	No	No
Arkansas	No	Yes
California	Yes	Yes
Colorado	No	No
Connecticut	No	Yes
Delaware	No	Yes
District of Columbia	No	Yes
Florida	No	No
Georgia	No	No
Hawaii	Yes	Yes
Idaho	No	No
Illinois	Yes	Yes
Indiana	Yes	Yes
Iowa	No	Yes
Kansas	No	No
Kentucky	No	No
Louisiana	No	No

State	Franchise Investment Law?	Franchise Relationship Law?
Maine	No	No
Maryland	Yes	No
Massachusetts	No	No
Michigan	Yes	Yes
Minnesota	Yes	Yes
Mississippi	No	Yes
Missouri	No	Yes
Montana	No	No
Nebraska	No	Yes
Nevada	No	No
New Hampshire	No	No
New Jersey	No	Yes
New Mexico	No	No
New York	Yes	No
North Carolina	No	No
North Dakota	Yes	No
Ohio	No	No
Oklahoma	No	No
Oregon	No	No
Pennsylvania	No	No

State	Franchise Investment Law?	Franchise Relationship Law?
Rhode Island	Yes	No
South Carolina	No	No
South Dakota	Yes	Yes
Tennessee	No	No
Texas	No	No
Utah	No	No
Vermont	No	No
Virginia	Yes	Yes
Washington	Yes	Yes
West Virginia	No	No
Wisconsin	Yes	Yes
Wyoming	No	No

Glossary

Arbitration. Formal dispute resolution process that is legally binding on the parties.

Business Format Franchise. See the definition of "franchise."

Business Opportunity. A package of goods and materials that enables the buyer to begin or maintain a business. The Federal Trade Commission and 25 states regulate the concept.

Copyright. The legal right protecting an original work of authorship that is fixed in a tangible form.

Earnings Claim. A statement by a franchisor regarding the financial performance of existing franchisees or a projection of how a particular investor/franchisee will perform. Earnings claims may be made by a franchisor, but if so, they must be presented in item 19 of the UFOC.

Federal Trade Commission's Franchise Rule. The 1979 trade regulation rule by which all franchisors in the United States are required to deliver a presale disclosure document.

First Personal Meeting. A disclosure trigger under the Federal Trade Commission Rule; not a casual or chance meeting but a detailed discussion about a specific franchise opportunity.

Franchise. The law defines a franchise as the presence of three factors: 1) the grant of trademark rights, 2) a prescribed marketing plan, or significant control or assistance in the operation, or a community of interest, and 3) payment of a franchise fee for the right to participate. In business terms, the franchisee receives full training in the operation, follows a detailed set of business techniques, uses the franchisor's trademark and pays a continuing royalty for participation in the program.

Franchise Agreement. The contract by which a franchisor grants franchise rights to a franchisee.

Franchisee. One who receives the rights to a franchise. The owner and operator of a franchised business.

Franchise Fee. The money a franchisee is required to pay for the right to participate in the franchise program. Under the federal rules the minimum amount of franchise fee payment allowed before disclosure is required is $500. A franchise fee includes any lump sum initial payment and ongoing royalty payments.

Franchise Investment Laws. The laws of the Federal Trade Commission and 14 states that regulate the sale of a franchise.

Franchise Relationship Laws. State franchise statutes in 19 jurisdictions that generally restrict terminations or nonrenewals of franchise agreements in the absence of "good cause." See appendix A.

Franchisor. The person or company that grants franchise rights to a franchisee.

Limited Liability Company. A relatively new form of business organization with the liability-shield advantages of a corporation and the flexibility and tax pass-through advantages of a partnership.

Mediation. Professionally assisted negotiation. Now frequently used as a first step to resolve a dispute between a franchisor and franchisee. Mediation is generally nonbinding, unless the parties agree to a resulting settlement.

Patent. An inventor's right protecting an invention, new device, or innovation.

Product Franchise. The legal definition is the same as a "franchise." In business terms, it is a system for the distribution of a particular line of products, usually manufactured and/or supplied by the franchisor.

Renewal. Most franchise agreements grant the franchisee the right to renew the initial contract term for additional time at the end of the initial term. The contract may impose conditions on the right to renew, such as providing timely written notice, signing a new form of agreement, and paying a renewal fee.

Royalty Fee. The continuing payment paid by a franchisee to the franchisor. Usually calculated as a percentage of the franchisee's gross sales.

Territory. The rights granted to a franchisee that offer a restriction on competition within a stated area.

Trademark. A word, phrase, or logo design that identifies the source or quality of a product. A service mark means the same thing, but identifies a service.

Trade Show. An exhibition of businesses offering franchises and/or business opportunity packages.

Transfer. The sale of franchise rights by a franchisee to the buyer of all or a portion of the franchisee's business.

UFOC. Uniform Franchise Offering Circular, the specialized franchise disclosure statement that franchisors must deliver to prospective franchisees at the earlier of (1) the first personal meeting for the purpose of discussing the sale or possible sale of a franchise, or (2) ten business days (14 calendar days in Illinois) before the prospect signs a franchise agreement or pays money for the right to be a franchisee.

Index

Listings Index

Key: 🏠 = Homebased; $ = Low cost

Key: 🏠 = Homebased; ∮ = Low cost

Key: 🏠 = Homebased; $ = Low cost

Key: 🏠 = Homebased; $ = Low cost

Key: 🏠 = Homebased; $ = Low cost

Key: 🏠 = Homebased; ∮ = Low cost

Key: 🏠 = Homebased; $ = Low cost

Key: 🏠 = Homebased; $ = Low cost

Key: 🏠 = Homebased; 💲 = Low cost

Key: 🏠 = Homebased; ∮ = Low cost

Key: 🏠 = Homebased; $ = Low cost

Key: 🏠 = Homebased; ₷ = Low cost

Key: 🏠 = Homebased; $ = Low cost

Key: 🏠 = Homebased; $ = Low cost

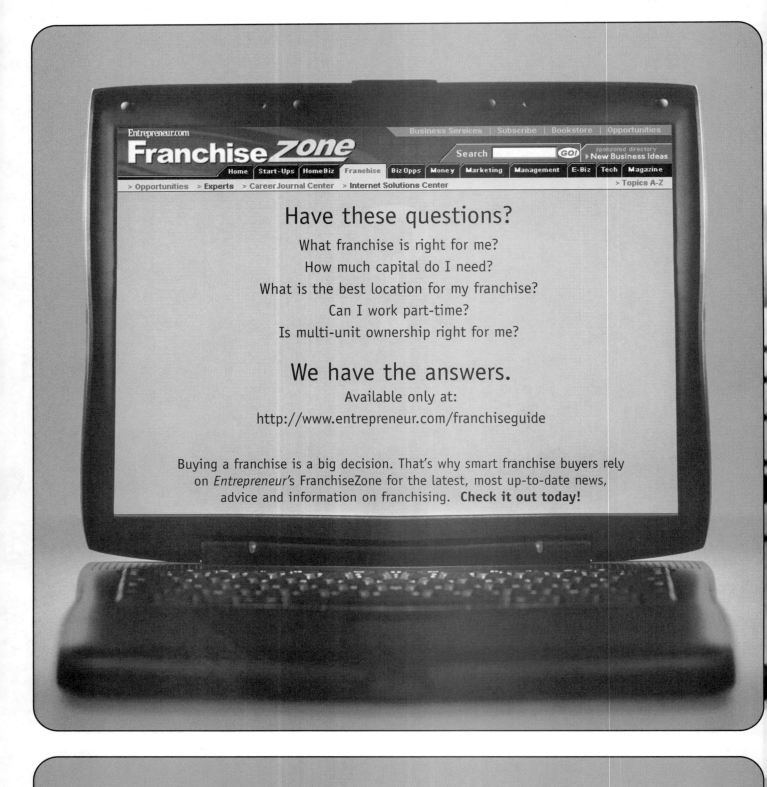